Supply Chain Innovation for Competing in Highly Dynamic Markets:

Challenges and Solutions

Pietro Evangelista
IRAT-CNR & University of Naples Federico II, Italy

Alan McKinnon
Heriot-Watt University, UK

Edward Sweeney
Dublin Institute of Technology, Ireland

Emilio Esposito
University of Naples Federico II, Italy

BUSINESS SCIENCE Reference

Published in the United States of America by
Business Science Reference (an imprint of IGI Global)
701 E. Chocolate Avenue
Hershey PA 17033
Tel: 717-533-8845
Fax: 717-533-8661
E-mail: cust@igi-global.com
Web site: http://www.igi-global.com

Library of Congress Cataloging-in-Publication Data

Supply chain innovation for competing in highly dynamic markets: challenges and solutions / Pietro Evangelista ... [et al.], editors.
p. cm.
Includes bibliographical references and index.
Summary: "This book investigates the role of innovation in the management of supply chains of today, focusing on supply chain integration from both strategic and operational perspectives and the impact of information technology-related innovation in supply chain and logistics service industries"--Provided by publisher.
ISBN 978-1-60960-585-8 (hbk.) -- ISBN 978-1-60960-586-5 (ebook) 1. Business logistics. 2. Business logistics--Information technology. 3. Business logistics--Technological innovations. I. Evangelista, Pietro, 1963- II. Title.
HD38.5.S8954 2012
658.7--dc22

2011013907

British Cataloguing in Publication Data
A Cataloguing in Publication record for this book is available from the British Library.

Table of Contents

Section 2
ICT Supply Chain Innovation

Section 3
Sustainability Innovation

Preface

Recent years have seen major changes in the logistics and supply chain management (SCM) landscape. Firstly, markets have become more competitive and complex and customers have become more discerning. Secondly, changes in the international economic and business environment have resulted in supply chain configurations becoming more international, and sometimes genuinely global, in complexion. Thirdly, as firms have focused on their core competencies, the outsourcing of supply chain activities deemed to be "non-core" has taken place resulting in a process of vertical disintegration in many supply chains. Finally, successful firms are increasingly recognizing that the supply chain itself represents a potentially major source of competitive differentiation. This point is critical. The key objectives of SCM relate to the consistent achievement of the customer service levels demanded in target markets and the optimization of total supply chain costs. As customer service is becoming an order winning criterion in an increasing number of sectors, the role of SCM as a key source of strategic differentiation has become more critical. The continuous quest by firms to become more cost competitive has also sharpened the focus on the need for robust SCM given that a large proportion of the cost base of organizations is in the supply chain. Leveraging the supply chain as a key source of competitive advantage has, therefore, become a more critical and urgent task.

In this competitive and highly dynamic environment organisations that fail to deal proactively with these challenges will not succeed. The key to success is based on developing competitive supply chain strategies that provide a basis for meaningful change across the supply chain. Failure to change will almost inevitably result in decline (i.e. "standing still = falling behind"). However, it is not about change for the sake of change; rather, it is about carrying out supply chain processes in a different and more innovative manner. The word "innovation" - derived from the Latin "novus" meaning "new" - is about identifying new and better ways of doing things in all aspects of an organisation's activity.

This book identifies some of the key challenges and solutions when it comes to applying innovative approaches across the supply chain. In particular, it focuses on the barriers to success, as well as on the critical success factors, in identifying the key challenges and implementing appropriate solutions aimed at improving the efficiency and effectiveness of supply chains.

Four main areas of innovation have been identified given their role in the overall SCM philosophy. Firstly, supply chain integration (SCI) has long been regarded as the central tenet of SCM thinking. Any meaningful attempt at innovating supply chains must, therefore, have a strong focus on this area. Section 1 of this book identifies challenges and possible solutions in this area. Recent years have seen rapid developments in supply chain technology based in particular on information and communications technology (ICT). There is little doubt that these tools have the potential to generate significant supply chain improvement if implemented in an integrated and strategic manner. Innovation in the application of these emerging technologies is the key to ensuring that this potential is realised in practice. This is the focus of Section 2 of this book. The contribution of logistics and supply chain activities to environmental degradation has highlighted the need for more sustainable approaches to the design and management of supply chain operations. Legal, market and financial considerations have brought this issue to the fore in recent years. Section 3 of this book explores innovation in the context of the environmental sustainability, identifying a range of challenges and proposing a number of possible solutions to these challenges. Finally, all supply chains comprise a large number of discrete organisational entities each of which plays a specific role in the value creation process. Effective SCM relies heavily of the ability of firms to properly manage their suppliers in a proactive and strategic manner. Innovation in this complex supply system provides the focus of Section 4 of this book.

Section 1: Innovation in Supply Chain Integration

The contemporary supply chain management (SCM) paradigm focuses heavily on the notion of integration. Integration in this context is primarily concerned with replacing traditional supply chain configurations that were often characterised by high levels of fragmentation with more innovative approaches that are characterised by different supply chain elements working together in a more seamless fashion. The integration concept can be considered at many levels. The two primary levels considered in this book are internal and external. The former refers to the integration of activities and processes within organisations, with the latter referring to interaction between different entities upstream and downstream in the supply chain. Given to centrality of supply chain integration (SCI) in the wider SCM approach, it is clear that any worthwhile attempt at improving supply chain capability and performance should focus on innovation in this regard.

Challenges can only be identified by fully understanding the dynamics of the business environment, as well as the strengths and weaknesses of existing supply chain architectures. In relation to solutions, it is important to recognise that all supply chains are unique and require innovation that is appropriate to the situation under consideration. This uniqueness relates to products, processes, people and much else besides. Identifying the appropriate form of supply chain change must pay attention to detailed issues associated with the distinctive characteristics of an organisation and its operating environment. This is particularly the case with regard to SCI. Identifying the appropriate solution requires that the process of supply chain analysis and planning is carried out in a logical and systematic manner with proper attention to detail. It further required that integration plans are properly implemented, paying particular attention to cultural and other people-related aspects of the change process.

Section 2: ICT Supply Chain Innovation

Although many technological innovations have affected logistics and SCM in recent decades, there is no doubt that developments in information and communication technology have been the main driver of change in the field. Both academics and managers have emphasised the potential role of ICT to pervade the whole supply chain, enabling not only the integration of functions and processes of a single company, but also those of suppliers and customers with broad and long-term implications for an organisation's competitive advantage.

ICT is considered one of the most prominent innovation domains in the supply chain. A growing number of companies have adopted new information systems and technologies for supporting their logistics and SCM operations. Examples include Dell, Wal-Mart, Cisco Systems, Intel, Celestica and General Electric. The main benefits achieved by these companies relate to end-to-end visibility, reduced cycle time and inventories, minimization of the bullwhip effect, and improvements in the effectiveness of distribution channels. This supports the view that ICT has a profound impact on the management of supply chains as new technologies greatly facilitate the flow of information, extend control over remote operations and across organisational boundaries and automate processes.

As result, the adoption of new technology innovations and the benefits associated with specific types of ICT-related innovations are of paramount interest to the different kinds of companies operating in supply chain networks. The chapters included in this part of the book deal with challenges and solutions concerning technology innovations particularly with reference to the adoption of new technologies in the logistics service industry, radio frequency identification (RFID) supply chain applications and intelligent freight transportation systems (IFTS).

Despite information technology capabilities being critical for logistics service differentiation and a tool to cut costs and effectively serve clients through better service customization, the adoption of ICT is a great challenge for logistics service providers, particularly for small and medium-sized logistics service providers. Due to a lack of resources, these companies show difficulties in investing and using ICT. The analysis of a number of case studies of small Italian logistics service companies provides implications for supply chain innovation. Firstly, closeness to customer is a relevant source of collaborative innovation. Secondly, the combination between "service strategy" and "technology strategy" is an important factor stimulating supply chain innovation. Thirdly, in order to obtain differentiation advantages from ICT usage, the focus of small logistics service providers' technology investment have to be on the way ICT used rather than on technology itself.

A further challenge faced by logistics service providers relates to rapidly changing service requirements. Visibility, capacity and equipment utilization, reduction in inventory and transportation costs, monitoring of supply chain security and environment control are increasingly demanded by buyers of logistics services. As documented by two leading case companies based in an Asian country, the adoption of ICT innovations in these areas may provide solutions at both operational (functions and processes) and strategic level (human, knowledge and technology capital development), at firm and industry levels, and more importantly, some of these innovations may have environmental ramifications.

A key challenging area in SCM concerns uncertainty. Shortening product lifecycles and fast changing customer demand for products or services result in more uncertain and complex environment. ICT applications may provide solutions in mitigating and managing uncertainty in a supply chain context. This is the case with radio frequency identification (RFID) in retail industry. This sector is facing a paradigm shift in managing perishable items characterized by limited shelf-life that make supply chain decisions even more difficult, leading to high loss rates. RFID may provide relevant information in order to make the good's deterioration process more predictable and visible at the early stages of supply chain. Innovative retailers can use RFID applications to reduce costs and the risk associated with fluctuations in demand and energy costs. Interesting aspects of this innovation might be the positive impact on accountability of losses along the supply chain and implications for contracts and buy-back options.

Uncertainty also affects inventory management. It is considered a challenging task in SCM due to difficulties in estimating demand, especially in the case of new products. In addition, unpredictable demand and dynamic consignment locations make stock control challenging. These issues frequently result in high inventory costs, inadequate resource allocation and slow response to the customer. An innovative solution for enhancing inventory management should be based on a mix of technology and theory. Combining RFID application for colleting data (to optimize inventory level along the supply chain) and artificial neural network for data analysis (to forecast future demand), it is possible to achieve lean and economically efficient supply chain management.

In recent year, intelligent freight transportation system (IFTS) has been widely used to optimize transport and logistics operations. IFTS opens up possibilities to face many challenges in this area by increasing monitoring, control and planning capabilities. Nevertheless, the strategic potential of IFTS has not been analysed beyond purely operational benefits. Integrating the key IFTS components (smart goods, smart vehicle, and smart infrastructure) may provide solutions to better exploit these innovative systems and provide the base for a more solid evaluation of their effects on transport and logistics operations

Section 3: Sustainability Innovation

The pressure on companies to improve their environmental sustainability is steadily mounting. It is coming from various sources. Government agencies at multi-national, national, regional and local levels are tightening environmental regulations, introducing new forms of green taxation and offering more incentives for companies to clean up their operations. Consumers have become much more aware of environmental issues and are taking greater account of them in their buying decisions. Other stakeholders, particularly investors and employees, also have a strong interest in ensuring that their companies meet high environmental standards.

While the corporate drive to become greener is affecting most aspects of the business, particular attention is focusing on logistics and SCM because these activities are geographically extensive and environmentally intrusive. The movement of freight is a major emitter of greenhouse gases and other air pollutants, is one of the main causes of noise disturbance and is responsible for a significant proportion of traffic accidents. Many of the related costs are external to companies' balance sheets and borne by the community at large and ecosystems. People enjoy having the goods that logistics systems bring them, but generally perceive the delivery process as being bad for the environment.

Many people hold this negative view despite the fact that there have been impressive improvements in the environmental performance of logistical activities over the past few decades. For example, in Europe and North America truck exhaust emissions are an order of magnitude cleaner today than were in the early 1990s. Vehicles are much quieter, safer and less damaging to the road surface. These environmental improvements have resulted from the application of a range of technical and operational innovations. Green logistics has proved to be a fertile area for such innovation and this is likely to continue. This is illustrated by the four chapters in this part of the book which show how a range of new systems, practices, regulations and technologies can reduce the environmental impact of logistics even more.

A first challenge in this field concerns effective ways of increasing the environmental sustainability of road freight transport. Relaxing legal restrictions on truck weights and dimensions allow companies to consolidate freight in a smaller number of deliveries. The experience of companies which permit the use of longer and heavier vehicles (LHVs) demonstrates that they offer a combination of economic, environmental and safety benefits. Proposals to extend the use of LHVs in Europe has, however, proved to be extremely controversial and met with strong resistance from railway interests and environmental groups. Reviews the available published evidence on this issue show how the diffusion of a major transport innovation can be obstructed by government regulation and political lobbying.

The role of the public sector also features prominently in assessing the potential of urban consolidation centres (UCCs) to rationalise the movement of freight in urban areas. Although the earliest UCCs emerged in the 1970s and they have been the subject of numerous feasibility studies since then, it is only over the past few years that their commercial and operational viability has been demonstrated, both in the retailing and construction sectors. A general overview of the UCC concept and its related benefits have been outlined and four case studies in different urban contexts have been used. From the review of the literature and analysis of the case studies, a series of critical success factors have been identified that need to be present for this city logistics innovation to meet its economic and environmental goals.

Another challenge analysed focuses on the return movement of waste products from urban areas. A range of reverse logistics innovations that can improve the efficiency and reduce the environmental impact of the return flow of waste for recycling, reuse or disposal have been analysed. If successfully implemented, these measures can make recycling more commercially attractive, increasing its uptake and yielding additional environmental benefits. The proposed solution is based on various operational, regulatory and equipment innovations, ranging from the integration of commercial and household waste streams to the introduction of 'smart' bin technology.

Finally, the contribution logistics service providers can make to raising environmental standards in this sector has been explored. As a large proportion of logistics expenditure is now outsourced, logistics service providers directly control much of the movement, storage and handling of goods across supply chains. Some logistics service providers now recognise that environmental innovation can be a competitive differentiator, but survey evidence suggests that many are disappointed by their client's lack of interest in environmental initiatives. Logistics service providers need to be given stronger incentives to develop green service portfolios and closer collaboration between logistics service providers and their clients on environmental programmes is recommended.

Section 4: Innovation in Supply System Management

Customer-supplier relationships have been undergoing massive changes at a national and international level. These changes concern various aspects of such relationships: the object of transactions between customer and supplier (such as parts, components, complex systems); the firms' functions involved in the supply relationship (such as production, design, planning, marketing); the supplier's skills required by the customer (such as technical, logistics, managerial); and the level of trust and collaboration which sustain the relationships. From the analysis of the literature emerges that it is not easy to summarise the evolution of the customer-supplier relationships. Nevertheless, it is possible to identify four main evolving phases: 1) traditional supply (1960s - 1970s); 2) supply system development (1980s); 3) strategic alliance (1990s); and 4) globalisation (2000 and beyond). In line with this evolution, customer-supplier relationships are involved both in radical processes of innovation and new challenges oriented to the search of greater efficiency and effectiveness. The chapters included in this part of the book deal with five main challenges related to innovation in supply system management.

The first concerns the problem of the implementation of discontinuous innovation in supply chain relationships. The solution proposed indicates that it is necessary to look beyond the individual psychological barriers and organisational issues that have traditionally been discussed in the relevant literature. A multilevel analysis is needed in order to fully appreciate the complexity of the phenomenon of discontinuous innovation implementation in supply chain relationships.

The second challenge relates to the potential use of formalized supply evaluation models for the strategic management of the supply system. There are at least four good reasons to use formalized models rather than qualitative approaches; these relate to learning, transparency, motivation, and managerial issues. In this way, the customer is facilitated to manage the whole supply chain and constantly re-align the suppliers' objectives with its own goals.

The third challenge involves the concept of preferred customer status as a means for creating supply-side induced advantages in highly competitive supplier markets. This stresses the importance of being a preferred customer, particularly in a new product development context. The implication here is that implementing a preferred customer policy in buying firms this may improve the conditions for innovating with suppliers.

The fourth challenge concerns the human side of the supply chain and its role in supply chain risk management. Starting from a behavioral perspective, innovative approaches that include behavioral analysis in supply chain design and management can significantly contribute to supply chain risk reduction by taking into account the individual attitudes and biases of the decision maker.

The last challenge concerns risk management as a strategic approach to improving logistics outsourcing. The implication is that risk management could be an innovative tool facilitating the success of logistics outsourcing by securing future performance and relationships between supply chain partners.

Organization of the Book

The book is organized into four parts and includes 20 chapters. Each part is dedicated to one of the four supply chain innovation areas indicated previously. This section provides a brief description of chapters included in each of the above four areas.

The first part of the book deals with innovation in supply chain integration (SCI) and includes six chapters.

Chapter 1 analyses the concept of SCI on the basis of an extensive literature review. It focuses on identifying the main challenges associated with the implementation of an integrated business paradigm. The chapter focused on the effective management of both internal and external customer/supplier relationships as prerequisite for achieving the benefits connected with supply chain integration.

Chapter 2 discusses the barriers to SCI. The author notes that relevant literature has analyzed the many possible forms of SCI that may take place but that little progress has been achieved in its practical implementation. For these reasons, the chapter is focused on analyzing three obstacles to SCI: terminology/definitions; information systems and technology; and, organization design. These barriers have been identified as the most are critical challenges improve SCI in the next few years.

Chapter 3 deals with strategies for SCI in electronic product supply chains. The chapter investigates the main similarities and differences between the distribution models of digital and physical products. Using a number of case studies, the authors show how the software and hardware supply chain elements may be integrated within the hi-tech supply chain in order to deliver continuously innovative value to customers.

Chapter 4 is focused on challenges connected with supply chain integration in a mature industry. The work examines the level of SCI in the Thai textile and garment industry. The results of the analysis provide a road map for orienting integration processes in the textile and garment supply chains.

Chapter 5 provides an application of the SCI approach in maritime ports. The authors proposed a new theoretical model aimed at identifying the sources of value creation in port environments. The model may be used to support port authorities in defining strategies on the basis of a pro-active role for ports in an SCI context.

Chapter 6 deals with challenges in the implementation process of SCI in a public hospital in Ireland. The author points out that innovative SCI approaches must be incorporated into the implementation process in this complex environment. Using the action research approach, the work identifies critical success factors and inhibitors to success in relation to SCI in this environment.

The second part of the book is focused on ICT innovation in supply chains and comprises five chapters.

Chapter 7 is focused on the adoption of ICT in small transport and logistics service providers. In this context, technology adoption and investments are particularly challenging. Through a case study analysis conducted in the Italian logistics service market, the work analyses the role of ICT in service customization together with inhibitors and enabling factors influencing ICT related innovation.

Chapter 8 examines innovative ICT applications in transport and logistics in Asia. The work provides examples of effectively usage of ICT tools and applications and how these have shaped the innovation landscape of Asian supply chains.

Chapter 9 discusses challenges in using technology to reduce supply chain uncertainty and losses in the supply chains of perishable goods. Using the example of strawberries in Switzerland, the authors investigate how and under what conditions the value of information provided by the RFID technology may provide increasing efficiency in logistics operations and lowers the environmental footprint of supply chains.

Chapter 10 deals with the challenges posed by demand uncertainty and the bullwhip effect in the supply chain and how to mitigate this effect through the use of technology. The authors discuss the use of RFID to minimize the potential impact of the bullwhip effect through information symmetry across the supply chain and increasing visibility of goods and material flows, keeping track of the location and quantity at distribution centers and warehouses. The work proposes a new framework that, combining the strengths of RFID and neural networks, allows for more accurate inventory analysis and demand forecasting in fast moving consumer products' supply chains such as electronics and automobiles.

The third part of the book presents four chapters focused on environmental sustainability innovation in the supply chain.

Chapter 11 addresses the challenge of analyzing the effects of intelligent freight transportation system (IFTS) in the economic, environmental and social areas. Several effects were found that may increased performance of transport operations including automatic item identification, safety and security prevention, real-time navigation, traffic situation notification and carbon footprint registration. The possible solutions relate in most instances to advanced ICT components that allow more sophisticated ways of planning, monitoring and controlling transportation operations.

Chapter 12 reviews recent studies on size and weight of trucks as a way to improve road freight transport efficiency and reduce its environmental impact. The author presents an analytical framework based on two key benefits that may be achieved through consolidating loads in fewer vehicles: reduction in vehicle operating costs; and, reduction in lorry traffic levels which helps to alleviate environmental impacts and congestion.

Chapter 13 discusses the role that urban consolidation centres (UCCs) can play in helping to reduce goods vehicle traffic and its environmental impacts in urban areas. The authors analyze freight transport and the logistics advantages offered by UCCs. They provide empirical evidence based on four case studies of recent UCCs trials in the UK comparing objectives, operational and financial aspects and impacts of these UCCs. Critical success factors are also identified.

Chapter 14 presents some of the innovative approaches that have been taken by businesses involved in reverse logistics for the removal of waste from urban areas. This chapter reviews some of these approaches and suggests which could be used more widely based on their specific limitations.

Chapter 15 is focused on the role of transport and logistics service providers in developing sustainability innovation in a supply chain context. The author reviews options available to transport and logistics service providers wishing to market their green logistics capabilities and discusses the potential for them to assume a pro-active role in promoting a more sustainable supply chain.

The fourth part of the book concerns innovation in supply system management and it includes five chapters.

Chapter 16 deals with discontinuous innovation in supply relationship management focusing on its implementation process. The authors present a literature review on motivation, barriers and enablers connected with the implementation of discontinuous innovation. The literature review has been used to analyze the implementation process of discontinuous innovation in two case examples. The results allow the identification of future research avenues in this field.

Chapter 17 addresses the issue of methodology for supplier evaluation. There is a gap between theory and practice in this field. The chapter attempts to bridge this gap proposing a new methodology based on the Analytical Hierarchical Process (AHP) that has been empirically tested in a number of case studies. The results allow identification of the strengths and weaknesses of surveyed suppliers and demonstrate the potential of the method as a strategic tool for managing the supply chain.

Chapter 18 explores the concept of preferred customer status and how this concept may have a positive impact on the generation of innovation upstream the supply chain. This chapter focuses on the importance of being a preferred customer particularly in a new product development context by empirically testing the impact of preferred customer status on the level of supplier innovation in a buyer-seller relationship. The results indicate that implementing a preferred customer policy in buying firms may contribute to improving the conditions for innovating with suppliers.

Chapter 19 discusses behavioral research relevant to supply chain risk management. The work provides an overview of the extant literature on behavioral issues in SCM and outlines opportunities for future research in this area.

Chapter 20 explores the effect of risk management on logistics outsourcing. The authors propose a model for risk management in logistics outsourcing relationships. The model has been tested using a case study. The findings show that risk management may be an innovative tool in managing supply chain relationships as it has positive impact on the various determinants of outsourcing success.

Section 1
Innovation in Supply Chain Integration

Chapter 1
Supply Chain Integration:
Challenges and Solutions

Edward Sweeney
Dublin Institute of Technology, Ireland

ABSTRACT

Since its introduction by management consultants in the early 1980s, supply chain management (SCM) has been primarily concerned with the integration of processes and activities both within and between organisations. The concept of supply chain integration (SCI) is based on documented evidence that suggests that much of the waste throughout businesses is a consequence of fragmented supply chain configurations. However, there is also evidence to suggest that the achievement of higher levels of intra- and inter-firm integration presents an array of managerial challenges. The need for innovation in all aspects of SCM is widely recognised. Given the pivotal role of the integration paradigm within SCM, any meaningful innovation in this area must focus heavily on this issue. This chapter outlines some of the challenges by exploring the evolving SCM business context. It goes on to relate SCM theory to the widely cited Porter value chain concept. The core of the chapter provides a detailed description of SCI based on a wide variety of literature. It does so with particular reference to the challenges inherent in implementing an integrated business paradigm with a view to identifying a range of possible innovative solutions. The adoption of more integrated supply chain structures raises questions regarding the nature of both internal and external customer/supplier relationships. The effective management of such relationships is, therefore, given particular focus.

DOI: 10.4018/978-1-60960-585-8.ch001

INTRODUCTION

Since its introduction in the early 1980s, supply chain management (SCM) has attracted a lot of attention in both business and academic circles. Recent years have seen a proliferation of literature with its origins in a range of academic disciplines and industry sectors. This has prompted scholars to classify the literature in various ways. For example, Tan (2001) illustrates the evolution of SCM from both a purchasing and supply perspective, as well as a transportation and logistics perspective. However, one theme that is a characteristic of much of the scholarly work in the field is that of integration.

Integration in this context refers to the extent to which various supply chain activities and processes work together in as seamless a manner as possible. It has long been recognised that traditionally managed businesses and supply chains, often characterized by high levels of fragmentation, have failed to achieve their true potential in terms of profitably meeting customer expectations. Supply chain integration (SCI) is, to a great extent, concerned with the development of more integrated approaches that hold out the prospect of eliminating many of the inefficiencies directly attributable to supply chain fragmentation. A plethora of supply chain management (SCM) definitions have been developed in recent years. There is evidence of differences in emphasis and approach between different industrial sectors, geographical areas and functional backgrounds. Furthermore, a variety of associated terminologies have also been developed which has added to the complexity. As noted by Ross (1998), this can limit management's understanding of the SCM concept and the practical effectiveness of its application, particularly in relation to the implementation of more integrated supply chain configurations.

The overall aim of this chapter is to provide the reader with insights into the essence of SCI, with a view to identifying both challenges and possible innovative solutions. Following this introduction, a overview of the evolving SCM business context is set out. This points to some of the challenges that need to be addressed in putting SCI concepts into practice. This theme is developed by relating SCM theory to one widely used approach to the formulation of business strategy—the value chain concept and value chain analysis. The core of the chapter then provides a detailed description of SCI based on a wide variety of literature. It does so with particular reference to the challenges inherent in implementing an integrated business paradigm with a view to identifying a range of possible innovative solutions. The adoption of more integrated supply chain structures raises questions regarding the nature of both internal and external customer/supplier relationships. The effective management of such relationships is, therefore, given particular focus. Based on the foregoing some future research directions are proposed and a number of conclusions drawn.

THE EVOLVING SUPPLY CHAIN MANAGEMENT ENVIRONMENT

The literature suggests that a number of key issues are changing the supply chain management (SCM) and logistics strategic landscape. Arguably, the three most significant such issues are:

1. Internationalisation (or globalisation) of supply chains
2. Vertical disintegration
3. The changing role of the supply chain as a source of strategic leverage

This is in line with much of the published work (Sweeney, 2007). For example, Storey et al. (2006) point out that their work "concurred with the literature in identifying globalisation, outsourcing and fragmentation as three major drivers". Vertical disintegration is largely a consequence of outsourcing and fragmentation in this context refers to strategic leverage, particularly in the context of product strategy. More specifically, fragmentation refers to issues such as proliferation of stock keeping units (SKUs), shortening product life cycles and the requirement for increased customisation. Internationalisation is being driven by changing structures in the international economic and business environment. Vertical disintegration and the changing strategic view of the supply chain are both parts of the strategic response of firms to competitive pressures in the marketplace. The author recognises that these three issues are in many ways interrelated and interdependent: for example, outsourcing of manufacturing to lower labour cost economies is facilitated by economic liberalisation in these countries. Nonetheless, the following sections discuss each of these issues in detail.

Internationalisation

The structure of the international economic and business environment has changed significantly in recent years. The growth of trade blocs throughout the world has resulted in increasing global economic integration. This evolution, largely based on the reduction of barriers to the movement of capital, goods, services, people and information internationally, has facilitated increased international trade and foreign direct investment (FDI). The value of world merchandise trade reached about US$13.6 trillion in 2007. In 1990 it was less than US$2.85 trillion (UNCTAD, 2008). According to the World Trade Organisation (WTO), international trade flows multiplied by a factor of 25 between 1950 and 2003 (WTO, 2004). Annual foreign direct investment (FDI) expanded over 19-fold between 1973 and 2004, that is from US$21.5 billion to over US$410 billion (UNCTAD 2004). These trends have resulted in the increasing internationalisation of supply chains. This can be related to the 'buy–make–move–sell' model of product supply chains (New 1997; NITL 2000).

Buy

Global sourcing of raw materials and other inputs has now become a reality for many organisations as the structure of the international economic and business environment has evolved (Fagan, 1991; Trent and Monczka, 2003). The WTO provides an interesting example in its 1998 annual report (WTO, 1998). In the production of an 'American' car, 30 per cent of the car's value originates in Korea, 17.5 per cent in Japan, 7.5 per cent in Germany, 4 per cent in Taiwan and Singapore, 2.5 per cent in the United Kingdom and 1.5 per cent in Ireland and Barbados. That is, "… only 37 per cent of the production value … is generated in the United States". This phenomenon is large enough to be noticed in aggregate statistics. Feenstra and Hanson (1996) used US input–output tables to infer US imports of intermediate inputs. They found that the share of imported intermediates increased from 5.3 per cent of total US intermediate purchases in 1972 to 11.6 per cent in 1990. Campa and Goldberg (1997) found similar evidence for Canada and the UK.

Make

Access to lower cost manufacturing worldwide is now possible. For example, the expansion of China in recent years, based to a large extent on outsourcing (or 'offshoring') of labour-intensive manufacturing by companies from developed countries, is indicative of this. No other country has attracted as much FDI as China. In 2004, approximately US$60 billion of FDI was absorbed; between 1979 and 2004, the total was approximately US$560 billion (UNCTAD 2004). As a result China is growing rapidly and attaining pre-eminence in global manufacturing in certain sectors. For example, by early in the last decade the country already produced 50 per cent of the world's cameras, 30 per cent of air conditioners and televisions, 25 per cent of washing machines and

20 per cent of refrigerators (Pinto, 2005). Similar trends have occurred in central and eastern Europe as the European Union (EU) expanded eastwards.

Move

The above has implications for the logistics and distribution strategies of companies (Waters, 2004). Increased trade volumes globally have created the need for new logistics pipelines. The growth in the international 3PL sector is a reflection of this. The large number of mergers and acquisitions in the sector has been driven significantly by the desire of companies to have a stronger global presence (Eyefortansport 2001). With specific reference to the European freight industry, Peters (2000) notes that growth in the 1990s has offered a lesson that "the country-by-country model for logistics is no longer valid; companies have begun to reorganize themselves into continental operations based on integration and rationalisation".

Sell

Furthermore, as markets have opened up internationally for a range of products and services, international (and in some cases global) selling has become the reality. The cases of China and India are worthy of particular comment. As pointed out in a survey in *The Economist* (2005), the two countries are home to nearly two-fifths of the world's population and are two of the world's fastest-growing economies. A recent report by America's National Intelligence Council (2004) likened their emergence in the early 21st century to the rise of Germany in the 19th and America in the 20th century, with impacts potentially as dramatic. The liberalisation of markets has sharpened the focus on the need for more robust approaches to international marketing strategy (Bradley, 2004; Cateora and Graham, 2004). For example, the term 'glocalisation' (from 'global' and 'localisation') has been used to refer to the creation of the local (country or regional) market presence of a global enterprise (Fan and Huang, 2002).

In short, as economic and business globalisation has happened, supply chain architectures have become more global. The resulting challenges in terms of SCM and SCI have been the subject of significant research, debate and discussion (e.g., Arntzen et al., 1995; Gourdin, 2000; Simchi-Levi et al., 2002; Bolstorff and Rosenbaum, 2003; Ayers, 2003).

Vertical Disintegration

Companies are increasingly focusing on what they regard as their core activities or competencies. Oates (1998) defines core competencies as the central things that organisations do well. The corollary of this is that activities regarded as 'non-core' are often being outsourced. Greaver (1999) states that "non-core competencies take up time, energy and workspace, and help management lose sight of what is important in an organisation". Furthermore, the trend towards economic and business globalisation has facilitated the outsourcing of various activities to overseas locations (offshoring – see above). Key supply chain activities are increasingly being outsourced to third-party organisations. This can again be related to the 'buy–make–move–sell' model of product supply chains.

Buy

Purchasing and procurement activities have generally not been outsourced in the traditional sense but the development of purchasing consortia has meant some sharing of responsibility for this activity between companies. Hendrick (1997) defines a purchasing consortium as:

A formal or informal arrangement, where two or more organisations, who are separate legal entities, collaborate among themselves, or through a third party, to combine their individual needs for products from suppliers and to gain the increased pricing, quality and service advantages associated with volume buying.

Essig (1999) notes that a purchasing consortium is often just one element of an overall supply strategy.

Make

The classic 'make versus buy' decision has been a central theme in the field of manufacturing strategy for decades (e.g. Hayes and Wheelwright, 1984). The traditional focus was largely on the financial and economic analysis of in-house versus outsourced options for particular processes within a manufacturing operation. Manufacturing outsourcing decision-making processes now tend to take a broader and more strategic view (e.g. Hill, 1999). Many large manufacturers have outsourced significant parts of their production activity to third parties (e.g. Edwards and Edwards, 2000; Hassey and Lai, 2003). For example, in the electronics sector, the trend is one of original equipment manufacturers (OEMs) outsourcing significant amounts of manufacturing to contract manufacturing companies. Companies in the electronic manufacturing services (EMS) sector, such as Flextronics, Foxconn and Celestica, have grown rapidly as a result.

Move

Transport and a range of other logistics activities are increasingly being outsourced by manufacturers and retailers (Scott and Westbrook, 1991; McKinnon, 1999). The 3PL sector has developed rapidly as it has responded to its customers' requirements for the supply of tailor-made services (Razzaque and Sheng, 1998; Skjoett-Larsen, 2000). The European Union PROTRANS project (PROTRANS, 2003) developed a definition of 3PL based on a wide number of definitions which have appeared in the literature:

Third-party logistics are activities carried out by an external company on behalf of a shipper and consisting of at least the provision of management of multiple logistics services. These activities are offered in an integrated way, not on a stand-alone basis. The co-operation between the shipper and the external company is an intended continuous relationship.

This definition reflects the manner in which shippers' requirements have evolved in recent years. The emphasis now is on the provision of integrated multiple services and the development of relationships.

Sell

Selling as a process has generally not been outsourced in the traditional sense. Nonetheless, many of the individual activities which comprise sales channels may be owned by other companies. The actual selling of products to consumers may be carried out by retailers, who may in turn obtain the products from wholesalers; third-party owned and managed call centres may be an integral part of the selling process; third-party agents, franchisees or distributors may also have some responsibility (e.g. Friedman and Furey, 1999).

The above has resulted in a shift away from the traditional model of 'control through ownership' towards models which are based on management and control through effective supply chain relationship management. The former is based on the strategic logic of vertical integration. Vertical integration is the degree to which a firm owns its upstream suppliers and its downstream buyers (Greaver, 1999). Harrigan (1999) provides a good description of the logic underpinning this approach to strategic development. The latter, effectively a process of vertical disintegration, has taken place as a result of the trends outlined above (Mpoyi, 1999; Langlois, 2001). Recent developments in information and communications technology (ICT), in particular Internet technologies, have facilitated this process and laid the foundations for the 'network economy model' (Reddy and Reddy, 2001). According to Hugos (2002) traditional supply chain models have "given way to virtual integration of companies". In short, as outsourcing of various elements of supply chain functionality takes place, supply chain architectures are becoming more virtual. The traditional *fully vertically integrated* approaches are being replaced by contemporary *fully virtually integrated* approaches - a new FVI is evolving.

Strategic Leverage

Classically in the field of strategic management, the generic approaches of cost leadership, differentiation, and focus have been identified (Porter, 1985). Porter's classic text described these alternatives, as follows:

- A cost leadership strategy requires a company to be a low cost supplier, and to sell either at below average industry prices to gain market share, or at industry average prices to earn a profit higher than that of rivals.
- A differentiation strategy requires a product or services that offers unique attributes that are valued by customers, thereby allow premium pricing.
- A focus strategy concentrates on a narrow segment and within that segment attempts to achieve advantage through either cost leadership or differentiation.

A significant proportion of the overall cost base of companies is in the supply chain. In the automotive industry, for example, A.T. Kearney (1999) report that typically component (30 per cent), manufacturing and assembly (28 per cent) and distribution (four per cent) costs together represent 62 per cent of sales price. Hence, any worthwhile cost leadership approach needs to focus on the optimisation of total supply chain costs and the elimination of non-value-adding activities (NVAs). The author's definition of an NVA - based on Jones et al. (1997), Goldrat and Cox (1992), Womack and Jones (2003) and others is: *any activity (or resource or asset) that adds cost (or time) to any supply chain process without adding value from a customer perspective*. Much of this lean thinking has its origins in the Japanese automotive industry, in particular in the Toyota Production System (TPS) and the just in time (JIT) paradigm (Ohno, 1988; Womack and Jones, 2003). The main objective of this thinking was the elimination of waste (or 'muda' in Japanese).

Customer service is becoming a key source of differentiation or an order winning criterion in many sectors (Christopher, 2005). An order winning criterion (or 'order winner') is a feature of the product or service offering which differentiates it from the competition and is, therefore, likely to be a source of increased market share; an order qualifier, on the other hand, is a feature which must exist to ensure that a product or service gets into the market in the first instance and stays there (Hill, 1999). The latter tend to have order losing rather than order winning characteristics. In many sectors the importance of customer service relative to product quality (now largely an order qualifier) and price (largely determined by the dynamics of supply and demand in the market and subject to downward pressure in many sectors) has increased (Sweeney, 2004). Customer service is delivered by the supply chain. In this way, the supply chain itself has become a key factor in the development of a differentiation strategy.

As pointed out earlier, a focus strategy concentrates on a narrow segment and within that segment attempts to achieve advantage through either cost leadership or differentiation. The points made above in relation to the role of SCM in strategy formulation and implementation are, therefore, equally relevant in the context of a focus approach.

In short, a company pursuing a cost leadership, a differentiation or a focus strategy can leverage the supply chain as a fundamental element of its effort to improve competitive performance. The role of SCM in strategy formulation and implementation is given extensive treatment in the literature (e.g. van Hoek and Harrison, 2004; Simchi-Levi and Kaminsky, 2003; Cohen and Roussel, 2004). Two approaches are worthy of particular mention.

Firstly, Christopher and Ryals (1999) argue that SCM has a central position in the creation of shareholder value. In this context, shareholder value is defined as the financial value created for shareholders in the companies in which they invest. The four basic drivers of enhanced shareholder value (i.e. revenue growth, operating cost reduction, fixed and working capital efficiency) are "directly and indirectly affected by logistics management and supply chain strategy". The framework of value-based management (VBM) plays a potentially important role in achieving these improvements in practice. The paper concludes by noting that: "By seeking out opportunities for partnership in the supply chain combined with an emphasis on the reduction of non-value-adding time, the evidence suggests, enduring improvement in shareholder value can be achieved" (Christopher and Ryals, 1999). The emphasis on time compression is important as it has the potential to reduce cost and improve customer service.

Secondly, a graphical representation of Gattorna's 'Strategic Alignment Model' is shown in Figure 1 (Gattorna et al., 2003). He argues that empirical evidence is mounting to suggest that if organisations are to achieve sustained high levels of financial and operating performance, the four elements shown in the diagram must be dynamically aligned.

Alignment in this context means:

- An understanding of customers' buying behaviour;
- Corresponding value propositions to align with the dominant buying behaviours;
- The appropriate capabilities (or cultural capability) embedded in the organisation to underpin the delivery of these specific value propositions; and,

Figure 1. The strategic alignment model

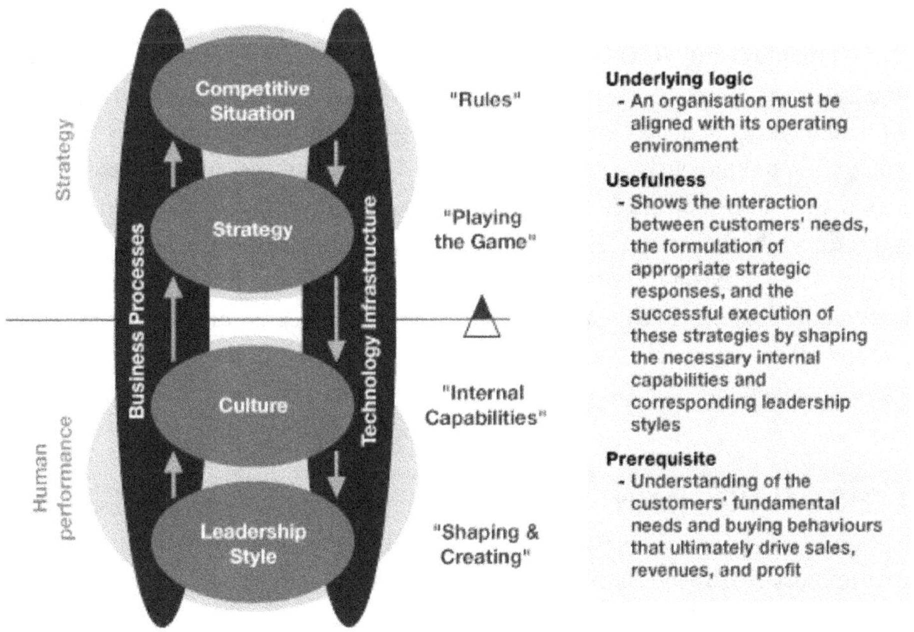

- A composite leadership style at the executive level to ensure the appropriate subcultures are in place as required.

Organisations seeking superior performance must be both very aware of their customers' expectations and of their own internal capability. If these two dimensions are addressed adequately, then an organisation is fully aligned with its marketplace. This is in line with classical approaches to strategy formulation – for example, Porter (1985) points out that the essence of formulating a competitive strategy is relating the company to its environment – but with a strong focus on the role of SCM in ensuring that strategic plans are realised in practice.

Key Challenges from the Evolving Environment

Economic and business globalisation is happening. Companies are increasingly focussing on their core competencies and as a result, vertical disintegration is happening. Finally, more and more companies are coming to regard the supply chain as a source of strategic leverage. In short, supply chains have become more global and more virtual (and, therefore, their management has become more complex) and SCM – with the concept of integration at its core - is becoming a more integral and integrated part of overall corporate strategy. Simultaneously, customers have become more discerning and are demanding better quality products, higher levels of service and reduced prices. This increasingly competitive business environment has sharpened the focus on the need for more robust approaches to supply chain design and management.

SCM AND THE VALUE CHAIN

One well-known approach to strategic thinking and strategy formulation, based on the concept of the value chain, was introduced a quarter of a century ago by Michael Porter (Porter, 1985). The idea of the value chain is based on the process view of organisations, the idea of seeing a manufacturing (or service) organisation as a system, made up of subsystems each with inputs, transformation processes and outputs. Inputs, transformation processes and outputs involve the acquisition and consumption of resources, such as money, labour, materials, equipment, buildings, land, administration and management. How value chain activities are carried out determines costs and affects profits.

Most organisations engage in hundreds, even thousands, of activities in the process of converting inputs to outputs. These activities can be classified generally as either primary or support activities that all businesses must undertake in some form. According to Porter (1985), the *primary* activities are:

1. **Inbound Logistics**, which involve relationships with suppliers and include all the activities required to receive, store and disseminate inputs.
2. **Operations** are all the activities required to transform inputs into outputs (products and services).
3. **Outbound Logistics**, which involve relationships with customers and include all the activities required to collect, store and distribute the output.
4. **Marketing and Sales** are activities that inform buyers about products and services, induce buyers to purchase them and facilitate their purchase.
5. **Service** includes all the activities required to keep the product or service working effectively for the buyer after it is sold and delivered.

The *support* activities are procurement, human resource management (HRM), technological development and infrastructure. A graphical representation of Porter's value chain is shown in Figure 2.

Jacobs (2003) notes that:

The value chain disaggregates a firm into its stratgeically relevant activities in order to understand the behaviour of costs and the existing and potential sources of differentiation. A firm gains competitive advantage by performing these strategically important activities more cheaply or better than its competitors.

One implication of Porter's thesis is that firms need to examine each activity in their value chains to determine whether or not they have a real competitive advantage in the activity. One consequence of this is that activities which are not a source of real competitive advantage are often being outsourced (see above) thus creating more vitual supply chain architectures.

The relationship between this chain and SCM has been the subject of discussion in several papers (e.g. Barney, 1997; Lazzarini et al., 2001). As noted earlier, supply chains are sets of activities representing successive stages of value creation. The literature on SCM suggests that vertical interdependencies require a systemic approach to the management of material and information flows between firms engaged in the chain. On the other hand, Porter's original value chain analysis was primarily an approach that described a set of sequential activities creating value *within* firms. However, outsourcing of supply chain functionality and the resulting creation of more virtual configurations has had the effect of extending the value chain beyond the boundaries of individual firms. As noted by Christopher (2005, p. 14), 'the supply chain becomes the value chain'. In other words, the distinction often traditionally espoused between the *value chain* and the *supply chain* has become inconsequential. As succinctly suggested by Christopher (2004): "Now the focus has widened as the move to outsourcing non-core activities in the value chain accelarates. Thus, we are seeing, in effect, the supply chain become the value chain."

THE ROLE OF INTEGRATION IN SCM

It is evident that the concept of integration lies at the heart of SCM philosophy (see, e.g. Christopher, 1992; New, 1996; Lambert, 2004). Cooper et al. (1997) specifically describe SCM as "an integrative philosophy". Storey et al. (2006) in their discussion of the interlocking ideas and propositions

Figure 2. Porter's value chain

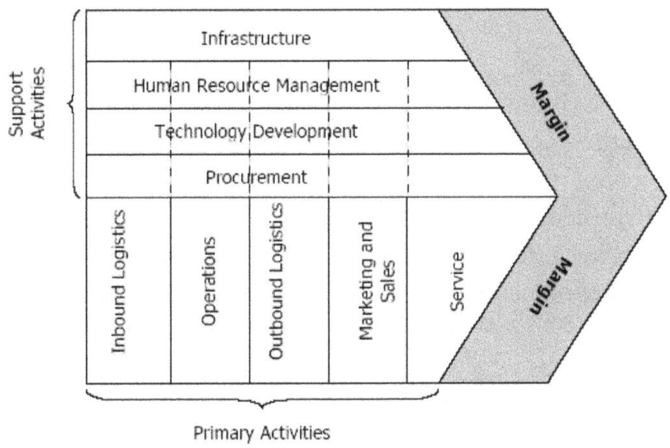

of SCM declare that, "the central underpinning ideas relate to alignment and integration" (p. 758). Perhaps most tellingly, Pagell (2004) declares that "in its essence the entire concept of SCM is really predicated on integration" (p. 460). If, as Mentzer et al. (2001) suggested, SCM can be regarded as a management philosophy then this philosophy is concerned first and foremost with integration. The widely cited work of Bowersox and his collaborators at Michigan State University (see, for example, Bowersox et al., 1999), which describes a framework of six competencies (the *Supply Chain 2000Framework*) that lead to world class performance in logistics and SCM, supports this view. The six competencies, grouped into three areas (operational, planning and relational) are all concerned with integration.

The work of Fawcett and Magnan (2002) identified four levels of integration in practice:

1. Internal cross-functional integration.
2. Backward integration with valued first-tier suppliers.
3. Forward integration with valued first-tier customers.
4. Complete backward and forward integration ('from the supplier's supplier to the customer's customer').

Furthermore, and as noted earlier, Harland et al. (1999) classifies research in this area according to the level of integration between supply chain activities. The four levels are:

1. Internal level, which considers only on those activities which are entirely internal to the focal company.
2. Dyadic level, which considers single two-party relationships (between, for example, supplier and manufacturer or manufacturer and distributor/retailer).
3. Chain level, which encompasses a set of dyadic relationships including a supplier, a supplier's supplier, a customer and a customer's customer.
4. Network level, which concerns a wider network of operations.

In each of these cases, the first level relates to integration of activities and processes which are carried out within a single organisation (i.e. *internal* or *micro-* or *intra-firm* supply chain integration). The others describe varying degrees of integration of activities which span the boundaries of organisations (i.e. *external* or *macro-* or *inter-firm* supply chain integration), with the last one of Fawcett and Magnan (2002) often being viewed as the theoretical ideal. The following sections discuss internal and external integration in more detail.

Internal Chain Integration

The phrase 'internal supply chain' has appeared in the literature (Huin et al. 2002) to describe work aimed at breaking down the barriers between functions within organisations. To establish a framework for describing the key functions of a typical internal supply chain, New's comment (1997) that SCM "revolves around the buying, making, moving and selling of 'stuff' " is quite instructive. It is in line with the 'buy–make–move–sell' model of product supply chains (NITL 2000) introduced earlier. For the purposes of this section the author has added a fifth element, namely the 'store' activity. This has been done to ensure that all activities associated with the design and management of warehouses and other storage locations is given due recognition in the framework. Warehouse management has long been regarded as an integral element of the logistics activity of firms (see below) and a significant amount of specialist knowledge and expertise in this area has been developed over the years. Essentially, 'move' has been disaggregated into separate 'move' and 'store' elements, reflecting the specific characteristics of each of these activities.

Most businesses – certainly manufacturing-based business – can be described in terms of the five functions: buy, make, store, move and sell. This is what is referred to as the internal (or micro- or intra-firm) supply chain as shown in Figure 3.

Traditionally these functions have often been measured, and therefore managed, in isolation, often working at cross purposes. As succinctly noted by Storey et al. (2006) this traditional approach is analogous to a relay race with responsibility being passed from one function to another. SCM means thinking beyond the established boundaries, strengthening the linkages between the functions, and finding ways for them to pull together. A recognition that the 'whole is greater than the sum of the parts' calls for more effective integration between purchasing and procurement (buy), production planning and control (make), warehouse management (store), transport management (move) and customer relationship management (sell), as illustrated in Figure 4.

This shift, away from a functional orientation towards a more company-wide focus, is in line with the early stages of the various models of SCM historical evolution. It is also analogous to the supply chain orientation (SCO) approach of Mentzer et al. (2001) in the sense that SCO at firm level, as manifested in high levels of internal integration, could be regarded as a prerequisite for SCM, as manifested in high levels of external integration. Nonetheless, the desirability of achieving seamless integration is not something which is unique to SCM. As noted earlier, organisations have long realised the need for company-wide approaches to organisational design and redesign. The development of systems engineering approaches to manufacturing system redesign in the 1970s and 1980s (see, e.g. Hitomi, 1996) was followed by the focus on organisational re-engineering, often based on business processes, in the 1980s and 1990s (Hammer and Champy, 1993). A common feature of these approaches was recognition that 'the whole is greater than the sum of the parts'. In other words, optimising subsystems (whether those subsystems are functional departments, production sites or individual processes in the manufacturing cycle) can result in a sub-optimised total system. Lack of efficiency and/or effectiveness is often a result of the poorly designed interfaces between subsystems rather than any inherent subsystem weaknesses. There are numerous examples of companies which have generated significant improvements in competitive advantage as a result of the application of this 'total systems' thinking (see, e.g. Checkland and Scholes, 1999; Sweeney, 1999).

External Chain Integration

Every product or service is delivered to the final consumer (the only source of 'real' money in the chain) through a series of often complex movements between companies which comprise the complete chain. An inefficiency anywhere in the chain will result in the chain as a whole failing to achieve its true competitive potential. In other

Figure 3. The internal supply chain

Figure 4. Integrating the internal supply chain

words, supply chains are increasingly competing with other supply chains rather than, in the more traditional axiom, companies simply competing with other companies. The phrase 'supply chain' is used to indicate that the chain is only as strong as its weakest link. Lambert et al. (1998) suggested that "much friction, and thus waste of valuable resources results when supply chains are not integrated, appropriately streamlined and managed". (p. 14). This concept of inter-company 'friction' is useful in conceptualising the need to replace fragmentation with integration.

The simplistic representation in Figure 5 of the external (or macro- or inter-firm) supply chain shows materials flowing from the raw material source through the various stages in the chain to the final consumer. Money (i.e. funds) then flows back down the chain. The point is that every link matters and that value is added, and profit generated, at each link along the way.

This aspect is central to most widely cited definitions of SCM. As Houlihan (1988) notes, "the supply chain is viewed as a single process". In other words, the various links in the chain need to function in as seamless a manner as possible. Monczka et al. (1998) refer to the use of "a total systems perspective across multiple functions and multiple tiers of suppliers". The reference to 'multiple functions' alludes to internal integration;

Figure 5. The external supply chain

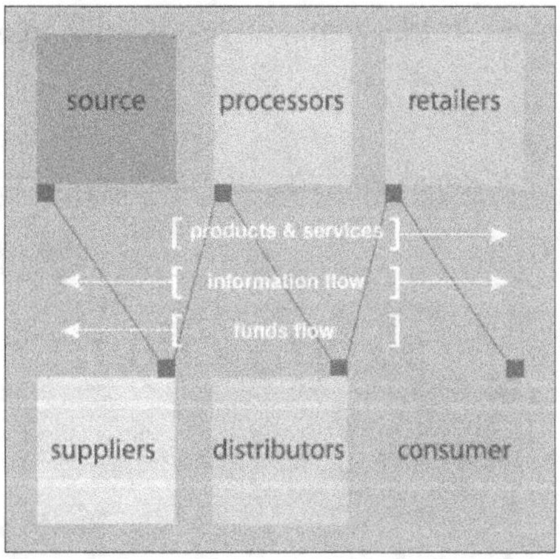

extending this to 'multiple tiers of suppliers' introduces the external integration concept, albeit in the rather limited sense of backward integration with suppliers. As noted earlier, the theoretical ideal is complete backward and forward integration ('from the supplier's supplier to the customer's customer').

It is important to note that the representation in Figure 5 corresponds to the 'chain level' in the classification of Harland (1996). In reality most 'chains' are more like the 'network level' with multiple suppliers and customers across the various tiers in the 'chain'. Lambert et al. (1998) made reference to:

- **Horizontal structure:** this refers to the number of tiers across the supply chain
- **Vertical structure:** this refers to the number of suppliers/customers represented within each tier
- **Horizontal position:** this refers to where the focal company is positioned within the chain (e.g. close to the initial source of supply or nearer to the ultimate customer)

Thus, most 'supply chains' are in reality three dimensional networks of organisations. In view of this, Lambert and Cooper (2000) suggest that "the ultimate success of the single business will depend on management's ability to integrate the company's intricate network of business relationships" (p. 65).

It was noted earlier that 'complete backward and forward integration' as postulated by Fawcett and Magnan (2002) might be viewed as the theoretical ideal. However, in reality various degrees of integration between upstream and downstream organisations will exist. In this context, Frohlich and Westbrook (2001) proposed the concepts of 'arcs of integration' with the direction of the arc referring to the direction of integration (i.e. upstream or downstream) while the degree of the arc indicates the level or extent of integration (from 'no integration' to 'extensive integration').

Similarly, Bask and Juga (2001) proposed the concept of 'semi-integrated' supply chains. They suggest that "a fully integrated supply chain sounds impressive but says little" (p. 150). By way of illustration they note that:

The relationships between organisations are subtle and complex and no one recipe exists on how the supply chains achieve best performance. For some companies, tight integration is the answer under regimes like efficient consumer response, quick response, etc. For others, intensive integration may be the goal in selected areas of SCM, while in other areas it can be beneficial to strive for limited integration. Simultaneous properties of tight and loose control are needed as is suggested in the notion of semi-integrated supply chains. (p. 149)

The work of Fabbe-Costes and Jahre (2007) is in line with this concept. They identify a "differentiated" approach to supply chain integration which "can help companies to identify and then to focus on a limited number of integration factors" (p. 847).

Performance Measurement

It was noted earlier that traditionally supply chain activities have often been measured, and therefore managed, in isolation. The contention implicit in this statement is that fragmented approaches to measurement result in fragmented approaches to management. This is line with the "what gets measured gets done" axiom. In relation to internal integration, Ellinger (2002) reinforces this point by contending that:

If functions are very interdependent in their work, it is counterproductive to base evaluation and reward systems on individual performance. The nature of such work demands compatible systems such as team-based pay and compensation, performance appraisal and accountability at the team level, and recognition for team results. (p. 87)

One of the case companies studied by Storey et al. (2006) provides a good illustration of this point in relation to external integration. The company in question had measures in place that showed that they consistently achieved their three-day delivery target. However, the large majority of orders were delivered after the date the customer had originally requested, and on average they were 16 days late. The problem was that only that part of the supply chain over which they had control was being measured. As Brewer and Speh (2000) noted, performance metrics 'are not always focused on measuring, motivating, and optimising inter-firm and intra-firm performance' (p. 82). Gunasekaran et al. (2004) capture the challenge very effectively by noting that:

Many companies have not succeeded in maximizing their supply chain's potential because they have often failed to develop the performance measures and metrics needed to fully integrate their supply chain to maximize effectiveness and efficiency. (p. 335)

Buisness performance measurement generally, and supply chain performance measurement specifically, are subjects which have been the subject of extensive discussion in the literature for many years. The amount of work in the area of supply chain performance measurement specifically is illustrated by Fabbe-Costes and Jahre (2007) who note that a search in EBSCO-Business Source Complete identified over 700 peer-reviewed articles with a combination of 'performance' and 'supply chain management' in the title, abstract and/or keywords. An examination of the historical development of this domain over time suggets that the general trend has involved a shift away from the use of purely financial metrics with the importance of the supply network emerging in the final and current phase. This recognises that customer satisfaction can only come from the supply chain functioning effectively in totality (both processes and process interfaces).

Several authors have pointed out some of the challenges associated with effective supply chain performance measurement and some of the weaknesses inherent in current approaches. Chow et al. (1994) discuss how logistics performance has been and could be conceptualised. Van Hoek (1998) suggested that vertical disintegration has resulted in a new scenario as much of a firm's competitive capability is no longer under its direct operational control. Beamon (1999) notes that "current supply chain performance measurement systems are inadequate because they rely heavily on the use of cost as a primary (if not sole) measure" (p. 280). Gunasekaran et al. (2001) note the lack of a "balanced approach" and the lack of a "clear distinction between metrics at strategic, tactical and operational levels" (p.72). Lambert and Pohlen (2001) suggest that "in most companies, the metrics that management refer to as supply chain metrics are primarily internally focused logistics measures' and that 'these metrics do not capture how the overall supply chain has performed" (p. 1).

In 1994, Caplice and Sheffi (1994) presented a taxonomy of logistics performance metrics, organized by process rather than by function, with the metrics evaluated using established criteria. Since then, a number of frameworks have been proposed which aim to address fragmentation in supply chain performance measurement, as well as some of the other weaknesses noted above. Three such approaches provide some useful foundations for effective measurement in a SCM context.

Balanced Scorecard

Brewer and Speh (2000) demonstrated how the balanced scorecard framework developed originally by Kaplan and Norton (1996) could be adopted in a SCM context. The balanced scorecard is an attempt to balance the inclination to overemphasise purely cost and other financial metrics with measures related to other drivers of long-term profitability. It does this by using customer satisfaction, innovation and learning and business process metrics, along with purely financial metrics. Brewer and Speh (2000) propose that the supply chain perspective can be embedded within the internal business process dimension of the scorecard through the use of both 'integrated' and 'non-integrated' measures. They cite cash-to-cash cycle time as an example of the former in that it embraces several functions across several organisations. The latter, in contrast, provide diagnostics on where problems are occuring within individual functions and firms.

Lambert and Pohlen Framework

Lambert and Pohlen (2001) proposed a framework that aligns performance at each dyadic link (i.e. supplier-customer pair) within the supply chain. The framework begins with the linkages at the focal company and moves outward a link at a time. The link-by-link approach provides a means for aligning performance downstream and upstream "with the overall objective of maximizing shareholder value for the total supply chain as well as for each company" (p. 8). The framework comprises seven steps:

1. Map the supply chain from point-of-origin to point-of-consumption to identify where key linkages exist.
2. Use the customer relationship management (CRM) and supplier relationship management (SRM) processes to analyse each link (customer-supplier pair) and determine where additional value can be created for the supply chain.
3. Develop customer and supplier profit and loss (P&L) statements to assess the effect of the relationship on profitability and shareholder value of the two firms.
4. Realign supply chain processes and activities to achieve performance objectives.
5. Establish non-financial performance measures that align individual behaviour with

supply chain process objectives and financial goals.

6. Compare shareholder value and market capitalisation across firms with supply chain objectives and revise process and performance measures as necessary.
7. Replicate steps at each link in the supply chain.
8. This framework represents a methodology for overall supply chain improvement with a novel approach to performance measurement at its core.

Gunasekaran et al Framework

Gunasekaran et al (2004) proposed a measurement framework by considering strategic, tactical and operational measures for the four supply chain activities/processes of plan, source, make/assemble and deliver. The authors suggest that this framework provides "a starting point for an assessment of the need for supply chain performance measurement" (p. 344). In other words, the framework does not provide a usable tool but rather provides a foundation which can be developed and built upon.In this context, Beamon (1999) presented four characteristics of effective performance measurement systems, which should be: inclusive (i.e. measure all pertinent aspects); universal (i.e. allow for comparison under various operating conditions); measurable (i.e. data is available); and, consistent (i.e. measures used should reflect organisational goals).

Integrating The Supply Chain: Challenges And Solutions

Virtually all contemporary definitions of SCM place a strong emphasis on the need for a shift from traditional supply chain architectures, which were often characterised by fragmentation, to more effective configurations, which need to replace fragmentation with integration. This is true both in relation to internal and external chains. The achievement of high levels of integration has implications for the design of organisational structures and supply chain architectures. Kemppainen and Vepsalainen (2003) suggest that in the future this is "expected to result in a new structure of demand-supply networks, in this paper called the encapsulated network, with shared technology and systems, extended decision rights and non-territorial services" (p. 716). While 'leading edge' companies may well have adopted this philosophy to varying degrees, there is a need to understand its role and impact in the wider business community. For example, the recent work of Fabbe-Costes and Jahre (2008) concludes that:

In going behind the rhetoric of "integration is always best", we have shown that "evidence" cannot be taken for granted and that much more research is needed in particular with regard to the impact of extended inter-organisational SCI on supply chain performance. (p. 145)

Finally, moving from fragmented to more integrated approaches inevitably requires changes to the ways in which both internal and external customer and supplier relationships are created and managed.

SUPPLY CHAIN RELATIONSHIP MANAGEMENT

The need to replace fragmentation with integration and the holistic approach to flow management requires a re-appraisal of the way in which both internal and external customer/supplier relationships are created and managed. As noted by Sweeney (2005): "SCM is not a 'zero-sum' game based on adversarial relationships. Rather, it needs to be a 'win–win' game based on partnership approaches". This point is relevant to the interactions between the key *internal* supply chain functions of buy, make, store, move and sell, as well as to relationships between an organisation and its external customers and suppliers. Several of the SCM definitions in the literature highlight the importance of relationship management. For example, Monczka et al. (1998) refer to the requirement for "joint relationships with suppliers across multiple tiers". La Londe and Masters (1994) suggest that supply chain strategy includes, "… two or more firms in a supply chain entering into a long-term agreement; … the development of trust and commitment to the relationship; … the integration of logistics activities involving the sharing of demand and sales data". The CSCMP definition of SCM (CSCMP 2009) specifically embraces the concept of "co-ordination and collaboration with channel partners". Lambert et al. (1998) go even further by suggesting that: "Increasingly the management of relationships across the supply chain is being referred to as supply chain management (SCM)".

Types of Relationships

Lamming (1993) highlights the need to move from 'zero-sum' to 'win–win' games; from competitive to collaborative approaches; and, from adversarial to partnership relationships (and beyond - as suggested in the title of his book *Beyond Partnership: Strategies for Innovation and Lean Supply*). As noted above, various degrees of integration between upstream and downstream organisations exist depending upon a range of factors. It is not surprising, therefore, that in reality many different possible relationship types exist. Quinn and Hilmer (1994) categorised relationships based on the trade-off between the need for flexibility and the need for control, as shown in Figure 6. Choosing the appropriate relationship model is a key issue in any given situation.

Croom et al. (2000) identify ten variables which influence the nature of relationships between actors in a network. These include the attitude and commitment to collaborative improvement programmes, legal issues and the degree of power and influence of each party. It is widely recognised that, as noted by Lambert and Cooper (2000), "the closeness of the relationship at different points in the supply chain will differ" (p. 69). In other words, it is not a case of 'one size fits all'. A key management decision involves determination of the appropriate relationship that best suits a particular set of circumstances.

The Impact of Vertical Disintegration

As noted earlier, companies are increasingly focusing on what they regard as their core activities or competencies. The corollary of this is that activities regarded as 'non-core' are being outsourced. Key supply chain activities such as transportation, warehousing and manufacturing are increasingly being outsourced to third-party organisations. This has resulted in a shift away

Figure 6. Categories of customer/supplier relationship

from the traditional model of 'control through ownership' towards models which are based on management and control through effective supply chain relationship management (Christopher, 2005). In short, as this process of vertical disintegration has taken place, supply chain architectures have become more virtual. As noted earlier, the traditional *fully vertically integrated* approaches are being replaced by contemporary *fully virtually integrated* approaches. This has sharpened the focus on the need for the creation of appropriate relationship forms throughout the supply chain, as well as on their effective management.

Strategic Partnering

Much of the literature presents the partnership approach as an ideal. For example, Harland et al. (1999) argue that: "The search for closer co-operation and integration is evident not only with customers; suppliers are increasingly being viewed as partners, becoming more deeply involved in co-operative problem solving". In a truly strategic partnership approach a number of features should be evident (Rothery and Robertson 1995), as follows:

- Senior management from both firms meet regularly.
- Payments relate to specified business outcomes or pre-agreed levels of performance rather than fixed work volumes.
- Outsourcing contracts usually last for five years or longer.
- Disclosure takes place of costs and margins between both the parties.
- Each in involved in the other partner's strategic planning.
- Partner is not chosen on the basis of a competitive tendering process.
- Each partner searches for ways to reduce total costs of the partnership.
- Each partner must genuinely add value.

However, as noted by Stone (2002): "In reality, few partnerships are arrangements between equal parties". Fernie (1998) goes further by noting that, "there is an impression that companies enter some form of partnership but in many cases lip service is being paid to the idea". Lamming (1993) also referred to the 'lip service' trap in relation to customer/supplier partnerships by noting that, if companies talk about it for long enough, they begin to believe they are doing it.

The People Dimension

It is important to note that relationships are in essence about people. For example, Grieco (1989) recognised that effective SCM "rests on the twin pillars of trust and communication". Ellinger (2000) indentifies the role of "predominantly informal processes based on trust, mutual respect and information sharing, the joint ownership of decisions, and collective responsibility for outcomes" (p. 86). Lambert et al. (1998) proposed that the fundamental management components of SCM can be classified into 'physical & technical management components' and 'managerial and behavioral management components'; the former might be characterised as the 'hard wiring' of the supply chain while the latter relate to the 'soft-wiring'. The latter components are all concerned with the people dimension of SCM and the model indicates their important role in the overall SCM paradigm and to SCI particularly.

Another important aspect of the people dimension relates the the role of management in supply chains. As noted by Lee (2004) in the *Harvard Business Review*, "there are no technologies that can do those things; only managers can make them happen" (p. 11). Mangan and Christopher (2005) suggest that contemporary SCM requires managers with a 'T-shaped' profile. This recognises the need for in-depth expertise in one discipline combined with sufficient breadth of understanding to facilitate interactions with others. In line with this and with specific reference to future skill requirements for supply managers, Giunipero et al (2006) suggest that communication skills, as well as technical and financial skills, will be important.

A number of authors have proposed the concept of supply chain learning (Bessant at al, 2003, Sweeney et al, 2005). This involves leveraging the supply chain as a mechanism for inter-firm competency development. Bessant et al (2003) outline several possible benefits of this type of approach but recognise that inter-firm learning is not necessarily a natural feature of business networks.

The people dimension in SCM is important from many perspectives (including relationships, management development of the potential role of supply chain learning). However, Storey et al. (2006, p. 754) acknowledge the "crucial importance of the behavioural and people dimension but the relative neglect of this in any substantive form". In relation to supply chain learning specifically, Bessant at al (2003) acknowledge that "it is still at an early stage and being made with faltering steps" (p. 182). Similary, Mangan and Christopher (2005) recognise that "there is still some way to go" in building the required SCM skills and competencies (p. 189).

Supply Chain Relationship Management: The Key to Effective SCI

Based on the foregoing, the creation and management of partnerships with all customers and suppliers (internally and externally) is not what SCM is about. As stated earlier, it is about recognising that putting SCM philosophy into practice requires a reappraisal of such relationships. There is no 'one size fits all' approach to this. There are many possible relationship forms and choosing the right ones in specific situations is the key. Nonetheless, one of the biggest manifestations of the application of SCM in recent years has involved the move away from adversarial relationships with key external suppliers towards relationships which are based on mutual trust and benefits, openness and shared goals and objectives. As noted by Harland et al. (1999), "there has been an observed shift away from multi-sourced adversarial trading with suppliers, towards single or dual sourcing, resulting in a reduction (or 'rationalisation') of supplier bases used by firms".

SOLUTIONS AND RECOMMENDATIONS FOR SUPPLY CHAIN INNOVATION

The foregoing sections suggest that the concept of integration lies at the heart of the contemporary SCM paradigm. Any worthwhile attempt to improve supply chain capability and performance must, therefore, focus on innovation in this area. As noted earlier, the evidence in relation to experience at firm and supply chain levels indicates that there are many barriers and challenges that must be addressed. It is important to recognise that no panacea exists when it comes to being innovative in achieving higher levels of integration. However, there is a logical and systematic way of addressing the challenges in holistic manner in line with the underpinning principles and concepts of SCM. What is required above all is the commitment of senior management teams to developing and implementing the required strategies.

As noted throughout this chapter, integration can be considered on at least two levels – i.e. intra-firm and inter-firm – and it is essential that both dimensions are considered. The author's experience suggests that without relatively high levels of internal integration any attempt at innovation externally is likely to be difficult. This is in line with the SCO/SCM approach of Mentzer et al. (2001) in the sense that SCO at firm level, as manifested in high levels of internal integration, could be regarded as a prerequisite for SCM, as manifested in high levels of external integration. Approaching the issue in a logical and systematic manner is likely, therefore, to begin with addressing issues of fragmentation within organisations. This requires a multi-disciplinary approach with an emphasis on the identification of NVAs in a cross-functional manner. Once improvement has been achieved internally by supply chains firms then efforts at inter-organisation collaboration are more likely to succeed.

Recent years have seen rapid developments in ICT thus providing the technological basis for improvement. There can be little doubt that the effective implementation of technology has the potential to radically enhance SCI through better management of information both within and between firms. However, for the real potential of technology to be realised its potential must be considered as an integral part of the overall innovation process of organisations. Other chapters in this book deal with some of these technological issues in more detail. What is arguably more important and more difficult is the 'soft wiring' dimension of SCI, in particular issues related to relationship management.

Innovation in SCI is most of all about improving the manner in which individual components within the overall supply chain architecture interact with each other. This often requires that existing mindsets are challenged and that innovative approaches to communication are adopted. This issue is about the people dimension of SCM with innovative models, particularly in the area of supply chain learning, likely to play a more pivotal role in the coming years. This in turn raises issues in relation to education and training – it is only with the right competencies in place throughout the supply chain that sustainable innovation can be achieved.

FUTURE RESEARCH DIRECTIONS

SCM, and its core philosophy of integration, is not new. The term may be relatively new but supply chains have existed for a very long time – in fact they have probably always existed! For example, Forrester's often cited article from the *Harvard Business Review* in 1958 (Forrester, 1958) states that:

Management is on the verge of a major breakthrough in understanding how industrial company success depends on the interactions between the flows of information, materials, money, manpower, and capital equipment. The way these five flow systems interlock to amplify one another and to cause change and fluctuation will form the basis for anticipating the effects of decisions, policies, organisational forms, and investment choices. (p. 37)

His article introduced the demand amplification concept using a computer simulation model. If, as Forrester suggested, management was on "the verge of a major breakthrough" over half a century ago, it seems pertinent to raise questions concerning how this breakthrough – mainly in relation to integration and managing relationships between supply chain companies – has impacted on companies in reality. In fact over 40 years after Forrester's article first appeared, Mentzer et al. (2001), in concluding their paper, ask the specific question: "How prevalent is SCM?" This is a key question to which ongoing research needs provide some answers.

A number of authors have raised serious questions about the real impact of SCM in practice. Cousins et al (2006) suggest that:

SCM still appears to suffer from an underlying frustration or perception of being largely ignored; practitioners feel they have a great deal of value to add, but the organisation is not concerned with them. (p. 699)

Storey at al (2006) raise doubts about the "more full-blown claims of many of the advocates (of SCM)" and suggest that "the pretence that SCM is a discipline which is effectively grappling with these forces is a exaggeration" (p. 771). They also state that the SCM literature tends "move rather imperceptibly between description, prescription and trend identification". This results in what New (1997) referred to as 'normative tension' between the *is* and the *ought*:

The rhetoric of managerial folklore tells managers to feel that they should take a broad, integrative approach and "manage the whole chain", and this often clouds practitioner reports, with both overstatement and yet profound cynicism. (p. 16)

He goes on to suggest that "academics too are often guilty of perpetuating a type of breathless hyperbole" and to note that "researchers must grapple with the fact that (SCM) exists in the netherworld of the imperative and the actual" (p. 16).

Empirical research is needed to disentangle the rhetoric from the reality, with particular reference to SCI concepts and principles. Much of the earlier empirical research in this field has focussed on specific elements of the overall SCM concept rather than on wider cross-functional and inter-organisational integation. A key aspect of this research involves moving beyond these specific foci and examining SCI in a more *holistic* manner. Current research being undertaken by the author is attempting to to address these issues by adopting an integrated research design based on the principles of triangulation.

CONCLUSION

There is significant evidence that the effective implementation of integrated SCM has the potential to generate significant improvements in the performance of firms. For example, on the basis of a study of 196 firms Li et at., (2006) concluded that higher levels of SCM practice "can lead to enhanced competitive advantage and improved organizational performance" (p. 107). Similarly, the work of Frohlich and Westbrook (2001) based on a survey of 322 global manufacturers strongly supported the hypothesis that "the companies with the greatest arcs of supplier and customer integration will have the largest rates of performance improvement" (p. 193). This is significant given the centrality of integration in SCM philosophy. This chapter has discussed the role of integration as part of the overall SCM paradigm.

However, the adoption of SCI concepts and principles is not without its challenges. For example, Fabbe-Costes and Jahre (2008), based on a systematic review of 38 papers on the subject of SCI note that:

Even though half of the papers of our total sample conclude that SCI has a positive effect on performance, the variety of empirical bases and the research design of the studies suggest that caution is advisable. (p. 140)

In a similar vein, Storey et al (2006) assert that, "while there is an emerging body of theory which ostensibly offers a relatively coherent and compelling prescriptive narrative, predominant practice is at considerable odds with this conceptualisation" (p. 755). Future research needs to address this conundrum if the true potential of the integrated SCM narrative is to be realised in practice.

REFERENCES

Arntzen, B. C., Brown, G. G., Harrison, T. P., & Trafton, L. L. (1995). Global Supply Chain Management at the Digital Equipment Corporation. *Interfaces*, *25*(1), 69–93. doi:10.1287/inte.25.1.69

Ayers, J. B. (2003). *Supply Chain Project Management: A Structured Collaborative and Measurable Approach*. Los Angeles, CA: CRC Press. doi:10.1201/9780203501474

Bask, A. H., & Juga, J. (2001). Semi-integrated Supply Chains: Towards the New Era of Supply Chain Management. *International Journal of Logistics: Research and Applications*, *4*(2), 137–152. doi:10.1080/13675560110059434

Beamon, B. (1999). Measuring supply chain performance. *International Journal of Operations & Production Management*, *19*, 275–292. doi:10.1108/01443579910249714

Bessant, J., Kaplinsky, R., & Lamming, R. (2003). Putting supply chain learning into practice. *International Journal of Operations & Production Management*, *23*(2), 167–184. doi:10.1108/01443570310458438

Bolstorff, P. & Rosenbaum, R. (2003), *Supply Chain Excellence: A Handbook for Dramatic Improvement Using the SCOR Model*, New York; American Management Association.

Bowersox, D. J., Closs, D. J., & Stank, T. P. (1999). *21st Century Logistics: making supply chain integration a reality*. Oak Brook, IL: Council of Logistics Management.

Bradley, F. (2004). *International Marketing Strategy* (4th ed.). London: Prentice Hall.

Brewer, P. C., & Speh, T. W. (2000). Using the balanced scorecard to measure supply chain performance. *Journal of Business Logistics*, *21*(1), 75–93.

Campa, J. M., & Goldberg, L. S. (1997). The Evolving External Orientation of Manufacturing: A Profile of Four Countries. *Federal Reserve Bank of New York Economic Policy Review*, *3*, 53–81.

Caplice, C., & Sheffi, Y., A. (1995). Review and Evaluation of Logistic Metrics. *International Journal of Logistics Management*, *5*(2), 11–28. doi:10.1108/09574099410805171

Cateora, P. R., & Graham, J. L. (2004). *International Marketing* (12th ed.). New York: Irwin.

Checkland, P., & Scholes, J. (1999). *Soft Systems Methodology in Action* (2nd ed.). Chichester, UK: John Wiley & Sons.

Chow, G., Heaver, T. D., & Henriksson, L. E. (1994). Logistics Performance: Definition and Measurement. *International Journal of Physical Distribution & Logistics Management*, *24*(1), 17–28. doi:10.1108/09600039410055981

Christopher, M. (1992). *Logistics and Supply Chain Management: Strategies for Reducing Costs and Improving Services*. London: Financial Times/Pitman.

Christopher, M. (2005). *Logistics and Supply Chain Management: Creating Value Adding Networks* (3rd ed.). Harlow: FT Prentice Hall.

Christopher, M., & Ryals, L. (1999). Supply Chain Strategy: Its Impact on Shareholder Value. *International Journal of Logistics Management*, *10*(1), 1–11. doi:10.1108/09574099910805897

Cohen, S.& Roussel, J. (2004). *Strategic Supply Chain Management: The Five Disciplines for Top Performance.* New York: Higher Education.

Cousins, P. D., Lawson, B., & Squire, B. (2006). Supply chain management: theory and practice – the emergence of an academic discipline? *International Journal of Operations & Production Management*, *26*(7), 697–702. doi:10.1108/01443570610672194

Croom, S., Romano, P., & Giannakis, M. (2000). Supply chain management: an analytical framework for critical literature review. *European Journal of Purchasing and Supply Management*, *6*(1), 67–83. doi:10.1016/S0969-7012(99)00030-1

CSCMP. (2005). *Council of Supply Chain Management Professionals*. Retrieved from http://www.cscmp.org

Economist, The (2005). Survey: India And China. 3 March.

Edwards, P., & Edwards, S. (2000). What's Your Problem? *Entrepreneur*, *28*(7), 150.

Ellinger, A. E. (2000). Improving marketing/ logistics cross-functional collaboration in the supply chain. *Industrial Marketing Management*, *29*, 1–6. doi:10.1016/S0019-8501(99)00114-5

Essig, M. (1999).Cooperative Sourcing as a New Strategic Supply Concept: Theoretical Framework and Empirical Findings.*Perspectives on Purchasing and Supply for the Millennium (Proceedings of the 8th International IPSERA Conference)*, March, 245–256.

Eyefortransport (2001). *Digital Logistics – Value Creation in the Freight Transport Industry* [online].Eyefortransport – First Conference. Available from: http://www.eyefortransport.com.

Fabbe-Costes, N., & Jahre, M. (2007). Supply chain integration gives better performance – the emperor's new suit? *International Journal of Physical Distribution & Logistics Management*, *37*(10), 835–855. doi:10.1108/09600030710848941

Fabbe-Costes, N., & Jahre, M. (2008). Supply chain integration and performance: a review of the evidence. *International Journal of Logistics Management*, *19*(2), 130–154. doi:10.1108/09574090810895933

Fagan, M. L. (1991). A Guide to Global Sourcing. *The Journal of Business Strategy*, (March–April): 21–25. doi:10.1108/eb039398

Fan, I. S., & Huang, C. P. (2002).Aligning Local Office Management Plan to Global Corporate Strategy. *Restructuring Global Manufacturing – Towards Global Collaborative Supply Networks (Proceedings of the 7th Annual International Manufacturing Symposium)*, 12–13 September, Institute for Manufacturing, Deptartment of Engineering, University of Cambridge.

Fawcett, S. E., & Magnan, G. M. (2002). The rhetoric and reality of supply chain integration. *International Journal of Physical Distribution & Logistics Management*, *32*(5), 339–361. doi:10.1108/09600030210436222

Feenstra, R. C., & Hanson, G. H. (1996). Globalization, Outsourcing, and Wage Inequality. *The American Economic Review*, *86*, 240–245.

Fernie, J. (1998).Outsourcing Distribution in UK Retailing. *Research Paper 9801*, Institute of Retail Studies, University of Stirling.

Friedman, L., & Furey, T. (1999). *The Channel Advantage*. New York: Butterworth-Heinemann.

Frohlich, M. T., & Westbrook, R. (2001). Arcs of integration: an international study of supply chain strategies. *Journal of Operations Management*, *19*(2), 185–200. doi:10.1016/S0272-6963(00)00055-3

Gattorna, J., Ogulin, R., & Reynolds, M. W. (2003). *Handbook of Supply Chain Management* (5th ed.). London: Gower.

Giunipero, L., Handfield, R. B., & Eltantawy, R. (2006). Supply management's evolution: key skill sets for the supply manager of the future. *International Journal of Operations & Production Management*, *26*(7), 822–844. doi:10.1108/01443570610672257

Goldratt, E. M., & Cox, J. (1992). *The Goal: A Process of Ongoing Improvement*. New York: North River Books.

Gourdin, K. G. (2000). *Global Logistics Management: A Competitive Advantage for the New Millennium*. New York: Blackwell.

Greaver, M. F. II. (1999). *Strategic Outsourcing – A Structured Approach to Outsourcing Decisions and Initiatives*. New York: Amacon.

Grieco, Jr., P. L. (1989). Why supplier certification? And will it work? *Production and Inventory Management Review* with *APICS News*, May, 38-40.

Gunasekaran, A., Patel, C., & McGaughey, R. E. (2004). A framework for supply chain performance measurements. *International Journal of Production Economics, 87*(3), 333–347. doi:10.1016/j.ijpe.2003.08.003

Gunasekaran, A., Patel, C., & Tirtiroglu, E. (2001). Performance measures and metrics in a supply chain environment. *International Journal of Operations & Production Management, 21*(1 & 2), 71–87. doi:10.1108/01443570110358468

Hammer, M., & Champy, J. (1993). *Re-engineering the Corporation: A Manifesto for Business Revolution*. New York: HarperCollins.

Harland, C. M. (1996). Supply chain management: relationships, chains and networks. *British Journal of Management, 7*, 63–80. doi:10.1111/j.1467-8551.1996.tb00148.x

Harland, C. M., Lamming, R. C., & Cousins, P. D. (1999). Developing the Concept of Supply Strategy. *International Journal of Operations & Production Management, 19*(7), 650–673. doi:10.1108/01443579910278910

Harrigan, K. R. (2003). *Vertical Integration, Outsourcing, and Corporate Strategy*. New York: Beard Books.

Hassey, P. & Lai, L. (2003). Outsourcing in the Manufacturing Sector – Where Is It At? *IDC Research*, November.

Hayes, R. H., & Wheelwright, S. C. (1984). *Restoring Our Competitive Edge: Competing Through Manufacturing*. New York: Wiley.

Hendrick, T. E. (1997). *Purchasing Consortiums: Horizontal Alliances among Firms Buying Common Goods and Services. What? Who? Why? How?* Tempe, AZ: Center for Advanced Purchasing Studies/National Association for Purchasing Management.

Hill, T. J. (1999). *Manufacturing Strategy: Text and Cases* (3rd ed.). London: McGraw-Hill/Irwin.

Hitomi, K. (1996). *Manufacturing Systems Engineering: A Unified Approach to Manufacturing Technology and Production Management* (2nd ed.). London: Taylor and Francis.

Houlihan, J. B. (1988). International Supply Chains: A New Approach. *Management Decision, 26*(3), 13–19. doi:10.1108/eb001493

Hugos, M. H. (2002). *Essentials of Supply Chain Management*. New York: Wiley.

Huin, S. F., Luong, L. H. S., & Abhary, K. (2002). Internal Supply Chain Planning Determinants in Small and Medium-Sized Manufacturers. *International Journal of Physical Distribution and Logistics Management, 32*(9), 771–782. doi:10.1108/09600030210452440

Jacobs, D.G. (2003). Antonomy of a supply chain. *Supply Chain Technology News*, March.

Jones, D. T., Hines, P., & Rich, N. (1997). Lean Logistics. *International Journal of Physical and Logistics Management, 27*(3/4), 153–173.

Kearney, A. T. (1999). *The Future of Automotive Distribution. Report published by international consultants A.* T. Kearney.

La Londe, B. J., & Masters, J. M. (1994). Emerging Logistics Strategies: Blueprints for the Next Century. *International Journal of Physical Distribution and Logistics Management, 24*(7), 35–47. doi:10.1108/09600039410070975

Lambert, D. M. (2004). Supply Chain Management. In Lambert, D. M. (Ed.), *Supply Chain Management: Processes, Partnerships, Performance* (pp. 1–23). Sarasota, FL: Supply Chain Management Institute.

Lambert, D. M., & Cooper, M. C. (2000). Issues in supply chain management. *Industrial Marketing Management, 29*(1), 65–83. doi:10.1016/S0019-8501(99)00113-3

Lambert, D. M., Cooper, M. C., & Pagh, J. D. (1998). Supply chain management: implementation issues and research opportunities'. *International Journal of Logistics Management, 9*(2), 1–19. doi:10.1108/09574099810805807

Lambert, D. M., & Pohlen, T. L. (2001). Supply chain metrics. *International Journal of Logistics Management, 12*(1), 1–19. doi:10.1108/09574090110806190

Lamming, R. (1993). *Beyond Partnership: Strategies for Innovation and Lean Supply*. London: Prentice Hall.

Langlois, R. N. (2001).The Vanishing Hand: The Changing Dynamics of Industrial Capitalism (September 14). University of Connecticut Center for Institutions, Organizations, & Markets Working Paper No. 01-1 (http://ssrn.com/abstract=285972).

Lee, H. (2004). The Triple-A Supply Chain. *Harvard Business Review, 82*(10), 102–112.

Li, S., Ragu-Nathan, B., Ragu-Nathan, T. S., & Subba Rao, S. (2006). The impact of supply chain management practices on competitive advantage and organizational performance. *Omega, 34*(2), 107–124. doi:10.1016/j.omega.2004.08.002

Mangan, J., & Christopher, M. (2005). Management development and the supply chain manager of the future. *International Journal of Logistics Management, 16*(2), 178–191. doi:10.1108/09574090510634494

McKinnon, A. (1999). The outsourcing of logistical activities. In Waters, D. (Ed.), *Global Logistics and Distribution Planning: Strategies for Management* (4th ed., pp. 215–234). London: Kogan Page.

Mentzer, J. T., DeWitt, W., Keebler, J. S., Min, S., Nix, N. W., Smith, C. D., & Zacharia, Z. G. (2001). Defining supply chain management. *Journal of Business Logistics, 22*(2), 1–25. doi:10.1002/j.2158-1592.2001.tb00001.x

Monczka, R., Trent, R. & Handfield, R. (1998). *Purchasing and Supply Chain Management*. Cincinnati: South-Western College Publishing.

Mpoyi, R. T. (1999). Changing Corporate Strategies: Restoring Competitive Advantage Through Vertical Disintegration. *Global Competitiveness, 7*(1), 26–34.

National Institute for Transport and Logistics (2000).Supply Chain Management Made Simple. Technical Fact Sheet Dublin: NITL.

National Intelligence Council (2004).Mapping the Global Future. Report of the National Intelligence Council's 2020 Project, NIC 2004-13.

New, S. (1997). The scope of supply chain management research. *Supply Chain Management: An International Journal, 2*(1), 15–22. doi:10.1108/13598549710156321

Oates, D. (1998). *Outsourcing and Virtual Organisation – The Incredible Shrinking Company*. London: Century Business.

Ohno, T. (1988). *Toyota Production System: Beyond Large-Scale Production*. Portland: Productivity Press.

Pagell, M. (2004). Understanding the factors that enable and inhibit the integration of operations, purchasing and logistics. *Journal of Operations Management, 22*(5), 459–487. doi:10.1016/j.jom.2004.05.008

Peters, M. (2000). {AQ: Please note the discrepancy in year – 2000 is correct}.Europe's 3PL Industry Consolidates on the Road to Pan-European Services. *Achieving Supply Chain Excellence through* [ASCET]. *Technology (Elmsford, N.Y.)*, *2*(April).

Pinto, J. (2005).The China Manufacturing Syndrome. *Automation World*, January, 62–66.

Porter, M. E. (1985). *Competitive Advantage: Creating and Sustaining Superior Performance*. New York: Free Press.

PROTRANS. (2003). *The Role of Third Party Logistics Service Providers and their Impact on Transport*. The Netherlands: NEI Transport B.V.

Quinn, J. B., & Hilmer, F. G. (1994). Strategic Outsourcing. *Sloan Management Review*, (Summer): 43–55.

Razzaque, M. R., & Sheng, C. C. (1998). Outsourcing of Logistics Functions: A Literature Survey. *International Journal of Physical Distribution and Logistics Management*, *28*(2), 89–107. doi:10.1108/09600039810221667

Reddy, R., & Reddy, S. (2001). *Supply Chains to Virtual Integration*. New York: McGraw-Hill.

Ross, D. F. (1998). *Competing Through Supply Chain Management*. New York: Chapman and Hall.

Scott, C., & Westbrook, R. (1991). New Strategic Tools for Supply Chain Management. *International Journal of Physical Distribution & Logistics Management*, *21*(1), 23–33. doi:10.1108/09600039110002225

Simchi-Levi, D., & Kaminsky, P. (2003). *Managing the Supply Chain: The Definitive Guide for the Business Professional*. New York: McGraw-Hill.

Simchi-Levi, D., Kaminsky, P., & Simchi-Levi, E. (2002). *Designing and Managing the Supply Chain* (2nd ed.). New York: McGraw-Hill/Irwin.

Skjoett-Larsen, T. (2000). Third Party Logistics – From an Interorganizational Point of View. *International Journal of Physical Distribution and Logistics Management*, *30*(2), 112–127. doi:10.1108/09600030010318838

Stone, T. (2002). Critical Appraisal of Implications of Partnership Arrangements on Employees and Companies. *Logistics Solutions*, *5*(2), 24–28.

Storey, J., Emberson, C., Godsell, J., & Harrison, A. (2006). Supply chain management: theory, practice and future challenges. *International Journal of Operations & Production Management*, *26*(7), 754–774. doi:10.1108/01443570610672220

Sweeney, E. (1999).The Systems Approach to Analysing Supply Chains and Improving their Performance.*Perspectives on Purchasing for the New Millennium, Proceedings of the 8th International Purchasing and Supply Education and Research Association (IPSERA) Conference*, Belfast, March, 739–744.

Sweeney, E. (2004). Making Supply Chain Management Work for You! *Logistics Solutions*, *7*(4), 21–25.

Sweeney, E. (2005). Managing the Supply Chain: The Role of Information and Communications Technology (ICT) As a Key Enabler of the Process. *Business Ireland*, Summer Issue, 105–109.

Sweeney, E. (2007). Perspectives on Supply Chain Management and Logistics: Creating Competitive [st *Century*. Dublin: Blackhall Publishing.]. *The Organ*, 21.

Sweeney, E., Evangelista, P., & Passaro, R. (2005). Putting supply chain learning theory into practice: lessons from an Irish case. *International Journal of Knowledge and Learning*, *1*(4), 357–372. doi:10.1504/IJKL.2005.008357

Tan, K. C. (2001). A framework of supply chain management literature. *European Journal of Purchasing and Supply Management*, *7*(1), 39–48. doi:10.1016/S0969-7012(00)00020-4

Trent, R. J., & Monczka, R. M. (2003). Understanding Integrated Global Sourcing. *International Journal of Physical Distribution & Logistics Management*, *33*(7), 607–629. doi:10.1108/09600030310499286

United Nations Conference on Trade and Development (2004). *Handbook of Statistics* Geneva: UNCTAD.

United Nations Conference on Trade and Development (2008). *Handbook of Statistics* Geneva: UNCTAD.

van Hoek, R. (1998). Measuring the Unmeasureable - measuring and improving performance in the supply chain. *Supply Chain Management*, *3*(4), 187–192. doi:10.1108/13598549810244232

van Hoek, R., & Alan Harrison, A. (2004). *Logistics Management and Strategy*. London: FT Prentice Hall.

Waters, C. D. J. (2004). *Global Logistics and Distribution Planning: Strategies for Management* (4th ed.). London: Kogan Page.

Womack, J. P., & Jones, D. T. (2003). *Lean Thinking: Banish Waste and Create Wealth in Your Corporation* (2nd ed.). London: Free Press.

World Trade Organisation. (1998). *Annual Report*. Geneva: WTO.

World Trade Organisation. (2004). *Annual Report*. Geneva: WTO.

Chapter 2
From Integration to Alignment:
Challenges and Solutions

John Gattorna
Gattorna Alignment, USA

ABSTRACT

Supply chain integration in its various forms has been talked about in the literature for nearly two decades. But the impediments to improved integration have been difficult to overcome, and progress has therefore been painfully slow. This chapter examines three of the most powerful obstacles to integration: terminology/definitions; organization design; and, systems/IT; and traces developments in these areas since the mid-1990s.

INTRODUCTION

There have been a lot of changes in the jargon in the four decades since the term physical distribution management (PDM) burst on the scene in an article by Robert Neuschel (Neuschel, 1967). Definitional issues have plagued this space as different schools of thinking want to have their terminology universally accepted.

I come from the school that has resisted changing terminology as the related concepts developed over time, because I thought we should avoid yet more jargon on top of that which already exists. In my view we just need to keep redefining what goes inside the various terms, and more recently this has meant a particular focus on the 'supply chain'.

However, despite my efforts and those of like-minded individuals, we have failed to have the term 'supply chain' recognized as having both revenue and cost reduction dimensions; most business managers still think of it in cost-down terms, much as they did with its forerunner, 'logistics'. And despite years of trying to get executives to understand that there is a big difference between

DOI: 10.4018/978-1-60960-585-8.ch002

'logistics' and 'supply chain', few have changed their mental model to factor in the potential riches that 'supply chain' end-to-end thinking can bring.

And as for including human behaviour and relationships, the business world is still largely in denial. Something has to change and maybe that is the way we need to present the full idea of the supply chain to top management- we simply have to get it accepted as a multi-disciplinary term, not of one functional specialism.

The term '*supply chain management*' was originally coined by the consulting house Booz Allen & Hamilton circa 1982. It never was a good term anyway, because it immediately conjured up in one's mind the 'supply' side of the enterprise. The 'chain' descriptor didn't help either, as it implies we are dealing with linear chains or strings of enterprises, when in fact the real world involves 3-dimensional arrays of enterprises. Indeed, our future world, whether we like it or not, is moving inexorably towards a '*network of networks*', and we had better get on board with that reality.

Over the last decade, various commentators have broken ranks in search of more meaningful terminology. For example, *value chain*; *demand-chain*; *demand-networks*. I raised this at a 'thought leadership' forum in Sydney in February 2010, and the term which ultimately emerged from the debate was *'value networks'*. However, although it is probably too early to move straight to this vernacular, I forecast that it will become widely adopted within 10 years. Why? Because the term 'value networks' beautifully encompasses everything we want in scope; supply-side supply chains; demand-side supply chains; and the idea that enterprises have many supply chains (or pathways) flowing through them. It also allows us to explain the concept of 'alignment' and describe the *dynamism* involved as combinations of different supply chain configurations mix and match to form aligned 'value networks'.

By ultimately embracing 'value networks' as the accepted vernacular in the future we automatically include all parties on the supply-side, all parties on the demand-side, and all parties in between, e.g., service-providers. When that happens we will have finally cracked the terminology and definitional problems that has bedevilled us for decades and been one of the primary inhibitors to the development of this relatively new sub-field of management science. We still have to overcome other impediments to end-to-end integration, and we will address these later in the chapter.

In this chapter I will refer to other components such as supply chains (plural); supply chain configurations; and 'hybrid' supply chains, but the over-arching albeit subliminal concept will be 'value networks' because this is the end-game. That's where I am heading in the future. What about you?

ORGANIZATIONAL DESIGN

In the end, supply chains are driven by people in various guises; customers, suppliers, third parties, and employees inside the enterprise, and everyone must fit into some type of organization structure. And herein lays the second big problem that has held back the development of supply chain thinking for decades—organizational design.

Unfortunately, we seem to have become wedded to the conventional functional silo design, whose origins date back as far as the Industrial Revolution. And over the years this functional design, with its emphasis on specialisms, has served us well, but that all stopped abruptly with the onset of the Internet in the early 1990s and the corresponding convergence of a plethora of new software applications. Consumers and businesses alike are now demanding responsiveness that was unheard of two decades ago. Hence, the organizational designs we became so comfortable with over time are now clearly outmoded. And the fact they still remain is a statement about how slow we as humans are to adapt; and how unwilling we are to accept reality, and look for creative solutions.

Customers are becoming frustrated at the inability of large organizations to respond to their needs because very often the sheer volatility in modern markets makes it impossible to do so with the outmoded organizational structures we still have in place. But simply gyrating from central designs to de-centralized designs is insufficient. The fact is, while we persevere with vertical silos we will always be at least 90 degree out of phase with customers, and they will no longer cut suppliers the slack of yesteryear. Relatively little experimentation has been undertaken in the last 50 years, and that in itself is an indictment on the organizational theorists who seem to have been devoid of ideas.

After significant field work, we have developed an over-arching theory of the firm called 'dynamic alignment'. This in turn has helped us find a solution to the organization structure conundrum, which is written up in detail in Gattorna (2010). Essentially, we need two components of the enterprise, each with specific roles, to work in synch if customers are to be satisfied under most if not all market conditions, much as depicted in Figure 1, which features the Agile supply chain configuration.

The vertical functions remain as always, but their specific role going forward is to focus on developing specialisms through the use of best-practices.

Running at 90 degrees to these functions we have a number of different 'supply chains' that are configured specifically around particular types of customer (behavioural) segments. These 'supply chains are driven by clusters of personnel, all seconded from the corresponding vertical functions, and tied together with joint KPIs and particular leadership styles. There may be up to four clusters of 20-30 personnel each driving a similar number of 'supply chains', each with different operating

Figure 1. Agile supply chain clusters

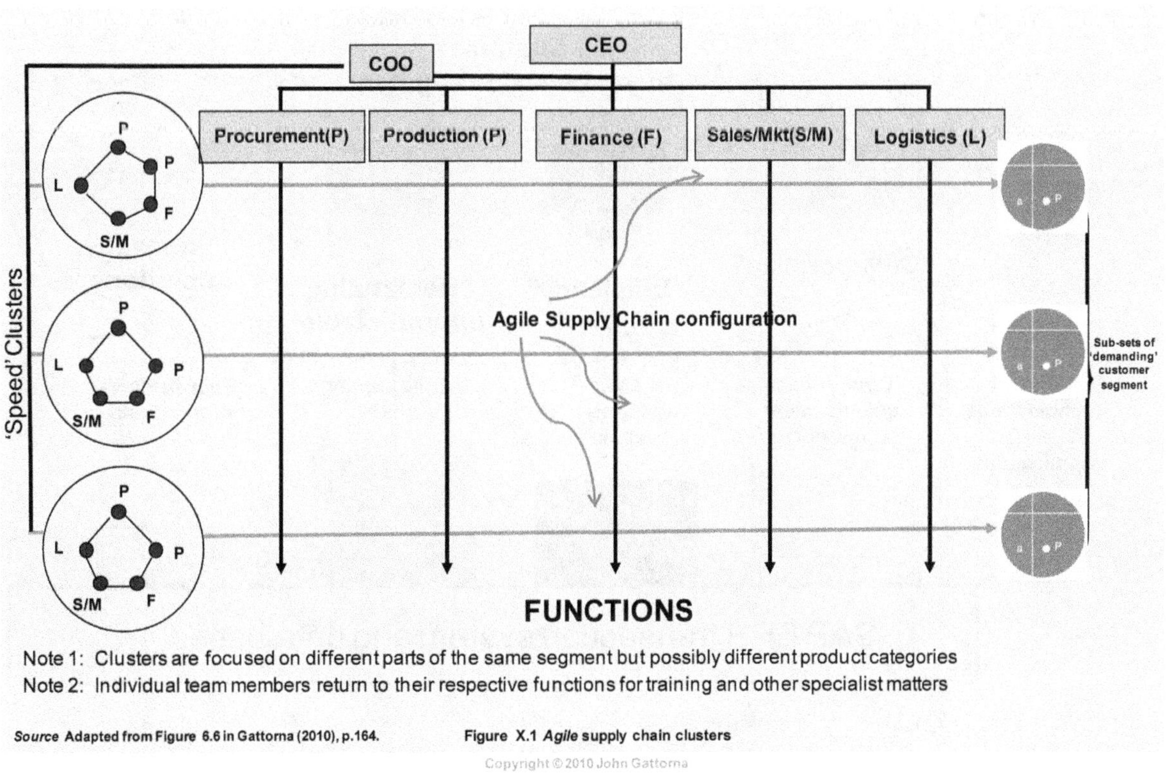

characteristics. These 'clusters' then report to a line executive, such as a Global Customer Operations VP or similar. This is definitely not a matrix organization we are suggesting here. Li & Fung, the Hong Kong based supply chain service company, and Zara, the global fast fashion manufacturer-retailer, have adopted a variant of this organization design, and are doing tremendously well as a direct result. They are just two organizations that have recognized the benefits of harnessing people power, and focusing it in the right places.

SYSTEMS/IT

During the 1990s when the push for improved integration really started, technology was more of an inhibitor than enabler. Thankfully, this situation has reversed in the last fifteen years, although information technology (IT) systems, and how they are best used in a supply chain context, is still not universally understood.

In our work developing the dynamic alignment model, it became obvious that IT systems should not be just thrown at every facet of the business, but instead, should be carefully packaged in different combinations to power the different supply chain configurations that we discovered, i.e., *Continuous Replenishment; Lean; Agile; and Fully Flexible*. We ideally should have in place an ERP transactional system, but it is best to select IT applications that do the specific job we want them to do, much as indicated in Figure 2.

In Figure 2 we have simply highlighted the specific case of a *Continuous Replenishment* supply chain serving the 'Collaborative' segment of customers, using the SAP suite to demonstrate. In this situation, perhaps the most important application is the SAP CRM module, which would help to systematically manage the expectations

Figure 2. Requisite technology for continuous replenishment supply chains

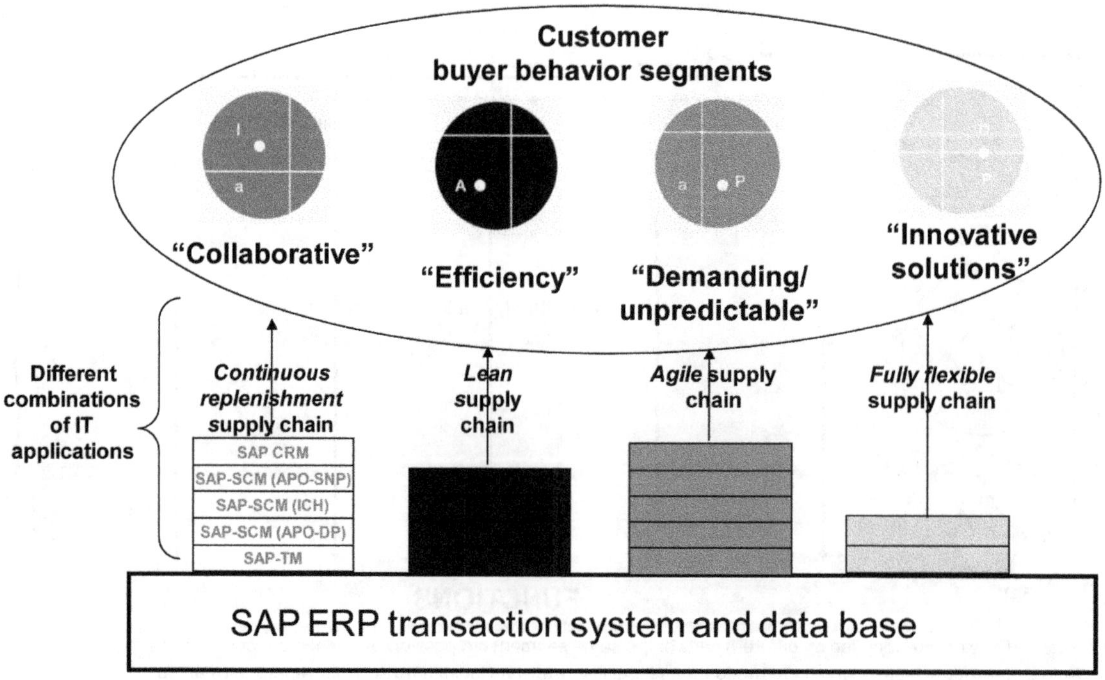

Source Adapted from Figure 7.3 in Gattorna (2010), p. 184.

of a customer group that is biased towards close and trusting relationships. Other modules in the same stack will also assist in this aim as well.

THE OTHER ROLES OF ORGANIZATION DESIGN AND IT SYSTEMS

If you follow the logic of the *Dynamic Alignment* model, it is also obvious that both organization design and IT/Systems have a major influence in shaping culture inside an enterprise, which in turn shapes the behaviours of personnel. See Figure 3 for the full list of 13 levers that shape internal subcultures.

By configuring the organization into functions and clusters as mentioned in an earlier section, the personnel have a clear mandate and know what is expected of them. Furthermore, if we carefully select these personnel on the basis of their individual values as well as their technical expertise, we are in effect building in the desired bias. So in the case of Figure 3 where we are featuring the Continuous Replenishment supply chain configuration, the idea is to embed a bias towards 'feeling' or relationships, since this cluster is managing customers in the 'Collaborative' segment with like values.

The same applies to IT/systems. As indicated above, the Continuous Replenishment supply chains features a combination of applications including customer relationship management (CRM), vendor-managed inventory (VMI) and collaborative planning forecasting and replenishment (CPFR), all designed to link the enterprise closely with particular customers who value relationships.

Figure 3. Continuous replenishment supply chain configuration (demand side)

MARKET SEGMENT	COLLABORATIVE	CLOSE WORKING RELATIONSHIPS SOUGHT WITH SELECTED SUPPLIERS
FULFILMENT STRATEGY	VALUE PROPOSITION	STRATEGIES • Share information • Seek *strategic partnerships* • Seek long-term stability • Build mutual trust Collaboration Zone
INTERNAL CULTURAL CAPABILITY	CULTURAL LEVERS 1. Org design 2. People positioning 3. Processes 4. IT/systems 5. S&OP 6. KPIs 7. Incentives 8. Job design 9. Internal comms. 10. Training & devel. 11. Role modelling 12. Recruitment	GROUP SUBCULTURE • Relationship cluster • Ensure bias in cluster is towards personnel with "F" in their MBTI profile • Standard processes, eg. Customer Account Management • CRM; VMI; ECR; CDP; CPFR • S&OP processes relatively simple in this collaborative environment • Emphasis on loyalty and retention • Encourage participative schemes • Authority/autonomy negotiated by consensus • Consultative; face-to-face • Team building • Managers with ESFP/MBTI profile are ideal • Recruit team players
LEADERSHIP	13 LEADERSHIPSTYLE	COACH • Conscientious • Lead by teaching • Concerned for others • Loyal, committed, politically astute • Seeks agreement by consensus

CONCLUSION

We started out this chapter explaining that the much sought after condition of 'end-to-end' integration had proved elusive in the 1990s as the very parameters that we sought to enable integration in enterprises, were the very ones that were acting as inhibitors. Over time, the terminology issue has receded to some extent, and with the coming of the Internet, so has the IT/Systems issue, although as pointed out we still need to think in terms of "requisite" technology rather than throw everything at the issue.

Organization design has been the last and perhaps the hardest inhibitor to remove, but there are signs in some of the leading companies that this is now happening.

Overtaking this move towards improved integration however, we have discovered that the bigger game is 'alignment' between the enterprise and its marketplace. Indeed, given the speed of change and the propensity for customers to change their buying behaviours as conditions change, we have seen the need to address this by adding a 'dynamic' capacity to 'alignment'. This we have done with our new *Dynamic Alignment* model, which ushers in a behavioural model of the firm, and by taking a holistic approach, informs us about the design and operation of the firm's supply chains. After all, it is now clear that enterprises of all types are simply an aggregation of the supply chains flowing through them, from source to consumption markets, and for most enterprises therefore, supply chains are the business.

REFERENCES

Gattorna, J. (2010). *Dynamic Supply Chains; delivering value through people*. Saddle River, New Jersey: FT Prentice Hall, Harlow (UK); and FT Press.

Neuschel, R. P. (1967). Physical distribution-forgotten frontier. *Harvard Business Review*, *45*(2), 125–134.

Chapter 3
Integration Strategies for Electronic Device Supply Chains

Claudia-Maria Wagner
Dublin Institute of Technology, Ireland

Colm Ryan
Dublin Institute of Technology, Ireland

ABSTRACT

The growth in the manufacture and distribution of electronic devices is one of the most significant sources of continuing innovation of the last half-century. These products are notable in that they integrate physical elements (i.e. hardware) and virtual elements (e.g. software) to deliver value to customers. This chapter examines the role of innovation in electronic product supply chains by exploring the commonalities and differences between the distribution models of digital and physical elements and examining alternative frameworks from which digital and physical distribution methods can be merged. A number of contemporary case studies are presented that highlight how the different elements can work together to deliver continuously innovative value to customers.

INTRODUCTION

One of the most significant trends of the last thirty years has been the massive increase in the number of digital devices in use. Products in this category are notable in that they need to seamlessly incorporate physical and virtual elements, often referred to as hardware and software. These elements are quite different, but nevertheless they need to work together in a closely integrated way.

From a supply chain (SC) perspective, hardware and software are dissimilar in many ways. Hardware is relatively expensive to procure, manufacture and distribute. It requires long lead times and strict management of yields and inventory, as well as compliance with multiple directives such as electromagnetic interference and waste disposal. Its design and functionality is difficult to change and product lifecycles can be

DOI: 10.4018/978-1-60960-585-8.ch003

comparatively long. Software, on the other hand, is primarily a creative, person centred activity. Once released, it is relatively easy to distribute and change. Lifecycles can be much shorter, and issues such as product returns or inventory management do not apply.

The challenge, therefore, is how best to integrate these two heterogeneous factors in the context of relentless and rapid innovation. The incorporation of the software supply chain into the hardware supply chain is a key concern for device manufacturers, particularly as the Internet and online software distribution continues to gain greater prominence.

This chapter looks at ways these different elements can be integrated within hi-tech supply chains in order to maximise value for customers and consumers in a cost effective way. It starts by contrasting dimensions of traditional physical product supply chains and the wider concept of supply chain management (SCM) with digital product supply chains and the distinctive ways of managing them and outlines potential interfaces for integration and innovation. Very little research has been published that links innovation management to digital products. To close this gap, new approaches for management of innovation in the context of digital products are presented. Although digital products potentially offer considerable advantages to innovators as they are less constrained by physical constraints, they also present significant challenges for innovators. Hybrid approaches are therefore explored, where the best of both worlds, physical and digital, can be applied. The authors conclude their theoretical framework by outlining some current physical and digital supply chain integration examples and by determining likely innovative supply chain scenarios on how these strategies might develop over the coming years.

BACKGROUND

This section sets out the background to this chapter by introducing traditional physical supply chain concepts and contrasts them to digital product supply chain frameworks. It outlines the importance of supply chain integration in a physical and digital context and sets the scene for the effective management of supply chain innovation cycles as a critical component.

Physical vs. Digital Product Supply Chain Frameworks

A myriad of different definitions of supply chains and their effective management exist in literature. Supply Chain Management in a traditional sense is concerned with the strategic management of a firm's activities, which together provide customers with the appropriate level of service at optimum cost (Christopher, 2005; Lambert et al., 1998; Sweeney et al., 2005). Chou and Ruchika (2006) note that the aim of supply chain management is to ensure that a product moves down the chain in the most effective manner, so as to maximise profits earned by the whole chain as well as minimise wastage of raw materials, labour and time. Supply chains can be external (macro) or internal (micro) in nature. Pant, Sethia and Bhandari (2003) define the supply chain in a macro-perspective as *"a connected series of (networked) organisations (suppliers, original equipment manufacturer, distributors, transporters, etc.), resources, and activities involved in the creation and delivery of value, in the form of both finished products and services to end customers"*. An organisation's external supply chain is further interlinked with the micro or intra-firm supply chain that addresses the integration of different functions within an organisation. Supply chain integration (SCI) aims to facilitate the flow between all organisations in a supply chain and thus positively affects operational performance (Naylor et al., 1999; Bagchi et al. 2005). The sharing of information is a critical success factor if seamless product and money flows between initial suppliers and end-consumers are to be achieved. Supply chain management as such allows value-add to customers starting from product design to delivery through the planning, implementation and monitoring of the various flows.

Figure 1 exhibits a simplistic representation of an extended supply chain. In the macro or external supply chain materials flow from the raw material source (n-tier supplier) through the various stages in the chain to the final consumer (n-tier customer). Money (i.e. funds) then flows back down the chain. The integration of fragmented parts of a supply chain into an extended single system leads to proactive measures rather than preventive action, where organisations tied in it derive a number of benefits (Baltacioglu et al., 2007). As a result, at every link in the supply chain each producer purchases inputs and then adds value, which then becomes part of the cost of the next stage of production. The sum of the value added equals the final product price (Linden, Kraemer and Dedrick, 2009).

Traditionally, a value chain is the combination of nine generic value-added activities that provide (product and service) value within an organisation to be passed on to a customer. However, Ramsay (2005) notes that value is a perceived quality that is associated with the benefits that can occur at various points along a supply chain. Thus, value chains can operate in both directions.

The supply chain framework focuses on industries with traditional (manufacturing) supply chain architectures of physical goods. Physical goods possess mass and occupy volume; they can break down and degrade. It is not possible to create products without first sourcing appropriate materials. Energy is expended in transformation and transportation and the physical transportation element plays a major role in moving the product from its various stages. However, with the rise

Figure 1. Traditional supply chain framework

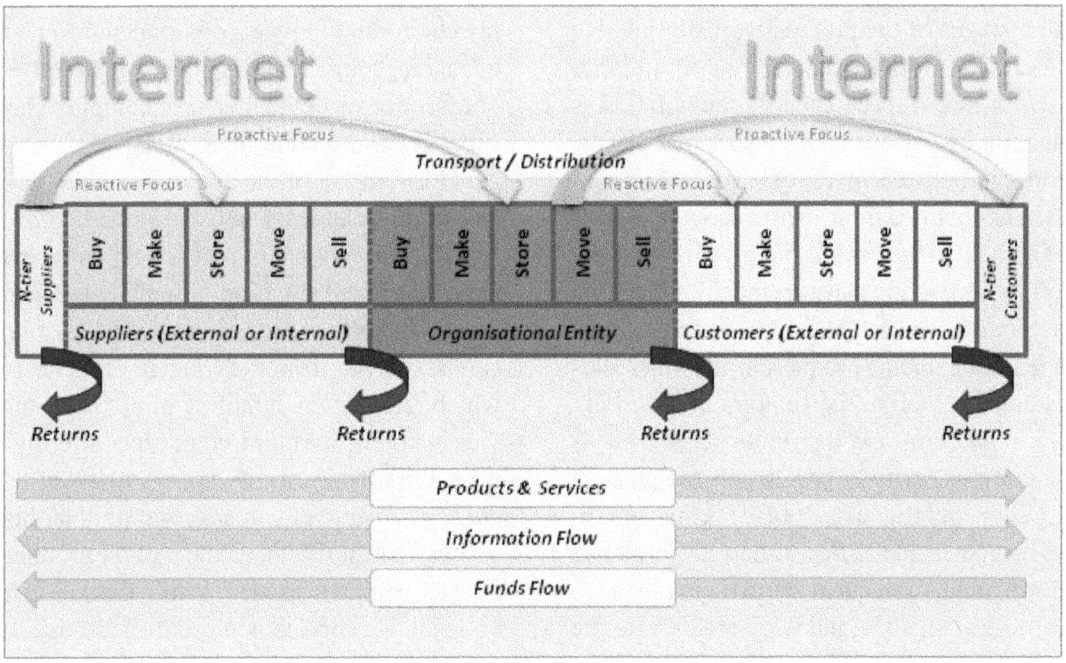

of information and communication technology (ICT), many products have no longer physical properties, but are described as digital products, virtual goods or information goods (Shapiro and Varian, 1999). The co-ordination and integration scenario surrounding digital goods is much different. Ryan and Wagner (2009) note that some elements of traditional supply chain co-ordination are less of an issue as the distribution of the product happens online. Due to the fast reproducibility (the ease by which digital products can be reproduced, stored and transferred), transmutability (the ease by which a digital product can be modified) and indestructibility (the tendency of a digital product to maintain its form ad-infinitum) of digital products, there are no critical inventory or purchasing issues to contend with. However, other issues, such as restrictions to copying create new and complex co-ordination challenges, for example the supply of activation keys and the monitoring of software assets remotely to ensure that copyright is not being breached.

There are generally several stages in a digital product planning and production process. Figure 2 illustrates an example of a digital supply chain. The first stages of the process typically involve design and development and testing of a digital product. In that respect, each digital solution is a collection of various components that can be developed in-house, acquired or licensed through a supplier, or obtained from an open-source repository. The next stages entail the preparing of the support infrastructure that accompanies the main digital product. This might include a user-guide or documentation, media production and other add-on features, as well as the final product rollout. Finally, marketing and distribution, as well as retailing and security efforts to sell the product ensue (Chou and Ruchika, 2006). Formal and informal reverse feedback flows allow performance monitoring and subsequent system maintenance and improvement. Ryan and Wagner (2009) argue that a digital product can be characterised as a movement of value. Thus, key flows represent information, ideas and innovation, from requirements into development, from release through to distribution and finally to the end-consumer. Information is shared through integrated electronic means within and outside of an organisation. The abolition of the trade-off between richness and reach of information means that everybody can communicate with everybody at almost zero cost, without constraints on the richness of information. (Evans and Wurster, 1997).

Parallels to physical product supply chains can be adopted in managing the various flows of information exchanges and processes within the above described digital framework. A bill of materials can help organising the hierarchy of virtual product components. Process mapping can be used to identify all business activities associated with customer demand satisfaction, from the initial idea generation through to final product delivery. In a similar sense to physical product supply chains, three major functions exist along the digital supply chain: (1) supplier sourcing (buy), (2) product development and testing (make) and (3) product distribution and delivery (sell). This simplified structure of a digital product supply chain can often be a component in a network of a larger solution and each manufacturer is only one vendor or developer in a complex chain of suppliers and system integrators.

The merging of the above discussed physical and digital elements into an integrated product creates a supply chain that is very different to a purely physical situation. Supply chain management principles of such a hybrid product approach can be derived from the concept of servitisation, which refers to the bundling of products and services into one harmonised product offering. Services and software are two very much overlapping concepts. Typically, in a hybrid product bundle, software as the digital element of the product is an enabler behind a service. While the software can be copied, a service is more difficult to emulate because it often incorporates non-digital elements. Therefore it seems worthwhile to outline factors

Figure 2. Digital product supply chain

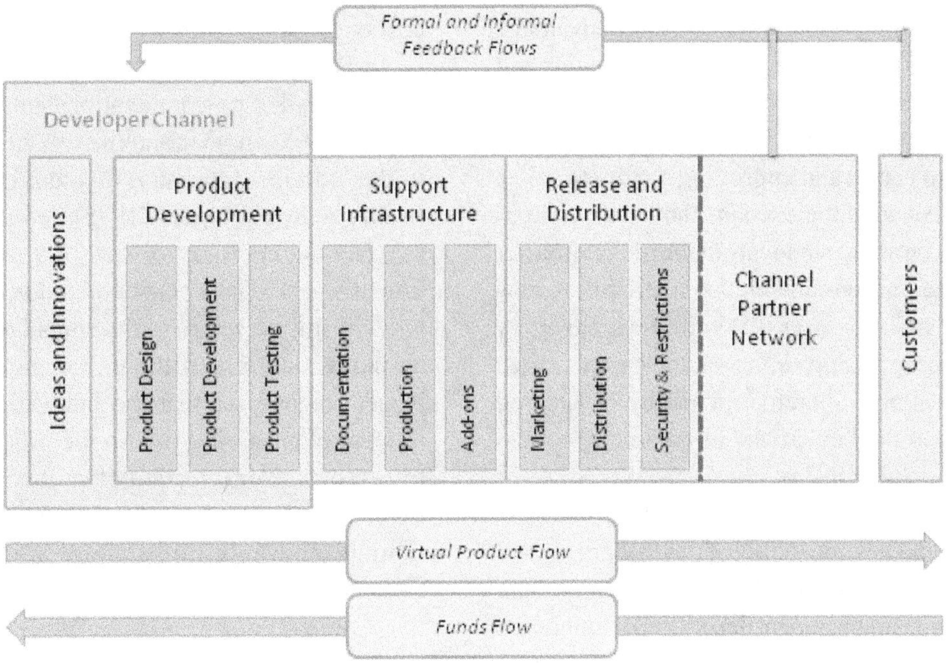

derived from research on servitisation strategies that are contributing to the competitiveness of hybrid approaches. We list four such factors that are derived from Johnson and Mena (2007):

- Software that enable services tend to be tailored and the holistic concept tends to be more difficult to imitate and locks the user into a long-term relationship (Vandermerwe, 2000);
- Software as a closed-loop service providing reverse feedback can improve knowledge through an increased insight into how products are used and potentially enhanced (Alonso- Rasgado et al. 2004);
- Software as a service can provide a differentiating factor from traditional manufacturing (Penttinen and Palmer, 2007);
- Manufacturers that utilise hybrid product approaches can increase revenues (Oliva and Kallenberg, 2003) as software enabled services tend to have higher margins and can provide a stable revenue stream throughout the life of the product (Cohen et al., 2006).

A hybrid supply chain requires the careful synchronisation of physical and digital supply chains. The effectiveness of this integration will determine to a large extent how competitive the product will be in the market. Another key factor is the extent to which the process of integration is amenable to continuous innovation. This is the focus of the next section of this chapter.

INNOVATION MANAGEMENT IN SCM

Innovation has been defined as the *"(...) adoption of an internally generated or purchased device, system, policy, program, process, product, or service that is new to the adopting organisation"* (Damanpour, 1991). According to Rogers, *"an innovation is an idea, practice, or object that is perceived as new by an individual or other unit of adoption."* The most viable strategy for both generating and sustaining a competitive advantage has become one of both continuous innovation and corporate renewal (Merrifield, 2000). Porter and Stern (2001) argue that, in the past, firms focused on reducing costs and improving quality to gain a competitive advantage. Today, however, companies must be able to innovate at the global frontier and create and commercialise a stream of new products and processes that shift the technology frontier, progressing as fast as their rivals catch up. Innovation is therefore generally considered to be one of the key drivers of corporate success (Cardozo et al., 1993).

Modern definitions of supply chain management expand beyond the activities that are related to working capital as outlined in the traditional supply chain management definitions (Lummus et al., 2001). Innovative creation and promotion of value and the maximisation of this value over the longer term is becoming more and more critical elements in supply chain management (Ryan and Wagner, 2009). Roy, Sivakumar and Wilkinson (2004) emphasize that innovation generation, as multidisciplinary activity, has increasingly been recognized as an outcome of interaction between a firm and various outside entities and does not originate from the buyer alone. In such a context, supplier involvement and alliances are routes to innovation generation. The generation of an innovation typically occurs in the development phase of a new product. This includes the generation of initial ideas, their critical evaluation, the testing of derived concepts, the product development, and final launch (Crawford and Di Benedetto, 2000). Roy, Sivakumar and Wilkinson (2004) argue that nevertheless, fundamental changes in the configuration of an existing product may as well be considered as radical for the affected supply chain members. If the innovations involving less radical or incremental changes entail for example quicker delivery periods, or reduction of material thickness and cost. Innovation generation in a supply chain context involves changes in product, process, or service that either reduce cost or improve efficiency.

In Roger`s (1995) seminal research the process is detailed how innovations move from one population to another and the role of key factors in the individual decision to adopt is discussed. In this context, Rogers (1995) defines adoption as *"(...) the decision to make full use of an innovation as the best course of action available"*, while diffusion refers to the spread over time of an innovation within the unit or to other units. Rogers recognises that the innovation decision process plays a vital role in the process leading to acceptance or rejection of an innovation. The explicit motivators for the organisational adoption and innovation diffusion are described by the following set of variables:

- **Relative advantage:** the extent to which the innovation is perceived to have significant advantages over current alternatives.
- **Compatibility:** the degree to which the innovation is seen as being consistent with past practices, current values and existing needs.
- **Complexity:** the extent to which the innovation can readily be understood and easily implemented.
- **Trialability:** new ideas that can be tried out at low costs before wholesale adoption are more likely to be taken up.
- **Observability:** the degree to which the use and benefits of the innovation are visible to others, and therefore act as a further stimulus to uptake by others.

In this context it is worthwhile to mention the theory of S-curve in innovation adoption (Rogers, 1995). It suggests that technologies are a conceptualisation of S-curve sequences that drive various new product introductions. The S-curve emerges because a new technology or product is rather limited to a small group of early adopt-ers and small niche markets that derive benefits from this early introduction (Chandy and Tellis, 2000). With its diffusion to a wider user group, the product or technology gains ascendancy and new capabilities are introduced and refined. During this middle phase a dominant allegiance of the product or technology in the market place emerges, which is effecting standardization from design to manufacturing. This in turn allows heightened competition as new entrants realize opportunities for further innovation based on cost and scale as well as product performance. This is the period of rapid and greatest growth. During the final phase the product reaches market saturation and hits a plateau. Successful companies begin to consolidate their market share, seek further economies of scale, but also shift focus by targeting other growth opportunities (Essa, 2005). Harrison and Waite (2005) therefore argue that the extent to which adoption of an innovation can yield a competitive advantage is relatively short-lived. As the innovation becomes more widespread, competitive advantage diminishes and innovation becomes a necessary competitive requirement. Dos Santos and Peffers (1995) argue that in today's hypercompetitive markets, even if an innovative ICT application enables a firm to reduce costs or increase product value, it may not provide a long-term competitive advantage if competing firms can introduce similar, or highly substitutable applications. This means that new product development, its maintenance and updates need to be effectively and flexibly managed from the initial idea through to final delivery to the customer in a closed loop fashion. The management of closed innovation cycles is seen as a key component in sustaining competitive advantage within supply chains (Utterback, 1994; Tidd et al., 2005). Few companies have achieved mastery over their innovation cycles. Highly innovative companies are characterised by regular updates of new products and the ability to introduce new products that alter the basis of competition (Anthony et al., 2008).

In their research on understanding the evolution of value chain innovations through the perspective of biological evolution models, Graeml, Engelbert and Weiler (2008) point out that parallels can be drawn between how companies evolve, and the way they co-ordinate their activities to produce goods and services, to the way species evolve in the animal world. In that context, these authors point out that fruit flies are studied much more often by biologists than any other animal due to their short life-cycle. This allows researchers to study many generations and being able to follow up changes over time. 'Corporate genetics' focuses on studying organisations that belong to the fastest evolving industries as any phenomenon observed may lead to a better understanding of 'difficult to notice' changes that are happening in other industries at a slower pace. Fast evolving companies are for example electronic device manufacturers in the infotainment industry. The Internet in particular has accelerated this sectors' evolutionary speed and consumers of digital infotainment devices are experiencing a true revolution in the supply and distribution chains for many of such products. The reason for this rapid change can be attributed to groundbreaking developments in conductor technologies, such as increased transmission capacities in broadband, together with the evolution of so called boxes, including DVD players, digital recorders, digital TV decoders, music and video digital players, PDAs and digitally enabled mobile phones. This gave rise to develop hybrid devices that combine physical and digital product innovations to create a market-leading product idea, which is able to dictate the alignment of conductor and content providers to its own standards (Graeml, Engelbert and Weiler, 2008). Graeml, Engelbert and Weiler (2008) describe Apple's iPod (box) and the iTunes (conductor) store as one such example.

Ryan and Wagner (2009) point out that digital product manufacturers must work with customers and developers in a tightly managed cyclical fashion. While original ideas may be generated internally within the developer network, once those ideas are transformed into products the customer takes a central role in the future direction of the product and the further changes that ensue from there. Within this extended concept, the role of partnership remains paramount. Product developers operate within complex webs and networks of players – engineers, product managers, developers, industrial designers etc. – each of whom need to work together to turn around new products quickly and efficiently. Information management is required to connect producers to customers, thus ensuring that the products meet changing customer requirements. A kind of reverse logistics flow needs to be factored into digital supply chain – the movement of customer feedback into the hands of the manufacturers in order to enable products to be updated and improved. Customer responses will inevitably form part of the development of subsequent versions of the product, so mechanisms that gather feedback from the customer, be it formal (for example, surveys or automated bug-reporting) or informal (for example, phone calls, emails, web postings), need to be in place. In essence the key to competition in the digital realm is not really a single sale, but the long-term relationship with the customer base and the securing of a profitable income stream over time.

Innovation cycles need to be incorporated when considering supply chains for products that require physical and digital elements. Changes required by customers from a software perspective may force modifications to the hardware. More commonly, changes in the hardware may require further software development and careful consideration of software roadmaps in the light of rapid advances in physical technology. Software and hardware developments need to be closely aligned for the lifecycle of the product because the customer may not be as concerned by the distinction between the two as the developers might be.

The following section of this chapter describes different examples of hybrid product innovations. It is, however, necessary to point out that sectors that experience constant technological innovation evolve at a much faster pace. Competition in particular speeds the development of products and processes. A fairly practical consequence of the increased evolutionary pace is that the concept of sustainable competitive advantage becomes irrelevant. Any of such advantages is at most temporary in nature.

VIRTUAL / PHYSICAL SUPPLY CHAIN INTEGRATION CASE STUDIES

This book chapter examines the role of innovation in electronic product supply chains by exploring the commonalities and differences between the distribution models of digital and physical elements and examining alternative frameworks from which digital and physical distribution methods can be merged. To complement the theoretical frameworks of the above sections, a number of contemporary mini case studies are presented that highlight how companies manufacturing electronic devices integrate their physical products with digital entities. Up through the 1980s, the majority of electronics companies' innovative products were manufactured within their vertically integrated operations. From then on, supply chains in the global electronics industry have steadily disaggregated across separate companies and become more and more a global phenomenon. The creation and maintenance of a successful innovative product incorporates value far beyond the lead firm and includes partners in the supply chain as well as firms that offer complementary products or services, each of which has its own chain of input and service providers. A successful lead firm understands that the creation of value through innovation is not a zero sum game, and profits are needed all along the supply chain for a business model to be sustainable (Linden, Kraemer and Dedrick, 2007). In the electronics industry each product has typically a large number of low-value components. Although the manufacturers of these components earn profits, they account for a small share of the total value added along the supply chain. Most electronics products further contain a small number of high-value components, such as visual displays, hard drives or key integrated circuits. These components most likely embody proprietary knowledge that helps differentiating the final product and to command a commensurately high margin. By virtue of their high cost, these inputs will usually account for a relatively large share of total value added. Innovation is rapid in these components, and accounts for much of the short product cycles for final products (Linden, Kraemer and Dedrick, 2009). By combining such high value physical components with innovative digital products, such as software, new lines of innovative products emerge that represent new challenges for supply chains. In this scenario, the supply or availability of digital product becomes integrated into a more comprehensive supply chain strategy involving physical supply and service-based elements. Hybrid distribution leverages the advantages of digital products to improve the performance of more traditional supply chains. The following describes three industry examples of such approaches and illustrates the benefits and challenges of hybrid innovations.

Case A: Computer Manufacturer

Company A is a global hardware and systems software company, selling a wide variety of software and hardware solutions to enterprise customers and general consumers. The products sold by Company A are much more open and mainstream in terms of the general computer market. They are designed on open standards and thus can integrate easily with multiple third-party systems. Access to the Internet is a given, and multiple different updating approaches are available.

Alongside Company A's hardware supply chain there is a digital supply chain, focusing on the distribution of software over the Internet. Company A's key strategy is to maximise the sales of hardware using software to enhance this value proposition. Therefore, many key software packages are free to all users and have commanded large market share in some niche areas. The approach to software distribution is simple. Customers log in, share details that can be used by Company A for marketing purposes, and then they receive the software over the Internet for free. (If customers want a DVD they need to pay a premium to cover postage and other incurred costs). Some high end software licenses require payment and in this case a standard "shopping cart" e-commerce process is used. Few software controls such as DRM (Digital Rights Management) are imposed, as payment is primarily used to provide customers with extended warranty contracts and customer services.

The biggest challenge faced by Company A relates to the size of the downloads (often many gigabytes). Very large downloads require specialised software to manage file corruption or a breakdown in internet access during the download process itself. More intelligent download mechnisms can be used to limit the amount being downloaded, particularly if the files being downloaded are updates to already installed software. Management of newly launched software can generate enormous stresses on the infrastructure so third party Content Distribution Networks (CDNs) are engaged to assist with the process.

Case B: Computer Manufacturer

Company B is a global Software and IT Hardware company, selling IT focused software and hardware solutions to enterprise customers. Company B's core systems are sophisticated high end units that are often pre-configured to each customer's exact specification prior to shipping. Pre-configuration involves selecting different options in both hardware and software elements.

A key feature of these systems is that they are in regular contact with the manufacturer over the Internet. Configuration management software residing within the manufacturer keeps track of all software on each system and will alert if new versions of software become available. When the systems contact the manufacturer using a pre-arranged polling schedule, any updates to the base software configuration can be downloaded automatically to the systems over the Internet. Customers purchase a software contract from the manufacturer when buying the systems. This contract can be renewed after a number of years, often involving the purchase of a new hardware system. In this way a regular stream of revenue is maintained while the payment process is separated from the downloading process, greatly simplifying the updating process.

Another advantage of the approach used by Company B is that the manufacturer can quickly identify if there are any problems associated with the hardware system, i.e. if any key components are not working correctly. A regular diagnostic check is carried out and if any aspect of the system fails the check, a technician is automatically deployed to the customer with a replacement component ready to install. This has significant implications inventory management benefits for Company B's service division while also providing large supply chainale customer service benefits. New software packages can be installed onto the systems (based on changes to the software contract). This can be carried out based on remote downloads or (because of the large size of some software packages) on-site update using optical media. The systems themselves will register the installation and update the configuration management system. The key concern with this approach is the sophistication of the configuration management infrastructure which requires a cradle-to-grave approach for the lifetime of the hardware system.

Case C: Automotive Device Manufacturer

This manufacturer (Company C) provides diagnostic devices to aftermarket automotive technicians. The devices require the latest servicing information on the newest vehicles in the market, so there is a requirement to update the devices frequently.

There are a number of challenges associated with this particular market. First of all, the working environment is prone to significant wear and tear. Diagnostic devices and their update mechanisms need to be able to handle grease and grime, wildly fluctuating outdoor temperatures and rough treatment by customers. An automotive workshop is not necessarily the best place for thumb-drives and DVD updates. Secondly, the information content requiring update can be very large, amounting to gigabytes of information during each update. Thirdly, internet access is patchy in the target market. Many areas of the USA and Europe – the principal target markets – do not have reliable access to high-speed broadband. Clearly, there is a need for a combined physical / digital supply chain. The physical supply chain will cover the manufacture, distribution and repair of the hardware, while a digital supply chain is required to manage the software update process.

Company C's original approach to managing this problem was to provide hard-wearing cartridges (akin to the cartriges used in old-style video gaming devices) each time there was a software update. This approach was very expensive, limiting in terms of sales, requiring its own separate manufacturing and distribution process, and difficult to manage, so Company C invested in a new approach that would enable the dealer (the principal sales and service contact with the customer) to download the software onto the customer devices themselves. CD's were provided to the dealers and from there the software could be downloaded to the customer's device.

This process has simplified the process of delivering software updates as it does not require an intensive manufacturing process other than the burning of CD's and free distribution of this media through the postal system. Work is ongoing to make the updates available to dealers over the Internet. There are a number of complexities associated with the process. Special computer software tools are required to ensure that revenue is collected from every customer download. Because an unlimited number of downloads can take place from each dealer's laptop, it is important that a high level of security is implemented to prevent non-revenue downloads from taking place. In addition, the process requires significant dealer involvement. This is a technical task requiring training and it takes time away from the dealers when they could be selling. The company has more recently implemented subsupply chainriptions packages to separate the revenue gathering process from the downloading process. This further removes complexity and provides the opportunity of a further income stream for the company.

SOLUTIONS AND RECOMMENDATIONS FOR SUPPLY CHAIN INNOVATION

The above case studies lead the authors to recommend a number of approaches to improving supply chain innovation.

a. Internet access and Internet updating should be central to the development strategy of electronic devices. As much software and firmware as possible should be amenable to Internet updating. The benefits are a decoupling of the product lifecycles, the obvious reduction in updating costs associated with an upgrade and the improvement in customer service effectiveness as updates and bug-fixes can be addressed more quickly. While hardware development should be primarily focused on developing and improving connectivity, reliability and performance; software should focus on functionality in all its forms). Hardware development, in so far as is possible, should not dictate how software should function.
b. Strong processes are required for integrating customer feedback into the product development cycle. These processes must incorporate Internet based feedback and can be both explicit (customers contacting manufacturers and developers directly, and implicit - software contacting product developers about usage and performance). Feedback integration strategies need to keep in mind privacy and aspects.
c. Software enables innovation to be an ongoing, continuous process and not an infrequent, intermittent activity. New innovations can now be introduced on the basis of hours and days, not months and years. Developers should work to eliminate many of the barriers to ongoing innovation, such as revenue systems that are decoupled from the innovation process or waterfall methodologies that can result in long turnaround timelines.

FUTURE RESEARCH DIRECTIONS

The research presented in this chapter is rather exploratory and qualitative in nature and thus has limitations in terms of its generalisability. Therefore, further research using a mix of alternative quantitative and qualitative approaches that allow a larger and more diverse population would improve reliability. The main focus of this chapter concentrated mainly on software and neglects other types of hybrid products including music and video players, video-game consoles, vehicles and industrial control systems. Further research is necessary to understand the particular supply chain management implications for each product type. Different customers and industrial sectors may further affect the hybrid approaches employed by electronic device manufacturers. A number of key factors may be derived from an analysis of different market sizes and dynamics, supply chain lead times and innovation cycle periods.

A more recent advent in supply chain related innovation is mobile supply chain management (mSCM). It refers to the use of mobile applications and devices to monitor the running of supply chain activities and enables real-time reverse feedback flows. The integration of mobile technology enabled products into existing IT systems and thereby replacing dependence on wired systems provides organisations the flexibility to apply wireless technology to any IT-enabled supply chain functions, and thus extends existing supply chain management capabilities. With such real-time information broadcasts and updates there is no waiting time and supply chain transactions are instantaneous and efficient (Eng, 2006). Thus, a further research direction would be to explore the extent of use of mobile enabled supply chain technologies within the realm of hybrid products.

CONCLUSION

In order to compete in a highly innovative market, electronic products manufacturers increasingly require hybrid supply chains that integrate digital products and physical products to create long-term customer value. There are a number of approaches possible, depending on the degree to which the products are updateable via the Internet and the extent to which the producer wishes to manage intellectual property. As electronic devices become more widespread and sophisticated, hybrid supply chains will increase in prominence and importance.

REFERENCES

Alonso-Rasgado, T., Thompson, G., & Elfstrom, B.-O. (2004). The design of functional (total care) products. *Journal of Engineering Design, 15*(6), 515–540. doi:10.1080/09544820412331271176

Anthony, S. D., Johnson, M. W., Sinfield, J. V., & Altman, E. J. (2008). *The Innovator's Guide to Growth: Putting Disruptive Innovation to Work*. Boston, MA: Harvard Business Press.

Bagchi, P. K., Chun, B., Skjoett-Larsen, T., & Soerensen, L. B. (2005). Supply chain integration: A European survey. *International Journal of Logistics Management, 16*(2), 275–294. doi:10.1108/09574090510634557

Baltacioglu, E. A., Kaplan, M. D., Yurt, O., & Kaplan, C. (2007). A new framework for service supply chains. *The Service Industries Journal, 27*(2), 105–124. doi:10.1080/02642060601122629

Cardozo, R., McLaughlin, K., Harmon, B., Reynolds, P., & Miller, B. (1993). Product- market choices and growth of new businesses. *Journal of Product Innovation Management, 10*, 331–340. doi:10.1016/0737-6782(93)90075-2

Chandy, R. K., & Tellis, G. J. (2000). The incumbent's curse? Incumbency, size, and radical product innovation. *Journal of Marketing, 6*, 1–17. doi:10.1509/jmkg.64.3.1.18033

Chou, M., & Ruchika, A. (2006). *An in-depth study of the software supply chains*. IEEE International Conference on Industrial Informatics.

Christopher, M. (2005). *Logistics and Supply Chain Management: Creating Value-Adding Networks*, London: FT Prentice Hall.

Cohen, M. A., Agrawal, N., & Agrawal, V. (2006). Winning in the aftermarket. *Harvard Business Review, 84*(5), 129–138.

Crawford, C. M., & Di Benedetto, C. A. (2000). *New Product Management*. Boston: McGraw-Hill.

Damanpour, F. (1991). Organizational innovation: a meta-analysis of effects of determinants and moderators. *Academy of Management Journal*, *34*(3), 555–590. doi:10.2307/256406

Dos Santos, B.L., Peffer, K. (1995). Rewards to Investors in Innovative Information Technology Applications: First Movers and Early Followers in ATMs. *Organization Supply chainience, 6* (3), 241-259.

Eng, T. Y. (2006). Mobile supply chain management: challenges for implementation. *Technovation*, *26*, 682–686. doi:10.1016/j.technovation.2005.07.003

Essa, A. (2005). *Innovation Life Cycle and the S-Curve*. Retrieved: 28 June 2010 from: http://tatler.typepad.com/nose/2005/11/innovation_life.html.

Evans, P. B., & Wurster, T. S. (1997). Strategy and the new economics of information. *Harvard Business Review*, (Sept-Oct): 69–82.

Graeml, A. R., Ebgelbert, R., & Weiler, A. L. G. (2008). *Understanding value chain strategies for the iPod through the perspective of Fine's evolutionary model*. Proceedings of the 15th Annual International Conference of the European Operations Management Association (EurOMA), Gronigen, Netherlands, 15-18 June, 2008.

Harrison, T., & Waite, K. (2005). Critical factors affecting intermediary web site adoption: understanding how to extend e-participation. *Journal of Business and Industrial Marketing*, *20*(4/5), 187–199. doi:10.1108/08858620510603864

Johnson, M., & Mena, C. (2008). Supply chain management for servitised products: a multi-industry case study. *International Journal of Production Economics*, *114*, 27–39. doi:10.1016/j.ijpe.2007.09.011

Lambert, D. M., Cooper, M. C., & Pagh, J. D. (1998). Supply chain management: implementation issues and research opportunities. *International Journal of Logistics Management*, *9*(2), 1–20. doi:10.1108/09574099810805807

Linden, J., Kraemer, K., & Dedrick, G. (2009). Who profits from innovation in global value chains? A study of the iPod and notebook PCs. *Industrial and Corporate Change*, 1–36.

Lummus, R. R., Krumwiede, D. W., & Vokurka, R. J. (2001). The relationship of logistics to supply chain management: developing a common industry definition'. *Industrial Management & Data Systems*, *101*(8), 426–432. doi:10.1108/02635570110406730

Merrifield, D. B. (2000). Changing nature of competitive advantage. *Research Technology Management*, *41*(1), 41–45.

Naylor, J. B., Naim, M. M., & Berry, D. (1999). Leagility: Integrating the lean and agile manufacturing paradigms in the total supply chain. *International Journal of Production Economics*, *62*(1–2), 107–118. doi:10.1016/S0925-5273(98)00223-0

Oliva, R., & Kallenberg, R. (2003). Managing the transition from products to services. *International Journal of Service Industry Management*, *14*(2), 160–172. doi:10.1108/09564230310474138

Pant, S., Sethia, R., & Bhandari, M. (2003). Making sense of the e-supply chain landscape: an implementation framework. *International Journal of Information Management*, *23*(3), 201–221.

Penttinen, E., & Palmer, J. (2007). Improving firm positioning through enhanced offerings and buyer–seller relationships. *Industrial Marketing Management*, *36*(5), 552–564. doi:10.1016/j.indmarman.2006.02.005

Porter, M. E., & Stern, S. (2001). Innovation: location matters. *MIT Sloan Management Review*, *42*(4), 28–36.

Ramsay, J. (2005). The real meaning of value in trading relationships. *International Journal of Operations & Production Management, 25*(6), 549–565. doi:10.1108/01443570510599719

Rogers, E. M. (1995). *Diffusion of innovations.* 4 ed. New York: The Free Press.

Roy, S., Sivakumar, K., Wilkinson, I.F. (2004). Innovation generation in supply chain relationships: a conceptual model and research propositions. *Journal of the Academy of Marketing Supply chainience, 32* (1), 61-79.

Ryan, C., & Wagner, C. (2009). Innovation Cycle Management of Digital Supply Chains, Chapter 13 in Sweeney, E. (ed.) *Supply Chain Management and Logistics in a Volatile Global Environment,* Dublin: Blackhall Publishers, 169-182.

Ryan, C., Wagner, C., Sweeney, E., Esposito, E., & Evangelista, P. (2009). *Digital supply chains: towards a framework for software distribution.* Annual Conference of International Purchasing and Supply Education and Research Association (IPSERA), European Business Supply chainhool (EBS), Wiesbaden, Germany, April 6-8.

Shapiro, C. & Varian, H. (1999). *Information Rules*. Boston: Harvard Business Supply chainhool Press.

Sweeney, E., Evangelista, P., & Passaro, R. (2005). Putting supply-chain learning theory into practice: lessons from an Irish case. *International Journal of Knowledge and Learning, 1*(4), 357–372. doi:10.1504/IJKL.2005.008357

Tidd, J., Bessant, J., & Pavitt, K. (2005). *Managing innovation: integrating technological, market and organizational change*. Chichester: Wiley.

Utterback, J. M. (1994). *Mastering the dynamics of innovation: how companies can seize opportunities in the face of technological change*. Boston, MA: Harvard Business Press.

Vandermerwe, S., & Rada, J. (1988). Servitization of business: adding value by adding services. *European Management Journal, 6*(4), 314–324. doi:10.1016/0263-2373(88)90033-3

Chapter 4
Supply Chain Integration in the Textile and Garment Industries:
Some Observations from Thailand

Ruth Banomyong
Thammasat University, Thailand

ABSTRACT

Supply chain integration has been theoretically posited as a key requirement that enhances supply chain competitiveness and innovation. However, there has been a lack of empirical evidence related to the level of supply chain integration and its benefit. This chapter provides an illustration of the level of integration observed in the Thai textile and garment supply chain. The supply chain integration analysis was done through the use of the quick scan audit methodology and it was observed that there was no integrated supply chain in the Thai textile and garment industry. The majority of the existing textile and garment supply chain relationship in Thailand was mostly limited to internal functions within member firms with some dyadic relationships. This means that most Thai textile and garment firms are still struggling with internal integration and are still not able to integrate their respective supply chain thus affecting innovation capability of Thai textile and garment supply chain. Governmental support may be needed to develop the facilitating environment for supply chain integration.

DOI: 10.4018/978-1-60960-585-8.ch004

INTRODUCTION

The purpose of this chapter is to describe the status of supply chain integration found in the textile and garment industry in Thailand. A quick scan audit methodology (QSAM) was used to measure the integration of Thai textile and garment supply chains. It was observed that total supply chain integration remains part of utopia. However, it was noticed that dyadic integration is slowly emerging within the Thai textile and garment supply chain members. The output of the QSAM provides insights on the potential development of a roadmap for the integration of textile and garment supply chains not only in Thailand but possibly in other countries as well.

This chapter is separated into 4 main sections. After the introduction, a general background of the Thai textile and garment industry is presented to provide readers with a better understanding of the context and issues faced by the industry. The following section briefly discusses supply chain integration in the literature and the observed gaps. The methodology and findings are then presented to describe the current state of supply chain integration in the textile and garment industry in Thailand. Solutions and recommendations for supply chain innovations are then further explored.

THE THAI TEXTILE AND GARMENT INDUSTRY

Thailand has had a long history of textile and clothing production. The so called "modern" garment and textile industry was established relatively late compared to other East and Southeast Asian countries. The Thai Ministry of Defence first imported textile machinery from Germany in 1936 for military purposes. Private textile mills emerged shortly after the Second World War in response to local textile shortages. Production, which greatly expanded by the 1950's, suffered at the time from the low cost of imported cotton textile from Pakistan resulting in government protection in the form of import quotas and restrictions.

The Thai Investment Promotion Act in 1960 saw the takeover and expansion of military owned mills. Local entrepreneurs and Chinese investors from Shanghai and Hong Kong became key players in consolidating the textile and garment industry. This was coupled with Japanese firms forming joint ventures with Thai textile companies a few years later.

The 1970's found the Thai government mixing protection, promotion and restriction policy together. Import tariffs were extremely high, up to 100 percent, protecting the industry from external subsidised products and regional competitors. Throughout the decade, restrictions were placed on the industry prohibiting capacity expansion and the establishment of new textile firms. While the laws were not entirely effective in limiting capacity or expansion as companies imported machinery without registering it with the Thai Ministry of Industry, the abolishment of restrictions in 1987 resulted in large increases in investment, machinery imports and establishment of new companies.

The importance of textile and clothing manufacturing to Thailand's economy is apparent. The industry currently consists of approximately 2000 garment firms, 250 weaving and textile firms and 150 spinning companies employing over 1 million workers.

The export of garments and textiles from Thailand was heavily influenced by membership in the Multi-Fibre Agreement (MFA) and Agreement on Textiles and Clothing (ATC). The MFA, which started in 1975, oversaw a textile quota system in place for the export of garments and textile from developing countries to the United States, Canada, the European Union (EU) and Norway. The ATC, signed in 1995, started a 10-year transition period, which incrementally raised quotas on textiles and clothing, until full elimination by the year 2005, integrating the sector fully into General Agreement on Tariff and Trade (GATT) principles. The MFA initially proved to be beneficial to Thailand as it curtailed the exports of clothing and textiles from Hong Kong, South Korea and Taiwan, allowing local firms to develop markets.

By the 1980's, Thailand was using its full quotas and the agreement started to hinder exports, particularly with the United States, which placed embargos on Thai clothing for exceeding quotas in 1985. The Department of Foreign Trade (DFT) at the Thai Ministry of Commerce administered the textile quota allocation to Thai exporters by granting textile export licenses for products entering the American, Canadian or European markets. The available quotas were divided into two parts: the basic quota and the residual quota. The principal quota, usually 70 to 80 percent of the export quota available, was distributed free annually to exporting firms on the basis of their past export performance. The residual quota, usually the remaining 20 percent, was allocated on a monthly basis and can be sought by new firms, or ones already holding principal quotas. This system favoured large exporting firms who could monopolise quotas because of their historical performance, and forced new firms to concentrate on non-quota markets including Japan, and ASEAN countries[1].

The clothing and textile industry in Thailand was originally founded on low cost labour and its future depended very much upon more modernisation and change. Low cost producers in China, Indonesia and Turkey are providing significant competition to Thailand in labour intensive production, while Hong Kong, Korea, Italy, the USA and other countries have a strong holds on the higher technology, higher value garment and textile market.

The Thai government responded to the problem by borrowing from the Asian Development Bank and the World Bank to finance industrial rehabilitation. A Thai Textile Institute was set up to stimulate the upgrading of the industry and manage the distribution of funds in the form of soft loans to finance renovation. This Thai Textile Institute has been focusing its efforts on improving the competitiveness of local garment and textile businesses. Emphasis has been put on the upgrading of existing machinery with modern technology for greater efficiency along with human resource development to improve knowledge, and competency of textile industry management and workers through seminars, training and education. The Thai Textile Institute has tried to guide Thai textile and clothing manufacturers to operate in a similar fashion to those in countries with developed industries by improving Thai design capability, brand-name development, and by establishing industrial clusters through integrated supply chain management.

The success of such initiative to modernise the clothing and textile industry along with the adaptability of individual companies will largely determine if this industry remains an integral part of the national economy, or if it is indeed a 'sunset' industry as some have predicted. The survival of Thai textile and garment industry requires public and private cooperation in building strength and finding niche markets.

TEXTILE AND CLUSTER SUPPLY CHAIN DEVELOPMENT

Thai authorities readily admit that there is an urgent need to create industrial clusters to support the local textile and garment industry. These industrial clusters need to be linked through the integration of supply chain management processes and practices. This rationale was developed because of the changes occurring in the competitive landscape. Stand-alone Thai textile and garment factories that preferred to have nothing to do with anyone else are not able to survive much longer as they simply cannot compete in today's cut-throat environment, particularly when dealing with overseas buyers who have a variety of choices and enormous bargaining power. This is particularly true at the lower end of the market where buyers are very cost conscious and want speedy delivery. The most important thing for today's buyer is the ability to deal with suppliers who can provide everything in one place.

As an example, a customer would like to order 1 million shirts from a given company X in Thailand with delivery scheduled within 45 days. The order will come with complete specifications for the raw materials, colour and size. Company X in Thailand would then need to immediately manage the order with the other textile firms in its supply chain. This means ordering the cutting at the same time as ordering fabric and other accessories. Supply chain management therefore becomes a key success factor for company X to successfully respond to customer's order.

This approach is totally different from what had happened in the past when buyers usually indicated that they wanted to use certain fabrics from certain countries. Today, orders from buyers are placed based on the basis that the supplier has strong supply chain capability. As a result, only the emergence of a strong cluster can lead to an integrated supply chain and solid links with outside stakeholders. A strong cluster means smooth trading processes throughout the supply chain with the elimination of bottlenecks. This will further reduce cost and lead time. In addition, with the introduction of sophisticated information and communication technology (ICT), the flow from securing raw materials through the production process to the end product being ready for delivery to the customer will be even faster and more accurate while internal communication between parties within the supply chain more precise.

If the Thai textile and garment industry can integrate their supply chains then Thai manufacturers would be able to respond faster to market demands than their competitors. Only with such speed would the Thai textile and garment industry survive.

The main problem from a policy perspective is how long it will take to build strong textile and garment industrial clusters through supply chain integration?

SUPPLY CHAIN INTEGRATION

Supply chain integration (SCI) is an important research area as such integration is claimed by many authors to be akin to supply chain excellence (Christopher, 1998; New, 1996). Indeed, in the current climate of global supply chain competition, integration is regarded as a prerequisite for enabling winning performance (Lee, 2000; Margetta, 1998). Published studies have mainly focused on power position in the supply chain (Cox, 2001); purchasing integration (Narasimhan and Das, 2001); impacts of simplified material flow (Childerhouse and Towill, 2003); barriers to implementation (Pagell, 2004); and shared resources (van Donk and van Vaart, 2005).

Despite over 25 years of academic publications, there remains a significant gap between SCI theory and practice. This might be partly due to the natural tendency to mostly highlight 'best practice' where presented supply chains are often perceived to be in better shape than is the reality. For example, a comprehensive site-based study by Towill *et al.* (2000) of the European automotive sector, found that only 10 percent of supply chains could be regarded as fully integrated. A survey by Poirier and Quinn (2003) likewise concluded that just 10 percent of supply chains in North America had achieved external integration.

The literature on supply chain integration is vast and varied but it was observed that the gap between theory and practice has not been filled yet. It is therefore important to utilise an analytical tool that can provide an assessment of supply chain integration level as well as linkage strengths between supply chain members.

THE QUICK SCAN AUDIT METHODOLOGY

A Quick Scan Audit Methodology (QSAM) is a supply chain oriented business diagnostic. It is designed to take a snapshot of the present operation of the supply chain. It focuses on the product delivery process and the associated information control process. It identifies key improvement opportunities with respect to supply chain issues and is geared towards understanding and documenting the business process. These improvement opportunities can then be ranked for implementation in terms of economic value added (EVA) benefit, time and cost to implement. Hence, a road map for supply chain improvement is generated indicating both "Quick Hits" and longer term actions. At the end of the supply chain diagnostic there are three possible outcomes:

- The supply chain exhibits best practice. No need to improve but use the QSAM as a tool to transfer best practice.
- The supply chain can be greatly improved with a few simple actions by implementing the most critical "Quick Hits".
- The supply chain needs major re-engineering. Need to set up a dedicated task force to design and implement the change.

Figure 1 illustrates the scope of the QSAM while Figure 2 describes the process involved when conducting a QSAM. The scope of the QSAM is based on the Understand, Document, Simplify and Optimise (UDSO) framework and it should be understood that the QSAM is not a miracle tool that can address all supply chain problems. It can be seen that the QSAM primarily focused on the first two stages: understand and document. Although any identified high-impact, quick-hit opportunities tend to be tackled early in the simplification stage, in order to demonstrate in-house capability and an early return on the QSAM investment, nevertheless the ultimate aim of QSAM is to identify the types of soundly underpinned and customised supply chain integration recommendations that tend to require persistent implementation effort and longer term company commitment.

QSAM team members frequently take on a steering group role for such endeavours. By closing the gap between researcher and subject, QSAM yields consistent results and provides close, customised supply chain integration support to practising supply chain professionals. In essence, it helps managers to identify the root (Tillman, *et al*, 2008a). The QSAM is akin to being diagnosed initially by a generalist medical doctor and if specific symptoms require expert advice then referrals can be made to the most appropriate specialist.

The unit of analysis for QSAM is a value stream, which was popularised by Womack and Jones in 1996. In many respects 'supply chain' and 'value stream' are synonymous; a practical interpretation is that a supply chain consists of a bundle of value streams. During a typical QSAM: material and information flows are process-mapped; key managers are interviewed; company archive information is evaluated; and attitudinal questionnaires are completed concerning the interfaces of each value stream.

Figure 1. Scope of QSAM in the UDSO Model

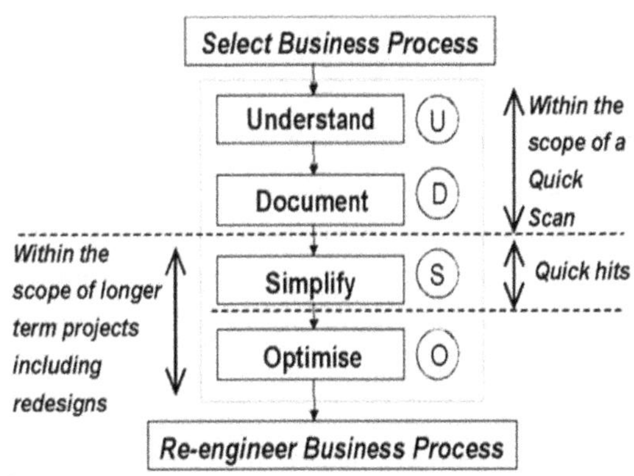

The QSAM process itself is conducted by experienced supply chain academics in a structured approach designed to fit around the limited time availability of busy managers and employees, see Figure 2. To this end, typically four researchers will spend three days actually on site, assisted by an in-house business champion.

QSAM adopts the most common supply chain perspective: that of a focal organisation and its integration into the wider supply chain. At its heart lies an assessment of supply chain integration maturity.

Many authors have identified the need to minimise and remove uncertainties in order to increase control and co-ordination, and improve decision-making effectiveness. Supply chain uncertainty has been classified into four general types in order that root causes and methods for minimisation can be developed, namely process uncertainties, supply uncertainties, demand uncertainties and control uncertainties, in what Mason-Jones and Towill (1997) termed the "uncertainty circle".

Supply uncertainty results from an inability of a company to order raw material efficiently and can be evaluated by looking at supplier delivery performance, time series of orders placed, call offs, deliveries from customers, lead-times, supplier quality reports and raw material stock time series.

Demand uncertainty is associated with a specific customer in relation to schedule variability and can be visualised as the difference between the end customer demand and real orders placed by your customer also an indication of how well you meet your customer requirements. Developing a time series of customer orders, call-offs, deliveries and forecasts identifies this uncertainty.

Process uncertainty affects company's ability to meet a production target. Understanding yield ratios and lead-time estimates in the operations of each business process identifies this uncertainty. Also, if the value stream is competing against others for resources, then the interaction between these value streams must be identified.

Control uncertainty affects company's ability to manage its activities and to transform customer orders into production targets and supplier raw material requests and can be investigated via the time series of customer requirements and supplier requests to deliver. Additionally, a time series of production targets and a thorough understanding of the decisions or control systems that are used to transfer the customer orders into production targets and supplier raw material requests are required.

Figure 3 provides a conceptual illustration of the "uncertainty circle" and its relationship with supply chain uncertainty.

Each of these uncertainties creates a drag on operational performance, and supply chain professionals often are so busy dealing with the fallout they do not have time to attack the root causes of the problem (Tillman, et. al., 2008b). If managers could just understand which of the four areas was causing greatest uncertainty, they could prioritise resources when embarking on a supply chain integration programme.

SUPPLY CHAIN INTEGRATION IN THE THAI TEXTILE AND GARMENT INDUSTRY

The QSAM was utilised to study the Thai textile and garment supply chain in order to assess its level of integration. The scope of the supply chain under study reflects a basic or direct supply chain with 3 levels. The 3 levels are the textile industry, the garment industry and the clothes retailing industry. Figure 4 describes the scope of the supply chain under study.

In order to refine the unit of analysis, a number of supply chains were analysed to reflect the information and physical flow that occurs within textile and garment supply chains. A total of 8 supply chains were selected and an understanding of supply chain processes involved had to be clarified. Figure 5 describes the common flows moving within the Thai textile and garment sup-

Figure 2. The quick scan audit methodology process

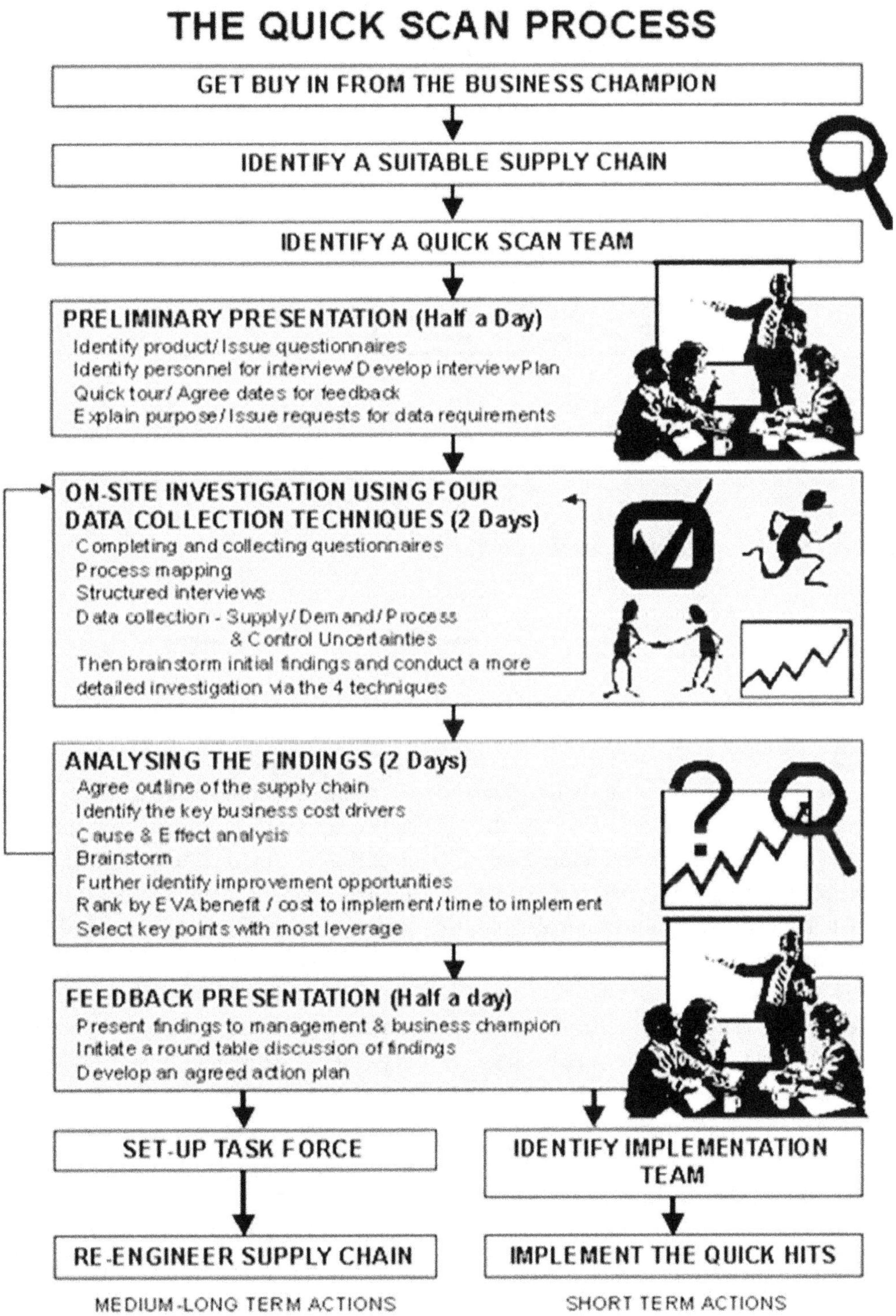

Figure 3. The "uncertainty circle"

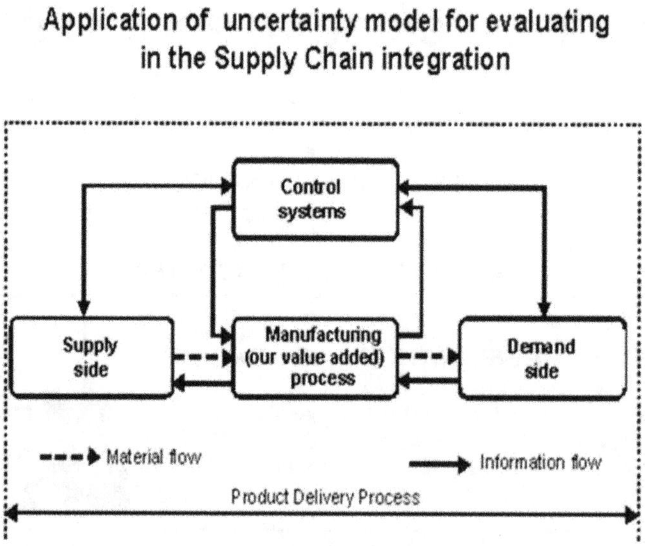

Figure 4. Thai textile and garment supply chain scope

ply chain. The information flow starts from the order generated by the clothe retailer while the physical flow in the supply chains under study starts from the textile manufacturer. It must not be forgotten that the textile manufacturer also has suppliers but they are not considered within the scope of this audit.

A value stream analysis was further conducted to identify activities in the supply chain processes that were either value added or non value added as per the lean paradigm. This value stream analysis was done on a number of textile and garment supply chains. Table 1 hereunder describes the value stream from the textile manufacturers to the garment manufacturers to the clothe retailers. Value-added activities only represent 7.87% of all activities conducted to produce and sell clothe to consumers starting from the textile manufacturers.

A more detailed breakdown of the value added activities highlights that the value added activities for the textile manufacturer is 4.72%, for the garment manufacturer is 2.75% and for the clothe retailer 0.40%. It was observed that in this supply chain, the more one moves up the value chain the more activities add values.

The number of necessary but non value added activities is extremely high. This is in itself not surprising as the highest ratio is taken by the clothe retailer whose main value adding activities relates to making the product available to consumers. It is often observed that in a non manufacturing environment, the highest ratio of activities are those that are considered necessary but non value added. The most common non value added activities relates to the waiting time between each supply chain links and if Thai textile and garment supply chains are able to reduce the overall waiting time

Figure 5. Information and physical flow in Thai textile and garment supply chain

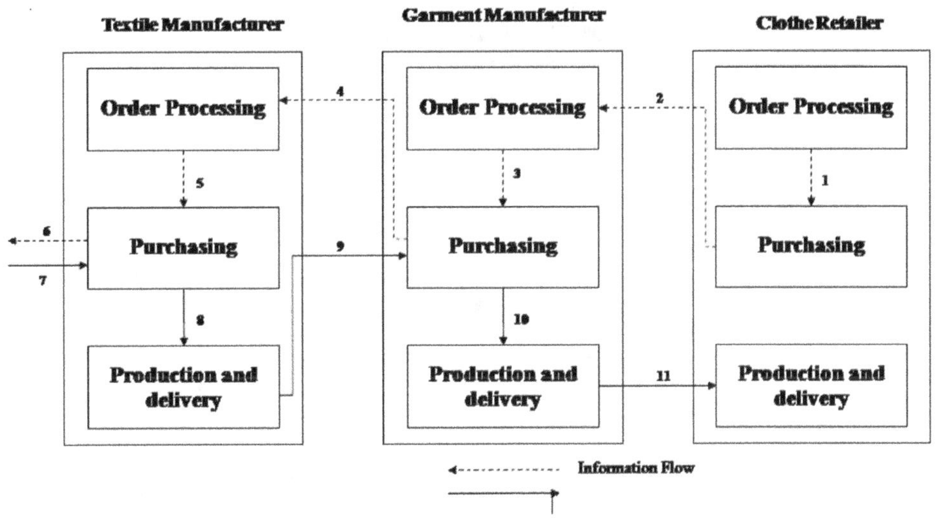

this could help reduce not only its response time but also increase the ratio of value added activities.

The capability to reduce or eliminate non value added activities in supply chains is not sufficient. It is important for supply chains when managed are subject to minimum uncertainty. The rationale behind such statement is derived from Tillman et al (2008b) as low levels of uncertainty have shown to correlate directly with best-in-class practice in which supply chains are highly integrated.

The Thai textile and garment supply chain "uncertainty" cycle highlighted that control uncertainty impacted the most the supply chains under study. In many instances, there was a lack of control capability which was reflected by a lack of visibility within supply chains, lack of mid-level management skills and poor labour discipline.

Table 1. Value stream analysis on Thai textile and garment supply chain

Type of activities	No. of Occurrences	%
Value Added	20	7.87
Non Value Added	42	16.54
Necessary but Non Value Added	192	75.59
TOTAL	254	100

Source: The Author

In order to obtain increase visibility it is possible to enhance the use of information system. Many mid-level managers in the studied supply chains have in fact started from the factory floor and are therefore very good in terms of quality control or production efficiency but they have not been trained to manage production lines effectively. The issue of poor labour discipline is mostly derived from the fact that the majority of factory workers in the Thai textile and garment supply chains are day labourers with no real job security. Figure 6 summarises the supply chain uncertainty circle in the Thai textile and garment supply chain.

Process uncertainty was ranked the 2nd highest uncertainty to impact the Thai textile and garment supply chain followed by supply and demand uncertainty. However, it is interesting to note that uncertainties that impact the most Thai textile and garment supply chain are in fact internal uncertainties not external uncertainties.

Figure 6. Thai textile and garment uncertainty circle

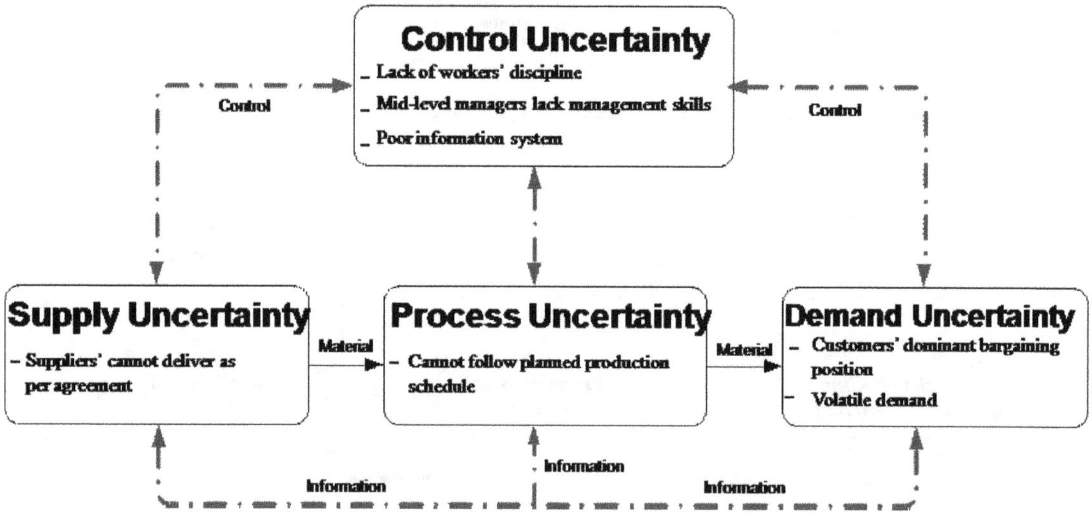

Based on the QSAM, supply chain integration key performance indicators (KPIs) were identified to reflect the level of external integration with suppliers and customers. These KPIs are related to:

- Contract length
- Joint Research and Development Programme
- Trust
- Dependence
- Commitment
- Communication
- Information sharing
- Cost transparency

The following Figure 7 and 8 reflects the level of relationship between the focal firm with his main supplier and customer. There exist in the studied supply chains, cases where main supplier and customer belong to the same conglomerate and cases where the main supplier and customer are both external.

Figure 7 describes the relationship between supplier and customers that are from the same conglomerate. It is interesting to note that even though members of this given supply chain belong to the same business group, there are discrepancies in terms of their relationship levels. Information sharing is done with the supplier but not with the customer while there is more cost transparency with customers than with suppliers. Information sharing and communication are different concepts as communication relates to the frequency of communication between supply chain members What is surprising is the fact that there is no joint research and development within this particular supply chain even though supply chain members are from the same conglomerate.

Figure 8 illustrates the relationship of the focal firm with external suppliers and customers. There is still no joint research and development between supply chain members while it seems that the focal firm is more integrated with its supplier than its customer. This is reflected in the level of commitment, communication, and information sharing as well as cost transparency. There is no cost transparency with the customer.

These relationships related KPIs provided reference on the level of integration between supply chain members. The studied supply chains demonstrated only 2 related integration level. The first level is the baseline, see Figure 9. The baseline refers to the fact that there is no integration within the studied supply chain as all members

Figure 7. Integration with supplier and customer within the same group

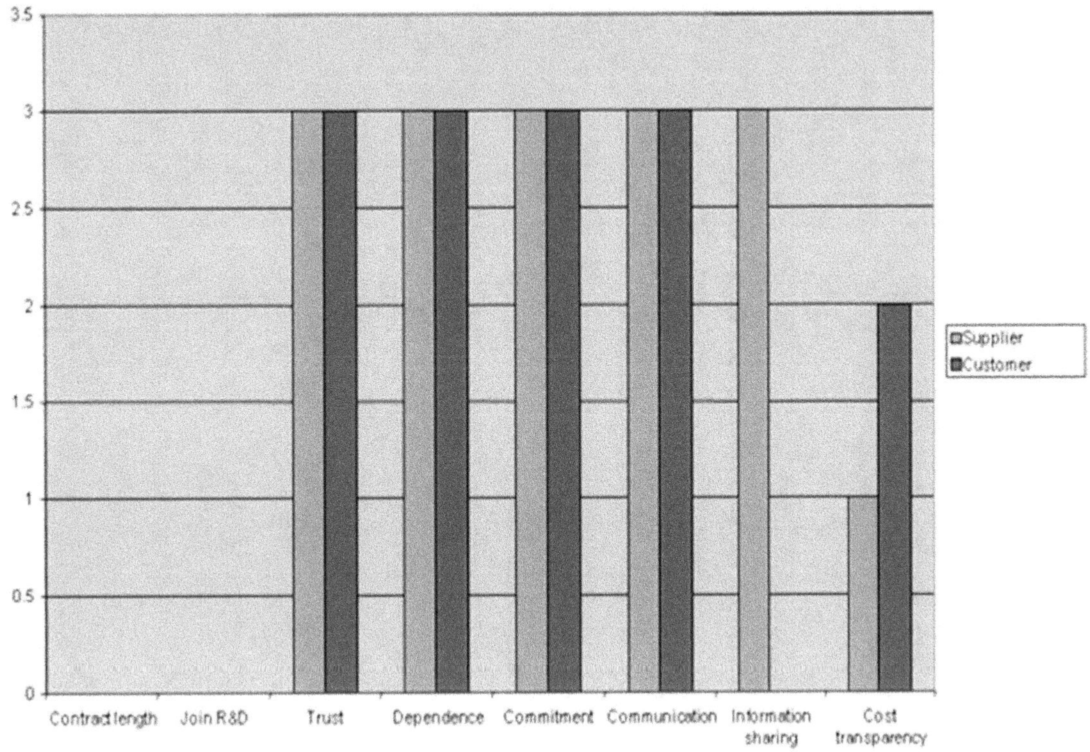

are in fact linked on a transactional basis. The majority of the studied Thai textile and garment supply chains are at the baseline level.

However, it was also observed that some Thai textile and garment supply chains were starting to integrate themselves with key partners. Integration was either found to exist between textile and garment manufacturers or between garment manufacturers and clothe retailers. Figure 10 illustrates the types of existing integration found in Thai textile and garment supply chains.

Currently there is no integrated textile and garment supply chains in Thailand as described in Figure 11. Based on the sample of the Thai textile and garment supply chains studied integrated supply chains are non-existent. Some supply chains are moving in the right direction with dyadic integration but the integration process is not holistic at the present moment. It is based on the power relationship between members within the Thai textile and garment supply chains where the supply chain member with the most bargaining power tries to have either its supplier or customer integrate more into their business process. Maybe this is one of the reasons why industrial clusters in the textile and garment industry have never materialised.

Integrated supply chains remain an elusive goal for most organisations despite a wealth of documented knowledge and ready availability of enabling technologies. Uncertainty is endemic and best practice adoption is patchy at best, despite research that supports the view that a seamless supply chain is not just a theoretical construct but can be achieved in practice (Tillman, et. al. 2008b).

Figure 8. Integration with external supplier and customer

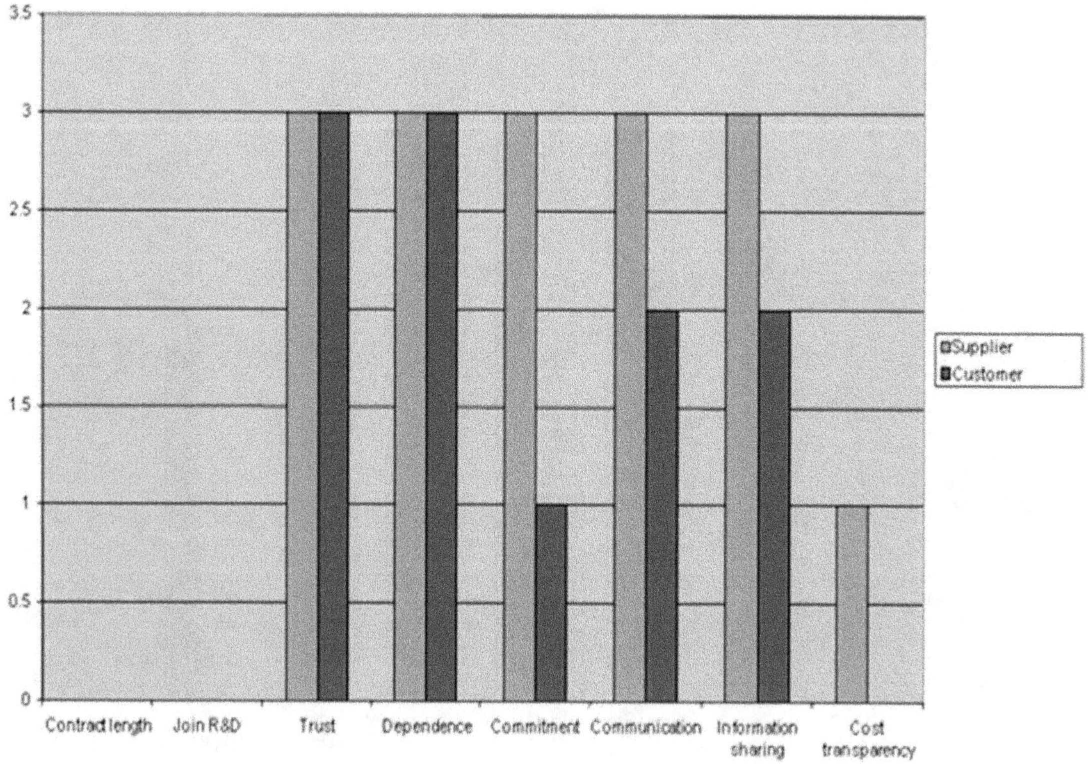

Figure 9. Level 1 baseline

Figure 10. Level 2 dyadic integration

Figure 11. Integrated supply chain

SOLUTION AND RECOMMENDATIONS FOR SUPPLY CHAIN INNOVATION

It is important that these Thai textile and garment supply chains are integrated if supply chain innovation capability is to be enabled. Currently this is not the case as most of the Thai studied firms in the industry are still very much focused on improving their internal supply chain without having the capability to integrate their external supply chains.

Supply chain innovation requires an enabling environment where supply chain integration plays a key driving role. Currently it is too early to state that supply chain innovation exists in the Thai textile and garment supply chain as the necessary preconditions are not in place.

Expanding the knowledge of supply chain integration will provide further basis to understanding the foundation required for supply chain innovation. Sustainable supply chain competitiveness remains an elusive goal that requires innovation capability derived from total supply chain integration.

FUTURE RESEARCH DIRECTIONS

Supply chain integration is a very popular topic in supply chain research. However, there have been limited empirical findings of actual supply chain integration levels described in the literature. Most of the discussion has been focused on the importance of supply chain integration with limited real life examples. This chapter has illustrated a situation related to supply chain integration in the Thai textile and garment industry. This case study is not sufficient to confirm the gap related to the dissemination and implementation of integrated supply chain and further research is needed to validate such observation. It is necessary not only to look at cross-country comparison but also conduct cross-industry analysis on integration levels.

CONCLUSION

The development of industrial clusters through supply chain integration requires close and tight connections between supply chain stakeholders. One of the objectives of such integration is to increase competitiveness and use focused marketing to improved local and international market access. In addition, technology need to be introduced and applied to create higher quality products and better processes while public and private agencies will be encouraged to provide better support in order to improve textile and garment industry responsiveness. Specific policies need to be implemented in order to facilitate the supply chain integration of the Thai textile and garment industry. Hereunder are 4 proposed key supply chain integration policies specific to the Thai context.

- The Thai textile and garment industry will need to focus on the development of both local and international markets. Industry stakeholders must collaborate with regards to domestic markets research in order to obtain a more precise picture of local customers' requirement. In international markets, the industry will need to collaborate on issues such as foreign market penetration, marketing activities, developing niche market and creating merchandise brand.
- The Thai textile and garment industry must focus on developing products that respond better to customers' needs. These include the development of high-performance raw materials such as fibre, special-blended yarn, multi-functional textiles and technical textile where the latter can link this industry with other related industry such as the cluster that develops textile for use in the automotive industry.
- The Thai textile and garment industry must improve its production methods by changing from mass production to mass customization. This can only be realized through

a move into integrated supply-chain management where there will be enhanced collaboration between suppliers and raw material users. In addition, there will be integration in production planning, information system updating, logistics, and last but not the least the alignment of management vision.

- The Thai textile and garment industry will need to cooperate with the Government and other supporting industries as well as integrate the industry with educational, financial institutions, R&D units and other government agencies in order to develop more effective support policies and practices for supply chain integration. This will finally lead to supply chain innovation.

These policies need to be considered carefully as the Thai textile and garment industry currently suffers from a lack of supply chain integration even though there is some dyadic integration within certain level of the industry. Supply chain integration is difficult to achieve due to numerous internal and external barriers. A proposed supply chain integration roadmap jointly developed by the Thai textile and garment industrial associations with the support from the Thai Government could facilitate such integration with the implementation of pilot supply chain integration projects.

REFERENCES

Childerhouse, P., & Towill, D. R. (2003). Simplified material flow holds the key to Supply Chain Integration. *Omega*, (31): 17–27. doi:10.1016/S0305-0483(02)00062-2

Christopher, M. (1998). *Logistics and Supply Chain Management* (2nd ed.). London: FT Prentice Hall.

Cox, A. (2001). *Supply Chains, Markets and Power: Mapping Buyer and Supplier Power Regimes*. London: Routledge.

Lee, H., (2000). Creating value through supply chain integration. *Supply Chain Management Review*, September, 30-36.

Margetta, J. (1998). Fast, global and entrepreneurial: supply chain management Hong Kong style, an interview with Victor Fung. *Harvard Business Review*, (Sept-Oct): 103–114.

Mason-Jones, R., & Towill, D. R. (1997). Information enrichment: designing the supply chain for competitive advantage. *Supply Chain Management: An International Journal*, *2*(4), 137–148. doi:10.1108/13598549710191304

Narasimhan, R., & Das, A. (2001). The impact of purchasing integration and practices on manufacturing performance. *Journal of Operations Management*, *19*(5), 593–609. doi:10.1016/S0272-6963(01)00055-9

New, S. J. (1996). A framework for analysing supply chain improvement. *International Journal of Operations & Production Management*, *16*, 19–34. doi:10.1108/01443579610114059

Pagell, M. (2004). Understanding the factors that enable and inhibit the integration of operations, purchasing and logistics. *Journal of Operations Management*, *22*, 459–487. doi:10.1016/j.jom.2004.05.008

Poirier, C. C., & Quinn, F. J. (2003). A survey of supply chain progress. *Supply Chain Management Review*, *7*(5), 40–48.

Tillman, B., Childerhouse, P., Deakins, E., Potter, A., & Towill, D. (2008a). Supply chain diagnosis. *Operations Management*, *2*, 12–17.

Tillman, B., Childerhouse, P., Deakins, E., Potter, A., & Towill, D. R. (2008b). Why diagnosis supply chain uncertainty. *Operations Management*, *3*, 19–23.

Towill, D. R., Childerhouse, P., & Disney, S. M. (2000). Speeding up the progress curve towards effective supply chain management. *Supply Chain Management: An International Journal*, *5*(3), 122–130. doi:10.1108/13598540010338866

van Donk, D. P., & van der Vaart, T. (2005). A case of shared resources, uncertainty and supply chain integration in the process industry. *International Journal of Production Economics*, *96*, 97–108. doi:10.1016/j.ijpe.2004.03.002

Womack, J. P., & Jones, D. T. (1996). *Lean Logistics*. New York: Simon and Schuster.

ENDNOTE

1 The Association of South East Asian Nations (ASEAN) is composed of Brunei, Cambodia, Indonesia, Lao PDR, Malaysia, Myanmar, Philippines, Singapore, Thailand and Vietnam.

Chapter 5
Supply Chain Integration and Port Competitiveness: A Network Approach

Marcella De Martino
National Research Council, Italy

Alessandra Marasco
National Research Council, Italy

Alfonso Morvillo
National Research Council, Italy

ABSTRACT

The chapter addresses the issue of port value creation from a supply chain integration (SCI) perspective. Based on the concept of supply chain management (SCM), a theoretical model is proposed aimed at identifying the sources of value creation in port environment. The model views the port as a network of actors, resources and activities that co-produces value by promoting a number of interdependencies and assumes that the competitiveness of this port supply network increasingly depends on its "organisational component" as it affects the quality of services including range of logistics services, information and communication technology (ICT) solutions, know-how, and relationships in the port network itself. The final purpose of this model is the definition of a pro-active role of port in supply chain integration and therefore to support port authorities in defining their strategies in the context of growing complexity affecting both the port community and the external competitive arena.

INTRODUCTION

Supply chain management (SCM) literature has highlighted the benefits deriving from logistics integration, meant as the coordination and integration of activities devoted to planning, managing, and controlling the flow of goods, services and related information from the point of origin to destination (transportation, inventory management, order processing, etc.). Integration is the core concept of SCM and all definitions emphasize, to different extents, the need to integrate processes and flows between organisations within a supply chain through inter-organisational relationships,

DOI: 10.4018/978-1-60960-585-8.ch005

with the aim of increasing value for the final customer. According to some authors, the higher the level of integration between actors of the chain, the more potential benefits for all the actors (including the final customer) and thus, the more competitive the whole supply chain (Hines *et al.*, 2000; Lambert, 2001). From an empirical perspective, studies on SCM have analysed the effects of integration on three interdependent levels: (1) intra-organisational, i.e. among the different departments and company activities; (2) dyadic, i.e. among activities of the company and its suppliers or customers; and, (3) inter-organisational (the supply chain), i.e. among the activities of the company, its direct suppliers and its customers (Harland, 1996). The relatively recent incorporation of the term network into SCM research can be seen as an attempt to widen the concept so as to describe the complex reality more appropriately (Dubois *et al.*, 2003). Obviously, the whole complexity cannot be captured but what particular structures and patterns are exploited for value generation and how these are managed by the organisations require consideration. This can be explained by the fact that most of SCM models emphasize the linear relationships between a focal firm, a supplier, and a customer. One of the major overlooked issues is that any focal organisation is normally part of several supply chains and, therefore, efforts to optimise individual supply chains without considering multiple interdependencies among chains may hamper the efficiency elsewhere in the network (Hakansson & Peerson, 2004).

The application of the network concept in the SCM literature has resulted in the definition of supply network, i.e. "the set of supply chains that describe the flow of goods and services from its original source to its end customer" (Lamming *et al.*, 2000, p. 676). This concept considers the companies to be like open systems, influenced by the actors in the environment in which they operate and dependent on the resources supplied by other organisations; through different forms of interactions, the companies can have access to and make use of external resources owned by other network actors. The actors are defined by the activities they carry out and by the resources they control; they are connected to the other network actors through relationships. The identity of an actor is therefore made up of the unique combination of resources it owns and the activities it manages (Hakansson & Shenota, 1995).

The supply network structure is a field of study of considerable importance, as it includes the identification and description of relationships among actors in the same network and the process of creating value for the end customer, through different mechanisms of coordination (Lazzarini *et al.*, 2001). Every company is a member of a set of supply chains with different roles and decision-making powers. In this environment, the inter-organisational relationships are considered to be the most relevant strategic resources and viewed as "bridges of value" (Hakansson, 1982) in that they give companies access to other actors' resources in the network and strongly contribute to value co-production (Normann & Ramirez, 1993).

With reference to port competitiveness, some authors have referred recent contributions and conceptual categories within SCM literature to re-define strategic positioning and port strategies. Indeed, consistent with the spread of the new paradigm by which real competition is not company against company but rather supply chain against supply chain (Christopher, 1992), it has been stated that also for port, competition is between logistic chains (Huybrechts *et al.*, 2002).

From a review of recent studies (Huybrechts *et al.*, 2002; Robinson, 2002; Paixão & Marlow, 2003; Carbone & De Martino, 2003; Bichou & Gray, 2004; Tongzon *et al.*, 2009), the role of ports in supply chains has been analysed by addressing the strategies and integration processes undertaken by terminal operators and shipping companies that undoubtedly play a key role in determining port competitiveness. Thus, these studies have mainly focused on the contribution of a single port actor in the process of value creation, without considering the interdependences among different actors of the port community. Despite having brought to light the traditional conflictuality within port communities and the need to integrate the port and its hinterland, these studies have not dealt with integration among actors as a source of competitive advantage.

Starting from this gap, the definition of a proactive role of port in supply chain integration is the purpose of this chapter that presents a new framework for port competitiveness based on a network perspective (Hakansson & Snehota, 1995), adopting the concept of value chain constellation (Normann & Ramirez, 1993). In particular, the framework takes into consideration all the possible interaction modalities among port actors in the management of business activities and resources in the process of creating value for final clients. The way in which resources are "activated" and activities performed largely depends on the inter-organisational relationships among port operators and other actors in the supply network. Indeed, relationships are the means by which port actors access to, mobilize and combine critical resources and processes, creating value and promoting innovation within the company and in the network.

Thus, the theoretical model focuses on the issue of coping with multiple interdependencies among supply chains, contributing to the scientific debate on supply chain innovation in the port environment. In this respect, though acknowledging the critical role of new technologies for innovation and integration of ports in supply chains, it is believed that prior attention should be dedicated to the collaborative networks that represent the "fertile ground" in which any improvement can take place effectively.

The chapter is structured as follows. In the first section a literature review on port studies adopting a SCM approach is presented with the aim of highlighting the main problematic issues for its application in the port context. Then, the network model for port value creation is described in its main features, while the third section is dedicated to the definition of the methodological pathway in order to apply the framework. Finally some solutions and recommendations for supply chain innovation in ports are provided, followed by future research directions and concluding remarks.

SUPPLY CHAIN INTEGRATION FOR PORT COMPETITIVENESS

In the recent debate on port competitiveness, a growing number of studies have focused on the integration of port activities in companies' supply chains in an attempt to frame the port as a whole in the process of creating value for the end customer.

The concept of integration in the port context has essentially concerned intermodality and organisational integration undertaken by global carriers in order to meet the changing requirements of industrial and commercial firms and, at the same time, improving their own efficiency. In particular, the literature on intermodality has mainly concentrated on the conditions for efficiency and effectiveness of intermodal container transport chains, with specific reference to the management of port logistics (Morash & Clinton, 1997; Janic & Reggiani, 2001). Literature on organisational integration, however, has dealt with the process of logistics re-organisation of large global players, created by means of different forms of vertical and horizontal integration (Evangelista & Morvillo, 1999; Heaver *et al.*, 2000; Cariou, 2001; Notteboom & Winkelmans, 2001; Slack & Fremont, 2005). With reference to this issue, the debate on the competitive struggle between large terminal operators and shipping companies for the control - through mergers and acquisitions - of the container market, and the role the port authority should play in order to avoid dominant positions in the port (Notteboom, 2004), is particularly interesting. These two areas of study extend the field of analysis to the role and integration modes of ports within global transport systems, but they underline the passive role traditionally played by ports in relation to the strategic choices of other port community operators, with obvious effects on their bargaining power and, more in general, on their development strategies. In this respect, it has been shown that ports are mere "pawns in the game" within global transport systems and that the power of liner shipping affects port development (Slack, 1993).

Under this perspective, terminals and their management, though crucial for port competitiveness, should not represent the only element in the development of port policies, as they link the success or failure of the port to the strategic choices of global players such a terminal operators and shipping companies. Such a passive position of the port does not guarantee a long term and sustainable positioning and should be replaced by a dynamic and more proactive role in this new competitive scenario.

In re-defining port positioning and strategies, Robinson (2002) proposes a new paradigm based on the concept of value constellation (Normann & Ramirez, 1993). The author considers a port as a Third Party Logistics (TPL) provider that intervenes in a series of different companies' supply chains. Specifically, the port is a market focused firm, where all businesses are managed to provide superior value to target customers. By using the theoretical considerations elaborated by Cox *et al.* (2002), he believes that also with reference to ports, strategic positioning choices involve two key issues: what supply chain resources a port should own or control; and, how it should defend its ability to accumulate the value so derived. The proposed framework is highly innovative for its conceptual base of reference and offers interesting insights into the port value creation process in the supply chain. However, it neglects the great number of interactions within the port context. Indeed, the empirical application of the framework only centres on the practices of shipping companies aimed at integrating their complex logistical services, from intermodal transport to goods handling.

Paixão & Marlow (2003) provide a framework for the development of a proactive rather than reactive role of ports in the supply chain. The paper deals with the agile strategy in the port sector, starting from managerial strategies undertaken by port players (mainly terminal operators) aimed at tackling the high levels of market uncertainty. The methodology, based on strategic logistics tools already experimented within other industrial sectors, is structured into two different stages: the first concerns internal integration, while the second relates to the external integration of ports with other actors in the supply chain. Also in this case, the analysis focuses on terminal operating companies with reference to both internal and external integration.

Carbone & De Martino (2003) contribute to the scientific debate on port SCM through an empirical analysis carried out by interviewing various port operators involved in the Renault supply chain. The purpose of the study was to analyse the contribution of the port of Le Havre in the Renault supply chain, according to the model developed by Lambert (2001). The work takes a client perspective (that of the Renault) and proves how the performance of traditional port's components (terminals, infrastructures of connections, etc.) are considered pre-requisites for port competitiveness. Indeed, it is more relevant the ability of the port operators to set up relationships with other actors of the port community in supplying valued-added logistics services in the process of satisfying Renault's requirements.

A further conceptualization of ports from a SCM perspective is from Bichou & Gray (2004), who define a new framework for measuring port performance. To this end, they identify three different channels: the trade channel, the logistics channel and the supply chain channel. The logistics channel consists primarily of specialists that facilitate the efficient progress of cargo through a supply chain (e.g. shipping companies, freight forwarders). The trade and supply chain channels are both related to the ownership of goods moving through a system of interacting organisations. While the trade channel is perceived to be at the sector or industry level (e.g. the oil trade), the supply chain is at the firm level. The interaction of these three channels affects the level of port integration and, hence, its performance. As to the results of their exploratory investigation, it is interesting to note that respondents belonging to the port community showed a lack of familiarity with logistics and SCM concepts, especially those related to logistics integration. This is mainly due to the lack of a "competitive community spirit" among the actors, both public and private. Some authors (Bichou & Gray, 2004; Carbone & Gouvernal, 2007) have indeed demonstrated the scarce sensitivity of port operators and public authorities towards the pursuit of new forms of integration entailing cooperation with other actors and hence mutual trust.

A recent empirical work on the port of Incheon (South Korea) analyses the port's supply chain orientation using two different perspectives: the port's services providers (i.e. the terminal operators) and the port's services users (i.e. the shipping companies) (Tongzon *et al.*, 2009). The authors measure the extent to which shipping companies perceive terminals to be supply chain oriented and investigate whether there is a convergence of perceptions between terminals and shipping companies. According to our point of view, shipping companies, though being key port actors, cannot represent the only subject of analysis because the port should build its success by developing activities and resources that do not exclusively favour shipping companies' distribution networks, but also other port users, including freight forwarders, third party logistics and manufacturing companies in its hinterland.

In conclusion, all reviewed contributions have the merit of triggering the debate on the use of the SCM approach that proves to be particularly complex to apply to the port environment. In this regard, Bichou & Gray (2005) have identified a set of motivations: (1) multi-firm dimensions, namely the wide range of actors involved in and across port supply chains (shippers, ocean carries, port operators, logistics operators, etc); (2) multi-functional dimensions, that is to say the differences of operational/strategic viewpoints in a traditional port setting, often typified by institutional fragmentation and conflict over channel control and management; and, (3) multidisciplinary dimensions of port research and SCM, with the first extending across manufacturing, trade and service industries, and the latter intersecting wide subjects ranging, inter alia, from engineering and operational research, marketing and quality management.

Given the state of the art of SCM and port competitiveness, and considering that the port represents a complex reality, it is believed that models based on a network perspective, adopting the concept of value chain constellation, can set the framework to determine port competitiveness (De Martino & Morvillo, 2008; De Martino, Morvillo & Marasco, 2010). In particular, these models allow the limitations of previous studies to be addressed by taking into consideration all the potential interaction modalities among a multiplicity of network actors, by analysing the development of inter-organisational relationships in the management of business activities and resources in the process of creating value for the client. A first, simple application of the industrial network approach in the port environment has been carried out by Harrison & Håkansson (2006). Through two case studies on a Norwegian airport and seaport, they provide an example of how the value of single resources can be enhanced when they are combined in new ways. It is shown that the value of resources is closely connected to how actors are able to activate networks of existing yet passively connected resources. In this respect, a fundamental role is played by the port authority in coordinating the network of previously passively connected resources and in widening the range of port's users by considering also the private industry.

However, according to our point of view, this active role of the port authority can be effectively played only on the basis of an overall understanding of existing and potential relational patterns, governance structures and power positions of the different actors in the port community. The network model presented in the next section is aimed at addressing these issues.

A NETWORK MODEL FOR PORT VALUE CREATION

Studies on the network approach are characterised by a holistic perspective in the definition of strategies and strategic positioning, and starting with the concept of value constellations, they have highlighted the aspects of interdependence and interaction among different actors involved in the value creation process. In particular, they attempt to overcome what is considered to be a traditional vision of value creation, based on the Porter value chain concept, trying to develop alternative models of interpretation, such as the value net, value network, or value-creating network (Stabell & Fjeldstad, 1998; Huemer, 2002; Holzle *et al.*, 2002). According to this view, the value for the client is not created by a single company, but it is co-produced in combination with other actors in the network. The greater the degree of interdependence between the network's actors, the more potential co-produced value (Hakansson & Waluszewski, 2001).

A general model based on the concept of the supply network has recently been proposed by De Martino & Morvillo (2008). In this model, the port is represented as a network of actors that carry out a number of activities, sharing different resources. The features of supply chains in the network have to be considered in both *assessing, and then eventually redefining*, port development policies, because they determine the resources to be controlled and the activities to carry out in the port in order to achieve higher integration and consequently better performance. More in detail, the analysis of activities, resources, and inter-organisational relationships allows the determination of port actors' interaction in the management of port activities and the relative resources exploited in the value generation process. Naturally, resources and activities are completely intertwined, because resources are necessary for the undertaking of activities and have no value unless they are activated. And the way in which resources are "activated" and activities performed largely depends on the inter-organisational relationships among port operators and other actors of the supply network. The activities carried out by these actors can be divided in three macro-categories (Teurelincx, 2001): (1) activities related to its foreland (maritime transport and maritime access); (2) activities within the port sector itself (such as transhipment, warehousing, value added logistics, manufacturing, forwarding and distribution); and, (3) activities in relation to its hinterland (road transport, rail transport and inland navigation).

With reference to resources, some of these prove to be more important than others, as they are essential to create and supply services to the customer. These key resources, defined in literature as critical assets (Cox *et al.*, 2002), hold a central position for the acquisition and accumulation of value in the supply chain. Within ports, resources are those necessary to perform both transport and value-added logistics activities. These can be subdivided into (Huybrechts *et al.*, 2001): infrastructures, such as terminals, quays, modal connections, etc; superstructures, i.e. assets for the supply of transport and logistics services (cranes, depots, equipments, etc.); human capital and competences; and, ICT solutions.

Traditionally, terminals have represented the key resource for creating value, especially from a shipping company's perspective. However, in combination with these physical resources, the intangible (i.e. human capital and IT systems) are becoming increasingly source of competitive advantage, as they determine competencies hard to imitate (Winkelmans, 2003) and encourage the development of collaborative relationships in the port community, and between port actors and other actors of the local economic system.

Finally, with reference to different types of relationships, recent third party logistics literature shows that outsourced logistics activities are ever less limited to traditional transport and warehousing, but they include a wide range of additional and added value activities; moreover they are increasingly managed by long term collaborative relationships (Marasco, 2008). Typically, the relationships between shipping companies and terminal operators can be consortia, joint ventures, strategic alliances, mergers and acquisitions, aimed at optimising the management of intermodal and maritime transport services (Heaver *et al.*, 2000). Although transport and storage remain the main activities managed in the port, these are not sufficient to guarantee its active role, which is instead increasingly dependent on the ability of the port authority to strengthen its linkages with its economic hinterland. This can be achieved by encouraging port actors to form relationships for the management of a wider range of added value logistics activities. "Collaborative spirit" and mutual trust are therefore fundamental in order to create reciprocal benefits and a higher level of involvement of the port in the supply network.

Port Value Creation: A Focal Net's Perspective

Starting from the conceptual categories previously described, a methodological pathway has been defined on the basis of the scheme proposed by Hakansson & Snehota (1995) for the analysis of development effects of business relationships according to the Activities Resources Actors (ARA) model. In this analytical framework, two dimensions are combined in order to describe the elements being connected in business relationships and to capture the effects of these connections: the "substance", which regards what the relationship affects, and the "function", which concerns who is affected by the relationship. As to the former, the authors distinguish three layers of substance concerning the activities performed by the companies involved in the relationship, the resources needed and controlled by them and the bonds between the actors that arise as they become connected. With regard to the second dimension, three different "functions" are distinguished for identifying the different parties that are affected by the relationship: single companies, the dyad as a conjunction of two actors and the broader network of other players.

According to the authors, this scheme can be used as a conceptual framework to analyse the factors that affect the possibilities of development of a relationship as well as to identify where and how to intervene in relationships in order to get some desired effects. According to our point of view, the port should build its success by developing relationships concerning activities and resources not exclusively with shipping companies, but also with all the other port actors, including intermediaries such as freight forwarders, multimodal transport operators, logistics operators, other services suppliers and, finally, manufacturing companies in its own hinterland. Therefore, given the complex nature of the port environment, in a first phase the analysis will be developed by using the concept of a focal net; subsequently single focal nets will be analysed within the broader relationship context of the supply network.

According to Moller & Halinen (1999), a focal net is a central construct that describes the environmental context of actors. From the perspective of an individual firm, a focal net consists of those actors that are within its network horizon and that management perceives as relevant. From strategic perspectives, the focal net concept is also used to refer to an interrelated group of actors pursuing a joint strategy within a network. Tikkanen (1998) emphasizes that a focal net is always part of a broader network and thus could be viewed as a local network or micro network. However, the difference is that a focal net is studied from the viewpoint of a certain, single network actor, which usually is a company. The central aim in focal net analysis is to take into account all parts of the broader network that are relevant from the single actor's perspective.

According to the ARA model, the focal net can be constructed by analysing all the dyads considered strategic from the focal firm perspective (Håkansson & Johanson, 1992). With reference to the port context, terminal operator can be considered as the focal firm (De Martino, Morvillo & Marasco, 2010). Starting from this, in a first stage all the dyads between terminal operators and their direct clients (shipping companies) will be analysed. In the subsequent stages all the strategic dyads will be examined in order to highlight all the relationships, thus identifying focal nets in terms of web of actors, activity patterns and resource constellations.

Table 1 describes three simplified configurations of port focal nets, characterised by different final clients that are shipping company (column **α**), multimodal transport operator (column **β**) and freight forwarder, logistics operator and manufacturing firm (column **γ**). Shifting from **α** to **γ**, a growing extension and complexity of the web of actors, activity patterns and resource constellations can be observed. This extension reflects the importance of the port in the process of creation and appropriation of value through an increasingly complex set of services, the involvement of a growing number of specialised actors and the use and combination of a broader typology of resources. From a different perspective, these focal nets can represent a potential development path that a port can follow on the basis of the ability of port management to catch the opportunity offered by its economic and politic context.

In the case **α**, the port shows an approach mainly focused on internal logistics, based on the supply of cargo handling services as the main client is represented by shipping companies. In this case, strategic options are aimed at maximizing throughput, improving shipping companies' satisfaction and increasing the efficiency of port operations. This is the typical and traditional focal net in the port environment.

Focal net **β**, which obviously comprises the previous case, is characterised by a focus on the cargo flows optimization and on the improvement of transport chain's efficiency through the supply of handling, storage and inland transport services to multimodal transport operator. Ports' strategic options are oriented toward the improvement of modal connections so as to allow the supply of intermodal services and to expand the port hinterland. Examples can be found in an increasing number of ports such Genoa, Algeciras, Rotterdam, etc., where port authorities have invested in adequate network of railway and road connections in order to favour the growth of container traffic and to overcome the lack of space within the port perimeter.

Finally, in focal net **γ**, the port approach is aimed at satisfying the needs of logistics operators and manufacturing firms through the supply of further services – the value added logistics services - other than the ones related to transport. In this case, the port further extends its influence beyond the traditional boundaries towards the hinterland, including activities, resources and actors of the local economic context. In this scenario, ports represent the springboards for economic development of the hinterland and therefore their strategic options are oriented to strengthen the integration with those business actors of its territory that can perform their supply chain activities more conveniently in the port environment. For example, the port of Rotterdam established three distriparks in order to provide value-added logistics with compre-

Table 1. Port value creation: a focal net perspective

	α Shipping Company	β Multimodal Transport Operator	γ Freight Forwarder Logistics Operator Manufacturing firm
Activities patterns	Maritime transport; Cargo handling and storage.	Maritime transport; Cargo handling and storage; Inland transport; Warehousing.	Maritime transport; Cargo handling and storage; Inland transport; Warehousing; Value added logistics (VAL); Manufacturing Distribution
Resource constellations	Infrastructures, such as terminal, quay Superstructures: assets for the supply of maritime transport and cargo handling Traditional competences in port maritime services and cargo handling	Infrastructures, such as terminal, quay, modal connections; Superstructures: assets for the supply of maritime, cargo handling and transport services; ICT system; Competences in different transport chain stages	Infrastructures, such as terminal, quay, modal connections, logistics area, dry port, Distripark; processing area; Superstructures: assets for the supply of transport and value added logistics services; facilities for import and export goods; ICT system Competences in VAL and highly skilled workforce
Web of Actors	Terminal operating company; Shipping company.	Terminal operating company; Shipping company; Railway transport operator; Road Haulier	Terminal operating company; Shipping company; Railway transport operator; Road Haulier; MTO; Freight forwarder

Source: De Martino, Morvillo & Marasco (2010)

hensive facilities for distribution operations at a single location, connected directly to container terminals and multimodal transport facilities for transhipment, employing the latest in information and telecommunication technology. The port provides a comprehensive range of value-added services to fulfil highly heterogeneous customer demand. These value-added services include assembly, labelling, testing/examination, packaging and repackaging, sorting and invoicing.

The different strategic options have impacts on all focal net layers determining, from **α** to γ:

- The development of new activities such as warehousing, distribution, value added logistics and manufacturing;
- The use and combination of different typologies of resources - terminal, quay, modal connections, logistics area, dry port, distripark, processing area, assets for the supply of transport and value added logistics services, facilities for import and export goods, ICT systems; competences in value added logistics and a highly skilled workforce; and,
- The involvement of a great number of specialised operators in the field of transport and logistics.

The described focal nets are not mutually exclusive as in a same port there could be contextually several focal nets characterised by different interdependences based on the role of port actors, activities and resources. Indeed, the set of embedded focal net constitute the port supply network (PSN). This allows the effective representation of port complexity through the identification of narrower and more local "networks" that, although interdependent, have the capability to autonomously explain the sources of port value creation.

Figure 1. A simplified port supply network

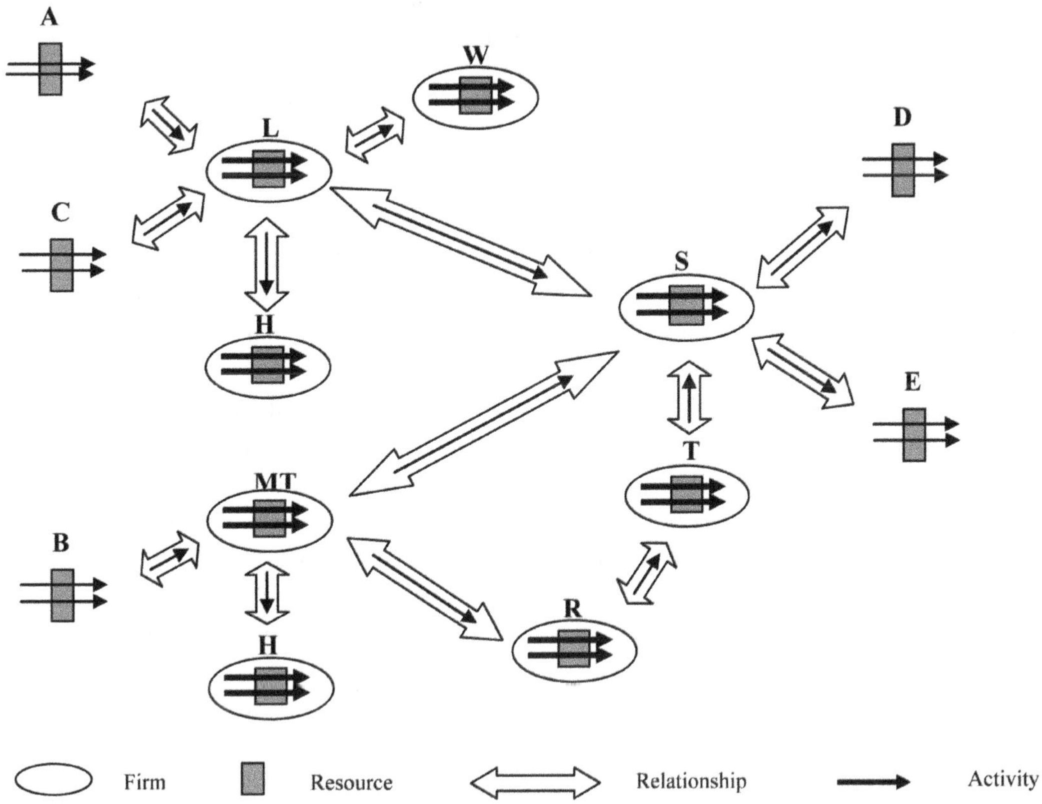

Figure 1 provides a simplified representation of a possible configuration of a Port Supply Network, including examples of focal nets **α** and **β**.

In particular, in the first case, the availability of modal connections between the terminal and road and railway network are critical resources that allow the multimodal transport operator (MT) to provide intermodal services to firm B. In detail, the main relationships in this focal net are centred on the MT in charge of the transport chain organization by involving haulier (H) for road transport services, railway operator (R) for railway services and, shipping company (S) for maritime transport services to the final destination. In the second case, port provides also value added logistics service through a warehouse owned by a logistics operator (L) and located in the port area. More specifically, this actor collects different cargoes from the hinterland (A and C) and performs a number of transport and logistics activities through a set of relationships haulier and shipping company in order to deliver cargoes to the final destinations (D and E). Moreover, the dyad between the shipping company (S) and the terminal operator (T) is a key linkage within the port supply network but the higher port value stems from resources controlled and activities performed by other network actors such as multimodal transport and logistics operators. Indeed, intermodal connections and warehouses represent alternative sources of port value generation, as they can influence the port's ability to be more supply chain oriented.

The use of focal net allows identifying those relationships having higher impacts on value creation and, at the same time, the lack or the particular configuration of some relationships can constrain the value creation process of the port. This approach is particularly effective from a strategic perspective as it provides focal firms of both port focal nets (i.e. business operators) and port supply network (i.e. port authorities) proper tools to diagnose their performance and to intervene in the networks according to well defined strategic options. In this respect, port authorities as main governance actor of the port supply network (PSN) can affect significantly the role of single port focal net in value creating process through the definition of policy actions. Only through the understanding of the whole PSN, can the port authority define policies sustainable under economic, social and environment perspectives.

SOLUTIONS AND RECOMMENDATIONS FOR SUPPLY CHAIN INNOVATION

Given its focus on the complex port environment, the model contributes to the scientific debate on supply chain innovation by focussing on the problem of coping with multiple interdependencies among supply chains that can not be addressed through traditional frameworks emphasising linear, vertical relationships. This model substantially differs from the traditional approaches based on the port strategic planning rationale; indeed, by exploiting conceptual categories of the network approach, the model: (a) offers the opportunity to highlight different and new sources of value generation from interactions among actors of the port community whose boundaries expand towards its hinterland; (b) allows evaluation of the effectiveness of a variety of strategic options in relation to their impact on value creation; and, (c) addresses resource optimisation, generally overlooked in the analysis of port value creation. For these reasons, it is believed that the model contributes to supply network innovation as it considers innovation as a collective process which increasingly depends on the formation of collaborations and alliances.

Shifting our consideration to the real world, current port dynamics are determined by the role of global players (shipping companies and terminal operators) having dominant positions by incorporating port's assets into their own organizations. In particular, they integrate vertically or horizontally, and become "owners" of a large part of the port supply network; in this way, they potentially increase efficiency and effectiveness of their own business, leaving little rooms for other members in the network to develop their own assets and operations. As a consequence, improvement, growth and innovation of port network are limited, with clear consequences for value creation. In this scenario, the port authority has a passive role as it cannot incisively affect competitive dynamics; indeed port strategic positioning is out of the control of port authority as well as the value distribution among actors of the port community.

The recognition of ports as networks of actors, resources and activities represents a critical and fundamental issue for spreading innovation in the port, especially from a culture perspective, as it allows interpretation and consideration of collaboration as a means of value creation This innovative interpretation should encourage the spread among port actors of a sense of belonging to the territory and therefore the development of a real port community. Collaborative spirit and mutual trust are fundamental in order to create reciprocal benefits and a higher level of involvement of the port actors in the network. In contrast, port complexity remains a major problematic issue to which neither the academic literature nor the business world has found a persuasive and effective solution. In this respect, the reviewed models of port literature are still in the phase of the theoretical elaboration and showed their limits in addressing port complexity (De Martino, Morvillo, 2008).

According our point of view, the introduction of the concept of focal net can offer a significant contribution in this respect as it makes port complexity more intelligible through the identification of narrower and more local "networks" that, though being interdependent, have the capability to autonomously explain the sources of port value. In this way, the port authority can understand existing, but not always clearly evident, governance structures and the power positions of the different actors in the port community, getting key information for designing more effective policy actions directed to enhance port value creation.

Only based on a proper understanding of the features and rationale for the formation of relationships among actors of port community and all actors involved in the process of value creation for the final client, can new and more effective networks be fostered and developed. These networks should be characterised by the development of relationships not exclusively between shipping companies and terminal operators, but also among all port community's actors including manufacturing companies in its own hinterland.

It is now acknowledged that relationships can determine greater value co-production in the supply of integrated services, a common and shared strategic thinking among network actors and, finally, a greater spread of innovation within the network. Only provided that the port community recognises the value of relationships, the port authority will concretely play a crucial role as the main governance actor of port supply networks by: promoting innovation through policy actions aimed at improving the efficiency of port infrastructures and their connections within existing transport systems, according to environmental, social and economic sustainability criteria; favouring and stimulating free competition among port operators, through a proper concession of both terminal and land management to private business actors for the supply of value added services; enhancing the collaboration and coordination of port activities through the so called services-enhancing activities, such as EDI systems, marketing and performance benchmarking; and, contributing to the development of its own hinterland by creating economical, relational and social connections between the port and the market place.

At the same time, the active role of the port authority should also be directed to making port actors aware of the existence of a network of interconnections and interdependencies among the activities they perform, and therefore that cooperation can be an important lever to improve performance in the competitive scenario.

FUTURE RESEARCH DIRECTIONS

Future research should be aimed at addressing several research questions. Those that are most relevant at this stage of research are the following: (1) can the proposed model ensure the coherence/convergence of value propositions between the port authority and port business operators?; (2) with reference to the interpretation of port as networks of actors co-producing value, can the relationship between the level of interdependence and innovation be confirmed?; and, (3) under what conditions does the port authority have the "power" to affect the development of relationships in the port community?.

In order to answer to these questions, several theoretical problems have to be addressed.

A first issue concerns the conceptualisation of value to be used in order to assess the contribution of port actors within focal nets and the whole supply network and thus the effectiveness of policy choices for network reconfiguration. Indeed, actors involved in the port community are typically motivated by opposing interests and non-convergent objectives in terms of expected value. The presence of public and private operators in the port community requires a deep understanding the different value propositions as these affect the efficacy of the proposed model in defining appropriate and shared policy actions.

According to the paradigm that competition is shifting from the level of single firms to the level of interorganisational networks, our view is that that innovation occurs in collaborative interaction among network actors. At this stage, most of the academic works have addressed how innovation drives competitive advantage at the level of single firms. Recently, the academic debate has shifted focus to what drives innovation at the interorganisational level. With reference to the port context, it is very challenging to examine how knowledge is exchanged between port actors and the role of the port authority in boosting innovation in port supply network.

Another important consideration concerns the variables to be used for the quantification and assessment of relationships that are generally of a qualitative nature (e.g. trust, commitment, goal sharing, etc.) and therefore cannot be directly used for measuring value contribution. This issue increases in complexity when shifting from the dyad level to the network one. In this respect, a set of quantitative indicators for the assessment of relationships at both focal net and supply network levels is required. In particular, these indicators will have to be used in order to analyse different sources of the port value and evaluate the policy actions impacts at different network layers. This set of variables, of course, will have to take into account not only the economic but also the social and environment perspectives.

Finally, the delimitation of network boundaries, frequently stressed within network literature, appears to be particularly problematic in relation to the high complexity of the port community in terms of number of actors, resources, activities and relationships. In this respect, focusing on a limited set of port actors makes model implementation easier, as well as more cost and time efficient, but reduces its effectiveness as it overlooks the potential contribution of other actors in the value creation process.

Once these issues are addressed adequately, the next step in the research design will consist of the validation of the model through an empirical analysis. According to our point of view, the model should be applied in several port contexts characterized by different levels of complexity in terms of activity patterns, web of actors and resources constellations. In this respect, the range of chosen ports will vary from Naples to Antwerp.

CONCLUSION

SCM has been increasingly recognized as a lever for improving firm performance and building a competitive advantage. This approach prescribes a close working relationship beyond traditional organizational boundaries with an emphasis on inter-firms co-operation across supply chains. This requires the creation of different forms of co-operation among network actors, based on mutual trust and on shared strategic objectives to improve the end customer satisfaction.

This chapter starts with the consideration that in the current scenario, ports should define their strategies and competitive positioning on the basis of a new paradigm that views the port as a network involved in a multiplicity of supply chains. Starting from the current situation in which the port is passively linked to the strategic choices of the global players, the objective of this chapter is to hypothesize an active role for the port authority in orienting all the relationship in the network in order to enhance the value co-production for the final client.

From a review of the most relevant contributions on this topic, it is clear that there is a substantial "gap" between the available theoretical frameworks and the concrete possibility that such frameworks are shared and implemented in the port community, at least in the short run. Some of the reviewed contributions, in fact, pointed out the scarce sensitivity of port operators and public authorities towards the pursuit of new forms of integration entailing cooperation with other actors and hence mutual trust.

Given such a background, the core of this chapter is the presentation of a new theoretical model based on the network approach, aimed at identifying the sources of value creation in an innovative way. It assumes that the traditional approaches to port competitiveness—strongly related to structure-type variables (geo-economic context, institutional model and the port-hinterland infrastructures)—are not enough to cope with current market dynamics. Instead, according to a new systemic view, the competitiveness of ports increasingly depends on its "organisational component" as it affects the quality of services including: range of logistics services, ICT solutions, know-how, level and intensity of relationships. Indeed, the model allows viewing the port as a network of actors, resources and activities, which co-produce value by promoting a number of interdependencies in which the port itself is embedded.

REFERENCES

Bichou, K., & Gray, R. (2004). A logistics and supply chain management approach to port performance measurement. *Maritime Policy & Management*, *31*(1), 47–67. doi:10.1080/0308883032000174454

Bichou, K., & Gray, R. (2005). A logistics and Supply Chain Approach to Seaport Efficiency – An Inquiry Based on Action Research Methodology. In Kotzab, H., Seuring, S., Muller, M., & Reiner, G. (Eds.), *Research Methodologies in Supply Chain Management* (pp. 413–428). Heidelberg: Physica-Verlag. doi:10.1007/3-7908-1636-1_27

Carbone, V., & De Martino, M. (2003). *The integration of port operators in the automotive supply chain: the port of Le Havre and Renault.* Paris, France: Les Collections de l'INRETS, n. 251.

Carbone, V., & Gouvernal, E. (2007). Supply Chain and Supply Chain Management: appropriate concepts for maritime studies. In Wand, J., Oliver, D., Nottebbom, T., & Slack, B. (Eds.), *Ports, Cities and Global Supply Chains*. London, UK: Ashgate.

Cariou, P. (2001). Vertical Integration Within the Logistic Chain: Does Regulation Play Rational? The Case for Dedicated Container Terminals. *European Transport*, *7*, 37–41.

Christopher, M. (1992). *Logistics and Supply Chain Management*. London, UK: Pitman Publishing.

Cox, A., Ireland, P., Lonsdale, C., Sanderson, J., & Watson, G. (2002). *Supply Chains, Markets and Power*. London, UK: Routledge.

De Martino, M., & Morvillo, A. (2008). Activities, resources and inter-organisational relationships: key factors in the Port competitiveness. *Maritime Policy & Management*, *35*(6), 571–589. doi:10.1080/03088830802469477

De Martino, M., Morvillo, A., & Marasco, A. (2010). *Value Creation within Port Supply Network: Methodological Issues*. Paper presented at the 26th IMP Conference, 2-4 September, Budapest, Hungary.

Dubois, A., Hulthén, K., & Pedersen, A. C. (2003). *Interdependence within and among supply chain.* Paper presented at 12th International IPSERA Conference – Budapest.

Evangelista, P., & Morvillo, A. (1999). Alliances in Liner shipping: an instrument to gain operational efficiency or supply chain integration? *International Journal of Logistics: Research and Application*, *2*(1), 21–38. doi:10.1080/13675569908901570

Hakansson, H., & Johanson, J. (1992). A Model of Industrial Networks. In Easton, G. (Ed.), *Industrial Networks: A New View of Reality*. London: Routledge.

Hakansson, H., & Persson, G. (2004). Supply Chain Management: the logic of supply chain and networks. *The International Journal of Logistics Management, 15*(1), 11–26. doi:10.1108/09574090410700202

Hakansson, H., & Snehota, I. (1995). *Developing relationships in business networks*. London, UK: Routledge.

Hakansson, H., & Waluszewski, A. (2001). *Co-evolution in technological development – the role of friction*, Paper presented at the 17th IMP Conference, Oslo.

Hakansson, H. Y. (1982) (Ed), *International Marketing and Purchasing of Industrial Goods: an interaction approach*, Chichester: Wiley.

Harland, C. (1996). Supply chain Management: relationships, chain and networks. *British Journal of Management, 7*, 63–80. doi:10.1111/j.1467-8551.1996.tb00148.x

Harrison, D., & Håkansson, H. (2006). Activation in resource networks: a comparative study of ports. *Journal of Business and Industrial Marketing, 21*(4), 231–238. doi:10.1108/08858620610672597

Heaver, T., Meersman, H., Moglia, F., & Van de Voorde, E. (2000). Do Mergers and Alliances Influence European Shipping and Port Competition? *Maritime Policy & Management, 27*, 363–373. doi:10.1080/030888300416559

Heumer, L. (2002). *Value creation strategies in supply networks: the case of logistics service providers*. Paper presented at the 18th IMP Conference, Dijon, France.

Hines, P., Lamming, R., Jones, D., Cousins, P., & Rich, N. (2000). *Value Stream Management: Strategy and Excellence in the Supply Chain*. London, UK: Prentice-Hall.

Holzle, K., Ritter, T., & Walter, A. (2002). *Relationship function and customer trust as value creators in relationships: a conceptual model and empirical findings for the creation of customer value*. Paper presented at the 18th Annual IMP Conference, Dijon, September.

Huybrechts, M., Meersman, H., Van De Voorde, E., Van Hooydonk, E., Verbeke, A. and. Winkelmans, W. (2002). *Port Competitiveness: an economic and legal analysis of the factors determining the competitiveness of seaports*. Antwerp, Belgium: Editions De Boeck Ltd.

Janic, N., & Reggiani, A. (2001). Integrated transport systems in the EU. *Transport Reviews, 21*(4), 469–497. doi:10.1080/01441640110042147

Lambert, D. M. (2001). The supply chain management and logistics controversy. In Brewer, A. M., Button, K. J., & Hensher, D. A. (Eds.), *Handbook of logistics and supply chain management* (*Vol. 2*, pp. 99–125). Oxford: Pergamon.

Lamming, R., Johnsen, T., Zheng, J., & Harland, C. (2000). An initial classification of supply networks. *International Journal of Operations & Production Management, 20*(6), 675–691. doi:10.1108/01443570010321667

Lazzarini, S. G., Chaddad, F. R., & Cook, M. L. (2001). Integrating supply chain and network analyses: the study of netchain. *Chain and Network Science, 1*(1), 7–22. doi:10.3920/JCNS2001.x002

Marasco, A. (2008). Third-party logistics: A literature review. *International Journal of Production Economics, 113*(1), 127–147. doi:10.1016/j.ijpe.2007.05.017

Möller, K., & Halinen, A. (1999). Business Relationships and Networks: Managerial Challenge of Network Era. *Industrial Marketing Management*, *28*, 413–427.

Morash, E. A., & Clinton, S. R. (1997). The role of transportation capabilities in international supply chain management. *Transport Journal*, *36*(3), 5–17.

Normann, R., & Ramirez, R. (1993). From Value Chain to Value Constellation: Designing Interactive Strategy. *Harvard Business Review*, (Jul/Aug): 65–77.

Notteboom, T. E. (2004). Container Shipping and Ports: an overview. *Review of Network Economics*, *3*(2), 86–106. doi:10.2202/1446-9022.1045

Notteboom, T. E., & Winkelmans, W. (2001). Structural changes in logistics: how will port authorities face the challenge? *Maritime Policy & Management*, *28*(1), 71–89.

Paixao, A. C., & Marlow, P. B. (2003). Fourth generation ports- a question of agility? *International Journal of Physical Distribution & Logistics Management*, *33*(4), 355–376. doi:10.1108/09600030310478810

Robinson, R. (2002). Ports as elements in value-driven chain systems: the new paradigm. *Maritime Policy & Management*, *29*(3), 241–255. doi:10.1080/03088830210132623

Slack, B. (1993). Pawns in the game: ports in a global transport system. *Growth and Change*, *24*, 579–588. doi:10.1111/j.1468-2257.1993.tb00138.x

Slack, B., & Frémont, A. (2005). The Transformation of Port Terminal Operations – From the Local to the Global. *Transport Reviews*, *25*(1), 117–130. doi:10.1080/0144164042000206051

Stabell, B. C., & Fjeldstad, O. D. (1998). Configuring value for competitive advantage: on chain, shops and networks. *Strategic Management Journal*, *19*, 413–437. doi:10.1002/(SICI)1097-0266(199805)19:5<413::AID-SMJ946>3.0.CO;2-C

Teurelincx, D. (2001). Functional analysis of port performance as a strategic tool for strengthening a port's competitive and economic potential. *International Journal of Maritime Economics*, *2*(2), 119–140.

Tikkanen, H. (1998). The Network Approach in Analyzing International Marketing and Purchasing Operations: A Case Study of a European SME's Focal Net. *Journal of Business and Industrial Marketing*, *13*(2), 109–131. doi:10.1108/08858629810213333

Tongzon, J., Chang, Y.-T., & Lee, S.-Y. (2009). How supply chain oriented is the port sector? *International Journal of Production Economics*, *122*, 21–34. doi:10.1016/j.ijpe.2009.03.017

Winkelmans, W. (2003). *Port Competitiveness and Port Competition: two of kind?* Paper presented at IAPH Congress, Burdan.

Chapter 6
Implementing Integrated Supply Chain Management

Dermot Carey
MRM-Global, Ireland

ABSTRACT

The concept of supply chain integration (SCI) has been widely set out in the academic literature in recent years. The advantages associated with the integrated approach have been articulated, as have possible approaches to planning for SCI. However, there is a dearth of literature in the area of SCI implementation. This chapter describes a piece of action research that aims to identify some of the critical success factors and inhibitors to success in relation to SCI. The action research was carried out in a complex hospital environment. Implementing anything that is new is typically met with resistance. Resistance to change is a natural response and the only way to get buy-in is to impress. That usually means presenting something of benefit and interesting. SCI in this regard requires that innovation is present in both concept and output. Innovative ideas, approaches and re-invention is a constant requirement for operational and strategic efficiencies. Similarly in SCI new and challenging ways must be incorporated into the implementation process.

INTRODUCTION

Integrated supply chain management (ISCM) is widely advocated and accepted as the desired best state for effectiveness and overall efficiencies in providing enhanced service levels and improved contribution or profit. However, for many organisations, despite their efforts to adopt best practice, supply chain management (SCM) principles and practices in reality remain an aspiration. The shortfall in reaching this objective is influenced by a number of obstacles and challenges, including the time to focus and implement the necessary elements. Furthermore, this can be exacerbated by

DOI: 10.4018/978-1-60960-585-8.ch006

the lack of a clear method that encompasses the stakeholders' interests both internal and external to the organisation. Too often responsibility for the implementation of the integrated concept is passed to the head of supply chain. This on top of normal everyday pressures is usually impractical. There is also an assumption that, because knowledge is understood, that the transfer is possible. This is not always the case as it involves many other vital skills including change management, process re-design, project management, innovation and communications. This chapter comments on some of the major aspects and key considerations of the implementation process. It will refer to a piece of action research on the application and implementation of integrated procurement and SCM in an acute public hospital in Ireland.

A hospital environment is a complex supply chain environment. Typical supply chain activities include dealing with emergency response times, life and death scenarios against a backdrop of public sector systems and traditions. The effective implementation of ISCM in this type of organisation encounters many of the challenges that may prevail in any other business sector. The study was initiated by the author, whose interest and motivation for the initiative was grounded in his belief that the application of ISCM principles would bring benefits to both the patient and the hospital. The project was breaking with tradition as it was the first time that a public acute hospital in Ireland challenged the traditional role of the supplies function. A traditional supplies role was mainly re-active in nature i.e. it responded to requests. Demand planning and forecasting was the exception and not the norm. Boardroom representation by SCM personnel was rare. Organisational structures and systems were fragmented and mainly administrative as distinct to strategic in nature. This is despite the fact that the annual spend on goods and services had a value greater than €50 million annually. When considered against this criterion alone one would think that the function would merit strategic attention.

This chapter highlights some of the key approaches to the application and implementation of ISCM systems and structures. The author is an advocate of the ISCM concept and has worked around the world with major organisations in delivering this objective. It is from this experiential perspective that some practical ideas are put forward.

To appreciate what is required to achieve an integrated procurement and supply chain system and structure the following equation is illustrative:

$$\text{Integration} = (c^5 + p^1) \times 3DI$$

For ISCM to be achieved, it requires an end-to-end process (p^1) with the visibility and capability to communicate enterprise wide and evaluate options at each stage of the supply chain from demand to fulfilment. This will involve the introduction of change incorporating, consolidation, collaboration, classification and contracting methods (c^5). These facets for supply chain decision making need to be further supported by three dimensional intelligence (3DI) based software. The absence of any one of these vital elements will result in only a partial solution and perpetuate the fragmented model. The implementation challenges require the ability to provide intelligence for procurement and supply chain decision making. For this to have any commercial or corporate value, it requires innovativeness in the ability to transfer the integrated concept to all stakeholders and to obtain their buy-in. This is best achieved in the early stages in the form of incentivising the stakeholders through added value benefits. Added value can manifest itself in many different forms. However, it is vital to be able to demonstrate and measure these benefits for credibility and continuous support. Consequently all aspects presented in the formula are essential to build a process and communicate the benefits. Very often access to vital information is limited and cumbersome and can slow down the progress of integration and result in the loss of vital momentum.

BACKGROUND TO ACTION RESEARCH

A proposal was submitted to the board of management of the hospital following a brief review of its expenditure, as well as its supply and storage activities. The findings were numerous and the recommendations were radical when compared with ISCM methods. This is not surprising since working to an integrated SCM system is not common in either the private or public sectors. The hospital has seven hundred and fifty beds on a fifty-two acre campus with a budget of approximately €150 million per annum and over 3,000 staff. It is a prestigious teaching hospital. The study involved the examination and transformation of how the hospital managed and executed its non-pay spends activities, which accounted for approximately €50 million. This project was high profile, underwritten by both the hospital's management and the relevant government ministry – the Department of Health and Children (DOHC). It carried with it both the opportunities and the risks associated with change in a traditional and politically sensitive environment. ISCM was one vehicle to introduce change in a sensitive environment. It required trust and professional respect by the researcher and the CEO for their respective objectives to be realised. This project would bring the political kudos associated with success, while the converse would be the case if things did not work out quite so well. The hospital was widely regarded as a flagship for other hospitals to follow on many of its undertakings. The development and application of a programme of change concentrating on ISCM in a public hospital environment gained the interests of many, both internally and externally. This section details the approaches to, and the events associated with, the implementation and application of ISCM.

The project was planned following initial research to gain an understanding of the wider issues that were likely to present themselves. It is often overlooked at the beginning of a project what the end result might look like. In this particular case the author had a vision of what the ISCM model would require in terms of infrastructure, systems support and resources on an enterprise-wide scale. A sanity check in terms of where to start from is a pre-requisite in the first steps of a long journey. If one has an idea of the end destination, plotting the journey can be focused. The first piece of work was a review of change management, procurement and supply chain management, and business process re-engineering's latest thinking and practices. This is an essential part of the preparation not only to ensure familiarity with the latest practice and thinking but also to help in prioritising actions in a structured and informed manner. After this phase it was possible to develop a proposed project framework and to test it against the reality in the hospital. At this stage one should have an idea of the difference between the vision and the reality. At this point, the project can be proposed, and potential buy-in from stakeholders could be sought out. Without the framework backed up with innovative, verifiable and credible benefits the project could be in danger of not capturing the interests of the wider hospital community. This is a work in progress and will change a number of times as new information unfolds. It is essential in any major project that comprehensive documentation is maintained. It is important also that notes are updated on an ongoing basis commenting on observations, conclusions drawn and recommendations proposed for the integrative element of the study.

CHANGE

The successful implementation of the integrated paradigm requires drawing information from a number of management disciplines:

- Change Management;
- The Learning Organisation;
- Business Process Re-engineering; and,
- Procurement and Materials Management.

Change management is central to most projects applying new concepts and it involves new learning. This aspect should take cognisance of an organisation as a learning entity, which is a realm unto itself when it comes to techniques and method of implementation. There is no shared meaning of what constitutes a learning organisation; rather, it develops organisational learning capabilities, it is important to be aware of these dynamics. In the context of implementing ISCM or indeed any other new concept these fundamentals cannot be ignored. The transfer of learning has to be flexible and achieved by whatever format is most suitable. These can include meetings, workshops, training sessions, coaching, demonstrations, lectures and communicating the changes. These inclusive methods encouraged teamwork, continuous learning, employee participation and development. The learning was an important part of the project and it required openness by all. Sometimes this was achieved through facilitation to ensure that the learning was maximised. The project had a hospital-wide impact. However, not everybody actively interacted with purchasing and supply chain management. As a consequence, decisions had to be made as to what level of learning was necessary to complement the vision of the project and the depth of integration required.

The hospital is best described as a set of inter-related, interdependent and interacting subsystems. However, they lacked the required ISCM systems and structure to enhance patient services and consequently acted as independent units. By working closely with the independent divisional cultures, specific tactics were developed so as to achieve the strategic objectives. This approach formed the basis of the methods developed to enable the integration to be achieved. In simple terms, it outlined the advantages of supporting and working towards the integrated process in a positive co-operative and benefits-related manner. At this point it is worth summarising the key steps in the implementation phases.

1. Examine the concept and the beneficial relationship across multiple management disciplines.
2. Be aware of the different types of learning transfer methods to be employed.
3. Engage positively with the stakeholders with multiple benefits for them as the goal.
4. Re-visit and communicate regularly the implementation plan and its key milestones.
5. Continuously provide training on new developments.
6. Inform and encourage managers to enable change enterprise-wide.
7. Develop group and team work.

An important objective in any project is to facilitate the transfer of knowledge and skills back to the job, so that there is improved job performance. All of the above are important for alignment and process development. The learning gained and the transfer of knowledge and skills needed are vital in the longer term to continue beyond the project. This is achieved in an environment of continuous improvement and requires a commitment with the project team to take a long-term view.

At this point we have hardly touched on the specifics of SCM. The ISCM philosophy cannot be implemented successfully without the management of change supporting the integration process. Processes deliver outputs and ISCM processes will deliver enhanced outputs. The shortfalls of a non-integrated process are well understood and are aptly described by Senge (1990, p. 68) where he says that "…the un-healthiness of our world is in direct proportion to our inability to see it as a whole". This is particularly appropriate to a hospital.

Crossing the boundaries of tradition in the hospital encountered many complex challenges some of which included resistance to change, culture and politics. Whilst the ISCM initiative was new to the hospital and was ground breaking, change management was well tried in similar environments. The author drew from the experience of a number of experts. They highlighted many of the challenges facing the project not least of which would be the age old problem and the continuing reluctance of consultants to become involved in management. There is of late a shift in the clinician's perception of management and this is cited as an example of similar resistance that will be encountered in other sectors. It is vital to establish cross working initiatives and in an ISCM model it is important to create an environment and understanding where there is a culture that everyone is a customer of each other interdepartmentally.

Change is a permanent feature of life and the main power groups that are typically encountered include politicians, bureaucrats, professionals and the administrators or managers. These power groups all had an influence in the hospital and featured in how change was implemented. Adapting to change is essential for the performance of the organisation and for it to have a positive impact. Change, however, is usually met with resistance and can be represented in such features as rigid structures and systems, closed mindsets and entrenched cultures. Some of these resistances were endemic characteristics in the hospital. Change in one part of the hospital based on the ISCM approach without knowledge and acceptance of it throughout the organisation would have limited value. It is essential that the values of change are incorporated into the ethos and culture of the organisation and in a structure that manifests itself in an innovative, positive and progressive way for all staff.

Change and learning experiences need to be proactively managed; it would be foolhardy to undertake the project without acknowledgement of the particular standpoints and to expect a professional outcome from one's own perspective.

EXPECTATIONS

The expectations of management in the adoption of any new system or structure will be unique to each business. In the context of ISCM it is likely that those expectations may include improvement in costs and services through the supply chain functions, with measurement and accountability as an accepted principle and practice.

This outcome requires as a basis an informed approach to the identification and structuring of solutions to a complex business problem. It will involve the incorporation of the influences on SCM from the management initiatives associated with business process re-engineering (BPR), the learning organisation and change management. ISCM involves - in broad terms - the transformation from an independent reactive based process to a fully integrated and planned corporate business system and structure. The project is an example of where the theory needed to be tested and reformed to fit a diverse and complex environment. The principles and values envisaged for the integrated structure had to meet and complement the exacting standards and ethos of the hospital.

There was little value in promoting at an early stage what ISCM stood for until the wider hospital community had some tangible evidence of the benefits associated with its use. Their appreciation was similarly developed at a later stage through gaining their support and involvement in various initiatives. The theories of ISCM, change management, BPR and others would remain theories unless they were transformed into workable practices and this requires the buy-in of everyone. All views were therefore important regardless of their origins for any sustainable changes to emerge. The research of the hospital environment included all of the interface functions including the supply base. It examined their traditional roles, cultures, expectations, standards and positions of power and their potential reaction to change in an ISCM context. This is relevant in any business environment.

BUSINESS PROCESS RE-ENGINEERING (BPR)

The implementation of a fully integrated SCM system and structure into a complex organisation would not be possible without commenting on business process re-engineering (BPR). The author does not rely on BPR processes alone to arrive at the 'best of best' solutions; however, some process models are worth considering for ISCM implementation. BPR has been embraced by many businesses for years now. Typically this is brought about when there is the need for improvement in performance, service and costs. In the context of ISCM this is particularly relevant. A study worth mentioning was undertaken at Caterpillar Inc. (Khosrow-pour, 2006) and the findings cut across many of the issues experienced in an implementation programme such as ISCM. They included:

1. Providing a road map for systematically migrating from a silo culture to a process culture.
2. The methodology to guide cross-functional teams towards effective solutions to process problems.
3. Process thinking is made easier because teamwork and facilitation are at the core of the methodology.
4. Creativity training is provided to promote "out of the box" thinking and help dislodge a status quo mentality.

These points are directly relevant to ISCM and should be considered at a process level. Other studies should also be considered to provide ideas for the implementation of best practices. People usually want to give their best and it is important to encourage and empower them to do so - this can be facilitated with good practical examples of success elsewhere. Empowerment is part of the culture change that cuts across the supply chain functions. The integrated nature of an ISCM project also demands the creative use of information technology (IT) systems.

INTELLIGENCE BASED SOFTWARE

IT in the procurement and supply chain arena is predominantly supported by enterprise resource planning (ERP) systems. There is a requirement now for major IT re-structuring to support the ISCM process. Many SCM specialists reading this will relate to systems that support the transactional activities of their organisation. These ERP systems are mainly designed for financial reporting purposes and not designed for SCM decision making. It is a challenge to find systems designed to provide integrated intelligence at each stage of the supply chain. Instead there are many packages providing independent elements. This is in contrast to the quest for many to aspire to ISCM as a system and structure. Business/SCM integration will drive systems integration. This is because there is very little to be gained from restructuring IT without modifying business processes and, in turn the organisational structure. ISCM requires radically revised IT systems supporting dynamic decision making.

The hospital management decided to implement SAP as a corporate system with a materials management module. The introduction of SAP/R3 was a traumatic experience for the staff of the materials function. The weights of these comments are important as an appreciation of the amount of work needed when undertaking change from a mainly clerical practice to an automated process. It involves in-depth training on an on-going basis in the theory of SCM. The changes in work practices involve each facet of the supply chain. Many of the changes required the development of new manually-based approaches for ultimate transfer to automated processes. There was a natural relationship between SCM and IT in the conversion from manual to automated systems and new ways of doing things. ISCM requires the radical redesign of strategic value added business processes and the organisational structure. When handled effectively the strategic use of ISCM improves customer service and competitiveness. Organisations should take a look at the entire supply chain and identify areas for revolutionary or evolutionary change. In the hospital there was the belief from many sections that the introduction of SAP would speed up the process. This was naive but nonetheless a commonly held misconception. Whilst SAP was a major improvement over the previous system it did not provide the essential intelligence to support an ISCM process. It is another illustration of where there is a need for radical change in IT for SCM. Technology is important to support the successful integration of the functions to share varied and voluminous forms of data across all functions. Full integration requires the technology that provides information in real-time. The combination of management techniques employed in any complex change project vary in nature and application. The expectation for the investment and effort is typically weighed against improvements over the status quo, regardless of the sector or organisation.

MATERIALS MANAGEMENT AND ISCM

For some organisations, materials management could have several areas of responsibility attributed to it. Procurement, supply, purchasing, logistics, shipping, warehousing, inventory control, materials handling, supplier management and customer service have all been variously assigned to this function. Here we will refer to it as ISCM. These variations were influenced by several factors. They can be individual or idiosyncratic interpretations of the function where an individual would typically have a bias towards a particular field of expertise. This in turn influenced the position of the functions within the structure. These various interpretations contributed to a misunderstanding of the integrated message. It typically led to an incomplete or partial understanding and therefore an inadequate materials management function being introduced. The multidisciplinary nature of a hospital has been a major influence on the independent nature of the structure that was employed. Moves to improve performance led to the establishment of Clinical Directorates – often referred to as Business Units in the private sector. This had the result of the further compartmentalisation of the disciplines. This in turn increased their accountability as budget holders and enhanced the independence of these functions. The quest for ISCM is made more difficult when decisions of this nature are taken in isolation from the whole.

When ISCM is practiced, costs can be reduced substantially. For an integrated system and structure to improve performance, it is reliant on quality and enterprise-wide participation. Materials management in the health services generally has a low profile and consequently rarely features in strategic matters. This view was to change. The DOHC Materials Management Advisory Group, following a review of materials management practices throughout the hospitals and regional health boards in Ireland, issued a report that gave recognition to materials management now and for the future (DOHC, 1996). This was further complemented later by the DOHC as part of the new National Health Strategy which outlined the framework for changes including the development of human resources, reform of the acute hospital system and wider organisational reform. A shared definition for SCM was important if a common understanding were to be developed. The variations were as many as the variable number of activities often attributed to the materials management function as cited earlier.

While materials management typically had purchasing as one of its functions, SCM is the extent of vision required on the part of managers, with respect to their value adding systems. This brought into focus the various aspects of added value. These demanded the reduction and containment of costs, which were an important area of management in the supply chain. There still remains a profusion of varying terms describing materials management or SCM, which appear to mean the same thing. This inter-changeability of terms and definitions continues to lead to confusion. For the concept of materials management or SCM to be promoted in an integrated way requires a standardisation of terms and a cohesive message across the disciplines. There has been a move in recent years away from using the term 'materials management' and towards 'supply chain management' as a more comprehensive term. Presenting the function in so many ways runs the risk of confusing the non-supply chain person. It also creates the possibility of the definitions being misinterpreted and indeed of the professional responsibilities being misunderstood. These misunderstandings were present in the hospital because no single definition of the role was provided. By extending the integrated philosophy as a means to create lowest costs, the concept of lean thinking and the elimination of waste were of interest. This concept of lean thinking was not practiced in the hospital and was dismissed by the hospital materials staff as inappropriate to a hospital environment. This was also true in relation to planning and the introduction of ISCM because these were thought of as production or manufacturing related methods only.

RELATIONSHIPS

The relationship between purchaser and supplier requires the understanding of each other's reciprocal needs. This is of particular interest in the effective integration of suppliers into the organisation. For ISCM to have any sustainable value and contributions for the future it is essential that measurement matrices (key performance indicators or KPI's) are agreed, introduced and managed. Sustainable improvements will be achieved where there are strong supplier relationships and these are central to demonstrating to the wider community the value of their co-operation and collaboration. ISCM takes into account the whole supply chain as a single entity rather than a series of different entities. This is consistent with the concept of collaboration. A large part of SCM involves the management of relationships to achieve enhanced performance and outcomes for all parties. Each entity in the supply chain affects the performance of the other supply chain members. It is therefore vital that strong relationships are developed. Consolidation and commonality are just two areas that can be a focus for improved service levels and reduced costs where relationships are founded on strong commercial grounds. Collaboration is core to achieving reduced costs and risk. This opens a new territory for many businesses where the traditional model was one of secrecy and single minded competitiveness. Trust and greater transparency between competing entities will become the new norm as supply chains compete with one another. Those organisations that adopt the integrated approach will have a greater chance of success than those that retain the independent model. The new model will rely upon enhanced three dimensional intelligence (3DI). Furthermore it will capitalise on deeper and broader relationships improving the benefits of consolidation, collaboration, commonality, and communications with better contracts (C^5). This will be supported for sustainability and consistency by an integrated SCM process (P^1). Hence the equation: $I = (C^{5} + P^{1}) \text{ X } 3DI$.

THE HOSPITAL SYSTEM

The over-riding caring ethos of the hospital's culture influenced the approach adopted in the implementation of ISCM. This will be different and unique to each environment. For any improvement to emanate from ISCM it requires buy-in from all the key stakeholders and budget holders to the proposed change. The belief in the ISCM concept must be understood as vital to the nature of the processes and structural changes being introduced to achieve the integrated system and structure. In the hospital this was done with the development and implementation of a closed loop supply chain model where the patient is placed at the core. This draws on the logic and practice of knowing your core activities or business. It is important to mention at this point that the prevailing belief in the hospital was that forecasting or demand planning was not practical because of the variable nature of the business. This is a widely held view in many businesses and too often goes largely unchallenged.

For the purposes of demand planning and forecasting, the patient base in the hospital is broadly made up of 40% elective and 60% emergency, of which there are repeated demands for goods and services in greater than 98% of the cases. As soon as a patient arrives at the hospital, depending on where the arrival started, it is from that point that patient-specific requests for goods and services are generated. These requests are typically passed to the supplies department for stock items and ordered directly or via a requisition if they are non-stock items. This process was custom and practiced despite the cumbersome and time related consequences of continuing such an ad-hoc process. In the majority of cases the demands were generated from the nursing and medical staff. This process perpetuated a reactive identification of needs. Nothing would happen without the written or oral request. In the interim the patient may be subjected to delays related to whether the requested items were stock items or not. This is anathema to the philosophy of ISCM. There was no consistency in the way in which requests were raised. In some cases they would be routed through the supplies department; in other cases they were ordered directly from the supplier. Data on the transactions hospital-wide were fragmented and unreliable. The discontinuous nature of the processes required that any future changes would require the involvement and support of users, IT, finance, administration and suppliers to ensure accuracy and sustainability. This process involved data collection and the closing of the loop across the interfaces as shown in Figure 1.

Communications with all of the internal parties was essential to establish their perception of their various needs and to clarify the ultimate relationship required with SCM. Following the initial analysis of the system there emerged an appreciation of the need for some concept of an integrated data flow. This would involve the centralisation of all existing data on non-pay spend. A cross section of data from across all of the functions allowed for the development of an integrated data-base. This was the first stage at which the requirement for the introduction of policies to support the integrated model was conceived of. This data was converted into information, relevant to each of the functions, from which centrally driven performance improvement initiatives could emerge. This centralised integrated information highlighted the need for improved inventory management and demonstrated the improved financial benefits to be derived from its introduction. Thereafter, from improved information there emerged a growing appreciation of the non financial benefits that were attendant on the changed system: a planned approach, more frequent meetings and a willingness to challenge the old ideas as well as the new. A further development was the emergence of a more highly developed and more focused form of group behaviour with more sharing, supporting and questioning taking place. A modified closed loop model of ISCM was adopted. In an attempt to draw these ideas together from the efforts of the stakeholders a model emerged which was loosely based on the application of the concept of Porter's value chain model (Porter, 1985).

The emergent model identified the key stakeholders in the hospital who had influence on the cost drivers in the supply chain and this model again placed the patient at the centre, not least

Figure 1. Closed loop data transactions and interfaces

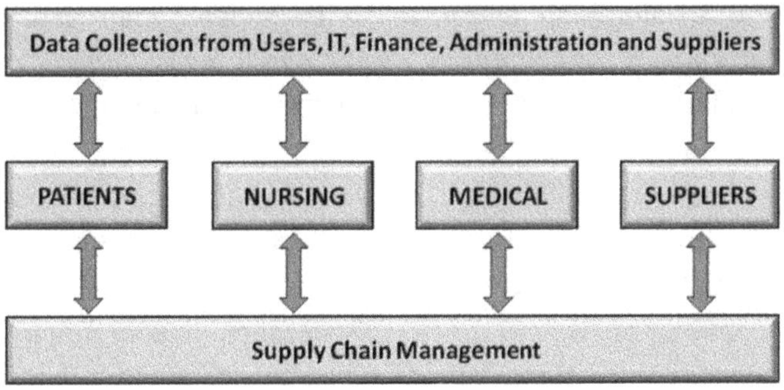

because the patient influences the cost by the severity of their complaint and the duration of their stay. The closed loop approach brought the key stakeholders into contact with each other with the intention of enhancing patient care in a supply chain context. This framework demanded total integration of effort throughout the supply chain for optimum results. This is done to support the objectives of all the functions acting as a unified whole to fulfil its basic responsibility to optimise service levels. This was a radical departure from the endemic systems, structures and processes in the hospital. Getting each of the stakeholders to participate and actively support the integrated concept was of great importance. Three fundamental steps were followed for the integration to succeed

1. Speak to the decision makers in each of the constituencies of the hospital.
2. Get them on board from a knowledgeable perspective that they could see the potential benefits.
3. Keep them engaged through delivering against promises and providing an improved professional service.

Each decision maker from all the constituencies had to be identified. Records with this information were not easily obtained and it meant building on personnel information to identify the population. It was important that everyone was involved, particularly those who actually did the work but may not have had the recognised authority. Following this was a series of information gathering on each of the constituencies in terms of any history that may be relevant and, in particular, what they would want from any proposed change. To facilitate the gathering of this information this effort was preceded by the development of a profile of the personalities: whether they were difficult, friendly, impatient and so on. Contact with the key players was undertaken after the CEO announced at the Executive Management Group (EMG) meetings that interviews were to commence and that he wanted their full support. This announcement by the CEO and the provision of information on the personalities involved was very useful as it was often the difference of saying and doing the right thing at the appropriate time which typically determined whether you got to see the people or not. All of these facets of communicating the ISCM concept became important as integration evolved.

The model brought the patient into the centre, from which all services and product demands were driven. This positioning was to be the basis for all thinking and subsequent processes that would emerge. From a supply chain perspective, understanding the cost drivers at each stage of the supply chain was important in order to identify how added value may be achieved through improved processes. For added value to be achieved it required new process development to reduce the number of tasks and the time taken to procure and deliver products and services to the patient at a reduced price. It was at this point that a major misinterpretation of materials management's role was uncovered. Two main aspects were to feature prominently and became focused parts of the project: power and the politics of change. From these focal points a framework evolved with measurement criteria coming to the fore for the first time from the perspective of SCM.

The integration process involved three key phases:

1. The integration of the old supplies department into the proposed new integrated SCM function.
2. The integration of SCM practices across the hospital's user community.
3. The integration of SCM practices and wider hospital's needs into the external supply chain to create the integrated supply chain.

The need for performance measurement is important since it is necessary to assess progress against each of the phases outlined above. This also supports the concept of integration because progress in the areas targeted would involve results being measured from an integrated value perspective. The absence of such measurement would result in unnecessary costs and risks, which was traditionally the case in the hospital. Immediate price savings are usually the focus area. SCM should make it known that demand-planning ability is a factor in supplier choice. This was contrary to the custom and practice found in the hospital. The widely held view was that because of the unique and varying nature of patient care, planning was not a feasible option. This stance perpetuated the reactive nature of purchasing or - to be more precise - ordering, that operated in the hospital. Thus many opportunities for price reductions were lost. Strategies involving matters of product standardisation and supplier rationalisation require a vision of the integrated supply chain and cannot be determined effectively from a fragmented approach. The supplier should be able to forecast and manage the flow of products to the end customer. Without an adequate planning function being in evidence this desired situation would not be reached in the hospital. This ability to plan was of vital importance to the project. For the objectives of ISCM to complement patient service, and value for money to be delivered, change had to occur. This required strategic planning, which was a new way of thinking for the staff. The revised importance of the planning function is that it focuses on patient needs and supplier choices. This fact revised the starting point by focusing on the patient and determined the costs incurred in the supply chain, while at the same time enhancing patient service.

Professional SCM measurements were not a feature of the activities, nor were materials management represented at senior management level. Consequently performance was evaluated from a different perspective, most notably on the basis of annual expenditure trends from the budget holders. Table 1 is an example of the measurement criteria adopted across each of the functions. Each element had an impact on the performance of the other functions. This was also the first time that measurement had featured as part of the work ethos within the supplies department.

The philosophy of putting the patient at the centre became one of the streams from which everything would flow. This is illustrated in a model that enables the developmental integrated supply chain system and structure to emerge (see Figure 2).

This model introduced radical change from the previous structure. It had two new added dimensions. The first change was the introduction of measurement against targeted performance and expectations against each of the criteria outlined in Table 1. The second change introduced a planned approach from each of the disciplines. This planned approach was the most radical departure. It im-

Table 1. Sectional performance measurement criteria

Purchasing	Inventory Control	Distribution & Customer Service
Budgets	Inventory Investment	Logistics Costs
Strategic Plan	Strategic Plan	Strategic Plan
Supplier Cases	Stock Turn	Service Fill
Price Cases	Benchmarks	Improvements Plan
Inventory Cases	Policy Drivers	Policy
Product Cases	Procedural Changes	Communications
Contract Cases	Results	Customer Management

pacted directly on all interfaces in terms of information flow, communications and ensuing procedural changes. For improved benefits to be derived on a sustained basis it required that specific measurements for each phase of the supply chain that had an impact on patient care be introduced, managed and adjusted in accordance with demand and learning. The measurement criteria remained under the same management headings but were adapted for the particular disciplines. The measurement criteria were also a focus for planning and forecasting activities that were required to develop and improve.

AUDIT PROCESS

The emergence of the integrated model was the result of an audit process that was followed closely to ensure that the ISCM concept was understood by all key interfaces. The alignment of the concept into the individual functions had to be debated in depth, and this required many meetings. It was after joint agreement and with full commitment to maximising patient care and service that changes for integration were introduced. This process was repeated with each group to ensure that individual requirements and nuances were fully appreciated. The audit process had to test the new measures and processes introduced in a practical and results-driven nature. These measures and processes had to be audited as workable and beneficial throughout the supply chain internally and externally if patient care and service was to be improved on a sustainable basis. The audit was designed to ensure that the new integrated model and the patient's needs were complemented by the combined medical units and ISCM processes adopted. It was also vital that the assessment tested that both the medical and commercial aspects of the processes adopted were developed so as to enhance patient care. The audit also assessed that the processes introduced were detailed and rigorous to ensure that agreed measures were in place to satisfy both medical and

Figure 2. Partially integrated hospital supply chain model

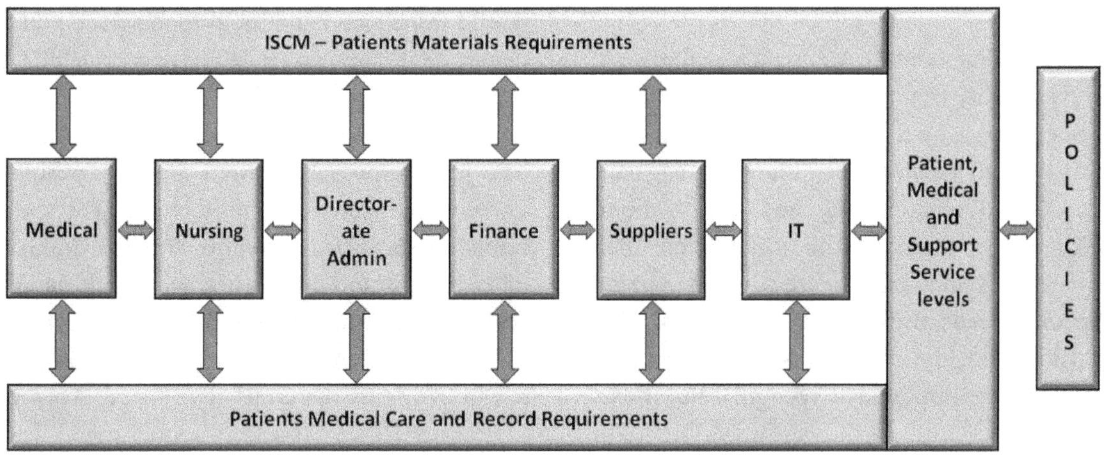

commercial controls. This audit would primarily probe that there was detailed and inclusive agreement to processes and controls to create confidence and to encourage open dialogue on issues, thus reducing incidences of failures and conflict. The audit procedure focused on the following:

- ISCM principles;
- Procedures;
- Process; and,
- Policy.

ISCM Principles

The principles of ISCM had to be communicated, clarified, repeated and then tested to ensure that the concept was understood. There were a series of lectures, workshops and meetings held to communicate these principles hospital-wide and the audit established that each unit had been involved in all of these activities. Once there was knowledge and acceptance of the concept, the principles of alignment in relation to their operations were explored. These discussions were conducted in the main as mini projects. Typically this resulted in the exploration of potential procedural improvements with SCM involvement. This activity enabled the relationships to develop and to reduce previous barriers. The next step focused on the procedures adopted in expenditure related activities.

Procedures

This stage of the contact was typically the most sensitive. It was vital that time was given to the staff to explain why they did what they did. Frequently the staff had this expenditure duty as a part of their overall responsibility and often without any support or training. It was inevitable that the procedures undertaken were adopted to meet the specific needs of the unit and these typically would not be developed from a SCM perspective. However, it was important to recognise that those procedures typically were designed to complement the unit's needs for effectiveness. It was therefore essential that a reciprocal appreciation and understanding of these needs were considered by the SCM department staff before any proposed changes were tabled. In the majority of cases these duties, while taken seriously, were time consuming and not considered seriously from a commercial standpoint. It was here that opportunities to introduce changes in the process became apparent.

Process

The expenditure processes in place with the budget holders were specific to each unit and bore the characteristics of the individuals who developed them and the specific requirements of the unit. The processes typically focused on providing documentary evidence of authorisation to commit to expenditure and to justify payment. Quotations were also sought on occasions from three suppliers. There was not one process followed by all of the budget holders. Consequently there were various levels of detail and controls. What was constant was that none managed the expenditure activities from a planned SCM perspective. This was because the function of SCM had not developed nor were specific professional results or measures expected. Any proposed changes to these well-established processes would have to be sensitive to the traditional processes in place and demonstrate that any changes proposed would introduce benefits to themselves and the department. These exercises were conducted after rigorous scrutiny of the information gathered and were run jointly between SCM staff and the unit. The joint approach ensured that any problems encountered were recognised by both parties and remedies identified at source. This was done on a phased basis and pilot tested with each function for up to two months until there was confidence in the new processes. Only after this period would a hand-over to materials take place. This was then confirmed with process documentation being written up and agreed between materials and the units. These changes were radical but were essential for the values of the integrated concept to be realised by the patients and the hospital. Once the processes were formally adopted, the collective agreements across the units would form the basis of a policy document to be developed, agreed and issued. It is on this issue that the next part of the audit process would focus.

Policy

There was no hospital or departmental policy in existence for the expenditure of approximately €50 million in the hospital. At best there was an observance of an authorised paper trail by the budget holders. This was accepted as custom and practice in the absence of an ISCM function. With the shift to the integrated paradigm and the acceptance by each of the units of the newly introduced ISCM function and processes there was now the need to develop and introduce an ISCM hospital policy. This was not only a first for this hospital but also for the rest of the hospitals in Ireland because no such integrated paradigm existed up to the commencement of this project. Policy document templates were developed and promulgated in accordance with the change necessary to implement the integrated concept. There was still ongoing integration taking place in some departments after the contract for the study had expired. It was agreed to wait until the requirements of the integration processes were understood by all before the policy was formalised. It was also proposed that each budget holder would be involved with the SCM section or department in formulating the final document. This approach would secure a hospital-wide acceptance of the new policy and of the new functional responsibilities.

Each of the stages outlined above were audited on an ongoing basis and continue to be audited today at regular intervals to incorporate any changes in patient care that may have occurred. This audit process was detailed in nature addressing the key phases of the supply chain and the interfaces required. Through validation of the changes introduced and the associated improvements towards patient care and service it enabled the development of the fully integrated model to emerge with confidence.

FULLY INTEGRATED SYSTEM

There was a general agreement that there was a need for measurement. This extended to a need to improve the elapsed time between awareness of patient need and the satisfaction of that need. Because this produced a change to a planned holding of inventory, this activity now became central to the ISCM structure. This enabled the enhancement of the integrated model shown in Figure 3 to be developed specifically in terms of service levels to the patients. This was in the form of information flow from a medical perspective and planned materials availability for each patient from an SCM perspective. This integration of information and communication resulted in the emergence of a revised framework as illustrated in Figure 3.

This model was developed so as to integrate the key aspects of the value chain concepts into the service flow in the hospital environment. The marriage of these two concepts led to the application of the integrated supply chain approach. Furthermore, the importance of supplier association was particularly significant in arriving at the adoption of time-based principles for the delivery of care to the patient within the shortest possible time frame. This was considered because of the need to include elements of production, administration, development and integration into the framework for the strategic management of delivery of service to the patient.

Communications provided the basis of interaction with all parties in the supply chain at all levels whether strategic or on an operational basis

Figure 3. Fully integrated closed loop integrated supply chain management model

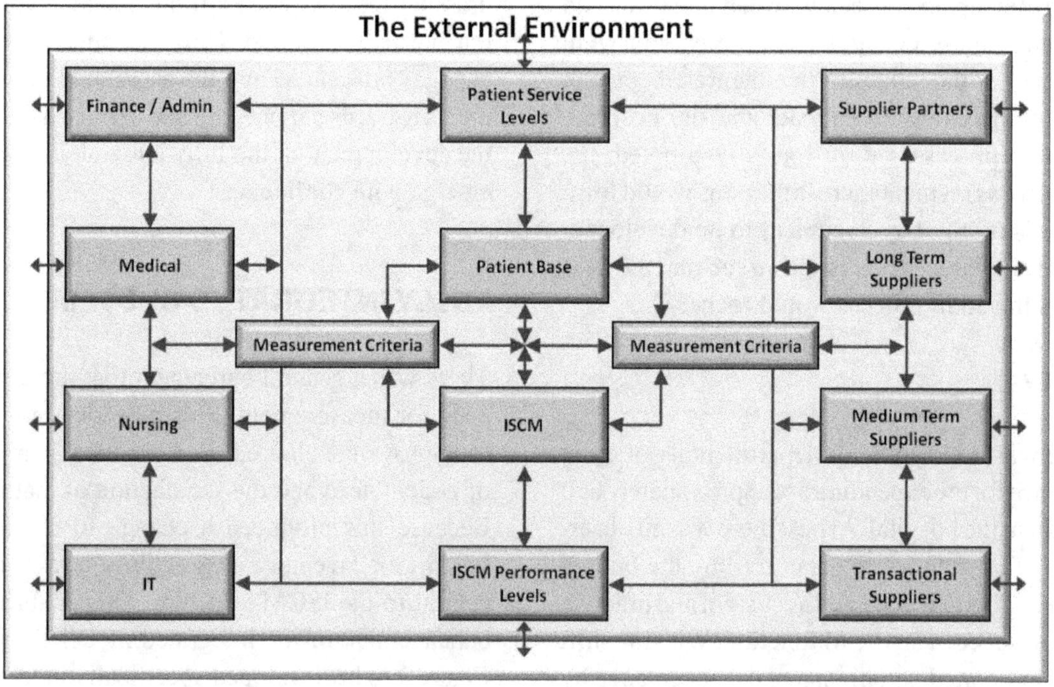

in the existing system. The revised system would have to preserve the best of the old and eliminate the sources of misunderstanding or delay in the new. By operating from this changed perspective, policies to support a total quality patient service could then emerge. These would only be as good as the people who operated them. Getting the most through people, by the utilization of organisational development techniques, together with the ideas of total quality management (TQM) were useful guidelines to ensure that the important human dimension of the project was not lost.

A vibrant planning and forecasting culture is necessary and implicit to the achievement of the ISCM model. MRP is a technique used to determine future inventory requirements. It provides a means of reducing the risk of stock-outs and also provides feedback on the accuracy of the planning process. Feedback was necessary to sustain improvements. The importance of the benefits to be derived from the introduction of MRP still held in the hospital scenario. The principles of forecasting with a SCM emphasis needed to be developed as part of the change to the new system and structure. The predominant view in the hospital at the beginning of the assignment, however, was that planning and forecasting were a function of a manufacturing environment and as a result were not relevant in their case. This extended the thinking into adopting and considering many other proven approaches other than healthcare-based examples. The approach adopted was eclectic: not all elements of BPR or traditional industrial engineering were utilized. However, the need for a holistic approach based on systems theory was accepted particularly if the loop were to be closed by the provision of feedback on improved patient welfare based on cost saving in the system as a whole.

Strategy development was not a common practice. This aspect had to be developed if enhanced performance was to be achieved. For example, the importance of a planned approach to purchasing was fundamental to strategic supply performance and costs. The use of information and tools for the transformation from a reactive function to a strategic proactive entity were pre-requisites for success. The use of Pareto profiling was one such method that was introduced to the hospital. This tool gave information from so many different perspectives that it was the enabler for many strategies to evolve. The performance activity headings were common to all functions (planning, forecasting, staffing, budgeting etc.) but the measurement criteria were specific to each of the functions. However, the targets were professionally specific to each function as shown in Figure 3. This changed emphasis required the adoption of leadership strategies and processes for each function to be adapted to enable planning and forecasting to be set against performance measures specific to each functional area. Communications across the functions were essential to ensure that there was a synergy between objectives and target setting, and these affected both internal and external interfaces. Measuring SCM as a profit centre supported the new direction and culture of measurement even in the not-for-profit health care environment. Within each of the functional areas it was important to test the level of understanding across the hospital community regarding the basic elements of the supply chain approach. The supply base and - perhaps most important of all - the SCM units, required measurement against professional criteria of performance i.e. effective SCM. The external involvement of the supplier, working with the buying organisation, also had to be introduced as an approach to be considered. This was necessary so as to highlight the need to capitalize on the improved relationship of a professional nature that was being fostered. Prior to the project starting expenditure decisions were made in isolation. The framework developed was the first major step towards the introduction of ISCM concepts. Decisions on expenditure and consideration of the systems impacts of these decisions flowed from the introduction of the model at the conceptual level and this had to be monitored at the practical level.

REORIENTATION OF THE OLD ROLE TO ISCM

This was a new concept for the hospital and one of the challenges presented at the outset was the lowly status afforded to the supplies department and to the purchasing department within the hospital. Even these titles were a significant improvement on the earlier focus that saw the function as stores. This ensured that the department was not represented at the bargaining table or seen as a power broker in the organisation. This had to change, not only for the benefit of the incumbents in the department, but was necessary to raise the profile of the function to a professional managerial status if the project were to succeed. This became one of the many items on the checklist of things to do. The need for structural change and the attendant power in this area focused the mind on the competencies required of the desired SCM manager. These competencies were identified as follows:

1. Strategic SCM;
2. Functional budget development and management;
3. Supplier development and relationships;
4. Contract development and partnership management; and
5. Cost and price management.

This resulted in the selection of a professionally qualified supply chain manager and the elevation of the function to new heights. What was important for SCM management and staff alike was that they could demonstrate early benefits through their methods in order to gain support for the change. It required the confidence of the SCM staff to introduce new improved ways in a structured manner that the wider hospital community could see and appreciate. Confidence in, and recognition of the contribution made by, SCM required a movement from the traditional viewpoint and the methods and procedures that this viewpoint produced. The importance of the interaction by the budget holders with the SCM department was central to the improvements of integration being experienced. The potential will be realised through the connections between the component parts of the supply chain.

PURCHASING

Purchase market research, new product developments and the introduction of such new products and supplier capability studies were not a feature of the traditional supplies function. These aspects were pivotal in the integration process and brought traditionalists out of their normal comfort zones. Reliable supplier research techniques for the selection of new and potential suppliers were vital for focused supplier selection. The professionally determined elimination of poorly performing suppliers to improve overall standards throughout the supply chain was also necessary. The importance of supplier selection would not have been considered in a professional context in the past within the hospital. Instead they would typically have been taken on a superficial assessment basis in their capacity of having goods and services to offer. Professional supplier selection is critical in meeting the objectives of SCM. Traditional purchasing practices tended to rely on the market to determine price through tendering and quotations. This process, however, would at best generate an understanding of price comparisons in the market. There was the need to understand costs more. This was important so that the significance of prices was understood so as to determine whether they were economically advantageous or not. Supply chain managers should know the ingredients and behaviour of product costs as part of overall cost control. Essentially the management had to learn the significance of the difference between cost and price. This approach challenged the very core of purchasing practices and it was necessary to develop a new understanding of not only cost knowledge of products but also the additional cost drivers in the supply chain in determining ultimate costs. This demanded a radical shift in thinking and also required them to accept planning as an integral part of the process. It took more than a year to arrive at a stage where the data collected was formatted to give information in a manner that was usable from an SCM perspective. This was a consequence of the poor and inappropriate electronic systems in operation. The use of Pareto analysis, with the management information developed, proved invaluable in identifying high spend areas by product, department, supplier and volumes. The same was true from an inventory investment perspective and it was from this area that many of the initiatives for change were generated.

Quality could not be compromised. This demanded that all support processes complemented the integrated objective. A planned approach to inventory investment for a comprehensive range of stock to be available in the supply chain was essential. This represented a major departure from previous practice. Supplier involvement and adopting time–to-market principles were important in getting product properly positioned in the supply chain. This would enable the attainment of the fastest time–to-customer with the lowest cost. Lean thinking principles led to the adaptation of lowest inventory investment practices to maximise customer service and minimise obsolescence. Techniques such as consignment stocking, furthering the lean thinking concept, were also introduced into SCM in the hospital.

CONTRACTUAL RISK

Contracting in a manner that minimised risk and reflected the exact requirements of the organisation was a desired objective. Communication and clear specification development with user departments were required for these to be transferred into the market place in a manner that would optimise commercial results whilst observing EU directives. There is a paucity of writing on contractual risk management from a supply chain perspective. This is surprising given that any major contractual undertaking has varying degrees of risk at each point of the supply chain. From a legal point of the view it would be far better for supply chain managers to proactively manage this by being involved early and protecting against risk by establishing and defining the contractual obligations of each party.

SOLUTIONS AND RECOMMENDATIONS FOR SUPPLY CHAIN INNOVATION

Implementing SCI is a complex process. The degree of complexity will be a product of the nature and maturity of the organisation in question. There is no simple solution to implementing SCI. The programme of events must be well planned and take account of all stakeholders, both internal and external to the organisation. It requires leadership, vision of the end state, continuous proof of concept, flexibility, willingness to make mistakes and the ability to engage all communities to be part of one initiative. With these characteristics as integral requirements for successful implementation the benefits of change must also transfer to the wider community. These benefits must also be measurable in terms of value for money and/or improved efficiencies. In the case of the hospital benefits were measured on the basis of improved quality of service and products to patients. The solution to implementing SCI requires drawing on many management disciplines beyond SCM. These will include: change management, project management and business process re-engineering to mention a few.

FUTURE RESEARCH DIRECTIONS

When SCM is well managed and correctly aligned to its core business offerings then positive performances are usually the result. SCM decisions are core to business performance and yet many decisions are taken in the absence of reliable information. Future research will need to analyse and provide market intelligence for optimal supply chain approaches. This will need to look at the wider factors influencing decisions, such as the impact of outsourcing, collaborative opportunities, access to and sharing information. Wider market information will need to be provided in a format to enable aligned strategies. This will mean a change in how IT supports this vital decision making aspect of business.

CONCLUSION

A consistent SCM theme is the need for an aligned or integrated approach to the management of supply chains. With the criteria proposed by these approaches correctly applied and adopted in an integrated manner, performance will be enhanced.

The necessary changes in the hospital incorporated changes in thinking, processes and in the use of technology. The capabilities and interfaces were assessed against the emerging processes and systems changes and adapted accordingly. These included hand-held scanners introduced and managed by SCM offering live data downloads. This information would then automatically trigger a replenishment activity from the planned inventory system. Change required them to move to a new level of corporate thinking and a transfer of this new approach into the market place in a meaningful professional manner. This was a profound change to the practices of the past. The focus was now on improved costs and performance on a corporate basis.

The need for integration of the organisation to be consistent in its activities was a prerequisite to capturing the benefits of partnerships. This required the breaking down of traditional barriers between departments and the adoption of a different set of values on performance. No partnership agreement existed in the hospital which was further confirmation of the limited value put on supplier relationships. This non-aligned association with the supply base perpetuated the individual reactive price-based trading relationship with little or no attention to the value chain. As long as these barriers and independent business decisions were reached in isolation from the ISCM approach the increased probability of not realising the integrated objective was increased. This point was of particular relevance where the patient was put at the centre from which all demands would flow and to whom benefits would accrue as shown in the conceptual framework in Figure 3. By the introduction of such change the work of the supply chain professional would become more complex. It would require a detailed understanding of the supply chain in the hospital. It also required a different set of performance related values for a successful outcome to be assured. The argument for improved performance was dependent on the lean integrated approach and required the collective contribution of each element of the supply chain for improvements to be realised.

The final links in the chain were the conversion of the collective needs into procurement plans and contracts reflecting the key measurement criteria across the entire supply chain while achieving lowest ultimate cost and minimum contractual risk. For the purposes of this project the work concentrated on the application and implementation of ISCM in a hospital environment. The significance of the culture of power and politics in the hospital were seen as two of the major factors that would either facilitate the introduction of the systems change or ensure its failure. Irrespective of sector there will always be unique differentiators to the actual method employed in the implementation of ISCM. Most of the circumstances illustrated in this Chapter will present themselves as features of any implementation programme. It is not a straight forward task and cannot be entered into lightly. However, with the move to the integrated paradigm the benefits far outweigh the effort involved.

REFERENCES

Department of Health and Children. Ireland (1996), *Report of the Materials Management Advisory Group*: established by the Minister for Health / Department of Health.

Porter, M. E. (1985). *Competitive Advantage*. New York: Free Press.

Senge, P. M. (1990). *The Fifth Discipline: The Art and Practice of the Learning Organization*. New York: Currency Doubleday.

Section 2
ICT Supply Chain Innovation

Chapter 7
Adding Value to Logistics Services using ICT:
A Case Study Analysis of Small Logistics Companies in Italy

Pietro Evangelista
IRAT-CNR & University of Naples Federico II, Italy

ABSTRACT

The adoption of information and communication technology (ICT) is one of the most critical areas of innovation for third-party logistics service providers (3PLs). ICT is seen as tool for achieve service differentiation and improving connectivity with other supply chain partner. Nevertheless, many logistics service companies had failed to use ICT to gain competitive advantage as the implementation of technology innovation is a challenging and risky process involving huge resources. In the context of small 3PLs, technology adoption is particularly critical and ICT investments need to be carefully planned. The objective of this chapter is to investigate ICT adoption in small 3PLs through a case study analysis conducted in the Italian logistics service market. The role of technology in supporting service customization together with inhibitors and enabling factors influencing technology innovation are explored. Implications are derived from the research and supply chain innovation perspectives.

DOI: 10.4018/978-1-60960-585-8.ch007

INTRODUCTION

It is widely recognized that innovation is a key ingredient in the business success as it provides a number of benefits including the enhancement of process quality and revenues that may be able improving the competitive position of companies. The ability to be innovative has become one of most important issues for companies in the 21st century forcing them to re-think their products, their services and their processes (Tidd et al., 2001).

Both academics and practitioners have traditionally viewed innovation as key to productivity in manufacturing firms and studies on the innovative process have been dominated by manufacturing-based paradigms (Gallouj and Weinstein, 1997). The role and the impact of innovation in services companies have been neglected as innovation has been perceived to play a limited role in the performance of these firms (Miles, 1993). In more recent years, innovation in service attracted the attention of an increasing number of scholars of technological change (Barras, 1986; Gallouj and Weinstein, 1997; Metcalfe and Miles, 2000) and two interesting trends have been identified. Firstly services are becoming more R&D intensive (Pilat, 2000; Cainelli *et al.*, 2004; European Commission, 2007). Secondly, services are increasingly innovative than in the past and are generating more innovations over time (Tether, et al., 2001).

Many studies indicate that the identification of the types of innovation is extremely important to understand how an innovation is adopted and the factors affecting its adoption process (see for example Damanpour, 1991; Sinha and Chandrashekaran, 1992; Wolfe, 1994). A large number of classifications and typologies of innovation have been proposed in the relevant literature (see for example Schumpeter, 1939; Knight, 1967; Henderson and Clark, 1990; Christensen, 1997; Garcia, Calantone, 2002). However, the distinction among technological and non-technological innovations is one of the most commonly used. According to Knight (1967) and Damanpour and Evan (1984), technological innovation relates to products, services and production process technology and it may concerns either product or process. It differs from administrative (non-technological) innovations that mainly involve organizational structures and administrative processes. Howells (2000) also distinguishes innovations between technological and non-technological innovation. The first type of innovation often consists of a new product or service, while non-technological innovation focuses on process and organizational elements that can improve service customization, network capabilities of the company, procurement and distribution and management practices.

The focus of this chapter is on the adoption of a specific type of technological innovation (ICT related innovation) by specific service companies (small transport and logistics service providers).

In today's turbulent supply chain environment characterised by ever-increasing level of competition and customer demands for higher service level at lower costs, 3PLs are required to offer new and innovative ways to improve logistics effectiveness. As result, ICT is considered increasingly important in the management of the 3PL business as technology may contribute to add value to logistics services through improving cost-efficiency and customer service simultaneously. This is contrasted by the findings of a number of studies that suggest that 3PLs are not very innovative (e.g. Wilding, Jurado, 2004; Wagner, 2008; Wallenburg, 2009). However, when specifically focusing on ICT adoption and implementation in logistics companies, the literature is incomplete. This is particularly true when the size of logistics companies is considered. ICT application in large logistics service companies has been widely investigated (van Hoek, 2002; Larson and Gammelgaard, 2001; van Hoek, 2000; Berglund et al., 1999; Peters et al., 1998), but ICT adoption in small 3PLs has attracted little attention. This is reflected in a shortage of research with little empirical surveys. In fact, the existing studies have seldom focused on small logistics service providers in general (Gunasekaran and Ngai, 2003) and ICT usage in particular (Pokharel, 2005).

Large logistics firms have heavily invested in ICT and have actively developed information systems to support their operations for a long time. Small and medium-size transport and logistics companies, on the other hand, have more difficulties in setting up ICT applications. Moreover, competition among small providers is generally cost-based and service quality is still considered less important compared to other factors. Such behaviour reduces the innovative potential associated to the use of ICT complicating the competitive positions of these companies.

This is critical particularly for those markets populated by a high number of small 3PLs such as the Italian logistics industry. The Italian 3PL market is one of the largest in the European Union (EU) with a growing expansion rate. Unlike many other countries in Europe, the Italian logistics service market show a lower level of logistics outsourcing. According with Datamonitor (2006) survey, the vast majority of Italian manufacturing companies outsource general haulage and distribution but not much else. Another important feature of the Italian logistics market is the high level of fragmentation that is evident when considering employee data. According to KPMG report (2003), about 50% of Italian logistics service providers employ less than 50 people and that 35% of them employ less than nine people. In addition, this fragmentation facilitated the entry of large multinational logistics groups in recent years.

Based on the above picture, the Italian logistics service market appears a suitable context for this research. Therefore, the purpose of this chapter is to investigate ICT innovation adoption in small logistics service companies through a case study analysis focused on a set of companies operating in the Italian market.

The chapter is organized into eight sections. Following this introduction, the relevant literature on the theme of this study is reviewed. This is followed by the description of the methodology used. The main findings achieved are then presented and discussed. On the basis of research results, some recommendations for supply chain innovation have been provided. Finally, future research avenues and concluding remarks have been given.

LITERATURE REVIEW

ICT Innovation in the Logistics Service Industry

Information and communication technology is considered one of the most important and fast growing technological innovations that provide companies with a wide range of opportunities to improve efficiency and effectiveness and even gain competitive advantage (Porter and Millar, 1985). Employ ICT as a means to enhance competitiveness is an ongoing challenge for any firms operating in a supply chain environment. Transport and logistics service providers are no exception. Over the last years, technology has been considered increasingly important in the management of 3PLs' business as its adoption may provide operational benefits and improve firm's performance (Speakman, 2002). Closs et al., (1997) argued that ICT related innovations have also the potential to leverage the overall firm's logistics competencies. Accordingly, there has been a proliferation of ICT applications on the market and several 3PL companies have implemented information technologies. This trend is reflected by a number research that analyzed different aspects of ICT related innovation in the 3PL industry including advantages associated with the use of general or specific applications and impact of technology on 3PLs' performance.

LaLonde and Auker (1973) suggest that technology may have the potential to enable the transformation of the supply chain role of logistics companies. The authors argue that the adoption of ICT by these companies facilitates the change from the operational and material-handling approach to a decision-making and activity-planning approach.

Langley *et al.* (1988) argue that 3PLs must carefully select ICT tools to be implemented. ICT may improve the strategic and operational profile of the firm if technology is selected considering overall business needs first. The authors conclude that priority in selecting ICT tools should be given to the value they may provide to the customer and other supply chain partners, rather than looking at the benefits that may be obtained by the company itself.

The work of Stock (1990) demonstrates how logistics companies may improve their competitive advantage through the use of a number of specific logistics ICT applications such as stock picking, bar code and automated warehouse systems.

Lewis and Talalayevsky (2000) discuss how the usage of ICT by logistics service companies has allowed manufacturers and retailers to better focus on their core competencies and contract out logistics activities. Product proliferation and shorter product life cycles require an efficient logistics management that is beyond the reach of many companies. Thanks to ICT improvements, logistics companies are able to manage this complexity and serve the customer more effectively.

Another stream of research focussed on assessing the impact of technology on 3PL's performance. These studies show a general consensus on the fact that ICT adoption affects positively 3PLs' performance. In particular, some of these works indicate that the enhancement of customer service and increased productivity and process quality is dependant on ICT adoption (Bowersox and Daugherty, 1995; Calder and Marr, 1998; Speakman, 2002; James et al., 2004; Lau et al., 2006, Chow et al., 2007; Liu et al., 2010). Wang et al. (2008) successfully linked 3PL financial performance to ICT advantage and involvement. A positive relationship between ICT adoption and company performance has been found by a study conducted on the transport and logistics service sector in the EU (e-Business Watch, 2008). This study ascertained that 3PL companies that have introduced ICT-enabled innovations were more likely to experience sales growth and an increased market share. More recently, the work of Lai et al. (2008) suggest that the range of logistics service offered might be have a mediating role in the relationship between ICT adoption and 3PLs' performance.

Despite the potential benefits associated with the use of ICT in logistics operations, many 3PL companies failed to obtain significant improvements. This is particularly true in the area of customer relationship. A recent Capgemini (2009) study provides a detailed analysis of the existing gap between shippers' expectations for 3PLs' ICT capabilities and their satisfaction with those capabilities. This misalignment may be attributed in part to the lack of continuous, ongoing use of ICT for improving service offerings. On the other hand, 3PL companies underestimate motivators and barriers that may affect their technology investment. These two critical elements in the 3PLs' approach to technology investment and adoption have seldom been the focus of the existing studies.

In relation to the first element, Nixon (2001) suggests that logistics service providers should employ new information technologies to raise their service capability in the e-commerce age. Van Hoek (2002) assigns a specific role to ICT for 3PLs, aiming to perform customising operations for service users. The author pointed out that the use of specific technological capabilities may leverage transport and logistics services and facilitates more effective integration across companies in the supply chain. For 3PLs, ICT capabilities can ensure the rapid customisation of products and maintain competitive lead-times. On the other hand, Sauvage (2003) stresses the key role of technology for logistics providers operating in a highly competitive context characterised by time compression. He argues that, in this environment, technological effort becomes a critical variable and a significant tool for differentiation of logistics services. As a consequence, technological innovation may be considered a vector of emancipation for small logistics suppliers (e.g. road haulage companies) who aspire to move away from their status of simple subcontractors. Finally, Chapman *et al.* (2003) identify ICT, knowledge and relationship networks as the main factors influencing innovation in the logistics service industry. The authors argue that innovation *per se* is of limited significance. To achieve competitive advantage, logistics companies have to anticipate and innovate service to meet the evolving customers' needs.

As far as determinants of ICT adoption is concerned, Lin (2008) provides empirical evidences of factors influencing technological innovation processes of logistics service providers in China. He identified the three following potential influencing factors: technological, organisational and environmental factors. The results of the survey confirmed that all the above three determinants influence significantly technological innovation processes of logistics companies.

Technology Adoption in Small Logistics Companies

The low level of customer satisfaction in using 3PLs' ICT capabilities evidenced by the Capgemini (2009) study reinforces the fact that ICT adoption is a risky process, particularly in the case of small and medium-sized logistics companies. While, large logistics companies have heavily adopted ICT, technology investment and adoption is a great challenge for small 3PLs. These companies show reluctance in investing in ICT due to insufficient human and financial resources (Colin, 1989). In addition, ICT is often perceived by these companies as an additional cost as its adoption involves company re-organization actions and skills updating. This situation is confirmed by a recent report of the European Commission (e-Business Watch, 2008) that documented a huge digital divide between large and small 3PL companies in the European Union logistics service market.

From the research point of view, little has been written in relation to the role of ICT innovation in small 3PLs (Evangelista and Sweeney, 2006). Three papers reporting empirical evidences concerning ICT usage in small logistics companies have been retrieved and they have been summarised below.

In their paper, Gunasekaran and Ngai (2003) examine a case study of a successful small logistics company based in Hong Kong. The authors argue that small 3PLs are flexible and innovative in executing logistics operations but they have problems in acquiring enough capital, resources and skills. Moreover, due to the lack of resources and budget available for technology investment, such companies tend to lag behind in the implementation of information systems such as electronic data interchange (EDI), Internet, extranet and enterprise resource planning (ERP). The authors also identify a number of key areas for future development of small logistics companies. Among these, web-based information may reduce communication barriers and both tangible and intangible factors should be considered when justifying investments in ICT projects.

The second paper relates to the study carried out by Pokharel (2005). It deals with ICT perception by transportation and warehousing companies in Singapore. The survey investigates 45 logistics companies (33 of them are small companies) and explores a number of interesting issues related to ICT usage and perception through comparing small and large 3PL companies. The analysis shows that large companies have a higher status of ICT implementation. Significant differences between the perception of ICT in small and large companies have been found. In general, smaller companies tend to serve a few customers or a small market area. Therefore, these companies have a lower perception of ICT implementation in comparison with large companies. The author also noted that large companies have more motivation to adopt ICT than small firms. Finally, concerning barriers, the perception differs significantly between large and small transport companies in terms of management support, compatibility and quantifying intangible benefits. Small transport companies perceive the lack of management support as a more serious barrier than their larger counterparts.

Finally, the research conducted by Kilpala, et al. (2005) on ICT usage by small 3PLs in the Barents region focused on the cooperation practices and the ICT implementation. The results achieved are based on a questionnaire survey involving 168 3PLs in Finland, Norway and Sweden. The survey results among the 3PLs in Finland and Sweden show similarities in most aspects regarding the overall development, cooperation practices and ICT implementation status. The 3PLs surveyed in Norway show some differences in comparison with the companies operating in the other two countries as the Norwegian 3PLs showed a higher overall ICT implementation status. In all three countries, the 3PL sector consists of a large number of small and medium-sized companies. The results indicate that the majority of the 3PLs surveyed are familiar with computer technology and have some ICT tools available. EDI implementation is in a very early stage in Finland and Sweden, whereas Norwegian 3PLs show a higher usage of this technology. Route planning tools were also more common among the surveyed 3PLs in Norway. The GPS technology implementation made an interesting exception: among the generally less "technology-oriented" 3PLs in Finland GPS systems were more common. Another issue investigated by the survey is motivators and barriers to ICT adoption. Improving control and planning was found to be an important motivator, while the most important barriers are the low level of compatibility with current system, a lack of adequate employee training and system not being flexible enough. Difficulties in system acceptance by customer and difficulties in achieving the planned level of work efficiency are considered barriers of less importance by the surveyed companies.

Summary of Literature Review

The literature review indicates that technology may enable innovation processes in the logistics service industry contributing to shifting the supply chain role of logistics service companies from simply operational asset-providers toward a more strategic supply chain orchestration position. On the other hand, while the literature emphasises a number of potential benefits associated with 3PLs' ICT adoption, there is still a gap between customers' expectations for 3PLs' ICT capabilities and their satisfaction in using those capabilities. This has critical implications for the success of 3PLs that will increasingly depend on the ability of such companies to deliver integrated, end-to-end solution that provides significant improvements in financial and operational performance of customers. The literature review highlights that research on ICT usage is predominantly focused on large logistics companies and research in this field are generally not based on empirical investigations as indicated by recent extensive 3PL literature surveys (Selviaridis, Spring, 2007; Maloni, Carter, 2006). A substantial void of research investigating the role of technology in small logistics service companies has been identified and very few empirical studies have been done in this area. This gives rise to the need to develop research and investigation in order to acquire a deeper understanding and in-depth knowledge in relation to a number of important components of ICT innovation in small 3PLs such as the level of ICT adoption, the role of technology in supporting the customisation of services provided, and the factors influencing ICT adoption.

METHODOLOGY

This chapter is aimed at exploring ICT innovation adoption in small logistics service companies via a series of case study companies operating in the

Italian market. The specific research objectives are as follows:

a. to define a technological profile of the surveyed companies
b. to analyze the role of ICT in supporting service customization
c. to identify factors influencing ICT adoption.

Despite the use of case study methods has increased significantly in logistics research over the last few years, the need for more case study analysis has been emphasised by several scholars. Chow *et al.* (1994) pinpointed how "... the predominance of the mail survey as data collection method raises some concern in light of its inherent limitations." In her pioneering work, Ellram (1996) observed that the case study method is not well understood, particularly in the field of purchasing and logistics management research. Meredith (1998) noted that the case study method continues to be rarely used in operation and logistics management and he documented the advantages and rigor of case study research. Gammelgaard (2003) analysed a selection of 17 case investigations published in leading logistics scientific journals to derive a framework for understanding and conducting case study analysis in logistics research. In order to increase the value for logistics research, she pointed out that the importance to choose and discuss an appropriate strategy for case study analysis. Juga (2003) argued that in logistics research, case studies can be considered a valuable tool to stimulate the dialogue between practitioners and academics and promote improvement in logistics competencies. Finally, Maloni and Carter (2006) on the basis of their literature survey covering leading academic logistics and supply chain journals, indicate that logistics service literature is dominated by survey-based research (almost 57% of articles analysed from 1989 to 2004). The weight of qualitative-based research papers is still limited with case study accounting for 21.5% only. The authors concluded advocating an increasing use of qualitative data collection methods (e.g. case study and focus group) for complementing quantitative survey data in this field.

The use of case study in this research is also motivated by the fact that ICT adoption in small 3PLs is an emergent issue with limited discussion on the subject in the logistics and supply chain management (SCM) literature. Therefore, as this research is exploratory in nature, case study method appears particularly appropriate. The case study survey has been carried out mainly to gain insights into "how" and "why" ICT is used in small logistics companies and in-depth information to identify factor affecting technology usage (Voss et al., 2002). The main advantage of case study is that the researcher can adapt the questions as necessary, clarify doubts, and ensure that the responses are properly understood. However, case study as a method relies heavily on the perceptions, opinions, and perspectives of respondents and is hence susceptible to response bias (Yin, 1998). Another important reason for using the case approach in the context of this research is that case study is a suitable method when small companies are investigated (Chetty, 1996).

Finally, the use of case study is justified by the qualitative nature of most of research objectives b) and c) above. The case study analysis has been conducted in a set of seven small Italian logistics service providers and it was carried out using a methodology based on four different stages (see Figure 1).

Case Study Selection

A preliminary important decision in the case selection process concerns the number of cases to be investigated. The basic choice is between single case and multiple case studies. Single, in-depth case studies are frequently used in longitudinal research. Operations management literature offers several examples of single cases of this type (Narasimhan, Jayaram, 1998; Karlsson, Ahlstrom, 1995). In the field of logistics and SCM research,

Figure 1. The case study research method

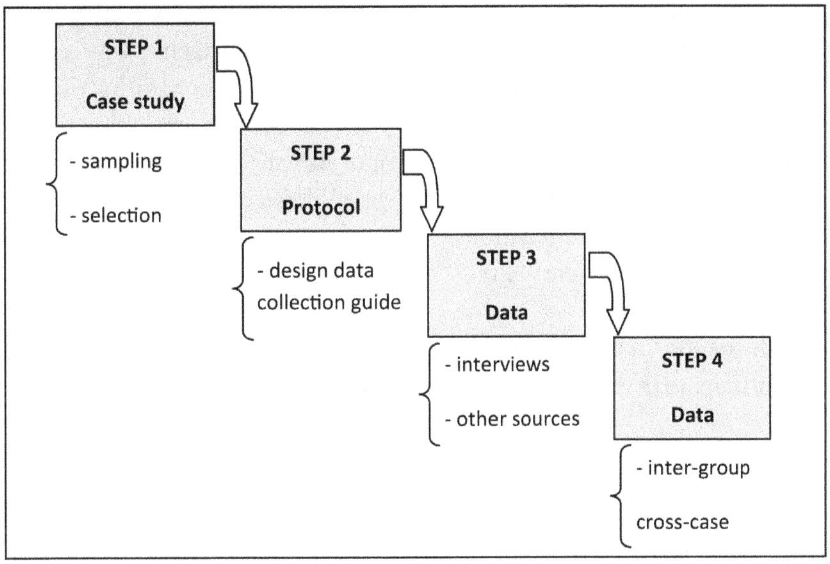

Koulikoff-Souviron and Harrison (2005) argued that a single case may be chosen in order to research exemplary practices in great depth. Nevertheless, the use of the single case approach is strongly constrained by the limited generalisability of results. Conversely, the comparison of two or more cases allows to overcome this constraint (Bryman and Bell, 2003, p. 56). When comparative logic is applied, it generally takes the form of multiple case studies that usually involve two or more organisations as cases for comparison. One the main benefit associated to multiple case study research is that it supports exploratory research (Ellram, 1996). In addition, multiple case study approach improves theory building (Meredith, 1998). These advantages made evidence from multiple cases more compelling and the overall study more robust.

It is difficult to determine what is an adequate number of cases to include in multiple case survey. Yin (2003) indicates that 6 to 10 cases should provide evidences to support or reject propositions, while Eisenhardt (1989) recommend 4 to 10 case studies. Koulikoff-Souviron and Harrison (2005) review of a number of papers based on case study, they found that the number of cases used ranging from 3 to 11. The review of papers carried out by Voss *et al.* (2002) provides evidence that the number of cases used range from 3 to 30. Finally, although multiple case study research is a relatively common research design in the field of management and business, Seuring (2005) noted that there are few papers based on case study in the field of logistics and operations management in which data have been collected at two or more stages of the supply chain.

Considering the purposes of this study, a multiple case study approach was chosen for the following reasons:

- given the lack of studies, multiple case study setting may be considered a more appropriate research design to increase the body of knowledge in the field;
- by analysing more case studies it is possible to obtain better insight into the way in which small logistics companies use ICT;
- using a multiple case study approach it is possible to increase both the reliability of the overall research process.

Another critical element in case study research is the appropriate selection of case companies to include in the survey. In this study, the selection process has been organised in the following two phases:

a. selection of a set of companies from the sample firms of the previous questionnaire survey that was ended on early 2005 (Evangelista, Sweeney, 2006);
b. phone inquiry to secure the agreement of companies to participate in the case survey.

The traditional way of sampling is to extract a random or stratified sample from a population. By contrast, in case research, the definition of the sample is often realised according to different criteria. In this study the population consisted of the 153 companies that participated in a questionnaire survey. The selection of case companies has been based on the following small 3PLs groups (Evangelista, Sweeney, 2006):

1. *Full Haulage Providers*: those companies for which transport activities represent 100% of turnover;
2. *Basic Logistics Providers*: those companies for which transport and warehousing together comprise over 50% of turnover; and,
3. *Advanced Logistics Providers*: those companies for which transport and warehousing together comprise less than 50% of turnover (e.g. where more than 50% of the total turnover is generated by value added logistics and SCM services).

According to such taxonomy, three sets of companies have been selected from the sample firms using the two following criteria:

a. the breakdown of the company turnover by the type of service provided; and,
b. the level of ICT in the company in terms of number and sophistication of tools adopted.

In the case of Full Haulage companies, the 100% of turnover is generated by pure haulage, so the level of technology adopted has been the single criterion used to discriminate between these companies. In the case of Basic Logistics Providers and Advanced Logistics Providers, the different breakdown of turnover associated with transport/warehousing and other services provided (value added services and SCM services) has been used to select the companies.

The basic aim in this step was to select case companies with sharply contrasting characteristics capable of highlighting the differences being studied. Accordingly, within each group of provider type, two subsets of companies have been further selected with extremely different profiles in terms of both range of service provided and technology adopted. For example, within each provider type, one subset of companies showed a low level of technology in place and a limited breadth of service provided, while the second subset has a higher level of technology adoption and a wider range of service provided.

A set of 43 companies has been selected in total from the questionnaire survey mailing list. The selected companies were distributed according to the small 3PL taxonomy as follows: 10 Full Haulage Providers, 21 Basic Logistics Providers and 12 Advanced Logistics Providers. Subsequently, a phone inquiry has been conducted to secure the acceptance of companies to participate in the survey and to check both the breadth of service provided and the level of technology in place. Seven companies agreed to participate in the survey divided by provider type as follows:

- 2 Full Haulage providers (FH),
- 3 Basic Logistics providers (BL), and
- 2 Advanced Logistics providers (AL).

Within the Basic Logistics providers, 3 companies were selected because this category has the largest number of companies in the sample frame. These companies have a different combination of turnover allocated to service provided and technology adopted. Table 1 shows a summary profile of the studied companies.

Protocol Development

After selecting the case companies to include in the survey, the subsequent step in the research process consisted of building up the protocol and the research instrument. Yin (2003) argues that a well-designed protocol is particularly critical in multiple case study as it enhances the reliability and validity of case research.

The core of the protocol consists of the set of questions to be asked during interviews. Accordingly, the primary sources of data and information in this study have been unstructured interviews. To this end, a semi-structured data collection guide has been designed. The data collection guide contained both open-ended and closed questions which allowed informants to discuss related issues outside the interview structure also. It has been organised into the following four sections:

- Section A: General company profile
- Section B: Technological profile
- Section C: The role of ICT in service customisation
- Section D: Factors influencing ICT deployment

Each section of the data collection guide starts with broad open-ended questions, while more specific and detailed questions come last. The questions in each section were non-directive in order to minimise unplanned, leading questions while interviewing.

Data Collection

The data collection phase consisted of many activities. The first was to contact case companies to agree dates for the interview meetings. After that

Table 1. Characteristics of the case study companies

Case company	Size*	Customer industry	N. of customer	Customer Concentration**
Full Haulage 1	micro	Fertilizers for agriculture, food & beverage	20	85%
Full Haulage 2	small	Hazardous goods, food & beverage	200	10%
Basic Logistics 1	medium	Electrical device and machinery, electronics, chemical and oil, textile and clothing, automotive, paper	150	40%
Basic Logistics 2	micro	Raw material for plastic products	30	80%
Basic Logistics 3	small	Biomedical, publishing textile-clothing-shoes and food packaging	200	90%
Advanced Logistics 1	small	I.T., electronics, telecom, pharmaceutical, automotive, banks and insurance, fashion, promotional and publishing	120	50%
Advanced Logistics 2	medium	Coffee, metals, cellulose, rubber and perishable goods	6,000	30%

* The company size has been measured using the latest European Commission definition of small and medium sized enterprise (European Commission, 2005). According with this definition, firms with less than 10 employees are considered "micro", firms whose employees range from 10 to 50 are "small", while firms employing less than 250 people are considered "medium."

**Customer concentration: company's turnover percentage generated by the largest 5 customers a letter outlining survey objectives and data collection guide, were sent via e-mail or fax to make sure that interviewee(s) were properly prepared.

As interviews focused on ICT and logistics service issues, two "key informants" were invited to take part in the interview: the IT manager (or other manager when there was no IT manager) and the manager with overall responsibility for transport and logistics operations of the case company. The reason for this is that no single person has all the required knowledge concerning the research topics.

In-depth interviews were conducted at the company site in summer 2005. The average time spent on each interview was approximately two hours and each interview was conducted on a face-to-face basis, so as to stimulate a broad discussion and break down any barriers between the interviewer and interviewee.

After the interview, a tour of the company's facilities and IT department (when it exists) took place. Such tours allowed for a visual check and comparison of each company's facilities (e.g. warehouse) and technologies adopted to support related activities (e.g. radio frequency, bar code, etc.). These tours provided an additional opportunity to clarify some interview responses.

All interviews were tape-recorded and subsequently transcribed to minimise researcher bias and support data quality and reliability. Informants were re-contacted many times by phone to clarify and confirm data and information gathered during interviews.

In order to corroborate and augment evidences, data obtained through interviews have been supplemented and integrated with information from other sources such as: company documentation (brochures and internal reports), company websites, articles published in industry magazines, records obtained from on-line archival resources of industry associations and chambers of commerce.

Because a multiple case study involves collection of a large amount of documentary evidence, these data need to be organised and filed to make them easily retrievable for later use. A case study database was created to store interviews and other relevant information with regard to each single case company. Finally, contact records have been maintained, listing all contact detail of informants, date and location of interviews. Data and information collected were finally included into the case study database. This amount of information has been used for executing a structured analysis as detailed in the next section.

DATA ANALYSIS AND FINDINGS

Due to the depth of data and information gathered, the analysis of case studies is challenging and it demands particular care. Analyzing case study data is the most complicated and least codified part of the process.

The approach adopted for this study consists of comparing the case companies to each other within each group (between-company comparison) of the small 3PLs categorization proposed above. This approach is based on detailed case study description of each company surveyed containing all the information gathered during interviews. Such case study descriptions are critical to the generation of insight as they help the analysis process when a large amount of data is involved. The aim of this approach is to understand, explain and interpret critical aspects of the phenomenon investigated by identifying similarities and differences within each of the three categories of small 3PLs defined as detailed in the following sections below.

Comparison of Full Haulage Providers

The two companies in this category show a different basic profile. The Full Haulage 1 (FH1) was a small size pure haulage company operating a small fleet of vehicles with a focus on the domestic market. It is specialized in the transportation of commodities, food and beverage. The Full Haul-

Table 2. Technological profile of full haulage

Case company	ICT dep./ ICT manager	ICT expenses	ICT integration	e-Marketplace usage
Full Haulage 1	no/no	**Decreasing due to reduction in communication costs**	No integration with both customer and 3PLs	No - considered not reliable
Full Haulage 2	no/yes	Increasing due to update technology in place (HW & SW) particularly in the communication area and website	Low integration with both customer and 3PLs	Yes - use very low as the company considers e-marketplace not so reliable and it needs to retain the full control over the shipment (as in the case of hazardous goods)

Table 3. Role of ICT in supporting the services customization in full haulage

Case company	Software usage	Track & trace
Full Haulage 1	No - no need for specific applications to support company activities	No - not currently required by customer
Full Haulage 2	Yes - to manage the several specific aspects of the business. Standard software package integrated with specific modules	No - service not required by customer

age 2 (FH2) was a freight forwarding company mainly focused on foreign markets. It provides a range of full door-to-door express transport services using all modes of transport but with an emphasis on air transport. The company manages a small distribution centre. FH2 was specialized in transporting perishable and hazardous goods, but it also supports the internationalization process of small local manufacturing firms, providing services such as import/export and organization of trade fairs.

The two companies also showed substantial differences in their technological profile as shown in Table 2. FH2 has shown an advanced technological profile in comparison with FH1. This is evident considering a number of findings. FH2 was much more willing to invest in technology, particularly in the communication area and to improve its website. FH2 had a higher level of information integration with customers and other logistics companies in comparison with FH1. Finally, FH2 used transportation e-marketplace to some extent, while such portals are not used at all by FH1.

No significant difference emerged in relation to future ICT plans. Neither of the companies has planned to implement technology and this reflects the low importance attributed to technology as a driver for developing the business. Certified e-mail was the only tool that will be adopted by both companies in the near future. GPS (for both companies) and EDI (only for FH2) could be adopted depending on evolving business conditions (e.g. increase in the number of trucks operated and customer demand). This may be interpreted as further evidence of the "wait and see" approach characterizing this group of providers. Other differences emerged looking at the use of ICT for services customization (see Table 3). FH2 used software packages and the company was willing to invest in this area as the modularization of software packages facilitated the provision of tailor-made service solutions for the customer. Surprisingly, the company did not provide any track & trace service because of such functional-

Table 4. Source of ICT innovation in Full Haulage

Case company	ICT innovation driven by the case company		ICT innovation driven by supply chain partner	
	toward customer	*toward other 3PLs*	*from customer*	*from other 3PLs*
Full Haulage 1	No initiatives due to the low ICT usage and technological sensibility of customer	No initiatives due to the low level of cooperation	No stimuli received due to their scarce technological sensibility	No stimuli received due to the low level of cooperation
Full Haulage 2	No initiatives as price and service quality are the most important elements in the selection process	No initiatives due to the low level of cooperation	No stimuli received to develop ICT cooperation	No stimuli received to develop ICT cooperation

Table 5. Factors influencing ICT usage and impact on performance in full haulage

Case company	Main ICT inhibitors	Main ICT stimulators	ICT impact on performance
Full Haulage 1	• ICT may negatively influence truck drivers' performance	• ICT embedded in new truck generations	• No impact on company performance
Full Haulage 2	• ICT supply as ICT products and services are often inconsistent with small 3PLs needs	• Financial and cost factors • Price reduction in ICT tools	• Turnover improvement • Customer service • Operational activities

ity was not required by customers. FH1 did not use ICT to customize its services. This is mainly due to the nature of the business it operates (point-to-point road transportation service).

Technological capability of customers played an important role. Customers did not consider important to conduct transactions electronically. They still preferred paper-based transactions and to "hear" the voice of their logistics provider. This situation is reflected in the lack of initiatives to promote ICT innovation (see Table 4). The two companies had no projects in place aimed at improving ICT usage with either customers or other logistics providers. The reasons given to justify this were quite similar for the two companies: the low level of customer technological capability and the low level of cooperation with other logistics companies.

Relevant differences between the two companies were evident when considering factors affecting ICT usage (Table 5).

For FH1, technology may had a negative effect on truck drivers as they can be used to control their performance. The main innovation stimulator was new ICT tools embedded in new truck generations.

FH2 considered ICT supply side as the main inhibitor as technology products and service did not reflect the real business needs of small logistics companies. Cost factor and price reduction of ICT tools were considered the main stimulators for wider use of ICT. Moreover, the two companies attributed to ICT a completely different impact on company performance. For FH1, technology had no impact on company performance. FH2 attributed to ICT the improvements in several areas such as turnover, customer service and operations to ICT.

Table 6. Technological profile of the basic logistics

Case company	ICT dep./ ICT manager	ICT expenses	ICT integration	e-Marketplace usage
Basic Logistics 1	no/no	Increasing technology costs to adjust technical standard to different ICT requirements of customer sectors	Very low integration with both customer and 3PLs	Yes: • to fully exploit the capacity of its trucks • to serve new geographic areas
Basic Logistics 2	no/yes	Stability in technology costs due to price reduction in ICT products and service	Very low integration with both customer and 3PLs	Yes: • to reduce empty trips and to optimise vehicles capacity
Basic Logistics 3	yes/yes	**Decreasing ICT costs due to reduction of the budget devoted to external consultancy**	• High customer integration • Low 3PLs integration	No: • considered not reliable

Comparison of Basic Logistics Providers

The three companies selected in this category all had different backgrounds. Basic Logistics 1 (BL1) was a road haulage and courier company operating a fleet of vehicles and warehouse. The company served several manufacturing sectors and it is mainly focused on the domestic market.

Basic Logistics 2 (BL2) was a freight forwarding company (focused on land and sea transport). It also offered warehousing and some value added logistics services. BL2 was specialized in the logistics of raw material for plastic product. It geographical range is within the domestic market.

Basic Logistics 3 (BL3) was a logistics company with a focus on providing value added logistics and SCM services. The service focus was on supply chain design and management, while transportation was predominantly outsourced. Service customization and information management played an important role in the overall company strategy. BL3 served both manufacturing and service sectors and the geographical range of their service was global, thanks to a wide warehousing and distribution network exploited through a number of partnerships.

Differentiated technological profiles emerged from data gathered, as shown in Table 6. BL3 had the most advanced technological profile in comparison with the other two companies. BL3 had an ICT department in place managed by an ICT manager, while BL2 had a responsible for information systems but there was no ICT department in place. The level of ICT expenses was increasing for BL1 and stable for BL2. In the case of BL3, the decrease in ICT expenses was due to a strategy developed to increase the exploitation of internal technological capabilities, thereby reducing resources allocated to external ICT consultancy.

From the ICT integration point of view, BL3 shown a high level of integration, particularly with customers. A very low level of integration emerged for the other two companies. The usage of electronic transportation markets paints an interesting picture. BL1 and BL2 shown intensive use of such portals, while BL3 did not use such new intermediaries as they are considered unreliable. This situation may be explained considering that BL1 and BL2 provided transport-intensive services and e-marketplaces are mainly used to fully exploit the capacity of vehicles and reduce empty trips. As the focus of BL3 was on the overall management of supply chain and the physical movement of goods was mainly outsourced, the use of e-marketplace was considered redundant.

No evidence emerged with regard to future technology implementation plans in any of the three companies. Considering the differentiated ICT profile of these companies, this is surprising.

Table 7. Role of ICT for services customization in basic logistics

Case company	Software usage	Track & Trace
Basic Logistics 1	Yes - to manage more effectively different transport operations	No - not required by customer
Basic Logistics 2	No - software is costly and with low level of flexibility and friendliness	No - not required by customer
Basic Logistics 3	Yes - to increase the effectiveness of service delivery and to provide a higher value to customer	Yes - to provide higher value to customer through T&T functionality

Table 8. Source of ICT innovation in basic logistics

Case company	ICT innovation driven by the case company		ICT innovation driven by other supply chain partner	
	toward customer	*toward other 3PLs*	*from customer*	*from other 3PLs*
Basic Logistics 1	No initiatives as price and other service attributes (e.g. punctuality, reliability, etc.) play a major role	No initiatives to stimulate ICT improvements	No stimuli received to develop ICT cooperation	No stimuli received to develop ICT cooperation
Basic Logistics 2	No initiatives as service and price still play a major role	No initiatives to stimulate ICT improvements	No stimuli received to develop ICT cooperation	No stimuli received to develop ICT cooperation
Basic Logistics 3	Yes initiatives implemented particularly in the area of data exchange through collaborative benefits analysis	No initiatives implemented due to the poor level of technology adoption	Yes, initiatives generated to design and implement specific technology solutions in the area of shipment document delivery	No stimuli received due to the poor level of technology in place

The implementation of some specific applications over the next three years was planned: certified e-mail and bar-code for BL1, radio frequency for BL2 and certified e-mail for BL3. Some additional tools, such as EDI, tracking and tracing (T&T), radio frequency identification (RFID), customer relationship management (CRM) and ERP was planned to be adopted if customer requires such functionalities. This highlights how ICT innovation is "customer driven" in this group of companies.

The emphasis of BL3 on information management was also evident considering the role of ICT in service customization (Table 7). BL3 used software extensively to support administration, warehousing, transportation and distribution operations through different packages. Also BL1 used software to manage transport operations in a more effective way. BL2 did not use software at all. BL3 provided T&T applications with a great level of detail to increase the value for customers. BL1 and BL2 did not provide any T&T service as it was not required by customers.

Data concerning sources of ICT innovation provides an interesting picture (Table 8). BL1 and BL2 had no initiatives in place to stimulate innovation in relation to either customers or other 3PLs. This may be motivated by the fact that service price was the main area of improvement, while innovation in technology was not considered important. Neither of the two case companies had received stimuli to innovate in ICT from either customer or other 3PLs, due to low level of existing cooperation.

BL3 adopts a different approach. The company had closely involved customers in a technol-

Table 9. Factors influencing ICT usage and impact on performance in basic logistics

Case company	Main ICT inhibitors	Main ICT stimulators	ICT impact on performance
Basic Logistics 1	- Financial and cost factors - Lack of funds	- ICT supply - Technology standards	- Customer service - Operational activities
Basic Logistics 2	- ICT supply - ICT products and services are generally not in line with small 3PLs needs	- Better market knowledge	- Customer service - Operational activities
Basic Logistics 3	- Financial and cost factors - Technology "myopia" of small companies	- ICT supply - Advancements achieved in ICT and related benefits	- Customer service

ogy project aimed at sharing and exchanging information. On the other hand, customers proposed that the case company design a specific project to make shipment documentation electronically available. Due to the poor level of technology adoption, no technology innovation projects or initiatives were in place with other 3PLs.

In relation to factors inhibiting ICT usage, BL1 and BL3 indicated financial and cost factors, while BL2 identified ICT supply as the main source influencing negatively the use of technology (Table 9). It is interesting to note that BL3 indicated the technology "myopia" of small companies as one of the most important inhibitors. ICT supply was considered by two companies (BL1 and BL3) as the source of stimulation for wider usage of technology in the sector. BL2 identified the possibility to improve market knowledge as the main ICT stimulator.

Information gathered on ICT impact on company performance demonstrated how all three companies interviewed attributed ICT with the potential to improve customer service, while BL1 and BL2 also attributed technology with a positive impact on operational activities.

Comparison of Advanced Logistics Providers

The case company Advanced Logistics 1 (AL1) is a logistics company providing a wide range of logistics and SCM services. It is focused on the domestic market and it serves a number of both manufacturing and service sectors.

The case company Advanced Logistics 2 (AL2) is specialized in the commodity logistics, particularly coffee and metal. It provides a range of transportation, warehousing and handling services and it has a strong focus on international markets.

The technological profile of each of the two companies shows many similarities (see Table 10). They both have an ICT department in place, ran by a manager. Both companies shown an increase in technology expenses, mainly due to updating of hardware and software. Both companies do not use transportation e-marketplaces for a number of reasons. AL1 do not use e-marketplaces due to the good level relationships with other logistics companies. AL2 do not participate in electronic markets as their main supply chain partners are not involved in them. AL2 plans to build-up its own e-marketplace to optimize relationships with customers, suppliers and other logistics service providers.

Both companies have a high degree of technology integration with customers, but they show different levels of information integration with other logistics companies. AL1 was highly integrated with large logistics companies with notable technological capability, but the degree of integration is low when counterparts are small logistics companies. AL2 had a low level of integration with other logistics companies because it changed

Table 10. Technological profile of the advanced logistics

Case company	ICT dep./ ICT manager	ICT expenses	ICT integration	e-Marketplace usage
Advanced Logistics 1	yes/yes	Increasing ICT costs in hardware and software costs and decreasing consultancy and communication costs	- High customer integration - The level of integration with 3PLs varies according with the size providers	No - the company do not use e-marketplace as it is satisfied with regard to the relationships with other 3PLs
Advanced Logistics 2	yes/yes	Increasing ICT costs in hardware and software	- High customer integration - Low 3PLs integration	No - customer and supplier of the company does not participate in such electronic markets

Table 11. Role of ICT in supporting the customization of services in advanced logistics

Case company	Software usage	Track & trace
Advanced Logistics 1	Yes - improving the effectiveness of services provided	Yes - on the base of future customer needs analysis
Advanced Logistics 2	Yes - improvement of effectiveness of services provided	Yes - offered through other partner companies

logistics provides very frequently and, generally, their average size was very low. These two reasons inhibited specific investment for integrating logistics partners.

Both companies have a formal plan to improve ICT in the near future. In both companies the plan has been validated by top management and a budget has been allocated to implement it. Adoption of specific tools is also planned: certified e-mail, wireless local area network (LAN) and RFID in the case of AL1 and certified e-mail, EDI and RFID for AL2. This evidences confirm the "proactive" approach to technology adopted by these companies.

Similarities also emerged in relation with the role of technology in service customization, as reported in Table 11.

Both companies used software extensively to support their service provision and both companies adopted point solutions due to specific supply chain requirements of customers operating in different industries, as in the case of AL1 or the lack of integrated solutions available on the market, as in the case of AL2. The provision of T&T service is based on various motivations. AL1 decided to start the provision of this functionality on the basis of customer needs analysis. As the company serves many customers operating in different supply chains, the T&T service has been designed to provide full supply chain visibility of product along its own supply chain. In addition, the T&T service is highly integrated in the customer information system. On the other hand, AL2 did not provide its own T&T service, but it provided information concerning shipment using the service provided by logistics company partners (e.g. large container shipping company).

Many similarities also emerged between the two companies in the area of ICT innovation (see Table 12). Both companies exerted and received pressure from customers for innovating in the ICT area. AL1 designed a technological solution to solve the specific needs of some of their customers. At the same time, the company has been stimulated to cooperate in the technology field by some of its customers, particularly in the design of specific software solutions. AL2 tried

Table 12. Source of ICT innovation in advanced logistics

Case company	ICT innovation driven by the case company		ICT innovation driven by other supply chain partner	
	toward customer	*toward other 3PLs*	*from customer*	*from other 3PLs*
Advanced Logistics 1	Yes - co-designing technology solutions to address customer specific needs	No initiatives implemented due to the poor level of technology adoption	Yes - customer asked for developing specific software applications and collaborative technology projects	No stimuli received due to the poor level of technology in place
Advanced Logistics 2	Yes designing a solution to better integrate small customer systems into the company system	Yes some initiatives implemented only with large 3PLs in the area of information exchange	Yes initiatives implemented with large customers in the area of system integration	No stimuli received to develop ICT innovation

Table 13. Factors influencing ICT usage and impact on performance in advanced logistics

Case company	Main ICT inhibitors	Main ICT stimulators	ICT impact on performance
Advanced Logistics 1	Sector issues - high fragmentation of industry	- ICT supply - New technological infrastructure	- Customer service - Operational activities
Advanced Logistics 2	Sector issues - uncertainty characterizing the competitive scenario	Changing in legislation (as traceability law for food product)	Low impact as ICT has an enabling role

to integrate some of its customers (small coffee roasting companies) in the company ICT platform.

Some customers have also encouraged the company in the area of information systems integration. Innovation activities involving other logistics service companies present a different landscape. Generally, neither of the two companies had initiatives in place for developing collaborative technological solutions with other logistics service providers, and neither do other 3PLs stimulated either of the two companies to initiate some form of innovation. Only AL2 has developed some forms of technological cooperation/integration with some large 3PL company partners.

With regard to inhibiting factors, both companies indicated sector issues (Table 13). The fragmentation of the Italian logistics service industry and the low level of technological culture were the main factors preventing a wider diffusion of ICT in the sector according to AL1. The uncertainty concerning the future evolution of the competitive scenario has been identified by AL2 as the main inhibiting factor.

Differences emerge in relation to factors stimulating technology diffusion. AL1 stressed the role of the ICT supply side and the development of new technological infrastructures as the main factors that may stimulate the use of ICT in the sector. For AL2 the changing legislation in different sectors (e.g. food supply chain traceability) could have positive effects in further stimulating technology adoption by logistics service companies. Significant differences appear with regard to the impact of ICT on company performance. AL1 recognizes that ICT is having a positive impact on both customer service and operations, while AL2 believes that ICT is simply an enabler and does not produce significant effects on company performance.

DISCUSSION

The comparison of full haulage companies shows substantial differences in their technological profile from the organizational, cost and supply chain integration points of view. Despite these differences, neither of the companies used technology to support service customization. A possible reason for this may be found when the source of innovation is considered. It emerges that customers play a fundamental role in limiting the technological efforts of these companies. Neither of the two companies have initiatives in place to stimulate customers to improve technology adoption but, most importantly, customers do not require any shift toward the usage of ICT for conducting their business (e.g. electronic rather than paper-based transactions). Surprisingly, significant differences emerged in relation to factors affecting ICT usage. Full haulage 1 did not considered ICT important for its business. In addition, technology innovation was considered an exogenous factor, to the extent that innovation is expected to come from new technology embedded in new truck generations. Full haulage 2 recognizes that ICT may have a positive impact on company performance and considers the lack of ICT solutions for small companies the main inhibiting factor. In conclusion, full haulage companies are generally small firms and tend to serve few small customer firms in a limited geographical area. In addition, the characteristics of their business (the main focus is on transportation) and their small turnover capacity, have a significant influence in limiting their need for ICT implementation.

The analysis of basic logistics case companies provides a different picture. Basic logistics 3 case company shows a higher technology profile in comparison with the other two companies. This is reflected in greater attention to service customization in terms of both software usage and track and trace service provision. Moreover, this company had a two-way innovation channel in place with customer in order to continuously improve technology adoption and share advantages. In addition, current and future initiatives for improving technology usage with other 3PLs were adopted. Factors influencing ICT usage reflected this approach. According to this company, one of the most important barriers to further ICT adoption was the technology "myopia" of most small and medium sized firms, while ICT supply side was seen as an important ICT stimulator. Finally, customer service was the area in which ICT has the most critical impact.

The case companies in this group have shown a higher perception and usage of technology. Probably, the provision of wider range of services (transport and warehousing) required a higher importance of cost efficiency for the achievement of economies of scale. Consequently, these factors may determine a positive perception of ICT usage. In addition, ICT was also perceived as a tool to improve customer service and this may explain the involvement of customers in ICT innovation initiatives.

A more homogeneous situation emerges from the analysis of advanced logistics case companies. The two case companies have a structured ICT department in place, a good level of integration with customers (although integration with other 3PLs is still low) and high level of ICT expenses. More importantly, the two case companies have a formal future ICT implementation plan to improve their technological capability. ICT is widely used to support the service provision. Both companies have involved customers in technology innovation initiatives, and, at the same time, clients request technology improvement from the two case companies. Only AL company 2 involved other (large) 3PLs in initiatives finalized to enhance information exchange. In this scenario, it is not surprising that the two case companies identified exogenous factors as both inhibitors (such as industry fragmentation and uncertainty in the competitive scenario) and stimulators (ICT supply side, new technological infrastructures and changes in legislation) of ICT usage. The two case companies have shown a prominent level of ICT adoption in comparison with the other two groups. The focus on value added service provision and their role as supply chain orchestrators emphasize the importance of information management for their customers. This may explain the customer demand for higher visibility in areas such as easy access to shipment and payment information and on-line status of inventory. This, in turn, allows to innovate operations for further improvements in service offering.

SOLUTIONS AND RECOMMENDATIONS FOR SUPPLY CHAIN INNOVATION

The case study findings allow drawing a number of implications for supply chain innovation.

Firstly, depending on the specific supply chain role, ICT have a differentiated impact on different type of small logistics companies. Small 3PLs more close to customer are in a better position to provide services supported by technology solutions. These companies have the potential to design innovation in collaboration with customer and other supply chain actors in comparison with companies that function as tier suppliers in the supply chain.

Secondly, to fully exploit the potential of ICT for developing supply chain innovation the combination between "service strategy" and "technology strategy" is an important factor. For example, advanced logistics companies tend to proactively develop supply chain solutions for customers. The implementation of this strategy is based on the following three components that may provide distinctive edges: customer service, supply chain integration, and visibility.

Finally, the case study findings indicate that, when planning their technology investment, the focus of small 3PL have to be on using ICT to change supply chain relationships rather than on technology itself. ICT is a valuable, but no longer rare resource. Technology investments may be easily replicated by competitors and thus provide temporary advantages. The way technology is used can enable differentiation advantage. To this end, ICT innovations have to be used by small 3PLs to building up non-imitable supply chain coordinated and collaborative strategies.

FUTURE RESEARCH DIRECTIONS

A number of areas would merit further investigation. Firstly, further case study analysis would enlarge the qualitative information base established by the present research. In particular, a larger number of case companies will allow to overcome the limitation of this study in order to achieve a higher degree of generalisation of results. Future case studies could focus on the analysis of ICT costs/benefits in the selection of technology investment projects and the need for technological skill and knowledge in small 3PLs. Another important topic that needs to be explored in more depth is the ICT impact on performance of small 3PLs. Research should concentrate on the analysis of the ICT implementation process and its impact on company performance.

In addition, future research should focus on ICT costs in order to explain why small 3PLs invest so little in technology innovation. Next, by using longitudinal data, future research could investigate the process of ICT adoption and trace its impact on company operations through time. Longitudinal study will be of help in formulating more appropriate policy recommendations for managers, ICT vendors and governmental bodies.

Given the importance of small 3PLs in the development of the logistics service industry, comparative studies between small logistics service companies operating in different countries/markets may be beneficial. The cross-country analysis could be of help in understanding differences and commonalities of ICT adoption as well as motivators and barriers in investing in ICT by small logistics service providers located in different countries. Considering the existing gap in knowledge, such analysis could stimulate further research in this field. In addition, the results could help managers of logistics service companies in comparing the business attitude and cultures of small 3PLs operating in different countries.

It will be important to include a customer perspective in future studies of this kind. The challenge for researchers will be to match service user and provider perspectives. This will provide deeper insights into the mechanisms that influence ICT usage and customer expectation associated to technology adoption. This will allow more appropriate recommendations could be made to managers of small 3PLs, ICT vendors and policy makers.

CONCLUSION

Although the present study is exploratory in nature, the findings presented help managers of small logistics service companies to understand the status of ICT implementation, as well as opportunities and obstacles connected to technology usage.

The study findings suggests that companies with a longer term strategic view of the business tend to adopt more proactive ICT solutions aimed at reinforcing and sustaining the firm's competitive position. On the other side, less developed providers have no clear appreciation of the role of technology in achieving their business objectives. These evidences confirm that ICT innovation in small 3PLs sector is not homogeneous diffused and contrast the idea that small 3PLs are less innovative than larger counterparts. The study also support the importance attributed by Busse (2010) to industry-specific innovation research as innovation activity and performance in logistics service industry differs substantially from other service industries.

REFERENCES

Barras, R. (1986). Towards a theory of innovation in services. *Research Policy*, *15*(4), 161–173. doi:10.1016/0048-7333(86)90012-0

Berglund, M., van Laarhoven, P., Sharman, G., & Wandel, S. (1999). Third-party logistics: is there a future? *International Journal of Logistics Management*, *10*(1), 59–70. doi:10.1108/09574099910805932

Bowersox, D. J., & Daugherty, P. J. (1995). Logistics paradigms: the impact of information technology. *Journal of Business Logistics*, *16*(1), 65–80.

Bryman, A., & Bell, E. (2003). *Business Research Methods*. New York: Oxford University Press.

Busse, C. (2010). A procedure for secondary data analysis - the example of innovation by logistics service providers. *Journal of Supply Chain Management*, *46*(4), 44–58. doi:10.1111/j.1745-493X.2010.03205.x

Cainelli, G., Evangelista, R., & Savona, M. (2004). The impact of innovation on economic performance in services. *The Service Industries Journal*, *24*(1), 116–130. doi:10.1080/02642060412331301162

Calder, R., & Marr, P. (1998). A beef producer initiative in traceability: Scottish borders TAG. *Supply Chain Management: An International Journal*, *3*(3), 23–126. doi:10.1108/13598549810230822

Capgemini. (2009). The state of logistics outsourcing 2009 third party logistics. Results and findings of the 14th annual study, available at www.3plstudy.com.

Chapman, R. L., Soosay, C., & Kandampully, J. (2003). Innovation in logistic services and the new business model. A conceptual framework. *International Journal of Physical Distribution & Logistics Management*, *33*(7), 630–650. doi:10.1108/09600030310499295

Chetty, S. (1996). The case study method for research in small- and medium-sized firms. *International Small Business Journal, 15*(1), 73–85. doi:10.1177/0266242696151005

Chow, G., Heaver, T. D., & Henriksson, L. E. (1994). Logistics performance: definition and measurement. *International Journal Physical Distribution and Logistics Management, 24*(1), 17–28. doi:10.1108/09600039410055981

Chow, H. K. H., Choy, K. L., Lee, W. B., & Chan, F. T. S. (2007). Integration of Web-Based and RFID Technology in Visualizing Logistics Operations - a Case Study. *Supply Chain Management: An International Journal, 12*(3), 221–234. doi:10.1108/13598540710742536

Christensen, C. (1997). *The Innovator's Dilemma*. Boston: Harvard Business School Press.

Closs, D. J., Goldsby, T. J., & Clinton, S. R. (1997). Information technology influences on world class logistics capability. *International Journal of Physical Distribution & Logistics Management, 27*(1), 4–17. doi:10.1108/09600039710162259

Colin, J. (1989). Du conteneur a la logistique: vers la dissolution des modes de transport? *Culture Technique, 19*, 216–224.

Damanpour, E. (1991). Organizational innovation: a meta-analysis of effects of determinants and moderators. *Academy of Management Journal, 34*(3), 555–590. doi:10.2307/256406

Damanpour, E., & Evan, W. M. (1984). Organizational innovation and performance: the problem of organizational lag. *Administrative Science Quarterly, 29*(3), 392–409. doi:10.2307/2393031

Datamonitor. (2006), *Logistics in Italy - Industry Profile,* May. e-Business Watch. (2008), *The European e-Business Report - The Impact of ICT and e-Business on Firms, Sectors and the Economy*, 6th Synthesis Report of the Sectoral e-Business Watch, DG Enterprise & Industry, European Commission.

Eisenhardt, K. M. (1989). Building theories from case study research. *Academy of Management Review, 14*(4), 532–550.

Ellram, L. M. (1996). The use of case study method in logistics research. *Journal of Business Logistics, 17*(2), 93–138.

European Commission. (2005). *The New SME Definition. User Guide and Model Declaration*. Bruxelles: European Commission, DG Enterprise & Industry.

European Commission. (2007), *Fostering Innovation in Services,* Report of the Expert Group on Innovation in Services for the European Commission, available at: www.europe-innova.org/servlet /Doc?cid=7550&lg=EN.

Evangelista, P., & Sweeney, E. (2006). Technology usage in the supply chain: the case of small 3PLs. *The International Journal of Logistics Management, 17*(1), 55–74. doi:10.1108/09574090610663437

Gallouj, F., & Weinstein, O. (1997). Innovation in services. *Research Policy, 26*(4/5), 537–556. doi:10.1016/S0048-7333(97)00030-9

Gammelgaard, B. (2003). Case studies in logistics research, *Proceedings of the 15th Annual NOFOMA Conference for Nordic Researchers in Logistics*, (ed. by Juga J.), Oulu (Finland), Faculty of Economics and Business Administration, 12-13 June.

Garcia, R., & Calantone, R. (2002). A critical look at technological innovation typology and innovativeness: a literature review. *Journal of Product Innovation Management, 19*, 110–132. doi:10.1016/S0737-6782(01)00132-1

Gunasekaran, A., & Ngai, E. W. T. (2003). The successful management of a small logistics company. *International Journal of Physical Distribution & Logistics Management, 33*(9), 825–842. doi:10.1108/09600030310503352

Gunasekaran, A., & Ngai, E. W. T. (2004). Information systems in supply chain integration and management. *European Journal of Operational Research, 159*(2), 269–295. doi:10.1016/j.ejor.2003.08.016

Henderson, R., & Clark, K. B. (1990). Architectural innovation: the reconfiguration of existing product technologies and the failure of established firms. *Administrative Science Quarterly, 35*(1), 9–30. doi:10.2307/2393549

Howells, J. (2000). Innovation & services: new conceptual frameworks, Discussion paper No. 38, Centre for Research on Innovation and Competition (CRIC), University of Manchester & UMIST.

James, M., Grosvenor, R., & Prickett, P. (2004). e-Distribution: internet-based management of a merchandiser supply chain. *Supply Chain Management: An International Journal, 9*(1), 7–15. doi:10.1108/13598540410517539

Johnson, M. E., & Wang, S. (2002). E-business and supply chain management: an overview and framework. *Production and Operations Management, 11*(4), 413–423. doi:10.1111/j.1937-5956.2002.tb00469.x

Juga, J. (2003). Case study in logistics organization analysis. In Ojala L., Hilmola O.P. (eds. by), *Case study research in logistics,* Series B-1, Turku: Turku School of Economics and Business Administration, 73-82.

Karlsson, C., & Ahlstrom, P. (1995). Change processes towards lean production: the role of the remuneration system. *International Journal of Operations & Production Management, 15*(11), 80–99. doi:10.1108/01443579510102918

Kilpala, H., Solvang, W. D., Widmark, J., Bagaeva, A., & Tuohinto, P. (2005). *Analysis of ICT use in the Barents region: research findings from logistics service providers and forest industry,* STBR (Sustainable Transport in the Barents Region) Publications 11/2005, available at: http://www.barentsinfo.fi/stbr/

Knight, K. E. (1967). A descriptive model for intra-firm innovation process. *The Journal of Business, 40*(4), 478–496. doi:10.1086/295013

Koulikoff-Souviron, M., & Harrison, A. (2005). Using case study methods in researching supply chains. In Kotzab, H., Westhaus, M., Seuring, S. A., Muller, M., & Reiner, G. (Eds.), *Research Methodologies in Supply Chain Management* (pp. 267–282). Heidelberg: Physica-Verlag. doi:10.1007/3-7908-1636-1_18

KPMG. (2003), *Logistica integrata ed operatori di settore: trend e scenari evolutivi del mercato Italiano.,* KPMG Business Advisory Services, Milan, Italy (in Italian).

Lai, F., Li, D., Wang, Q., & Zhao, X. (2008). The information technology capability of third-party logistics providers: a resource-based view and empirical evidence from China. *Journal of Supply Chain Management, 44*(3), 22–38. doi:10.1111/j.1745-493X.2008.00064.x

Lai, K. (2004). Service capability and performance of logistics service providers. *Transportation Research Part E, Logistics and Transportation Review, 40*(5), 385–399. doi:10.1016/j.tre.2004.01.002

LaLonde, B. J., & Auker, K. (1973). A survey of computer applications and practices in transportation and distribution. *International Journal of Physical Distribution, 3*(5), 292–301. doi:10.1108/eb014285

Langley, C. J., Carlisle, D. B., Probst, S. B., Biggs, D. F., & Cail, R. E. (1988). Microcomputers as a logistics information strategy. *International Journal of Physical Distribution & Materials Management*, *18*(6), 11–17.

Larson P.D., & Gammelgaard B. (2001), "Logistics in Denmark: a survey of the industry", *International Journal of Logistics Research and Applications*, 4(2), 191-206.

Lau, H. C. W., Lee, C. K. M., Ho, G. T. S., & Ip, W. H. (2006). M-commerce to support the implementation of a responsive supply chain network. *Supply Chain Management: An International Journal*, *11*(2), 169–178. doi:10.1108/13598540610652564

Lewis, I., & Talalayevsky, A. (2000). Third-party logistics: leveraging information technology. *Journal of Business Logistics*, *21*(2), 73–185.

Lin, C. Y. (2008). Determinants of the adoption of technological innovations by logistics service providers in China. *Journal of Technology Management and Sustainable Development*, *7*(1), 19–38. doi:10.1386/ijtm.7.1.19_1

Liu, X., McKinnon, A. C., Grant, D. B., & Feng, Y. (2010). sources of competitiveness for logistics service providers: a UK industry perspective. *Logistics Research*, *2*, 3–14. doi:10.1007/s12159-010-0024-7

Maloni, M. J., & Carter, C. R. (2006). Opportunities for research in third-party logistics. *Transportation Journal*, *45*(2), 23–38.

Meredith, J. (1998). Building operations management theory through case and field research. *Journal of Operations Management*, *16*(4), 441–454. doi:10.1016/S0272-6963(98)00023-0

Metcalfe, J. S., & Miles, I. (2000). *Innovation Systems in the Service Economy*. Dordrecht: Kluwer Academic Publishers.

Narasimhan, R., & Jayaram, J. (1998). Reengineering service operations, a longitudinal case study. *Journal of Operations Management*, *17*(1), 7–22. doi:10.1016/S0272-6963(98)00029-1

New, S. J., & Payne, P. (1995). Research framework in logistics. Three models, seven dinners and a survey. *International Journal of Physical Distribution & Logistics Management*, *25*(10), 60–70. doi:10.1108/09600039510147663

Nixon, M. (2001). Innovation in logistics technology: generating top-line value and bottom-line ROI. *World Trade*, *14*, 62–64.

Peters M., & Jockel O. (1998). The day of the mega-carrier. *Logistics Europe,* June, 16-25.

Pilat, D. (2000). Innovation and productivity in services: state-of-the-art. *OECD/Australia Workshop on Innovation and Productivity in Services,* Sidney, October.

Pokharel, S. (2005). Perception on information and communication technology perspectives in logistics - A study or transportation and warehouse sectors in Singapore. *The Journal of Enterprise Information Management*, *18*(2), 136–149. doi:10.1108/17410390510579882

Porter, M. E., & Millar, V. E. (1985). How information give you competitive advantage. *Harvard Business Review*, *63*(4), 149–160.

Sauvage, T. (2003). The relationship between technology and logistics third-party providers. *International Journal of Physical Distribution & Logistics Management*, *3*(33), 236–253. doi:10.1108/09600030310471989

Schumpeter, J. A. (1939). *Business Cycles: a Theoretical, Historical and Statistical Analysis of the Capitalist Process*. New York: McGraw Hill.

Schumpeter, J. A. (1942). *Capitalism, Socialism and Democracy*. New York: Harper.

Selviaridis, K., & Spring, M. (2007). Third party logistic: a literature review and research agenda. *The International Journal of Logistics Management*, *18*(1), 125–150. doi:10.1108/09574090710748207

Seuring, S. (2005). Case study research in supply chains - An outline and three examples. In Kotzab, H., Westhaus, M., Seuring, S. A., Muller, M., & Reiner, G. (Eds.), *Research Methodologies in Supply Chain Management* (pp. 235–250). Heidelberg: Physica-Verlag. doi:10.1007/3-7908-1636-1_16

Speakman, J. P. (2002). Innovation leads to new efficiencies. *Logistic Management*, *41*, 71.

Stock, J. R. (1990). Managing compute, communication and information system strategically: opportunities and challenges for warehousing. *Logistics and Transportation Review*, *26*(2), 133–148.

Tether, B. S., Miles, I., Blind, K., Hipp, C., de Liso, N., & Cainelli, G. (2001). *Innovation in the Service Sector: Analysis of Data Collected under the Community Innovation Survey (CIS-2),* Report for the European Commission DG12 within the Innovation Programme, Manchester, Centre for Research on Innovation and Competition (CRIC), University of Manchester, available at: http://www.kiet.re.kr/files /econo/20021230-inno.pdf.

Tidd, J., Bessant, J., & Pavitt, K. (2001). *Managing Innovation - Integrating Technological, Market and Organizational Change* (2nd ed.). New York: John Wiley & Sons.

Tilanus, B. (ed. by) (1997), *Information Systems in Logistics and Transportation,* Oxford: Pergamon.

van Hoek, R. (2000). The role of third-party logistics providers in mass customization. *The International Journal of Logistics Management*, *11*(1), 37–46. doi:10.1108/09574090010806056

van Hoek, R. (2002). Using information technology to leverage transport and logistics service operations in the supply chain: an empirical assessment of the interrelation between technology and operation management. *International Journal of Information Technology and Management*, *1*(1), 115–130. doi:10.1504/IJITM.2002.001191

Voss, C., Tsikriktsis, N., & Frohlich, M. (2002). Case research in operations management. *International Journal of Operations & Production Management*, *22*(2), 195–219. doi:10.1108/01443570210414329

Wagner, S. M. (2008). Innovation management in the German transportation industry. *Journal of Business Logistics*, *29*(2), 215–231. doi:10.1002/j.2158-1592.2008.tb00093.x

Wallenburg, C. M. (2009). Innovation in logistics outsourcing relationships: proactive improvement by logistics service providers as a driver of customer loyalty. *Journal of Supply Chain Management*, *45*(2), 75–93. doi:10.1111/j.1745-493X.2009.03164.x

Wang, Q., Lai, F., & Zhao, X. (2008). The Impact of Information Technology in the Financial Performance of Third-Party Logistics Firms in China. *Supply Chain Management: an International Journal*, *13*(2), 138–150. doi:10.1108/13598540810860976

Wilding, R., & Jurado, R. (2004). Customer perceptions on logistics outsourcing in the European consumer goods industry. *International Journal and Physical Distribution & Logistics Management*, *34*(8), 75–93.

Wolfe, R. A. (1994). Organizational innovation: review, critique and suggested research directions. *Journal of Management Studies*, *31*(3), 405–431. doi:10.1111/j.1467-6486.1994.tb00624.x

Yin, R. K. (2003). *Case Study Research: Design and Methods* (3rd ed.). Thousand Oaks, CA: Sage.

Chapter 8
Innovative ICT Applications in Transport and Logistics:
Some Evidence from Asia

Mark Goh
University of South Australia, Australia & National University of Singapore, Singapore

Kym Fraser
University of South Australia, Australia

ABSTRACT

This chapter examines the applications of innovative information and communication technology (ICT) applications in transport and logistics in Asia. Specifically, the authors examine two case studies of how a Logistics Service Provider (LSP), and a public sector agency based in Asia who acts as a regulator of ports and maritime services and facilities have effectively used ICT tools and applications to their advantage and how this has shaped the innovation landscape of the supply chain in Asia.

INTRODUCTION

To thrive in today's competitive global markets, managers need to keep an eye on a multitude of activities within the firm and across the supply chain. These activities include the critical functions of procurement, production operations, employee productivity, load utilization, and ultimately profitability and cash flow. Many companies, including medium sized firms, have adopted modern, integrated Enterprise Resource Planning (ERP) systems to help provide a holistic view of a company's activities. Such an ICT application mounted on an SAP platform has helped to give managers and decision makers the requisite information needed to do the job effectively, and to stay ahead of the competition. However, such applications do not come cheap.

As the world becomes increasingly globalised, there is in reality a renewed call for greater innovation especially in the areas of services, technology and practices so that the delivery of goods and

DOI: 10.4018/978-1-60960-585-8.ch008

services are up to speed vis-à-vis competition. Already, we note that two dimensions of business, namely, speed to market and product life cycles, are getting shorter with each passing business cycle, and with knowledge (both tacit and explicit) aging rapidly. In the context of the supply chain, it has been well recognised and accepted that ICT engenders the integration of supply chain activities which enables the seamless globalisation of services and can afford greater specialisation for the service provider as operations become more sophisticated. Indeed, the innovative use of ICT in the supply chain context can be referred to as the use of ICT applications that support the supply chain's objectives of improved efficiency and responsiveness, based on the needs of the current stakeholders in the supply network. Today, in Asia, we see ICT innovations continually driving down costs, with the quality of logistics service standards being simultaneously raised. Indeed, in many industries today, most services are characteristic of continuous innovation with limited shelf and user life. Based on the Clark-Fisher hypothesis, the redeployment of people from the less productive to the more productive sectors stimulates innovation, competition and growth (Botten and McManus, 1999). This in turn fuels the trade in services.

This paper seeks to describe the state of progress of innovative ICT applications in the LSP sector in Asia where there is now a greater need to drive for better innovation solutions and delivery so as to maintain the rate of business evolution mentioned earlier. We will focus on two cases, one of a global LSP competing in an increasingly competitive marketplace in Asia and the other of a public sector agency acting as a ports and maritime regulator where innovation has played a big part in driving the continued relevance for the organisation and the relevant community as a whole, respectively.

The rest of this chapter is organised as follows. In the interest of space and time, a short literature review on ICT applications and supply chain innovation is provided in the next section. Thereafter, we discuss ICT diffusion in supply chain management in Asia. This is then followed by a presentation of two case studies, one a public sector agency involved directly in maritime logistics, and the other a global LSP with a significant footprint in Asia. Next, we provide a discussion highlighting the managerial implications, followed by some managerial recommendations.

LITERATURE REVIEW

Over the past two decades, the nature of international trade operations and international logistics practices has changed by leaps and bounds. Innovations in transport, information and communications technologies as well as the liberalisation of trade tariffs and finance have brought to life a global production structure (e.g. Dicken, 2003) that is highly dependent on reliable and robust ICT applications and their delivery. As mentioned by Grainger (2007), with global supply chain and networks at work, there is now an imperative for a robust ICT system to bring the supply chain system to fruition, as in any cross border operations interfacing with the regulatory authorities at the national borders, without pre-emptive technologies in place would mean excessive documentation requirements and a lack of transparency in the goods inspection requirements and objectives. Hence, there is a need to bring about greater and quicker modernisation to the flow of cross border trade and hence the case for greater innovation in ICT applications in logistics as this type or family of applications brings business to the heart of the supply chain, namely, speed, efficiency, and transparency in cross border flows. On another note, innovation in ICT applications if appropriately applied can also bring to bear a real reduction in trade compliance costs. Grainger (2007) rightly identifies the following uses for ICT applications, which are still unevenly applied and enforced throughout Asia, namely,

1. Standardisation of documents and electronic data requirements
2. Automation of business processes
3. International electronic exchange of trade data
4. Single window for customs clearance

In the literature, much has been done to empirically examine the role of ICT in improving supply chain performance through better collaboration (e.g. Salam, 2009). Indeed, ICT has been shown to support the exchange between trading partners (Pramatari, 2007). This finding is not new, rather it is a reinforcement of Nohria and Eccles (1992) who have suggested that electronically mediated exchanges such as those in modern ICT applications contribute to increased collaboration because it empowers front-line workers with information, enables direct communication between individuals at the operational levels in the organization across time and space, and blurs organizational boundaries. These electronically mediated exchanges refer to the extent to which supply chain partners communicate through an electronic media such as the Internet, intranets, electronic mail or Electronic Data Interchange (EDI) systems (Kulchitsky, 1997). In the supply chain context, we know through the learnings of the beer game (Chopra and Meindl, 2009) that integrated information flows often reduce uncertainty (Allaire and Firsirotu, 1989) as well as reduce any supply chain system volatility induced by unnecessary information delays (Towill, 1992). The ICT applications that support electronically mediated exchange encourage inter-organizational collaboration by facilitating interaction and dissemination of information at all organizational levels. Myhr and Spekman (2005) have found that collaborative partnerships can be achieved both via trust and through electronically mediated exchange. Because electronically mediated exchange assists people at the operational level who need up-to-date information to carry out their roles effectively in the supply chain relationships, ICT applications are likely to have an immediate impact on the construction of this collaboration.

Each change or innovation in one of the above mentioned areas will have an influence on the supply chain system as a whole, in relation to improved performance in the materials flow, transport units, and management control of the entire supply chain. There is no doubt that ICT innovations if managed properly and diffused pervasively can effectively support an optimized supply chain especially in the last mile context (Gevaers, Van de Voorde, & Vanelslander, 2009), and this is useful for ensuring a sustainable logistics system.

The literature also reports that in the role as a supply chain manager and developer, the LSP has partial (sometimes more) responsibility of the tactical or strategic management of the supply chain or supply network (Fulconis, Saglietto, & Paché, 2006). In many ways, the LSP develops new operational models, which enhance the performance of the supply chain. This role differs from the earlier role of a value adder in a way that supply chain innovations are originated by the LSP instead of the manufacturer or the subcontractor. To be able to be in this role, the LSP has to have a deep understanding of the industry environment in which they are working and be proactive in innovating their ICT applications intended for use on the shippers so as to sustain long-term business relationships with them. The case of DHL being constantly involved in ICT innovations helps to put this thinking in its proper perspective.

At the same time, it has been recognised in the literature that direct intervention by the state especially in the arena of global trade is found to be detrimental to the market efficiency of business (Stiglitz, 1991; Markham and Millar, 2009). Hence, in the case of Singapore and other progressive Asian countries, the role of the government agencies in assisting innovation and technology applications for logistics facilitation is to only proactively dismantle and minimise the barriers and restrictions to trade and business (Goh, 2005). As such, we will present the case of the Maritime and Ports Authority of Singapore (MPA) to highlight how such an agency has proactively invested in ICT applications to create seamlessness in the passage of goods through the port of Singapore.

There are other reasons cited in the literature for the public sector engaging in innovative ICT applications. Hülsmann and Berry (2004) argue that the LSPs have to face complex and perpetually changing settings of environmental requirements. Thus, the LSPs have to engage in innovative ICT applications to ensure the relevance and longevity of technology based competitive advantages, particularly when the profit margins are rapidly eroding with time and industry maturity. However, as pointed out by Hülsmann, Korsmeier, and Cordes (2009), the innovation capabilities also depend on the technological savvy-ness of the firm, which has to balance eroding profit margins with the rising cost of ICT investments. This necessitates bringing an independent higher hand to introduce new larger scale innovative ICT applications for the common good of the community, namely, the public sector agencies.

To date, there few studies on how innovation in ICT applications has been managed strategically in an Asian context to improve supply chain performance. This paper therefore contributes to the literature by highlighting two specific cases of how innovative ICT applications have been employed to integrate the various logistics activities in the supply chain, to create sustained competitive advantage (Watson, Kelly, Galliers, & Brancheau, 1997).

ICT DIFFUSION IN SUPPLY CHAIN MANAGEMENT IN ASIA

In Asia, the landscape of logistics/supply chain management is becoming competitive and challenging. For one, the logistics and transport functions are becoming more complex, and better coordination is needed from a control tower perspective. In this regard, the astute observer will notice a greater diffusion of ICT applications in the logistics industry in Asia in the past decade. There are two reasons for doing so.

First, Cette and Lopez (2008) recently reported, in an empirical study of eleven OECD countries that the extant literature has shown that the level of ICT diffusion has a favorable effect on productivity. Further, they showed that the use of ICT applications generally requires labour with a higher degree of skills than other production technologies. In the case of Asia, a similar phenomenon is observed. In terms of ICT diffusion, Table 1 below shows the state of ICT diffusion in some of the major economies in Asia. Table 1 shows the low base that the key economies in Asia, particularly China, India and Indonesia, are starting from. Thus, it is worthwhile examining the approach taken by the logistics industry in fostering innovative ICT applications to help drive greater productivity improvement and ensure business success.

We now present two case studies to showcase how each has exploited and adapted innovative ICT applications for competitive advantage and for the common good of the business community in Asia. We first present the case of the MPA to show specifically how it has strategically deployed innovative ICT applications to improve the business and operational processes in and around the port area. The second case company we analyze, our focus on innovative ICT applications adopted by DHL, a global LSP targeted at improving functional productivity and greater customer satisfaction among Asian clients.

Maritime and Ports Authority of Singapore (MPA)

It has been reported that 90% of non-bulk cargo worldwide moves by containers stacked on transport ships (Ebeling, 2009). Of this amount, 26% start their journey from the ports of China (The

Table 1. ICT diffusion fact sheet

	China	India	Indonesia	Malaysia
ICT expenditure in 2001				
Total ICT (USD mil)	66,612	19,662	3,540	6,325
ICT as % of GDP	5.7	3.9	2.2	6.6
ICT business and government environment in 2002				
Local specialized ICT services availability	4.3/7	5.8/7	4/7	3.9/7
Government online services availability	3.5/7	3.9/7	2.0/7	3.3/7
Government prioritization of ICT	5.3/7	5.6/7	3.7/7	5.9/7

Note: ICT business and government environment in 2002 is measured on a 7-point Likert scale where 7 indicates the highest or best rating.
Source: Promoting ICT for human development in Asia: realizing the millennium development goals, UNDP 2005.

World Bank, 2010), an important export source for the world. Another half of this amount pass through the Straits of Malacca calling on the Port of Singapore for transshipment. In all, there are more than 18 million containers which make at least 200 million trips each year since 2005. Considering this massive scale for maritime and logistics, the maritime industry is at the core of the logistics sector.

Hence it makes good sense to study the maritime logistics sector to appreciate the ICT innovations that have taken place to the extent that it encourages more trade between nations and we choose Asia as the context as highlighted by the high percentage container movement to and from China annually. Thus, we will discuss the case of the MPA, a public sector agency located in Singapore.

The maritime industry in Singapore is vibrant and contains more than 5,000 maritime establishments and businesses, contributing about 7% each year to Singapore's Gross Domestic Product and provides jobs for more than 120,000 workers. Maritime Singapore is a thriving ecosystem of maritime and port services, with an entrenched and growing base of ship owners and operators, supported by a broader and deeper suite of maritime services and capabilities. It is Singapore's desire to be a leading global integrated logistics hub, with robust maritime, aviation, and land transport capabilities supporting the global economy. This vision rides on 3 key enablers: political, economic and regulatory stability; excellent infrastructure; and a critical mass of professionals. Part of this responsibility in ensuring the sustainability of the enablers lies in the judicious use and development of suitable ICT applications for maritime logistics. The agency responsible for making this initiative happen is the MPA.

Profile of MPA

The MPA was established on 2 February 1996, with the original mission to develop Singapore as a premier global hub port and International Maritime Centre (IMC), and to advance and safeguard Singapore's strategic maritime interests. The MPA is the driving force behind Singapore's port and maritime development, taking on the roles of port authority, port regulator, port planner, an IMC champion, and a national maritime representative. The MPA partners the logistics industry and other agencies to enhance safety, security and environmental protection in Singapore's port waters, facilitate port operations and growth, expand the cluster of maritime ancillary services, and promote maritime R&D, and manpower development.

Supply Chain Challenges for MPA

Being responsible for the above activities around the shore of Singapore practically means that the MPA has to manage expeditiously the more than 26 million TEUs that transit through the Port of Singapore. This translates to tracking and providing visibility for the 471 million tonnes of cargo, the 36 million tonnes of bunker fuel and the more than 130,000 vessels that visit Singapore each year. The efficiency needed to clear these ships ultimately means that the MPA has to engage in innovative ICT applications to be efficient, productive and competitive lest the ships venture to neighbouring ports for cargo clearance and so on.

Innovative Logistics ICT Applications

Further, the MPA is responsible for port development and investments in systems and technologies to raise the speed, productivity and reliability of port operations. Indeed, ICT continues to play a big part in the hub port of Singapore, and the MPA continues to leverage on ICT through the IT Master Plan and the Infocomm@SeaPort programme. Specifically, the Infocomm@SeaPort programme set up in September 2007 by the MPA and the Infocomm Development Authority in which both agencies have each provided S$6million serves to enable the maritime community to create more efficient business and operational processes using ICT, and has given rise to several projects. We report some of these in this case study.

WIrelesss-broadband-access for the sea port, or WISEPORT, is one of them, which puts in place the mobile WiMAX infrastructure to provide vessels operating within the port vicinity with wireless mobile broadband connectivity. This innovation allows for faster and cheaper short range communications with the port area and is a world first. Other projects involve the use of radio frequency identification or RFID technology to improve car transshipment operations at PSA terminals. This innovation draws from the concept of asset tracking used in the typical warehouse, except now it is used in the open yard.

Yet another innovative ICT application is the BunkerNet system which draws heavily on ICT innovations to improve bunker supply chain visibility by enhancing the work processes. This system simplifies and accelerates the electronic reporting of bunker barge movements within the waters of Singapore, facilitates the ease and speed of calculation of bunker quantities on board the ships, and expedites the billing cycle for the ship owners, not to mention the usual benefits of ICT applications such as streamlining document flow, enhancing the planning and deployment of bunker craft, increasing the operational efficiency and reducing data errors by automating information flow, and serving as a gateway for bunkering operations and information, thus leading to better accuracy, reliability and timeliness of operational data, as well as boost safety and security.

In terms of the other ICT applications, the MPA has adopted a number of measures and applied state-of-the-art technology to ensure that vessel traffic in the busy waterways of the Singapore port and the Singapore Strait flows smoothly. Chief among these is the radar-based Vessel Traffic Information System (VTIS). The MPA currently operates two fully integrated port operations control centres, and both centres employ the VTIS, which can track up to 5,000 vessels in real-time to provide accurate navigational information to ships plying around Singapore, and is integrated with electronic navigational chart displays, synchronised voice, track and data recording, and the computerised Port Traffic Management System.

The use of the VTIS and other navigational safety measures not only allows for effective command and control of all vessels involved in dealing with emergencies, it also allows the MPA to keep an eye on the other vessels in the port and to keep them clear of the affected areas, if necessary, and this has enabled the MPA to maintain its excellent port safety record at a very low 0.03 incidents per 1,000 vessel movements, in spite of the busy daily traffic. Apart from managing the larger vessels, the MPA has also taken steps to secure the port waters in terms of regulating smaller vessels, through the ship self-security assessment checklist, harbour craft security code and pleasure craft security code, as well as the Harbour Craft Transponder System (HARTS), which became fully operational in 2007.

HARTS enables the automatic identification of all powered harbour and pleasure craft plying in Singapore waters. This allows the security agencies to focus on marine craft without an identification tag, which greatly simplifies the task of monitoring and control of smaller vessels within Singapore waters. Doing so practically reduces the opportunity for pirate ships to slip into Singapore waters from the Straits of Malacca, which has one of the highest incidence of piracy. The HARTS set-up comprises three main components, namely, the transponders fitted onboard the craft, the wireless communication link, and a shore-based tracking system. Through this system, real time data from the transponder such as vessel identity, position, speed, course and other information are transmitted to a shore-based system via the wireless communication link using either GSM/GPRS (Global System for Mobile communications/General Packet Radio Service) offered by the local telecommunications service providers to provide the most cost effective solution requiring a minimum set up cost as the onshore base station is already in place. Locally-registered craft known as harbour craft operating within the port would be required to carry the low-cost transponder system (HARTS).

At a strategic level of ICT innovation and application, the MPA has also established a S$100 million Maritime Innovation and Technology (MINT) Fund to support development programmes for the maritime technology cluster, in particular to support the main area of offering development research funding for proof-of-concept projects, test-bedding and establishing commercial viability. This platform for Test-bedding, Research, Innovation and Development for New-maritime Technologies is known as TRIDENT.

Through this supply chain technology-related funding in April 2009, Global-I Pte Ltd, a Singapore-based company, developed a groundbreaking container tracking solution, with the support of the MINT Fund. Called G-Track, the tracking device is designed to improve the visibility and security of high-value perishable cargo requiring cold chain logistics. Complete with GPS, GPRS, GSM, Zig-bee modules, a RFID reader and temperature sensors, the G-Track device assures security as well as proper product temperature throughout the entire transport chain, from packing to delivery. The technical details of these innovations can be found on the MPA website.

DHL

For many logistics service providers in Asia, the past decade has witnessed huge leaps in logistics technologies due to the corresponding advances made in ICT development and applications such as wireless, GPS, GPRS, RFID and so on. Indeed, today many logistics players see ICT applications as a tool that enables them to build and operate new, more efficient logistics structures for its internal workflow processes and its customers. Integrated tracking and tracing systems, originally implemented by the international parcel and express cargo service providers represented a breakthrough for the transport and logistics service industry. With the help of better and faster computers, the tracking (control) and real time routing (scheduling) as well as the locating and monitoring (tracing) of shipments has led to greater productivity improvement of a logistics network. Shippers are now able to query on the status of their shipments at any time and at any location. This system coupled with vehicle asset tracking using GPS makes it possible for full-coverage utilization.

With the advent of the contactless RFID technology, such shipment monitoring will be even faster and more widespread than previously possible with barcodes and scanners. The location and the processing history of millions of parcels and cargo items, exchange pallets, swap bodies and containers can thus be automatically called up at any time and be made available to other applications, such as load optimizers and slot optimizers.

Another innovative direction is evident in the advances in the supply chain event management (SCEM) systems. The fundamental idea behind such systems is to rely on ICT applications to eliminate the need for persons responsible for a supply process (or other processes) to perform tracking and tracing for all shipments or objects (such as vehicles and containers) and instead automatically provide them with information, should something unforeseen occur as the result of an unplanned event during transit. The SCEM system, with sufficient rules or knowledge built into it, can also suggest remedial measures for the unforeseen situation and initiate the necessary corrective measures. The new opportunities made possible by ICT applications are enhancing the ability of the LSPs to offer their customers better rationalization (which is important for yield management), quality assurance and new value added services.

Profile of DHL

We now turn our attention to DHL. DHL is a part of the Deutsche Post DHL group, one of the largest employers in the world with 300,000 employees, with a global network covering more than 220 nations (www.dhl.com). DHL provides innovative, reliable logistics services and solutions in international express, air and ocean freight, road and rail transportation, contract logistics and international mail to multinational shippers. DHL serves a wide range of products from the traditional automotives and retail goods sectors to the more demanding time sensitive sectors of life sciences and healthcare.

Supply Chain Challenges for DHL

Being in a service oriented industry, DHL faces challenges on several fronts. First, As DHL expects Asia to contribute to almost 40% of global trade by 2028 (Mahalingam, 2011), there is an immediate need for DHL to be ready for this growth through the smarter use of ICT, equipping DHL's regional offices in Hong Kong and Singapore to handle the increase in traffic volume. Second, while more free trade agreements are being established between countries in Asia, such as that between China and North Korea and between ASEAN and China, the manpower needed for the highly service oriented logistics industry has not increased correspondingly. Again, DHL has to rely on innovative ICT applications to cope with the anticipated traffic increase and the shortfall of human capital. Third, related to the above two reasons, there is an increasing request from the shippers to have better visibility of the supply chain for better control tower planning of the product lifecycle of emerging products such as healthcare products, and other perishables. Fourth, in line with DHL's corporate policy on sustainability, DHL is actively working to reduce the amount of documentation needed for cargo freight to reduce the cost of trading by up to 30% by 2020.

Innovative ICT Applications by DHL

DHL employs three different ICT systems in Singapore to support the Asia Pacific's logistics operations, namely the Real Time Shipment Management System (RTSMS), the Crisis Management System (CMS), and the Regional Security Centre System (RSCS).

The RTSMS monitor DHL's shipments continuously, from freight pickup to delivery. It comprises two sub-systems; one is used for monitoring line haul services while the other is for shipment itself. Both systems are real time, governed by separate applications and working on the same principle of the traffic light mechanism. Put simply, the application uses simple visual identifications similar to the traffic light system: green for on-time delivery, amber for potential or slight delay and red for delays in shipment and actions are required. If nothing goes wrong, the systems will show a green light. Sometimes, an "amber threshold" or a "red threshold" may not necessarily mean there is a problem. It could be a potential problem. For example, the system may generate an "amber alter" if it does not have the confirmation on the departure of an aircraft. Using the RTSMS, DHL's country stations can assess the situation and decide on the necessary actions to take. As a rule of thumb, country stations will handle all "amber thresholds" while the staff in the regional office will handle all the "red" situations. The contingency procedures will be decided by each station and validated by the regional office. The movement of flights is displayed on a large screen and shows the real time location of the flight. These visual cues allow the service centre at DHL to respond to any potential delay and prevent the problem from escalating to an alert status. In the case of a red alert, the incident within any service centre will be escalated to the country level, and from country level to the Asia Pacific level.

The metric used in the RTSMS is "saved shipments", referring to those shipments which could have incurred a delay without this system. In a two-week pilot test, DHL achieved 2,000 saved shipments by implementing the RTSMS. The RTSMS was developed specifically for DHL's operations and was deployed in the Asia Pacific. With this system, millions of shipments passing through the 17 country checkpoints were tracked and fed into the system. It helped DHL to track changes during the shipment process, allowing DHL to react pro-actively to any potential delays, to respond quickly to any unexpected crises and to make contingency plans to ensure timely shipments.

Unlike the RTSMS, CMS focuses on forecasting or trying to avoid any disasters. It helps DHL to manage natural disasters, such as earthquakes, typhoons and tsunamis. CMS, as an ICT application, monitors any crisis, including earthquakes, strikes, bombings or typhoons. The contingency plans are usually decided at the regional office. However, country stations have the authority to revise and improve such plans as most crises affect only local areas. The most common contingency plan is to bypass DHL's logistics hubs when a crisis occurs. For example, the decision to fly direct from origin to destination rather than hubbing, despite the lower load volume, is often made with the help of the CMS. In this way, DHL can perform service recovery in a timely manner, for example, by shifting particular shipments to other aircraft to recover lost time or reduce further delays. Customers are then informed so that they could plan their contingency plans in case of such delays.

The RTSMS and CMS both work together to provide advance information on shipment delays. This is critical in information management as DHL staff can now drill down to get specific information related to the information on the delayed shipment and the particular flight. A contingency plan is also generated by the system and information is kept for future learning.

The last integrated ICT system, RSCS, links the four DHL hubs in Asia: Tokyo, Bangkok, Singapore, and Hong Kong. Regional CCTV networks monitor the activities at the hub and gateways so that incidents such as the mishandling of shipments or other security risk issues can be mitigated. The high value shipments item can be tracked continuously through the CCTV network to protect goods against theft. Hence, shippers are assured that their shipment reaches their destinations safely. This is a simple yet innovative ICT application making use of cost effective CCTVs. As of now, other smaller players have adopted this innovation to their advantage in managing their business operations by remote.

As the development of DHL's ICT application is web based, they can be easily deployed to the other divisions globally. The application management is based on the operations structure and once that structure is established, the software can be fanned out to the other regions such as Europe or the US.

Further, as the systems are portable and scalable, DHL is now able to extend its service offering to the supply chain partners who also require similar visibility albeit on a fee paying basis. In this way, the real-time logistics visibility systems developed for DHL's internal use is now packaged as ICT support solutions for external providers too as a value-added component of DHL's service offerings. This potentially creates a new revenue stream, leveraging on DHL's ICT experience in the supply chain arena.

The provision of real-time visibility to its customers forces an impetus for DHL to ensure the most efficient and streamlined operations. This serves to enhance its competitive edge against its competitors. It can also serve as a powerful branding and marketing collateral that can be capitalized upon to DHL's benefit and advantage. Having such a centralized system built for Asia can help DHL to re-look at its operating structures in areas where there is no real-time system yet. This can help to streamline global operations and lead to cost-savings along the supply chain. The strategic investment by DHL in ICT capability and support systems serve to add value to both the value chain as well as the supply chain of DHL and by extension, to those of DHL's customers as well. More importantly, DHL realises that continuous innovation, sometimes incremental, is crucial in maintaining the competitive advantage in the face of constantly changing global business conditions and stiff competition.

DISCUSSION

As the supply chain becomes more global to meet the growing globalised world and marketplace, the battle cry is for better, smarter and more innovative ICT applications which can help to achieve the desired overall productivity levels in transport and logistics. In this regard, the past decade has witnessed many quantum leaps in ICT applications, from those that employ simple bar-coding technology to those that rely on RFID related applications. Moving forward, innovative ICT applications in this arena will continue to dominate discussion, both academic and practice wise. The reason is simple. ICT applications have transformed this sector from a labour intensive one to one which can be highly automated, intelligent and proactive. In the future, with a greater need for visibility in the supply chain, ICT applications will seek out greater innovations in order to meet the requirements of greater visibility, security and environmental sustainability. In short, the new perennial question is to determine if there are smart intelligent agents which can miniaturized onto the palm of a hand to track and trace, and clear container movements, just like the electronic drones that are currently used in sophisticated warehouses for cycle counting.

However, we have also noticed that the implementation of large scale, general use ICT applications such as those afforded by the MPA requires a push approach in that an over-arching player e.g. the government or her related representative (in this case, the MPA) has to provide the application and users have to suggest the innovation direction of such applications. Nevertheless, these innovative ICT applications, if used strategically, can have immense value add to the community and provide a potential stream of revenue to the service provider just as the case of DHL has alluded. We leave this discussion to another forum.

Theory-wise, there are several explanations provided by the literature to understand this phenomenon. For instance, Corrocher, Malerba, and

Montobbio (2007) who have looked at the growth and technological pervasiveness of ICT-related innovations mention that ICT applications are dependent on a number of factors, two of which are the high rate of entry of new innovators and the high concentration of technological activity across firms. In the case of DHL, the situation depicted in this case study here resembles the Schumpeterian Mark II or "deepening" pattern of innovation, which is typical of the major role of the existing set of service providers engaged in innovative ICT applications and the customer's desire to see greater improvements in supply chain visibility probably explains for the incremental innovation done on the DHL's visibility system which has also since been replicated quickly by DHL's competitors. This phenomenon is supported by Carr's (2003) argument and that is competitive advantage (in this case DHL's logistics visibility system) driven by ICT is not sustainable unless the ICT application strengthens the existing competitive advantage. While the risk of failure in this situation is minimal, however, mimetic pressures would force competition to mimic DHL's innovation or risk losing customers. Doing so can only make the application more ubiquitous, which is not necessarily a bad thing from the perspectives of cost, usage and familiarity.

In the case of the MPA, the proactive step undertaken by the MPA to build innovative ICT applications for the general good of the community and hence the environment also helps to promote a similar set of innovative ICT applications downstream. This represents the Schumpeterian Mark I or "widening" pattern of innovation whereby taking the first step in creating such applications, MPA has indirectly fostered a higher concentration of innovative and technological activity in the space of logistics service providers and technology platform providers. With a public sector agency, given its sense of openness and neutrality, taking the lead in boosting the overall productivity levels of actors in the supply chain, the smaller players in the supply chain can now afford to leap-frog onto a higher plane of technology driven solutions in transport and logistics, which is really good news for all concerned as this will widen the network of firms who will embrace new technologies and strengthen the security and visibility fabric of the supply chain in Asia.

SOME SOLUTIONS AND RECOMMENDATIONS FOR SUPPLY CHAIN INNOVATION

From the two case studies presented in this chapter, we observe that innovative ICT applications are needed in response to a dynamic business landscape. Clearly, as the supply chain grows in tandem with global trade, there is an obvious need for better visibility, better capacity and equipment utilisation, further reduction in inventory and transportation costs, better monitoring of supply chain security and better stewardship of the environment, and finally an increase in sustainable competitive advantage.

The solutions for supply chain innovation as provided by DHL and the MPA occur at both the operational level (functions and processes) and the strategic level (human, knowledge and technology capital development), at the firm and industry levels, and more importantly, some of these innovations have longer term environmental ramifications.

Moving forward, clearly, some of the recommendations for companies and countries wishing to stay at the forefront of competition and business could include those innovative ICT applications already rolled out by the MPA and DHL. For instance, interested companies (and governments) could undertake the following improvements in their supply chains by:

1. Using system wide ICT applications to improve supply chain visibility events by exception e.g. DHL's RTMS and CMS.

2. Using ICT applications innovatively to reduce asset pools and fleet sizes, and to improve the returns on asset investments e.g. DHL's RSCS.
3. Using ICT applications to communicate across countries and organisations to monitor an asset's known location relative to where it is supposed to, e.g. MPA's G-Track, VTIS, and HARTS for vessel movement around harbours.
4. Harnessing innovative ICT applications to increase competitive advantage by realising that new technologies can enable material improvements to operating models e.g. MPA's TRIDENT and WISEPORT.

CONCLUSION

This chapter has attempted to highlight the use of innovative ICT applications to bring to bear better productivity for the logistics and transport sector in Asia, better visibility and hence security especially in maritime transport where a large percentage of global piracy acts take place in the neighbouring Straits of Malacca. Further, we have attempted to show how the use of such ICT applications lend itself to greener and more sustainable supply chains in Asia, through less documentation flow and greater collaboration between the shipping and service provider communities. We have especially highlighted two distinct case studies. The first is that of DHL which has applied innovative ICT applications in response to a push factor from increasingly sophisticated customers in Asia, and to distinguish itself from the competition. The other is that of the MPA which has deliberately provided and established holistic innovative ICT applications for the maritime sector so as to pull in the maritime service providers and improve productivity for the industry.

REFERENCES

Allaire, Y., & Firsirotu, M. E. (1989). Coping with strategic uncertainty. *Sloan Management Review, 30*(3), 7–16.

Botten, N., & McManus, J. (1999). *Competitive strategies for service organisations*. Purdue: Purdue University Press.

Carr, N. (2003). IT doesn't matter. *Harvard Business Review, 81*(5), 41–49.

Cette, G., & Lopez, J. (2008). What explains the ICT diffusion gap between the major advanced countries? An empirical analysis. *International Productivity Monitor, 17*, 28–39.

Chopra, S., & Meindl, P. (2010). *Supply chain management: Strategy, planning, and operation* (4th ed.). Upper Saddle River, NJ: Pearson.

Corrocher, N., Malerba, F., & Montobbio, F. (2007). Schumpeterian patterns of innovative activity in the ICT field. *Research Policy, 36*(3), 418–432. doi:10.1016/j.respol.2007.01.002

DHL. (n. d.). Retrieved from http:/www.dhl.com on 15 Oct 2010.

Dicken, P. (2003). *Global shift: Reshaping the global economic map in the 21st century*. London: Sage.

Ebeling, C. E. (2009). Evolution of a box. *Invention and Technology, 23*(4), 8–9.

Fulconis, F., Saglietto, L., & Paché, G. (2006). Exploring new competencies in the logistics industry: The intermediation role of 4PL. *Supply Chain Forum: An International Journal, 7*(20), 68–77.

Gevaers, R., Van de Voorde, E., & Vanelslander, T. (2008). *Technical and process innovations in logistics: Opportunities, barriers and best practices*, Paper presented at the European Transport Conference, Leeuwenhorst, The Netherlands.

Gevaers, R., Van de Voorde, E., & Vanelslander, T. (2009). Innovations in last-mile logistics: The relations with green logistics, reverse logistics and waste logistics. In K.S. Pawar and C.S. Lalwani (Eds.), *Proc. of ISL 2009: Global supply chains and inter-firm networks* (pp. 451-458). Istanbul, Turkey: Nottingham University Business School.

Goh, A. L. S. (2005). Promoting innovation in aid of industrial development; The Singaporean experience. *International Journal of Public Sector Management, 18*(3), 216–240. doi:10.1108/09513550510591524

Grainger, A. (2007). Supply chain security: Adding to a complex operational and institutional environment. *World Customs Journal, 1*(2), 17–29.

Hülsmann, M., & Berry, A. (2004). Strategic management dilemmas: Its necessity in a world of diversity and change. In R. Lundin, R. Wolff, & S. Jönsson (Eds.), *Proc. of the SAM/IFSAM Seventh World Congress on Management in a World of Diversity and Change*. Göteborg, Sweden. CD-Rom, 18pp.

Hülsmann, M., Korsmeier, B., & Cordes, P. (2009). Longevity of technological competitive advantages for logistics service providers? A complexity science based analysis of autonomous co-operation technologies. In K.S. Pawar and C.S. Lalwani (Eds.), *Proc. of ISL 2009: Global supply chains and inter-firm networks* (pp. 634-642). Istanbul, Turkey: Nottingham University Business School.

Kulchitsky, J. D. (1997). *The effects of information and technology on the relational orientation of marketing channels: Impact on structure and performance.* (Unpublished doctoral dissertation). University of Alberta, Edmonton.

Mahalingam, E. (2011, November 22). *DHL expands Asia-Pacific network.* Retrieved from http://biz.thestar.com.my/news/ story.asp?file=/2010/11/22/business/7441222&sec=business on 19 Jan 2011.

Markham, D., & Millar, T. (2009). Global trade liberalisation continues, but risks abound. *Backgrounder (Washington, D.C.)*, (2320): 1–9.

Myhr, N., & Spekman, N. M. (2005). Collaborative supply-chain partnerships built upon trust and electronically mediated exchange. *Journal of Business and Industrial Marketing, 20*(4/5), 179–186. doi:10.1108/08858620510603855

Nohria, N., & Eccles, R. G. (1992). Face to face: Making network organizations work. In Nohria, N., & Eccles, R. G. (Eds.), *Networks and Organizations: Structure Form and Action* (pp. 288–308). Boston, MA: Harvard Business School Press.

Pramatari, K. (2007). Collaborative supply chain practices and evolving technological approaches. *Supply Chain Management: An International Journal, 12*(3), 210–220. doi:10.1108/13598540710742527

Salam, M. A. (2009). The role of trust and technology on collaboration and supply chain performance. In K.S. Pawar and C.S. Lalwani (Eds.), *Proc. of ISL 2009: Global supply chains and inter-firm networks* (pp. 116-123). Istanbul, Turkey: Nottingham University Business School.

Stiglitz, J. E. (1991). The invisible hand and modern welfare economics. *NBRE Working Paper*, #W364.

The Maritime and Ports Authority of Singapore. (n. d.). Retrieved from http://www.mpa.gov.sg on 15 Oct 2010.

The World Bank. (n. d.). *Container port traffic (TEU: 20 foot equivalent units)*, retrieved from http://data.worldbank.org/indicator /IS.SHP.GOOD.TU on 15 Sep 2010.

Towill, D. N. (1992). Industrial dynamics simulation models in the design of supply chains. *International Journal of Physical Distribution & Logistics Management, 22*(5), 3–13. doi:10.1108/09600039210016995

United Nations Development program Report (UNDP). (2005). *Promoting ICT for human development in Asia: Realizing the millennium development goals*. India: Elsevier.

Watson, R. T., Kelly, G. G., Galliers, R. D., & Brancheau, J. C. (1997). Key issues in information systems management: An international perspective. *Journal of Management Information Systems*, *13*(4), 91–115.

ADDITIONAL READING

OECD. (2004). *The economic impact of ICT: Measurement, evidence and implications*. Geneva: OECD.

Chapter 9
Using Sensor-Based Measurement Technology to Reduce the Environmental Impact of Perishable Goods

Alexander Ilic
ETH Zurich, Switzerland

Thorsten Staake
ETH Zurich, Switzerland

Elgar Fleisch
ETH Zurich & University of St. Gallen, Switzerland

ABSTRACT

Perishable goods are still a major challenge for supply chains. Temperature fluctuations and other disruptions can occur at various stages of a distribution network. Without sensor technologies, these disruptions are often not detectable in early stages of the supply chains. As a result, losses accumulate at the end of supply chains where a lot of energy as already invested for delivering these goods up to this point. This chapter shows how sensor technologies can enable a new way of data-driven decision making at the distribution stage of a supply chain. It demonstrates when and how sensors can be used for smart removal and sorting decisions. The results indicate that these decisions can reduce the environmental impact and even increase profits significantly.

INTRODUCTION

The literature sends a clear message that loss rates in supply chains of perishable goods are significant. Statistics by the U.S. Department of Agriculture report that average yearly loss rates at the retail level alone can be as high as 51% for specific commodities. When reviewing the loss figures from a quality management perspective, it is hard to think of any industry that could survive with such high defect rates.

The limited shelf-life of perishable goods and their susceptibility to fluctuations in environmental parameters often force managers to make

DOI: 10.4018/978-1-60960-585-8.ch009

decisions under uncertainty, leading to high loss rates. In order to achieve the same desired output, additional input resources are often required for compensation.

A solution could be low-cost measurement technologies such as Radio Frequency Identification (RFID) tags and sensors. They could provide the necessary information to make the quality deterioration process more predictable and to make problems visible even at earlier stages of supply chains.

This chapter shows when and how sensor information can help increasing efficiency in logistics operations and lowers the environmental footprint for supply chains.

The next section provides background information about sensor-based condition monitoring and product-level carbon footprinting. Sensor-based condition monitoring allows to track information pertaining to individual goods. With this information, each item can be assigned with an individual carbon footprint value. The combination of these two concepts is necessary to quantify the environmental impact of food losses and the potential improvement due to sensor-based decision making.

The main part of this chapter is based on a case study that stems from a research project with a Swiss retailer. We use the example of strawberries in Switzerland to investigate the value of sensor information for profit increase and carbon-footprint reduction on the distribution level. As a primary analysis method, we apply computer simulation. This allows us to explore, evaluate, and analyze parameters of a complex system such as a supply chain in a very cost efficient way. The insights provide also inputs for full-scale roll-outs of sensor technologies and help to determine the economic feasibility. As a starting point for practitioners, we provide a framework to determine the business case for such a scenario.

Finally, this chapter reviews future research directions and trends.

The goal of this chapter is to analyze the impact of sensor based condition monitoring to reduce the chance of food spoilage by making informed sorting and removal decisions at the distribution stage. The hypothesis is that this can lead to significant reductions of greenhouse gas emissions due to waste reduction and better load utilization.

The objectives of this chapter are 1) to provide insights on data-driven decisions for perishable goods at the distribution stage, 2) to show how these decisions can help to reduce the environmental impact at low cost, and 3) to understand the critical factors when and how to apply sensor technologies for managing perishable goods.

BACKGROUND

Sensor-Based Condition Monitoring

The goal of sensor-based condition monitoring is to predict the condition of a good based on the collected temperature information. More accurate temperature measurements lead to the better prediction of shelf-life. A study of Jedermann, Emond, & Lang (2008) indicates that the confidence levels for condition monitoring with current sensor technology is already high enough for supply chain applications. More details on the most suitable implementation for monitoring perishable goods with sensors be found in Jedermann, Ruiz-Garcia, & Lang (2009).

The focus of this section is on applying low cost sensors (such as semi-active RFID tags) to track the temperature of goods. The schematics of such a tag are depicted on Figure 1. The left side of Figure 1 shows the antenna of the tag and the radio frequency front-end. This part is usually powered by the reader in order to conduct a data transfer from the tag memory to the reader. The semi-active tag also contains a battery. The battery enables the microcontroller to continuously measure and store sensor data (e.g., temperature) in the memory for later read-out. RFID readers that are deployed at certain parts of the supply chain (or mobile readers) can retrieve the stored sensor data history (e.g., temperature) and make it available for processing in a computer system. In the case of perishable goods, this information is usually a time-temperature history that is used together with a shelf-life prediction model. The shelf-life prediction model gives an estimate of the good's actual quality level.

In general, there are sensor tags for two different monitoring approaches: continuous monitoring and discrete monitoring. The two approaches and their application areas are described below.

Continuous Monitoring

In continuous monitoring, the sensor measures and stores the current temperature in pre-defined intervals (e.g., every 10 seconds). Figure 2 shows an example for continuous temperature monitoring in a supply chain. The top shows the time-temperature history with a critical temperature threshold at 5 degree Celsius. The bottom shows RFID read events that happen whenever the good passes through a reader gate on the way from supplier downwards the supply chain. As the figure shows, when and where the threshold was exceeded can be clearly identified. Moreover, since the full temperature history is available, the remaining shelf-life can be re-calculated at every RFID read point. Therefore, this approach is well suited for decision-making during the distribution of goods.

Discrete Monitoring

The second popular way of monitoring is discrete monitoring. A typical example is a shock sensor that detects whether a box of fragile items has been dropped. Figure 3 shows this example. The threshold in this case is defined on the sensor. The sensor thus delivers only 1-bit data (shock occurred, yes or no) to every read point. The time-resolution depends on the frequency of RFID read points. Therefore, it is not possible in this case to provide an assessment of remaining shelf-life. However, 1-bit sensors are usually less complex and thus quite cheap. This makes their application possible for several product groups.

Foundations for Measuring the Environmental Impact of Food Losses

Food losses have a negative impact on the environment. Depending on how much energy was already invested into preparing, packaging, processing, cooling, or transporting an item to a specific stage, the environmental impact can differ

Figure 1. Schematics of a semi-active RFID tag with sensor (Bowman, Harrison, Ilic, & Ng, 2009)

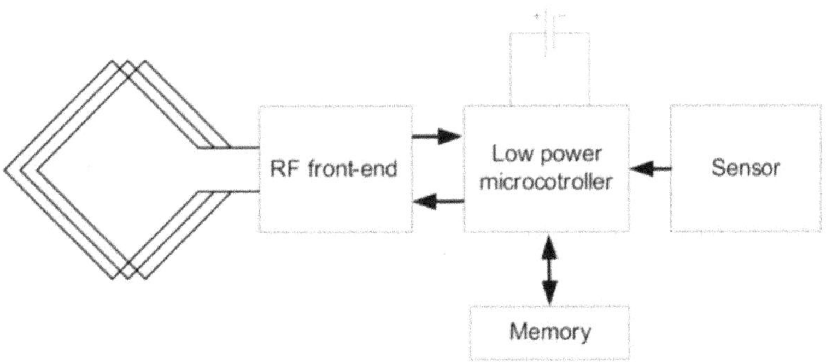

Figure 2. Data plot example for a continuous monitoring approach (Bowman et al., 2009)

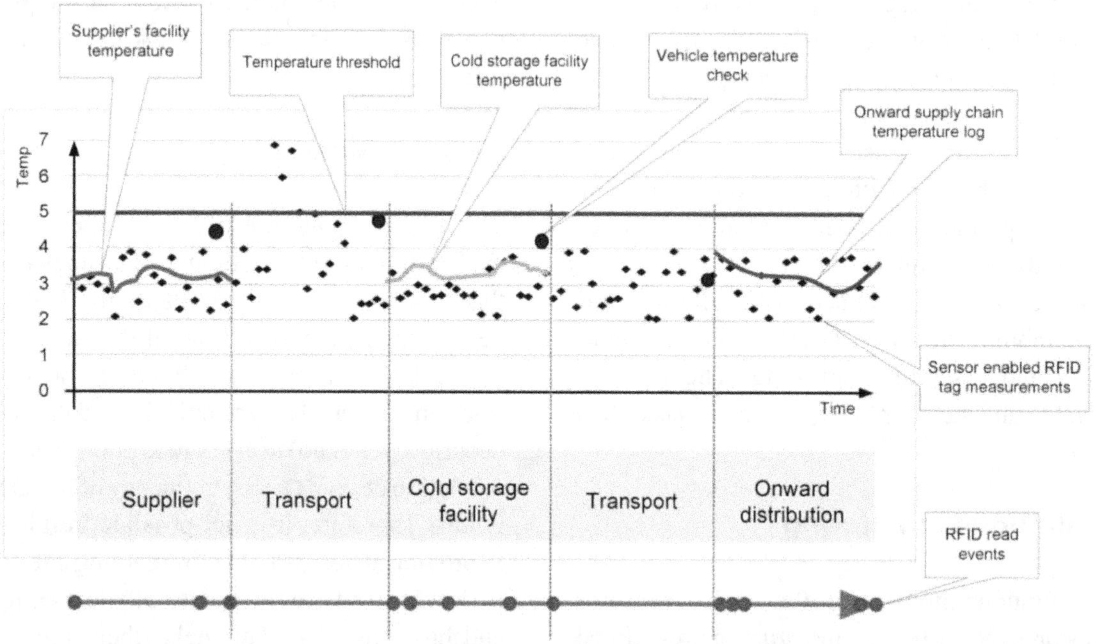

Figure 3. Data plot example for a discrete monitoring approach (Bowman et al., 2009)

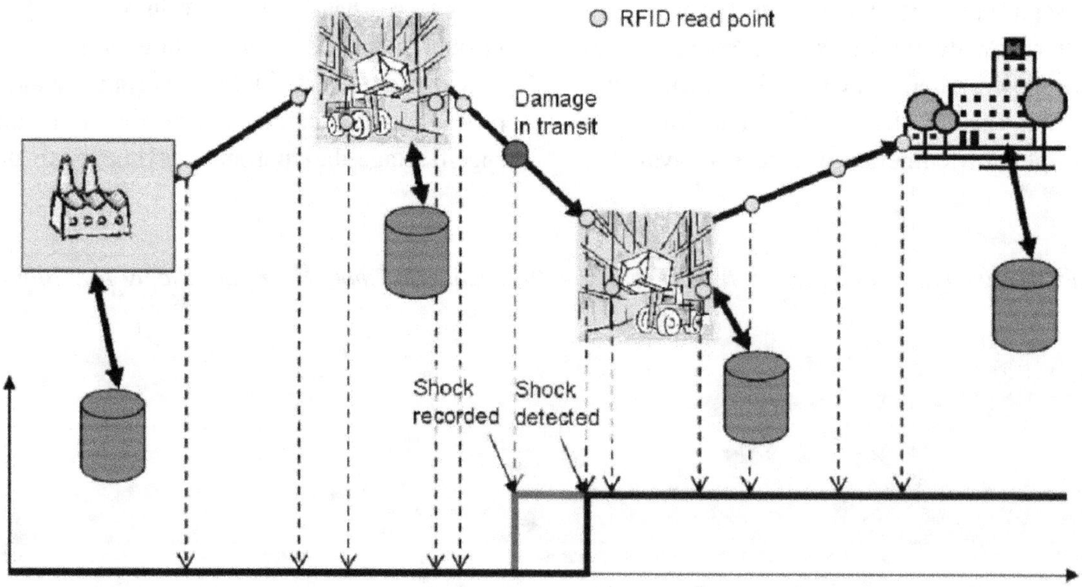

greatly. This section describes the fundamentals of how the environmental impact for these losses can be assessed.

Carbon Accounting

Depending on the product category and the targeted consumer group, companies are used to optimizing their supply-chain processes for cost, speed, quality, safety, and other key performance indicators. Greenhouse gas (GHG) emissions only recently appeared on the list of important target figures. Due to the growing concern over climate change, an increasing number of companies have adopted carbon accounting practices. Carbon accounting refers to the corporate practice of collecting and analyzing the emission data that result from the production, operations, or service provision of a given organization. The total set of these emissions for a given product, event, or organization is called carbon footprint. For simplicity, the carbon footprint is usually expressed in CO2-equivalents. A CO2-equivalent is the amount of carbon dioxide with the same global warming potential as a given mixture of GHGs with respect to their global warming potential over a specified timescale (generally, 100 years).

To facilitate carbon accounting, emission databases such as GEMIS or ecoinvent exist. These databases maintain a repository of emission factors of all sorts of different process steps and allow for a modular and fast analysis of carbon footprints (modular lifecycle analysis). One key issue that remains is the topic of accounting boundaries and the issue of granularity. Therefore, for this chapter, we will consider the approach of product-level carbon footprinting instead of a single company's corporate perspective.

Product-Level Carbon Footprinting

A product-level carbon footprint typically includes emissions related to production, transportation, storage, use, recycling and disposal, and loss rates. The carbon footprint can be determined using modular lifecycle analysis by dividing the lifecycle of a product into different process steps and phases. An example for strawberries based on (REWE Group, 2009) for the lifecycle of strawberries is given on Figure 4.

For each of these steps, the emissions can be calculated using an emission database and the quantities for the given scenario. The output of the analysis in the previous example is shown on Figure 5.

Of course, these emissions can greatly vary throughout the year. For instance, a retailer might change the source of out-of-season fruits from local to long-distance suppliers. Another example would be the carbon footprint of losses at different stages which must be distributed among the remaining sellable items.

Novel approaches such as those described by Dada et al. (2008) aim to make this information available to the consumer. The idea is that the transparency can help consumers to make better buying decisions and thus reward environmentally friendly practices in an effective way. As the study of (Kimura et al., 2010) shows, this can even lead to an increase of the willingness to pay for consumers actively seeking information related to environmental friendliness. Environmentally aware consumers might also consider changing their dietary habits based on this information to reduce their carbon footprints (Pathak, Jain, Bhatia, Patel, & Aggarwal, 2010).

Abatement Costs

In the context of emission reductions, CO2 abatement costs represent another important measure. These costs express how much a stakeholder must invest to lower emissions by a certain amount. For some investments, the abatement cost can be negative. Energy-saving lamps, for example, might reduce GHG emissions and save the consumer money due to lower electricity bills, which compensate for the initial high one-time costs. The

Figure 4. Relevant lifecycle modules and stages of strawberries as input for the modular LCA (REWE Group, 2009)

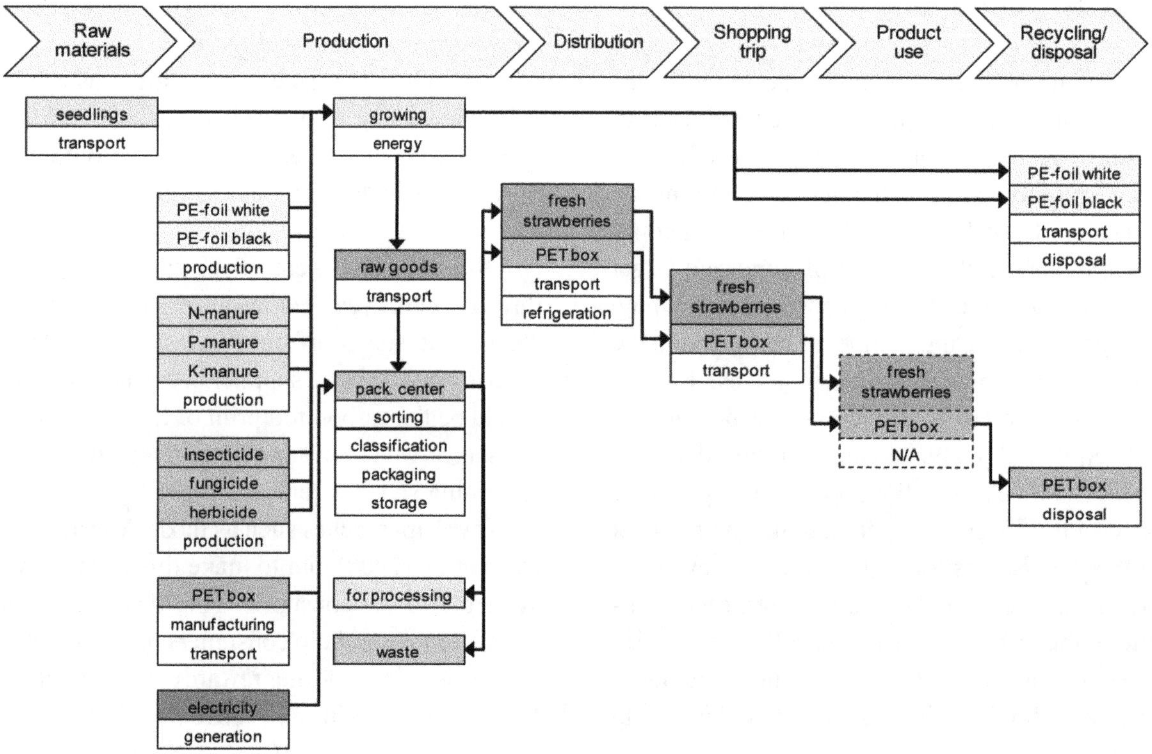

CO_2 abatement cost concept is relevant for supply chain partners in order to determine if taking certain measures for reducing the environmental impact require an investment or even generate more profits.

THE VALUE OF SENSOR-BASED DECISION MAKING

Limitations of Current Practices

With temperature being the main cause for spoilage, the current practice is to track the temperature within a container with a temperature logger. Frequently, the industry uses analog Partlow recorders (Figure 6) to measure the return air flow to get an indication of the cargo's state. The recorder's display is usually located on the outside of a container. Today, decisions whether to accept or reject shipments are often made on the basis of the Partlow recorder chart.

One problem with the current practice of using a Partlow recorder is that it implicitly assumes that the temperature distribution within a container is uniform. As Figure 7 shows, the placement of goods within a container can in itself result in a violation of this assumption. For example, Chiquita Brands International discovered (O'Connor, 2006) that the temperature distribution within a single container can vary up to 35 percent between pallets. These variations, which are often referred to as microclimates, sometimes were responsible for the rejection of entire loads of

Figure 5. Total greenhouse gas emissions for strawberries resulting from the modular LCA example (REWE Group, 2009)

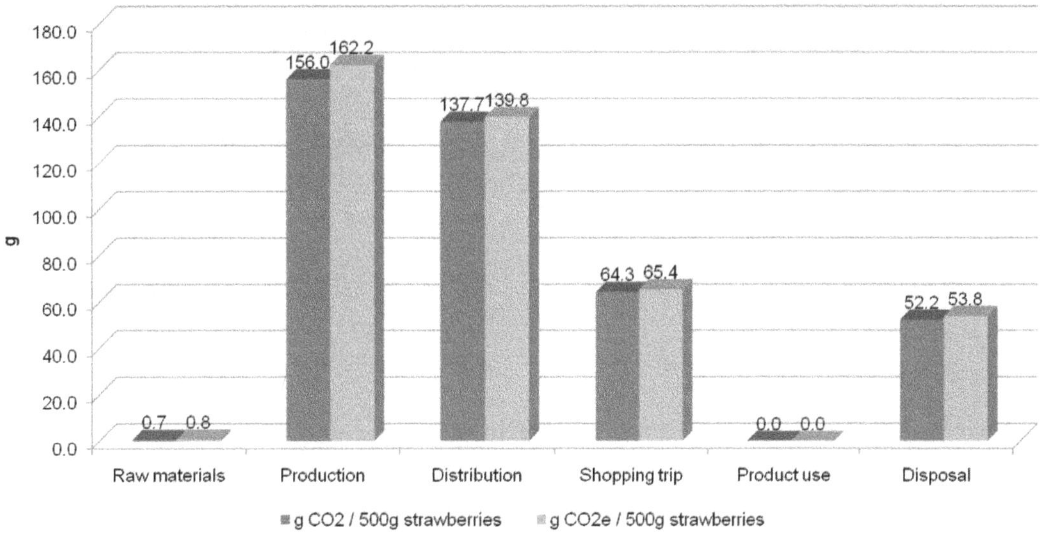

incoming shipments. In fact, the spread in temperature depends on various factors such as the ambient temperature, the total rate and distribution of air circulation, sun exposure, and the goods' respiration heat. Therefore, ambient temperature measurement does not provide sufficient information on the condition of goods during transport and storage. The industry needs a more fine-grained temperature-tracking method to assess the impact on individual cases.

Figure 6. Partlow recorder for tracking the temperature for a whole container (GDV, 2008)

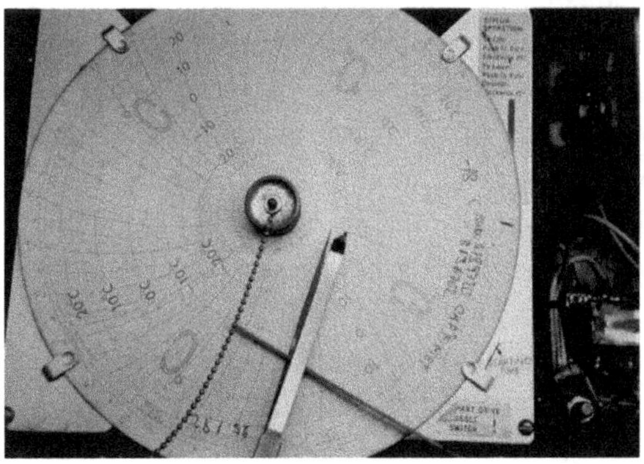

Basically, the problem of perishable goods comes down to the problem of matching supply with demand in food supply chains. This often materializes as waste. Waste is an inefficiency that can be described with loss rates based on the initial supply.

There is data available about how well the industry currently performs. The USDA maintains statistics on the loss rates of individual perishable products. Figure 8 shows an excerpt of a report of loss rates (Buzby, Wells, Axtman, & Mickey, 2009). On average, 8.4% of all fresh fruits are lost per year at the retail level. This figure, however, neglects aspects such as seasonality and different sourcing options for goods. For some specialty foods such as papayas, the loss rate can be as high as 58.7%. As a conclusion, a lot of energy can be saved if goods with overly low quality are removed earlier in the supply chain.

Figure 7. Self-heating problems due to incorrect storage within a container (GDV, 2008)

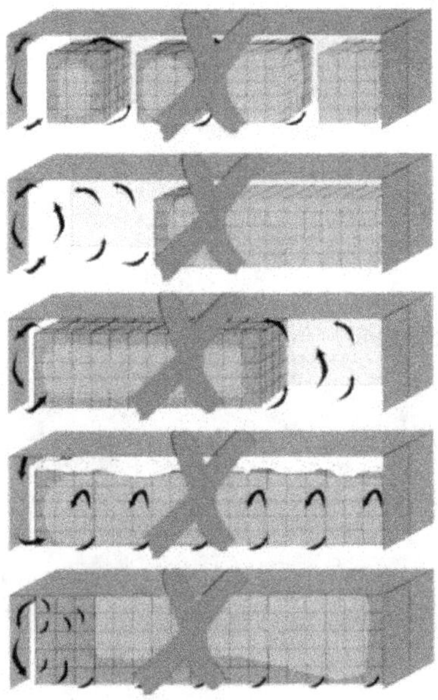

Smart Removal and Sorting Decisions Based on Sensor Data

One approach of improving the current situation is to detect failures early in the supply chain. Sensors provide the means for making these decisions already at the distribution stage. In the following, we look at a case study for smart removal and sorting decisions based on better data.

Research Question and Solution Approach

We assume that the temperature of goods is tracked on a case level by sensors starting at the production stage of the supply chain. This data is available at a later supply chain stage to make decisions. We simulate a scenario where two types of sensor-based decisions can be made by the retailer at the distribution center (DC) level:

- Active removal of goods with overly low quality
- Sorting of the stock-depletion order according to a First-Expiry-First-Out (FEFO) strategy

The three key questions we want to answer with this study are 1) what is the impact of these decisions on the environmental footprint and profits, 2) how does the performance compare to the traditional non-sensor case, and 3) for which supply routes would we recommend a sensor-based monitoring approach.

Methodology

This chapter focuses on discrete-event simulation. Discrete-event simulation allows modeling an existing or proposed system with its key characteristics and parameters (Murty et al., 2008). The model's behavior and performance respond to events that take place over time.

Next to observing an actual implementation, simulation modeling is the best quantitative methodology available for investigating operational problems (Taha 2006). Simulation allows analyzing a system without requiring substantial investments for actual roll-outs or making risky changes to existing systems. Moreover, it is nearly impossible to precisely capture all relationships and interactions of the system parameters in strict mathematical equations, as is required by other mathematical modeling techniques. Instead, simulation focuses on the most relevant characteristics and key factors. It allows these characteristics to be explored in a flexible and cost-efficient way. Because actual implementations for the advanced operational models that are proposed in this thesis are scarce, simulation modeling was considered the optimal choice for answering the previously stated research questions.

Figure 8. Loss rates of selected perishable goods on the retail level (Buzby et al., 2009)

Fruit	2005	2006	2005-06 percentage-point change	2005-06 average
	Percent		*Number*	*Percent*
Papayas	58.7	51.0	-7.7	54.9
Apricots	37.5	32.6	-5.0	35.1
Honeydew melons	20.9	24.6	3.7	22.8
Tangerines	19.5	21.4	1.9	20.4
Pears	19.7	15.4	-4.3	17.6
Plums	20.7	14.0	-6.7	17.3
Watermelons	18.7	14.9	-3.8	16.8
Pineapples	16.8	12.5	-4.3	14.6
Mangoes	21.2	7.7	-13.5	14.5
Grapefruits	12.9	12.8	-0.1	12.8
Kiwis	15.7	9.6	-6.0	12.7
Cantaloups	11.1	13.3	2.3	12.2
Peaches	14.8	9.1	-5.7	11.9
Oranges	12.8	10.3	-2.5	11.6
Strawberries	10.0	9.5	-0.4	9.8
Avocados	9.7	9.0	-0.7	9.3
Apples	9.5	7.8	-1.7	8.6
Limes	10.9	5.7	-5.2	8.3
Bananas	9.4	6.5	-2.8	8.0
Grapes	8.1	7.1	-1.0	7.6
Lemons	8.1	5.9	-2.2	7.0
Cranberries	7.1	4.8	-2.3	6.0
Blueberries	5.9	4.6	-1.3	5.2
Cherries	2.8	4.9	2.1	3.9
Average	10.7	8.4	-2.3	NA[1]

[1]When the impact of incorporating the new estimates on ERS Loss-Adjusted Food Availability data was analyzed, the estimate of the overall average supermarket loss for fresh fruit was 11.4 percent.

Source: Adapted from the Perishables Group final report to ERS. September 28, 2007.

Objective Function

The variables V^x are ex post count variables for sold units V^s, units held at the retail level V^H, total waste V^W, and total number of replenishment orders V^R for the simulated period. We assume no penalty for perished goods other than the lost margin.

Cost parameters are shown in Table 1.

We measure the performance of the simulated scenarios by using the following profit function:

$$\text{Profit }(X)=(C_p - C_w - C_s)V^s - C_h V^w - C_k V^R$$

We define Profit*(X) as the profit-optimal configuration of a scenario X (whereas U_1 is the conventional and U_2 is the sensor-based approach). We obtain the optimal configuration of Profit*(X) with a full search over the replenishment parameter pair (s, S) with a sufficiently large maximum stock level for the selected demand and product life time parameters (our search range is $0 < s \leq S \leq 40$).

Table 1. Cost parameters and values

Description	Variable
Selling price per item	C_p
Purchasing costs per item	C_w
Rental costs for RPC without sensor[1]	C_s
Rental costs for RPC with sensor[i]	C_s
One-period holding costs per item at the retail level	C_h
Fixed costs per order	C_k

For a given optimal replenishment configuration Profit*(X), CF(X) is the resulting carbon footprint per product. We define CF*(U_2) as the emission-optimal configuration of U_2 with the lowest carbon footprint and a profit greater than or equal to U_1.

The calculation of the carbon footprint is based on the sum of emissions generated at each step of the supply chain. V^P is the number of purchased trade units, and V^{IW} is the number of units wasted due to in-store spoilage. f_x represents the specific emission factors per trade unit for food production f_p, f_{R1} represents the transport from the supplier to the distribution center, f_{R2} represents the transport from the distribution center to the retail store, f_H represents the cool storage per item per day, and f_W represents disposal due to spoilage. We divide the sum of these emission steps by the number of sold products to obtain the carbon footprint:

$$CF(X) = \frac{f_p V^p + f_{R1} V^p + f_{R2}(V^s + V^{iw}) + f_H(l_1 V^p + l_2[V^s + V^{iw}] + V^h + f_w V^w}{V^s}$$

The emission factors follow the modular LCA approach (Table 2). We use two different emission factor sets for the conventional and the sensor-based approach. All emissions required for producing and transporting the sensor are taken into account. The emission factors base on the Ecoinvent database:

Case Study

We use the example of strawberries in Switzerland to investigate the value of sensor information for profit increase and carbon-footprint reduction in retail supply chains.

The Swiss consume approximately 16,500 metric tons (t) of strawberries per year. Because the domestic crop yield only satisfies 5,500 t of that demand and the product is seasonal, imports from other countries must fill the resulting 66% gap. Suppliers and distribution routes change frequently and quality drops are likely to occur between the supplier and retailer. Strawberries are so fragile that retailers perceive them as a difficult product class with high loss rates. Figure 9 shows how the main sourcing focus switches throughout the year.

Our exemplary case is based on a research project with a major Swiss retailer. Data was changed for confidentiality reasons. For this study, we assume that the retailer has a market share of 10%. We selected computer simulation as our primary analysis methodology because it is a powerful and flexible way to explore, evaluate, and analyze parameters of complex systems such as supply chains for which a full-scale roll-out of sensor technologies is too costly. Following an iterative process, we elicited and validated our simulation parameters in several discussions with industry experts.

Simulation Model and Flow of Goods

The simulation model is depicted on Figure 10. A retailer sells a perishable commodity, in our case strawberries, through retail stores (R_1, … R_n) to consumers. We assume that all stores are homogenous and therefore model them as one big virtual retail store in our simulation.

The basic unit of goods is a trade-unit (TU) that comprises a Reusable Plastic Container (RPC) capable of containing 10 sellable consumer units. The time resolution of the simulation is set to seconds.

Demand arrival is random and follows a Poisson distribution with mean $\mu_d = 6\frac{TU}{day}$. Replenishment occurs according to a continuous (s, S) policy (Porteus, 2002) which automatically triggers orders to the distribution center (DC).

The DC ships the goods to the retail store whereas the distance $d_2 = 100km$ and the lead time $l_2 = 1\ day$. The DC itself gets automati-

Table 2. Emission factors used for LCA calculation

Supply chain phases for a full TU of strawberries[2]	U_1	U_2
Production	$f_p = \frac{1632.25861 gCO_2}{trade\ unit}$	$f_p = \frac{1706.67524 gCO_2}{trade\ unit}$
Transportation (3.5-7.5t truck EURO3)	$f_{R1} = \frac{4.20710 gCO_2}{km}$	$f_{R2} = \frac{4.23340 gCO_2}{km}$
Transportation (7.5-16t truck EURO3)	$f_{R1} = \frac{1.86125 gCO_2}{km}$	$f_{R2} = \frac{1.87288 gCO_2}{km}$
Transportation (16-32t truck EURO3)	$f_{R1} = \frac{1.07494 gCO_2}{km}$	$f_{R2} = \frac{1.08166 gCO_2}{km}$
Transportation (air freight)	$f_{R1} = \frac{7.33952 gCO_2}{km}$	$f_{R2} = \frac{7.38539 gCO_2}{km}$
Refrigeration during transport and storage per day	$f_H = \frac{6.13993 gCO_2}{d}$	$f_H = \frac{6.17830 gCO_2}{d}$
Waste management/disposal (excluding RPC and sensor disposal emissions)	$f_w = \frac{206.027 gCO_2}{trade\ unit}$	$f_w = \frac{206.027 gCO_2}{trade\ unit}$

Figure 9. Main sourcing options for strawberries throughout the year

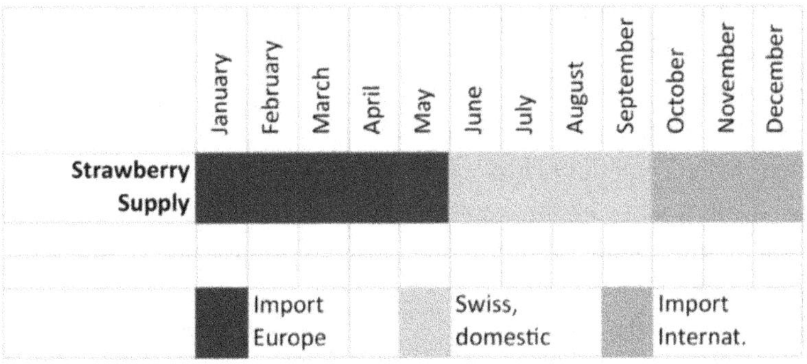

Figure 10. Simulation model

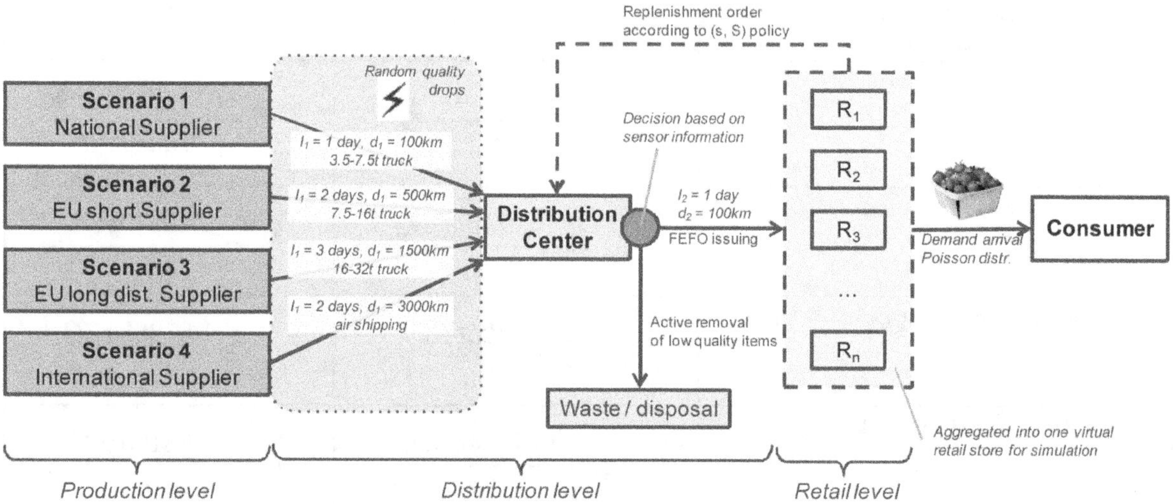

cally replenished by suppliers. Depending on the time of the year, a different supplier might be selected. Basically, there are four different sourcing scenarios, each with a different mode of transportation, different lead time, and a different transportation distance (see left side of Figure 10). The initial quality of goods is set for all sourcing scenarios to $M = 8$ *days*. We assume that the TUs are equipped with sensors and record temperature fluctuations in the transport link from supplier to DC. The random quality drops are modeled with an exponential distribution with mean $\mu q =$ 0.75 *days*.

In the non-sensor approach, items are simply moved through the supply chain.

In the sensor-based approach, there is a decision point at the DC. At this decision point, a decision is made based on the temperature history of individual goods. If the quality of the items is too low for being sold at the retail store after shipment, the item is immediately discarded at the DC level. If the quality of the item is only lower than expected to be, the stock depletion order is changed. Items are scheduled according to a First-Expiry-First-Out (FEFO) strategy. This means that items that will be unsellable earlier get more priority to being moved to the retail store.

For the present case study, we assume that these costs occur for items moving through the supply chain (Table 3).

Simulation Results

Based on the previously described parameter sets, we conducted 4,680 experiments with 10 replications per experiment. We compared the U1 and U2 profit-optimal configurations. Table 4 shows the simulation results with respect to profit increase and emission reduction relative to the non-sensor approach. Although both mea-

Table 3. Assumption for cost parameters in case study

Description	Variable	Value
Selling price per item	C_p	\$60
Purchasing costs per item	C_w	\$30
Rental costs for RPC without sensor[3]	C_s	\$0.75
Rental costs for RPC with sensor[i]	C_s	\$1.5
One-period holding costs per item at the retail level	C_h	\$1 per day
Fixed costs per order	C_k	\$12

sures were substantial in the base case (scenario 2), we can see that the emissions caused by the sensors' carbon footprint outweigh the achieved reduction in scenario 1. On the contrary, the sensor costs and emissions are nearly negligible for scenarios 3 and 4.

In all scenarios the sensor-based approach yielded more profits. For scenarios 2-4, there is also a positive effect on the total emission level. Only for scenario 1, the emissions generated due to the sensor use outweigh the achieved savings. The total profit increase due to sensor information is \$0.66 million per year (8%) and the achieved emission reduction amounts to 36 t CO2 (2%).

The results show that introducing sensor technology into supply chains can have a positive effect on emission levels while at the same time increasing profits. The reason is that sensor information reduces uncertainty in quality levels for distribution decisions. This in turn leads to additional profits by enabling a better replenishment configuration. The retailer can optimize its replenishment parameters (s, S) for the reorder point and the order-up-to level in particular. When determining the optimal choice of these parameters, a retailer can aim to maximize the profit gain or maximize emission reductions under the assumption of at least some positive profit gain in comparison to the traditional approach.

Our results show that emission reductions induced from avoiding waste and reducing the number of shipments more than compensate for the emissions related to sensor production and usage. A particularly valuable lesson is that in certain but highly relevant scenarios, the abatement costs are negative; that is, companies that use sensor technology effectively can save money and lower their carbon footprint. Our study does not even include other beneficial environmental effects (such as less land use) and monetary effects (such as better company image and charging a premium for suitably handled products).

For the retailer in our case study we would therefore recommend to use sensor-based condition monitoring for all non-regional supply links.

Implications

The case study of this chapter can be seen as an example on how to review the performance of retail supply chains. Companies can run similar simulations with their specific parameters to

Table 4. Simulation results by scenario

		Scenario			
	Total	1 Regional	2 EU short	3 EU long	4 Internat.
Consumer demand p.a. (t)	1650	5500	4290	4290	2420
Market share of retailer	165	550	429	429	242
Expected demand p.a. (in 1000 trade units)	330	110	86	86	48
Profit U_1 (in \$1000)	8098	3027	2214	1608	1249
Profit increase *U2* (in \$1000)	660	105	146	328	82
Emissions U_1 (t of CO_2)	2105	228	255	389	1233
Emission reduction U_2 (t of CO_2)	–36	36	–16	–185	–194
Purchasing volume U_1 (t)	1825	555	458	554	258
Purchasing volume reduction U_2 (t)	–52	-4	–11	–31	-6

quickly determine the potential of using sensors in their case. It helps companies in their decision making to determine product groups or supply links bear the most potential to "go green and save money".

This chapter provides a starting point for a business case analysis for deploying sensor-based condition monitoring in practice. The results of the previous section primarily reviewed the profit side of using sensor technology. In addition, the technology costs including sensor tag costs, implementation costs, and roll out costs need to be considered. Typically, this is done with a Return-On-Investment (ROI) calculation, which can be visualized with an ROI tree structure (Figure 11).

To calculate the ROI based on the proposed structure (Figure 11), the following steps are necessary:

1. Adapt the simulation input parameters to match the company's supply chain and product characteristics
2. Profit: Conduct simulation runs to determine the profit gains of the sensor-based approach
3. Costs: Select the appropriate sensor technology, and determine the costs of sensor tags
4. Investment: Determine the costs of initial setup and roll-out
5. Calculate the ROI period

In the case that sensors are attached to Reusable Transport Items (RTIs) as in the case study of this chapter, the costs of an individual sensor tag can be distributed over the number of cycles for the lifetime of the tag and RTI. Doing this will lead to a quick amortization of the costs and thus facilitate a deployment decision. For an example of such a cost calculation, please refer to (Ilic, Ng, Bowman, & Staake, 2009).

CHALLENGES AND TRENDS

The case study showed that there is some potential for a slight improvement of a single product with regards to profitability and sustainability. Some of the assumptions of the previous case study, however, might change significantly in the future. There might be a change from rather fixed to more uncertain and complex environments. The key trends of increasing demand and product scarcity, dynamics in energy costs, and the consumers increasing requirements for transpar-

Figure 11. ROI tree structure

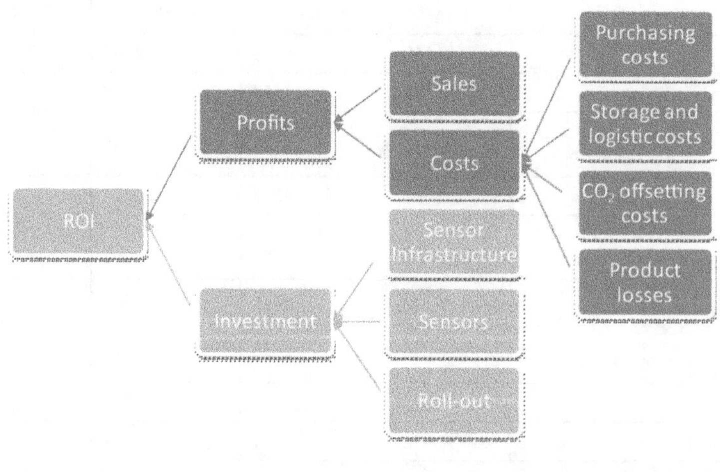

ency support this hypothesis and will be outlined below. Measurement-based approaches as the one outlined in this chapter will therefore gain more importance and get on top of the retailers' agenda.

Growing Demand for Fresh Fruits and Vegetables

Chronic diseases and conditions (such as diabetes, overweight, and obesity) affect the quality of life and well-being of more than 90 million Americans. A key reason for this large impact on Americans is that they still fall short of government recommendations in the quantity of fruits and vegetables consumed (USDA, 2005). On average, Americans consumed 1.03 cups of fruits and 1.58 cups of vegetables per day in 2004, compared with the recommended 1.80 cups of fruits and 2.60 cups of vegetables (Dong & Lin, 2009). The following sections discuss problems associated with growing demand and how the results of this chapter could help to mitigate them.

Some proposals suggest subsidizing prices in order to stimulate more demand. As the paper (Dong & Lin, 2009) shows, a 10-percent subsidy (requiring an annual investment by the Government of $580 million) would lead to an increase in consumption by approximately 2.1 to 5 percent of low-income consumers. The approach outlined in this chapter could be another way of reducing the costs of fruits and vegetables. Given the current potential of loss-rate reduction and the promising results of this chapter, a reduction of food prices seems feasible. This reduction would in turn stimulate demand and thus help low-income consumers to be able to consume more fruits and vegetables.

Another question concerns what would happen to the food supply if all Americans meet their dietary targets. The consequence would be an increase in demand by 75% for fruits and by 65% for vegetables. Because the results of this chapter provide means to reduce input resources by using better information for decision-making. This means that for instance less area of farm-land is needed to fulfill the same amount of demand. Therefore, sensor information can help address increasing demands faster than traditional, slower approaches of doubling the agricultural land-use.

Rising Energy Costs and CO2 Costs

Today's global food systems depend heavily on cheap transportation methods. This dependence makes them quite vulnerable to increases and fluctuations in energy costs.

Oil is the basis for today's fuel and is a limited resource. Several sources indicate that we might be already beyond "peak oil" and thus that production will diminish faster than anyone expected. Only recently did the International Energy Agency (IEA) recognize that oil prices are unlikely to be constant over the next 20 years.

It is more likely that oil prices will continue to increase and that unpredictable fluctuations of prices will happen. In fact, the unforeseen peak of fuel prices in the summer of 2008 has already resulted in several breakdowns in food supply chains, hitting small farmers in particular quite hard (Connelly, 2008). For example, the supply of strawberries from the western to the eastern coast of the US was interrupted. Sensors can contribute to a better visibility on an item-level.

Fuel prices are not the only energy-related price impact felt by food supply chain companies. The costs of CO2 abatements will also rise, given that environmental costs of climate change are converted to market costs. Political regulations such as the Kyoto Protocol, the Robust European and Asian renewable energy mandates, California's AB 32 Global Warming Solutions Act, the Regional Green House Gas Initiative and incentive programs such as the EU Emissions Trade Scheme and the 2005 U.S. Energy Bill (PV and BioFuel tax credits) will foster this development and force companies to consider this topic as one of their key priorities.

By applying a more granular management approach as discussed in this chapter, supply chains become more efficient and thus less prone to fluctuations.

Information Transparency Required by Consumers

The consumer is a powerful player in retail supply chains. By executing buying decisions, the consumer supports certain suppliers and products. There is an increasing demand for more transparency regarding product origin and environmentally friendly production processes. In particular, there are several projects that aim to communicate the carbon footprint (Dada et al., 2008) to the consumer to enable more environmentally friendly decisions.

With a sensor-based condition-monitoring approach as described in this chapter, the data base required to enable an increased transparency to consumers would already be in place. The costs of infrastructure will thus be lower.

IMPLICATIONS FOR SUPPLY CHAIN INNOVATION

The retail industry will likely face a paradigm shift in how to manage perishable items. Instead of relying on fixed assumptions, actual data can be used to make informed decisions already at early stages of supply chains in order to increase their eco-efficiency.

Using sensors for certain products and supply chains already makes sense today. The costs for sensors will likely continue to go down and their accuracy will go up. This increases the application areas significantly and will lead to more visibility of goods in the supply chain. Innovative retailers can apply the measurement driven management methods to differentiate themselves from the competition, drive down costs and reduce the risk against fluctuations in demand and energy costs. Interesting aspects of this innovation might be the implications the accountability of losses along supply chains and their implications for contracts and buy-back options.

CONCLUSION

Sensor data enables a new way of decision making in supply chains. Problems become visible earlier and thus can be mitigated more efficiently.

This chapter showed that already simple removing and sorting decisions at the distribution level can have a significant impact on an entire supply chain's performance – not only on profits, but also on carbon footprints. By achieving a "pre-filtering" of waste at the distribution level, a significant waste reduction and the better utilization of truck loads can be achieved. In the case study, the sensor-based approach resulted in faster reordering and increased efficiency. As a result a profit increase of 8% was achieved while simultaneously reducing the carbon footprint by 2%.

For practitioners, this chapter can be seen as a framework to review their operations, to establish new key performance indicators, and to identify critical product groups for an evaluation with sensor-based monitoring.

As a key contribution to theory, these results show that sensor information can improve the management of perishable goods and can replace additional input resources with better information. This result underlines the relevance of integrating item-level quality modeling into the research stream of supply chain research.

REFERENCES

Bowman, P., Harrison, M., Ilic, A., & Ng, J. (2009). *Serial-Level Supply Chain Control: Sensor-based Condition Monitoring*. Brussels, Belgium: BRIDGE Deliverable D-3.6.1.

Buzby, J. C., Wells, H. F., Axtman, B., & Mickey, J. (2009). *Supermarket Loss Estimates for Fresh Fruit, Vegetables, Meat, Poultry, and Seafood and Their Use in the ERS Loss-Adjusted Food Availability Data (No. EIB-44)*. Washington, D.C.: U.S. Department of Agriculture, Economic Research Service.

Connelly, E. A. (2008). *Fuel price hikes squeeze farmers at local markets*. New York, USA.

Dada, A., Staake, T., & Fleisch, E. (2008). *The potential of UbiComp technologies to determine the carbon footprints of products*. Paper presented at the Sixth International Conference on Pervasive Computing.

Dong, D., & Lin, B.-H. (2009). *Fruit and Vegetable Consumption by Low-Income Americans: Would a Price Reduction Make a Difference?* Washington, D.C.: Economic Research Report No. 70, U.S. Department of Agriculture, Economic Research Service.

GDV. (2008). *Container Handbook – Cargo Loss Prevention Information From German Marine Insurers*. Berlin, Germany: GDV.

Ilic, A., Ng, J., Bowman, P., & Staake, T. (2009). The value of RFID for RTI management. *Electronic Markets*, *19*(2), 125–135. doi:10.1007/s12525-009-0011-5

Jedermann, R., Emond, J.-P., & Lang, W. (2008). Shelf Life Prediction by Intelligent RFID – Technical Limits of Model Accuracy. In *Dynamics in Logistics* (pp. 231–238). Bremen, Germany: Springer. doi:10.1007/978-3-540-76862-3_22

Jedermann, R., Ruiz-Garcia, L., & Lang, W. (2009). Spatial temperature profiling by semi-passive RFID loggers for perishable food transportation. *Computers and Electronics in Agriculture*, *65*(2), 145–154. doi:10.1016/j.compag.2008.08.006

Kimura, A., Wada, Y., Kamada, A., Masuda, T., Okamoto, M., & Goto, S.-i. (2010). Interactive effects of carbon footprint information and its accessibility on value and subjective qualities of food products. *Appetite*, *55*(2), 271–278. doi:10.1016/j.appet.2010.06.013

Murty, K. G., Trafalis, T. B., Gilbert, R. C., Weng, M., Yildirim, M. B., & Masud, A. S. M. (2008). *Operations Research Methodologies*. Boca Raton, FL: CRC Press.

O'Connor, M. C. (2006). *Cold-Chain Project Reveals Temperature Inconsistencies*. Hauppauge, USA: RFID Journal.

Pathak, H., Jain, N., Bhatia, A., Patel, J., & Aggarwal, P. K. (2010). Carbon footprints of Indian food items. *Agriculture Ecosystems & Environment*, *139*(1-2), 66–73. doi:10.1016/j.agee.2010.07.002

Porteus, E. (2002). *Foundations of Stochastic Inventory Theory*. Stanford: Business Books.

REWE Group. (2009). *Fallstudie "Best Alliance" - Frueherdbeeren der REWE Group*. Cologne, Germany: Product Carbon Footprinting Project.

USDA. (2005). *Dietary Guidelines for Americans*. Washington, D.C.: U.S. Department of Health and Human Services and U.S. Department of Agriculture.

ENDNOTES

1 We calculated that the RPC was rented from a container pooling provider for \$1.5 per rotation with the sensor attached and for \$0.75 per rotation without the sensor. These costs are based on current market prices (including transportation, collection, and cleaning), assuming 10 rotations per year, an RPC life of 5 years, a sensor life of 5 years, sensor costs of \$35, and a loss rate of 0.5% per rotation.

2 Emission factors are GWP100 and base on EcoInvent data V2.1 16.12.2007; The basis for the calculation is one TU consisting of 10x500g strawberries, 10x20g cardboard box, 1x1.2kg RPC, and optional a 40g sensor on the RPC; emissions for sensor and RPC are proportionate emissions per rotation;

3 We calculated that the RPC was rented from a container pooling provider for $1.5 per rotation with the sensor attached and for $0.75 per rotation without the sensor. These costs are based on current market prices (including transportation, collection, and cleaning), assuming 10 rotations per year, an RPC life of 5 years, a sensor life of 5 years, sensor costs of $35, and a loss rate of 0.5% per rotation.

Chapter 10
Managing Uncertain Inventory in Supply Chain with Neural Network and Radio Frequency Identification (RFID)

CKM Lee
Nanyang Technological University, Singapore

Ng Wenwei Benjamin
Nanyang Technological University, Singapore

Shaligram Pokharel
Qatar University, Qatar

ABSTRACT

Demand uncertainty leads to fluctuations in inventory position at each echelon of a supply chain causing bullwhip effect, which can lead to significant cost and loss of efficiency and waste of resources. One of the aspects that can reduce potential bullwhip effect is the sharing of real time information for which the recently mass produced Radio Frequency Identification (RFID) can be of great value. The use of RFID technology can also help in increasing the visibility of the flow of goods and material, keeping track of the location and quantity at each distribution centre and warehouses. This will also help in the periodic and near real time optimization of inventory level of goods and material. The data collected with RFID can be analysed in artificial Neural Network (NN) to forecast the future demand. In this chapter, a framework is proposed by combining RFID with artificial neural network so that lean logistics can be realized in the supply chain.

DOI: 10.4018/978-1-60960-585-8.ch010

INTRODUCTION

Inventory management is a critical issue of supply chain management. An efficient inventory management system can enhance the service level and improve the responsiveness of the customer requests. However, inventory management is a challenging task and it is difficult to estimate the demand quantity especially for the products that are newly introduced to the market. The unpredictable demand and dynamic consignment location leads to the difficulty in keeping track of the stock. As a result, it leads to high inventory cost, inadequate resource allocation and slow response to the customer request.

One of the ways to tackle uncertainty is to increase stock levels but it will increase the total cost of operation as well when the demand fluctuates and when there is a time lag in terms of collating sales figures and estimating demand. Such a situation can lead to bullwhip effect, which can be minimized through information symmetry across the supply chain. This will not only help in the visibility of inventory in terms of stock and usage rate on a real time basis but it can also support in demand analysis and forecasting.

In this chapter, logistics framework is proposed by combining the strengths of RFID and neural network (NN) for inventory analysis and demand forecasting of fast moving consumer products such as electronics and automobiles. Neural network has been widely used for pattern recognition and it can help in recognizing and predicting the changing demand pattern so as to formulate a better inventory management strategy. Therefore, we adopt this technique to develop the forecasting framework in this study.

This book chapter consists of nine main sections. The next section focuses on reviewing current methods on inventory management and related technologies. RFID-based inventory management system and its architecture are presented in third section. The use of NN for demand forecasting is shown in the fourth section. A case example to illustrate the use of the proposed model is given in the fifth section, while results are discussed in the sixth section. The seventh section provides solutions and recommendation for supply chain innovation emerging from the study. The last two sections are dedicated to future research directions and concluding remarks

THE TREND IN RFID BASED MODELLING

The quantitative forecasting method can be generally classified as time-series model and causal model. Time series model includes naïve forecast, moving average (MA) and autoregressive (AR), exponential smoothing (ES), double exponential smoothing (DES) and triple exponential smoothing (TES). In causal forecasting method, a forecast of the quantity of interest (the dependent variable) is obtained by relating it to one or more of independent variables such as lead time, customer satisfaction and product reliability.

Saygin (2006) has proposed the use of forecast-integrated inventory model under simulation environment and showed that the model combined with RFID can produce the desired level of system performance in terms of lowering manufacturing costs and inventory levels. RFID can also be used for managing ordnance inventory with multiple attribute utility structure to realize the non-cost benefit such as safety, manpower issues and ROI analysis (Doeer et al., 2006). Choy et al. (2009) use a case based reasoning method for selecting material handling equipment and the shortest order picking path by using RFID. The use of RFID for inventory accuracy was examined by Uçkun (2006) and Uçkun et al., (2008) and showed that RFID investment can be highly beneficial for sharing inventory information within entities in a supply chain.

Demand and lead time are most uncertain factors for inventory management. Croston's model (1972) was claimed as unbiased and has better performance than simple exponential moving. Eaves and Kingsman (2004) have further studied the demand forecasting method and compared with Croston model with approximately unbiased modification which can outperform Croston's estimator. The calculated demand forecasting result is based on demand of last period and assumption of demand distribution. It's not easy to predict changing demand pattern and it always leads to the error factor. As neural network is good at pattern recognition, researchers adopted NN for lumpy demand forecasting (Gutierrez et al., 2008) and short term demand forecasting with temporal features(Tsai et al., 2009). Under stochastic environment, Gumus and Guneri (2009) propose to use deterministic/stochastic-neuro-fuzzy cost models for inventory management to determine demand, lead time and expediting cost variables of the models. NN relies on demand data feed in the system so as to have accurate demand forecasting. Although many research studies have already been done on using various approaches to forecast demand (Cervellera et al., 2007; Tsai et al., 2009), the research related to the use of NN for inventory management together with RFID has not received much the attention. The use of NN brings about promising interesting solutions that would be further analysed in the subsequent sections. A combination of NN and RFID is investigated in this chapter to enhance the supply chain effectiveness and efficiency.

RFID BASED INVENTORY MANAGEMENT SYSTEM

An integrated information system proposed in this chapter helps in tracing and tracking inventory and storing the real time data in the supply chain. Therefore, based on the consumption patterns and information shared among retailers the decision makers can adjust and determine the ordering quantity. Obtaining the order quantity is a complex issue due to many interactions among the organizational functions and forecast variables. Therefore, data on actual sales captured by RFID system are feedback to NN for aggregated analysis of the inventory and demand in the supply chain. Aggregation of inventory can reduce the safety stock and allow logistics practitioners to reduce the stock levels in the supply chain. Bowersox et al (2010) have shown that demand pooling of this type allows an organization combine the demand and variability for multiple locations and forecast accurately for the total demand.

The basic framework proposed in this chapter is given in Figure 1. The figure shows that RFID captures the data from different locations and the systems updates the consumption (or sales) data in each location. RFID provides retailers and manufacturers more visibility into the movement of goods at item level at different stage of supply chain. The proposed system, incorporating RFID middleware in inventory management system, captures the data and calculates the forecasted demand to prepare sufficient stock for meeting changing customer demand.

RFID can capture the actual demand data in certain period and those data are the input for NN to calculate the forecasted demand. By using NN, the demand pattern is analysed and aggregated demand for the product is obtained where the fluctuation or change of demand pattern can be easily captured and detected with RFID. The objective of forecasting method with NN is to predict the systematic component of demand and estimate the random component. In general, systematic component of data include level, trend or seasonal factor. Without RFID, the demand data with the form of level, trend or seasonal may not be acquired immediately which in turn will affect the accuracy of NN output. Accurate demand forecasting can help supply chain parties to reduce excess inventory and alleviate the bullwhip effect by combining RFID and NN. Apart from accurate demand forecasting, quick replenishment is also essential to reduce the inventory level without losing the service level. In this case, RFID becomes

Figure 1. Overview of NN in RFID based inventory management system

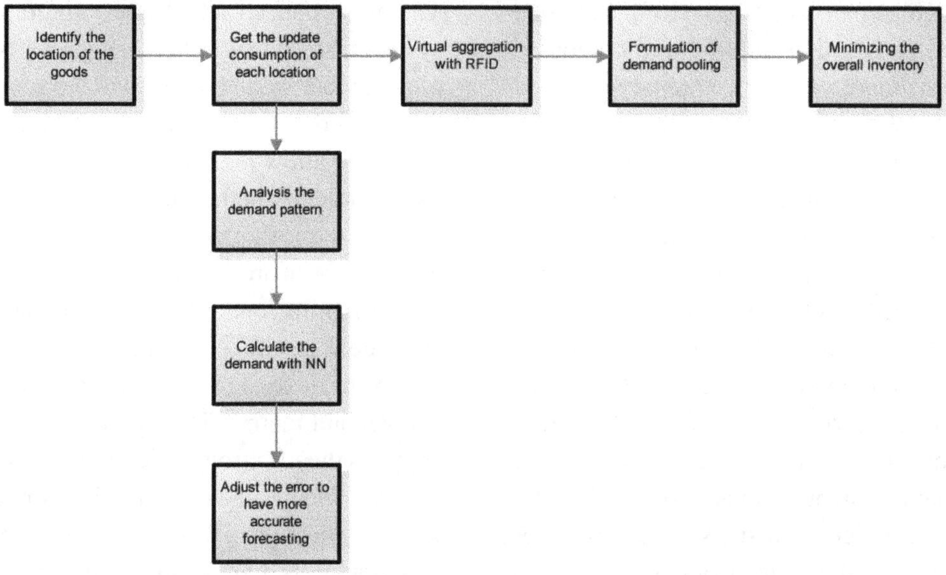

useful as it helps to enhance the visibility of the supply chain operations. The real-time data related to consumption rate can be directly transferred by RFID and those data can be analysed with NN so as to further analyse the demand patterns and replenish the inventory from a nearby warehouse or supply chain entity.

NEURAL NETWORK FOR DEMAND FORECASTING

Demand forecasting play a crucial role in the supply chain and accurate demand forecasting can provide high value for push/pull supply chain planning. Organization takes various factors to predict the demand of the product with past demand, lead time, price, quality of the products, economic environment, and competitors' price and supply. In general, forecasting methods are classified as four types which are qualitative, time series, causal and simulation. Neural network can be used as time series or casual forecasting. Neural network can take the past demand data as input and update knowledge over time as long as more training data sets are provided. The neural system can also learn new demand pattern not previous available in the training data set where the demand can vary as level, trend, seasonal, cycle and random. Figure 2 shows the representations of an artificial neural network and real (biological) neuron respectively. Neural networks offer a mathematical model that attempts to mimic how the human brain operates. Complex nonlinear input-output relationship can be modelled and knowledge is represented by layers of interconnected processors. The processor nodes indicate a relationship with the neurons of the brain. Each of these nodes is assigned a weighted connection to several other nodes in adjacent layers. Individual nodes would take the input (i.e. past demand) received from connected nodes and use the weights together with a simple function to compute the output values (i.e. forecast demand). Compared with other qualitative forecasting, neural network has less exhaustive computing and processing time. Neural network can model the input-output relationship without formulating the complex mathematical model which may further reduce the development time.

Figure 2. Comparison between artificial neuron and biological neuron

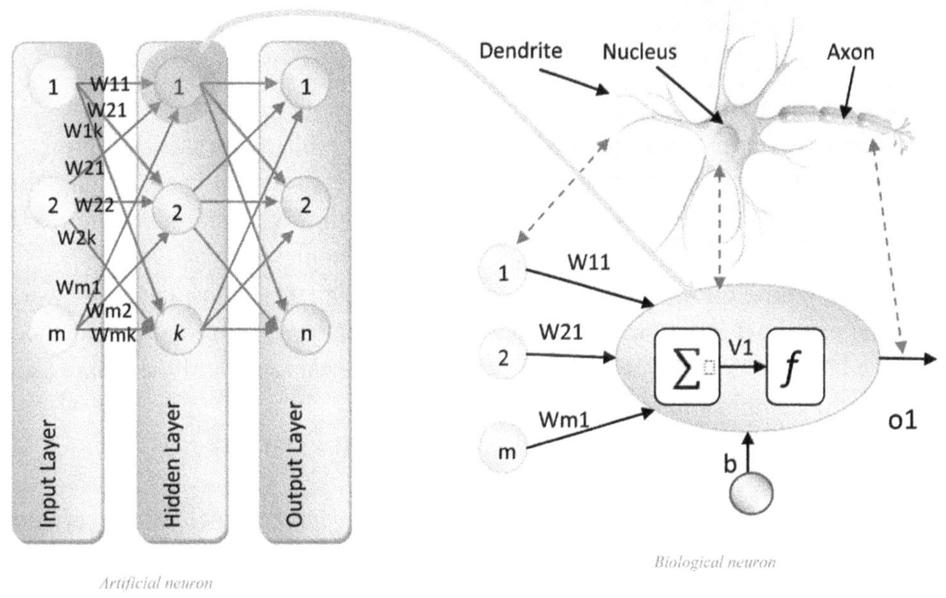

Artificial Neuron Model

An artificial neural network typically consists of several components:

1. A set of neurons
2. Pattern of connectivity
3. Propagation Rule
4. Activation Rule /Transfer Function and
5. Learning Rule.

(1) Neurons are simple processing units that send and receive signals from the external environment. They could also be inter-connected with other neurons. (2) These neurons form a network by linking to one another in a pattern of connectivity. (3) A propagation rule is used to aggregate input signals from the other neurons and once these input signals are aggregated, the neuron applies an activation rule to convert the weighted input with its previous level of activation into a new level of activation. (4) A transfer function maps the activation value of the neuron into an output signal which would be sent to other neurons. (5) Learning in a neural network involves a process of changing the pattern and strength of connectivity among neurons.

Transfer Function

Transfer function convert weighted sum for the output neurode (a neuron and a node with several inputs and one output) and it can control how the degree or the sum will lead to neuron activation. There are many transfer functions that could possibly be used for the NN such as the competitive transfer function (that provides null value except that for one significant output), hard-limit transfer function (for identifying and mapping inputs) and the log-sigmoid transfer function (mapping inputs to 0/1 interval). The transfer function should be differentiable and the typical function is sigmoid function. Apart from sigmoid function, Gaussian and Tanh are commonly adopted.

For the hidden layer shown in Figure 2, sigmoid function is used and the shape of the function is S-shaped which means the output can be affected at different degrees with the range of input. In addition, the change of output also depends on the value of the weights. The number of nodes in the hidden layer may incorporate different value of weights between the nodes, which in turn, result in different output values. The complicated shape of the NN is due to the combination of various layers of sigmoid functions.

For the output layer, it is required to have suitable functions so the output value approximates to the target values. Logistic function is commonly used for binary output (0/1) and for continuous-valued target with a bounded range. Tanh function can also used for continuous-valued targets by scale-up or scale down the put to the range of the target or vice versa.

Error Back Propagation

Back-propagation is a common method of training artificial neural networks how to perform a given task. It is a form of supervised learning method and is an implementation of the Delta rule. It allows NN calculate the desired output for any given input, especially for feed-forward networks. As mentioned, back-propagation typically requires that the activation function used by the artificial neurons is differentiable.

The error back propagation function operates as follow:

- Present a training sample to the neural network
- Compare the network's output to the desired output from that sample. Calculate the error in each output neuron
- Calculate the target output for each neuron with a scaling factor. Adjust the amount so as to achieve the desired output by considering local error.
- Adjust the weights of each neuron to lower the local error.
- Assign blame for the local error to neurons at the previous level, giving greater responsibility to neurons connected by stronger weights.
- Repeat the adjustment of weights and thereafter on the neurons at the previous level, using each of the blame as its error.

Learning Process

The learning process includes perceptron learning and delta rule which are shown in the following two sections.

Perceptron Learning

The first generation of neural network single layer network has one single layer of output node. The simple feed-forward network is that the input is fed directly to output via a series of weights. The neuron process the calculation by summing the product of the weight and the inputs. The threshold is usually set as "0". The neuron will be fired when the activation value is 1 while the neuron will not be fired when the deactivated value is -1. Perceptron is regarded as the network with neuron that has activation function named as neurons of linear threshold unit. Analysts or decision makers can set the threshold value between activated and deactivated states where any values can be set for activated or deactivated states. In general, a perceptron with output from 1 to -1 can perform training efficiently. A learning algorithm called delta rule, as discussed below, train the perceptrons. The errors are calculated and the weights are adjusted by comparing the calculated output and target output.

Delta Rule

Delta rule is applied in training the network for finding out the difference between the actual output and the desired output. Connection weights are adjusted in proportion to the product of error and scaling factor for global accuracy. Those processes are operated in an individual node. It is important to identify the input that will lead to the largest error and to provide corrective action to minimize such an error. On the other hand, the error would not contribute from the inactive node. Therefore, it is not useful to adjust the weight of inactive node. During the learning process, the final output layer is computed with a forward sweep. Taking account with the difference between desired output and calculated output, the previous layer can be modified by the derivative of the transfer function and delta rules is used to adjust the connection weight. The process is back-propagated to the previous layers and it ceases at the input layer.

CASE EXAMPLE

The design and training process is very important for the assessment of demand using NN. Brief account on various steps that is required for the experiments for demand forecasting are discussed here. The required data for the purpose are used form *US Census Bureau Retail Trade and Food Services: Retail Trade Report 2009* as the report provides retail sales data of different industries in the US. For the purpose of this study, sampled sales data from the electronics, automobile and departmental stores are used. The performance parameter used for the experiments in this report is the percentage error between the actual and forecasted value. The simplistic formula is as follows: $\frac{\text{Forcasted Value}}{\text{Actual Value}} \text{x}100\%$

The approach of using NN as a forecasting tool is summarized as follows:

1. Tabulation and Graphical Representation of Sample Data: The demand of electronic sales for each month is collected in the enterprise database. Figure 3 shows the graphical representation of the sample data.
2. Inputs and Target Values (training phase): This data extracted from the main database is arranged systematically into the Matlab NN toolbox. The method that would be used is somewhat similar to the Moving Averages method. The values are arranged in such a way that every two data produces an output of the subsequent data. For example, the values for the data for January (i.e. 6692) and February (i.e. 7348) should produce an output of 7465 as the Target shown in Figure 4. The procedure would repeat itself until we reach the data just before the last sales data.
3. Comparing forecasted demand and actual demand: After the network is trained which enable a network to handle noisy input data, comparison is done to test for its accuracy in forecasting demand. Two intermediate values just before the last value of the selected sample data are used as the input. The last value of the selected sample data would be the data which the NN would forecast. For this same example, the values of October (i.e. 5612) and November (i.e. 4611) would be used to predict an output forecasted value for the December (i.e., 4731). The forecasted data is compared with actual data for assessing prediction quality.
4. Compilation of results: Traditional forecasting methods used for comparison of forecast includes naïve, moving averages (m=2 and m=3), exponential smoothing (alpha=0.2), double exponential smoothing (DES-1 step, DES-2 step and DES-3 step), and triple exponential smoothing (1-step).

Figure 3. The table and graphical representation of the sample data

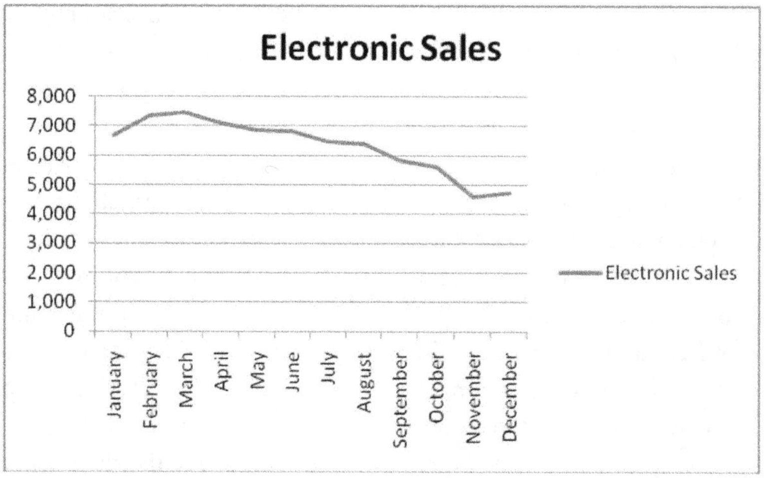

Figure 4. The arrangement of values into INPUT and TARGET dialog boxes

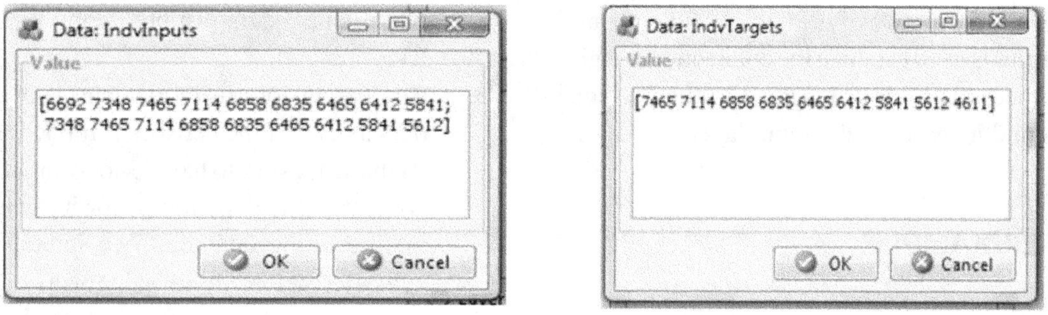

Data Selection and Data Reliability

The sales data from the electronics and departmental stores were used for this series of experiments. The demand trend obtained from the sample data for electronic industry was steady with a sharp rise during December and January of next year. This demand trend is expected because of the tendency for consumers to spend more on retail stores during the year end period, due to a number of reasons, including year-end bonuses and the occurrence of festive seasons. Similarly, the sample data for departmental stores also showed a cyclical pattern over the years. The trend however, is more erratic than that for the electronic industry. For this reason, the data provided for departmental store was also selected for analysis.

Selection of Neural Network Architecture

The selection of the Neural Network Architecture was largely determined by a series of organized tests on Mat lab NN toolbox. In general there are 6 aspects of the NN that is needed to be carefully selected.

1. **Network Type:** The type of network used for forecasting demand should be the most important issue. The feed forward back-propagation is the popular, effective, and easy-to-learn model for complex, multi-layered networks. Its greatest strength is in non-linear solutions to ill-defined problems. The typical back-propagation network has an input layer, an output layer, and at least one hidden layer. With an adequate amount of training, the network will mimic the function that it is demonstrating. Furthermore, with this type of NN, the network will learn to ignore any inputs that don't contribute to the output. Hence, the Feed Forward Back-propagation was chosen network type for the project experiments.
2. **Number of Hidden Layers:** There is no theoretical limit on the number of hidden layers for the Feed-forward back-propagation NN. Problems that require two hidden layers are rarely encountered as neural networks with two hidden layers can represent functions with virtually any kind of shape. There is currently no theoretical reason to use neural networks with any more than two hidden layers. In fact, studies have shown that for many practical problems, there is no reason to use any more than one hidden layer.
3. **Number of Neurons in each Hidden Layer:** It is important to find out the number of neuron in the hidden layers and the number of hinder so as to let the NN has good performance. Too few neurons in hidden layers will lead to under fitting while too many neurons in hidden layer will lead to over fitting. Therefore, the architecture should be designed properly to avoid under fitting and over-fitting. If the neurons are too few, signal cannot be detected in large amount of complex data and this may result in under-fitting. However, over fitting occurs when the number of neuron in hidden layer has high processing capacity than it is required for the training data set and the training data is not enough to train all the neurons in the hidden layer. On the other hand, the large number of neurons in the hinder layer may lead to longer computation time. Followins are the rule-of-thumb methods for determining the correct number of neurons to use in the hidden layers
    - The number of hidden neurons should be 2/3 the size of the input layer, plus the size of the output layer.
    - The number of hidden neurons should be between the size of the input layer and the size of the output layer.
    - The number of hidden neurons should be less than twice the size of the input layer.
4. **Adaptation Learning Function:** The Matlab NN toolbox™ allow for two types of learning functions for the Back-propagation network: LEARNGD and LEARNGDM. The function LEARNGD refers to the gradient descent weight and bias learning function. This function takes in several inputs to return an output matrix and a new learning state. The default value for LEARNGD's learning parameter is set at 0.01 learning rate. The function LEARNGDM, on the other hand, refers to gradient descent with momentum weight and bias learning function. It too takes in several inputs to return an output matrix and new learning state. LEARNGDM function makes use of two learning parameters. The default value is set at 0.01 learning rate and 0.9 momentum constant.
5. **Training Function:** Among the many training functions available in the Matlab toolbox, the default Levenberg-Marquardt (LM) was used. In mathematics terms, LM algorithm provides a numerical solution to the problem of minimizing a function, generally nonlinear, over a space of parameters of the function. The LM algorithm is suggested as the most efficient optimization algorithm

and is widely used for many applications as NNs. Therefore, LM algorithm was selected in the chapter as training function for the NN architecture.

6. **Pattern Recognition Network:** The default configuration on the Toolbox utilizes the Scaled Conjugate Gradient Algorithm as the pattern recognizing network. The Scaled Conjugate Gradient Algorithm divides the input and target vectors randomly as follows:
   60% - for **Training** purpose
   20% - for **Validation** purpose
   20% - for **Testing** purpose

The Neural Network Toolbox

The Neural Network Toolbox extends MATLAB with tools for designing, visualizing, simulating and implementing neural networks. Users can select the network paradigms supported with graphical user interfaces (GUIs) that enable user to design and manage the neural networks efficiently. The modular and extensible design of the toolbox also simplifies the creation of customized functions and networks (Beale et al., 2010). Figure 5 shows a three-layer neural network converted into Simulink blocks. Neural network simulation blocks for use in Simulink can be automatically generated with the appropriate simple commands.

Neural Network Toolbox enables users to identify and control of nonlinear systems. In addition, users can incorporate neural network predictive control blocks included in the toolbox into Simulink models. By changing the parameters of these blocks, the network's performance can be tailored accordingly as shown in Figure 6.

The Neural Network tool is a complex system which allows users to enter Input data, Target data, Input delay units and layer delay states. The results are displayed in Output window while the errors in Error window. The tool also allows users to easily change many parameters of the network. Further discussion of the NN architecture settings would be done in the subsequent section. Figure 7 shows the user interface for the NN tool for Mat lab version 2009.

NN Forecasting against Traditional Forecasting

To compare the accuracy of forecast between the NN tool and the traditional forecasting techniques, comparison of forecast values for a cyclical demand from data source name "Total Retail Sales 2008" is done and shown in the following figures.

The NN tool performed exceptionally well in this experiment. It was ranked first among the 8 other forecasting techniques used for this literature. The demand trend for this particular demand is

Figure 5. Simulation blocks for a sample neural network

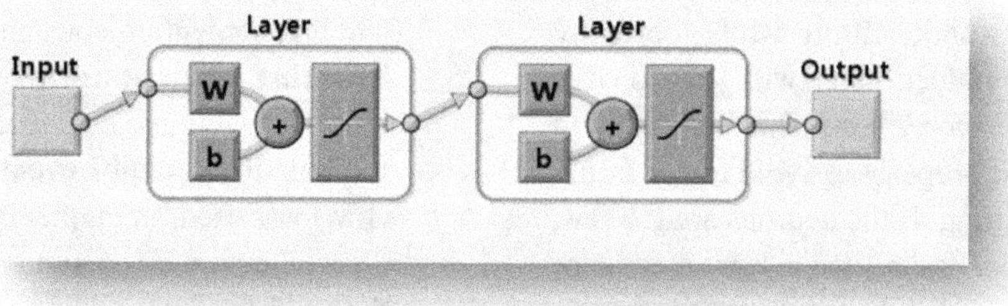

Figure 6. Result of the network training performance

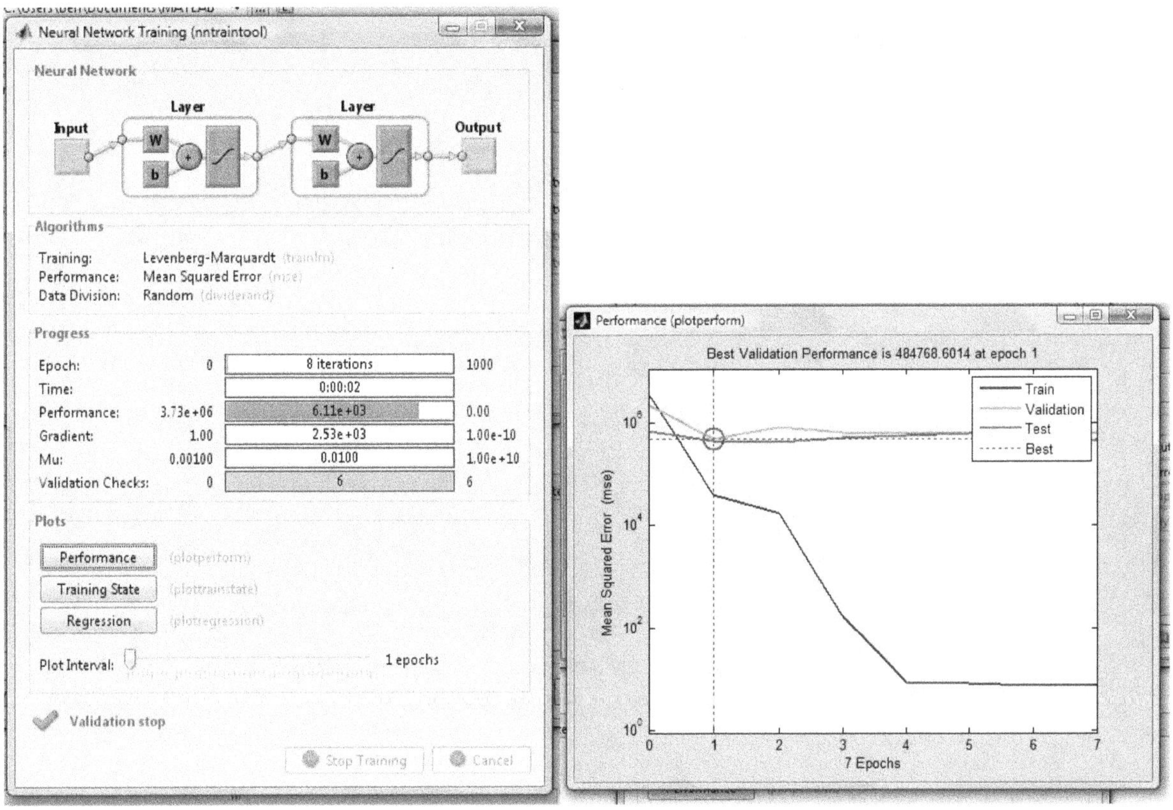

cyclical shown in Figure 8 and the demand data can be captured with RFID. Figure 9 shows comparison of forecast values for a Cyclical Demand.

The double exponential smoothing also performed relatively well with a percentage error of 0.77%. For this particular demand trend, there is only slight fluctuation in the demand all year round. As expected Naïve forecasting performed the poorest at a percentage error of nearly 13%. Figure 10 shows the Percentage Errors of the 8 traditional forecasting techniques versus the NN forecasting tool for the sample data: Total Retail Sales 2008

DISCUSSION

Neural networks are being used for knowledge analysis and management as they provide an efficient platform for recognizing the data pattern faster. As sales data change frequently over the supply chain, ability to capture such a pattern on a real time or near real time basis can help us to understand the consumer demand behaviour for implementing a real time demand response. The combination of RFID and NN proposed in this paper helps to extract the advantages of both real time data capture and demand analysis. The combination of RFID and NN not only helps in demand analysis but also helps in moving stock from one entity of the supply chain to another.

Figure 7. The user interface for the NN tool for Mat lab version 2009

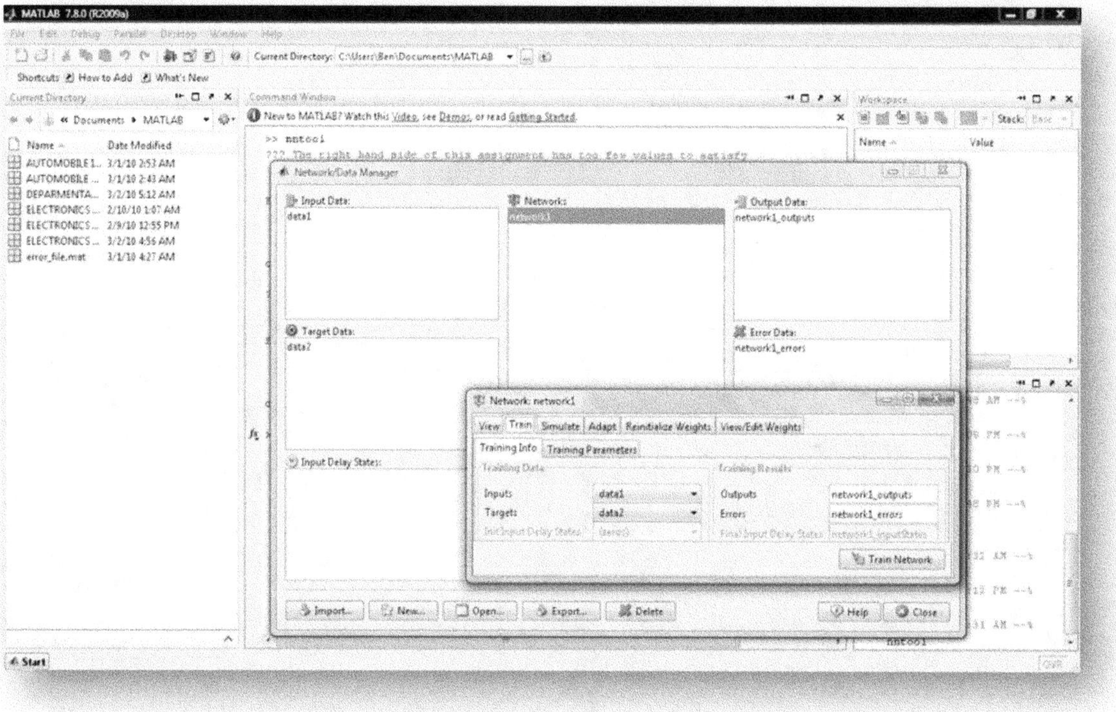

Figure 8. Demand of electronic product from total retail sales 2008

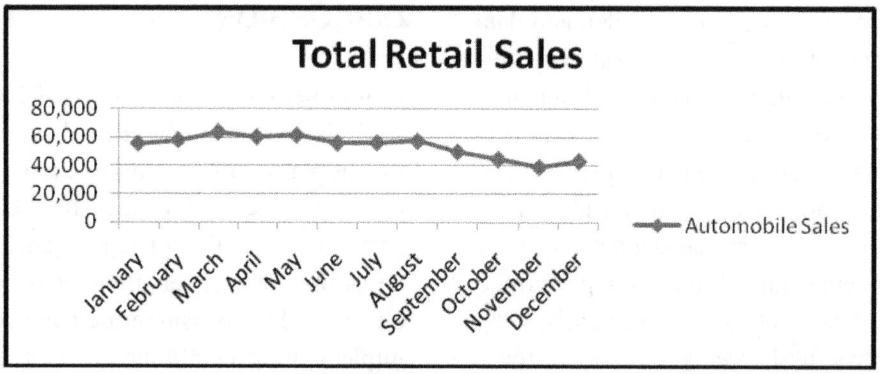

The analysis presented in this chapter compares traditional time series methods with NN and it shows that the forecast from NN was much closer to the actual sales. The value of the proposed method is in its ability to provide a faster and closer demand forecast in supply chain. However, the gap between the forecast and actual sales can increase significantly if sales pattern is erratic. Although the framework provides the visibility of inventory at each echelon, optimal redistribution or echelon inventory is another aspect that needs addition of optimization module with the framework. This will pose another challenge for a broad-based strategic decision making in the

Figure 9. Forecasting result of neural network vs. traditional forecasting method

Period	Actual	Naive	MA m=2	MA m=3	ES (Alpha=0.2)	DES 1-Step	DES 2-Step	DES 3-Step	TES 1-Step	Neural Network
1999	6,595									Training Data
2000	6,864	6594.83			6,595	6,595				Training Data
2001	6,700	6863.58	6729.21		6176.40	6659.33	6594.83			Training Data
2002	6,991	6699.58	6781.58	6719.33	6217.72	6679.74	6670.08	6,595		Training Data
2003	7,246	6991.42	6845.50	6851.53	6293.18	6766.90	6692.10	6680.83	6,595	Training Data
2004	7,901	7246.42	7118.92	6979.14	6340.34	6906.81	6791.73	6704.46	6726.168463	Training Data
2005	8,457	7900.92	7573.67	7379.58	6511.67	7189.41	6950.82	6816.56	6627.648919	Training Data
2006	9,023	8457.08	8179.00	7868.14	6731.34	7577.42	7273.18	6994.83	7130.165877	Training Data
2007	9,324	9022.58	8739.83	8460.19	7088.27	8058.74	7711.90	7356.95	7023.532076	Training Data
2008	9,257	9324.42	9173.50	8934.69	7428.22	8554.79	8251.02	7846.38	8235.264053	Training Data
2009	8,059	9256.75	9290.58	9201.25	7716.97	8966.17	8797.70	8443.31	8409.559844	9201.6253
% Error		14.86	15.28	14.18	4.24	11.26	9.17	4.77	4.35	14.18
										RANKED 6th!

Figure 10. The percentage errors of the 8 traditional forecasting techniques vs. the NN forecasting tool for the sample data: Total Retail Sales 2008

Total Retail									
Percentage Errors	Naïve	MA m=2	MA m=3	ES (Alpha=0.2)	DES 1-Step	DES 2-Step	DES 3-Step	TES 1-Step	Neural Network
Monthly Sales Data for 1999-2009	12.68	10.91	10.32	7.15	4.06	1.51	0.77	2.89	0.30

supply chain. To conclude, with fluctuations in world's economy, demand for goods would tend to be more discontinuous and random. The chapter provides the value that, the growing use of RFID and development in NN can help to overcome some of these challenges and the proposed approach could possibly revolutionize the way of demand forecasting for the future supply chain.

SOLUTIONS AND RECOMMENDATION FOR SUPPLY CHAIN INNOVATION

The development of new methodology in supply chain visibility and forecasting for commercial application is the main contention of this chapter. Such a combination of theory, technological (framework based approach) and proposed potential to use in a commercial application is mentioned as an innovative approach by Trott (2004) as well.

This chapter has introduced a theoretical concept of NN for demand forecasting and the technical invention of RFID automates the data capturing of product codes and data transfer, the inventory status is monitored and the data can show the flow from one process to another. The idea of process integration proposed in the framework here directly helps in elimination of waste and promotes lean and economically efficient supply chains. As enterprises realize the value added on the processes, it can further extends the exploitation to different echelon of the supply chain.

To enable the adoption of latest ubiquitous technology and artificial intelligence system, firms are required to make process reengineering so as to enhance the effectiveness of resource allocation. Process redesign and reengineering may improve the productivity in supply chain and reduce the operation cost. To achieve supply chain innovation, companies, are require wide scale collaboration with entities of supply chains. With the advent of data exchange technology, the demand pattern can be more visible for multiple echelon of supply chain and it can help to reduce the bullwhip effect. The flow of product can be trace and track with RFID so as to realize the inventory on hand and in-transit. With accurate and update data, logistics practitioners can analysis the data with NN. Data exploration and visualization can help top management to make decision judiciously for developing mutually beneficial business opportunities.

FUTURE RESEARCH DIRECTIONS

Although the framework proposed here takes a pragmatic view of supply chain situation, the integration of methodology with the existing information infrastructure can pose a real challenge. The research should therefore be focussed on the impact of the framework especially handling exponential data. Additional real time data cleaning and data mining methodologies might have to be researched for adoption in the proposed framework.

As demand is affected by marketing promotion, like quantity discounts or bundling, and sales strategy, like deferred payments or warranties, the demand prediction and response to such impromptu demand changes might strain the supply chain system. Therefore, further study on the impact of marketing strategy on demand should be conducted to understand the blitz situations on demand.

CONCLUSION

As product lifecycles are getting shorter and the need to improve the products in terms of quality, cost and delivery has increased, companies have to look for ways to make order fulfilment process as swift as possible so that opportunity cost for the lost sales and cost of obsolescence due to overstocking is minimized. Traditionally, preplanning and post planning were applied to understand the demand pattern and to act accordingly. In such a situation, the time lag for planning and execution would be rather large to be able to design an agile system for an effective supply chain. The proposition in this paper is that if real time data on sales, moving stocks and stationary stocks could be made visible, then it can help the companies to respond faster to demand changes so that the losses due to overstocking and understocking are minimized. This helps to increase the economic and delivery efficiency. As the cost of RFID is decreasing and RFID application is penetrating the markets, more companies can use this technology to store; update and access real time data for inventory and sales visibility of the supply chain. The contribution of this chapter is on the proposal to integrate RFID with NN to enhance inventory management through the adoption of NN methodology for integration with RFID technology. The proposed method will prompt applications and further research to enhance supply chain efficiency.

REFERENCES

Beale, M. H., Hagan, M. T., & Demuth, H. B. (2010). *MATLAB: Neural Network Toolbox 7 Users Guide: MathWork.* Retrieved 10 Nov 2010, http://www.mathworks.com/help /pdf_doc/nnet/nnet.pdf

Bowersox, D. J. Closs, David J. & Coooper, M. Bixby.(2010). Network design. In *Supply chain Logistics Management* (3 ed., pp. 302-326). New York: McGraw-Hill.

Cervellera, C., Wen, A., & Chen, V. C. P. (2007). Neural network and regression spline value function approximations for stochastic dynamic programming. *Computers & Operations Research, 34*(1), 70–90. doi:10.1016/j.cor.2005.02.043

Croston, J. (1972). Forecasting and stock control for intermittent demand. *Operational Research Quarterly, 23*, 289–303.

Doerr, K. H., Gates, W. R., & Mutty, J. E. (2006). A hybrid approach to the valuation of RFID/MEMS technology applied to ordnance inventory. *International Journal of Production Economics, 103*(2), 726–741. doi:10.1016/j.ijpe.2006.03.007

Eaves, A. H. C., & Kingsman, B. G. (2004). Forecasting for the ordering and stock-holding of spare parts. *The Journal of the Operational Research Society, 55*, 431–437. doi:10.1057/palgrave.jors.2601697

Gumus, A. T., & Guneri, A. F. (2009). A multi-echelon inventory management framework for stochastic and fuzzy supply chains. *Expert Systems with Applications, 36*(3, Part 1), 5565–5575. doi:10.1016/j.eswa.2008.06.082

Gutierrez, R. S., Solis, A. O., & Mukhopadhyay, S. (2008). Lumpy demand forecasting using neural networks. *International Journal of Production Economics, 111*(2), 409–420. doi:10.1016/j.ijpe.2007.01.007

Poon, T. C., Choy, K. L., Chow, H. K. H., Lau, H. C. W., Chan, F. T. S., & Ho, K. C. (2009). A RFID case-based logistics resource management system for managing order-picking operations in warehouses. *Expert Systems with Applications, 36*(4), 8277–8301. doi:10.1016/j.eswa.2008.10.011

Saygin, C. (2007). Adaptive inventory management using RFID data. *International Journal of Advanced Manufacturing Technology, 32*(9), 1045–1051. doi:10.1007/s00170-006-0405-x

Trott, P. (2004). *Innovation Management and New Product Development* (3rd ed.). London: Prentice Hall.

Tsai, T.-H., Lee, C.-K., & Wei, C.-H. (2009). Neural network based temporal feature models for short-term railway passenger demand forecasting. *Expert Systems with Applications*, *36*(2, Part 2), 3728–3736. doi:10.1016/j.eswa.2008.02.071

Uçkun, C. (2006). *Modeling and analysis of RFID technology within the supply chain*. Koc-University.

Uçkun, C., Karaesmen, F., & Savaş, S. (2008). Investment in improved inventory accuracy in a decentralized supply chain. *International Journal of Production Economics*, *113*(2), 546–566. doi:10.1016/j.ijpe.2007.10.012

Chapter 11
Intelligent Freight Transportation System:
The Effects on Transportation Operations Performance

Gunnar Stefansson
Chalmers University of Technology, Sweden & University of Iceland, Iceland

ABSTRACT

The purpose of this chapter is to identify the necessary components of Intelligent Freight Transportation System (IFTS) and analyze the potential effects on transport operations performances in all the three pillars of sustainability, namely the economics, environmental and social impacts. In order to achieve this objective, a literature study was conducted, looking for relevant up-to-date literature within the fields of transportation, logistics, and information and communication technology (ICT) and environmental impacts of freight transportation. In addition, two separate rounds of empirical studies were made. From literature, as well as from part of the empirical data collection, a requirement analysis was done to understand issues and problems in transport operations that can be addressed with more sophisticated information and communication systems. The second round of empirical data collection was done to identify potential solutions of the identified issues. Finally an analysis was made to understand the functionalities of possible IFTS solutions. Many effects were found that can contribute to increased performance of transport operations including automatic item identification, safety and security prevention, real-time navigation, traffic situation notification and carbon footprint registration.

DOI: 10.4018/978-1-60960-585-8.ch011

INTRODUCTION

In recent years, the transport industry has been exposed to various challenges related to different operational issues. Some of the major challenges have been to deal with the increased globalization in the two last decades of the 20th century involving longer supply chains and increased complexity; capacity limitations due to increased freight volume in the beginning of the 21st century for more or less all transportation modes; increased congestion on roads, rail tracks and in ports that reduces efficiency of the transportation infrastructure and increases travel time, fuel consumption and air pollution; more attention on risk issues as a consequence of the terrorist attack in September 2001; increases in cost of transportation operations due to increase in fuel price and taxes; increased requirements on environmental and social impacts; and now the sudden decrease in freight volume due to the wide spread economic recession in last years.

At the same time opportunities have surfaced with increased knowledge in the transportation industry that allows better design of transportation solutions and new technologies that opens up possibilities to face many of these challenges by increasing monitoring, control and planning capabilities. Without any doubt, ICT can create many utilities, but it does not come free of charge. A particular case is the transport operators who are currently subjects of significant pressure to incorporate new ICTs into their operations from vehicle suppliers, government as well as their customers directly or via their contracted logistics service providers (LSPs). Transport operators are often not able to employ or develop own technical competence, as they are generally very small companies operating at very small profit margins.

Although transport operators and logistics service providers are at the heart of the current development of distributed data capture, processing and communication in supply chains, most literature in the field of logistics and ICT takes the perspective of the transport buyers e.g., (Landers, 2000; Spekman, 2006), LSPs e.g., (Stefansson, 2006; Durr, 2003) or government e.g., (McKinnon, 2006; Tsai, 2006). Very few publications analyze effects of advanced ICT beyond operational benefits, i.e. not taking into consideration the three different sustainability impacts.

The purpose of this chapter is to identify the necessary components of intelligent freight transportation system and analyze the potential effects on transport operations performances in all the three pillars of sustainability, namely: economics, environmental and social impacts.

BACKGROUND

The relevant literature related to the transportation, logistics, information and communication technology (ICT), environmental impacts of freight transportation will be discussed in this section.

Information and Communication Systems

Different types of information systems (ISs) are available and used by industry today. These include proprietary legacy systems, off-the-shelf systems provided by major enterprise resource planning (ERP) system suppliers, and single user simple office applications (Stair *et al.*, 2008). Off-the shelf systems provide a certain degree of integration capability, not the least if the applications are from the same supplier. Although middleware is needed, the implementations are likely to have experience with these systems, so it makes integration easier even if the applications come from different suppliers, assimilar database approaches can be used in most instances (Narasimhan and Kim, 2001; Edwards *et al.*, 2001; Helo and Szekely, 2005). In addition to the variety of different systems that exists, communication systems are a vital enabler oforganisations' integration efforts. Large organisations use electronic data interchange

(EDI) applications to automate their data exchange (Stair *et al.*, 2008) while others, often smaller organisations, use less cutting-edge methods, such as phone and fax. Technology is emerging that allows Internet based approaches to follow the extensible markup language (XML) data exchange methods. This method allows organisations of all sizes to participate in a relatively inexpensive data exchange setup where one or more actor in a supply chain establishes an Extranet web page for others to use without needing any backbone IS (Stair *et al.*, 2008). This is of possible interest for mobile applications where data exchange partners can be on the move, i.e. carrying out transportation assignments or assignments in distribution centers (Wang, 2009).

Advanced information and communication technologies and information systems have been available for decades that aim at improving business operations for different industries. The number of implementations of software applications for the purpose of operational planning including warehouse operation, inventory planning, production planning, material requirement planning and similar has mounted in recent years and still are (Jonsson et al., 2007). The benefits of such software has been proven by showing more efficient operations, lower inventory levels, better customer service through better inventory availability, decreased fulfillment time, and increased delivery reliability (Vaugan, 2003; Ustundag, 2009).

The same cannot be said about information and communication technologies (ICT) and information systems (IS) aimed for the transportation industry including mobile solutions for truck operations. The availability of various solutions on the market is greater than ever but companies hesitate to invest in the applications and associated equipment. One of the reasons may be that managers do not fully believe that promised benefits will be realized and a reasonable return of investment achieved. This attitude is logical, not much evidence exists that show the benefits of the technologies and the systems within the carrier industry. Hence, spite the availability, most transportation companies in Europe and the USA operate without much ICT and IS support (Stefansson, 2007) for their operation of mobile units. At the best, technologies and systems have been implemented to track vehicles as customers′ requirements in many industries today demand tracking and tracing capabilities and even more advanced event management to secure delivery precision and reliability (Engström, 2005).

Intelligent Transportation Systems

In the relevant literature, Intelligent Transportation Systems (ITS) is mainly associated with transportation of people. However, in recent years a new field has developed where ITS is associated with freight transportation as well. According to Crainic et al. (2009), the term is used to refer to the latest technologies, infrastructure, and services as well as the operations, planning and control methods that are used for the transportation of passengers and freight. Different technologies such as communication technologies, computing hardware, positioning systems, telecommunications, vehicle technologies, electronics and sensors have been integrated and fitted to build the concept of the ITS. ITS is being used in different areas related to freight transportation, including: fleet management and control; controlling the position, condition, placement and identification of the freight and vehicles; and city logistics.

Components of Smart transportation management (STM)

For a system to be considered intelligent, certain capabilities of being adaptive is necessary. i.e. to be able to adjust some system parameters based on the current or coming situation. To be able to build up such capabilities, several system components need to be in place, sub-components and connections between. For this purpose Stefansson and Lumsden (2009) identified the three major components of what they call Smart Transportation Management system. These are: Smart Freight, Smart Vehicle, and Smart Infrastructure. All these three components need to be working together simultaneously and only then a certain level of intelligence can be achieved. Complete and effective integration of these components are requisition for IFTS to work effectively.

Smart Freight

Smart freight, smart goods, and intelligent goods are used interchangeably in the literature and are partly synonyms. According to Holmqvist and Stefansson (2007) "Smart Goods" is characterized by a higher level of sophistication than traditional goods identification". This means that instead of using former technologies such as barcodes (to identify an item), it is now possible to furnish the freight, either individual items or the load unit, with new smart technologies, simply by using a modified RFID tag as a carrier of data. Holmqvist& Stefansson (ibid) further introduces and explain several technologies that are combined with each other, among others; RFID, GSM/GRPS and Web Technology (Kärkkäinen, 2003; Ghribi, 2000). When these technologies are combined together and the benefits from each are used, potential to reach maximum performance along with higher data exchange is possible.

Smart freight by itself has many components and relies on many technologies to enable operation. The use of RFID in the supply chain has the potential to provide real benefits in inventory management, asset visibility, and interoperability in an end-to-end integrated environment (Vaughan, 2003; Ustundag, 2009; Prater et al., 2005; Twist, 2005; Jones et al., 2005). By using RFID and other identification technologies supply chain visibility can be obtained (Lapide, 2004).

Smart Vehicle

A major issue in the IFTS system framework is the so-called Smart Vehicle. For this work, mainly distribution vehicles or trucks are in focus where the truck cabin is equipped with a vehicle computer system and identification of goods is done as freight is loaded or unloaded off the vehicle. Communication of this information to central systems is not necessarily carried out, in many cases the information is only stored in the vehicle computer system and in other instances, the information is communicated to a central information system, especially if deviations occurs or a pre-notification of arrival is needed.

Considering that information about the freight is captured while loading the vehicle and that the manifest is downloaded to the in vehicle computer gives the following:

- the possibility to minimize the risk of loading/unloading the wrong freight
- helps to load/unload in the right sequence
- makes it more visible to know how many assets which are used in the system
- proof of Delivery and Proof of Acceptance can be sent to the host system in real time

With such a solution, a link is established between the vehicle and the goods, something that is not seen in many operational systems today although exception occurs.

Smart Infrastructure

To complete the Smart setup in the IFTS concept, the Smart infrastructure needs to be introduced. Smart Infrastructure can be divided into two parts; digital and physical. It is important to distinguish between these two, as they are so different in characteristics. Physical infrastructure is not only the roads and bridges vehicles travel on. It consists of:

- roads
- tunnels
- ferries
- ports
- warehouses
- terminals and similar asset based facilities.

Towards this physical mart infrastructure, Smart Vehicles can have double directed information through the ICT systems that are part of the digital infrastructure. The smart digital infrastructure retrieves, manipulates, stores and communicates data and information from the physical infrastructure to and from the Smart vehicles using different digital technologies such as sensors, cameras, databases, and positioning technologies. The Smart infrastructure enables information exchange about the goods, vehicles and infrastructure to be transmitted between participants as needed (Jones et al., 2005; Alvergren et al., 2007).

There is no common standard or definition of how a smart infrastructure should be designed or built. However, there have been efforts to describe how a possible smart infrastructure could be designed. Spieß et al. (2007) have focused on identifying and explaining the technical requirements of a holistic "Smart items infrastructure" (SII). With a service oriented architecture (SOA) they suggest a more flexible and adaptable infrastructure for ubiquitous computing. This SII cannot only fulfill current and future demands on Auto-ID, but also scale provide a foundation for the next generation smart items. This includes items with locally embedded units with processing power.

Decentralization is a very important part of the entire Smart infrastructure concept, and this also applies to the Smart items infrastructure. Some of the benefits according to include scalability, improved data accuracy and response times (ibid). Through the decentralization and implementation of more units with processing power the reliance on centralized databases and backend systems decreases, and overall system performance is assumed to increase and become more reliable.

Environmental Impacts of Transportation

The environmental impacts and its relation with green house gases (GHG) is known and a growing global concern. The contemporary lifestyle of our societies is largely supported by multitude of transportation activities to supply demands of raw material and finished products to awaiting customers. The amount of GHG emissions caused by transportation operations globally is 14% of the total emissions (Stern, 2007). Compared to passenger transportation, freight transportation is rapidly increasing and does not show any tendency of decreasing. Also, freight transportation produce substantially more GHG of the total vehicle emissions compared to passenger transportation (Taniguchi, 2001). In the EU no less than 44% of the freight is transported by vehicles on roads, compared to 10% by rail, 4% by inland water and 42% by sea (EC 2006). Between 1990 and 2004 the transport sector increased its emissions by 28% (EC, 2006). At the same time, the European manufacturing industry decreased their emissions by 18%. Decreasing the emissions generated by transportation operations will be necessary to be able to reach long-term goals for reducing GHG both globally and in the EU. Requirements of estimating the impacts of transportation in form of carbon emissions have increased and it has become more common to find demand of estimation of products' carbon footprint (Stern, 2007), even if not fully realized in many industries.

The discussion in recent years on sustainability related to the transportation industry has been to a great extent focusing only on the environmental impacts, or the so called "green" issues, without taking into consideration other impacts such as operational, economical or social issues. However, the economical sustainability is as well very important. Only with long run economical sustainability, companies can take actions to lower environmental impacts and fulfill their social responsibility.

METHODOLOGY

The methodology used in this study is based on three main steps. First, a literature study was conducted, looking for relevant up-to-date literature within the fields of transportation, logistics, information and communication technology (ICT) and environmental impacts of freight transportation. In addition, two separate rounds of empirical studies were made. The first round of interviews was made to confirm findings from literature and eventually add new issues do not discovered previously. The purpose was to make a requirement analysis and to understand issues and problems in transport operations that can be addressed with more sophisticated information and communication systems. The second round of empirical data collection was done to identify potential solutions of the identified issues.

The first round of empirical data was collected through interviews with users of logistics and transportation services followed up with operators of logistics and transportation activities such as third party logistics service providers and transportation operators. The users are represented by logistics managers from large Swedish producers and retailers. In total, interviews were made in five different companies including eight different respondents.

Second round of interviews were made with vehicle producers, information systems and technology providers and finally infrastructure providers. The design of the study was inspired by the smart transportation management concept including the three different components; smart freight, smart vehicles and smart infrastructure. A system approach has been applied where not only was it important to understand the system components but also the relations between the components. To be able to do so, the components were studied in their natural relation to each other and not only in their causal relations (Arbnor, 1997). The study on smart freight included mainly secondary data as a lot of evidence can be found in the literature on automatic identification, RFID and decentralization of information. For the smart vehicle study, both truck manufacturer and suppliers of advanced transportation management systems were studied. The systems embedded in trucks today were considered and the providers of such system, including one of the major truck manufacturers in Sweden were included in the study. The vehicle information system providers were studied and the information systems they supply reviewed. This included a major Swedish provider of transport management and fleet management systems. Finally, the study of the smart infrastructure included experts in road administration as well as providers of system and technologies within the infrastructure area.

The interviews that have been carried out were in all instances based on semi structured interview template that was adapted to the two rounds and the different respondents. In addition, documentation was reviewed and when possible, direct observation done to accomplish a data triangulation (Yin 1994). The reason for choosing the semi-structured configuration was to increase the coherence between the interviews and make a within-case analysis easier (Eisenhardt 1989).

MAIN FINDINGS

To structure the effect analysis the fundamental components of STM; Smart Goods, Smart Vehicle and Smart Infrastructure have been poised against the areas of transport performance operation in this work. The structure was then used when looking for evidence of impacts from the literature as well as during the interviews with the experts.

Evidence from the literature was mainly found concerning transport operations and economics related to the three components of the STM setup. Much is found on identification technology and the benefits of quicker and more reliable identification that relates to Smart Goods. By automating time-consuming activities and removing the human factor, previously involved costs are reduced and errors are less likely to occur. In a supply chain perspective this leads to transparency and visibility throughout the chain and production (Lee &Özer, 2007; Boushka et al, 2002). With the use of RFID tags with sensors perishable or temperature sensitive freight can be monitored during the transport. Abusive and/or fluctuating temperature accelerates rapid growth of pathogens and specific spoilage organisms (Jol et al. 2005; Raab et al. 2008), causing safety problems and economic losses.

Advanced identification also allows transportation companies to monitor and adjust their operations to ensure that the goods is not damaged or spoiled in transit and further reduce claims for replacements. In relation to Smart vehicle, evidence of the need for track and trace applications are reported and the functions analyzed. The Smart freight is therefore preferably equipped with an automatic identification mechanism (such as RFID tag) that allows considerable amount of data to be stored and retrieved. In addition, read/write technology has to be in place and collected data needs to be submitted to a backbone system that is interoperable with the operators´ ERP systems. In addition, an enabler with embedded logic needs to be used to interpret the data and thereby support local decisions.

Much less is found in the literature on environmental impacts related to the different components of STM - more is found on general issues to decrease the impacts such as on fossil CO2 emissions including Eco driving, technology developments and similar.

A function that was mentioned by all respondents is a "Location" function. That function was considered to be very useful for many reasons. Some mentioned are to enable tracking of vehicles and thereby goods during logistics operations. Furthermore, the possible effects of having access to "Location" information would be to use it for road charging purposes and thereby having potential effects on the environment. For this function, technology was discussed but for the purpose of this research it was clearly stated that the technology is not relevant – the function of being able to locate a vehicle was in focus.

Related to the "Location" function was the "Carbon footprint" function mentioned. The possibility to track goods movements and then declare the carbon footprint was considered to be a future requirement and the location information together with effective tracking systems to enable vehicle – goods relations necessary for future environmental considerations.

Another function that was frequently mentioned was the "Routing" function. Having possibility to make more dynamic routing is considered positive and a clear overlap came across between traffic information and routing capabilities, as the function of "Routing" should take into consideration the traffic situation and even road situation. Together with this function, even a discussion of forecasting was mentioned so that routing could be done based on predicted traffic situation.

Still another function related to the previous "Routing" function was mentioned and that was goods related routing meaning that depending on the goods being moved, the routing mechanism would choose the most appropriated road or even based on limitations found such as forbidden dangerous goods movements in tunnels, etc.

A clear overlap between Smart vehicle and Smart infrastructure was experienced. Example is the "Routing" function, is it a part of the Smart vehicle only or does it include the Smart infrastructure. A common understanding is that it is part of the Smart vehicle as the hardware and software is part of the Smart vehicle capabilities but a dynamic routing cannot be done without an interaction towards the Smart infrastructure giving data on road and traffic situations, enforced limitations such as weight limitations, road work, etc.

When discussing environmental impacts "Routing" came again up as a function and furthermore a connection to forecasts of road situations in front of the vehicle in some hours. This function would make it possible to slow down the truck to prevent finding it in a congestion situation as it would anyway be delayed was mentioned as an alternative and a function that would safe fuel.

Summary of the first round of interviews are found in Table 1.

Table 1 shows the identified possible when IFTS is available and the necessary functions that are needed with the Smart freight and Smart vehicle areas to fully enable Smart infrastructure functionality. Many more functions are found within the Smart freight and Smart vehicle areas, but they are not in focus for this research.

SOLUTIONS AND RECOMMENDATIONS FOR SUPPLY CHAIN INNOVATION

The main solutions identified from this study is that the concept of ITS, that is mainly established in the area of person transport and it needs to be applied to freight transportation where it may labeled as intelligent Freight Transport System (IFTS). IFTS setups can be defined in different ways. In most instances it is related to advanced ICT components that allow more sophisticated ways of planning, monitoring and controlling transportation operations.

The underlying concept is theinnovative Smart Transportation Management concept has been developed out of several scientific contributions that have been published in recent years. The main contributions are Smart Freight concept given by Lumsden and Stefansson (2007) where the main

Table 1. Summary of the identified IFTS effects

Area	Smart freight	Smart Vehicle	Smart Infrastructure
Transport operation	Faster identification Logic for handling Delivery reliability	Load information Vehicle Routing Fleet management Real time communication Rest planning &Parking assistance	Location information Road situation Traffic situation Dynamic routing Infrastructure charging Two way communication
Environmental	Delivery reliability	Speed scheduling Variable speed Driving behavior Vehicle routing Carbon footprint registration	Vehicle routing Congestion prevention Carbon footprint registration
Safety/Security*	Dangerous goods Theft prevention	Theft prevention Collision prevention, Driver permission (ID)	GeoFencing Infrastructure access Saefty management Security management

characteristic of the decentralized concept is described. The concept is based on the assumption that the freight carries along considerable amount of data, preferable in a data tag. The participants in the supply chain have access to the relevant information by retrieving this data and use as needed. The introduction of this system has potential to reduce the actual mismatch between material and information flow. One of the advantages to move to a decentralized system is that many vertical transactions between a central system and the moving object will be avoided and this will contribute to the synchronization of material and information flow.

One of the major issues in the decentralized information and decision concept is that a local unit is supporting decision making and for that a unit with embedded logic needs to be provided. This has been called "enabler" in Stefansson and Lumsden publications (e.g. Lumsden and Stefansson, 2007). The role of the enabler is to collect data from RFID tags and interpret in a correct manner, store or send to the right database. This enabler can be situated in facilities such as warehouses or in mobile units such as trucks, forklifts, etc. An example of such application is shown in Figure 1 developed by Stefansson and Woxenius (2007). It describes the benefits of using all the three components of Smart transportation management, Smart goods, Smart vehicle, and Smart Infrastructure, integrated in an innovative way to constitute Intelligent Freight Transportation System.

Stefansson and Woxenius (ibid) divide the benefits of advanced information and communication systems into three categories; managing vehicles and driver, managing the freight flow and customer contacts, and managing authority contact.

The major characteristics of managing the vehicle and driver are: reducing fuel consumption and maintenance costs, better overview of driving hours, access information about road congestion or other relevant information about the traffic situation (such as delays reduction). All of these benefits affects the three impacts areas of sustainability; economics, environmental and social impacts.

The major characteristics of freight flow and customer contacts are: reduce waiting time by providing customers with notification of impending delivery, reduce delivery and invoicing errors, reduce delivery mistake, improved customer

Figure 1. Activities benefiting from IFTS support (Stefansson & Woxenius, 2007)

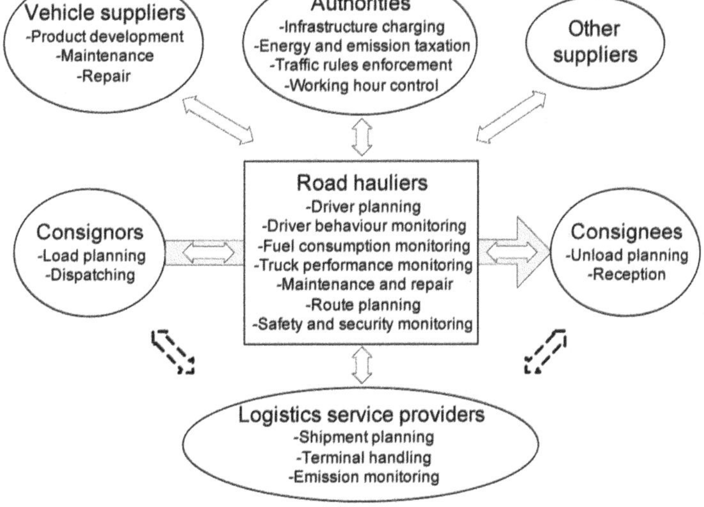

service through "real time" visibility of arrival and departure and identification of problems en route. These identified benefits affect mainly the economics and environmental impacts.

The major characteristics of managing authority contacts are reduced paperwork and administration costs, improved driving hour reporting and improved charging feasibility and common platform for charging policy. The identified benefits are strongly associated with economical impacts but also social as driving hours regulation can prevent accidents and improve drivers employment situation.

For the purpose of meeting some of the challenges and demands from authorities and society, the production and transportation industry needs to become more innovative. This does not only mean changes in business strategies, but also changes in supply chain and transportation systems design and in addition, implementation of more advanced technology. This technology should ensure increase in operational efficiency, lower environmental impacts and raise social responsibility.

FUTURE RESEARCH DIRECTIONS

This chapter has focused on intelligent freight transportation system and the integrated components that are needed to enable such systems. The identified components all exists and proofs can be found of their effects in many operational situations. Freight is equipment with tags that enables the smart functionality as discussed. Vehicles of all different transportation modes have embedded smartness by utilizing on-board information and communication systems. Finally the infrastructure is getting more advanced; the physical one by utilization of sensors, cameras and tag reading mechanism, and the digital infrastructure is being build in an ever increasing pace by introducing faster communication means, more advanced location services, satellite services, etc.

However, we do not see many large-scale solutions using all the three major components; smart freight, smart vehicle, and smart infrastructure in a IFTS setup. In most instances, the applied solutions are limited to one or two of the components, i.e. a warehouse operator using smart goods and smart infrastructure in the warehouse, transportation company using smart vehicle and smart infrastructure for fleet management purposes.

The logistics and transportation industry is obviously struggling with implementation problems and from the literature, as well as the interviews made, it can be understood that the reluctance relies on mainly two reasons; cost is too high and the operators doubt of reaping the benefits in a reasonable time. Other issues including standardization issues, mental resistance and more have as well been identified.

There is a need to quantify the various effects of the IFTS as it is important for the industry to understand the costs, the possible savings, and any implications including benefits and drawbacks. This research needs to focus on one or more of the three pillars of sustainability as the effects can be very different, possible operational savings can be realized by implementing IFTS, at the same time the systems and implementation costs can be substantial. The short-term as well as the long-term total effects need to be understood including the cost and revenue issues.

Further research within the area is needed and new studies including more interviews with new respondents is required for further insights into the functions and moreover the effects these functions result in for the transportation industry. Furthermore, the effects are seldom only beneficiary for one single stakeholder, i.e. decreased fuel consumption is not only benefit transport operators, but also society as it reduces environmental impacts. Further research will therefore also include wider range of stakeholders in the supply chain.

CONCLUSION

The purpose of this chapter is to identify the necessary components of Intelligent Freight Transportation System (IFTS) and analyze the potential effects on transport operations performances in all the three pillars of sustainability, namely the economics, environmental and social impacts. To prepare it, a literature study was conducted to search for relevant up-to-date literature within the fields and data was collected by interviewing representatives from companies and organizations that are considered experts in various aspects of transportation operations. The approach was to identify the functionality of Smart Infrastructure for transport operations and analyze the main impacts on transport operations and the environment.

The work has identified that IFTS needs to build on the three components of Smart Transportation Management components; Smart goods, Smart Vehicle, and Smart infrastructure. In addition, by integrating these components and introduce new information services, both by industry and authorities, an innovative IFTS system can be accomplished with many effects on transportation operations.

Some of the major effects of IFTS on transport operations can to be very valuable for many areas of transport operations such as managing the vehicle and the driver in more efficient way and by that reducing fuel consumption and maintenance costs, better overview of driving hours, access information about traffic situation, etc. The effects on freight flow and customer contacts are mainly to reduce waiting time, reduce delivery mistake, reduce invoicing errors, improved customer service, and more. Still another major effect is in managing authority contacts where administration costs can be reduced, driving hour reporting improved and charging feasibility. Most of the identified effects are strongly associated with all the three impact areas of sustainability; economics, environmental and social impacts, even though the degree of benefits differ.

REFERENCES

Arbnor, I., & Bjerke, B. (1997). *Methodology for creating business knowledge*. London: Sage Publications Ltd.

Dürr, E., & Giannopoulos, G. A. (2003). SITS: a system for uniform intermodal freight transport information exchange. *International Journal of Transport Management*, *1*(3), 175–186. doi:10.1016/j.ijtm.2004.01.003

Eisenhardt, K. M. (1989). Building theories from case study research. *Academy of Management Review*, *14*(4), 532–550.

Engström P. et al., (2005). *Stena Gotthard AB e-Effektivare logistik med hjälp av IT-system-*. BlekingeTekniskaHögskola (in Swedish).

European Commission. (2006). *Energy and Transport in Figures Statistical Pocketbook 2006*. Luxembourg: Directorate-General for Energy and Transport.

European Commission. (2007). *Panorama of transport*. Luxembourg.

Ghribi, B., & Logrippo, L. (2000). Understanding GPRS: The GSM Packet Radio Service. *Computer Networks*, *34*, 763–779. doi:10.1016/S1389-1286(00)00127-4

Holmqvist, M., & Stefansson, G. (2007). Mobile RFID a case from Volvo on innovation in SCM. *Journal of Business Logistics*, *27*(2), 251–272. doi:10.1002/j.2158-1592.2006.tb00225.x

Jones, P., Clarke-Hill, C., Hillier, D., & Comfort, D. (2005). The benefits, challenges and impacts of radio frequency identification technology (RFID) for retailers in the UK. *Marketing Intelligence & Planning*, *23*(4), 395–402. doi:10.1108/02634500510603492

Jonsson, P., Kjellsdotter, L., & Rudberg, M. (2007). Applying advanced planning systems for supply chain planning: Three case studies. *International Journal of Physical Distribution and Logistics Management, 37*(10), 816–834. doi:10.1108/09600030710848932

Kärkkäinen, M., Fräamling, K., & Ala-Risku, T. (2003). *Integrating material and information flows using a distributed peer-to-peer information system. Department Of Industrial Engineering and Management*. Helsinki: Helsinki University of Technology.

Landers, T. L., Cole, M. H., Walker, B., & Kirk, R. W. (2000). The virtual warehousing concept. *Transportation Research Part E, Logistics and Transportation Review, 36*(2), 115–126. doi:10.1016/S1366-5545(99)00024-1

Lapide, L. (2004). RFID: "What's in it for the forecaster? *The Journal of Business Forecasting Methods & Systems, 23*(2), 16–19.

Lumsden, K., & Stefansson, G. (2007). Smart Freight to Enhance Control of Supply Chains. *International Journal of Logistics Systems Management, 3*(3), 315–329. doi:10.1504/IJLSM.2007.012996

McKinnon, A. C. (2006). Government plans for lorry road-user charging in the UK: a critique and an alternative. *Transport Policy, 13*(3), 204–216. doi:10.1016/j.tranpol.2005.09.002

Miller, J. (2008). *Vehicle-to-Vehicle-to-Infrastructure (V2V2I) Intelligent Transportation System Architecture*. University of Alaska.

Prater, E., Frazier, G. V., & Reyes, P. M. (2005). Future impacts of RFID on e-supply chains in grocery retailing. *Supply Chain Management: An International Journal, 10*(2), 134–142. doi:10.1108/13598540510589205

Spekman, R. E., & Sweeney, P. J. II. (2006). RFID: from concept to implementation. *International Journal of Physical Distribution and Logistics Management, 36*(10), 736–754. doi:10.1108/09600030610714571

Spieß et al, (2007). Going beyond Auto-ID: a service-oriented smart items infrastructure. *Journal of Enterprise Information Management, 20* (3), Emerald Publishing Group Limited.

Stefansson, G. (2006). Collaborative Logistics Management. *International Journal of Physical Distribution and Logistics Management, 36*(2), 76–92. doi:10.1108/09600030610656413

Stefansson, G., & Lumsden, K. (2009). Performance Issues of Smart Transportation Management. *International Journal of Productivity and Performance Management, 58*(1), 55–70. doi:10.1108/17410400910921083

Stefansson, G., & Sternberg, H. (2007). Smart Logistics Systems – SLS. *The 11th WCTR– World Conference on Transport Research,* UC Berkeley, 24-28 June 2007.

Stefansson, G., & Woxenius, J. (2007).The Concept of Smart Freight Transport Systems – the road haulier's perspective. *Proceedings of the 19th NOFOMA Conference, Reykjavik, 7-8 June 2007*

Stern, N. (2007). *The Economics of Climate Change: The Stern Review*. New York: Cambridge University Press.

Taniguchi, (2001). *City Logistics - Network modelling and Intelligent Transport Systems*. Pergamon

Tsai, M. C. (2006). Constructing a logistics tracking system for preventing smuggling risk of transit containers. *Transportation Research Part A, Policy and Practice, 40*(6), 526–536. doi:10.1016/j.tra.2005.11.001

Twist, D. C. (2005). The impact of radio frequency identification on supply chain facilities. *Journal of Facilities Management*, *3*(3), 226–239. doi:10.1108/14725960510808491

Ustundag, A., & Tanyas, M. (2009). The impacts of Radio Frequency Identification (RFID) technology on supply chain costs. *Transportation Research Part E, Logistics and Transportation Review*, *45*(1), 29–38. doi:10.1016/j.tre.2008.09.001

Vaughan J. (2003). DoD, Wal- Mart push RFID. *Applications Development Trends magazine*, 11/19/2003.

Yin, R. K. (1994). *Case study research: design and methods*. Thousand Oaks, CA: Sage Publications Inc.

Section 3
Sustainability Innovation

Chapter 12
Improving the Sustainability of Road Freight Transport by Relaxing Truck Size and Weight Restrictions

Alan McKinnon
Heriot-Watt University, UK

ABSTRACT

Increasing legal limits on the size and weight of trucks allows companies to achieve a higher degree of load consolidation. This reduces the total number of vehicle-kilometres required to distribute a given quantity of goods, saving money and reducing environmental impacts. Proposals to legalise longer and heavier vehicles, (LHVs) have, nevertheless, generated intense debate, particularly in Europe where they are strongly resisted by railway and environmental organisations. This chapter reviews recent studies on this subject, presents an analytical framework and focuses on three critical issues: the extent to which loads can be consolidated in LHVs, their effect on the freight modal split and the possibility that the resulting reduction in road freight costs will stimulate additional traffic growth. Most of the recent studies support the development of LHVs, particularly those based on actual experience of their use in countries such as Australia, Sweden and the United States.

DOI: 10.4018/978-1-60960-585-8.ch012

INTRODUCTION

Consolidating loads in larger and heavier vehicles is one of most effective ways of improving the efficiency of road freight transport and reducing its impact on the environment. Governments around the world have therefore been under pressure from industry to relax truck size and weight restrictions and thereby reduce the number of trips required to move a given quantity of freight. There are, nevertheless, physical limits to the size and weight of trucks that be can accommodated within the existing road infrastructure and representatives of competing transport modes have strongly opposed the introduction of larger and heavier vehicles. This has made the maximum weight and dimensions of trucks one of the most controversial public policy issues to arise in the field of logistics for many years. The contradictory positions on this issue are well illustrated by the European Shippers Council (2007) and German Environment Ministry (Umwelt Bundes Amt, 2007). The former argued that LHVs will '*reduce fuel consumption and pollution, lower transport costs, contribute towards an increase in the available capacity utilisation of the primary road network, reduce the number of lorry trips per annum, and increase the competitiveness and sustainability of EU industry*'. The latter asserts that '*megatrucks do not contribute towards sustainable development of freight transport. Their use relieves neither the environment nor road infrastructure.*'

This chapter reviews the evidence that has accumulated on this issue from both desk-based studies and operational experience in countries where larger and heavier trucks are allowed to operate. It examines the problems that researchers experience when trying to assess the net effects of allowing these vehicles onto the road. The discussion relates mainly to EU countries though makes reference to the use of these trucks in other parts of the world. It focuses on operational, economic and environmental issues. For detailed discussion of the implications for road safety and transport infrastructure readers should consult Knight et al (2008), TML et al (2008) and Leduc (2009).

This chapter is mainly concerned with a combined relaxation of vehicle size and weight restrictions in trucks that are both longer and heavier. It is, of course, possible for length and weight limits to be increased independently. In the UK in 2001, for example, the government raised the maximum weight of an articulated lorry (running on six axles) from 41 to 44 tonnes. It is currently considering an extension to the length limit within current weight restrictions. To maximise the economic and environmental benefit of relaxing legal limits on truck capacity, however, it is often desirable to increase weight and size limits simultaneously.

The semantics of truck enlargement also requires some comment at the outset. Various terms have been used to describe bigger trucks. Some, such as 'megatruck', 'monster truck' and 'juggernaut', tend to be used by opponents of these vehicles and are fairly emotive. Others such as 'high productivity vehicle', 'high capacity vehicle', 'super truck' or 'load efficient vehicle' have much more positive connotations. Other expressions, such as the Australian 'road train', the US 'long combination vehicle' (LCV), the German 'gigaliner', European 'Eurocombi' and the British 'longer and heavier vehicle' (LHV) simply describe the vehicles. The last of these terms is now in common use and will be adopted in this chapter.

A BRIEF HISTORY OF LHVS IN EUROPE

LHVs with lengths in excess of 20 metres and gross weights of over 50 tonnes have been operating in Scandinavia for over 20 years. Sweden, for example, set a 24 metre length limit for trucks in 1968 and allowed them to run at weights up to

51.4 tonnes in 1974 (Vierth, 2008). At the time of Sweden and Finland's accession to the EU in 1996, special provision had to be made to allow these countries to continue to operate these vehicles which were much bigger and heavier than those permitted elsewhere in Europe. An EU Directive (96/53) was approved which granted all EU member states the right to operate longer vehicles so long as they conformed to the standard modular dimensions in existence at that time. This has since become known as the European Modular System (EMS). The main objectives of the directive were to avoid a proliferation of vehicle dimensions and promote the harmonisation of modules that could be transferred between modes. Although the 96/53 Directive allowed member states other than Sweden and Finland to legalise LHVs for use within their national borders, no country did so until recently.

Outside Scandinavia, the demand from hauliers and their clients for LHVs has arguably been greatest in the Netherlands. The Dutch government has responded by permitting two trials of LHVs, between 1999 and 2003 and 2004 and 2006. The results of the more recent trial were considered sufficiently positive to justify the general legalisation of LHVs in the Netherlands up to 25.25 metres long with maximum gross weights of 60 tonnes from 2008. Following a more limited trial in several German states (or 'lander') between 2006 and 2007, the federal government rejected the case for allowing LHVs to operate on German roads, ostensibly on safety grounds, though it is reckoned that this decision was also strongly influenced by plans to privatise half the country's rail system. A limited trial of LHVs was launched in Denmark in 2008. Following a desk-based study of seven regulatory options for LHVs published in 2008 (Knight et al, 2008), the UK government decided that only one option might be permissible involving the use of a semi-trailer 2 metres longer than the current maximum length of 13.5 metres. At the time of writing the government has still to make its final decision on this issue. In response to the growth of interest in LHVs at the national level, the European Commission has funded three studies of LHVs between 2007 and 2010 by TML et al (2008), Christidis and Leduc (2009) and one currently underway.

Despite all this research, wide consultation on the subject and the inclusion of changes in truck size and weight regulations in the EU's Logistics Action Plan (European Commission, 2007), no decisions have yet been made on modifications to the 96/53 Directive which would alter the maximum size and weight of trucks making international journeys across the continent. In the meantime, the Joint Transport Research Centre of the OECD and International Transport Forum have published the results of a global review of opportunities to '*move freight in better trucks,*' which is largely concerned with increases in vehicle carrying capacity (OECD / ITF, 2010).

Before examining the conclusions of these various studies it is important to identify the factors influencing public policy on truck size and weight and present an analytical framework within which the relationship between these factors can be mapped.

ANALYTICAL FRAMEWORK

Figure 1 shows the key elements in a cost and benefit analysis of an increase in truck carrying capacity. At its centre is the consolidation of loads in fewer vehicles, the source of all LHV benefits. This yields two streams of benefits: (i) a reduction in vehicle operating costs which are internalised by the carrier and / or shipper and (ii) a reduction in lorry traffic levels which helps to alleviate environmental impacts and congestion, cutting the external costs of road transport borne by the community at large. Against these benefits must be set a series of four potentially offsetting factors:

Figure 1. Inter-relationships in the cost-benefit analysis of LHVs

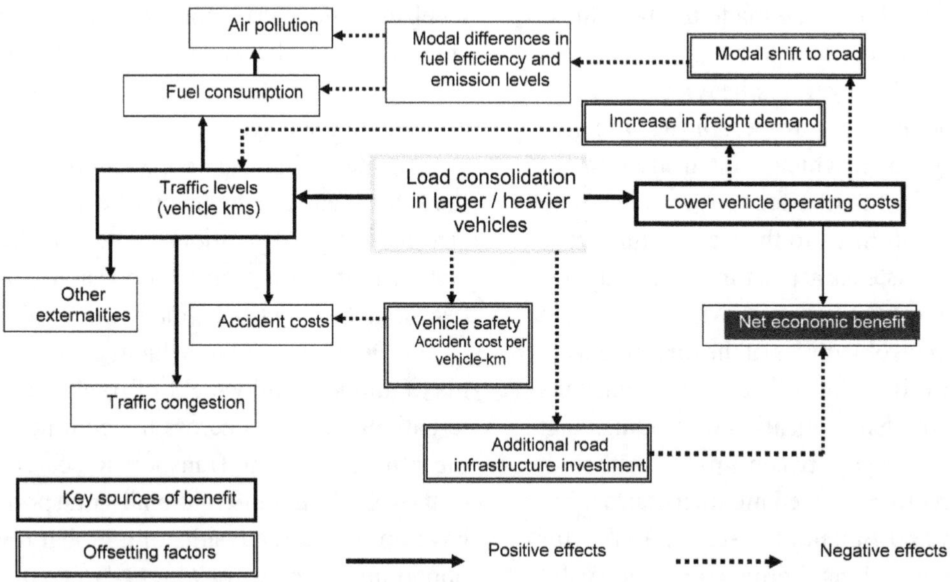

1. Possible shift of freight from less-environmentally-damaging modes (mainly rail and waterborne services) to LHVs to take advantage of the lower road freight costs they offer. As LHVs have higher external costs per tonne-km than these alternative modes, the environmental benefits from load consolidation must be scaled-down accordingly.
2. Possible generation of new freight traffic if companies respond to the reduction in freight costs by making their logistics operations more transport-intensive, by, for example, sourcing products from more distant suppliers or centralising their inventory. This can offset some of the vehicle-km, fuel and emission savings accruing from load consolidation
3. Possible increase in the severity of accidents as a result of the greater weight and size of LHVs. Accident costs per vehicle-km may therefore rise, though there will be an offsetting reduction in total vehicle-kms. Operational experience and simulation modelling, nevertheless, suggests the LHVs have a positive effect on safety. The OECD / ITF (2010) review concludes that '*the various studies and experiences from recent years agree that a transfer of goods to trucks with higher cargo capacity should result in a reduction in casualties per unit of goods moved*' (p.23).
4. Possible increase in expenditure on road infrastructure to accommodate LHVs. As it is normally assumed that maximum axle weights will remain unchanged and that any additional payload weight will be spread across more axles, 'wear and tear' on the road pavement is unlikely to increase. On the contrary, the reduction in truck-kms will be likely to reduce maintenance costs. The extra infrastructural cost is likely to be capital expenditure on modifications to road layouts and bridge strengthening.

The solid black lines in the diagram represent the positive / beneficial effects of LHVs while the broken lines show the offsetting negative effects. In assessing the case for permitting LHVs, researchers are therefore presented with a classic cost-benefit analysis problem whose solution depends critically on the weighting factors attached to the various positive and adverse effects and their monetary valuation.

In later sections of the paper we will examine the analytical problems that one encounters in trying to quantify three of the key variables in the cost-benefit analysis: degree of load consolidation, freight modal shift and induced traffic growth. The analysis is complicated by differences in the maximum length and weight proposed for LHVs and the diversity of LHV designs. These differences are considered in the next section.

DIFFERENT TYPES OF LHV

There are many types of LHV in commercial operation and in prototype form around the world, varying in design, size, weight and ability to meet infrastructural and safety requirements. In this chapter we are more interested in differences in the carrying capacity of LHVs than in their technical design features. A recent study compared the performance of 18 types LHVs in operation in nine countries (OECD / ITF, 2010). Thirteen of these LHVs combined a long trailer with a shorter one (up to a maximum combined length of 30 metres) and were described as 'higher capacity' vehicles. Five comprised either two full length trailers or three trailers and were classified as 'very high capacity' (with a combined length in excess of 30 metres). The 'higher capacity' vehicles typically offer 50% more cube than the standard 'workhorse' articulated truck, while the 'very high capacity' vehicles can increase the cube by 100% of more.

In Scandinavia the dominant type of LHV is a rigid vehicle hauling a 13.6 metre trailer with a maximum length of 25.25 metres and gross weight of 60 tonnes. Other European countries that have recently examined the case for LHVs have explored other configurations but focused mainly on this 25.25 metre maximum length (falling within the OECD / ITF's 'higher capacity' category). In the Netherlands 162 LHVs were trialled conforming to five LHV configurations, two-thirds of which operated at a maximum weight of 50 tonnes with the remainder at a 60 tonne limit. The sample of LHVs trialled in Germany (Lower Saxony) were 25.25 metres long but subject to the same weight limit as existing articulated trucks (40 tonnes). In the desk-based study conducted in the UK, seven LHV scenarios were tested (Figure 2). These were essentially regulatory scenarios relating to maximum lengths and weights. Each scenario could accommodate differing vehicle designs. The scenarios ranged from the *status quo* to a 34 metre road train with gross weight of 82 tonnes, which would be deemed 'very high capacity' by the OECD / ITF study. Three of the scenarios, for the longer semi-trailer and the 25.25 metre vehicle, introduced the concept of '*payload neutrality*'. This would have involved increasing the maximum gross weight of the vehicle in line with its tare (i.e. empty) weight but not permitting any increase in payload weight. It would allow companies moving low density products which currently '*cube out*' to take advantage of the additional space in LHVs without suffering a loss of weight-carrying capacity.

Several countries, such as Australia, Canada and South Africa, adopt a more flexible, 'performance-based' approach to regulating vehicle parameters. This involves defining the infrastructural, environmental and safety outcomes that must be achieved rather than quantitative size and weight limits. In other words it relates '*not to what the vehicle looks like*' but '*what the vehicle can do*' (Sullivan, 2010). In Australia, for example, '*performance based standards have been used to authorise access to suitable parts of the road network for vehicles that do not conform to prescriptive limits on mass or dimensions*' (OECD / ITF, 2010, p.8). This allows truck designers and manufacturers to be more innovative in develop-

Figure 2. Seven LHV scenarios tested the UK study (Source: Knight et al, 2008)

Scenario	Design	Length limit	Weight limit	Axles	Capacity change*
1		18.75m	44 tonnes	6	Increased cube Less weight
2		18.75m	45.8 tonnes (payload neutral)	6	Increased cube Same weight
3		25.25m	44 tonnes	8	Increase cube Less weight
4		25.25m	49.5 tonnes (payload neutral)	8	Increased cube Same weight
5		25.25m	60 tonnes	8	Increased cube Increased weight
6	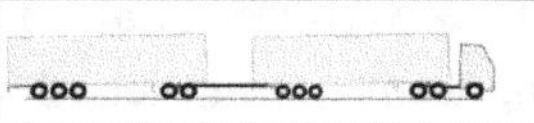	34m	63.2 tonnes (payload neutral)	11	Increased cube Same weight as 5.
7	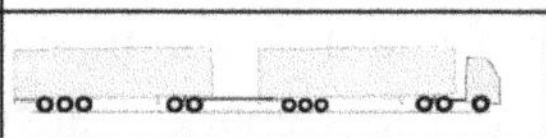	34m	82 tonnes	11	Increased cube Increased weight

ing vehicles which match particular traffic flows and the specific environmental and safety requirements of the areas through which they pass.

Reference is often made to the LHV as a single distinct type of vehicle. In practice it represents a heterogenous category of vehicles varying both in their maximum weights and dimensions and in their design. As the carrying capacity, operating costs, energy efficiency and emissions all vary with regulatory specification and design, it is difficult to generalise about the net economic and environmental effects of LHVs.

DEGREE OF LOAD CONSOLIDATION

The use of LHVs in those countries where their operation has been legalised indicates the actual degree of load consolidation that can be achieved. On the basis of Swedish and Finnish data, TFK (2002) estimated that the use of LHVs cut vehicle trip numbers by 32% and road transport costs by 23%. More recent research has reversed this analysis by assessing the likely impact of the removal of LHVs from Swedish roads and imposition of current EU regulations on truck size and weight (i.e. 18.75 metre and 40 tonne maxima). This indicates that vehicle numbers would have to increase by 37% and road freight costs by 24%, broadly corroborating the results of the TFK study. A study by Woodroofe and Ash (2001) in Alberta concluded that the use of single 'semi-trailer configurations' rather than 'long combination vehicles' would increase truck-kms by 80%, transport costs by 40%, fuel / CO_2 emissions by 32% and '*pavement wear on highways infrastructure*' by 40%. The Dutch trial, discussed earlier, indicated that '*depending on the level of the preconditions*' permitting LHVs could cut truck numbers by between 2000 and 5000 and raise fuel efficiency (expressed relative to tonne-kms carried) by around third (Aarts and Feddes, 2008). A study based on this trial assessed the wider impact of the legalisation of LHVs on traffic conditions and road transport costs in the Netherlands. It concluded that road congestion would be reduced by 0.7-1.4% and road transport costs by 1.8-3.4% (Arcadis, 2006).

Given the international differences that exist in the nature of freight markets, transport infrastructure and regulatory frameworks, one must exercise caution in geographically extrapolating on the basis of only a few countries' experience. Governments contemplating a relaxation of truck size and weight limits must therefore assess the likely impact of this regulatory change on their particular country's transport system. Increased load consolidation is a key element in this assessment.

It is possible to predict the extent to which loads will be consolidated in LHVs by:

1. measuring the proportion of loads that are capacity-constrained in trucks operating at the current maximum size and weight limits, and
2. estimating the proportion of these loads that will migrate to LHVs

Unfortunately very few countries compile the statistics required to make the first of these assessments. A recent review of available freight road data in the EU revealed a serious lack of statistics on vehicle loading (McKinnon, 2010). The UK government is exceptional in having collected data on truck load constraints since 1998. This differentiates the proportions of loads that are weight- or volume-constrained and has revealed that in the UK a much larger proportion of road tonne-kms are constrained by volume than by weight (Department for Transport, 2009). From this we can conclude that expanding the deck area / cubic capacity of trucks will offer greater load consolidation opportunities than increasing their weight limit. It is generally acknowledged too that the average density of freight is declining, partly as a result of the substitution of lighter materials for heavier ones, but also because of increased packaging. Unfortunately, however, no official data exists on the density of loads carried by road. If this information were available, one could analyse the statistical distribution of freight densities across all the loads surveyed. This would permit quantitative modelling of the migration of loads of varying density to LHVs with differing maximum weights and dimensions.

In an earlier UK study of the consolidation of loads in vehicles that were heavier but no larger (maximum weight raised from 41 tonnes to 44 tonnes), various percentage migration rates were applied to test the sensitivity of economic and environmental benefits to this variable (McKinnon, 2005). In the case of LHVs, this sensitivity analysis is much more complicated as vehicle dimensions can also be varied independently of the maximum weight. In the desk-based LHV study conducted in the UK by Knight et al (2008) for the Department for Transport, three maximum length and three maximum weight options were assessed. The three length options met the requirements of the EMS in conforming to existing modular lengths. The maximum weight options were (i) retaining the *status quo*, (ii) allowing a payload-neutral increase in gross weight and (iii) permitting an increase in gross weight commensurate with the increased number of axles[1]. In theory, the optimum gross weight for a particular modular length, offering the greatest load consolidation opportunities, could lie at an intermediate position between these three benchmark weights. Insufficient data exists, however, to model this empirically.

The load consolidation issue is further complicated by the likelihood that at least some categories of LHV would have their movements confined to particular classes of road. In Sweden and Finland, for example, where LHVs have operated for many years, they are denied access to most urban roads. The imposition of route restrictions on LHVs can be justified on several grounds, mainly their inability to negotiate local road layouts, the over-taking problems they create for other categories of traffic on single carriageways and public opposition in environmentally sensitive neighbourhoods. The tighter the network restrictions on LHVs, the less flexible will be their use and the lower the rate of load migration from existing trucks. In the course of the UK LHV study an attempt was made to model the effects of differing degrees of network restriction on the likely uptake of LHVs using trip-specific data from the main annual survey of road freight movements (Knight et al, 2008). This analysis was underpinned by numerous assumptions relating to vehicle loading, the compatibility of loads for consolidation and the coupling / decoupling of trailers at strategic locations on the road network. Table 1 summarises the results for one category of LHV, a 60 tonne 25 metre truck, and three levels of road network restriction. It shows the % reductions in traffic levels, cost and CO_2 emissions from operating this LHV rather than a standard articulated vehicle with a 13.6 metre trailer and gross weight of 44 tonnes. It can be seen how confining LHVs to particular categories of road significantly reduces these potential benefits.

Table 1. Effects on distance travelled, transport cost and CO_2 emissions of restricting LHVs to particular road networks (% savings relative to delivery by non-LHV, standard articulated truck)

Permitted categories of road	trips	vehicle-kms	cost	CO_2
motorways + roads within 20 kms	-10.4	-10.3	-6.5	-2.7
motorways and dual carriageways + roads within 20 kms	-24.8	-29.8	-19.3	-7.6
all roads	-34.6	-34.6	-22.9	-8.8

Not all journeys made by LHVs would move loads that are too large or too heavy to be transported in trucks meeting current regulations. Some will be run empty, while others will be only partially laden. In assessing the degree of consolidation, therefore, allowance must be made for the likely utilisation of LHV capacity. This too is very difficult to quantify in a desk-based study. It can simply be assumed that the average levels of empty running and lading will be the same as those achieved by trucks operating at the current maximum size and weight limits. This may underestimate the level of LHV utilisation, however, because, as these vehicles require additional capital investment, companies are likely to deploy them mainly on journeys which take advantage of their greater carrying capacity. This was a view strongly expressed by logistics managers consulted during the UK study (Knight et al, 2008 Appendix F). Another way of addressing this issue is to determine how high the vehicle utilisation factor would have to be for LHVs to yield a net economic and / or environmental benefit. A study conducted by the German Ministry of the Environment, for example, estimated that the average load factor[2] on LHVs 25.25 metres in length would have to be at least 77% for them to yield a net environmental benefit, well above the average achieved by trucks within current regulations (64%) (Umwelt Bundes Amt, 2007).

FREIGHT MODAL SPLIT

LHV impact studies have been criticised for not taking enough account of the effects of truck size and weight increases on the division of freight traffic between modes (Schulman, 2003). Railway trade bodies and their railfreight member companies have, nevertheless, commissioned several studies on the subject and strongly campaigned against wider introduction of LHVs in EU countries. They see LHVs as a major threat not only to the future growth of railfreight traffic but also to the existing railfreight market. UIC et al (2006), for example, argue that the '*advent of mega-trucks*' would result in the transfer of 7 bn tonne-kms per annum from road to rail in Germany (i.e around 16% of railfreight tonne-kms carried by rail in 2005). In the UK, the main railfreight operator, EWS (2007) has claimed that '*taking both the vulnerable bulk market sectors and the high-value intermodal sector, roundly half of all the freight moved by train in the UK is at risk from moving to road if LHVs were introduced.*' On the other hand, it is worth noting that in Sweden where LHVs have been operating for several decades, rail's share of total domestic tonne-kms in 2006 was roughly twice the EU25 average (35% as opposed to 17%) (Eurostat, 2009).

As discussed earlier, the displacement of freight from rail (and to a lesser extent water-borne modes) to road is considered to be one of the major disbenefits of LHVs. Some modal shift may be acceptable, however, so long as this disbenefit is more than offset by economic and environmental benefits accruing from load consolidation on the road network. As the Commission for Integrated Transport (2000) in the UK stated, '*encouraging freight consignors to use rail, canal or sea transport should be regarded as a means towards the end of environmental benefit, not as an end in itself.*' For many potential users of LHVs, transporting their goods by other modes is not an option. The nature of their products, the geography of their distribution operations and / or their delivery schedules often require the use of road transport. Such companies legitimately ask why they should be denied the opportunity of using LHVs to rationalise their road freight movements when the modal split issue has little or no relevance to them. As the OECD / ITF (2010) report explains, the impact of LHVs '*is limited by the fact that many freight markets are not contestable between modes*' (p.19).

Predicting the impact of LHVs on freight modal split is fraught with difficulty. This is partly because of a lack accurate, reliable and up-to-date modal cross-elasticity values. These values measure the extent to which changes in the price of one transport mode affect the demand for another. The LHV analysis undertaken in 2007 by Oxera for the UK railfreight operator EWS employed price elasticity values for freight transport quoted in a 1990 paper and largely based on North American experience (Oum et al, 1990). Christidis and Leduc (2009) reviewed road-rail cross-elasticity values cited in more recent studies and found that they ranged from '*0.3 to 2 depending on the trip length and commodity type*' (p.11). This suggests that a 10% reduction in the cost of road haulage could cut railfreight demand by between 3% and 20%. Dings (2007) quotes cross-elasticity values for rail of +1.8 to 3.0 which were derived by the Netherlands Economic Institute and CE Delft. On the assumption that the use of LHVs would reduce road freight rates by 20% he calculates that between 36% and 60% of railfreight would divert to LHVs. Given the broad spectrum of cross-elasticity values it is very difficult to generalise about the impact on modal split of the cost savings that would result from the use of even a single type of LHV.

To address this problem, cross-elasticity values should be derived for those sectors of the freight market within which rail and LHVs would be in direct competition. The nature of this competition partly depends on the maximum gross weight of the LHVs. As the railways tend to carry heavier, higher-density freight, competition from LHVs is particularly sensitive to their gross weight limits. If vehicle length were increased and maximum weight left unchanged, there is likely to be limited traffic erosion from rail. The main exception to this general statement would be containerised traffic. Although many commodities moved by rail in containers are relatively light, LHVs can still pose a major threat to the rail container market. 25.25 or 34 metre long LHVs, after all, permit the carriage of multiples of 40 ft and 20 ft containers and thus effect a step-change in the cost of moving containers by road. Research in the UK has suggested a price elasticity value of 2.5 for deep-sea container traffic moving by rail[3] (MDS Transmodal, 2006). If, as has been suggested by a UK railfreight operator, the use of a 25.25 metre LHV reduced the average cost of transporting containers by road by 15%, one might expect 37.5% of rail deep-sea container traffic to transfer to LHVs in the UK (Knight et al, 2008).

The Dutch trial suggested that the impact of LHVs on modal split was very limited with only 1.4-2.7% of railfreight diverting and 0.2-0.3% of inland waterway traffic switching (Aarts and Feddes, 2008). Given the wide differences in national freight markets it would be very unwise to extrapolate these modal shift estimates to other countries or to cross-border transport in Europe (Debauche and Decock, 2007). It is worth noting, however, that two studies undertaken for the European Commission of EU-wide LHV impacts yielded modal shift estimates of a similar magnitude. One of them, involving a Monte Carlo simulation analysis of the impact of allowing 60 tonne 25 metre LHVs to operate across the EU indicated that by 2020 railfreight traffic would be only 2.1% lower that would otherwise be the case (Christidis and Leduc, 2009). The other by TML et al (2008) which modelled the effects of allowing this type of LHV to run on EU motorways suggested that '*rail and waterway volumes would respectively decrease by 3.8% and 2.9%*' (p.72). On the other hand, a study commissioned by the rail sector (CER), using much higher cross-elasticity factors, estimated that within the EU rail tonne-kms would decline by, respectively, 11.6% and 12.9% if 60 tonne 25 metre LHVs cut trucking costs by 18% and 20% (Doll et al, 2008). This clearly illustrates the sensitivity of the modelling to the calibration of cross-elasticity values.

The modal split analyses conducted in the course of LHV impact studies have been largely confined to econometric modelling within a narrow set of parameters. Numerous studies have shown, however, that the mode choice decision is multi-dimensional, with cost being only one of a range of factors affecting the relative attractiveness of different transport services. Improvements in the marketing and quality of railfreight services could help to offset some of the loss in price competitiveness that would result from a wider use of LHVs. Opportunities also exist to increase the carrying capacity of freight vehicles on the railfreight network, for example by strengthening track to support heavier axle weights, expanding the loading gauge and lengthening sidings to accommodate longer freight trains, though exploiting them usually carries a high capital cost.

INDUCED ROAD FREIGHT TRAFFIC GROWTH

An argument regularly used against increases in vehicle capacity limits is that it will induce a '*rebound effect*' with the resulting transport cost reductions stimulating an increase in the demand for freight movement. It has been claimed that, in the case of LHVs in Europe, '*increased demand for road transport would cancel out any environmental gains from the increased efficiency*' (European Federation of Transport and Environment, 2007). Attempts to quantify this traffic generation effect are again frustrated by a lack of accurate and reliable price elasticity values, in this case solely for road freight transport[4]. Graham and Glaister (2004) and Christidis and Leduc (2009) reviewed the published estimates and found that most lie within the range -0.5 to -1.5, suggesting that a 20% reduction in road freight costs from the use of 60 tonne 25 metre LHV would generate 10-30% more freight movement.

A study conducted for the main UK railfreight company, Oxera attempted to estimate the strength of the '*market generating*' effect of LHVs (EWS, 2007). It predicted that the use of LHVs in the UK would cut road freight costs per tonne-km by 14.2-15.3% and that this would cause a surge in road tonne-kms. It gave no indication, however, of the likely sources of this large amount of additional freight traffic. Its econometric analysis was detached from the real world of production and logistics management. It merely asserts that '*over time the structure of supply chains will adapt to lower road haulage costs*' and that '*it would be naïve not to expect a substantial increase in the amount of freight transport (i.e. tonne-kilometres) in the UK as a result of the introduction of LHVs*' (p.16).

There is strong counter evidence to suggest that any freight traffic generation effect is likely to be weak. A retrospective analysis of the impact of the increase in maximum truck weight in the UK from 41 tonnes to 44 tonnes in 2001 could find little statistical evidence of this measure reinforcing the rate of freight traffic growth (McKinnon, 2005). Focus group discussions with logistics managers in the UK also challenged the premise that road transport savings arising from the introduction of LHVs would be likely to unleash a new wave of logistical restructuring (Knight et al, 2008). This concurs with the view of the OECD / ITF (2010) report that '*induced demand effects are likely to be small*' (p.9) The analysis undertaken by TML et al (2008) for the European Commission quantified this effect and found that it would be marginal. In its 60 tonne 25 metre LHV scenario '*road volumes are expected to increase by 0.99%*' (p.72).

NET ENVIRONMENTAL IMPACT

Several studies have conducted wide-ranging cost benefit analyses of the introduction of LHVs, taking account of the factors discussed above, plus others such as safety and the upgrading of road infrastructure, and applying monetary values to the various transport-induced externalities. Some of the results are not directly comparable as they differ in the range of factors included in the calculation, the definition of the LHV scenarios, the underlying assumptions and valuation of externalities. If one focuses on 60 tonne 25 metre LHVs, a consensus emerges in several of the main international studies that the use of these vehicles yields a net welfare benefit. For example, Christidis and Leduc (2009) place a '*mean value*' of 700 million Euro on the net welfare gain in 2020 from having 3.2% of EU road freight carried in these LHVs. Increasing this level of LHV useage raises the net benefit. Taking a global view of the use of LHVs, the OECD / ITF (2010) conclude that, '*Higher capacity vehicles have been operated extensively for a variety of freight tasks in some areas of the world without adverse impacts. The evidence available indicates significant safety, sustainability and productivity improvements' (p.10).*

FUTURE RESEARCH DIRECTIONS

One hesitates to recommend further research in a field that has already been extensively studied around the world. There are, nevertheless, several issues that merit more detailed investigation, such as:

- *Route-specific restrictions on LHVs*: it is generally acknowledged that it is desirable, for environmental, safety and infrastructural capacity reasons, to deny LHVs access to particular roads and districts. Advances in telematics now make it possible to monitor the movement of LHVs (and other trucks), providing route guidance to drivers and helping to enforce route restrictions. The costs and benefits of this application of telematics need to be more fully explored.
- *Price-elasticity of demand for freight transport:* As discussed earlier, analyses of the impact of LHVs have been inhibited by the lack of an agreed set of price elasticity values for freight movement within a single mode, in this case road, and between modes. A recent review of freight elasticities in European road freight transport by De Jong et al (2010) revealed a '*substantial*' variation in published elasticity values, only some of which they were able to explain. It would be a worthy research aspiration to derive, on a consistent and transparent basis, a broader suite of elasticity values for different freight markets. This would certainly help to make the modelling of LHV impacts more analytically robust.
- *Refining public policy on LHVs*: The aim of public policy in this arena is to maximise the economic, environmental and safety benefits of LHVs while minimising the disbenefits of modal shift and higher infrastructural investment. For some coun-

tries to meet this aim, public policy on this issue will have to be more finely tuned, striking a more delicate balance between conflicting objectives. This can be done, for example, by using the 'performance-based approach' to LHV regulation applied in Australia, Canada and South Africa, by adopting the principle of 'payload neutrality' where appropriate and finding more innovative ways of promoting the use of LHVs within rail- and water-based intermodal systems. The development of such policy refinements will be another fertile area for future research.

CONCLUSION

A large body of evidence now exists to confirm that increasing the maximum length and weight of trucks yield significant economic, environmental and safety benefits. On the basis of long experience of LHV useage in countries such as Sweden, Canada and Australia and the results of numerous trials and desk-based studies it is possible to build a persuasive case for relaxing current length and weight limits on trucks across the EU and elsewhere. Most of the evidence to the contrary is found in studies commissioned by railway organisations. They are naturally keen to defend their share of the freight market against the more intense competition that LHV would inevitably bring. Rather than allow the rail lobby to obstruct the consolidation of road freight in higher capacity vehicles, policy makers could use a combination of taxation and regulation to achieve a modal compromise that would maximise the net benefit to the economy, society and environment.

This chapter has focused on three issues at the heart of the current debate in Europe over the merits of LHVs: load consolidation, modal split and traffic generation. Space limitations have precluded detailed discussion of other important issues such as safety, energy efficiency, emissions, road investment and enforcement. This review of recent literature has, nevertheless, highlighted the difficulties of conducting research on this controversial subject and drawing general conclusions. First there is the lack of survey data on truck utilisation by weight and volume, the density of loads and the price elasticity of demand for freight services both within the road sector and cross-modally. Second, there is the diversity of LHV designs and capacities, each with a different cost-benefit ratio to be modelled. The third complication is the large number of operational, economic, environmental variables that must be factored into the analysis, many of which, as noted earlier, cannot be empirically calibrated. And finally, there is the need to 'customise' the analysis to the particular region, country or continent across which LHVs will operate, taking account of differences in its geography, transport infrastructure, industrial mix and freight market.

As the LHV issue combines analytical complexity and political sensitivity, there is a danger that it will never be resolved and that politicians will continually 'kick it into the long grass' of yet another study. At some point, however, policy-makers at both EU and national levels will accept that few other transport measures offer such large productivity and environmental benefits as increasing the maximum weights and dimensions of trucks.

REFERENCES

Aarts, L., & Feddes, G. (2010). *Experience with Longer and Heavier Vehicles in the Netherlands*. Presentation to the 10th International Symposium on Heavy Vehicle Transport Technology, Paris.

*Arcadis (2006).*Monitoringsonderzoek Vervolgproef LZV: Resultaten van de Vervolgproef met Langere of Langere en Zwaardere Voertuigcombinaties op de Nederlandse Wegen. *Arnhem.*

Christidis, P., & Leduc, G. (2009). *Introducing Mega-Trucks: A Review for Policy Makers*. Institute for Prospective Technological Studies, Seville.

Commission for Integrated Transport. (2000). *Interim Report: Permitting 44 tonne Lorries for General Use in the UK*. London: Commission for Integrated Transport.

De Jong, G., Schroten, A., van Essen, H., Otten, M., & Bucci, P. (2010). *Price Sensitivity of European Road Freight Transport – Towards a Better Understanding of Existing Results*. Report 9012-1, Significance / CE Delft.

Debauche, W., & Decock, D. (2007). *Working Group on Longer and Heavier Vehicles: A Multidisciplinary Approach to the Issue*. Brussels: Belgian Road Research Centre.

Department for Transport (2007). Road Freight Statistics. London.

Dings, J. (2008). *LHVs and the Environment – Addressing the Big Forgotten Issue*. presentation to LHV Stakeholder Meeting 4th March, Brussels: European Commission.

Doll, C., Fiorello, D., Pastori, E., Reynaud, C., Klaus, P., Lückmann, P., et al. (2008). *Long-Term Climate Impacts of the Introduction of Mega-Trucks*. Study for the Community of European Railways and Infrastructure Companies (CER) co-ordinated by Fraunhofer ISI, Karlsruhe.

European Commission. (2007). Freight Transport Logistics Action Plan. Brussels.

European Federation of Transport and Environment. (2007). *Longer and Heavier Lorries (LHLs) and the Environment*. Brussels.

European Shippers Council. (2007). *Road Transport Reduction through the European Modular System: the Challenges for European Transport Markets*. Brussels.

Eurostat (2007). *Panorama of Transport*. Luxembourg.

EWS. (2007). *Longer, Heavier Road Vehicles Study by TRL / Heriot-Watt University: A Response by English Welsh & Scottish Railway*. Retrieved from http://www.ews-railway.co.uk/news/ downloads/LHVs%20research% 20by%20EWS.pdf

Graham, D. J., & Glaister, S. (2004). Road Traffic Demand Elasticity Estimates: A Review. *Transport Reviews*, *24*(3), 261–274. doi:10.1080/0144164032000101193

Knight, I., Newton, W., & McKinnon, A. C. (2008). *Longer and / or Longer and Heavier Goods Vehicles (LHVs): a Study of the Likely Effects if Permitted in the UK. Report prepared for the Department for Transport*. TRL, Crowthorne.

Leduc, G. (2009). *Longer and Heavier Vehicles: an Overview of Technical Aspects*. Institute for Prospective Technological Studies, Seville.

McKinnon, A. C. (2005). The Economic and Environmental Benefits of Increasing Maximum Truck Weight: The British Experience. *Transportation Research Part D, Transport and Environment*, *10*(1), 77–95. doi:10.1016/j.trd.2004.09.006

McKinnon, A. C. (2010). *European Freight Statistics: Limitations, Misinterpretations and Aspirations*. Brussels: ACEA.

OECD / ITF. (2010). *Moving Freight with Better Trucks*. Paris: OECD.

Oum, T., Waters, W., & Jong, Y. (1990). *A Survey of Recent Estimates of Price Elasticities of Demand for Transport*. Working Paper, World Bank, Washington DC.

Schulman, J. F. (2003). *Heavy Truck Weight and Dimension Limits in Canada*. Ottawa: Railway Association of Canada.

Sullivan, P. (2010). *The PBS Model in Australia.* Paper presented at the 11th Heavy Vehicle Transport Technology conference, Melbourne, March.

TFK. (2002). *Improved Performance of European Long Haulage Transport.* Stockholm TML et al (2008). *Effects of Adapting the Rules on Weights and Dimensions of Heavy Commercial Vehicles as Established with Directive 96/53/EC.* Report for the European Commission, Brussels. UIC et al (2007). *Mega-trucks versus Rail Freight.* Paris.

Transmodal, M. D. S. (2006). *Impact of Track Access Charges on Rail Freight Traffic.* Chester.

Umwelt Bundes Amt. (2007). *Longer and Heavier on German Roads: Do Megatrucks Contribute towards Sustainable Transport.* Dessau.

Vierth, I. (2008). *The Effects of Long and Heavy Trucks on the Transport System.* Stockholm: VTI.

Woodrooffe, J., & Ash, L. (2001). *Economic Efficiency of Long Combination Transport Vehicles in Alberta.* Woodrooffe and Associates.

ENDNOTES

1 Most of the European studies have assumed that maximum axle weight will remain unchanged and that heavier weights will be distributed across more axles.

2 Measured in terms of loaded pallets per trip.

3 This elasticity value is expressed with respect to rail freight rates, though as road is the only competing mode and container volumes are relatively insensitive to inland transport rates, it can be applied to a relative reduction in road freight costs.

4 As there is an inverse relationship between road freight costs and the demand for haulage services, the elasticity values are negative. The cross-elasticity values discussed earlier were positive to reflect the direct relationship between road freight costs and the volume of freight carried by alternative modes.

Chapter 13
The Role of Urban Consolidation Centres in Sustainable Freight Transport

Julian Allen
University of Westminster, UK

Michael Browne
University of Westminster, UK

Jacques Leonardi
University of Westminster, UK

Allan Woodburn
University of Westminster, UK.

ABSTRACT

The chapter considers the role that urban consolidation centres (UCCs) can play in helping to reduce goods vehicle traffic and its environmental impacts in urban areas. A UCC is a logistics facility that is situated in relatively close proximity to the area that it serves. Goods destined for this area are dropped off at the UCC, and are sorted and consolidated onto goods vehicles for delivery to their final destinations, often using environmentally friendly vehicles such as electric and gas-powered goods vehicles, and electrically-assisted cycles. The development of UCCs since their first appearance in the 1970s is reviewed and the various types of UCC categorised. The freight transport and logistics advantages offered by UCCs are discussed. Case studies of four recent UCC trials are included. The objectives, operational and financial aspects and impacts of these UCCs are compared and their critical success factors identified.

DOI: 10.4018/978-1-60960-585-8.ch013

INTRODUCTION

This chapter considers the role played by urban consolidation centres (UCCs) in rationalising the movement of freight in urban areas to cut delivery costs and reduce environmental impacts. They not only permit greater consolidation of loads, but also permit greater use of electric and other alternatively-fuelled goods vehicles which emit less CO_2 and other, noxious gases.

The introductory sections provide an overview of the development of UCCs and the range of benefits that they offer. Case studies of four recent UCC trials and operations in the UK are then presented: the London Construction Consolidation Centre, the London Heathrow Retail UCC, the Bristol UCC and an urban 'micro-consolidation' Centre based in the City of London. The final two sections draw on the experience of these UCCs to highlight key issues and identify critical success factors and future research needs.

OVERVIEW OF UCCS

A UCC is a logistics facility that is situated in relatively close proximity to the urban area that it serves be that a city centre, an entire town or a specific site such as a shopping centre, airport, hospital or major construction site. Goods destined for these locations are dropped off at the UCC. The UCC operator sorts and consolidates these loads dropped off by logistics companies and makes deliveries to the final destinations, often using environmentally-friendly vehicles such as electric and gas-powered goods vehicles, and electrically-assisted cycles (Browne et al, 2005).

By improving the lading factor of goods vehicles making final deliveries in congested locations, UCCs reduce the total distance travelled by delivery vehicles in urban areas, as well as reducing greenhouse gas emissions and local air quality pollutants associated with these journeys (both through reductions in the total distance travelled, and through the use of low emission vehicles) (Browne et al., 2007). In addition the total kerbside time and space occupied by vehicles making on-street deliveries can be reduced through consolidation further reducing the impact of freight operations on traffic congestion. Other social and environmental advantages can include noise reductions through the use of quieter vehicles, reductions in conflicts between goods vehicles and other road users and greater pedestrian safety (Gonzalez-Feliu and Morana, 2008; WSP, 2008).

The logistics companies dropping their loads at the UCC benefit by avoiding the need to enter congested urban areas and thereby saving time and costs. Those receiving goods from the UCC benefit in terms of delivery reliability. In addition to consolidation and final delivery, a range of other value-added logistics and retail services can also be provided at the UCC.

Initial research into UCCs as an urban freight initiative commenced in the early 1970s and has continued ever since with levels of interest in this approach increasing during the last decade (see for example Browne et al., 2005; Institut für Seeverkehrswirtschaft und Logistik, 2005; McKinnon, 1998a; McKinnon, 1998b; van Duin et al., 2010).

An international literature review of UCCs carried out in 2005 identified 67 UCCs in 15 countries worldwide that had either been the focus of a feasibility study, trial or fully operational scheme. The earliest was a UCC study that took place in Columbus, Ohio in the early 1970s (McKinnon, 1998a). The majority of these UCCs had taken place in Europe, with France, Germany, Italy, the Netherlands and the UK accounting for 46 of the 67 identified (Browne et al., 2005).

The review indicated that 26 of the 67 UCCs had been the subject of a research study/feasibility project only, 13 had proceeded to a trial, and 28 had become fully operational schemes (Browne et al., 2005). At the time of the review (2005) 27 UCC schemes were understood to still be in operation, 14 of these dated from 2000 or later showing the growth in interest in setting up UCC operations in the last decade. Much of this had been driven by private sector involvement (including logistics service providers, property developers and landlords).

Three major categories of UCC can be defined:

1. ***UCCs serving all or part of an urban area.*** These UCCs are usually associated with the supply of retail products, but are also used for the supply of office products, and occasionally food supplies for restaurants and cafes. These UCC schemes are often used to serve locations with features such as narrow streets, historic layouts, and limited unloading facilities. The introduction of this type of UCC is usually initially suggested by the local authority on traffic and environmental grounds. Existing examples of such UCCs include Reglog in Regensburg, Cityporto in Padua, La Rochelle UCC, Nijmegen UCC and Bristol UCC.
2. ***UCCs serving large sites with a single landlord.*** These UCCs are most commonly associated with the supply of retail products and food supplies for restaurants and cafes. There are also examples of them being used for supplying hospital products. The types of large sites served by these UCCs include airports, shopping centres and hospitals. In some instances they serve only one large site (for example London Heathrow airport retail UCC and Meadowhall shopping centre UCC in Sheffield) and in other cases they serve several large sites (such as the Hospital Logistics Centre in London which delivers to several major hospitals). Although these UCCs only serve one or a few large sites, within the sites many different outlets may be served (such as many different retailers in a shopping centre or airport, or many different departments within a hospital). The interest in UCCs among developers and owners of airports and shopping centres usually stems from the desire to maximise retail space by minimising on-site storage and the need for multiple delivery bays (WSP, 2008). In the case of a hospital the interest is more commonly in reducing on-site stock levels and storage space. These UCCs can also be insisted on by the planning authority through the planning permission process in the case of new sites.
3. ***Construction project UCCs.*** These are UCCs that are used for consolidating construction materials for major building projects including housing, office blocks and hospitals. Examples include UCCs established at London Heathrow airport during major development work and in Hammerby in Stockholm for a major housing project. This type of UCC can serve either a single major building project or several. This type of UCC can either exist only for the lifetime of a building project or can be on-going serving new major building projects as they are established, but experience to date suggests that the former is more common. Either the site developer or the main construction contractor would decide to make use of a UCC, or it could be made mandatory through the planning permission process.

Each of these three types of UCC can offer either relatively basic consolidation and delivery services or offer a wider range of value-added logistics activities. In the 2005 literature review previously discussed 59 of the 67 UCCs identified served part or all of an urban area (type 1), five served large sites with a single landlord (type 2), and 3 were construction project UCCs (type 3) (Browne et al., 2005). This illustrates the predominance of UCCs serving part or all of an urban area over the other types.

Many additional UCC feasibility studies, trials and operations have been established since the 2005 literature review, especially in Italy, the Netherlands and the UK (see for example

Gonzalez-Feliu and Morana, 2010; JMP and TTR, 2010; van Duin et al., 2010; van Rooijen and Quak, 2010; Ville et al., 2010). A recent report lists ten UCCs that are operational in the UK alone in 2010, all of which opened since 2000 (TTR, 2010). All of these UCCs are operated by the private sector and several receive no public funding. Using the above categorisation approach, three are UCCs serving a town/city (Bristol, Regent Street in central London, and Snetterton which serves Norwich city centre), five are retail UCCs on single sites with a private landlord (three serve airports: Manchester, East Midlands and Heathrow, and two serve shopping centres: Meadowhall and Bluewater), and two of these are construction project UCCs in London. In addition, another UCC serving a town/city commenced operations in the City of London in 2009. This UCC handles office products and is the subject of the detailed case study in the next section. This indicates the current level of interest and activity in this city logistics innovation.

FREIGHT TRANSPORT AND LOGISTICS ADVANTAGES OFFERED BY UCCS

Impacts on Transport Operations

One of the primary reasons for considering the implementation of a consolidation centre is the potential to reduce freight transport activity and its associated social and environmental impacts. This is achieved through the improvements in vehicle load factor that can be attained through load consolidation at the UCC, together with the potential to use alternatively-fuelled vehicles (electricity or gas) for final delivery from the UCC. In addition some UCCs have made use of electrically-assisted tricycles (Attlassy and the University of Westminster, 2005; Transport for London, 2009). They are proving to be important test sites for these innovative vehicle technologies. UCC trials and operations that had been subject to evaluation show that reductions in vehicle kilometres can be up to 80 per cent, improvements in vehicle load factors range from 15-100 per cent, and reductions in greenhouse gas emissions range from 25-80 per cent as a result of the UCC.

In addition to the reduction in the total distance travelled per delivery in the urban area as a result of using a UCC, these schemes also offer an important operational advantage to freight transport operators using them. They allow a driver to drop their load at the UCC without having to make the final delivery in a congested urban area, and thereby save time and hence operating costs. In the case of a shopping centre, the use of a UCC removes the need for the driver to transport goods from shopping centre loading bays to receivers located long distances away as this is taken care of by UCC personnel (some of whom may be based in the shopping centre). Also, in the case of deliveries to construction sites, the use of a UCC means that the driver does not have to spend time searching for the correct location or person to deliver to.

UCCs also improve delivery reliability, as they are located in close proximity to the customers. Longer direct deliveries are more likely to experience delays, especially within urban areas. UCCs can also reduce the total kerbside time and space occupied in urban areas by vehicles making deliveries as they increase the quantity of goods delivered per stop.

Impacts on Other Logistics Activities

UCCs can also help to achieve other supply chain and logistics benefits. UCCs can offer a range of value-added logistics services including off-site stockholding, consignment unpacking, preparation of products for display and price labelling, goods return and waste collection services. These can benefit receivers by reducing their on-site space requirements, saving time by reducing the number of tasks that have to be performed on-site, and enhancing productivity and sales in core activities.

UCCs can also be used to offer community collection and delivery point facilities (for other consumer and business products), while home delivery operations can also be operated from the UCC.

Figure 1 illustrates the range of logistics and pre-retail activities that can be carried out by a UCC and the potential benefits of these activities.

Inventory Control and Associated Activities

A UCC can be used to offer stockholding services to users, subject to available capacity and appropriate storage conditions for the products

Figure 1. Range of potential logistics and pre-retail activities at UCC and possible benefits

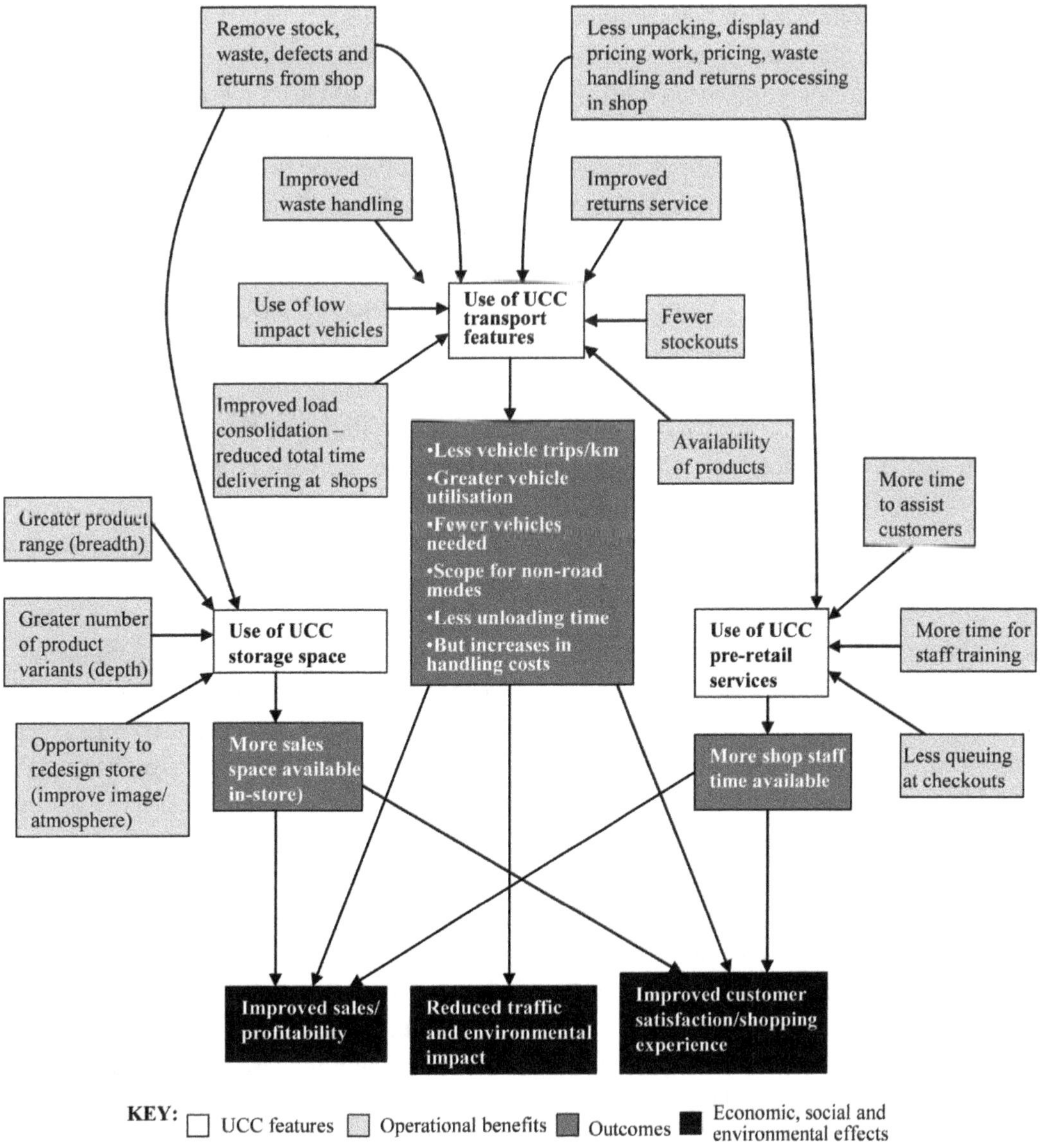

involved. In the main, only short-term storage tends to be envisaged, providing a useful local buffer stock that can be called off quickly when needed, thus reducing delivery lead times and improving product availability and customer service. For maximum benefit this depends on the UCC offering the flexibility for quick call-off of product as required. For certain products or customers, seasonal or peak storage can sensibly be provided by a consolidation centre so as to provide valuable additional space.

Other services can be offered, particularly by retail UCCs but perhaps also by other types of centre. Inventory monitoring and information collection and analysis, linked to in-store systems, can be provided. This can increase the visibility of the supply chain, again leading to better product availability and service levels, as well as reducing loss of stock. Product quality and quantity checking can be carried out upon consignments' arrival at the centre, giving advance notice to the customer of any problems with supplies. Various pre-retailing activities, such as consignment unpacking, preparation of products for display and price labelling, can also be carried out at the consolidation centre to reduce time and space requirements at the delivery point.

Impacts at the Delivery Location

As a result of the additional logistics services that can be offered by a UCC, space at the receiving establishment can be freed up for other activities that are more productive or profitable, such as retailing floor space or construction sites, which is likely to be particularly beneficial when space is at a premium or expansion is desirable. This can prove especially attractive to developers of shopping centres as the removal of storage space allows them to fit more retail space and units into the prime development.

If the UCC offers an enhanced delivery service, with more flexible and reliable delivery times, higher product or component availability may be achieved and, ultimately, sales volume or site productivity may be increased. Fewer deliveries to the destination may be required as a result of the load consolidation undertaken at the centre, thereby reducing the disruption and labour requirements associated with receiving multiple deliveries, leading to improvements in staff planning and productivity at delivery locations.

Off-site storage can also lead to reductions in damage and theft of stock, especially on construction sites, and thereby further reductions in development costs. The same benefit is true of the use of UCCs for hospital medical and equipment supplies.

Due to the reduction in deliveries associated with the use of UCCs it is also possible for developers of shopping centres and other major retailing centres to reduce the delivery bay requirements and thereby free-up this space for other, more profitable activities.

Impacts for Suppliers and Logistics Companies

UCCs may be open at more flexible times than city centre delivery points. Staff will be available to receive the consignment and the delivery company can avoid problems of congested loading bays found in many urban areas.

In some cases, the number of locations that a supplier has to deliver to may be reduced, since a particular UCC could be serving more than one customer location. In a broader sense, there may be some potential to ease skills shortages within the transport and related sectors (e.g. construction) through more efficient methods of working.

Product Flow

UCCs have a role in the handling of return and recycling flows, including product returns and the coordination of waste and packaging collection for reuse or recycling, instead of individual customers having to deal with this. As packaging waste regulations tighten, such coordinated approaches may offer greater benefits over time. UCCs may also offer a new distribution channel which, as a result of serving multiple customers, may offer opportunities to smaller suppliers to access new markets that are currently beyond their reach. Finally, UCCs may be in a position to offer B2B (business-to-business) and B2C (business-to-customer) services within their catchment area, perhaps including inter-store transfers, home delivery or customer collection of products purchased in town centres.

INTRODUCTION TO THE CASE STUDIES

This section contains case studies of four UCC schemes established in the UK in recent years. This includes two UCCs that serve part of an urban area, one UCC that serves a major site with a single landlord (retail outlets in an airport), and one construction project UCC. For each UCC, the objectives, operational characteristics, financial aspects and impacts are examined.

Table 1 shows basic details of the four UCC schemes. The sample comprises a range of UCC types, a mix of sectors and examples of optional and compulsory scheme participation.

Case Study: London Construction Consolidation Centre

Background and Objectives

A two-year trial project referred to as the London Construction Consolidation Centre (LCCC) operated from 2005 to 2007. The LCCC was a 5,000 sq. m. facility located in South Bermondsey, approximately five kilometres south of the City of London. Its objective was to serve four major construction sites in the City of London. It was intended for a rapid flow, on a just-in-time basis, of material from suppliers to site with storage time limited to ten days. The LCCC was intended to reduce the number of deliveries going directly to the construction sites and thereby reducing traffic congestion and vehicle emissions. The main reason for carrying out this LCCC project was to assess the potential benefits that such a scheme could bring (Transport for London et al., 2008).

Table 1. Key characteristics of case study UCCs

Centre	Location	UCC type	Product type	Trial or fully operational	Use of electric vehicles?	Current status	Terms of use
London Construction Consolidation Centre	London, UK	Construction	Construction	Trial	No	Closed *	Compulsory **
Bristol UCC	Bristol, UK	Part of urban area	Retail	Trial then fully operational	Partial	Active	Voluntary
City of London Micro-Consolidation Centre	London, UK	Part of urban area	Office products	Trial then fully operational	Yes	Active	Compulsory
London Heathrow UCC	London, UK	Airport	Retail	Trial then fully operational	Partial	Active	Compulsory

Notes: * - concept now applied to new site; ** - with certain exceptions (see case study)

Operational Aspects

Contractors working on the four construction sites placed orders for their material requirements with their suppliers in the normal way, but instructed that the delivery was made to the LCCC, not the construction site. Contractors then placed a delivery order with the LCCC for the materials they required. This was assembled at the LCCC and delivered to the sites. Approximately a sixth of all the deliveries requested from the LCCC by the construction sites were needed within less than 24 hours notice (i.e. on a just-in-time basis). This level of service would probably have been difficult to achieve if deliveries were made directly to site by suppliers. The delivery from the LCCC to the construction sites consolidated numerous contractors' orders onto each vehicle.

As well as delivering construction materials to the sites, the vehicles operating from the LCCC also collected recyclable packaging and unused materials and brought them back to the LCCC. This was then recycled, returned through the supply chain for re-use or collected by a waste operator. It is important to note that some supplies continued to be sent directly to the construction sites rather than via the LCCC. These included aggregates, structural steel, ready-mix concrete, escalators and furniture, all of which were usually delivered as a full vehicle load.

The LCCC employed 16 staff and had a fleet of six delivery vehicles. This comprised four flatbed rigid vehicles (ranging from 18 to 26 tonnes gross weight), one 7.5 tonne gross weight curtain-sider rigid vehicle and one 3.5 tonne gross weight van.

Financial Aspects

The project cost of £3.2 million was met by a partnership of private developers / construction companies and Transport for London (TfL), the public organisation responsible London's transport system. TfL funded £1.85 million, while the developers and construction companies funded the other £1.35 million. The companies participating in the LCCC project voluntarily agreed to use the LCCC for the four construction sites. Some of the costs of the LCCC were passed on to the individual building contractors (Transport for London et al., 2008).

Impact Assessment and Outcome

Operational targets were set for the performance of the LCCC. These are shown in Table 2 alongside the operational performance actually achieved. The performance targets were equalled or surpassed..

For those materials delivered via the LCCC, it is estimated there was a 60-70 per cent reduction in the number of vehicles delivering to the four construction sites. It is estimated that this resulted in a 70-80 per cent reduction in CO_2 emissions for these flows. Taking account of all de-

Table 2. LCCC targets and achievements

Key Performance Indicator	Target	Achieved
Reduction in freight journeys	40%	60-70% of journeys via LCCC 40% of journeys to construction site
Reduction in journey time of supplier deliveries to contractors	30-60 minutes	120 minutes
Delivery reliability	97%	97%

Source: Transport for London et al., 2008.

liveries from suppliers, there was a reduction of approximately 40 per cent in total vehicle deliveries to the Unilever House building site. This was considered the best managed site in that it had the lowest proportion of deliveries direct (Transport for London et al., 2008).

The vast majority of deliveries from the LCCC to construction sites were made in rigid goods vehicles. Consolidating goods at the LCCC eliminated the use of articulated goods vehicles for site delivery, and significantly reduced the use of vans. Two hours average reduction in supplier journey times were achieved by delivering to the LCCC rather than driving directly to the sites in the City of London (this included unloading time).

Deliveries from the LCCC to the sites achieved 97 per cent delivery reliability (i.e. 97 per cent materials of the correct type and quantity were delivered within 15 minutes of the scheduled time). In addition, productivity of the labour force on the construction sites increased by up to 25 minutes per person day as a result of the delivery reliability from the LCCC (Transport for London et al., 2008).

Negative impacts included some work scheduling problems at the construction sites caused by a lengthening of the order lead times for products channelled through the LCCC. There were also a few instances of incorrect components being sent from the LCCC to the sites and items being misplaced at the LCCC.

The LCCC trial was therefore judged to have been a success. While the original centre closed down at the end of the trial period, a 7,500 m^2 replacement construction UCC opened shortly afterwards in east London. This new UCC is operated by Wilson James, the operator of the trial UCC, on a commercial basis, highlighting the viability of the concept. It is serving a number of major construction projects, such as the redevelopment of Barts and the Royal London Hospital (Wilson James Ltd, 2008).

Case Study: London Heathrow Retail Consolidation Centre

Background and Objectives

Retail development within Heathrow airport increased dramatically over the decade up to 2000, but the capacity of road and unloading infrastructures was not expanded accordingly. Problems included traffic congestion on airport roads and at loading bays, and a lengthy and unpredictable delivery times. These issues, together with growing environmental pressures and the potential requirements of the planned Terminal 5, led to a re-examination of the supply system serving retail and catering outlets in Terminals 1-4.

A study reviewed the various retail delivery options. It concluded that the specific conditions would be best met by an urban consolidation centre through which all deliveries should pass with the exception of newspaper deliveries, cash and valuable items which should continue to be delivered directly to retail outlets.. A four-month trial was established in March 2000 in which the Heathrow Airport Limited (HAL) (the owner of Heathrow airport) contracted the logistics provider DHL Supply Chain to operate a consolidation centre, vehicle fleet and related goods reception and inventory management systems. Eight retailers with a total of 40 retail outlets across the four terminal buildings participated. Results showed a 66 per cent reduction in vehicle deliveries. Operations started in May 2001 (Department for Transport, 2002).

Operational Aspects

A 25,000 sq ft warehouse with cold store was established at Hatton Cross (2.5 km from Terminal 4) employing 20 operational and clerical staff. Deliveries by suppliers to the centre were subject to security checks, and then put into roll cages and sealed ready for dispatch to the retail outlets. By 2002 the delivery fleet consisted of three tractor units and three urban rear-steer 11 metre box van trailers with tail-lifts. Two trailers had dual compartments and were fitted with refrigeration to cater for chilled and frozen food deliveries. The delivery vehicles are also used to collect and remove empty roll cages, recyclable packaging waste, such as cardboard and plastic. In 2007 DHL introduced electric vehicles to the consolidation centre fleet (Avison, 2007a).

A new consolidation centre was developed in 2006 to cope with the growing space demands, higher product throughput and planning requirements for Terminal 5. This new centre is also based approximately 2.5 km from the airport and operates 24 hours a day, 7 days a week. Incoming deliveries are cross-docked onto the centre's vehicles and deliveries made to airside and landside stores from which other consolidation centre staff deliver orders to each retail outlet. These staff can also even stock shop shelves and carry out pre-retailing services such as pricing and ticketing.

By 2009 the consolidation centre was handling deliveries to 323 retail and catering outlets, pubs and restaurants based in the airport (DHL, 2009). The consolidation centre operation employs approximately 100 people (Avison, 2007b).

All retail and catering concessions operating at Heathrow airport use the consolidation centre as part of their rental agreement. It must therefore accommodate ambient, chilled and frozen goods. HCC operations have been effectively streamlined, increasing average accuracy to 99.9 per cent on all retail deliveries. Retail consolidation was a prerequisite for the planning permission to build Terminal 5 and is part of the future development of the airport including the renovation of Terminals 1 and 2.

Financial Aspects

The consolidation centre contract has a value to the operator DHL of approximately £9 million per year (DHL, 2009). By 2009 all retail and catering outlets based in the airport used the consolidation centre as part of their contractual agreement with HAL. Half of the income of the Heathrow consolidation centre is met by retailers and other outlets in the airport paying for the consolidated delivery service. 10 per cent of the income is generated from charges made for value added services such as pre-retailing and off-site storage. The remaining 40 per cent if income is met by the airport operator HAL (Hapgood, 2009).

Impact Assessment and Outcome

The Heathrow retail consolidation centre reduces vehicle deliveries to outlets in the airport by approximately 80 per cent (Bastien, 2007). It has been estimated that in 2008 these consolidated deliveries resulted in a saving of 218,000 km (DHL, 2009). This reduction in total distance travelled together with the use of an electric vehicle has been estimated to result in a 158,000 kg reduction in CO_2 emissions (DHL, 2009).

Case Study: Bristol Urban Consolidation Centre

Background and Objectives

The urban consolidation centre in Bristol was originally established as a trial in an EU-funded CIVITAS project. The objectives of the trial were to reduce goods vehicle activity in the central retailing area (Broadmead), thereby helping to relieve traffic congestion, improve air quality and minimise conflict between vehicles at loading areas/delivery bays. The trial was also intended to provide suppliers and retailers with improved logistics services, removing the need for suppliers to send their vehicles into central Bristol, increasing delivery reliability and offering a range of value-added services for such as pre-retailing, remote storage, and packaging and waste collection. The consolidation centre and delivery operations have been operated by DHL since it opened in 2004.

Operational Aspects

The trial commenced in May 2004. It has since become a permanent urban consolidation centre scheme. Retailer participation in the consolidation centre scheme is voluntary. The area served has been extended from Broadmead to the new Cabot Circus Centre retail development which opened in 2008 adding 40 per cent to the retail floorspace in the area. Also in 2008, new pedestrian areas were introduced and tighter loading time restrictions imposed (0500-0800 for the main pedestrian area of Broadmead). This has encouraged more retailers to make use of the consolidation centre (START, 2008). The catchment area comprises over 400 retail outlets approximately 70 of which currently use the consolidation scheme (Minihane, 2009).

The consolidation centre has a floorspace of 500 sq. m. and is located on an established industrial estate on the north western edge of Bristol, close to both the M4 and M5 motorways, 15 kilometres (25 minutes travel time) from Broadmead district, (Minihane, 2009).

Two delivery vehicles are operated from the centre, an 18 tonne diesel-powered vehicle with a Euro IV engine and a 9 tonne electric goods vehicle (Hapgood, 2009). The centre handles retail goods only and operates six days per week (Bastien, 2007). The local transport authority allows UCC vehicles to access a bus lane to and from the city centre on a trial basis to cut delivery times and improve reliability (Hapgood, 2009).

In addition to the consolidation and delivery services, other value-added services are provided including collection of waste cardboard and plastic for recycling, and pre-retailing activities.

Financial Aspects

The development and trial phase of the UCC from 2002-2006 was funded through the EC CIVITAS VIVALDI project. Some subsequent financial support has been provided by Bristol City Council. In 2007/08, the total UCC operating cost was £459,000, of which £285,000 came from Bristol City Council against income from retail users of £174,000. This represents a cost recovery rate of almost 40 per cent from users. In 2008/09, Bristol City Council contributed £225,000 (Hapgood, 2008). DHL Supply Chain is tasked with further increasing the cost recovery from retailers as public funding is planned to reduce progressively over time. This is intended to be achieved through signing up new retailers to use the service, and selling more value-added services to users. In addition, the UCC is to be offered to non-retail end users, and the scope of UCC services can also be expanded to include council deliveries (Minihane, 2009). However, despite the reduction in the proportion of total costs met from public funds it is likely that public support will be required on a continuing basis, especially as there is currently no mechanism for enforcing participation by retailers.

Impacts Assessment and Outcome

The UCC has resulted in a 77 per cent reduction in vehicle deliveries to participating retailers. This is equivalent to a total reduction of approximately 10,000 vehicle deliveries per annum, with a saving of 250,000 vehicle kilometres. It is estimated that the UCC scheme yields annual savings of approximately 30 tonnes of CO_2, 1,000 kg of NOx, and 30 kg of PM10. In addition 20 tonnes of cardboard/plastic are collected and recycled (Hapgood, 2009; Minihane, 2009).

Feedback from retailers has been positive, with 94 per cent stating that they would recommend the UCC service to another retailer. There have been no reports of losses or damage to stock, and a majority of retailers report that they are saving more than 20 minutes per delivery. As a consequence, 38 per cent say that this enables their staff to spend more time with customers, and 45 per cent state that staff morale has improved and stress levels have reduced (Minihane, 2009). Retailers generally seem to appreciate the improved service and cost reduction opportunities offered by channelling deliveries through the UCC.

While the scheme has been successful in operational terms, the main challenge is to improve the commercial viability of the scheme and to find further sources of income from potential users.

Case Study: City of London Micro-Consolidation Centre

Background and Objectives

Office Depot is a major supplier of stationary and other office products to businesses in the UK. In 2009 Office Depot made the decision to trial a new urban delivery system in the City of London in order to reduce the environmental impacts of their delivery operation. This decision was taken as part of the company's corporate social responsibility and environmental efforts (Office Depot, 2010a). However, it was also necessary for the new scheme to meet customer needs cost-effectively if it was to be adopted on a permanent basis (Office Depot, 2010b).

The City of London lies within the area of the Clear Zone Partnership serves as a testing ground for researching, trialling, monitoring and setting best practice for new transport technologies, innovations and physical measures. Since 1999 the London Borough of Camden, the City of London and the City of Westminster have worked jointly to achieve this.

Operational Aspects

The trial involved the use of an urban micro-consolidation centre located within the City of London together with electrically-assisted tricycles and electric vans. The customers to whom deliveries were made were all located in the City of London which is the historic core of London with an area of 2.9km^2. It is an area comprising a mix of very narrow streets and wider roads with double red lines on which no stopping is allowed, and have very heavy traffic flows in the morning peak. The urban micro-consolidation centre and the deliveries made from it were operated by Gnewt Cargo, a new company specialising in green urban freight deliveries.

Prior to the trial Office Depot operated a distribution system for deliveries in the City of London that involved using 3.5 tonne gross weight diesel-powered vans that were despatched from a warehouse located approximately 30 kilometres away in the London suburbs. A total of approximately 1,000 parcels were delivered per day, all to businesses addresses.

During the trial the micro-consolidation centre in the City of London was used as a transhipment facility for the transfer of parcels from the suburban depot onto electric vans and tricycles and for overnight vehicle storage. An 18-tonne goods vehicle was used to transport parcels overnight from the Office Depot warehouse in the suburbs of London to the micro-consolidation centre. Electrically-assisted tricycles and electric vans were used to make parcel deliveries from the micro-consolidation centre to customers in the City of London. Neither of these vehicles resulted in any fossil fuel consumption or CO_2 emissions as the electricity they used was produced from renewable sources.

Financial Aspects

The London Borough of Camden made a small financial contribution towards the costs of the trial as the City of London delivery area and much of the route taken from the suburban depot to the City of London was within the Clear Zone Partnership area. All the other costs were met by Office Depot, who expected the new delivery system to have similar costs to their existing system. The system was trialled in the City of London as it comprises a high density of Office depot delivery locations. This results in a relatively short travel distance between delivery locations and was therefore felt to be an appropriate setting in which to test the cost-effectiveness of using electrically-assisted tricycles for freight delivery (Office Depot, 2010b).

The trial proved successful from Office Depot's perspective in transport, environmental and financial terms. Office Depot has calculated that the new system with its electric vehicles and micro-consolidation centre has the same operating costs as the previous system using diesel vans dispatched the suburban London depot (Office Depot, 2010b).

Impacts Assessment and Outcome

The results show that the use of the micro-consolidation centre together with the complete replacement of the diesel van fleet by electrically-assited tricycles and electric vans led to a reduction of 20 per cent in the total distance driven per parcel delivered between the suburban depot and the customer delivery locations. Total CO_2 equivalent emissions per parcel delivered was 54 per cent lower in May 2010 than in October 2009 before the trial. This was due to the reduction in the total distance travelled per parcel and the use of electric vehicles whose batteries are charged with electricity from carbon-free sources.

The distance travelled between the suburban depot and the City of London per parcel delivered fell by 82 per cent due to the use of a single truck to transport goods between the suburban depot and the micro-consolidation centre in the City of London. However, within the City of London the total distance travelled per parcel delivered increased by 349 per cent by May 2010. This was due to the lower carrying capacity of the electric vans and tricycles compared to the diesel vans, thereby resulting in the need for more delivery activity per day. CO_2 emissions fell by 49 per cent, per parcel delivered between the suburban depot and the City of London, and by 83 per cent per parcel delivered within the City of London compared with the situation before the trial.

The results therefore reflect the trade-off between total distance travelled and CO_2 emissions associated with the use of electric vehicles replacing diesel vehicles with greater carrying capacity. The trial was of particular interest as the existing Office Depot delivery system prior to the trial already involved a high degree of product consolidation and hence high vehicle lading factors. It did not therefore typify the types of operation in which UCCs are usually considered beneficial – namely systems with poor load consolidation.

Due to the environmental and financial success of the trial, Office Depot decided to continue the operation beyond the end of the trial period. The scheme has now been made permanent (Office Depot, 2010b). Office Depot intends to implement the same delivery system in other cities, and is also considering the potential use of electrically-assisted tricycles in other environmentally sensitive locations or where noise pollution is an issue such as university campuses (Office Depot, 2010b).

FUTURE RESEARCH DIRECTIONS

A range of organisational, operational and financial issues have to be addressed in assessing the performance of UCC schemes. These include: the potentially high set up costs (and sometimes high operating costs) that need to be recovered; contractual issues concerning legal responsibility for goods; the loss of the direct interface between suppliers and customers possibly deterring some users; the relatively low rates of product throughput in the early stages; and the potential for local authorities to create monopolistic UCC situations, thus eliminating competition and perhaps leading to legal action.

Two factors appear to be decisive in the success of a UCC scheme. The first is the level of demand. Sufficient UCC users and product throughput is required to drive down the costs per unit handled thereby making the UCC highly competitive with traditional urban distribution systems. The second is the sharing of UCC costs and benefits between the various parties involved in the scheme. Although the UCC may result in total benefits that outweigh total costs (taking into account commercial, traffic, social and environmental impacts), each party must be prepared to share these costs and benefits fairly if the scheme is to succeed (Browne et al., 2005; TTR, 2007).

These two issues are less problematic in the case of UCCs that serve major sites with a single landlord and construction project UCCs as in these cases a single commercial party is typically responsible for financing the UCC. It either enjoys all the benefits or has leverage to recover some of the costs from the beneficiaries of the scheme.

The situation for UCCs that serve all or part of an urban area is more problematic. In these cases the decision of users to participate in the UCC is typically a voluntary one and there is no single private body responsible for financing the UCC or exploiting the benefits. Instead there are typically many business users, as well as a local authority that is keen to implement the UCC in its efforts to reduce traffic and environmental impacts. The financial costs in this type of UCC scheme tends to be largely borne by the local authority at least in the initial stages. This level of public subsidy is usually unsustainable in the longer term and therefore efforts to increase product throughput, and reduce unit costs become critical.

In the short-term the local authority can implement accompanying policy measures that encourage greater use of the UCC, such as allowing UCC vehicles access to bus lanes, or imposing tighter vehicle access or loading restrictions in the UCC catchment area. As new users are attracted to use the UCC and throughput increases, the level of public subsidy can be gradually reduced, until the UCC becomes financially self-supporting. It is important that mechanisms are put in place so that all users (carriers and receivers) make financial contributions in return for the commercial gains that the UCC offers them. The provision and marketing of value-added logistics services generates an additional stream of revenue and broadens the role of the UCC within the city logistics system.

There is a need for further research into the economic and environmental costs and benefits that arise from different types of UCC and the means by which these costs can be minimised and the benefits maximised. In addition, further consideration is required of how best to apportion the economic costs associated with the UCC between the various parties involved in order to ensure that the scheme is equitable and therefore attractive to all. In addition, it would be useful to understand the most promising and realistic actions that could be taken by various local authorities if they wished to encourage the use of a UCC approach.

CONCLUSION

This chapter has considered the role that can be played by UCCs in rationalising the movement of freight in urban areas. By increasing the consolidation of loads UCCs can assist in reducing delivery costs and environmental impacts. They also permit greater use of electric and other alternatively-fuelled goods vehicles which emit less CO_2 and other, noxious gases and help to reduce vehicle noise. UCCs should therefore be viewed as a potentially important innovation in helping to achieve greater sustainability in urban freight transport in both economic and environmental terms.

The case studies presented in the chapter have helped to demonstrate the various types of UCC that can be established and their attributes. As discussed the two key factors in the success of a UCC are the obtaining sufficient product throughput, and determining how the costs and benefits that arise from the use of a UCC will be shared fairly between the various parties involved in the scheme. UCCs can benefit from the public and private sectors working closely together to attempt to ensure their success. This is particularly necessary in the case of UCCs that serve all or part of an urban area, as operating incentives and some degree of public subsidy may well be required for a UCC to achieve viability, especially during its establishment.

REFERENCES

Attlassy, M. & University of Westminster (2005). *The tricycle experimentation in Paris "la Petite Reine"*. University of Westminster.

Avison, R. (2007a). *DHL hopes to expand airport consolidation centre, RoadTransport.com, 24 July 2007.* Retrieved December 18, 2010, from http://www.roadtransport.com/Articles/2007/07/24/127981/DHL-hopes-to-expand-airport -consolidation-centre.htm

Avison, R. (2007b). *Making consolidation centres work.* RoadTransport.com, 27 July 2007. Retrieved December 18, 2010, from http://www.roadtransport.com/ Articles/2007/07/27/128022/Making-consolidation-centres-work.htm

Bastien, O. (2007). *An Introduction to Retail Consolidation Centres*. presentation to the West London Freight Quality Partnership, 10th January 2007.

Browne, M., Woodburn, A., & Allen, J. (2007). Evaluating the potential for urban consolidation centres. *European Transport, 35*, 46–63.

Browne, M., Woodburn, A., Sweet, M., & Allen, J. (2005). *Urban Freight Consolidation Centres*. Report for Department for Transport, London: University of Westminster. Retrieved December 20, 2010, from http://www.freightbestpractice.org.uk/urban-freight-consolidation-centre-report

Department for Transport. (2002). *Heathrow Airport Retail Consolidation Centre*. Good Practice Case Study 402, Energy Efficiency Best Practice Programme. Retrieved December 18, 2010, from http://www.freightbestpractice.org.uk /heathrow-airport-retail- consolidation-centre

DHL. (2009). *DHL wins major contract extension for Heathrow Consolidation Center*. press release 16 November 2009, DHL. Retrieved January 5, 2011, from http://www.dp-dhl.com/en/media_relations /press_releases/2009/dhl_wins_contract_extension_for_heathrow_ consolidation_center.html

Gonzalez-Feliu, J., & Morana, J. (2010). Are City Logistics Solutions Sustainable? The Cityporto case. *Territorio Mobilità e Ambiente*, *3*(2), 55–64.

Hapgood, T. (2008). *Broadmead Freight Consolidation Scheme*. presentation made 28 July 2008 (provided by T. Hapgood).

Hapgood, T. (2009). *The Importance of Freight Management and the Role of Urban Consolidation Centres*. Paper presented at Seventh Transport Practitioners Meeting: Ideas and Reality, 13-15 July, University of Reading.

JMP & TTR. (2010). *Tactran Freight Consolidation Feasibility Study*. Draft Feasibility Report, Prepared for Tactran, JMP and TTR. Retrieved December 18, 2010, from http://www.tactran.gov.uk/documents/ TactranFreightConsolidationDraft FeasibilityReport280410.pdf

McKinnon, A. (1998a). *International Review of Urban Transhipment Studies and Initiatives*, Report prepared for the Retail and Distribution Panel of the UK Government's Foresight Programme, Edinburgh: Heriot Watt University. Retrieved December 20, 2010, from http://www.sml.hw.ac.uk/logistics /downloads/UKTranshipINT.pdf

McKinnon, A. (1998b). *Urban Transhipment: Review of Previous Work in the UK*. Report prepared for the Retail and Distribution Panel of the UK Government's Foresight Programme, Edinburgh: Heriot Watt University. Retrieved December 20, 2010, from http://www.sml.hw.ac.uk/logistics / downloads/UKTranshipUK.pdf

Minihane, E. (2009). *Bristol Consolidation Centre*. Presentation made at Chartered Institute of Logistics and Transport Seminar 14th October 2009. Retrieved January 5, 2011, from http://www.ciltuk.org.uk/pages downloadfile?d=52F89921-7B0D-4B0E-A8A7- 30462F93EFC7&a=stream

Office Depot. (2010a). *We all contribute: 2010 Corporate Citizenship Report*. Florida: Office Depot. Retrieved December 20, 2010, from http://www.officedepot.cc/environment t/downloads/OD-Corporate-Citizenship-Report-2010.pdf

Office Depot. (2010b). *Launch of Cargo Cycles*. Office Depot Briefing Document, Office Depot. Retrieved December 20, 2010, from http://www.officedepot.co.uk/ OD_content/data/documents/press-kit/ Cargo%20Cycle%20%20 briefing%20 doc1.pdf

START. (2008). *City of Bristol: Access Management and Priority Measures*. START project factsheet. Retrieved January 4, 2011, from http://www.start-project.org/download /fact%20sheets/START%20 Bristol%20WP3%20Dec08.pdf

Transport for London. (2009). *Cycle Freight in London – A Scoping Study*. London: Transport for London. Retrieved December 20, 2010 from http://www.tfl.gov.uk/assets/ downloads/businessandpartners/ cycle-as-freight-may-2009.pdf

Transport for London, Bovis Lend Lease, Constructing Excellence, Stanhope, Wilson James and the University of Westminster. (2008). *London Construction Consolidation Centre: Final Report*, London: Transport for London. Retrieved December 20, 2010, from http://www.tfl.gov.uk/microsites /freight/documents/publications / LCCC_final_report_July_2009.pdf

TTR. (2007). *South London Freight Consolidation Centre Feasibility Study: Final Report*. Report prepared on behalf of South London Freight Quality Partnership, TTR. Retrieved December 18, 2010, from http://www.londonsfqps.co.uk/ LinkClick.aspx?fileticket=1FSau5i7vTI%3d& tabid=188& mid=520&forcedownload=true

TTR. (2010). *Freight Consolidation Centre Study: Main Report*. Prepared for Department for Transport, TTR. Retrieved December 18, 2010, from http://www.dft.gov.uk/pgr /freight/research/freightreport/pdf /mainreport.pdf

van Duin, R., Quak, H., & Muñuzuri, J. (2010). New challenges for urban consolidation centres: A case study in The Hague, The Sixth International Conference on City Logistics. *Procedia Social and Behavioral Sciences*, 2, 6177–6188.

van Rooijen, T., & Quak, H. (2010). Local Impacts Of A New Urban Consolidation Centre – The Case of Binnenstadservice.nl, The Sixth International Conference on City Logistics, *Procedia Social and Behavioral Sciences,* 2, 5967–5979.

Ville, S., Gonzalez-Feliu, J., & Dablanc, L. (2010). *The limits of public policy intervention in urban logistics: The case of Vicenza (Italy) and lessons for other European cities*. At the 12th World Conference on Transport Research, 11-15th July, Lisbon, Portugal.

Wilson James Ltd. (2008). Personal communication from representative of Wilson James Ltd, July 2008.

WSP. (2008). *Freight Consolidation and Remote Storage*, BCSC Educational Trust. Retrieved December 18, 2010, from http://www.bcsc.org.uk/media/ downloads/FreightConsolidation2008.pdf

Chapter 14
The Role of Logistics Service Providers in the Development of Sustainability-Related Innovation

Maria Huge-Brodin
Linköping University, Sweden

ABSTRACT

Logistics service providers (LSPs) are important actors in the supply chain, and due to the transport intensive activities they manage, they can make a large contribution to the development of sustainable supply chains. They are often considered as reactive and quite passive in their role vis-à-vis their customers though many possess the critical logistics capabilities required to make distribution operations less damaging to the environment. Developing green logistics service offerings can be one way of greening the whole supply chain, though today there appears to be little demand for these services. In the longer term, however LSPs are likely to benefit from being an environmentally innovative and to apply their environmental knowledge more effectively inside their organisations. This will strengthen their competitive position in a future logistics market in which environmental capabilities become major selection criteria. Many of the innovative systems and practices may not be motivated primarily by a desire to preserve the environment but will, nevertheless, contribute to sustainable development. To make a major commitment to greening client's supply chain, an LSP will often require a longer-term contract that supports investment in more environmentally friendly technology and business processes.

DOI: 10.4018/978-1-60960-585-8.ch014

INTRODUCTION

Coordination between supply chain partners is often stressed as a pre-requisite for effective and efficient supply chain management. It is also argued that to achieve environmental and social sustainability in their logistics operations, companies must adopt a supply chain perspective to avoid sub-optimisation, and to avoid moving the problems around instead of reducing them (see e.g. Wu and Dunn, 1995). It is also common for supply chain initiatives to involve manufacturers, suppliers and retailers but exclude intermediaries like transport providers (Spens and Bask, 2002). This overlooks the fact that, Logistics Service Providers (LSPs) are crucial players in a co-ordinated and competitive supply chain.

Enhancing the sustainability of a supply chain should not only improve its performance in environmental and social terms, but also yield economic benefits. In this chapter, the focus is on the LSPs efforts to achieve sustainability across the so-called 'triple bottom line'. For LSPs, which normally participate in numerous supply chains simultaneously, a major challenge is to balance environmental, social and economic objectives across a range of clients. Many clients have traditionally regarded LSPs as being quite conservative, unresponsive and non-innovative companies. This characterisation of LSPs is often unfair and can be attributed to their client not giving them sufficient freedom and / or resources to innovate. Mounting pressures to make transport more sustainable are giving a new opportunity to demonstrate that they can be proactive and creative. In many business settings, after all, they are likely to be the player with most logistics-related knowledge resources, and hence to take lead in the development of sustainability initiatives. Many LSPs are keen to exploit this position and are now taking steps towards becoming more environmental sustainable and gaining the business opportunities available to early starters in a developing market. Many LSPs will, however, find it challenging to switch from a passive, responsive role to a more pro-active and innovative one. The aim of this chapter is to review different options available to LSPs wishing to develop and market a capability in environmentally sustainable logistics and to discuss the potential for them to take a leading role in the greening of supply chains.

LSPS AND SUSTAINABILITY-RELATED INNOVATION

It is now vital for LSPs to include environmental considerations in their overall business offering, and more specific business models targeted on particular market segments (Maack and Huge-Brodin, 2009). How are LSPs responding to the market demands for sustainable services today? An investigation among Swedish LSPs shows, in line with the findings of Wolf and Seuring (2010), that the LSPs are actually offering more environmental services than the market – the customers – demand (Martinsen and Björklund, 2010). As logistics is really their core business, LSPs' sustainability innovations are closely related to the logistics innovations. Flint et al. (2005) distinguish two types of logistical innovations: technological innovations and process innovations, and relate them to what can be included in a sustainable service offering from an LSP (Martinsen and Huge-Brodin, 2010).

Green service offerings from LSPs were described on the basis of literature reviews, a homepage scan, and a survey study among Swedish LSPs and logistics customers. They included choices relating to technology, emission- and energy reports as well as more complex issues like transport planning and environment-related network (Martinsen and Huge-Brodin, 2010). The investigation showed that the LSPs offerings exceed both the actual demand and the expectations from their customers, specifically in the areas of energy reports, mode choice, transport planning and network design (Martinsen and Björklund,

2010). On the other hand, the different groups' offerings and demands were more closely matched in their assessments of environmentally classified vehicles and fuels (Figure 1).

These findings can be interpreted in different ways. On the one hand, the LSPs' perception is that they over supply relative to the market demands, as represented by the customers' expectations. This would suggest that the LSPs are taking on a more proactive role, and that they present innovations before they are really demanded by the market. On the other hand, the gap between the LSP and the customer perceptions may partly be the result of differing interpretations of the levels of demand by the two groups. In fact, their opinions may be more closely aligned than the figures suggest. Such an interpretation would of course be less encouraging for the LSPs. However the interpretation that the LSPs would be more pro-active and innovative than demanded also presents the LSPs with some problems. As the logistics industry at large is cost-focussed and operates on relatively small margins, LSPs may doubt the benefit investing in greener services which their client are neither demanding or are prepared to pay for. In the short term, this might be the right conclusion to draw, however in this chapter the focus will be mainly on the more long-term options for innovating the logistics service industry from an environmental sustainability point of view. On this time-scale, LSP are likely to have a stronger incentive to green their service offering.

OPTIONS FOR THE DEVELOPMENT OF SUSTAINABILITY-RELATED INNOVATIONS BY LSPS

Even though there is some disagreement about the extent to which LSPs have greened their operations (Isaksson and Huge-Brodin, 2010), it appears that most companies have implemented at least some green measures. This chapter describes the different types of service innovation that have been applied that have yielded some sustainability benefit. It excludes carbon offset programmes, which may help neutralise of the carbon emissions from the transport- and logistics operations, but do not require business innovation. Attention will

Figure 1. The LSPs' green service offerings and the customers' demand, described per green item. The respondents were asked to rank each item according to which extent they included the item in their offering or demand (5 fully agree – 1 don't agree at all) (Martinsen and Björklund, 2010).

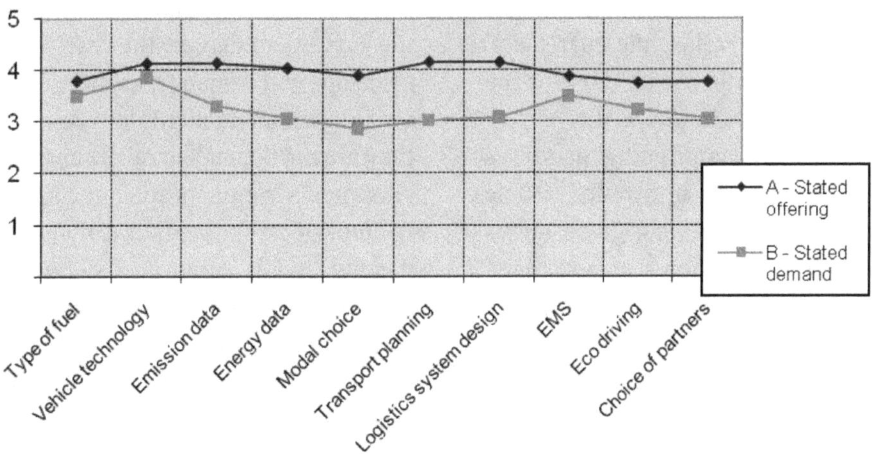

focus instead on those innovative service offerings that require more complex management and operation by the LSP and often include a company commitment on the strategic level.

This section starts with a brief description of the drivers and barriers encountered in the development of green service offerings among LSPs. It focuses on green service offerings that are available today. The section ends with an examination of the range of options for LSPs to further develop their green services. For those offerings that exist, and those that may emerge in the future, it is possible to differentiate several levels of innovation; in the management of resources, in the interactions with customers and in the strategic positioning of the LSPs with regards to environmental sustainability.

Within the logistics services sector, sustainability-related innovation is constrained, as discussed above, by cost pressures, low margins and doubts about customers' willingness to pay for environmental improvements. Very few investments are, therefore, made without evidence of a more definite customer requirement, including the willingness to share the investment. Other inhibiting factors are the transactional nature of the business relationships, which tends only to support investments with a quite short payback period. This, for example, discourages the adoption of new vehicle technology. It should be noted, however, this was one of the areas where, in the survey mentioned earlier, the customers' responses were closely in line with those of the LSPs (Martinsen and Björklund, 2010).

The customers apply conflicting pressures on some of the largest LSPs in Sweden. While some LSPs have been developing green initiatives primarily to attract the interest of customers, customers' lack of interest has become a major disincentive for others (Isaksson and Huge-Brodin, 2010). The customers are sceptical of the new service offerings and are not willing to pay a premium price for the greening of the logistics services that they procure. In fact, some customers have argued that those environmental measures that actually involve cutting costs – e-g- saving fuel – should not provoke increased prices, rather the opposite. These findings highlight a strategic dilemma for the LSPs in trying to determine when the new green services are likely to be required. They would also like to know to what extent they should be investing in 'green' knowledge in anticipation of a future growth in demand for greener logistics services. In the survey, top management support was stated as an important driver for green innovations among LSPs. This further underlines the strategic nature of their commitment to green issues. If, however, customer interest in these issues remains relatively low, sustainability may drop down the list of LSP's corporate priorities.

Current Efforts by LSPs to Green their Services

The offerings that we see today, and those that are emerging, concern both technical and process innovations. These different types of innovation seem to differ in complexity and the technical ones often need to be accompanied by some modification of processes. One of the aspects that the LSPs and the customers in the survey agreed upon was the level of demand and service offering in one aspect of environmental technology, namely the Euro-emission standards of vehicles and fuels (Martinsen & Björklund, 2010). One reason for the agreement may be the ease of defining these offerings and demands, as there exist established environmental standards for vehicles and fuels and they are not dependent on the customer's specific situation. Statements about the green technology content of an innovation can easily be communicated and is often posted on LSP's website (Martinsen & Huge-Brodin, 2010). However, in discussing the adoption of new technologies that stretch beyond the lowest acceptable level, LSP representatives often highlight the need for longer term contractual relationships with customers, which would allow for a longer payback period as well as enhancing the possibilities for sharing the related investment with specific customers (Martinsen et al. 2009). Respondents emphasised that it is not so much new technology that is needed; rather it is ways of increasing the adoption rate for these existing technological advances. This in turn would require innovation in the way LSPs do business with customers in the supply chain, specifically regarding the duration of contracts and sharing of investments.

A second issue that is highlighted by LSPs in their business communication (e.g. in their sustainability reports) is their willingness to provide customers with reports on the carbon emissions (Martinsen and Huge-Brodin, 2010). This is something which the customers in general appreciate, as they in turn are either obliged to, or choose to pass on details of their carbon footprint to their customers. These carbon reports can take different forms; some LSPs offer a free yearly carbon assessment, while others offer, as a supplementary, chargeable service, carbon declarations at an individual shipment level. There is also a variation in the way in which the disaggregated data is provided; it can either they be purchased in separate reports or treated as a value-enhancing feature, which the customer can either access via the internet or receive as additional information on the invoice. Whichever method of data delivery is used, the LSP still has the problem of ensuring the accuracy of the carbon assessment. There presents an innovation challenge for much of the organisation and not simply the environmental department or manager. The carbon assessment, after all, must span the full range of the LSP's activities. The LSP can choose to develop a special competence in carbon auditing or incorporate this environmental assessment within existing business systems. The latter approach still requires, beside the modification of existing software and reporting routines, a high level commitment by top management. For example, one of the largest LSPs operating in Sweden addresses the environmental reporting issue at board level, with directors receiving regular reports of the environmental performance of the company's transport operation.

A third problem that LSPs face when declaring information about their environmental performance is scepticism on the part of customers. The Swedish survey revealed that in the area of environmental report the level of trust between the LSPs and their customers is currently low (Isaksson and Huge-Brodin, 2010). This is a somewhat intriguing dilemma for the LSPs; they are expected to deliver expert logistics knowledge and high-performing logistics solutions to their customers, in a more proactive way than they have done in the past. But at the same time, when it comes to the green aspects of their service portfolio, they are often not trusted by their clients. Many of these clients place greater trust in some of the general environmental consultants who, in the past, have often proved themselves reliable to the customers in previous projects. One way of rectifying this trust problem would be for LSPs to form alliances with these environmental consultants treating them as partners rather than competitors. That would potentially earn more respect from the customers and increase the perceived value of their relationship with the LSP. It would also be a way of accessing more environmental knowledge and developing more unique capabilities for the LSPs, thereby increasing their competitive edge (Maack et al., 2010).

LSPs are at different stages in acquiring environmental knowledge and developing capabilities in green logistics. In many cases the challenge is not the acquisition of new knowledge but to better utilise the knowledge already possessed by the employees (see e.g. Maack & Huge-Brodin, 2010). While knowledge is one of many types of sustainability-related resources, it is vital for LSPs as it is one of the main reasons that companies outsource their logistics operations (Andersson, 1998). Knowledge can be defined at both the level of the individual employee and the organisation as a whole. At this higher level the company can marshal the individuals' knowledge and translate it into an important organisational asset (Maack et al., 2010). This presents a great challenge to LSPs, but also offers a great opportunity as they strive to gain competitive advantage through enhanced sustainability (ibid).

Future Efforts to Green Logistics Services

Some of today's innovations will take years to be implemented and refined. They will strengthen the LSPs competitiveness in a future possibly greener logistics service market in the medium to long term. In this section we will speculate on the future development of sustainability-related innovations by LSPs, which may strongly influence their future prosperity.

The pricing of more environmentally friendly services offered by LSPs, has been debated for some time. Research has been done on the extent to which the external costs of freight transport are internalised by taxation and its potential impact on logistics systems (Piecyk and McKinnon, 2008), but the market pricing of green logistics services by LSPs has so far attracted little attention. LSPs differ in their approaches to charging for green services, or the green content of their services. There is general consensus, however that the market is not yet mature enough for pricing green logistics services on a commercial basis (Isaksson & Huge-Brodin, 2010). However, should LSP's clients in the future value environmental performance more highly than they do today, a logical development would be that price models reflect this value. Sustainability would then exert some influence on rates alongside resource costs, service quality etc. The implementation of current proposals to internalise the environmental costs of freight transport in the EU would force LSPs to recover the higher taxes in higher rates. Whether more substantial taxes or more elusive customer value, LSPs could devise innovative pricing structures to try to capture some of the added value that customers attached to greener logistics services.

It has been observed that larger structural and strategic changes in the supply chain often offset the incremental improvements accomplished on a tactical or operational level (McKinnon, 2003). It has also been demonstrated, however, that structural changes, such as the centralisation of warehousing, can in turn increase the options for tactical and operational improvements (Aronsson & Huge-Brodin, 2006). Generally speaking, the larger the change to a system is, or the larger the domain it includes, the greater will be the sustainability impacts. For LSPs an important challenge for the future is to be able to enlarge their domain of responsibility and action. If they were allowed to take charge of their customers' entire logistics systems instead of just the transport operation, they would have more potential to apply their deep skill in the design and management of logistics systems. It would allow them to take a more holistic perspective of the environmental performance of the logistics system and avoid sub-optimisation, as discussed by Wu and Dunn (1995).

This type of innovation, requiring the extension of LSPs' control over a logistical system, is today inhibited by many of the obstacles discussed above. Playing a more active role in a customer's logistical system is not a short-term commitment, and therefore a longer-term contractual relationship is needed. To achieve this, the LSP would need to earn the trust of its customer to a higher degree than what is commonly the case today. Many companies would have to gain more confidence in an LSP's knowledge and capability in the development of green and profitable logistics solutions. More traditional logistics capabilities can also play a large role in this trust-building process (Maack and Huge-Brodin, 2009).

FUTURE RESEARCH DIRECTIONS

Overall, LSPs have not yet to any large extent been the topic in green logistics research. However their role in the green logistics innovation process is quite central. In this section we identify some areas of research, which could help LSPs to assume the central role more effectively and profitably. Priority should be given to research on the capabilities LSPs need to gain to be able to differentiate themselves as green operators.

The calculation and allocation of emissions in logistics systems is another fertile area for research. In the absence of detailed carbon measurement, it is far more difficult to decide which steps to take. For LSPs providing shared and groupage services the ability to divide carbon emissions from warehouses and vehicles between particular clients' consignments will become a basic requirement. This will also have to be done in a manner that conforms to national standards, such as those currently being developed by the European standards agency, CEN. Failure to do this on an accurate and consistent basis will be seen as a service deficiency by more environmentally-aware customers and may ultimately infringe law on the reporting of carbon emissions.

The development of sustainable logistics offerings by LSPs can find parallels in the application of the general concept of Supply chain management. The SCM literature highlights the need for longer-term relationships, and the sharing of burdens as well as profits. New sustainability initiatives by LSPs will similarly benefit from the existence of long-term relationships and an enlightened approach to the sharing of the resulting costs and benefits. Future research on green logistics, and specifically on LSPs' role in green logistics, should adopt this wider supply chain perspective.

CONCLUSION

In order to become more attractive for customers within sustainable supply chains, LSPs need to be a more fertile source of innovation. Despite that the LSPs exceed the expectations of their customers regarding green services, the lack of trust between the LSPs and their customers inhibits the development of green services. Ways to promote the level of trust include adopting a more pro-active approach to greening the logistics services, which in turn demand a vast range of innovation initiatives. The commitment to innovation needs to extend from the organisation as a whole to individual employee. Environmental assessment and reporting has been stressed as a crucial capability in the interaction between LSPs and other supply chain members.

LSPs need to incorporate the green initiatives into their business models, which will require top management support. This will extend the range of green service offerings to customers. These services can either be embedded in the general service, or come in the form of specific activities, targeted on customers with a higher environmental concern. Companies that procure the greener service alternative (or chooses the LSP with the greener overall offering) will gain a greener profile while the LSP with a greener service portfolio than its competitors will strengthen its position on a logistics market. Those LSPs with the strongest green capabilities will need both a longer-term relationship and extension control over a client's system to be able to fully exploit these capabilities. In some cases, this long term relationship could take the form of a joint investment in green logistics technology.

Through innovating their internal operations and environmental work, LSPs could take advantage of their position as intermediaries in the supply chain. Innovating their business offerings would enhance their supply chain position, allowing them to contribute substantially to the development of sustainable supply chains. While there are still few concrete examples of this occurring in practice, many LSPs are well aware of the potential role that they could play. And this poses a challenge to the companies in the supply chain that are potential LSP customers as well: are they ready to make the necessary modifications to their systems to accommodate the green logistics innovations offered by their LSPs? Are they also willing to enter into the types of contractual agreements with LSPs that gives them adequate incentive to develop innovative approaches to the greening of supply chains as strategic partners?

REFERENCES

Andersson, D. (1998). Outsourcing Logistics in Partnerships - Driving Forces and Effects. In Bask, A. H., & Vepsäläinen, A. P. J. (Eds.), *Opening Markets for Logistics* (pp. 23–34). Helsinki.

Aronsson, H., & Huge Brodin, M. (2006). Environmental impact of changing logistics structures. *The International Journal of Logistics Management, 17*(3), 394–415. doi:10.1108/09574090610717545

Flint, D., Larsson, E., Gammelgaard, B., & Mentzer, J. (2005). Logistics innovation: a customer value-oriented social process, in *Journal of Business Logistics,* 26(1), pp. 113-147.

Isaksson, K., & Huge-Brodin, M. (2010). Driving forces and barriers when pricing the environmental service offering – a cross case study of logistics companies. *Proceedings from the 15th LRN Conference* in Harrogate, pp. 303-311, Sept. 8-10

Maack, C., Huge-Brodin, M. & Abrahamsson, M. (2010). Greening logistics companies by utilizing employees' capabilities. In the *Proceedings from the 15th LRN Conference* in Harrogate, pp. 427-435, Sept. 8-10.

Maack, C., & Huge-Brodin, M. (2009). *Innovation in Logistics Companies: A Literature Review and Proposed Research Framework for Sustainable Business Models.* In the Proceedings from the 21st Annual Nofoma Conference, 11-12 June, Jönköping, Sweden, pp. 466-482.

Maack, C., & Huge-Brodin, M. (2010). Logistics companies' potential in greening their offered services. In the *Proceedings from the 17th EUROMA Conference* in Porto, paper No. SSC11, June 6-9 2010.

Martinsen, U., & Björklund, M. (2010). *Green Logistics Offerings and Demands - Matches and Gaps.* In Whiteing, T.,(ed). LRN, 8-10 September 2010 Harrogate, UK. 453-461.

Martinsen, U., & Huge-Brodin, M. (2010). *Greening the offerings of logistics service providers.* In Stentoft Arlbjörn, J., (ed). NOFOMA, 10-11 June 2010 Kolding, Denmark. 969-984.

Martinsen, U., Maack, C., Björklund, M., & Huge-Brodin, M. (2009). *Today's Challenges in Fostering Greener Logistics Systems.* In the Proceeding from the Logistics Research Network Conference 2009, 9-11 September in Cardiff, UK, pp. 925-928.

McKinnon, A. C. (2003). Logistics and the environment. In Henscher, D. A., & Button, K. J. (Eds.), *Handbook of transport and the environment.* Oxford, UK: Elsevier Ltd.

Piecyk, M. I., & McKinnon, A. C. (2008). External costs of road freight transport in the UK. *Paper presented to the NOFOMA conference*, Hanken University, Finland.

Spens, K., & Bask, A. H. (2002). Developing a Framework for Supply Chain Management. *The International Journal of Logistics Management, 13*(1), 73–88. doi:10.1108/09574090210806379

Wolf, C., & Seuring, S. (2010). Environmental impacts as buying criteria for third party logistical services. *International Journal of Physical Distribution & Logistics Management*, *40*(1), 84–102. doi:10.1108/09600031011020377

Wu, H., & Dunn, S. (1995). Environmentally responsible logistics systems. *International Journal of Physical Distribution and Logistics Management*, *25*(2).

Chapter 15
Reverse Logistics for Sustainable Waste Management Processes

Fraser McLeod
University of Southampton, UK

Tom Cherrett
University of Southampton, UK

ABSTRACT

This chapter highlights some of the innovative approaches that have been taken by businesses involved in reverse logistics for the removal of waste from urban areas. The chapter reviews some of these approaches and suggests which could be used more widely, recognising the specific limitations which may restrict their applicability. These innovative approaches include: the use of delivery vehicles to take-back waste/recyclate to out-of-town facilities such as a freight consolidation or recycling centre; combining commercial and household waste collections; deploying public transport vehicles to carry specialist recyclate; using multi-modal transport; 'smart' bin technology and pipelines for the removal of waste from buildings.

INTRODUCTION

This chapter is concerned with how waste management processes may be improved through the use of innovative ideas in reverse logistics. The main focus here is on the physical transportation of waste, rather than on the management and computer systems that may also be required to support these activities. The chapter begins by describing some of the basic concepts and typical methods found in waste management practice, highlighting the main practical, organisational, financial and legal issues. The chapter then describes a number of different innovative methods that have been introduced in recent years and assesses their advantages and disadvantages. The objective of

DOI: 10.4018/978-1-60960-585-8.ch015

the chapter is to provide a critical review of these innovative methods and to examine their scope for more widespread application.

BACKGROUND

Landfilling waste is generally considered to be unsustainable due to concerns about leachate contaminating ground water, the length of time needed to stabilize materials and the potential for methane to contribute to the global greenhouse effect (Das *et al.*, 2002). Recognising this, and driven by a series of European directives, the UK government produced a 'Waste Strategy for England 2007' (Defra, 2007), which promoted more sustainable waste management processes through reduction, re-use and recycling of waste, recovery of energy and reduced landfilling of waste.

Reverse logistics refers to the "planning, implementation and control of the movement of goods, raw materials and related items from the point of consumption to the point of origin, for the purpose of recapturing value or proper disposal." (Rogers and Tibben-Lembke, 1999). Typically, the starting points for waste (or return goods) are commercial premises in urban areas (e.g. High Street shops). The end points for waste depend upon the recycling or waste treatment options being used. Waste treatment options include incineration, pyrolysis, gasification, composting, anaerobic digestion and landfilling (Williams, 2005). Materials that are most commonly recycled include cardboard, paper, metals, plastics, textiles, wood and glass, with cardboard and paper typically comprising around two-thirds of the commercial waste from High Street retailers (Maynard and Cherrett, 2010). There are often intermediate points in the reverse supply chain for the consolidation of wastes which could be at regional distribution centres (RDCs), transfer stations, or other locations, before onward transportation to final disposal. The reverse logistics channels for return goods are likely to be different from those for waste, adding complexity to the combined problem.

The alternative disposition routes used for waste and for return goods tend to add to the overall transport burden associated with waste logistics, so innovative methods to reduce this are welcome. Improvements in terms of reduced transport costs or improved recycling performance may come from improved co-ordination of reverse logistics processes and greater co-operation between the parties involved (e.g. retailers). A lack of co-ordination, sub-optimal use of vehicles and low levels of waste/ recyclate backloading (use of delivery vehicles to collect waste), can result in unnecessary handling and associated increases in vehicle traffic (Shakantu *et al*, 2002).

EXISTING PRACTICE

In the UK, commercial waste is collected either by a national or local contractor, by the local authority, where they offer such a service, or in-house, using the business' own vehicles; in some cases, commercial waste may be taken, often illegally, to household waste recycling centres (Maynard and Cherrett, 2010). The frequency of collection depends on the size of the business, with the largest typically receiving daily collections and the smallest often requiring one collection each week; an average of 2.4 collections per week was estimated in a study of 83 businesses in the city of Winchester, UK (Maynard and Cherrett, 2010). The typical collection arrangements for commercial recyclable waste and residual waste from a survey of businesses on Winchester High Street are shown (Figure 1).

For returned goods, the main reverse logistics methods seen in practice (Mukhopadhyay *et al.*, 2006) are:

Figure 1. Summary of waste management systems used by businesses on Winchester High Street (Source: Maynard and Cherrett, 2010)

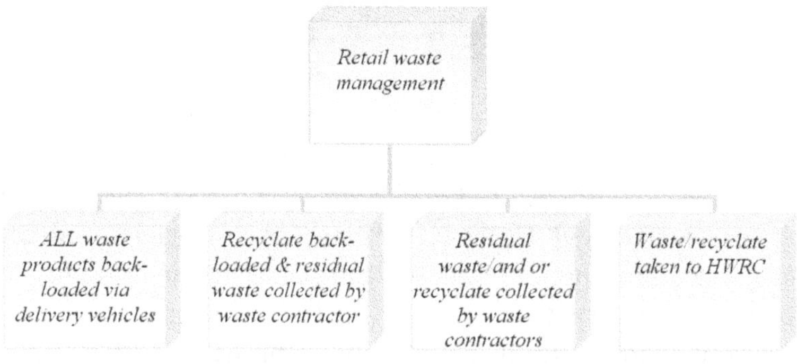

1. Use of delivery vehicles to take returned goods from stores to the RDC
2. Use of delivery vehicles to take returned goods from stores back to the suppliers, in exchange for credit
3. Use of a third party logistics (3PL) provider to take goods to the RDC
4. Outsourcing the entire returns management process to a 3PL, including refurbishment of the goods.

Where the retailer undertakes its own refurbishment of returned goods, the role of checking the goods to assess their initial status, suitability for resale and potential movement into the waste/material recovery stream may take place either at the individual store or at the RDC, depending on the level of expertise available, with the latter being most appropriate where the volume of return goods is high.

A perceived problem with existing practice is the fragmented nature of waste/recyclate collections, with a large number of waste contractors offering varying and competing waste collection services, resulting in many, part-loaded vehicles being used. In a study of businesses in Winchester (UK), 17 different waste contractors were observed operating within the city (Maynard and Cherrett, 2010). This is unlikely to be efficient from a transportation perspective and contributes to High Street congestion. The problem may be ameliorated by removing waste and/or returned goods using vehicles that already serve the city centre, such as delivery or service vehicles, e.g. refuse collection fleets used for serving domestic premises.

Levels of backloading, either for waste or return goods tend to be rather low, particularly for smaller businesses: a survey of 51 retailers across the county of West Sussex (UK) suggested that 31% of businesses 'always' had their packaging waste collected by delivery vehicles, 16% 'sometimes' and 53% 'never'; and, for return goods, 39% of businesses always had their return goods collected by delivery vehicles, 57% 'sometimes' and only 4% 'never' (Cherrett and Hickford, 2005); while across 83 businesses in Winchester (UK), 24% indicated that they used delivery vehicles to take back some element of waste and/or recyclate. Larger businesses, and, in particular, the major supermarket chains, are generally active in backloading. In most cases delivery vehicles are used to return packaging and, in some cases, other waste materials, to their depots for subsequent recycling or they can directly feed into recycling facilities either managed by supermarkets or by a third party.

There are a number of factors that determine whether backloading waste and recyclate using the delivery fleet is viable, including the size of the vehicle, vehicle utilisation, space and facilities at the location waste is to be taken to, and the frequency of vehicle deliveries in relation to the waste collection requirements. While it may be desirable to see levels of backloading increase, it should be recognised that there are a number of reasons why more backloading does not take place in practice, including: prioritising the outbound delivery service and not risking the possibility that backloading activities will cause delays; tight scheduling of return journeys; lack of knowledge of the backloading opportunities that may exist; and the use of specialised vehicles (e.g. temperature controlled compartments) or handling equipment that may be unsuitable for general backloading work (McKinnon and Ge, 2006). An analysis of grocery supply chains suggested that suitable backloads could be found for only 2.4% of empty journey legs, representing 2% of overall mileage (McKinnon and Ge, 2006). Multi-drop operations are often not well suited to returns management due to the numbers of time-critical deliveries made, the pressure on vehicle scheduling and possible cross-contamination (Fernie and Hart, 2001). Vehicle scheduling is a complex task, particularly where there are constraints such as delivery time windows. Incorporating backloading makes vehicle scheduling yet more complex and may act as a barrier to wider take-up but algorithms to solve variants of the combined 'backhauling and linehauling' problem have been proposed by Mitra (2005), Reimann and Ulrich (2006), Goetschalckx and Jacobs-Blecha (1989).

Another perceived problem is poor recycling performance, particularly for smaller businesses: the Winchester surveys indicated that 64% of businesses did not receive any dedicated recyclable waste collections. This may be due to financial reasons (cost of collection; cost of separating the waste), lack of space or difficulty in finding a suitable recycling service. Space issues may be influenced by the types and sizes of containers used to store waste. In Winchester, the most common receptacle used was an 1100L bin, while some businesses were required by their waste contractor to use sacks. It was observed that where waste contractors offered a recycling service, this was limited to a single day of the week, which may not suit all businesses. From the waste contractor's perspective, insufficient demand is often a core issue impacting on service frequency.

Legal Constraints

The waste management activities that retailers and waste contractors can undertake are governed by various national and European directives, laws and regulations. The main issues are summarised in this section.

Duty of Care

Retailers and carriers are under a 'duty of care' to ensure that waste is stored, treated and disposed of safely and that incompatible wastes are not mixed. All carriers of waste in the UK must be registered with the Environment Agency, with some exemptions (e.g. charities, local authorities). Where waste is transferred from one company (e.g. a retailer) to another (e.g. a waste contractor) then waste transfer notes describing the waste type and origin are completed, signed and required to be kept for a period of at least two years by both parties.

Pre-Treatment Requirements

As part of the Landfill Directive [1999/31/EC], all waste destined for landfill must first undergo treatment in the form of either a physical, thermal or biological process. Commercial waste producers can meet these requirements by either separating different waste streams for recycling, or by making arrangements for their waste contractors to treat the waste before disposing of it. In addition, co-disposal of hazardous waste with non-hazardous waste at landfill sites is banned, as is the disposal of liquid wastes, used tyres, healthcare and infectious clinical wastes, animal-by-products, explosive, corrosive, flammable, oxidising and chemical wastes (Triantafyllou and Cherrett, 2010a).

Hazardous Wastes

Producers of hazardous wastes must comply with stringent regulations ensuring safety and proper treatment and disposal. Hazardous wastes are defined on the basis of the 'European Waste Catalogue (EWC) 2002' and include fluorescent tubes (containing mercury), non-edible oil and fat, certain medicines and clinical waste, batteries and electrical and electronic equipment containing hazardous wastes. Hazardous waste often requires specialist collections and this can lead to a proliferation of vehicles used: in a study of Southampton's West Quay shopping mall, it was estimated that hazardous waste collections were made by 65 different waste contractors, although the vast majority (90%) of these were electrical/maintenance contractors replacing fluorescent tubes during routine maintenance visits a few times a year (Triantafyllou and Cherrett, 2010b).

Waste Electrical and Electronic Equipment

Under waste electrical and electronic equipment (WEEE) regulations, retailers and distributors are required to inform customers of how they can dispose of WEEE free of charge. The retailer/distributor can either do this by taking goods from customers directly (in-store, through the post, or collection from the customer) or by joining the Distributor Takeback Scheme (DTS), managed by Valpak Ltd on behalf of the UK government. This scheme allows customers to return WEEE to a designated collection facility (DCF), which comprise civic amenity sites (household waste recycling centres, waste transfer stations), not-for-profit/charity organisations and commercial sites. Although retailers/distributors who join the scheme must make financial contributions towards the provision of the WEEE collection facilities, this may be a more cost-effective option than organising their own reverse logistics. The treatment, recovery, recycling and disposal of WEEE is the responsibility of the producers of the goods, who are required to join a producer compliance scheme (PCS), approved by the Environment Agency. The PCSs are required to collect WEEE from all DCFs free of charge (Ongondo and Williams, 2011). The distances that WEEE has to travel are highly dependent on the goods type and location of the treatment facilities: as an example, mobile phones purchased from a shopping centre in Southampton were typically returned to a processing hub in Essex some 113 miles away (Triantafyllou and Cherrett, 2010b).

Packaging and Packaging Wastes

Packaging regulations set design standards with the aim of increasing recovery, reuse and recycling levels of commercial packaging and minimising use of hazardous materials. Packaging waste regulations require UK businesses with an annual turnover of more than £2 million and handling more than 50 tonnes of packaging annually to reach specified recycling and recovery targets and to set up systems to allow customers to return packaging. The targets for 2011 and 2012, set by Defra (2010), for various materials, are shown alongside the achieved recycling figures for 2009 (Figure 2). These latest available statistics show that recycling targets for wood, aluminium and paper are already being achieved, whereas improvements are demanded in the recycling of plastics, steel and glass.

Figure 2. UK business recycling targets (for 2011 and 2012) and achieved figures for 2009 (Source of data: Defra [2010])

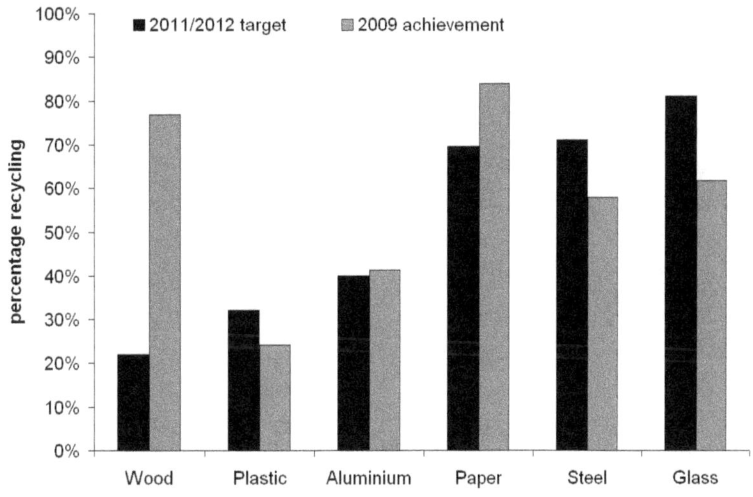

CONCEPTS FOR IMPROVING THE EFFICIENCY OF REVERSE LOGISTICS PROCESSES

Backloading to an Out-of-Town Facility

The UK Department for Transport has promoted backloading through its Freight Best Practice programme (Freight Best Practice, 2005), highlighting the potential efficiency gains to be made. Opportunities for backloading waste appear to exist, given the 2009 road freight statistics which showed that empty running across rigid lorries was 28.9% with an average 50% lading factor (ratio of actual goods moved to the maximum tonne-kms achievable if the vehicles, whenever loaded, were loaded to their maximum carrying capacity) (Department for Transport, 2010). Several online load matching companies have been created to facilitate backloading (e.g. www.truckspace.co.uk, www.haulageexchange.co.uk and www.courierexchange.co.uk). These allow hauliers and logistics providers to find and bid for backloading work by providing visibility of compatible loads across different supply chains.

Existing backloads most commonly involve a retailer returning goods or waste packaging from their own stores back to an RDC for subsequent re-use, recycling or disposal. However, an alternative option, which may reduce the transport footprint associated with waste management in urban centres, is to use delivery vehicles to take waste to an out-of-town facility, such as a consolidation centre, a recycling facility or a waste transfer station. There are already examples of this and in the UK, in 2008, it was reported that the Broadmead consolidation centre had received some 14.5 tonnes of consolidated cardboard and plastic from 64 retailers in Bristol (Hapgood, 2008).

The advantages and disadvantages of using consolidation centres have been described in detail by Browne *et al*., (2007), by the EU-funded BESTUFS project (2007) and by TTR (2010), among others, mainly from the perspective of the forward distribution channel, although similar considerations may also apply to reverse logistics. The main anticipated benefit is a reduction in the number of freight vehicles, particularly large and/or polluting ones, entering busy central areas. Reported statistics for the Bristol Broadmead consolidation centre, in 2007, included a 75% reduction in vehicle movements, equating to an annual savings of 178,000 vehicle kilometres, 20.3 tonnes of CO_2, 660 kg of NOx and 19.7 kg of PM_{10} (Hapgood, 2008). A potential drawback is that the location of the consolidation centre may require some vehicles to divert considerably from their normal routes, incurring additional cost and time.

To provide an example of the requirements for a consolidated take-back scheme, an analysis of the cardboard collection requirements of Winchester High Street businesses was made (Maynard and Cherrett, 2010). This indicated that each business generated around 1300 litres of cardboard each week, on average, equating to a total for the whole High Street of around 139,000 litres of cardboard, or 131 roll-cage equivalents. From this, it was then estimated that 15 collections per week would be needed to remove waste from the High Street, based on the use of rigid-bodied delivery vehicles with a gross vehicle weight of 18 tonnes and an average spare capacity of 26% of the deck area ($5.6m^2$), taken from Department for Transport (2006) statistics. The storage requirements, prior to collection, would depend on the frequency of collections: for example, if collections were only once a week then a minimum storage area of $83m^2$ (131 roll cages x $0.63m^2$ per roll cage) would be required. However, in practice, some businesses may choose not to participate in such a co-operative take-back scheme, as they may already backload their own waste or may be satisfied with their existing arrangements, so the collection requirements may be lower than this.

Consolidation of return goods, particularly small items, may also be facilitated through the emerging networks of attended and unattended collection-delivery points (McLeod and Cherrett, 2009). The use of attended premises, typically convenience stores, petrol stations and post offices (e.g. Kiala, Royal Mail, Parcel Force, Redpack Network) or unattended locker banks or boxes (e.g. ByBox, Bearbox) for returning products and recyclate back up the supply chain are already well established in the service industry. These systems are being used successfully by the service sector whereby used parts destined for reconditioning or cannibalisation can be returned to service centres via an attended or unattended collection point in the vicinity of the customer, reducing the amount of time the service engineer has to spend collecting and returning parts.

Coordinated Waste Collection from a High Street

The existing fragmented nature of waste collections from retailers in urban areas could be ameliorated with better co-ordination and centralisation of activities, similar in concept to the co-ordination that normally takes place at shopping malls, where all waste is centrally managed. If High Street retailers worked together, with support from the local authority, they could form common waste collection arrangements. This co-ordination would result in fewer waste collection vehicles being used and greater utilisation of those vehicles. Recycling performance may also improve as was seen for centralised co-ordination of returned goods at a shopping centre in Southampton which increased the amount of waste diverted from landfill from a mean of 26 tonnes per month to 143 tonnes per month between the periods January 2006 to April 2007 and May 2007 to August 2008, respectively, using a range of equipment to store and consolidate waste (pallets, roll cages, bins, balers and compactors) (Triantafyllou and Cherrett, 2010a).

A survey of 83 Winchester High Street business managers suggested that 45% of them would consider collaborating with their neighbours to improve material recovery (Maynard and Cherrett, 2010). Whether they would decide to do so would likely depend on:

- perception of the anticipated benefits in terms of cost savings or environmental performance
- availability of storage space and vehicle access
- organisational issues associated with how the scheme would be operated
- how the scheme meets their legal obligations
- their willingness to collaborate with other retailers who may be potential competitors
- financial values of recyclable materials (currently in decline)
- whether local or central government would provide incentives (e.g. tax breaks, priority access for delivery vehicles) to join such as scheme.

Collection of Commercial Waste alongside Household Waste

A potential way to improve waste logistics in an urban area is to combine waste collections from commercial premises, particularly small businesses, with household waste collections. Since household collections are the responsibility of waste collection authorities (WCAs) in the UK, this could only be undertaken by WCAs, or their appointed waste contractors. Such combined collections could be targeted towards recyclate or could also include residual waste. The main aims of combining collections in this way are to increase the amount of recyclable materials that are recovered, reduce the number of collection vehicles travelling in urban areas and to reduce the vehicle mileage associated with these collections. In a study of waste collections from 577 commercial premises and 25,600 households in Winchester, involving detailed modelling of existing rounds and development of new round designs, a vehicle mileage savings of 4.7% was estimated for combined collections compared to the existing separate vehicle rounds (McLeod and Cherrett, 2010). The results also suggested that the new round designs could accommodate collections from an additional 288 commercial customers per week, indicating scope for expansion of the existing business.

The number of WCAs offering commercial waste services (either collection and/or bring site provision) has increased in recent years with research suggesting that 65% and 43% of WCAs in England offered residual trade waste and recyclable trade waste services, respectively, in 2010 (WRAP, 2010). Perceived disincentives to collect trade waste are that while residual trade waste counts towards landfill targets, recyclable trade waste may not be directly counted towards recycling targets. This may change as the UK government has announced its intention to review definitions of commercial and municipal waste. Fully or near-fully integrated commercial and household collections in the UK are only undertaken by a few WCAs, including New Forest, Newham, Caerphilly and Ceredigion. The vast majority of WCAs undertake these collections separately from one another or only collect a small amount of commercial waste on the household rounds where it is expedient to do so (e.g. in remote areas) (Sanders, 2010). Although combining commercial and household collection rounds may have the potential to create more efficient vehicle rounds, this may not be suitable for all WCAs. For example, such a concept is not appropriate when a 'kerbside sort' system, using compartmentalised vehicles, is employed for household waste collections. Also, combined collections can be difficult to implement when an alternate weekly collection system (recyclable waste and residual waste collected from households in alternate weeks) is in use, since the commercial collections normally have to be made weekly, or more frequently. Other potential difficulties may arise if there are fundamental differences in how existing household and commercial rounds operate (e.g. start times, shift lengths, types of vehicle and lifting equipment).

Innovative Systems for Waste Logistics

Other innovative ideas for removing waste and recyclate from urban areas include:

Use of Public Transport Vehicles

There may be scope for using some public transport vehicles (trains, trams, buses) to carry certain elements of waste, thereby reducing the use of lorries in urban areas and conferring benefits in terms of fuel use, emissions and road congestion. Perhaps the best-known practical example is the Cargotram system in Zurich, introduced in 2003 (BESTUFS, 2005). The Cargotram system serves nine stations on the existing tram network, with a four-weekly service at each station, and carries bulky waste and WEEE, placed in standard refuse containers and loaded onto flat wagons, to a waste transfer station. The service is provided, free of charge, to public transport users, local residents, cyclists and pedestrians. The Cargotrams operate between 3pm and 7pm each day and are timetabled to avoid causing any delays to passenger trams. The main driving force behind this scheme was the municipal waste disposal and recycling authority, with the support of the public transport operators. Although this scheme does not take commercial waste, one can envisage the expansion of such a concept to incorporate carriage of commercial waste at non-peak times. Similar concepts can be envisaged for light rail systems. Trains are used to transport larger container-loads of waste and can support multi-modal operations. The concept of using buses for the dual purpose of transferring waste materials naturally raises legitimate concerns with regard to public safety. Such a system might only be suitable for the movement of specialist recyclate returns (e.g. small-sized engineering parts, as part of a service company returns network) but there will always be issues of segregating passengers and material on the same vehicle, available capacity and timetable compatibility. Dual use of rural buses to carry passengers and freight goods was reported in some regions of Germany (Schaefer, 2003), while in the UK the Royal Mail has a 'Postbus' service (www.postbus.royalmail.com) which allows passengers to travel on some of its postal vehicles; however, both of these cases are rather small scale (few routes, limited days of the year, restricted capacity, rural areas only) and it is difficult to assess the scalability of this concept to large urban areas.

Use of Inland Waterways or Short Sea Shipping

Existing examples of waste being moved by barges on inland waterways include use of canals and the River Thames in London (STRAW, 2006), with further plans to use inland waterways to remove waste from the Olympic Park during the 2012 Games (London2012.com, 2009), and on the River Meuse in Liege, Belgium (BESTUFS, 2005); however, there is considerable potential for waterborne transport, including short sea shipping, to be used more extensively for freight and this may become increasingly important in the future with the distances that waste has to be transported likely to increase as the number of waste management facilities grows (STRAW, 2006). Use of waterborne transport for carrying waste requires suitable loading/unloading areas, vehicles and lifting equipment (Figure 3). As with the use of public transport vehicles, the main perceived benefits are the reduction in truck use in city centres with associated reductions in emissions and energy use.

Use of Multi-Modal Vehicles

Where waste is to be transferred from a road vehicle to another mode of transport (e.g. train, barge) then an innovative and efficient way to do this is the use of a so-called multi-modal refuse collection vehicle (MMRCV), which has a demountable container and loads either from

Figure 3. Roll-on-off waste container being loaded onto a barge by a standard hook-lift vehicle (Source: Wood, Hall, Heward Ltd., London)

the side, front or rear. This type of vehicle was introduced in waste collection practice in 2003, most notably in the Netherlands and Germany, and, in 2008, was reported to be collecting around 40% of Germany's municipal waste (Transport for London, 2008). Use of such vehicles in the UK is not yet common, with fully-implemented examples only in Aberdeenshire and Bromsgrove and trials in London and Horsham (Transport for London, 2008). It was reported, by Transport for London (2008), that Aberdeenshire Council had been able to replace its fleet of 37 standard refuse collection vehicles with only 19 side-loading MMRCVs due to the efficiencies gained from being able to replace full containers with empty ones. In trials undertaken by Transport for London, a rear-loading MMRCV was preferred, as side-loading would be difficult in narrow streets full of parked cars. Their trials identified benefits in terms of reduced mileage, faster loading speeds and elimination of the need for waste transfer stations and 'double' handling of waste.

Use of Pipelines

A system introduced in Helsinki in 2001 by Puzair Ltd, a Finnish company specialising in environmental and building maintenance technology, used specially installed pipelines and pneumatic equipment to transport waste bags from apartment blocks and a neighbouring shopping centre to communal bins, with the installation taking place at the same time as the construction of the flats and shopping centre (BESTUFS, 2005). This rationalisation of waste collection was reported to involve fewer truck trips, improve working conditions for drivers and save residents the nuisance associated with trucks visiting their courtyards. Subsequently, a 'biowaste' version of this system was developed, designed to remove food and other biological waste from buildings such as restaurants, canteens, hospitals, shopping centres, airport terminals and residential apartment blocks (www.ecosir.com). Issues that would affect the suitability of such a system include cost (not reported) and how readily it can be installed in existing buildings.

Use of Smart Bins

Where waste collections are made from communal bins with varying fill rates, it would be useful to know the point at which bins are reaching capacity (>75% full) in order to schedule vehicle collections more efficiently. The aims are to avoid scheduling visits to bins that are under a threshold fill level (e.g. 50%) and to ensure that bins are visited before they overflow, as this can lead to waste being left outside the container, illegally dumped elsewhere or in the case of valuable recyclate, losing out on a potential donation to another recycler. This understanding has led to the innovative idea of equipping bins with some form of detection sensor and communications device to report this information to a central office. The advantages of dynamic waste collection schedules over fixed schedules were demonstrated, both analytically and using computer simulation, in Malmö, Sweden, where 3300 recycling containers were fitted with level sensors and wireless communication equipment (Johansson, 2006). For dense collection areas it was concluded that the best policy was to schedule bins to be collected when full, whereas for less dense areas it became more expedient to include collections from 'almost' full bins as well. The authors noted that, in practice, despite having sensor information available to them, many waste collection managers had not used the information to adapt their schedules, suggesting, perhaps, a need for training in being able to use dynamic information effectively. In the UK, similar technology was reported (www.smartbin.com) to have reduced vehicle trips by over 37% for a company making collections from textile banks. The data collected from such remote monitoring systems may also be useful for reporting purposes and in identifying occasions of theft, where materials have some value.

FUTURE RESEARCH DIRECTIONS

The 'Internet of Things' (Valhouli, 2010) means that, through ubiquitous forms of computing, all devices, items, products can be perpetually 'on' and connected to the internet. The developments in this area have significant implications for reverse logistics practices in the future. The ability to fit objects with smart tags and transmitters means that individual items (such as a bin, or a specific part in a photocopier) can have an IP (Internet Protocol) address, enabling them, with minimal processing power, to communicate with other 'things' in their vicinity (thing-to-thing), to be interrogated by users (person-to-thing) or inform of their situation/condition (thing-to-person). This means that the analogue bar code, used uniformly across the retail sector will enable 'things' to be tracked from cradle to grave using open platforms. Individual 'end-of-life' items will be able to report their status, identify the nearest refurbishment point and potentially find links with other similar items in the vicinity which could constitute a full load for collection.

As new treatment options for waste and return goods become available, there is an increased need for identifying and monitoring individual items within the reverse supply chain. The enhanced 'visibility' of 'things' within the reverse supply chain afforded by this technology could vastly improve when and how reverse movements occur, and further research into the impacts of this is warranted. This also creates a need for research to evaluate the most promising reverse logistics options from the point of view of feasibility, practicality, economic sustainability, material recovery, transport efficiency and environmental impact. In this regard, there will always be trade-offs between conflicting objectives. Increased recycling activity often results in increased transport, with negative impacts on fuel use and emissions and such negative impacts need to be accounted for in any scheme appraisal. Areas for future research should include assessment of collaborative transport mechanisms such as joint domestic and commercial waste collection schemes, co-ordinated take-back across centralised distribution systems, use of non-road transport and smart bin technology to improve waste collection scheduling.

CONCLUSION

This chapter has described innovative approaches for the removal of waste and/or returned goods from urban centres. Some of these have been based on technological innovations, such as smart bins, pneumatic pipes and multi-modal vehicles with demountable containers, while others have been based on improved collaboration and methods of working between retailers, waste contractors and local authorities, with central government also having a key role to play in enabling and/ or encouraging changes to be made. Redefining how commercial waste contributes to recycling and LATS targets could provide a greater incentive for local authorities to collect trade waste which may improve the currently fragmented nature of commercial waste collection. Similarly, this fragmentation may be ameliorated if there was improved co-ordination and co-operation between High Street retailers in organising how their combined wastes are dealt with.

For this to happen would most likely need the involvement of the local authority, or some other third party 'controller', to co-ordinate take-back of the consolidated waste streams through specific channels, so reducing the amount of separate contractor activity.

REFERENCES

Allen, J., & Browne, M. (2010). *Road freight transport and sustainability in Britain, 1984-2007.* Retrieved January 6, 2011, from www.greenlogistics.org/themesandoutputs /wm9/downloads/ Sustainablefreight transport-nationalfinal.pdf

BESTUFS. (2005). *Deliverable D2.1. Best Practice Handbook.* Retrieved November 19, 2010, from www.bestufs.net/download/ BESTUFS_II/ key_issuesII/ BESTUFS_BPH.pdf

BESTUFS. (2007). *Good Practice Guide on Urban Freight Transport.* Retrieved November, 2010, from www.bestufs.net/download /BESTUFS_II/ good_practice/ English_BESTUFS_Guide.pdf

Bridgewater, E., & Anderson, C. (2003). *CA Site WEEE Capacity in the UK. Network Recycling.* Retrieved January 6, 2011, from www.dti.gov.uk/ files/file30304.pdf

Browne, M., Woodburn, A. & Allen, J. (2007). Evaluating the potential for urban consolidation centres. *European Transport \ Trasporti Europei, 35*, 46-63.

Cherrett, T. J., & Hickford, A. J. (2005). *Freight and the economy.* The effects of freight movements associated with retailers common to Chichester, Horsham, Worthing and Crawley. Transportation Research Group, University of Southampton. Final report for West Sussex County Council.

Das, K. C., Smith, M. C., Gattie, D. K., & Hale Boothe, D. D. (2002). Stability and quality of municipal solid waste compost from a landfill aerobic bioreduction process. *Advances in Environmental Research, 6*(4), 401–409. doi:10.1016/ S1093-0191(01)00066-1

Defra (2007). *Waste strategy for England 2007.* Retrieved January 6, 2011, from www.defra.gov.uk/environment/waste /strategy/strategy07/documents/waste07-strategy.pdf

Defra (2010). *Packaging.* Retrieved January 12, 2011, from www.defra.gov.uk/environment/waste /producer/packaging/

Department for Transport. (2006). *Key Performance Indicators for Non-Food Retail Distribution.* Freight Best Practice Benchmarking Guide.

Department for Transport. (2010). *Road freight statistics, 2009.* Retrieved January 12, 2011, from www.dft.gov.uk/pgr/statistics/ datatablespublications/freight/ goodsbyroad/roadfreightstatistics2009

Fernie, J., & Hart, C. (2001). UK Packaging Waste Legislation; Implications for Food Retailers. *British Food Journal, 108*(3), 187–197. doi:10.1108/00070700110386737

Freight Best Practice. (2005). *Make backloading work for you.* Retrieved January 6, 2011, from www.freightbestpractice.org.uk/ make-backloading-work-for-you

Goetschalckx, M., & Jacobs-Blecha, C. (1989). The vehicle routing problem with backhauls. *European Journal of Operational Research, 42*(1), 39–51. doi:10.1016/0377-2217(89)90057-X

Hapgood, T. (2008). *Short term actions to reorganize transport of goods.* Presentation made at ITS Freight Interest Group meeting, University of Southampton, 27 May 2008.

Johansson, O. M. (2006). The effect of dynamic scheduling and routing in a solid waste management system. *Waste Management (New York, N.Y.)*, *26*, 875–885. doi:10.1016/j.wasman.2005.09.004

London2012.com (2009). *Recycling waste boosts sustainable transport target*. Press release 25 June 2009. Retrieved January 10, 2011, from www.london2012.com/press/media-releases /2009/06/recycling-waste-boosts-sustainable-transport-target.php

Maynard, S., & Cherrett, T. J. (2010). *Characteristics of Retail Waste Logistics on Winchester High Street.* Retrieved January 10, 2011, from www.greenlogistics.org/news/ retailwastelogistics.htm

McKinnon, A. C., & Ge, Y. (2006). The potential for reducing empty running by trucks: a retrospective analysis. *International Journal of Physical Distribution & Logistics Management*, *36*(5), 391–410. doi:10.1108/09600030610676268

McLeod, F. N., & Cherrett, T. J. (2009). Quantifying the environmental benefits of collection/delivery points. *OR Insight*, *22*(3), 127–139. doi:10.1057/ori.2009.2

McLeod, F. N., & Cherrett, T. J. (2010). Encouraging sustainable 'take-back': The scope for joint domestic/commercial waste collections. *Proceedings of the Logistics Research Network conference (CD)*, Harrogate, 8-10 September, 2010.

Mitra, S. (2005). An algorithm for the generalized vehicle routing problem with backhauling. *Asia-Pacific Journal of Operational Research*, *22*(2), 153–169. doi:10.1142/S0217595905000522

Mukhopadhyay, S. K., & Setaputra, R. (2006). The role of 4PL as the reverse logistics integrator. *International Journal of Physical Distribution & Logistics Management.*, *36*(9), 716–729. doi:10.1108/09600030610710872

Ongondo, F., & Williams, I. D. (2011). *A critical review of the UK household WEEE collection network. Accepted for publication in.* Waste and Resource Management.

Reimann, M., & Ulrich, H. (2006). Comparing backhauling strategies in vehicle routing using ant colony optimization. *Central European Journal of Operations Research*, *14*(2), 105–123. doi:10.1007/s10100-006-0163-8

Rogers, D. S., & Tibben-Lembke, R. S. (1999). *Going backwards: Reverse logistics trends and practices*. Pittsburg, USA: Reverse Logistics Executive Council.

Sanders, R. (2010). *Local Authority Commercial Waste Collections: A more sustainable approach to waste management?* Unpublished M.Sc. dissertation, University of Southampton, UK.

Schaefer, C. (2003). *MULTIBUS – A new and innovative approach for bus systems in rural areas. Association for European Transport.* Retrieved January 10, 2011, from http://etcproceedings.org/paper/download/888

Shakantu, W., Tookey, J. E., & Bowen, P. A. (2002). *Defining the role of reverse logistics in attaining sustainable integration of materials delivery with construction and demolition waste management.* In Proceedings of Creating a Sustainable Construction Industry. Conference of CIB W10: Creating a Sustainable Construction Industry in Developing Countries, South Africa. Retrieved January 10, 2011, from http://buildnet.csir.co.za/cdcproc/docs/3rd/shakantu.pdf

STRAW. (2006). *Sustainable Transport Resources and Waste*. Retrieved November 19, 2010, from www.massbalance.org/downloads /project-files/2150-00494.pdf

Transport for London. (2008). *Developing a multi-modal refuse collection system for London. Project report by the Freight Unit.* Retrieved January 10, 2011, from www.tfl.gov.uk/microsites/freight/documents/publications/multi-modal- refuse-system-london-nov-2008.pdf

Triantafyllou, M., & Cherrett, T. J. (2010a). *Waste Management and 'Take-Back' Processes in a Dedicated Shopping Centre - Results from the West Quay shopping centre Managers Survey.* Retrieved January 10, 2011, from www.greenlogistics.org/SiteResources /MT-Waste Report-2010.pdf

Triantafyllou, M., & Cherrett, T. J. (2010b). The logistics of managing hazardous waste – A case study analysis in the retail sector. *Proceedings of the Logistics Research Network conference (CD)*, Harrogate, 8-10 September, 2010.

TTR. (2010). *Freight consolidation centre study.* Report for the Department for Transport by Transport and Travel Research Limited. Retrieved January 10, 2011, from www.dft.gov.uk/pgr/freight/research/freightreport/

Valhouli, C. A. (2010) *The Internet of Things: Networked Objects and Smart Devices.* The Hammersmith Group Research Report, February 2010. Retrieved February 23, 2011 from http://thehammersmithgroup.com/images/ reports/networked_objects.pdf

Williams, P. T. (2005). *Waste Treatment and Disposal.* Chichester, UK: John Wiley & Sons, Ltd. Retrieved January 10, 2011, from http://onlinelibrary.wiley.com/doi/ 10.1002/0470012668.fmatter/pdf

WRAP. (2010). *Local authority trade waste and recycling survey 2010.* Retrieved January 10, 2011, from www.wrap.org.uk/downloads/ TW_survey_report_v1.9.a428e3e4.9521.pdf

Section 4
Innovation in Supply System Management

Chapter 16
Discontinuous Innovation in Supply Relationship Management:
Two Cases and a Future Research Direction

Richard Lamming
University of Exeter Business School, UK

Fu Jia
University of Exeter Business School, UK

ABSTRACT

Innovation may be divided into two types: incremental and discontinuous (Tidd et al. 2009). The first of these refers to 'doing what is already done but better.' The latter may come through the emergence of a new technology, a completely new market or a new business model and refers to decision making under uncertainty. The focus of this chapter is the implementation of discontinuous innovation (DI) in supply chain relationships. The authors review two research-led projects: the development and implementation of the SCRIA (Supply Chain Relationship in Aerospace) Relationship Evaluation Tool (RET) and the development of the concept of Value-Transparency (V-T). Both projects originated in the authors' academic research in the early 1990s and were aimed at subsequent implementation in the context of supply chain relationships. One was successfully implemented; the other was not. The authors introduce future research exploring some supply relationship context-specific barriers and enablers in the implementation of radical concepts or DI through case based research method.

DOI: 10.4018/978-1-60960-585-8.ch016

INTRODUCTION

Tidd and Bessant (2009) provide a useful differentiation between incremental and discontinuous innovation (DI). The former refers to doing what is already done but better. The latter may come through the emergence of a new technology, a completely new market or a new business model and refers to decision making under uncertainty. An example of this is contained in the well known case of the Lockheed Martin 'Skunk works' (Rich and Janos, 1996). The implementation of discontinuous innovation (DI) is the focus of this paper.

We review two research-led projects: the SCRIA (Supply Chain Relationship in Aerospace) Relationship Evaluation Tool (RET) and Value-Transparency (V-T) to illustrate the development of the two radical ideas and why they are radical. Both projects originated in academic research in the early 1990s and were aimed at subsequent implementation in the context of supply chain relationships.

First we shall provide some background for this research. This will be followed by reviewing literature on motivation, barriers and enablers for the implementation of discontinuous innovation. Then we shall use SCRIA-RET and V-T as two case examples, exploring the evolution of the two radical ideas. Finally we shall arrive at a further research direction.

BACKGROUND: MOTIVATIONS, BARRIERS AND ENABLERS TO IMPLEMENTING DISCONTINUOUS INNOVATION

In this section, we set out to discuss organisations' motivations in implementing DI and then move on to barriers and enablers to such implementation.

Motivation to Implement DI: The Organisation and Its Environment

Business organisations have often been be characterised as open, adaptive systems. This perspective originates in the 'organism' metaphor in organisational theory. Morgan and Smircich (1980) observe that the way organisational phenomena change over time is related to their organisational context: clearly this context must be included in our search for barriers and enablers to implementation of DI. Barriers and enablers are contextual variables that may affect the connection between organisation for implementation of DI and its success.

The organism metaphor is underpinned by contingency theory and new institutional theory. Galbraith (1973) notes two underlying assumptions of contingency theory. First, there is no one best way to organise and, second, ways of organising are not necessarily equally effective. Scott (1981) observes that 'the best way to organise depends on the nature of the environment to which the organisation relates.' Pfeffer (1997) adds that organisations having a structure more closely fitting the requirements of the context will be more effective than those which do not.

As long ago as 1967, Lawrence and Lorsch noted that organisations tend to develop separate specialist departments to address environmental factors (e.g. responding to or creating DI) but that forming these departments may itself create coordination problems. How well organisations can differentiate themselves, by organising to respond to the environment while integrating specialised departments into collective action, appears to be critical to their success.

Scott (1995) indicates that, in order to survive, organisations must conform to prevailing environmental norms. DiMaggio and Powell (1983) conclude that institutional isomorphism, both structural and procedural, will earn the organisation legitimacy. Later, the same authors provided cognitive and cultural explanations for social and organisational phenomena, Powell and DiMaggio (1991), recognising 'new institutionalism' as an emerging perspective in organisation theory. Rejecting the rational-actor models of classical economics, they describe supra-individual units of analysis that cannot be reduced to aggregations or direct consequences of individuals' attributes or motives.

Pfeffer's (1997) 'complex adaptive systems' concept was applied to supply networks by Choi *et al.* (2001). They conclude that greater levels of shared working norms, procedures and language among allied firms increase operational fit between the firms, i.e. in relationships and the network.

Summarizing the literature in the context of our research, we conclude that:

- Firms need to adapt to the environment in which they are embedded for survival.
- Firms need to coordinate internal functional departments for survival.
- These observations may be applied intra and inter-organisationally.

In other words, we suggest that what we know about organisational change can be applied to the management of supply chain relationships for DI.

Environmental, contextual and structural foci of contingency theory and new institutional theory provide insights on what drives firms to implement radical concepts. Putting these insights into a context of DI, Tidd and Bessant (2009) argue that factors such as copying, market signals, regulations, and competitors' behaviours may drive firms to adopt DI. We are interested in what promotes or inhibits DI implementation.

Barrier and Enablers to Implementing Discontinuous Innovation

Barriers

Charactering DI as a form of organisational change, we explore research on resistance to change in organisational behaviour literature, seeking barriers and enablers to implementation.

Buchanan and Huczynski (2004) identify polarized opinions regarding change management. The first is a 'blank sheet approach' advocating redesign from scratch, ignoring history and current practice, designing work to meet the needs of current customers. The second is the processual approach, proposed by contextual theorists. The practical nature of our focus suggests the latter approach may be more appropriate (i.e. rather than destruction of well developed supply relationships) and is considered next in terms of barriers and enablers.

Buchanan and Huczynski (2004) identified four common causes of resistance to organisational change:

- Parochial self-interest,
- Misunderstanding and lack of trust,
- Contradictory assessments of costs and benefits;
- Low tolerance for change

Eccles (1994) proposes the concept of 'readiness to change,' proposing eight questions:

- Is there a pressure for this change?
- Is there s a clear and shared vision of the goal and the direction?
- Do we have effective liaison and trust between those concerned?
- Is there the will and power to act?

- Do we have suitable rewards and defined accountability for actions?
- Have we identified actionable first steps?
- Does the organisation have a capacity to learn and to adapt?

Eccles considers these crucial: put simply, one should ask the people involved in a change management project before implementing it.

Eccles proposes thirteen possible sources of resistance, such as failure to understand the problem, fear of being unable to cope, and cost to implement it. Most are individual psychological reactions to change and may be attributed to parochial self-interest (Buchanan and Huczynski, 2004).

Focusing on resource-dependency, and discussing DI, Christensen and Bower (1996) conclude that inappropriate resource allocation routines (e.g. channelling resources into improvements in existing products to satisfy existing customers and investors) can contribute to the failure of strong and capably managed firms. In a similar vein, Utterback (1994) argues that a radical innovation may not initially address the needs of existing customers. An orientation toward existing customers may lead firms to invest hugely in continuously improving existing products or services, significantly increasing the potential difficulty in adopting a new idea.

Bessant *et al.* (2005) agree: traditional new product development routines - trusting accumulated knowledge to deliver success - may manifest themselves in management routines and processes that decide trajectories for the future (path dependence), perhaps because the strategic importance of DI is not understood as critical to survival (Christensen, 1997). Tidd and Bessant (2009) claim that inability to identify or generate a disruptive foothold against market and human barriers (e.g. ignorance, focusing on historical perceptions of success, and managers' concerns) may be barriers to DI.

Koberg *et al.* (2003) suggest that organisational age and size may be predictors of expected frequency of incremental rather than radical innovation. Bateman and Rich (2003) see workforce turnover as an inhibitor to process improvement. Soltani and Wilkinson (2010) identify incongruence in senior and middle managers' orientations as a key factor affecting the outcome of TQM programmes (arguably a case of DI) in the sense that middle managers tend to have a short-term tactical orientation while senior managers can see long-term benefits. The barriers to implementation are summarized in Table 1.

Enablers

As with barriers, it appears that enablers of one type of innovation may influence adoption of another in a different way. For example, employing a strategic alliance risk management perspective, Li *et al.* (2008) concluded that social control of an organisation may be beneficial to radical innovation while limiting incremental innovation. Conversely, formal control may facilitate incremental innovation while impeding radical innovation.

Organisational culture is widely considered a key contextual variable for managing innovation while organisational value is seen as a building block of an innovation-supportive culture. Khazanchi *et al.* (2007) suggest that paradoxical value profiles, including both flexibility and control, may be needed in order to have a successful implementation of process innovation. McLaughlin *et al.* (2004) agree: organisational cultures that facilitate radical innovation tend to be tolerant of risk taking and uncertainty.

Klein and Sorra (1996) present a model of determinants and consequences for innovation implementation effectiveness. They conclude that two determinants to implementation effectiveness are climate for implementation and fit of innovation to organisational and group values. A strong implementation climate is formed, they conclude, by ensuring employees are skilled in using inno-

Table 1. Summary of barriers to DI implementation

Researchers	Barriers	Category
Buchanan and Huczynski (2004), Eccles (1994)	• Parochial self-interest; • Misunderstanding and lack of trust; • Contradictory assessments of costs and benefits; • Low tolerance for change.	Individual psychological
Christensen and Bower (1996), Utterback (1994), Bessant *et al.* (2005)	inappropriate resource allocation routines	Organisational
Christensen (1997)	strategic importance of DI is not understood as critical to survival	Organisational
Tidd and Bessant (2009)	inability to identify or generate a disruptive foothold against market and human barriers	Organisational
Soltani and Wilkinson (2010)	incongruence in senior and middle managers' orientations	Individual
Bateman and Rich (2003)	Work force turnover	Organisational

vation, providing incentives for innovation use and disincentives for innovation avoidance, and removing obstacles to innovation use.

Tidd and Bessant (2009) propose the following components are crucial to building an innovative organization:

- Shared vision, leadership and the will to innovate
- Appropriate organisation structure
- Key individuals (champions)
- Effective team working
- High involvement innovation
- Creative climate (culture)
- External focus

Enablers to DI implementation are summarized in Table 2.

Barriers and enablers to DI appear to be focused on individual and organizational levels. This is understandable in that DI has typically been studied in a single organisation. No single comprehensive list exists of the factors affecting the implementation of DI.

Barriers and Enablers to the Implementation of DI in a Supply Chain Context

We focus on DI in supply chain relationships, borrowing from organisational and DI literature. Christenson (2006) makes the surprising proposition that the supply chain itself may be a disruptive technology as supply chains in the emerging market may 'hollow out' their customers in a developed market. Taken at a macroeconomic level this suggests that customers in the developed world may need a new way of managing in their supply chains compared to methods used in the past - a case of DI itself.

Flint *et al.* (2008) argue that the collaboration and coordination between functional departments lead to the inter-organizational learning and supply chain innovation. Following Mentzer *et al.* (2000), we propose that the barriers to implementing innovation in supply chain relationships may be manifested in such activities as sharing information and the coordination of strategies towards performance:

Table 2. Summary of enablers to DI implementation

Researcher	Enablers	Category
Eccles (1994)	• a pressure for change • a clear and shared vision of the goal • effective liaison and trust between those concerned • the will and power to act • suitable rewards and defined accountability for actions • actionable first steps • Learning capacity	Organisational and environmental
Khazanchi *et al.* (2007)	paradoxical value profiles: flexibility and control	Organisational
McLaughlin *et al.* (2004), Klein and Sorra (1996), Li *et al.* (2001)	organisational cultures: tolerant of risk taking and uncertainty; use both flexibility and control; social control	Organisational
Klein and Sorra (1996)	fit of innovation to organisational and group values	Organisational
Tidd and Bessant (2009)	• Shared vision, leadership and the will to innovate • Appropriate organisation structure • Key individuals (champions) • Effective team working • High involvement innovation • Creative climate (culture) • External focus	Organisational, individual and environmental

- An unwillingness to subordinate one organisation's goals to the good of the supply chain,
- Employees' resistance to change,
- Technological inadequacies,
- Weak relationships among trading partnership; and
- Not having the human and financial resources to invest in supply chain initiatives.

METHODOLOGY

Retrospective, multiple case studies were employed since our fundamental research question is why some radical ideas survive while others disappear. Case study method best answers 'why' and 'how' questions, which have not yet been thoroughly researched (Yin, 2003).

Rather than present solutions and recommendations in the following section, we present here the cases of two research-led projects in supply chain relationships carried out in the 1990s: the SCRIA-RET (Supply Chain Relationship in Aerospace, Relationship Evaluation Tool) and Value- Transparency (V-T) to illustrate the implementation of DI. Both projects originated in research work of one of the authors and were aimed at practical implementation.

It should be noted that the unit of analysis is the implementation process of the two projects: SCRIA-RET and V-T. Both were documented and explained as cases of DI (Richard *et al.*, 1996; Richard *et al.*, 2001). A table of description of the case companies is shown in Table 3.

TWO CASES: SCRIA-RET AND VALUE TRANSPARENCY

SCRIA-RET

Since the development of statistical quality control in the early part of the twentieth century, managers have sought to measure whatever they can within operating systems, repeating mantras such as 'what gets measured gets done' and if 'you can't measure it, it doesn't exist'. The manufacturing

Table 3. Overviews of four case companies involved

Project	Company	Brief company overview	Company size
SCRIA	Case A	defence, security and aerospace systems integrator	Turnover:£20Bn; employees: 100,000
	Case C	a total capability provider in the vertical lift market.	Turnover: Euro30Bn; employees: 70,000
V-T	Case B	A global power system integrator supplying aerospace industry	Turnover: £10bn employees:30,000
	Case D	the world's leading manufacturer of Electric, Pneumatic & Hydraulic Valve Actuators and associated Control Systems supplying defence sector	Turnover:£350million employees: 1,800

needs of the Second World War fuelled this development, resulting in widespread use of statistically based quality control systems in North America and Europe, and the influence of thinkers such as Deming, Juran, Feiginbaum and Garvin in Japan. The principle was 'company-wide quality control'- a system that left no stone unturned in its drive for installing quality in every part of a manufacturing firm.

In 1990s, these quality control methods were used in judging the inputs to the customers' operating systems and rolled out into the operations of the suppliers themselves (sometimes called 'vendors.'). Supplier/vendor assessment schemes flourished and spread to all sectors of industry- becoming the norm in leading sectors such as automotive and aerospace.

The assumption upon which supplier/vendor assessment is built is fundamentally challenged by the principles contained in the concepts of lean supply, first laid out in 1993 (Lamming, 1993; 2003). One of the observations upon which lean supply is built is that many traditional purchasing management practices and devices at the interface between a supplier and customer actually tend to inhibit rather than encourage effective supply, unless both parties are investing in the relationship, e.g. unless both customer and supplier are seen to be taking a risk in the interests of improving value transfer.

Typically, supplier/vendor assessment is based upon the customer setting up hurdles for the supplier to jump over, using the measurement data thus generated as a 'stick' with which to beat the supplier in negotiations. In other words, the data are used to show how bad the supplier is at, say, on-time delivery, in order to weaken their commercial reasoning during the inevitable confrontation on prices. If the buying firm tries to use political or economic power to manage its supplier, therefore, the supplier may be faced with commercial disaster. In practice, when faced with the ultimatum of 'supplier management' the supplier has to cheat, in order to survive. This is costly and creates excess work without adding value.

The theoretical argument of lean supply is that, in order to reduce costs in supply relationships, each side must respect the other's risk management. Considering lean supply in the context of long-term strategic supply relationships we might envisage an alternative approach to performance measurement, which focuses neither on supplier nor on customer performance but on relationship performance: the health of the relationship. This approach considers the supply relationship as a separate unit of analysis from either the customer or the supplier.

The Relationship Assessment Process (RAP) was developed as a practical application of this aspect of lean supply. The RAP model had its origins in the early work on lean supply (Lamming, 1993; Lamming, 1996). In common with other lean supply principles, the concept of relationship assessment represented a radical departure from established purchasing processes and it questioned the relevance of existing techniques such as supplier/vendor assessment and open-book negotiation (Lamming *et al.*, 2004). The RAP research project took place between 1994 and 1996. By 1996, the conceptual model had been developed by drawing on the findings from three in-depth case studies, which focused on the purchasing departments of three large commercial organizations (Shell, ICL and British Airways) and a selection of dyadic supply relationships.

The principle of relationship assessment is that the supplier and customer develop a framework that they can use for analyzing the relationship, using it together after first conducting in-house assessment of their own approaches to the relationship. An operational tool - the SCRIA-RET - was developed from RAP. This occurred as a result of an environmental factor that affected the aerospace industry.

When the Berlin wall came down in 1989 the world rejoiced. For the aerospace industry, however, it was followed by a slump in orders as "peace broke out." In the UK the civil aerospace development was intrinsically linked with that of military aircraft: passenger aircraft business would suffer as much as that in warplanes.

The Society of British Aircraft Companies (SBAC) decided a sector-wide national strategy was needed to maintain the industries competitiveness through this period – until military business picked up again. The approach was based upon improving supply chain relationships. SBAC built an initiative called Supply Chain Relationships in Aerospace – SCRIA. This contained a great deal of common sense and straight talking about relationships, with customers and suppliers in the industry committed to real change.

Companies in this industry were well aware of the lean manufacturing principles (that had been developed in the automotive industry in the previous decade) and were already implementing them. Key players in SBAC were also aware of the work under way in lean supply and knew about the academic *RAP* project. The academics were asked to develop a practical version of RAP for SCRIA. This became the SCRIA RET: a relationship evaluation tool. It embodied the principles of leanness in relationship and enabled problem solving through attention to specific improvements in the way relationships were managed – by customers and suppliers together.

As the century ended, the lull in military aerospace business abated. SBAC was inspired, however, by the power of sector-wide transformational initiatives and wished to continue the idea. The Lean Aerospace programme had brought major benefits to the sector and this was combined with SCRIA into "21st Century Supply Chains or SC21." The radical idea of relationship assessment was carried forward into SC21 and remains in use as the Relationship Management Matrix, ten years after its inception. The transfer from theory into practice was successful.

Value Transparency

Traditional management approaches in supply relationships emphasize the importance of employing economic power. Usually, this is presented as existing within the customer although it might as easily reside with the supplier. The resulting arrogance and myopia on the part of the customer have been labelled the 'vantage point syndrome' (Lamming, 1996). Organizations adopting this approach often behave as if they, and only they, have the full picture of the supply system and can require suppliers (and possibly customers) to follow their direction. In purchasing within such a firm, approaches such as supplier assessment, supplier development (or management), and open-book negotiation are generally popular, driven by the power resulting from the assumed vantage point.

The problem embedded in this phenomenon may lie in the cliché coined by the great retail pioneer, Gordon Selfridge, and the mind-set associated with it: "the customer is always right."

This is evident in 'open-book negotiation,' where the customer requires the supplier to disclose their real costs. The customer usually expects to take all the benefits while the supplier has to face price reduction, and often uses the intelligence it has gained with other suppliers.

The flaw in the logic of open-book negotiation lies in the customer requiring the supplier to take a risk, without hedge or security, in demanding the exposure of such sensitive data. This is incompatible with long-term survival for the supplier, who must therefore respond by hedging the risk, providing distorted or corrupt information, thereby protecting its economic position. Elsewhere (Lamming, *et al.* 2001), we have called this hedging 'cheating.' An extreme but commonplace example is the creation of entirely false books for the customer to inspect. Clearly, it would not be in a supplier's commercial best interests to reveal sensitive supply relationship information without some reciprocation. In seeking to hedge this risk (to cheat), the supplier is behaving entirely rationally.

First developed from research in the late 1980s as an alternative to traditional techniques, the concept of transparency in supply relationships arose (as *cost* transparency) during the development of the lean supply paradigm (Lamming, 1993). Originally based upon extensive work in the global automotive industry, the lean supply paradigm includes the application of radical techniques (i.e. doing things differently, rather than the old things better) in removing activities deemed wasteful (adding no value to the product or service, or the process of its delivery). No traditional factor is taken as *prima facie* necessarily wasteful by the lean approach. Indeed, apparently high inventory levels may be necessary for agility in responding to market dynamics, while idle time may be necessary for learning to take place in a system. Neither would necessarily detract from the leanness of the system. Early work on lean supply focused on less traditional concerns, questioning whether much so-called 'professional' purchasing was actually responsible for maintaining wasteful practices. These practices appeared to add cost and time to processes, reducing the ability of the organizations (customer and supplier) to respond to market signals (i.e., making them less lean and less agile).

In the mid-1990s, a second phase of research conducted in a variety of U.K. companies outside the automotive industry revealed the difficulties organizations might face in trying to implement cost transparency (Lamming *et al.*, 1996). The principal finding of this case based work was that inhibitors to transparency could be classed as *structural* or *operational*. The conclusion was that effective implementation of the concept would be facilitated by the *removal* of parts of a system, rather than introduction of new mechanisms. (It did not appear appropriate, for example, to introduce a "transparency manager".) This agrees with the lean principle of waste removal.

Conducted between 1998 and 2000, the third phase of the research involved working with a large high technology systems manufacturer in the aerospace industry. The practical outcome of this research contributed towards a clearer understanding of the conceptual and practical complexity and nature of transparency and a framework for discussion. In the third phase, further work was carried out on this framework, again working with manufacturing firms. Based on case studies in four high technology manufacturers (in a variety of industries), the framework was developed into a formal conceptual model and will lead to construction of a practical methodology for managers to use within supply relationships.

With its origins in lean supply, the concept of cost transparency was originally introduced as: "The sharing of costing information between customer and supplier, including data which would traditionally be kept secret by each party, for use in negotiations. The purpose of this is to make it possible for customer and supplier to work together to reduce costs (and improve other factors). Cost transparency is of no value … unless it is two-way" (Lamming, 1993 pp. 214-5).

It was proposed that the information sharing must be reciprocal, selective, and justified, but not necessarily symmetrical. It was central to the initial conceptualization that transparency should go beyond simply better 'communication.' Underlying the concept is the joint sharing or pooling of risk. This pooling of risk fundamentally distinguishes transparency (i.e., 'two-way' or 'reciprocal' sharing) from customer-driven approaches such as open-book negotiation.

The approach of lean supply principles to the problem is not based upon the conceptual debate, however, but on the observation that increased competitive pressures (including the Internet) are increasingly exposing previously hidden costs. Transparency suggests that hierarchy based responses to these competitive pressures (e.g., customer arrogance, open-book negotiation, and vantage points) may self-destruct. Transparency can forge a new bond between customer and supplier, which removes the costs and delays implicit in traditional poses. It may also challenge those who associate professionalism in both purchasing and sales with these postures: the ritualized deployment of the opening gambit, the hard-hearted partner, and the calculated delay of negotiation.

As in much of the lean supply paradigm, the key lies in unlocking the goodwill of the supplier. The hypothesis is that the risk taken on by the supplier in revealing sensitive information might be balanced by a similar advance by the customer. In this way, within a carefully bounded arena, the parties to the transaction become interdependent, for simple commercial reasons on each side and not as part of any philosophical standpoint (such as espoused partnering). To do this, the purchaser, in the person of the buyer, must manage risk in pursuit of improved added value. However, observations, corroborated by empirical research, reveal that risk management is not commonly found in the skill set of purchasing personnel.

The definition also proposed that transparency should be linked to value creation, reducing the cost of 'adding value.' Our research since that time has revealed that this point is actually critical to the process. Focusing on how implementing transparent ways of working in relationships might capture value developed the concept of cost transparency into 'value transparency' (V-T), defined as "the creation, nurture and delivery of value, for the benefit, and thus continued existence, of both parties" (Lamming *et al.*, 2004).

Going beyond the bilateral sharing of sensitive information, V-T involves managed risk for both parties, with identifiable additional returns that may be associated with that risk. Instead of limiting definitions for value (such as exchange or utility), it is more appropriate to consider operational forms that emerge from engagement in the relationship process. For example, within a supply base, V-T might be implemented in a tailored, project-by-project approach, with information and risk sharing limited to the scope of each project.

Exploring the concept of transparency with practitioners led to the adoption of a descriptive categorization borrowed from geology: that of the characteristics of minerals in terms of the amount light that can pass through them, used as an analogy for the transfer of information or knowledge in relationships. The three identified modes of transparency are clarity, translucency and opaqueness. Supply relationships are likely to contain elements of all three characteristics, in a variety of locations at different times.

These are the three modes of manageable exchange of sensitive information. Working with these in a project plan, it should be possible to decide jointly (i.e. supplier and customer together in a boundary-spanning project team) what type of sharing is necessary and possible at which stage of the project. In the first mode, clarity, information such as cost structures, forward volumes, design plans and other operating details may be entirely open. Where this is not possible or necessary, translucency might be employed - partial V-T where customer or supplier is able to 'ring fence' some factors and it is agreed that this is necessary. In the third manageable mode, opaqueness,' there is a 'no-go' area, the information pertinent to the stage of the project cannot be shared and other ways of working must be found. Removing the pressure to reveal such data should, we suggest, remove many hidden costs associated with protection, deception and concealment.

Two peripheral states were identified that appear unmanageable, at least in relationship terms. The first is 'Dazzle' - too much information is presented in response to a request and the receiver cannot effectively deal with it (this may be accidental or deliberate). The last is called 'Black Hole,' where it is claimed that the factors are so deeply buried or complex it is not possible to explain or share them. By employing this range of types it is possible to avoid referring to a specific relationship as 'transparent' or otherwise. Rather, a relationship may contain one, several, or all of these types and that the mix and consistency may vary, or be altered deliberately, over time (possibly in a very dynamic manner). The contingency approach gives a robustness and practicality to the concept.

In developing V-T, the researchers worked with a small number of companies in various industries to implement the concept in practice. It was well received but proved too radical a departure, or perhaps a threat to embedded practices, such as open-book negotiation. It remains on the agenda of the project companies but has not still been operationalised. Table 4 shows the key points emerged from the case descriptions.

FUTURE RESEARCH DIRECTION

It can be seen from the two cases that both projects were based on the tenets of lean supply but had different outcomes. It will be interesting to know what might have caused the success and failure in each case.

It has been found from literature review that research on DI has been predominantly in single organisations, focusing on individual and organisational variables; little work has addressed barriers and enablers for implementation of radical concepts in supply relationships, which was the case for V-T and SCRIA-RET projects. While change management literature provides some insights, research on DI says little about environmental variables of implementation processes, considered so important by contingency and new institutional theorists.

Our future research is therefore exploratory and inductive in nature: to test individual, organisational and inter-firm variables on one hand and explore environment and other variables emerging on the other. A grounded method will be chosen. This reflects the call by Binder and Edwards (2010) for more grounded theory method in Operations Management research. They see grounded theory method as particularly appropriate when research and theory are at their early stage and when the major research interests lie in the identification and categorisation of elements. This fits well with our research.

Table 4. Summary of emergent key points from two cases

Cases	Key points emerged
SCRIA	1. Lean supply is proposed to challenge the vendor assessment mindset and a radical innovation in supply relationship management 2. Propose long-term strategic supply relationship 3. Measure relationship rather than individual companies
V-T	1. Challenge open book negotiation 2. Information sharing must be reciprocal, selective, and justified, but not necessarily symmetrical 3. Three categories of transparency: clarity, translucency, and opaqueness; plus dazzle (too much information provided)

Retrospective, multiple case studies will be employed since our fundamental research question is *why* some radical ideas survive while others disappear. Case study methods best answer the 'why' and 'how' questions that have not yet been thoroughly researched.

Although both V-T and SCRIA-RET are action-based research, this future research takes a more objective view observing and exploring what had happened for these two projects.

Interviews are now being conducted with some managers involved in the SCRIA-RET and V-T projects, focusing on what happened before, during and after the implementation projects, and seeking to identify barriers and enablers. In research terms, these are 'stories.' They are effective in uncovering unspoken, perhaps unconscious, norms within an organisational subculture (Hansen and Kahnweiler, 1993). Gabriel (2000: 135) observes "stories are emotionally and symbolically charged narratives. They do not present information or facts about events but they enrich, enhance and infuse facts with meaning". We are clearly looking for meaning.

A small number of open questions were developed, enabling each interviewee to tell part of the overall story. Subsequently we are piecing together the fragmented narratives in order to represent a coherent reality. Other sources of information are documentation: reports, newsletters, SBAC case studies, journal papers and book chapters reporting findings from the projects. These provided comprehensive background information, vital for coherent stories

We believe it is necessary to look beyond the individual psychological barriers and organisational level factor traditionally discussed in the literature and a multilevel analysis is needed in order to fully appreciate the complexity of the phenomenon.

IMPLICATIONS AND CONCLUSION

In this chapter, we reviewed the literature on the motivation, barriers and enablers to the implementation of discontinuous innovation. We found that current research focuses on individual and organizational level factors affecting implementation of DI and that innovation and change management are usually based on a single organizational setting. This identifies a gap in the literature to which the future stage of our inter-organisational research could potentially contribute.

We also presented accounts of the evolution of two radical ideas - SCRIA-RET and V-T, explaining why they were considered radical, what radical change they brought to traditional purchasing practices, how they were developed, and their success and failure. Based on our reflection on the two cases, single organisational and individual factors alone can not explain the complex change processes like SCRIA and V-T. For example, what trigged the SCRIA to happy was the fall of Berlin Wall followed by a sharp reduction of orders for military aircrafts. This does not belong to organisational or individual categories and falls into the environmental category of factors.

There has an advocate for multilevel analysis in organizational research including innovation within organisations. Klein *et al.* (1999) argue that multilevel theory connects dots, making explicit previously unlinked constructs within organisational literature. Although multilevel theory is necessarily complex, their complexity may yield important practical insights. They also claim that multilevel analysis is dominated by two levels of analysis: individuals and organisations.

Kimberley and Evanisko (1981: 690) argue that organizational adoption of organisational innovation is influenced by "the characteristics of individual people—usually organisational leaders; by characteristics of the organisation itself; and by characteristics of the context in which it operates and out of which it emerged".

Building on Kimberley and Evanisko, Meyer and Goes (1988) carry out a multilevel analysis of innovation assimilation in hospitals and identify three categories of factors altogether accounting for 59% of total variance:

- Contextual attributes: characteristics of environment, organisations and leaders
- Innovation attributes: characteristics inherent in technological innovation
- Innovation-decision attributes: characteristics of innovation-context interaction

Based on above arguments, we propose that it is necessary to look beyond the individual psychological barriers and organisational level factors traditionally discussed in the literature and a multilevel analysis is needed in order to fully appreciate the complexity of the phenomenon of DI implementation in SCR.

REFERENCES

Bateman, N., & Rich, N. (2003). Companies' perceptions of inhibitors and enablers for process improvement activities. *International Journal of Operations & Production Management, 23*(2), 185–199. doi:10.1108/01443570310458447

Bessant, J., Lamming, R., Noke, H., & Phillips, W. (2005). Managing innovation beyond the steady state. *Technovation, 25*(12), 1366–1376. doi:10.1016/j.technovation.2005.04.007

Binder, M., & Edwards, J. S. (2010). Using grounded theory method for theory building in operations management research. *International Journal of Operations & Production Management, 30*(3). doi:10.1108/01443571011024610

Buchanan, D., & Huczynski, A. (2004). *Organisational Behaviour: An Introductory Text.* 5th ed., England: Financial Times/Prentice Hall.

Choi, T. Y., Dooley, K. J., & Ruanglusanathan, M. (2001). Supply networks and complex adaptive systems: control versus emergence. *Journal of Operations Management, 19*, 351–366. doi:10.1016/S0272-6963(00)00068-1

Christensen, C., & Bower, J. (1996). Customer Power, Strategic Investment and the Failure of Leading Firms. *Strategic Management Journal, 17*, 197–218. doi:10.1002/(SICI)1097-0266(199603)17:3<197::AID-SMJ804>3.0.CO;2-U

Christenson, C. (1997). *The innovator's dilemma.* Cambridge, MA: Harvard Business School Press.

Christenson, C. (2006). The supply chain as a disruptive technology. *World Trade*, December.

DiMaggio, P., & Powell, W. (1983). The Iron Cage Revisited: Institutional Isomorphism and Collective Rationality in Organisational Fields. *American Sociological Review, 48*, 147–160. doi:10.2307/2095101

Eccles, T. (1994). *Succeeding with Change: Implementing Action-driven Strategies.* Maidenhead: McGraw-Hill.

Flint, D., Larsson, E., & Gammelgaar, B. (2008). Exploring processes for customer value insights, supply chain learning and innovation: an international study. *Journal of Business Logistics, 29*(1). doi:10.1002/j.2158-1592.2008.tb00078.x

Gabriel, Y. (2000). *Storytelling in Organizations: Facts, fictions, and fantasies.* London: Oxford University Press.

Galbraith, J. (1973). *Designing Complex Organizations.* Reading, MA: Addison-Wesley.

Hansen, C. D., & Kahnweiler, W. M. (1993). Storytelling: An Instrument for Understanding the Dynamics of Corporate Relationships. *Human Relations, 46*, 1391–1409. doi:10.1177/001872679304601202

Khazanchi, S., Lewis, M. W., & Boyer, K. K. (2007). Innovation-supportive culture: The impact of organisational values on process innovation. *Journal of Operations Management, 25*(4), 871–884. doi:10.1016/j.jom.2006.08.003

Klein, K. J., & Sorra, J. S. (1996). The challenge of innovation implementation. *Academy of Management Review, 21*, 1055–1080.

Koberg, C. S., Detienne, D. R., & Heepard, K. A. (2003). In Empirical Test of Environmental, Organisational, and Process Factors Affecting Incremental and Radical Innovation. *The Journal of High Technology Management Research*, (14): 21–45. doi:10.1016/S1047-8310(03)00003-8

Lamming, R. C. (1993). *Beyond Partnership: strategies for innovation and lean supply*. Upper Saddle River, NJ: Prentice Hall.

Lamming, R. C. (1996). Squaring lean supply with supply chain management. *International Journal of Operations & Production Management, 16*(2), 183–196. doi:10.1108/01443579610109910

Lamming, R. C. (2003). *Oltre la Partnership: strategie per l'innovazione e la produzione snella*. Napoli: Edizione Scientifiche Italiane.

Lamming, R. C., Caldwell, N. D., & Harrison, D. (2004). Developing the concept of transparency for use in supply relationships. *British Journal of Management, 15*, 291–302. doi:10.1111/j.1467-8551.2004.00420.x

Lamming, R.C., Caldwell, N.D., Harrison, D.A. & Phillips, W.E. (2001). Transparency in Supply Relationships: Concept and Practice. *Journal of Supply Chain Management, 37* (4), Fall 2001.

Lamming, R. C., Jones, O. A., & Nicol, D. J. (1996). Cost Transparency: A Source of Supply Chain Competitive Advantage? *Proceedings of the 5th International IPSERA Conference*. Eindhoven

Li, Y., Liu, Y., Li, M., & Wu, H. (2008). Transformational offshore outsourcing: empirical evidence from alliances in China. *Journal of Operations Management, 26*(2), 257–274. doi:10.1016/j.jom.2007.02.011

McLaughlin, P., Bessant, J., & Smart, P. (2004). *Developing an Organisational Culture That Facilitates Radical Innovation in a Mature Small to Medium Sized Company: Emergent Findings,* Working paper. http://www.cranfield.ac.uk/som /research/working_ papers.

Mentzer, J. T., Foggin, J. H., & Golicic, S. L. (2000). Supply chain collaboration: enablers, impediments, and benefits. *Supply Chain Management Review, 4*(5), 52–58.

Morgan, G., & Smircich, L. (1980). The Case for Qualitative Research. *Academy of Management Review, 5*, 491–500.

Pfeffer, J. (1997). *New directions for organization theory*. New York: Oxford University Press.

Powell, W., & DiMaggio, P. (1991). *New institutionalism in organizational analysis*. Chicago, IL: The University of Chicago Press.

Rich, B., & Janos, L. (1996). *Skunk Works*. New York: Little, Brown & Company.

Scott, W. R. (1995). *Institutions and Organizations. CA*. Thousand Oaks: Sage.

Soltani, E., & Wilkinson, A. (2010). Stuck in the middle with you. *International Journal of Operations & Production Management, 30*(4).

Tidd, J., & Bessant, J. (2009). *Managing innovation* (4th ed.). England: John, Wiley and Sons.

Utterback, J. (1994). *Mastering the Dynamics of Innovation*. Boston: Harvard Business School Press.

Chapter 17
How to Use the Evaluation of Suppliers to Develop the Supply System

Emilio Esposito
University of Naples Federico II, Italy

Renato Passaro
University of Naples Parthenope, Italy

ABSTRACT

In recent decades several studies have highlighted that the competitive advantage of large customer firms arises significantly from their ability to achieve a successful supply system through the adoption of effective tools and methodologies for evaluating suppliers. Nevertheless it emerges that a gap exists between a growing number of applications and the scarce empirical evidence of the practical usefulness of such applications. The purpose of this chapter is to provide a contribution to bridging this gap through applying the Analytical Hierarchical Process (AHP) methodology suppliers' evaluation. The evaluation tree of the AHP assures transparency and traceability, features that allow using it as a tool for strategic management of the supply system. The AHP evaluation tree provides relevant indications for the strategic decision that both customers and suppliers have to adopt to reinforce the supply system and their competitive position. Relevant issues arising from the application and managerial implications for both customer and suppliers are discussed. In particular, we underline how the AHP methodology is not only a tool for supplier evaluation but also a strategic management tool to develop the supply system.

DOI: 10.4018/978-1-60960-585-8.ch017

INTRODUCTION

This chapter is aimed at proposing a methodology for supplier evaluation based on the Analytical Hierarchical Process (AHP), one of the most prominent methodologies used to address the evaluation problem (Saaty, 1980, 1994, 2001). The proposed methodology considers both aspects of evaluation: the customer's point of view (the perceptive aspect of supplier's performance) and the object of evaluation (the technical aspect of the supplier activity). These aspects are evaluated in relation to a specific transaction object consisting in a component of a complex product system. In this way the considered unit of analysis is the case of suppliers operating for a large customer on a particular component.

Considering the robust theoretical base of the AHP and illustrating its consistency through an empirical application to a case study, the purpose of this work is to provide a contribution to bridging the gap between a growing number of existing applications and the scarce empirical evidence of the practical usefulness of such tools. In fact, the evaluation tree system of the AHP assures transparency and traceability, features that allow using it as a tool for strategic management of the supply system.

To test the proposed method, a case study has been developed concerning the supplier evaluation process adopted by AnsaldoBreda a leading Italian railway manufacturing company. Four suppliers producing a component of the traction system have been considered. The analysis of the case study has allowed identification of strengths and weaknesses of suppliers, highlighting how AHP methodology can be used as a tool for strategic management of the supply chain (SC) by drawing actions and policies that both customers and suppliers may follow.

With these premises in mind, the chapter is organized into eight sections. Following this introduction, the second section illustrates the theoretical background of the work based on the analysis of the supplier evaluation problem. The third section deals with the methodological framework adopted, describing both the unit of analysis considered and the seven steps of the AHP methodology applied. The fourth section illustrates the empirical evidences achieved discussing the peculiar situation of each supplier emerging from the analysis. The fifth section proposes a discussion of the lessons learned during the design and implementation of the model, while solutions and recommendations for supply chain innovation derived from the exercise are proposed in the sixth section. In the last two sections future research perspectives are discussed and some managerial and policy implications are drawn.

THE THEORETICAL BACKGROUND

Several studies have shown that suppliers are increasingly essential contributors to building the competitive advantage of customers and that their actions have a positive impact on the performance of the entire supply chain (Vonderembse, Tracey, 1999; Sarkara, Mohapatrab, 2006; Shu et al., 2006). In the last decades an incresing number of scholars have focused on the issue of supplier selection methodologies (Weber et al, 1991; Bhutta, 2003; Cheraghi et al, 2004; Sonmez, 2006; Bruno et al., 2010) to develop supplier management process and supply relationship system able to rapidly react to market requirements and to innovation dynamics (Lamming et al, 1996; de Boer et al., 2001; Lee et al, 2001; Prahinski, Benton, 2004; Kamann and Bakker, 2004; Saen, 2007). In a general perspective, some scholars pointed out that, in recent decades, the evolutionary processes of supply chains also depend on the ability of large customer firms to adopt a proper suppliers' evaluation system (Esposito and Passaro 2009a, 2009b).

By analyzing the strategies of major competitors it emerges that they increasingly face a problem of selection of suppliers which consists of the identification of models and methods to analyze and measure the performance of a set of suppliers (vendors) to improve their own competitiveness. The problem is intrinsically multi-attribute since many qualitative and quantitative factors, often conflicting with each other, should be taken into account (Bhutta, Huk, 2002; Sonmez, 2006; Ramanathan, 2007; Ordoobadi, 2009). This has also led scholars to adopt multicriteria approaches (Dulmin, Mininno, 2003; Araz, Ozkarahan, 2007).

In fact, an increasing number of contributions has been devoted to the development of different kind of methodologies to cope with this problem over the past decades. Nevertheless, while the number of applications is growing, there is little empirical evidence of the practical usefulness of such tools (de Boer, van der Wegen, 2003; Hsu, 2006). It has been observed that the proposed models are very likely to be tested on generic applications, numerical examples and computational experiments (Ting, Cho, 2008; Ordoobadi, 2009; Bhutta and Huk, 2002; Dahel 2003; Saen, 2007), with scarce emphasis on problems emerging in the practical implementation of the methodology, strengths and weaknesses, and positive feedback from practitioners and managers involved in decision making processes (Bruno et al, 2010). In many cases qualitative factors impacting the decision process (incomplete information, imprecise preferences) are hardly taken into account (de Boer et al., 2003). Moreover, a large part of the literature deals with the problem considering the customer's point of view (Ali et al. 1997), neglecting both the importance of the collaborative relationship and the suppliers' key role within the supply system (Park, Krishnan, 2001).

In this scenario, despite there are a number of research works proposing empirical applications, the analysis of the literature reveals the low effectiveness of methods application and procedures. While the literature highlights a variety of methodologies and approaches for suppliers' assessment, little has been said about the use of these methodologies to improve the performance of the entire supply chain and how they can be used as a tool for the strategic management of the supply system. In this perspective, the evaluation system should be used for both identify a final position of a specific supplier in a suppliers ranking and transparent tool able to identify the strengths and weaknesses that determine the final score of all actors in the supply system. This tool should provide traceability of the procedures and factors that determine the final result. In this way, customer and suppliers may rely upon a clearer picture and take appropriate actions to reduce weaknesses and improve the efficiency and competitiveness of the entire supply system.

THE METHODOLOGICAL FRAMEWORK

The Unit of Analysis

The application of the AHP methodology is carried out within the context of the supply system of AnsaldoBreda (AB), a state-owned company, leader of the Italian railway industry and one of the world oligopoly players. AB outsources about 70% of parts and subsystems for the construction of railway locomotives and electric traction and its supply system consists of hundreds of medium and small sized suppliers located both in Italy and abroad (Esposito, Passaro, 2007).

The unit of analysis comprises the triangle formed by suppliers operating for the customer AnsaldoBreda on a particular component of the traction system (Figure 1). The component analyzed is the bogie (or wheel truck), which is the structure that supports the rail vehicle body, making it stable and ensuring comfort and safety. The bogie is characterized by a remarkable technological complexity and there are currently four potential AB suppliers of this component which later in this paper will be named as Alfa, Beta, Gamma, and Delta.

Figure 1. The unit of analysis

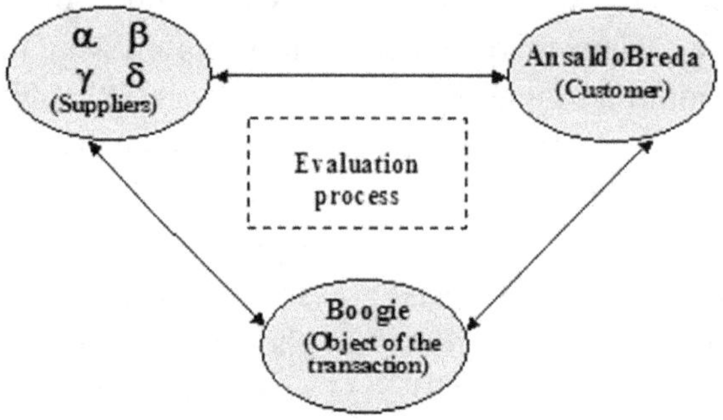

The supply system of AB encompasses suppliers belonging to different production systems characterized by diverse standards of quality, technology, cost and relationships with second tier suppliers. A supplier that provides a complex system typified by a high technological level cannot be evaluated with the same criteria of a supplier that provides capacity supplying. This brings about two main considerations. Firstly, the process of supplier evaluation cannot disregard the object provided. Secondly, it has to be able to adapt the process of evaluation to the customer's needs and the object in question. For this reason a methodology for suppliers' evaluation must present two characteristics:

1. specificity, the ability to evaluate suppliers operating in a specific production filière
2. flexibility, the ability to adapt the process of evaluation to the various activities outsourced by the customer.

The research strategy adopted was based on the interaction between the research group and company managers. For this reason, a working committee was created, including members from four different departments of AB (material planning, manufacturing, quality management, purchasing) in order to discuss critical attributes for supplier selection. The meetings took place at the company site and were moderated by members of the research group and it was aimed at building the research framework, developing the methodology and validating the research hypothesis.

In particular, during the meetings held with AB management, the logical process adopted to develop the methodology was identified. It consists of three main phases:

- Identification of the critical attributes
- Definition of the methodology
- Application of the methodology.

According to this methodology, entrepreneurs or production managers of the four suppliers operating on the bogie line were interviewed during *vis a vis* meetings at suppliers site using a semi-structured questionnaire to collect the required data and information.

The AHP Methodology

The AHP is a general theory of measurement that depends on the values and judgements of individuals and groups. More precisely, judgements are brought together according to a multilevel hierarchic structure to derive priorities. Among the major advantages of the hierarchical structure there are the features of transparency and traceability that allow for a detailed, structured and systematic deconstruction of the overall problem into its fundamental components and interdependencies,

Figure 2. The hierarchical structure of the evaluation process

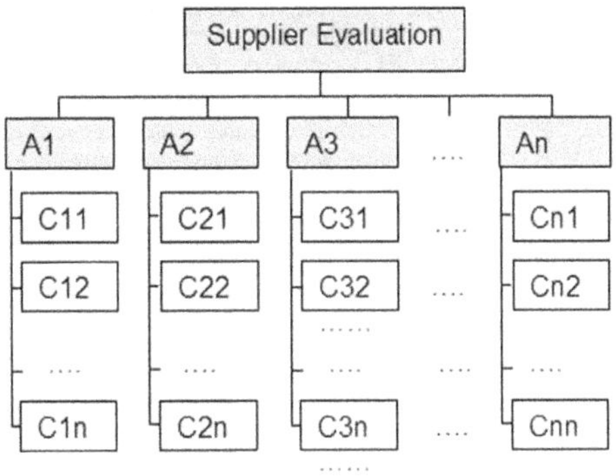

Table 1. Ratio scale of comparative judgements

Value	Interpretation
1: equal importance	*i* and *j* are equally important
3: weak importance over one another	*i* is slightly more important than *j*
5: strong importance	*i* is much more important than *j*
7: very strong importance	*i* is by far much more important than *j*
9: absolute or extreme importance	*i* is definitely much more important than *j*
2,4,6,8: intermediate values between 2 adjacent judgements.	

with a large degree of flexibility. The methodology adopted is organized into the following seven steps (Bruno et al, 2010):

a. *Structuring the problem into a hierarchy.* In general, hierarchies distribute a property (the goal) among the elements being compared (attributes and characteristics), to judge which one either influences or is influenced the most (Figure 2).

b. *Comparative judgements.* The aim is to measure the relative importance of the elements (attributes, characteristics) to the overall goal. When comparing two elements the question is "*how important is one of the two elements to the goal of the problem?*" Pairwise comparison matrices are associated with the set of attributes and each set of characteristics within each attribute. To compare two generic attributes and characteristics *i* and *j*, the ratio scale illustrated in Table 1 has been used.
At each hierarchical level the decision-maker establishes scores between elements by constructing a matrix of pairwise comparison judgements regarding relative importance or preference between any two elements. The a_{ij} value of the matrix represents the relative importance of the ith elements over the jth element. AHP allows for inconsistencies in pairwise judgements, i.e. a_{ij} x a_{jk} need not be equal to a_{ik}. Since each working committee member could have different knowledge and understanding of the supplier selection problem, input was expected to vary widely. However, several aggregation methods can be used for each judgement.

c. *Calculation of the vector of priorities.* Starting from the data obtained through the comparative judgement, the objective of this phase is to calculate the vector of priorities, which is the vector whose components are the priorities of each element of the hierarchy.

d. *Identification of indices for each element of the hierarchy.* The objective of this step is to identify a set of indices to measure supplier performance.

e. *Calculation of the vector of derived scores.* This step is addressed to build the value scale of the indices defined in the previous step for each hierarchical element in association with customer needs.

f. *Calculation of the vector of supplier performance.* Using the identified indices, the objective of this phase is to calculate the vector of supplier performance, that is the vector whose components are the performances of the supplier relative to each element of the hierarchy.

Table 2. Supplier selection attributes according to Ha and Krishnan (2008)'s framework

After sales service	Geographical location	Product appearance
Amount of past business	Impression	Production facilities and capacity
Attitude	JIT capability	Quality
Catalog technology	Labour relations	Reciprocal arrangements
Communication system	Maintainability	Reputation and position in industry
Delivery	Management and Organization	Response to customer request
Ease-of-use	Operational controls	Technical capability
E-commerce capability	Packaging ability	Technical support
Environmentally friendly products	Performance history	Training aids
Financial position	Price	Warranties and claims

g. *Calculation of the global score.* On the basis of the vector of priorities and the vectors of supplier performance, it is now possible to obtain a global score.

MAIN FINDINGS

To implement the AHP methodology the first step consists in structuring the problem into a hierarchy by defining attributes and characteristics. As regards the different attributes used in the literature to measure supplier performance and then to aggregate them in synthetic models, the first attempt to provide a general and comprehensive framework was provided by Dickson (1966) and also adopted by Weber *et al.*, (1991). Ha and Krishnan (2008) updated this set of attributes as shown in Table 2.

Price, Quality and Delivery are the three most used attributes; however, the list shows an extensive nature since the attributes are not always mentioned in a specific way and often no translation of these attributes into measurable characteristics is provided.

Starting from the list of 30 attributes identified by Ha and Krishnan (2008), during the first meeting, the managers of the four departments of AB were asked to choose the most relevant, without any restriction in the number selected. After a round of meetings, the managers agreed upon the four following attributes as those to be included in a hypothetical model to cope with the supplier evaluation problem:

1. *Process and Product Quality* (PPQ), expressing the efficiency and the effectiveness of the manufacturing processes and the quality of the final product;
2. *Service Level* (SL), expressing delivery punctuality and the respecting of other contract conditions;
3. *Management and Innovation* (MI), reflecting the supplier's attitude towards strategic R&D investments, HRM and capability of managing relationships with customers;
4. *Financial Position* (FP), expressing the firm's capacity to generate profits and liquidity.

Then, starting from the four attributes previously defined, three characteristics for each attribute were identified during subsequent meetings with AnsaldoBreda's management. Attributes and characteristics identified were translated into the hierarchical scheme described in Figure 3.

All the subsequent steps have been addressed to define the priorities (measure of the relative importance) of attributes and characteristics, identify the supplier performance for each element

Figure 3. Hierarchical structure of the evaluation process with attributes and characteristics

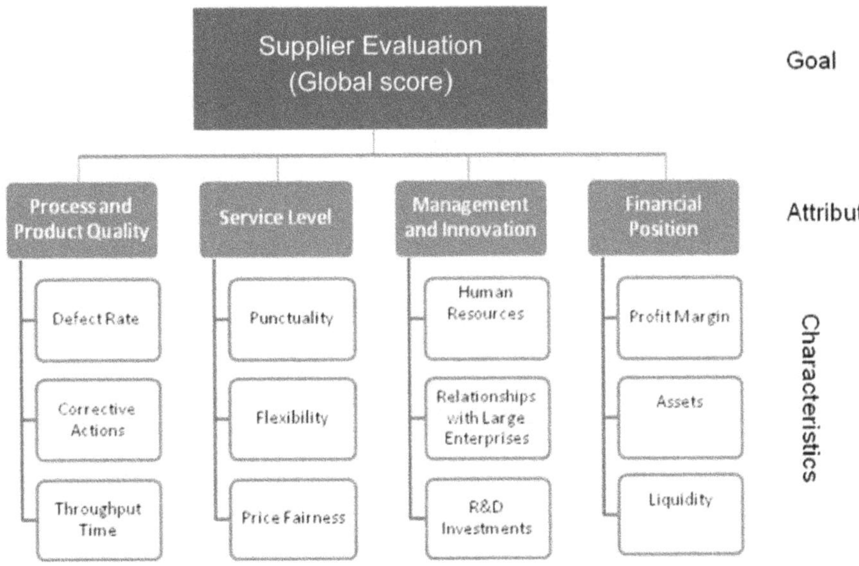

of the hierarchy and obtain the global score for each supplier.

The Figures 4 to 7 synthesises the findings derived by the implementation of the AHP methodology. They highlight that the supplier with the highest score is Beta (0.72) meanwhile the supplier Gamma has the lowest score (0,56). Suppliers Alfa (0,70) and Delta (0,68) are classified in an intermediate position, though placed immediately after Beta.

These positions are the result of the customer requirements and of different performances of the suppliers emerging from the combination of attributes and characteristics according to the evaluation of priorities. The evaluation tree allows to identify the different factors affecting the final score. Observing the score of the four suppliers we can trace both a performance profile of each supplier and a pathway to follow to improve the set of the supplier performance. The global score is the result of the combined impact of characteristics, attributes and priorities. This can be observed by means the hierarchical structure, which allows getting a detailed decomposition of the global score into its fundamental components and interdependencies. Moreover, the methodology allows customers and suppliers to get information about the partner perception and evaluation of their own choices and actions.

Looking at the evaluation tree we can observe both what strategies the customer company can follow to strengthen the supply system as a whole by supporting the supplier development and what behaviours and actions suppliers should take to improve their position in the supply system.

The Case of Supplier Beta

In relation to supplier Beta, the high value of the global score derives from the contribution of the maximum value (1,00) of the attribute PPQ associated with the highest priority (0,42). Also the attribute FP shows a high value (0,75) but the associated priority is quite low (0,13). From these two elements we can derive that, according to the customer, supplier Beta has reached the maximum level in terms of Quality of Process and Product, and, as a consequence, no effort to improve this position is needed. At the same time, this supplier could improve its FP attribute though this

Figure 4. The evaluation tree of supplier Alfa

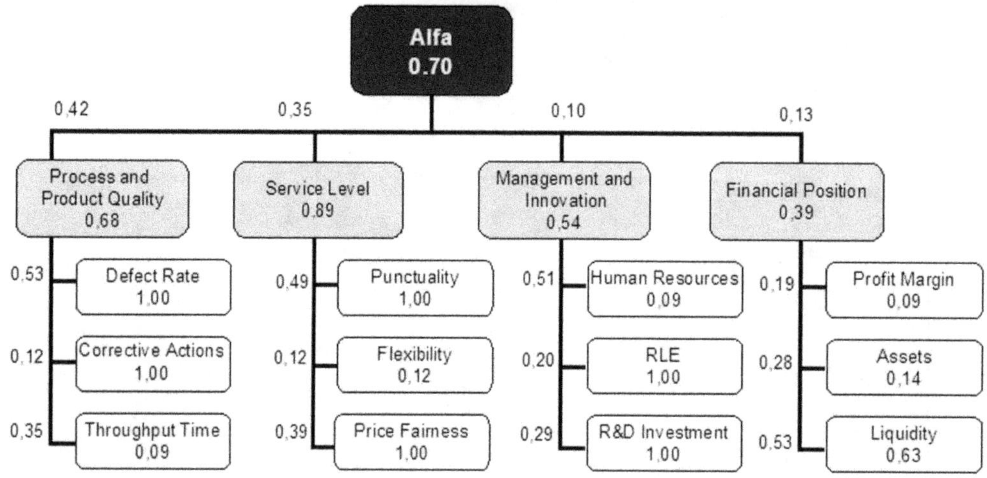

Figure 5. The evaluation tree of supplier Beta

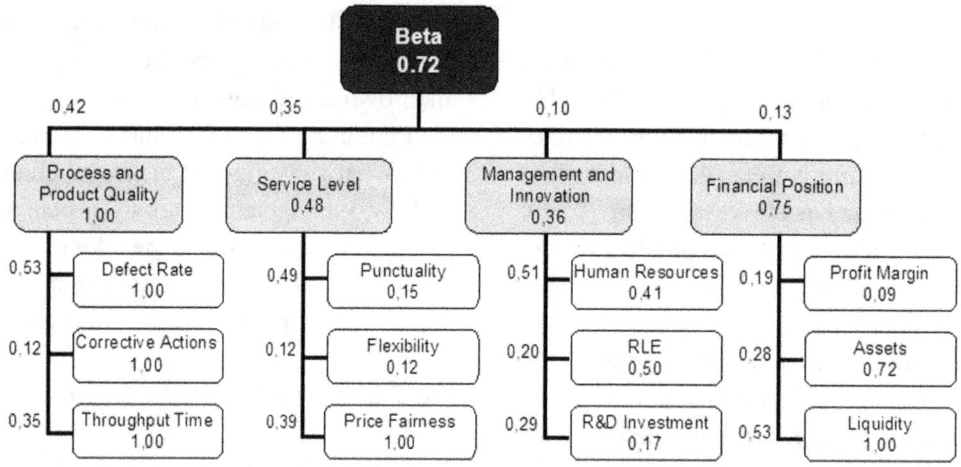

does not result in an effective behaviour since the company's efforts are greatly weakened given the quite low priority level.

A more suitable and effective behaviour would be to seek to improve the SL where the level of the attribute is low (0,48) but where the priority level (0,35) is higher than FP. In the SL case the efforts of the supplier might be more appreciated and valued by the customer as it is aimed at improving an attribute for which the supplier has shown a lower score and which is more important from the customer's viewpoint. At the same time the effort of the supplier is less demanding than that to be addressed to improve the financial position n.

The worst situation is apparently that of the characteristic MI. Here the lowest priority (0,10) is coupled with the lowest attribute (0,36). This means that while the supplier shows a large need

Figure 6. The evaluation tree of supplier Gamma

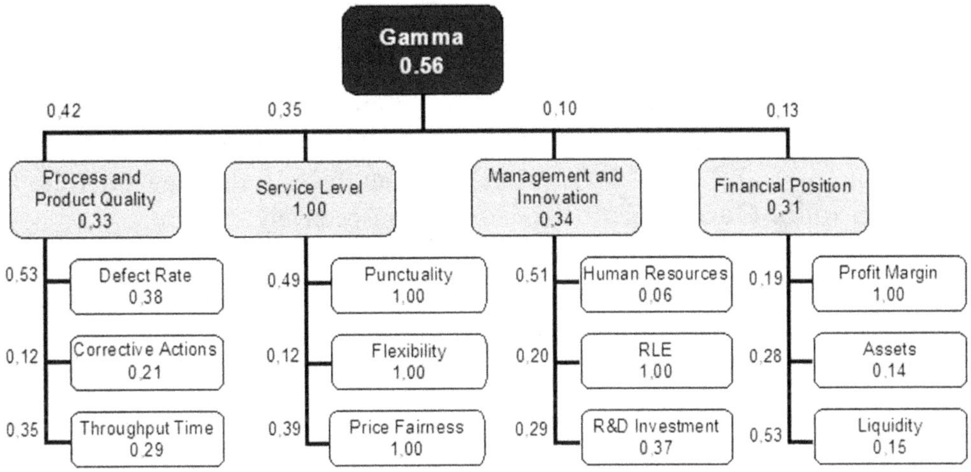

Figure 7. The evaluation tree of supplier Delta

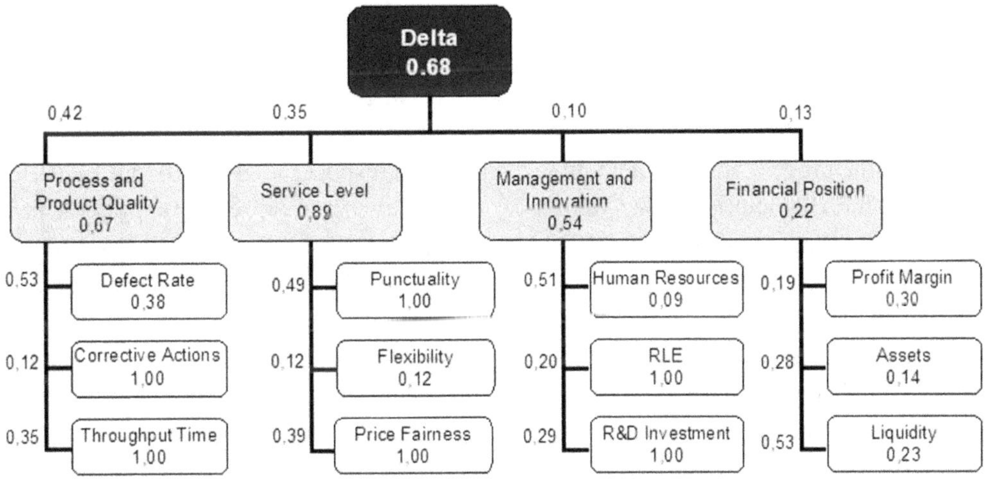

to improve this aspect of its whole performance, it has to produce a very robust engagement to obtain some sensible result, since this is not a priority from the customer's perspective.

On the basis of the described frame, it emerges that the more affordable strategy for the supplier Beta is the one addressed to improve the SL. The evaluation tree also provides relevant indications to the actions to be adopted to increase the global score by considering the characteristics (Punctuality, Flexibility and Price Fairness) determining the low level of SL attribute. As for the Price Fairness characteristic, the supplier shows the maximum performance. Given the low priority of Flexibility (0,12) with respect to Punctuality (0,49) the supplier has to consider that it is more effective to leverage the former characteristic than the latter in order to improve the low score of the

SL attribute. The above considerations lead the supplier Beta to consider that, in order to improve the overall score for the customer AnsaldoBreda, it is more suitable to adopt measures and practices to increase its capability to respect the scheduled Delivery time and to reduce late lines.

The Case of Supplier Gamma

Supplier gamma shows the worst global score (0,56). The evaluation tree underlines that the strength point of supplier Gamma is represented by the Service Level (whose score is 1,00), while other attributes are far enough away from SL. As a consequence, to improve its position Gamma must leverage on PPQ, MI and FP attributes, whose scores exhibit a low value of the score. About PPQ the supplier has to decide to invest to improve both quality procedures and production cycle, by addressing the characteristic Defect Rate (DR) that shows the highest score (0,38) and priority (0,53). Indeed, Gamma may also act on a different lever, since measures addressed to improve the time efficiency of the process are part of a viable strategy, whereas the characteristic Throughput Time (TT) has a score that can be improved (0,29) with a fairly high priority (0,35).

As regarding the attribute MI (whose score is the worst among the four considered), the supplier should improve its Human Resources characteristic (whose score is very low and whose priority is the highest) by adopting training/selection actions and/or a more appropriate HRM strategy addressed to increase the level of competencies of the company.

The attribute FP also has a very low priority (0,13). Between the two characteristics that can be leveraged, the one requiring the least effort is the Liquidity (LI) characteristic. This can be achieved by reducing the inventory level and the current liabilities.

Nevertheless, since the attribute PPQ exhibits the highest priority (0,42), improving it is likely to be the most effective choice.

The Case of Supplier Alfa

The evaluation tree shows that, in order to raise the global score, supplier Alfa has to improve the low score levels of MI and FP attributes. Pursuing this goal requires relevant efforts since both these attributes feature low priorities (0,10 and 0,13, respectively).

The most effective action to improve the low level of the FP is raising the Liquidity performance that shows the highest priority (0,53). The least effective action is to attempt to raise the very low level of Profit Margin (0,09), whose priority is 0,19.

To raise the MI level (0,54), the supplier is forced to improve the lowest score (0,09) of the Human Resources characteristic that is counterbalanced by the highest priority (0,51).

This decision is comparable to that of an intervention on PPQ. In fact, also in this case Alfa must act on a single characteristic, namely TT, that has the same priority of HR but a lower score (0.35).

Nevertheless, given the higher priority of PPQ (0,42) respect to MI (0,10) and FP (0,13), an effective action requires that supplier Alfa pursue an improvement of the global score acting on PPQ.

From the above consideration it emerges that, in order to improve the global score, supplier Alfa can adopt a potential of three different actions, respectively addressed to: diminish the inventory and current liabilities (in order to improve its liquidity level); raise the level of competencies of HR (whose situation is quite similar to that of supplier Gamma) by adopting training initiatives and/or a more appropriate HRM strategy; improve the time efficiency of the production process by overcoming the bottlenecks, re-programming the production cycles and adopting new investments in automation. The action addressed to raise the PPQ score emerges as the most effective.

The Case of Supplier Delta

Since the strength point of Delta is the attribute SL, and provided that its improvement requires a tough effort, since the only characteristic that can be leveraged is flexibility showing a very low priority (0,12), the firm should focus its attention on PPQ, MI and FP characteristics.

Intervening on FP is not an easy task, since it shows the lowest score (0,22) and a very low priority (0,13). At the same time, MI has a score that needs to be improved (0,54) and that is associated with the lowest priority (0,10). Based on these considerations, likewise supplier Gamma, the most effective choice for supplier Delta seems to be improving PPQ, since this attribute has the highest priority (0,42). In this case, there is no other option except to leverage Defect Rate characteristic. Moreover, this results in an effective choice since DR shows the lowest score and the highest priority.

In this case, the supplier has to adopt measures and practices to improve both the control of production process and the quality management procedures addressed to reduce the portion of defected items without wasting time and cost performances.

Alternatively, if supplier Delta decides to intervene on the MI attribute, it is obliged to raise the HR level, which has a quite high priority. If Delta decides to intervene on FP, then it is quite difficult to decide which characteristic has to be leveraged. In fact, all the FP characteristics should be improved, since they show low scores. Nevertheless, LI characteristic has the highest priority (0,53) and the actions on this aspect should result in a minimum effort.

DISCUSSION

Table 1 summarizes the result of the evaluation tree analysis of the four AnsaldoBreda suppliers for the production of the bogie. Among the four attributes considered, the one that shows the highest level of criticality to pursue effective actions aimed to improve the overall score is PPQ, which shows the highest priority. Among the characteristics, Defect Rate is the most critical one.

Both these results are consistent with the fact that, over the last few years, the railway industry has been characterized by both an increasing complexity of products and the search for processes' efficiency in order to satisfy the technological and quality standards imposed by the global competition and the increasing liberalization policy adopted by the European Union (Esposito, Passaro, 2009b).

Nevertheless, it emerges that the suppliers can follow different actions and strategies to improve their performance and to meet the customer requirements. Even though suppliers Alfa, Gamma and Delta have to improve the PPQ, they can achieve this goal through different actions. Alfa can leverage the throughput time and Delta can leverage the defect rate. On the other hand supplier Gamma may adopt a more flexible approach leveraging both defect rate and throughput time, though the former is more effective than the latter.

Supplier Beta has to adopt a different set of actions aimed to recover the SL score focusing its efforts on the improvement of time performance by leveraging the Punctuality characteristic.

The actions resulting from the analysis of Table 3 are the most effective and can be implemented in the short run and thus leading to alignment with the customer requirements.

Nevertheless, suppliers can decide to adopt actions that can be effective in the medium-long run to improve performances different from those indicated as critical in Table 3. These choices require a composite set of resources (human, organizational, technological, financial and knowledge-related) that imply a greater commitment and generate more uncertain results. Nevertheless, they reflect the attempt to improve the major weaknesses of the supplier, and addition-

Table 3. The positions of the four suppliers

Supplier	Alfa	Beta	Gamma	Delta
Critical attribute	PPQ	SL	PPQ	PPQ
Critical characteristic	Throughput Time	Punctuality	Defect Rate (Throughput Time)	Defect Rate
Actions	Eliminating bottle-necks, process automation, re-programming the production cycles	Complying to/Improving the scheduled delivery time and reducing late lines	Improving production processes control and quality management procedures	Improving production processes control and quality management procedures

ally can be useful to improve its position in front of other customers.

These considerations underline that the proposed approach is not only a tool for supplier evaluation but also a useful management tool for both customers and suppliers. From this point of view it may be considered a strategic approach for supply system government. A relevant advantage of the hierarchical structure is that it allows for a detailed, structured and systematic deconstruction of the overall problem into its fundamental components and interdependencies, with a large degree of flexibility.

This advantage is shared by both actors and can be observed from different points of view.

Adopting this methodology, the customer AnsaldoBreda may obtain the following results:

- a global score of the four suppliers for the object of the transaction
- a key to analyse the factors (attributes and characteristics) and mechanisms that have determined the suppliers' global score
- a tool to identify the suppliers' strengths and weaknesses points and improve the supply system.

On the other hand, each supplier may obtain the following results:

- better understand how it is assessed by the customer
- a key to analyse the factors and mechanisms that have determined the global score
- guidelines and suggestions to adopt appropriate corrective actions and practices to reinforce their position within the supply system.

SOLUTIONS AND RECOMMENDATIONS FOR SUPPLY CHAIN INNOVATION

The findings of this chapter highlight that formalized and explicit multi-criteria models for supplier evaluation may be useful tools to management innovation processes within the supply system. In fact, this chapter has shown that the customer may use the hierarchical structure of the evaluation tree to guide the suppliers' development program and to induce processes of innovation, concerning both the suppliers and the system of relationships. Furthermore, suppliers, by means of their involvement in the process, may adopt this tool to improve their capability of satisfying customer requirements by introducing specific corrective actions and innovation processes.

In both cases the transparency of the procedures and the flexibility of methodology adopted may induce the firms to adopt appropriate actions and decisions leveraging on the search for improvement of their competitive position.

In particular, two main managerial recommendations emerge from the work.

- As regards customer firms, the proposed methodology facilitates the management of the whole supply chain, beyond the dyadic supplier-customer relationship, by allowing a continuous realignment of the suppliers' aims to those of the customers and orienting their policies towards their own suppliers. To this end, appropriate programs for supplier development or early supplier involvement could be adopted.
- As regards small suppliers, they may be involved in the design of the evaluation methodology in order to comprehend how they are evaluated and improve their position within the supply system by adopting appropriate corrective actions and practices. To this end, they have to consider both external and internal aspects of the customer-supplier relationship. The former mainly relate to customer requirements while the latter concern constraints and capabilities affecting the supplier's decision to adopt specific measures and practices. The internal aspects of the matter are influenced by the specificity of the customer-supplier relationship. In fact, if the supplier has to satisfy the requirements of more customers having similar importance, the requirements of a specific customer will probably be less important. In this case, the key capability may be the adoption of a flexible approach to satisfy the requirements of more customers. On the other hand, if the supplier has to respond to the requirements of a specific prevailing customer, it is forced to adopt a hierarchical approach and will invest resources to improve those attributes and characteristics needed to satisfy only the prevailing customer's requirements.

FUTURE RESEARCH DIRECTIONS

The results of this paper are strictly connected with the unit of analysis, which concerns the large customer operating in a high-tech industry such as the railway (the assessor), a set of its suppliers (the assessed), and the object of transaction (the supply of the boogie). From this point of view, the following two main research questions emerge that may be investigated in future research:

- in what context the AHP models should be preferred to qualitative approaches that appear to be characterised by lower cost and higher flexibility?
- to what extent the results emerging from this analysis could be extended to others methodologies?

In relation to the first research question, it seems that AHP based models may be mainly applied in industries characterized by high technological and/or complexity level where the management of supply chain usually gives a robust contribution in terms quality and added value. In these industries customers have a strong interest to invest resources to improve their supply chain performance. By contrast, in industries where the supply chain gives a low contribution in terms of added value and where the object of supplying is not complex, qualitative models seem more appropriate since they are built on the basis of the experience of experts and qualitative judgments. Consequently they require neither high costs of development nor the involvement of huge resources in the decision making process. Future researches could explore this problem in depth.

As far as the second research question, research should be oriented to verify if strengths and weaknesses of the employed methodologies are related to any formal approach to the supplier selection problem and how other methodologies may overcome these shortcomings.

CONCLUSION

The results emerging from the implementation of the proposed methodology underline that the models based on the AHP approach require:

- a startup investment connected with substantial efforts in terms of time and training of personnel for its implementation;
- an ongoing maintenance, as changes in the customer strategy affecting the set of variables included in the process of evaluation and their relative importance.

For this reason the real implementations of these models need a startup period and, accordingly, their positive implications can be perceived only after this early phase. Consequently, there are good reasons to believe that these models can work successfully only if applied in industries where: i) investments in decision making models are considered worthwhile; ii) the added value associated to such investment is high; and iii) these models are adopted not only as static tools for suppliers evaluation, but also to support strategic tools for managing multi-criteria problem. These peculiarities fit well with high complex industries in which the supply systems are crucial for large firms to achieve competitiveness and suppliers provide a significant contribution to the value chain. By contrast, in industries where: i) decisions are made on the short term horizon; ii) well established relationships have a strong influence in vendors evaluation; and iii) few variables are computed to handle supplier assessment, qualitative methodologies could be the most effective approaches for suppliers' selection.

Nevertheless, whereas employing qualitative and not formalized judgments to select suppliers can present some advantages in terms of costs and flexibility, formalized supplier selection methodologies provide a number of benefits.

A first benefit concerns the development of learning processes, as setting up such a methodology allows both customer and suppliers to improve the knowledge of how a supply chain systems really works, identifying its strengths and weaknesses, pushing towards a formalized definition of the supply system capable of extending the supplier relationships beyond the classical dyadic view.

A second benefit consists in the involvement of various actors participating in the evaluation process. Such a model requires the involvement in the design phase of people from the purchasing department, managers from other departments and supplier firms. The main aim is to transform the supplier evaluation process from an operational to a strategic supply system management tool.

The growth of motivation resulting from the direct involvement of actors in the evaluation process is the third benefit. In this case, the presence of some clear attributes upon which the selection is based may force both suppliers and customers to achieve better performance all over the entire supply system. In their effort to improve performance for fulfilling customer's evaluation parameters, first tier suppliers could adopt and implement similar methodologies towards their vendors. In this way, the benefits of the adoption of formal methodologies can spread across the entire supply system. However, this could also lead to a side effect: firms could simply focus on the aspects considered relevant for the selection, completely disregarding the other ones.

The findings allow one important managerial implications. Once the effectiveness of formalized models as strategic tools for supplier selection has been displayed, the advantages related to their adoption can be easily transferred from one person to another without wasting expertise or knowledge of purchasing managers when job rotation policies take place. This imply several advantages for companies which, despite the initial efforts in term of money and time, may decide to implement the described model as a supporting tool for strategic supply chain management.

REFERENCES

Ali, F., Garet, S., & Saker, J. (1997). Developing buyer-supplier development. The buying-firm perspective. *European Journal of Purchasing and Supply Management, 3*(1), 21–31. doi:10.1016/S0969-7012(96)00003-2

Araz, C., & Ozkarahan, I. (2007). Supplier evaluation and management system for strategic sourcing based on a new multicriteria sorting procedure. *International Journal of Production Economics, 106*(2), 585–606. doi:10.1016/j.ijpe.2006.08.008

Bhutta, K. S., & Huk, F. (2002). Supplier selection problem: a comparison of the total cost of ownership and analytic hierarchy process approaches. *Supply Chain Management: an International Journal, 7*(3), 126–135. doi:10.1108/13598540210436586

Bhutta, M. K. S. (2003). Supplier selection problem: methodology literature review. *Journal of International Technology and Information Management, 12*(2), 53–72.

Bruno, G., Esposito, E., Genovese, A., & Passaro, R. (2010, May). *Supplier Evaluation in a Complex Industry: The Application of an AHP Based Model.* Proceedings of the 19th Annual IPSERA Conference, Lappeenranta, Finland.

Cheraghi S.H., Dadashzadeh M., Subramanian M. (2004). Critical Success factors for supplier selection. An update. *Journal of applied Business Research, 20*(4), 91-108.

Dahel, N. (2003). Vendor selection and order quantity allocation in volume discount environments. *Supply Chain Management: an International Journal, 8*(4), 335–342. doi:10.1108/13598540310490099

de Boer, L., Labro, E., & Morlacchi, P. (2001). A review of methods supporting supplier selection. *European Journal of Purchasing & Supply Management, 7*(2), 75–89. doi:10.1016/S0969-7012(00)00028-9

de Boer, L., van der Wegen, L., & Telgen, J. (2003). Outranking methods in support of supplier selection. *European Journal of Purchasing & Supply Management, 4*(2/3), 109–118.

de Boer, L., & van der Wegen, L. L. M. (2003). Practice and promise of formal supplier selection: a study of four empirical cases. *Journal of Purchasing and Supply Management, 9*(3), 109–118. doi:10.1016/S1478-4092(03)00018-9

Dickson, G. W. (1966). An analysis of vendor selection systems and decisions. *Journal of Purchasing, 2*(1), 5–17.

Dulmin, R., & Mininno, V. (2003). Supplier selection using a multi-criteria decision aid method. *Journal of Purchasing and Supply Management, 9*(4), 177–187. doi:10.1016/S1478-4092(03)00032-3

Esposito, E., & Passaro, R. (2007, April). *The evolution of the outsourcing strategy: the case of a vendor assessment process.* Proceedings of the 16th Annual IPSERA Conference, Bath, England.

Esposito, E., & Passaro, R. (2009a). The evolution of supply chain relationships: an interpretative framework based on the Italian inter-industry experience. *Journal of Purchasing and Supply Management, 15*(2), 114–126. doi:10.1016/j.pursup.2009.03.002

Esposito, E., & Passaro, R. (2009b). Evolution of the supply chain in the Italian railway industry. *Supply Chain Management: an International Journal, 14*(4), 303–313. doi:10.1108/13598540910970135

Ha, H. S., & Krishnan, R. (2008). A hybrid approach to supplier selection for the maintenance of a competitive supply chain. *Expert Systems with Applications, 34*(2), 1303–1311. doi:10.1016/j.eswa.2006.12.008

Hsu, C., Kannan, V. R., Leong, G. K., & Tan, K. (2006). Supplier selection construct: instrument development and validation. *The International Journal of Logistics Management, 17*(2), 213–239. doi:10.1108/09574090610689961

Kamann, D. F., & Bakker, E. F. (2004). Changing supplier selection and relationship practices: a contagion process. *Journal of Purchasing and Supply Management, 10*(2), 55–64. doi:10.1016/j.pursup.2003.12.002

Lamming, R., Cousins, P. D., & Notman, D. M. (1996). Beyond supplier evaluation. Relationship evaluation programmes. *European Journal of Purchasing and Supply Management, 2*(4), 173–181. doi:10.1016/S0969-7012(96)00013-5

Lee, E.-K., Ha, S., & Kim, S.-K. (2001). Supplier Selection and Management System. Considering Relationships in Supply Chain Management. *IEEE Transactions on Engineering Management, 48*(3), 307–318. doi:10.1109/17.946529

Ordoobadi, S. (2009). Application of Taguchi loss functions for supplier selection. *Supply Chain Management: an International Journal, 14*(1), 22–30. doi:10.1108/13598540910927278

Park, D., & Krishnan, H. A. (2001). Supplier Selection Practices among Small Firms in the United States: Testing Three Models. *Journal of Small Business Management, 39*(3), 259–271. doi:10.1111/0447-2778.00023

Prahinski, C., & Benton, W. C. (2004). Supplier evaluations: communication strategies to improve supplier performance. *Journal of Operations Management, 22*(1), 39–62. doi:10.1016/j.jom.2003.12.005

Ramanathan, R. (2007). Supplier selection problem: integrating DEA with the approaches of total cost of ownership and AHP. *Supply Chain Management: an International Journal, 12*(4), 258–261. doi:10.1108/13598540710759772

Saaty, T. L. (1980). *The Analytic Hierarchy Process*. New York: McGraw Hill International.

Saaty, T. L. (1994). *Fundamentals of Decision Making and Priority Theory with the Analytic Hierarchy Process*. Pittsburgh, PA: RWS Publications.

Saaty, T. L. (2001). *The Analytic Network Process: Decision Making with Dependence and Feedback*. Pittsburgh, PA: RWS Publications.

Saen, R. F. (2007). A new mathematical approach for suppliers selection: Accounting for non-homogeneity is important. *Applied Mathematics and Computation, 185*(1), 84–95. doi:10.1016/j.amc.2006.07.071

Sarkara A. Mohapatra, P. K. J. (2006). Evaluation of supplier capability and performance: A method for supply base reduction. *Journal of Purchasing and Supply Management, 12*(3), 148–163. doi:10.1016/j.pursup.2006.08.003

Sonmez, M. (2006). *A review and critique of supplier selection process and practices*. Occasional Papers Series, n.1. Loughborough University.

Ting, S., & Cho, D. I. (2008). An integrated approach for supplier selection and purchasing decisions. *Supply Chain Management: an International Journal, 13*(2), 116–127. doi:10.1108/13598540810860958

Vonderembse M.A., Tracey M. (1999). The Impact of Supplier Selection Criteria and Supplier Involvement on Manufacturing Performance, *Journal of Supply Chain management*, 35(3), 33-40.

Weber, C. A., Current, J. R., & Benton, W. C. (1991). Vendor selection criteria and methods. *European Journal of European Research, 50*(1), 2–18. doi:10.1016/0377-2217(91)90033-R

Chapter 18
Being a Preferred Customer of Leading Suppliers and its Impact on Supplier Contribution to Innovation

Holger Schiele
University of Twente, The Netherlands

Jasper Veldman
University of Twente, The Netherlands

Lisa Hüttinger
University of Twente, The Netherlands

ABSTRACT

In this chapter, the authors introduce the concept of preferred customer status as a means for creating supply-side induced advantages in highly competitive supplier markets. For the authors, being a preferred customer means that a buyer is awarded preferential treatment of important suppliers compared to what their other customers receive. Taking this into account, having Preferred Customer Status might also have a positive impact on the generation of innovation upstream the supply chain. As there is a lack of knowledge of what motivates suppliers to serve selected buyers better than others, the research presented here focuses on the suppliers' evaluation of customers and how it can be influenced by buyers. Based on an extensive literature review, an overview is provided of recent contributions on customer attractiveness and supplier satisfaction as the prerequisites for becoming a preferred customer of strategic suppliers. Furthermore, the authors stress the importance of being a preferred customer particularly in a new product development context by empirically testing the impact of preferred customer status on supplier innovativeness in a buyer-seller relationship. They conclude that implementing a preferred customer policy in buying firms can improve the conditions for innovating with suppliers.

DOI: 10.4018/978-1-60960-585-8.ch018

INTRODUCTION

The role suppliers play in business success of firms and - in connection - the importance their benevolence may have for buyers have substantially increased in the last decade. A prominent case here is the issue of innovation. Innovations are one of the basic ways in which a business can build and maintain a competitive advantage in the marketplace (Drucker, 1954). New product and process development has increasingly been analyzed from an 'open innovation' perspective, based on the argument that innovations are developed through the interplay of different parties from different organisations (Chesbrough, 2003; Edquist, 1997; Freeman & Soete, 1997; Steinle & Schiele, 2002; Trott & Hartmann, 2009; von Hippel, 1988). Still, the upstream part of open innovation (i.e., innovativeness of the supplier in the sense of successful early supplier integration in innovation processes with the buyer) has received less attention (Johnsen, 2009). To access external sources of technology, buyers strive for a network of 'innovation-suppliers' and willingly enter into close relationships with such suppliers (Clark, 1989; Handfield et al., 1999; Hartley et al., 1997; Primo & Admundson, 2002; Ragatz et al., 1997; Schiele, 2006; Tracey, 2004; Wagner, 2009; Wasti & Liker, 1997). However, identifying, cultivating and taking advantage of a wide variety of external sources for innovation poses several new managerial challenges:

The first challenge managers thereby face is to find suppliers who exhibit the required capabilities and expertise for innovation. As highly competent supplier markets are often characterized by an oligopolistic market structure, suppliers are scarce and hard to find.

The second challenge buying firms have to deal with is the problem that strategic collaboration increases supplier specificity. This is the case, when a supplier deepens his knowledge of the product or technology during innovation processes. The buyer and other competitors run the risk of gradually losing their full understanding of the progress that the supplier has made in solving the problem at hand (Cohen & Levinthal, 1990). This phenomenon eliminates potential competitors and alternative sources of supply and makes the (non)competitive market situation even worse (Laaksonen et al, 2008).

Due to the scarcity of high-skilled, innovative suppliers, the latter may not dedicate their resources equally to all customers, and become highly selective. In order to ensure that suppliers offer up innovative ideas in product development and manufacturing processes, buying firms must be more attractive for these suppliers than their competitors are. In this highly competitive environment, being a preferred customer is very important for buying firms and, potentially, essential for future success. This means that achieving preferred customer status with key suppliers could be one solution for the challenges the current supply market situation poses to upstream supply chain innovation. It creates the best conditions for innovating with supplier and competing with rivaling customers. We argue that a firm is preferred customer of its supplier, "if the supplier offers the buyer preferential resource allocation" (Steinle & Schiele, 2008, p. 11). Therefore, buyers may benefit from taking into consideration factors that motivate suppliers to award preferential treatment to selected customers and ultimately from answering the question of what can be done to become the preferred customer of leading suppliers.

Despite the apparent significance of preferred customer status, its drivers and impacts on supply chain performance remain largely unexplored in current literature. Although there have already been some attempts to study the antecedents of preferred customer status such as customer attractiveness or supplier satisfaction, there is still a lack of theoretical understanding and empirical analyses. Some authors show that a high level of customer attractiveness and supplier satisfaction helps to ensure the prime commitment of capable suppliers (Christiansen & Maltz, 2002; Ellegaard et al., 2003; Essig & Amann, 2009; Mortensen et al., 2008; Nyaga et al., 2010), but there is still no consensus on how preferred customer status can be achieved and what the impacts on the buyer-seller relationship and innovation, in particular, are.

Thus, the primary objective of this chapter is to provide a literature review highlighting important contributions on supplier satisfaction and customer attraction as the prerequisites for becoming the preferred customer of those suppliers considered to be important by the buying firm.

The second objective is to highlight the significance of being a preferred customer by empirically analyzing its impact on the generation of innovation in buyer-supplier relationships. Being the preferred customer for leading suppliers certainly can have several advantages for the buying firm and can positively influence factors such as quality, reliability, performance and prices. In this contribution, however, we concentrate exclusively on its impact on supplier innovativeness. Our work alert researchers and practitioners to the need to dedicate more effort to managing supplier portfolios in a way that guarantees preferential treatment by suppliers that represent an important strategic resource for the firm.

This chapter is structured as follows. First, we will give a comprehensive literature review on supplier satisfaction and customer attractiveness. Secondly, we will empirically evaluate what the impact of being a preferred customer is by testing its effects on supplier contribution to innovation. We will then draw several conclusions and give future research directions.

LITERATURE REVIEW

Since there is a void in research about the preferred customer concept we undertook a literature survey. It appeared that many publications on this topic lack a shared vocabulary and a clear articulation of the underlying constructs. Therefore, we classified the findings into categories, differentiating between papers on (1.) supplier satisfaction and (2.) customer attractiveness, which (3.) can be considered antecedents of the "preferred customer status" that suppliers award to selected buyers. In the next sub-section, we will give an overview of the relations between customer attractiveness, supplier satisfaction and preferred customer status.

The Connection between Customer Attractiveness, Supplier Satisfaction, and Preferred Customer Status

In cases where the supplier and buyer work closely together, for example in joint product development and innovation processes, interaction, mutual understanding and a high level of attractiveness are crucial (Mortensen et al., 2008). Attraction is an approach to managing business relationships in a relational mode based on the creation of voluntary motivation and commitment between the relationship partners, which differs from the traditional approach of managing relations by power and control mechanisms (Cox, 1999).

The concept of attraction has been described differently by a range of authors. Some find that the purpose of being attractive is to create the ability to manage and optimise value creation in the relationship and at the same time try to increase buyer-supplier commitment to ensure allocation of resources. For instance, Hald et al. (2009) "propose to understand attraction as the force fostering voluntarism in purchasing and marketing exchanges, and further pushing a buyer and supplier closer together in a mutual advantageous relationship" (p. 968). Mortensen et al. (2008) considered attraction "as a prerequisite for development of trust and commitment, not just in the initial stages of relationships but also in continuation and development throughout the relational duration" (p. 800). Thus, if the buyer is able to make himself attractive to the supplier, he can attract the necessary attention, which might create better innovative and operational performance, loyalty and proactiveness in the relationship. (Christiansen & Maltz, 2002; Cordon & Vollmann, 2002; Ellegaard & Ritter, 2006). We would like to maintain the notion of the dynamic character of attractiveness such as expressed before, but differentiate the construct to include two elements: *Customer attractiveness for a supplier describes a situation in which the supplier is (a) aware of the existence of the customer and knows his relevant attributes and (b) has a positive expectation towards this organisation.*

A necessary condition for customer attractiveness is that the supplier knows the buyer, which is a particular problem for small firms that might not a priori be known to their potential supplier. However, the awareness is not sufficient. The well-known customer can still be unattractive, which means that there are no positive but possibly even negative expectations associated with this organisation. Only if the two conditions are met, awareness and positive expectations, it is possible to speak about attractiveness.

If buyer and supplier enter into or intensify their business contact and the supplier's expectations are met, supplier satisfaction with this relationship is the likely outcome. Benton and Maloni (2005) established a definition of supplier satisfaction in the supply chain as a feeling of equity with the supply chain relationship no matter what power imbalance exists between the buyer and seller dyad. Essig and Amann (2009) had a similar understanding. They defined "supplier satisfaction as a supplier's feeling of fairness with regard to buyer's incentives and supplier's contributions within an industrial buyer–seller relationship as relates to the supplier's need fulfillment" (p. 104). The question that still remains open from this definition is: When does the feeling of fairness come into being? We suggest an answer to this question: *Supplier satisfaction is a condition that appears if costs and benefits from a buyer-supplier relation meet or exceed the supplier's expectations.* The exact nature of the expectations can remain open; as long as they are met, satisfaction is the outcome.

If the supplier, in turn, is more satisfied with the relationship to one customer compared to his other customers, he can award that buyer with preferred customer status. Adding a strategic element, it can be argued that customer attractiveness and supplier satisfaction are the necessary conditions for achieving preferred customer status; a strategic prioritization by the supplier is the sufficient condition. *A supplier awards a buyer with preferred customer status if he considers this customer attractive and is at the same time more satisfied with him compared to other buyers. As a consequence, a supplier reacts with prime commitment and privileged resource allocation for this customer.*

Thus, customer attractiveness and supplier satisfaction determine whether buyers are seen as preferred customer and, subsequently, awarded preferential supplier treatment. Once the buyer is aware of his preferred customer status, he can react by closer alignment to the supplier, therewith becoming even more attractive: a virtuous circle starts. The relation between the three concepts is illustrated in Figure 1.

From a buyer's perspective, thus, the main question is how he can become more attractive to the suppliers and increase supplier satisfaction within the relationship in order to become a preferred customer. To clarify this matter, we will provide insights from current literature in the following sub-sections.

Customer Attractiveness

As early as in 1988, Leenders and Blenkhorn mentioned the need to motivate a supplier to satisfy novel demands and labeled it 'reverse marketing'. It is based on the notion that the purchasing agent takes a marketing perspective and becomes the salesperson who actively seeks those suppliers that best meet their needs and expectations (Biemans & Brand, 1995; Larson & Kulchitsky, 1998; Plank & Francis, 2001). In other words, reverse marketing is a reversal of traditional buyer-supplier roles (Blenkhorn & Banting, 1991).

Figure 1. The virtuous circle of preferred customer status

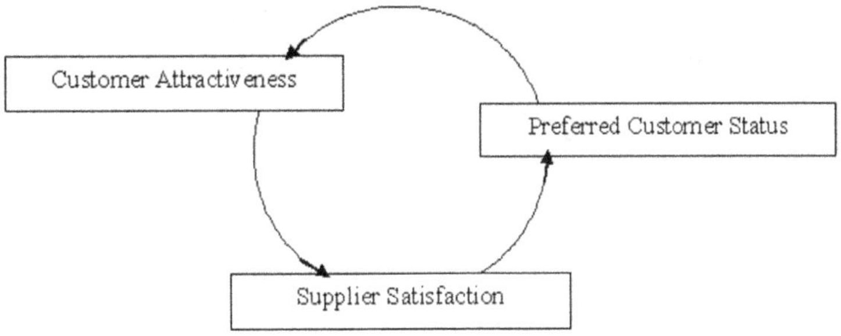

In a case study of new product development, Wynstra et al. (2003) concluded that the buyer should actively try to become interesting to the supplier. Christiansen and Maltz (2002) conducted case studies of several small Danish firms that were trying to do exactly this and to become 'interesting customers' to their large international suppliers. The authors argue that smaller customers must analyse which preferences their bigger suppliers have and focus on indirect value creation. In order to become attractive, they have to find areas, which bigger suppliers evaluate as compensating to lower economical attraction.

Ellegaard et al. (2003), again drawing on a case study, highlighted the particular importance of customer attractiveness in complex industrial buyer-supplier relationships. They viewed the concept as a way to attract the best qualified suppliers in competition with other customers. If buyers manage to be perceived as an attractive customer, they are in a better position to influence the supplier to act according to its wishes. Ellegaard and Ritter (2006) underlined the importance of customer attractiveness even more by arguing that suppliers will not improve processes, product technologies, etc. unless attraction is present. They see attraction as a prerequisite for mobilizing suppliers' resources and developing trust and commitment.

Mortensen et al. (2008) argued that customer attractiveness for suppliers may not be seen as a static condition but instead may change according to the maturity of the relationship. Therefore, the authors proposed a process model for attractiveness in supply chains containing five different relationship types determined by the complexity of the relationship and the maturity of the company.

Hald et al. (2009) focused on how dyadic relationships are managed in a relational way and how attraction is created between buyer and seller. They discussed attraction as the force drawing social exchange actors together and described it as being composed of the three components "expected value", "perceived trust" and "perceived dependence". Additionally, four mechanisms (investment, adaption, communication and institutionalization) are provided to influence the three dimensions of attraction in buyer-supplier relationships.

Assuming that the attractiveness of a buyer is given, the next issue would be to understand how supplier satisfaction can be achieved, because unsatisfied suppliers could find it difficult to award preferred customer status to any customer, regardless of its ex-ante attractiveness. The next paragraph, therefore, reviews the literature on supplier satisfaction.

Supplier Satisfaction

In marketing channel literature satisfaction is not a new term. Contrasting with the limited attention on supplier satisfaction, researchers have produced a wealth of studies exploring satisfaction within marketing and distribution channels since decades (Hunt & Nevin, 1974; Michie & Sibley, 1985;

Raven & Kruglanski, 1970). In particular in the relationship marketing literature, the processes of establishing and managing satisfactory relationships is studied, considering those relationships as a source of remarkable competitive advantage (Beekman & Robinson, 2004; Briscoe et al., 2005; Grönroos, 2000; Morgan & Hunt, 1994; Van der Haar et al., 2001; Varey et al., 2005). In this context, several authors have recognized the relevance of concepts such as perceived satisfaction (Anderson & Narus, 1990; Cannon & Perrault, 1999; Dwyer et al., 1987; Siguaw et al., 1998; Walter et al., 2003).

The ability to provide a high level of satisfaction has been considered an essential ingredient of business success (Morrisey & Pittaway, 2006). However, most publications in relationship marketing literature focus exclusively on the seller perspective. Consequently, mainly aspects of buyer–seller relationships that cause buyer satisfaction downstream the chain of value creation are well understood, i.e. answering the question of what the seller has to do in order to increase customer satisfaction.

Despite its apparent significance, supplier satisfaction has been widely neglected and remained largely unexplored, i.e. the question on what the buyer has to do to satisfy his suppliers has not been emphasized. Since purchasing is not a direct reflection of marketing, supplier satisfaction is not a mirror image of customer satisfaction.

Benton and Maloni (2005) stated that "a supply chain is only as strong as its weakest link. Thus, a manufacturer cannot be responsive without satisfied suppliers" (p.2). They empirically tested the assumption that supplier satisfaction benefits buyers and the entire supply chain through enhanced supplier performance and stressed the importance of a relationship-driven supply chain strategy rather than a performance based strategy. The quality of the buyer–supplier relationship seems to have a potent effect on supplier satisfaction.

Essig and Amann (2009) found that "industrial customers must be aware of the status of their supplier's satisfaction… [as] an unsatisfied supplier may produce poor quality output that lowers the quality of a buyer's products and thus influences the buyer's sale volumes and profitability" (p. 104ff.). They explored the construct of supplier satisfaction as a factor of buyer–supplier relationship quality and took into account interaction processes within buyer–supplier relationships (e.g., exchange of information) as well as the atmosphere within these relationships (e.g., power dependence).

Ramsay and Wagner (2009) analyzed organizational supplying behavior in order to inform buyers about suppliers' needs, wants and preferences. They contributed to a better understanding of suppliers' wishes and behavior by identifying various sources of supplier value. Buyers may be able to use this enhanced understanding of what creates value for suppliers in a relationship to increase supplier satisfaction and influence their behavior in a beneficial manner.

Suppliers often believe that they receive less from collaboration than they deserve. Corsten and Kumar (2005) found that there was greater feeling of inequity in the relationship on the part of suppliers. This made Nyaga et al. (2010) investigate whether buyer and supplier perspectives on collaborative relationships really differ. From each party's perspective, economic and relational factors that drive satisfaction and performance were determined. They found a dichotomy in the expectations of buyers and suppliers consisting of "buyers' focus on relationship outcomes versus suppliers' focus on collaborative activities" (p. 110). Buyers should, therefore, demonstrate an interest in collaborative activities such as information sharing and joint effort to signal their commitment to suppliers and strengthen supplier satisfaction. This is an important finding when it comes to adapting the relationship strategy for becoming a preferred customer.

What approaches can be undertaken by buyers to improve relationship quality is shown by Ghijsen et al. (2010), who examined the effects of direct and indirect influence strategies, promises and human- as well as capital-specific supplier development efforts on supplier satisfaction and commitment. They found that buyers "should attach more importance to indirect and other direct influence strategies and capital-specific supplier development efforts to stimulate supplier satisfaction" (p. 24). In addition, promises and human- and capital-specific development efforts can be used by buyers to enhance supplier commitment to the relationship.

If these efforts to achieve supplier satisfaction are successful, a satisfied supplier might award the buyer with preferred customer status.

Preferred Customer Status

Also the term "preferred customer" is not new, though its application from a purchasing perspective has received little attention. For instance, as early as 1970 Hottenstein argued that "Most businesses have preferred customer's lists, which may be based on past orders or expectations of future business." (p. 46). Hottenstein ran a simulation on order dispatching, in which he included an algorithm for privileged treatment of preferred customers, i.e. he analyses the phenomenon from the perspective of the selling firm which wants to optimize her deliveries.

From the perspective of the buying firm the preferred customer idea only recently started to emerge as a concept. Trent (2005), for instance, mirrored the idea of the "preferred supplier" list purchasers often establish suggesting being part of the "preferred customer" list of their suppliers. Schiele (2006) conceptualized that in order to get innovations from suppliers, a buyer may have to be their preferred customer. In 2007, Bew presented a practitioner paper at a conference in which he highlighted the importance of being a "customer of choice" of the suppliers, drawing back on a survey with sales personnel. In this survey 75% of the participants responded to give their preferred customers preferential treatment in allocation of materials, 82% gave first access to new product ideas and 87% argued that only the customer of choice gets unique cost reduction opportunities. Bew estimated that the total value of this package equates 2-4% of cost savings. Even though hints on the size of the sample and the surveying technique are missing, Bew's study provides some first indications on the benefits firms can achieve by being a preferred customer.

Steinle and Schiele (2008) used the preferred customer concept not to explain the benefits, but to explain the problems firms encountered in global sourcing when failing to get access to suppliers located in a foreign regional-sectoral industry cluster. Finally, Schumacher et al. (2008) developed a model urging firms to analyze their supplier portfolio and phasing out those strategic suppliers, which do not award them with preferred customer status and where they sense no realistic choice of ever becoming a preferred customer.

In sum, literature already provides some first hints on the benefits associated with preferred customer status and the risks involved in not being a preferred customer, but still miss a comprehensive empirical picture. The existing research gives valuable implications for the construct of preferred customer status, but as yet conceptual developments and quantitative verifications of the consequences of preferred customer status are scarce in literature.

Benefits of the Preferred Customer Concept

Table 1 provides an overview of the benefits mentioned in the above discussed papers on customer attractiveness, supplier satisfaction and preferred customer status. The papers are categorized according to the three cycle stages of the virtuous circle shown in Figure 1. There, we developed a model explaining how the constructs customer attractiveness, supplier satisfaction and preferred customer status are interlinked and which factors influence suppliers' decision making process as to whether preferential treatment is awarded or not. The benefits which can be achieved in the different cycle stages are listed in the second column. Customer attractiveness, supplier satisfaction and preferred customer status can have positive impacts on strategic and operational aspects, and on innovation. Strategic benefits are, for example, overall improved supplier performance, enhanced supplier commitment to the relationship and the creation of competitive advantages, whereas benefits in operations refer to the quality of goods received and the terms of delivery. Aspects like benevolent supplier pricing behavior fall into the category of other benefits. The methods used for exploring these consequences are shown in the third column.

It can be derived from the table that the benefits most often mentioned in current literature are strategic in nature. This might not be surprising bearing in mind that the preferred customer concept is a strategic instrument aimed at improving a company's overall competitiveness. Also, buyers applying a preferred customer oriented supply strategy intend to outperform competitors by positioning themselves better among strategic suppliers than their rivals do.

However, whereas existing research mainly concentrates on strategic benefits, having preferred customer status also influences the operational level of purchasing and has a positive impact on production and logistics.

Moreover, it can be seen in Table 1 that very few authors address the benefits preferred customer status has on innovation. Merely Christiansen and Maltz (2002) and Bew (2007) mentioned the positive impact preferred customer status can have on suppliers' contribution to innovation. However, their assumptions are not empirically tested or, at least in the case of Bew, not traceable. Therefore, we intend to present a short quantitative test, applying the preferred customer concept to the issue of supplier innovation in the next section. Supplier contribution to innovation is one of the expected and probably most important benefits buyers can derive from being a preferred customer of key suppliers.

EMPIRICAL STUDY

We conducted an empirical survey-based study to investigate the role of the preferred customer concept in collaborative innovation processes. In particular we tested the effects of supplier capability and preferred customer status on supplier innovativeness in collaborative innovation. By addressing these two variables simultaneously we are able to distinguish between the effects of technical factors (i.e. supplier capability) and preferred customer status.

Conceptual Model

In the literature it is relatively well-known that suppliers can complement buyer's internal capabilities in terms of cycle time, cost and quality problem reduction (Ragatz et al., 2002). Furthermore it has been found that a supplier's design capabilities, process and product expertise, R&D activities and other technological activities explain a supplier's innovativeness quite well (Cabral & Traill, 1999; Croom, 1999; Ellram, 1990; Koppelmann, 2000). Another important determinant of innovation outcomes is the willingness to engage in collaborative innovative activity (Krause et al., 2001; Schiele, 2006). The effective integration of willing suppliers into new product development teams provides an external source of ideas and solutions for the buying firm, which should facilitate problem-solving and enhance the innovation process, leading to the development of successful new processes and products (Chakrabarti & Hauschild, 1989; Smith & Reinertsen, 1991). Without

Table 1. Benefits analyzed in existing literature on preferred customer status

	Cycle Stage			Benefits					Methods		
	Customer attractiveness	*Supplier satisfac-tion*	*Preferred customer status*	*Strategic*	*Operations*	*Innovation*	*Other*	*None*	*Conceptual*	*Explorative*	*Empirical*
Christiansen and Maltz, 2002	■				■	■				■	
Ellegaard et al., 2003	■			■						■	
Ellegard and Ritter, 2006	■				■				■		
Mortensen et al., 2008	■			■						■	
Hald et al., 2009	■			■					■		
Benton and Maloni, 2005		■		■							■
Essig and Amann, 2009		■		■							■
Ramsay and Wagner, 2009		■		■						■	
Nyaga et al., 2010		■		■							■
Ghijsen et al., 2010		■						■			■
Bew, 2007			■		■	■	■				■
Steinle and Schiele, 2008			■					■		■	
Schumacher et al., 2008			■	■					■		

these suppliers' being sufficiently competent, the likelihood of integration efforts to fail increases. *We therefore expect supplier capability to have a positive influence on supplier innovativeness.*

In addition to the technical factor supplier capability, we are interested in the role of preferred customer status. As was stated above, several studies point out that being an attractive customer is a prerequisite for suppliers to dedicate the necessary attention and loyalty to the relationship (e.g. Christiansen & Maltz, 2002). Furthermore, customer attractiveness ensures the open exchange of knowledge and information. Although the importance of customer attractiveness in innovation and new product development has been pointed out by several authors (e.g. Ellegaard & Ritter, 2006; Schiele, 2006; Wynstra et al, 2003), the role of preferred customer status on innovation outcomes has been untouched. From that viewpoint, a supplier who is in a relationship with a preferred customer is more motivated to participate in and devote resources to product development and the improvement of manufacturing processes. The supplier might, for example, put his best employees at the preferred customer's disposal, adapt his capacity to his partner's wishes and give priority to his favorite buyer when offering up promising and innovative ideas. *Hence we expect preferred customer status to have a positive influence on supplier innovativeness.*

Research Design

We designed a quantitative study by means of a survey administered by the German and Austrian associations of materials management, purchasing and logistics - the BME and BMÖ, respectively. Respondents were mainly purchasing managers. To prevent bias that could result from respondents providing data of only their best or biggest supplier, we adopted the suggestion by Ulaga and Eggert (2006). The respondents were asked to assess a supplier with excellent performance in product and process innovation and a supplier who has exhibited disappointing innovativeness (i.e., a supplier who has failed to contribute according to expectations). The respondents were asked to write down the names of these two firms on a separate sheet of paper and then to answer the questionnaire for both suppliers. As a check of content validity, the instrument was pre-tested intensively with a sample of five academics knowledgeable in the field of buyer-supplier relations and with seven practitioners. The pre-test resulted in a few minor changes. The homepage containing the questionnaire was opened 440 times. We received 121 questionnaires (constituting a response rate of 27%) with data about 242 suppliers. However, we used case-wise replacement so that only fully completed questionnaires were used for analysis. This resulted in a final sample of 171 cases for analysis. The respondents represent the following industries: 26.8% mechanical engineering and machine-building; 22.2% electrical and electronic engineering; 9.2% chemical, rubber and plastics; 10.5% vehicles and 31.3% other industries (including 7.8% services). Respondent firms sizes were 4697 employees (median: 930 employees) with a yearly turnover of 1.475 billion Euros (median: 260 million). The sample can be considered high-tech; the average R&D expenditure was 8.1% of turnover.

To measure the preferred customer concept, we adopted an instrument developed by Ganesan (1994), who measured 'vendor's benevolence' in a retail channel study. As in Ganesan (1994) we use five items that, for example, refer to whether the supplier has made sacrifices in the past, cares for the buyer and dedicates his 'best resources' to the buyer. The items thus not only cover a certain emotion attached to the relation (e.g. 'caring' and 'being on the buyer's side') but also whether the supplier is willing to make an effort towards this relationship (e.g. 'sacrificing' and 'letting the best resources work for the buyer'). The four supplier innovativeness measures were based on a study by Krause et al. (2001). The measures are formulated in such a way that they focus on collaborative innovation rather than innovation that is fully detached from the buyer-supplier relationship. They emphasized, for example, willingness to use technological capability on behalf of the buyer, willingness to share important technological information and pro-activeness with respect to approaching the buyer with innovations. The constructs preferred customer and supplier innovativeness were reflective in nature. Supplier capability, however, was modeled as a formative construct composed of three items, which have been inspired by the study of Schiele (2006). R&D expenses were used as a way to capture suppliers' absorptive capacity. Previous studies have revealed a significant influence of R&D intensity on supplier innovativeness (Cabral & Traill, 1999). Similarly, the availability of required quality certificates has been included because the positive results of quality audits have been unveiled as antecedents of supplier innovativeness (Croom, 1999). As the third item of the construct 'supplier capability', finally, the project management capabilities of the supplier are included (Petroni & Panciroli, 2002). All items on the questionnaire were based on a five-point Likert scale except for one of the supplier capability items (size of R&D expenses). The complete list of items can be found in the appendix.

Results

To verify our assumptions, we used partial least squares (PLS) structural equation modeling (Fornell & Cha, 1994). Specifically, we used SmartPLS software (Ringle et al., 2005), which is a well-known software package for the simultaneous testing of both reflective and formative scales. PLS also allows the researchers to relax the stringent distributional assumptions generally imposed on other (co-variance-based) structural equation modeling approaches. To assess the measurement model we first examined the convergent validity of the reflective constructs 'preferred customer status' and 'supplier innovativeness'. The Average Variance Extracted (AVE) and Composite Reliability (CR) values exceed the recommended thresholds of 0.5 for AVE and 0.7 for CR (Bagozzi & Yi, 1988; Fornell & Larcker, 1981; Henseler et al., 2009). Discriminant validity was tested using the Fornell and Larcker criterion (Fornell & Larcker, 1981): the items all load higher on their intended constructs than on the other constructs. Furthermore, the smallest AVE exceeds the squared correlation between each pair of factors. This indicates a satisfactory level of discriminant validity. Cronbach's alpha values are far above the ordinary cut-off values: respectively 0.9224 (preferred customer status) and 0.9028 (supplier innovativeness)[1,2].

To assess our structural model we employed a bootstrapping procedure with replacement using 1000 rounds. The predictive validity within the model is fairly high; 62.9% of the variance in supplier innovativeness is explained by supplier capability and preferred customer status (i.e. R^2=.629). All estimates have high statistical power exceeding 0.9. Our first assumption was that supplier capability positively influences supplier innovativeness. We find that the path is indeed positive and significant (β=.367; t-value=6.82; $p \leq 0.01$). Furthermore we proposed that preferred customer status has a positive influence on supplier innovativeness. This path was also found to be positive and significant (β=.542; t-value=10.68; $p \leq 0.01$).

Our first finding supports the large body of literature that assumes that suppliers' innovative capabilities positively contribute to their innovativeness – more generally for the supplier itself as well as in particular buyer-supplier relationships (e.g. Cabral & Traill, 1999; Krause et al., 2001; Ragatz et al., 2002). Our second finding is that preferential customer treatment is important: preferred customer status has a positive influence on supplier innovativeness. Suppliers have to make choices with whom to partner and apparently tend to choose their preferred customers. The failure to consider preferred customer status with suppliers may also provide a new explanation for the often observed phenomenon of supplier obstructionism in collaborative development (Flynn et al., 2000; Hartley et al., 1997; Petroni & Panciroli, 2002; Primo et al., 2002; Rutten, 2003; Wognum et al., 2002; Zsidisin & Smith, 2005). This finding is in line with Christiansen and Maltz (2002) and Walter et al (2001), who also took on a view of what the buyer can offer to the supplier. They concluded that since close buyer-supplier relationships can benefit knowledge transfer and product innovation the buyer should therefore become interesting for the supplier.

Our findings show that the antecedents of supplier innovativeness are not purely technical in nature (i.e., supplier capability) but also depend on preferred customer status. Moreover, when we compare effect sizes, it can also be concluded that in our sample the technical factor supplier capability plays a less important role compared to preferred customer status.

RECOMMENDATIONS FOR SUPPLY CHAIN INNOVATION

Firms are not able to develop innovations merely by themselves, but increasingly rely on joint product development processes with suppliers as external sources of technology (Roberts, 2001). Howells (2008), for instance, showed that outsourced research and development (R&D) is growing twice as fast as the growth rate for in-house development.

As firms rely heavily on suppliers as external providers of innovation, the management of relationships with development partners should receive much more attention in the open innovation debate. Years of evaluating supplier working relationships in various manufacturing and service industries reveal that it is one thing for mechanisms to be available by which suppliers may transfer innovations to customers and quite another for suppliers to actually do the transferring (Henke & Zhang, 2010). In the automotive industry, for example, suppliers reserve their most advanced technological innovations for customers with which they have trusting working relationships. "Those customers with which suppliers have the closest working relations are more likely to be given access – sometimes exclusive – to supplier innovations before the supplier takes the technology to other customers" (Henke & Zhang, 2010, p. 43). Such innovations provide customers with superior manufacturing capacities, improved product performance and customization capabilities required for long-term competitiveness in the market place. Therefore, firms have to realize that their suppliers' prime commitment and willingness to invest in and share technology in joint development processes has to be secured. Since innovation related supplier activities enable the firm to differentiate itself from competitors, it is extremely important to establish successful customer/supplier collaborations that foster preferential supplier innovation transfer.

Previous research, however, has offered few insights into how relationship with innovative suppliers should be best managed. Firms seem to have only a limited understanding of how to choose and handle suppliers in NPD (Lakemond et al., 2006). There are many reports of suppliers' incompetence and even project obstruction when unsuitable suppliers were involved (Hartley et al., 1997; Flynn et al., 2000; Petroni & Panciroli, 2002; Primo & Amundson, 2002; Zsidisin & Smith, 2005). This may be due to the fact that firms did not pay enough attention to the management of such supplier relationships. As a consequence, suppliers did not treat the joint NPD projects preferentially, did not show enough commitment and, in doing so, contributed to their failure.

It can be seen that especially in open innovation approaches, having preferred customer status or not is particularly relevant. Achieving preferred customer status among key suppliers could well be one tool to influence the success of open innovation projects. Companies have to be aware that they are dependent on their suppliers' benevolence and that they can only be better than their rivals, if they get a better supplier treatment than their competitors do. Being the Preferred Customer of strategic suppliers is a major contributor to successful supply chain innovation and competitiveness, as it guarantees first access to the best resources available in global supply markets. Thus, it is advisable for firms to include a preferred customer oriented supplier strategy into their processes of early supplier involvement.

In doing so, firm strategy, innovation strategy and sourcing strategy would be interlinked. The purchasing department's role in this context would be to actively seek appropriate suppliers and to manage relationships with development partners in a way that motivates them to award preferred customer status. Thereby, a more innovative input and a higher supplier contribution to innovation are likely to be generated. We argue in line with Schiele (2010) that a stronger involvement of purchasing and an enhanced application of differentiated supply management strategies in NPD may improve the stagnating NPD success rate and the firm's overall competitive positioning.

FUTURE RESEARCH DIRECTIONS

The literature review has revealed a scarcity of research exploring the phenomena that lead to preferred customer status. At the same time, our empirical spotlight has unveiled the significance and the explanatory power of the preferred customer construct. In the context of explaining the innovative contribution of suppliers having preferred customer status or not, we could clearly differentiate between successful and disappointing buyer-supplier relationships. This encouraging result might ask for further exploration of the subject.

Drawing back on the conceptual model illustrated in Figure 1 a research programme could be organized alongside the three steps of (1) better understanding customer attractiveness, (2) understanding when a supplier is satisfied and finally, (3) how to profit from being a preferred customer:

1. The research on customer attractiveness still misses a strong theoretical basis. The transaction cost framework has been tentatively employed by some authors (Ellegaard et al., 2003; Nyaga at al., 2010), as well as social exchange theory (Hald et al., 2009; Nyaga at al., 2010), while the relational view of the firm or resource dependency theory might also contribute to the better understanding of the phenomenon. The latter theories also address the strategic dimension involved with customer attractiveness, i.e. the issue of not "only" being attractive, but of being *more* attractive than the competitors. Drawing back on a sound theoretical base, then, factors empirically explaining customer attractiveness could be tested in order to answer the question on how buying firms can become more attractive for their suppliers. A particular challenge might arise for firms located in peripheral regions or outside their main industry clusters (Steinle & Schiele, 2008).
2. Research is only beginning to discuss the antecedents of supplier satisfaction and how to measure it (Ramsay & Wagner, 2009). How do sellers determine the value of a particular relationship for them? And can supplier satisfaction, then, be linked to outcomes, such as satisfied suppliers contributing more to innovation, performing better in delivery or showing a more benevolent pricing behavior? Further, we are only beginning to understand when suppliers are so unsatisfied to discontinue business

relationships (Helm et al. 2006). Please notice that it could be conceptualized that a customer might be attractive for a supplier, but because of the buying firm's behavior the supplier nonetheless is not satisfied and does not award preferred customer status.

3. Such as demonstrated here and elsewhere (Schumacher et al. 2008) buying firms can assess whether they are a preferred customer of their key suppliers or not. The knowledge on the grace of the supplier asks to further elaborate on the issue how to profit from this status. Our findings suggest that the preferred customer concept could re-vitalize the stagnating research on early supplier integration in new product development (Cooper et al. 2004; Griffin 1997), by redirecting the attention from project management to partner selection issues. Recalling that preferred customer status had been defined in terms of preferential resource allocation to selected customers, it follows that buying firms can profit from resources needed for (collaborative) innovation, but also from production resources of the supplier or quality resources etc. Here again, a fruitful field of research opens.

CONCLUSION

The results of our study show that having preferred customer status with leading suppliers is a highly significant and relevant phenomenon, which positively influences suppliers' contribution and performance in buyer-seller relationships. By empirically testing its impact on innovation we were able to show its importance. However, there are certainly many other areas in operations and new product development which would be positively affected if buyers were treated as preferred customer and preferentially allocated supplier resources. A preferred customer oriented supply management strategy comprises the possibility to stand out from competitors and to create preferential relationships with satisfied suppliers.

We can identify several managerial implications. First and operationally, firms would profit from assessing their portfolio of suppliers identifying their status with the key suppliers. Since our data showed that being a preferred customer has a larger effect than the technical capabilities of the supplier, it could be concluded that the 'best' supplier is not always the best partner for every firm. Rather than trying to collaborate with world-leading suppliers without the opportunity of ever becoming a preferred customer of such a firm, it may be more advisable to team-up with a slightly less competent supplier, provided he honours the buyer with the privileges of preferential customer treatment. Carrying this line of thought forward, the ultimate managerial consequence would be to phase-out those suppliers where the buying firm sees no chance for achieving preferential treatment and closely integrating the rest of the strategic suppliers.

Second, the preferred customer phenomenon also has a strategic implication: In oligopolistic supply markets where a limited number of key suppliers is responsible for the bulk of innovations, being the first buyer to actively pursue a preferred customer policy may contribute to achieving sustainable competitive advantage. This pioneering firm will reorganize their portfolio of partners and establish a strong network with partners that award it with preferred customer status. A competing firm that recognizes the importance of preferred customer status too late may discover that in the meantime all key suppliers in the industry have committed themselves to their favorite customers and established close ties to that follower firm's competitors. In an open innovation environment a strategy of innovation leadership may no longer be possible, then.

REFERENCES

Anderson, J., & Narus, J. (1990). A model of distributor firm and manufacturer firm working partnerships. *Journal of Marketing, 54*(1), 42–58. doi:10.2307/1252172

Bagozzi, R., & Yi, Y. (1988). On the evaluation of structural equation models. *Journal of the Academy of Marketing Science, 16*(1), 74–94. doi:10.1007/BF02723327

Beekman, A., & Robinson, R. (2004). Supplier partnership and the small, high-growth firm: selecting for success. *Journal of Small Business Journal, 42*(1), 59–77. doi:10.1111/j.1540-627X.2004.00097.x

Benton, W. C., & Maloni, M. (2005). The influence of power driven buyer/seller relationships on supply chain satisfaction. *Journal of Operations Management, 23*, 1–22. doi:10.1016/j.jom.2004.09.002

Bew, R. (2007, May). *The New Customer of Choice Imperative: Ensuring Supply Availability, Productivity Gains, and Supplier Innovation.* Paper presented at the 92nd Annual International Supply Management Conference, Las Vegas.

Biemans, W., & Brand, M. (1995). Reverse marketing: a synergy of purchasing and relationship marketing. *International Journal of Purchasing and Materials Management, 31*(3), 29–37.

Blenkhorn, D., & Banting, P. (1991). How reverse marketing changes buyer-seller roles. *Industrial Marketing Management, 20*(3), 185–191. doi:10.1016/0019-8501(91)90016-9

Briscoe, J., Fawcett, S., & Todd, R. (2005). The implementation and impact of ISO 9000 among small manufacturing enterprises. *Journal of Small Business Management, 43*(3), 309–319. doi:10.1111/j.1540-627X.2005.00139.x

Cabral, J. E. O., & Traill, W. B. (1999). Determinants of a firm's likelihood to innovate and intensity of innovation in the Brazilian food industry. *Journal on Chain and Network Science, 1*(1), 33–48. doi:10.3920/JCNS2001.x004

Cannon, J., & Perrault, W. (1999). Buyer-seller relationships in business markets. *JMR, Journal of Marketing Research, 36*(4), 439–460. doi:10.2307/3151999

Chakrabarti, A. K., & Hauschild, J. (1989). The division of labour in innovation management. *R & D Management, 19*, 161–171. doi:10.1111/j.1467-9310.1989.tb00636.x

Chesbrough, H. W. (2003). The era of open innovation. *Sloan Management Review, 44*(3), 35–41.

Christiansen, P. E., & Maltz, A. (2002). Becoming an "interesting" customer: procurement strategies for buyers without leverage. *International Journal of Logistics: Research and Applications, 5*(2), 177–195. doi:10.1080/13675560210148678

Clark, K. B. (1989). Project scope and project performance: the effects of parts strategy and supplier involvement on product development. *Management Science, 35*(10), 1247–1263. doi:10.1287/mnsc.35.10.1247

Cohen, W. M., & Levinthal, D. A. (1990). Absorptive capacity: a new perspective on learning and innovation. *Administrative Science Quarterly, 35*(1), 128–152. doi:10.2307/2393553

Cooper, R. G., Edgett, S., & Kleinschmidt, E. J. (2004). Benchmarking best NPD practices – II. *Research Policy, 47*(3), 50–59.

Cordon, C., & Vollmann, T. E. (2002). The Next Game in Purchasing: Be the Most Attractive Customer to Key Suppliers. *IMD International, 86,* January, Lausanne.

Corsten, D., & Kumar, N. (2005). Do suppliers benefit from collaborative relationships with large retailers? An empirical investigation of efficient consumer response adoption. *Journal of Marketing, 69*(3), 80–94. doi:10.1509/jmkg.69.3.80.66360

Cox, A. (1999). Power, value and supply chain management. *Supply Chain Management: An International Journal, 4*(4), 167–175. doi:10.1108/13598549910284480

Croom, S. (1999). The dyadic capabilities concept: examining the processes of key supplier involvement in collaborative product development. *European Journal of Purchasing and Supply Management, 7*(1), 29–37. doi:10.1016/S0969-7012(00)00019-8

Drucker, P. (1954). *The practice of management.* New York: Harper & Row.

Dwyer, F. R., Schurr, P. H., & Oh, S. (1987). Developing Buyer-Seller Relationships. *Journal of Marketing, 51*, 11–27. doi:10.2307/1251126

Edquist, C. (1997). Systems of innovation approaches - their emergence and characteristics. In Edquist, C. (Ed.), *Systems of innovation. Technologies, institutions and organizations* (pp. 1–35). London: Pinter.

Ellegaard, C., Johansen, J., & Drejer, A. (2003). Managing industrial buyer-supplier relations - the case for attractiveness. *Integrated Manufacturing Systems, 14*(4), 346–356. doi:10.1108/09576060310469725

Ellegaard, C., & Ritter, T. (2006, September). *Customer Attraction and its Purchasing Potential.* Paper presented at the 22nd IMP Conference, Milan.

Ellram, L. M. (1990). The supplier selection decision in strategic partnerships. *Journal of Purchasing and Materials Management, 20*(4), 8–14.

Essig, M., & Amann, M. (2009). Supplier satisfaction: Conceptual basics and explorative findings. *Journal of Purchasing and Supply Management, 15*, 103–113. doi:10.1016/j.pursup.2009.01.001

Flynn, B. B., Flynn, E. J., Amundson, S. D., & Schroeder, R. G. (2000). Team characteristics as enablers of fast product development speed. *Advances in Interdisciplinary Studies of Work Teams, 5*, 133–169.

Fornell, C., & Cha, J. (1994). Partial least squares. In Bagozzi, R. P. (Ed.), *Advanced Methods of Marketing Research* (pp. 52–78). Cambridge, MA: Blackwell.

Fornell, C., & Larcker, D. F. (1981). Structural equation models with unobservable variables and measurement error: algebra and statistics. *JMR, Journal of Marketing Research, 18*(3), 382–388. doi:10.2307/3150980

Freeman, C., & Soete, L. (1997). *The economics of industrial innovation* (3rd ed.). London, Washington: Continuum.

Ganesan, S. (1994). Determinants of long-term orientation in buyer-seller relationships. *Journal of Marketing, 58*(2), 1–19. doi:10.2307/1252265

Ghijsen, P. W. T., Semeijn, J., & Ernstson, S. (2010). Supplier satisfaction and commitment: The role of influence strategies and supplier development. *Journal of Purchasing and Supply Management, 16*, 17–26. doi:10.1016/j.pursup.2009.06.002

Griffin, A. (1997). PDMA research on new product development practices: Updating trends and benchmarking best practices. *Journal of Product Innovation Management, 14*, 429–458. doi:10.1016/S0737-6782(97)00061-1

Grönroos, C. (2000). Relationship marketing: interaction, dialogue and value. *Revista Europea de Dirección y Economía de la Empresa, 9*(3), 13–24.

Hald, K. S., Cordón, C., & Vollmann, T. E. (2009). Towards an understanding of attraction in buyer-supplier relationships. *Industrial Marketing Management, 38*, 960–970. doi:10.1016/j.indmarman.2008.04.015

Handfield, R. B., Ragatz, G. L., Petersen, K. J., & Monczka, R. M. (1999). Involving suppliers in new product development. *California Management Review, 42*(1), 59–82.

Hartley, J. L., Zirger, B. J., & Kamath, R. R. (1997). Managing the buyer-supplier interface for on-time performance in product development. *Journal of Operations Management, 15*, 57–70. doi:10.1016/S0272-6963(96)00089-7

Helm, S., Rolfes, L., & Günter, B. (2006). Suppliers' willingness to end unprofitable customer relationships: an exploratory investigation in the German mechanical engineering sector. *European Journal of Marketing, 40*(3/4), 366–383. doi:10.1108/03090560610648101

Henke, J. W., & Zhang, C. (2010). Increasing supplier-driven innovation. *MIT Sloan Management Review, winter 2010*, 41-46

Henseler, J., Ringle, C. M., & Sikovics, R. (2009). The use of partial least square path modeling in international marketing. *Advances in International Marketing, 20*, 277–319.

Hottenstein, M. (1970). Expediting in job-order-control systems: a simulation study. *IIE Transactions, 2*(1), 46–54. doi:10.1080/05695557008974729

Howells, J. (2008). New directions in R&D: current and prospective challenges. *R & D Management, 38*(3), 241–252. doi:10.1111/j.1467-9310.2008.00519.x

Hunt, S., & Nevin, J. R. (1974). Power in a channel of distribution: sources and consequences. *JMR, Journal of Marketing Research, 11*(2), 186–193. doi:10.2307/3150557

Johnsen, T. E. (2009). Supplier involvement in new product development and innovation: taking stock and looking to the future. *Journal of Purchasing and Supply Management, 15*, 187–197. doi:10.1016/j.pursup.2009.03.008

Koppelmann, U. (2000). *Beschaffungsmarketing* [Supply marketing]. 3rd ed.). Berlin: Springer.

Krause, D. R., Pagell, M., & Curkovic, S. (2001). Toward a measure of competitive priorities for purchasing. *Journal of Operations Management, 19*, 497–512. doi:10.1016/S0272-6963(01)00047-X

Laaksonen, T., Pajunen, K., & Kulmala, H. I. (2008). Co-evolution of trust and dependence in customer-supplier relationships. *Industrial Marketing Management, 37*, 910–920. doi:10.1016/j.indmarman.2007.06.007

Lakemond, N., Berggren, C., & van Weele, A. (2006). Coordinating supplier involvement in product development projects: a differentiated coordination typology. *R & D Management, 36*(1), 55–66. doi:10.1111/j.1467-9310.2005.00415.x

Larson, P., & Kulchitsky, J. (1998). Single sourcing and supplier certification; performance and relationship implications. *Industrial Marketing Management, 27*(1), 73–81. doi:10.1016/S0019-8501(97)00039-4

Leenders, M. R., & Blenkhorn, D. L. (1988). *Reverse marketing: the new buyer-supplier relationship*. New York: Free Press.

Michie, D. A., & Sibley, S. D. (1985). Channel member satisfaction: controversy resolved. *Journal of the Academy of Marketing Science, 13*(2), 188–205. doi:10.1007/BF02729714

Morgan, R., & Hunt, S. (1994). The commitment-trust theory of relationship marketing. *Journal of Marketing, 58*, 20–38. doi:10.2307/1252308

Morrisey, J., & Pittaway, L. (2006). Buyer-supplier relationships in small firms; the use of social factors to manage relationships. *International Small Business Journal, 24*(3), 272–298. doi:10.1177/0266242606063433

Mortensen, M. H., Freytag, P. V., & Arlbjørn, J. S. (2008). Attractiveness in supply chains: A process and matureness perspective. *International Journal of Physical Distribution and Logistics Management, 38*(10), 799–815. doi:10.1108/09600030810926501

Nyaga, G. N., Whipple, J. M., & Lynch, D. F. (2010). Examining supply chain relationships: Do buyer and supplier perspectives on collaborative relationships differ? *Journal of Operations Management, 28*, 101–114. doi:10.1016/j.jom.2009.07.005

Petroni, A., & Panciroli, B. (2002). Innovation as a determinant of suppliers' roles and performances: an empirical study in the food machinery industry. *European Journal of Purchasing & Supply Management, 8*, 135–149. doi:10.1016/S0969-7012(02)00004-7

Plank, R. E., Francis, D. (2001). Does Reverse Marketing Reduce Conflict in Buyer-Seller Relations?. *American Business Review*, January 2001, 76-83.

Primo, M. A. M., & Amundson, S. D. (2002). An exploratory study of the effects of supplier relationships on new product development outcomes. *Journal of Operations Management, 20*(1), 33–52. doi:10.1016/S0272-6963(01)00080-8

Ragatz, G. L., Handfield, R. B., & Petersen, K. J. (2002). Benefits associated with supplier integration into new product development under conditions of technology uncertainty. *Journal of Business Research, 55*, 389–400. doi:10.1016/S0148-2963(00)00158-2

Ragatz, G. L., Handfield, R. B., & Scannell, T. V. (1997). Success factors for integrating suppliers into new product development. *Journal of Product Innovation Management, 14*(3), 190–202. doi:10.1016/S0737-6782(97)00007-6

Ramsay, J., & Wagner, B. A. (2009). Organisational Supplying Behaviour: Understanding supplier needs, wants and preferences. *Journal of Purchasing and Supply Management, 15*, 127–138. doi:10.1016/j.pursup.2009.02.001

Raven, B. H., & Kruglanski, A. W. (1970). Conflict and power. In Paul, S. (Ed.), *The Structure of Conflict* (pp. 69–109). New York: Academic Press.

Ringle, C. M., Wende, S., & Will, A. (2005). *SmartPLS 2.0 M3*. Retrieved June 13, 2010, from http://www.smartpls.de.

Roberts, E. B. (2001). Benchmarking Global Strategic Management of Technology. Survey of the word's largest r&d performers reveals, among other trends, a greater reliance upon external sources of technology. *Research Technology Management, 44*(2), 25–36.

Rutten, R. (2003). *Knowledge and innovation in regional industry: an entrepreneurial coalition*. London: Taylor & Francis Ltd.

Schiele, H. (2006). How to distinguish innovative suppliers? Identifying innovative suppliers as new task for purchasing. *Industrial Marketing Management, 35*, 925–935. doi:10.1016/j.indmarman.2006.05.003

Schiele, H. (2010). Early supplier integration: the dual role of purchasing in new product development. *R & D Management, 40*(2), 138–153. doi:10.1111/j.1467-9310.2010.00602.x

Schumacher, S. C., Schiele, H., Contzen, M., & Zachau, T. (2008). *Die 3 Faktoren des Einkaufs: Einkauf und Lieferanten strategisch positionieren* [The 3 factors of purchasing: Positioning purchasing and suppliers strategically]. Weinheim: Wiley-VCH.

Siguaw, J., Simpson, P., & Baker, T. (1998). Effects of supplier market orientation on distributor market orientation and the channel relationship: the distributor perspective. *Journal of Marketing, 62*(3), 99–111. doi:10.2307/1251746

Smith, P. G., & Reinertsen, D. G. (1991). *Developing products in half the time*. New York: Van Nostrand.

Steinle, C., & Schiele, H. (2002). When do industries cluster? *Research Policy, 31*, 849–858. doi:10.1016/S0048-7333(01)00151-2

Steinle, C., & Schiele, H. (2008). Limits to global sourcing? Strategic consequences of dependency on international suppliers. Cluster theory, resource-based view and case studies. *Journal of Purchasing and Supply Management, 14*(1), 3–14. doi:10.1016/j.pursup.2008.01.001

Tracey, M. (2004). A holistic approach to new product development: new insights. *The Journal of Supply Chain Management, 40*(4), 37–55. doi:10.1111/j.1745-493X.2004.tb00177.x

Trent, R. (2005). Why relationships matter. *Supply Chain Management Review, 9*(8), 53–60.

Trott, P., & Hartmann, D. (2009). Why 'open innovation' is old wine in new bottles. *International Journal of Innovation Management, 13*(4), 715–736. doi:10.1142/S1363919609002509

Ulaga, W., & Eggert, A. (2006). Value-based differentiation in business relationships: gaining and sustaining key supplier status. *Journal of Marketing, 70*(1), 119–136. doi:10.1509/jmkg.2006.70.1.119

Van der Haar, J., Kemp, R., & Omta, O. (2001). Creating value that cannot be copied. *Industrial Marketing Management, 30*(8), 627–636. doi:10.1016/S0019-8501(99)00128-5

Varey, R., Baxter, R., Brodie, R., Brookes, R., Plewa, C., Quester, P., & Schembri, S. (2005). Buyer-seller relationships: Australasian research and reflections. *Journal of Customer Behavior, 4*(1), 127–146. doi:10.1362/1475392053750289

Von Hippel, E. (1988). *The sources of innovation. New York etc.* Oxford University Press.

Wagner, S. M. (2009). Getting innovation from suppliers. *Research-Technology Management, 52*(1), 8–9.

Walter, A., Müller, T. A., Helfert, G., & Ritter, T. (2003). Functions of industrial relationships and their impact on relationship quality. *Industrial Marketing Management, 32*, 159–169. doi:10.1016/S0019-8501(02)00230-4

Walter, A., Ritter, T., & Gemünden, H. G. (2001). Value creation in buyer-seller relationships. *Industrial Marketing Management, 30*, 365–377. doi:10.1016/S0019-8501(01)00156-0

Wasti, S. N., & Liker, J. K. (1997). Risky business or competitive power? Supplier involvement in Japanese product design. *Journal of Product Innovation Management, 14*, 337–355. doi:10.1016/S0737-6782(97)00024-6

Wognum, P., Fisscher, O. A., & Weenink, S. A. (2002). Balanced relationships: management of client-supplier relationships in product development. *Technovation, 22*, 341–351. doi:10.1016/S0166-4972(01)00031-1

Wynstra, F., Weggeman, M., & van Weele, A. (2003). Exploring purchasing integration in product development. *Industrial Marketing Management, 32*(1), 69–83. doi:10.1016/S0019-8501(01)00197-3

Zsidisin, G. A., & Smith, M. E. (2005). Managing supply risk with early supplier involvement: a case study and research propositions. *The Journal of Supply Chain Management*, *41*, 44–57. doi:10.1111/j.1745-493X.2005.04104005.x

ENDNOTES

1 The various statistical measures normally reported are omitted for the sake of brevity; they can be obtained at the first author upon request.

2 Note that due to the formative nature of the supplier capability construct, no AVE, CR and Cronbach's alpha values can be given here.

APPENDIX

Measures

Supplier innovativeness (IS)	The level of technological capability the supplier possesses and is willing to use for our products is high	IS1
	The supplier is willing to share key technological information	IS2
	This supplier is capable of supporting collaborative processes in product development and process improvement	IS3
	This supplier is frequently proactive in approaching us with innovations	IS4
Supplier capability (SC)	The supplier obtained relevant quality certificates (e.g. ISO TS 16949 in the automotive industry)	SC1
	This supplier has well-developed project management capabilities	SC2
	Please indicate the magnitude of this supplier's R&D expenditure in relation to annual sales	SC3
Preferred customer (PC)	This supplier has made sacrifices for us in the past	PC1
	This supplier cares for us	PC2
	In case of shortages, this supplier has gone out on a limb for us	PC3
	We feel this supplier is on our side	PC4
	The best resources of this supplier work for us	PC5

Chapter 19
The Human Side of Supply Chains:
A Behavioural Perspective of Supply Chain Risk Management

Alessandro Ancarani
University of Catania, Italy

Carmela Di Mauro
University of Catania, Italy

ABSTRACT

The adoption of the behavioural approach for the study of OM and Supply Chain Management is still fairly novel. However, there is evidence that in order to improve supply chain management it is crucial to develop models that correctly describe human behaviour. Failure to account for behavioural components such as risk perception, time effects and social interaction may lead to models that are biased in their predictions. This chapter reviews extant behavioural research relevant to supply chain risk management. In particular, its implications for supply chain management are outlined, and opportunities for future developments of theory that is robust to behavioural effects are identified.

INTRODUCTION

In the past few years the attention towards supply chain risk management has increased significantly (Wagner and Bode, 2006). This attention has been triggered not only by the frequency and intensity of disruptions on a global scale but also by a number of events on the supply chain level, which resulted in serious problems for the firms involved (Sheffi, 2005). Today's supply chains are more complex than they used to be. There are various reasons for supply chain complexity, such as higher levels of R&D and manufacturing outsourcing, supplier–supplier relationships

DOI: 10.4018/978-1-60960-585-8.ch019

in supplier networks, increased dependence on supplier capabilities, new technologies, regulatory requirements, shorter product life-cycles due to rapidly changing customer preferences, and international market and production expansion (Wagner and Neshat, 2010). Moreover, as firms try to reduce costs through the rationalization and reduction of the supply base, the aim to secure an interrupt flow of materials has become more difficult to achieve (Harland et al., 2003).

Some scholars contend that modern supply chain management initiatives have great potential to make operations leaner and/or more agile in a stable environment but simultaneously amplify the fragility of supply chains (Zsidisin et al., 2005), due to increasingly complex and technology oriented processes that make organizations more prone to disruptions (Lee, 2004; Lin et al., 2006).

Several streams of research have addressed the issue of how to ensure continuity of supply, identifying the factors that drive supply risk (Sheffi and Rice, 2005; Tang, 2006), evaluating the negative implications of supply risk (Hendricks and Singhal, 2005; Wagner and Bode, 2006), and providing frameworks for analysing and reducing supply disruption risk (Kleindorfer and Saad, 2005; Tang and Tomlin, 2008).

While these contributions have provided important insights and have deepened our understanding about causes, effects, and management of supply risk, to our knowledge only little research has been devoted to the investigation of behavioural aspects of supply risk management.

The classical approach to risk in operations management has been to see risk as resulting from the product of probability of loss times the potential loss, i.e. the expected value of the loss. The goal to minimise expected losses accounts to assuming that the decision maker is risk neutral. However, this assumption may deviate from reality since, depending on the environment or the payoffs at stake, a rational decision maker may be either risk seeking or risk averse (Bendoly et al., 2006).

In addition, decision makers not only have attitudes towards risk different from neutrality, but also may depart from the rational model of behaviour. The investigation of these issues has received little attention by OM research so far, while, on the contrary, it has been an essential component of decision making research, at least since Simon (1957) and Kahneman and Tversky (1979). A large body of research is grounded in the evidence that, even when objective data could support rational decision-making, the subjective interpretation may bias the risk assessment process (Yates and Stone, 1992; Yates et al., 1994).

Thus, in the face of varying types and degrees of supply chain (SC) risk, managers' actions to protect against those risks and to reduce the vulnerability of the SC will likely depend on their individual characteristics, such as attitudes towards risk, on how perceptions of supply disruption risk are developed, and on the degree of confidence they assign to available risk information (Ellis et al., 2010).

Different approaches have been applied to the analysis of behavioural issues in OM. For instance, theoretical models have been developed providing suggestions on how managerial decisions are affected by risk attitudes and decision biases (Schweitzer and Cachon, 2000), and on how incentives should be modified to account for them (Croson et al., 2008). As far as empirical analysis is concerned, controlled human experimentation has become one of the most accepted methodologies for hypotheses testing, also in management and operations (Boyer and Swink, 2008). Experiments can supplement SC research by providing insights into how the human factor influences the SC management and by exploring how human characteristics interact with operational and organizational aspects, thus offering suggestions for theory revision and for improvement in management (Croson and Donohue, 2002).

The aim of this chapter is to provide an overview of the extant literature on the behavioural issues in supply chain management and to explore, on the basis of the stylised facts of behavioural research, some fruitful areas of application to supply chain risk management.

The remainders of the chapter is organised as follows. The next section provides an overview of the concept(s) of supply chain risk, making the case for the consideration of behavioural aspects. Then, we shall present the concept of behavioural Operations Management in the light of the main stylised facts of behavioural research. We then review the extant empirical literature on behavioural supply chain, focusing on experimental and survey studies. Finally, we discuss how behavioural research results can be relevant for supply chain risk related phenomena, andprovide suggestions for future research and SC management innovation.

SUPPLY CHAIN RISK AND VULNERABILITY

The concept of risk has been interpreted differently according to the field of research (Baird and Thomas, 1990; Jemison, 1987). In many fields of business research, including supply chain management, risk has been equated with the variance around the expected value of a performance measure (Paulsson, 2004).

In contrast, in most dictionaries as well as in the field of insurance, risk is viewed as the chance of injury, damage, or loss (Webster, 1983). The notion that risk inherits primarily negative consequences corresponds to the common human perception. This view too has been embraced by several scholars in supply management. Harland et al. (2003) for instance, discusses several definitions and concludes that supply chain risk is associated with the "chance of danger, damage, loss, injury or any other undesired consequences". According to another definition, supply risk is "the probability of an incident associated with inbound supply from individual supplier failures or the supply market occurring, in which its outcomes result in the inability of the purchasing firm to meet customer demand or cause threats to customer life and safety" (Zsidisin, 2003, p.222).

March and Shapira (1987) add a subjective dimension to the definition of risk based on the objective assessment of potential outcomes and of their probabilities. Risk is defined as the "variation in the distribution of possible outcomes, their likelihoods, and their subjective values". These authors examine empirically how managers perceive risk and react to it. They find that the majority of them tend to overrate the "downside" potential of risk.

Tang (2006) distinguishes two categories of supply chain risks, namely operational risks and disruption risks. An operational risk refers to those inherent uncertainties that inevitably exist in supply chains and therefore concerns high frequency events involving low-medium size of losses. Tang and Tomlin (2008) claimed that there are at least six major types of supply chain risks that occur regularly, namely supply risks, process risks, demand risks, intellectual property risks, political/social risks, behavioural risks. Supply risks include the risks associated with supply cost, supply quality, and supply commitment. Process risks include the quality, time, and capacity risks associated with in-bound and out-bound logistics and in-house operations. Demand risks include the risks associated with demand uncertainty. Intellectual property risks include the opportunistic behaviour and the contract weaknesses. Behavioural risks include the confidence and the reliability of the information available from suppliers. Political/social risks include the intrusion of political bargaining in the industrial logic. Classifications in the same vein are also provided by Svensson (2000), Juttner (2005) and Chopra and Sodhi (2004).

When the outcome of supply risk is an exceptional and anomalous situation in comparison to every-day business, the term disruption is used. A disruption is triggered by an underlying disruptive event (or a series of such events), that is unintended and unanticipated (Wagner and Bode, 2006; Craighead et al., 2007; Kleindorfer and Saad, 2005). Therefore, it concerns low frequency events involving large losses.

Extant literature has focused on identifying sources of uncertainty and the risks that emanate from them (Narasimahn and Talluri, 2009). Supply chain risks manifest themselves in the disruption of supply chain flows due to several reasons like disruptions to material flows, information flows, knowledge flows, and control and coordination flows. This perspective of supply chain risks requires that sources and types of risk be related to the flows that occur within the supply chain. The literature on this aspect of risk identification is not extensive (Juttner, 2005; Paulson, 2004).

Chopra et al. (2007) argue that bundling operational risk and disruption risk management may lead to erroneous decisions, higher inventories, and a higher supply chain cost than optimal. Even if executives and researchers have lately more attention to handling major disruptions, however, it remains critical to develop ways to manage supply chain risks arising from the problems of coordinating supply and demand because these risks are omnipresent. Atkinson (2006) reports the results of a survey on purchasing executives that demonstrates that only half of all respondents monitor supply chain risks.

While a supply chain disruption is the situation that leads to the resulting detriment, also the susceptibility of the supply chain to this situation is of significant relevance. This leads to the concept of supply chain vulnerability. Christopher and Peck (2004) define supply chain vulnerability as "an exposure to serious disturbance". Svensson (2000, 2002, 2004a, b) distinguishes between atomistic vulnerability (of a part of the supply chain) and holistic vulnerability (across the entire supply chain). In the literature on natural hazards and crisis management, vulnerability has been defined as a person's (or a group's) capacity to anticipate, cope with, resist, and recover from the impact of a natural hazard (Blaikie et al., 1994). In the context of maritime supply chains, Barnes and Oloruntoba (2005) describe vulnerability as "a susceptibility or predisposition to loss because of existing organisational or functional practices or conditions".

One important source of SC vulnerability has been the recent trend in SC management to reduce the supply base and, at the same time, to establish closer relationships with the suppliers in the reduced supply base. Various benefits of supply base reduction efforts are cited in the literature such as improved product (Kekre et al., 1995) or relationship quality (Ellram, 1991). However, relying on few and external sources affects supply chain vulnerability (Cavinato, 2004; Choi and Krause, 2006). When a firm concentrates its sourcing activities on a small number of suppliers, it loses the ability to switch to contingency suppliers in disruptive situations. Moreover, the buying firm is exposed to a heightened risk of organisational hold-up (Yu et al., 2009). Based on the findings from an exploratory quantitative survey and qualitative group discussions with supply chain managers, Juttner (2005) shows that 44% of the responding companies expected the vulnerability of their supply chains to increase within the following five years.

In addition to the tangible risks elements discussed so far, supply chain risks encompass also intangible elements (Wilding, 1998). Intangible elements are important in supply management but are often underrated. Intangibles not only interact with tangible sources of risks modifying their impact in case of disruption, but also may constitute a separate source of risk that may increase the supply chain vulnerability. As Bendoly et al. (2006) aptly summarise "A common factor in this breakdown is people. When it comes to implementation, the success of operations management tools and techniques, and the accuracy of its theories, relies heavily on our understanding of human behaviour (p.737)".

A wide definition of intangible elements refers to psychological effects tied to individual cognition and emotions, social interactions, and organizational culture. In SC risk management, intangible elements include the risk attitudes and risk perceptions of the users and members of the supply chain. Another example of intangible element is mistrust, i.e. the lack of confidence between actors in a supply chain that leads to actions and interventions which collectively could lead to cost escalation (Tang and Tomlin, 2008).

The subjective dimensions may affect both the design of SC and the SC management. Implications for SC design include the perception of long-term costs and benefits of contracts, the attitude towards fairness in the distribution of the contract benefits, the suboptimal enlargement of the supply base due to risk and loss aversion, or, on the contrary, its suboptimal reduction due to overconfidence. Implications for SC management include the possibility that prior relationships bias choice behaviour, thus inducing a sort status quo effect. Further, complexity and uncertainty within a supply chain can increase the "chaos" risks within the supply chain. These chaos effects result from over-reactions, unnecessary interventions, second guessing, mistrust, and distorted information throughout a supply chain (Childerhouse and Towill, 2003). The well-known "bullwhip" effect, i.e. the increasing fluctuations of order patterns from downstream to upstream layers of the SC, illustrates how a standard operational risk (such as demand uncertainty) gives raise to chaotic effects (Dooley et al., 2010; Anderson et al., 2000). The existence of nervousness and chaos in a supply chain also means that it is difficult to make optimal decisions at each stage in the supply chain. The risks of making the wrong or ineffective decisions, or decision risks, become the inevitable consequence (Tang and Tomlin, 2008).

All these examples illustrate the relevance of investigating aspects other than operational ones that may impact on risk management decisions. In this direction, supply chain management is one of the earliest areas of OM in which the behavioural approach has been applied (Sterman, 1989) and one where the contributions of psychology and sociology appear most promising.

To this now we turn, with the aim to present first some stylized facts from behavioural research that may be relevant in the general context of operations management.

BEHAVIOURAL OPERATIONS MANAGEMENT

Insights from Behavioural Research

The concept of *Homo Oeconomicus* underlying the standard theory of the firm in microeconomics refers to a perfectly rational, fully informed economic agent, who has perfect foresight, and is capable of identifying the optimal solution, however difficult the decision problem at hand. In a way, the economic man is non-human in this unlimited ability at problem solving.

At least since Simon (1957), economists have started to recognise the need for a theory of economic action that is not only normative but it is also behaviourally grounded. Following the failure of standard theory to account for many empirically observed regularities, behavioural economics developed as a sub-discipline seeking to make prediction of behaviour more accurate by drawing on the findings of social sciences such as psychology and sociology. Simon's concept of bounded rationality is perhaps the first milestone of behavioural economics. The limitations in the cognitive ability of man give rise to biases in judgement and decision making and lead individuals to act on the basis of heuristics.

One of the most far reaching contributions of behavioural research in the investigation of bounded rationality has been provided by Prospect Theory (Kahneman and Tversky, 1979). Prospect

Theory has shown that many empirical findings can be explained by a decision model whereby individuals act on the basis of reference points (one reference point may be the status quo) and calculate gains and losses with respect to it.

According to the standard decision theory of choice under risk, Expected Utility theory (EU henceforward) (Von Neumann and Morgestern, 1992), risk attitudes are simply due to the shape of the utility function, which is linear in payoffs if the decision maker is risk neutral, and concave/convex under risk aversion/loving preferences. Expected utility is the product of the utility and the probability of payoffs, and thus it is linear in the probabilities.

According to Prospect Theory (Kahneman and Tversky, 1979), utility under uncertainty is the joint effect of a value function, which is concave for gains and convex for losses, and of a weighting function, which is a nonlinear transformation of objective probabilities. Gains and losses are calculated with respect to a subjective reference point, which may be represented, for instance, by the decision maker's status quo. The shape of the value function implies that individuals are loss averse: a one euro loss entails a decrease in utility larger than the increase in utility brought about by a gain of one euro.

Thus, whereas the classical theory of behaviour under risk (Von Neumann and Morgestern, 1992) assumes that preferences for outcomes are linearly weighted by the probabilities of those outcomes, Prospect Theory and several subsequent theories (Quiggin, 1982; Schmeidler, 1989; Tversky and Wakker, 1995) have shown that individuals mentally transform probabilities.

By looking inside the toolbox of psychologists and sociologists, economics has discovered a series of general and systematic violations of the standard paradigm. More precisely, individuals are bounded not only as far as their rationality is concerned, but also as regards to their self-interest and self-control (Diamond and Vartiainen, 2007).

The pursue of self-interest has been put into question by the empirical observation of cooperative behaviour much more often than game theoretic models would predict (Ledyard, 1995), and by the strong tendency of individuals to reciprocate (Fehr and Gachter, 2000).

Lack of self-control is manifest in herding behaviour, whereby individuals passively follow the choices of others (Banerjee, 1992), and in the role emotions play when individuals take decisions in the face of risk (Loeweinstein, 1996).

Behavioural Operations

Operations Management (OM henceforth) is rooted in the standard theory of the firm and therefore embraces the paradigm of the rational man. OM scientists have been reluctant to concede that attributes of decision makers may play a role in the success of operations, in spite none would deny that "people may significantly influence how operating systems work, perform, and respond to management interventions" (Gino and Pisano, 2008). For instance, notwithstanding the importance of risk aversion in many settings (financial and investment decisions, occupational choice, insurance purchasing among others), preferences have played practically no role in OM (Bendoly et al., 2006), and the over-ruling paradigm in modelling and simulations is expected cost minimisation. According to Boudreau et al. (2003) OM models are normally built under the assumptions that human beings are not relevant in the model, are deterministic and predictable in their actions, act independently of others, and their decisions are emotionless, observable, and independent of the product.

Behavioural Operations Management is a framework that seeks to extend standard OM so to encompass features of human behaviour not present in the traditional approach. Operations are highly complex and dynamic settings in which individuals are called to solve complex decision problems in order to secure the goals of effectiveness, efficiency and quality. Further, decisions concerning operations are very often group decisions, and thus require attention not only to the cognitive foundations of choice but also to issues such as communication, coordination, network formation and social norms (Camerer and Malmendier, 2007). In short, it is important that prescriptive models accurately reflect all elements relevant for choice, and this calls for models with sound behavioural bases.

The literature on behavioural OM is still limited albeit rapidly expanding (Bendoly et al., 2010). Bendoly et al. (2006) provide an interesting framework for thinking about the behavioural assumptions to be used in OM models and for identifying potential OM problems to be subject to the behavioural lens. These assumptions are divided into Intentions, Actions and Reactions. Intentions refer to the model's hypotheses about the objective function of the decision makers. For instance, the assumption of expected cost minimization in inventory management (which corresponds to risk neutrality) may deviate from reality because the decision maker could be either risk seeking or risk averse or because the objective function may incorporate non-monetary values such as trust, fairness or prior relationships with sellers and buyers.Actions refer to the behaviour of human players in the model. In a behavioural model Actions include a variety of heuristics used as a consequence of cognitive limitations, communication methods, motivation and work. For instance, in supplier-buyer relations a buyer may evaluate the goodness of a contract according to the perceived equity of the distribution of the gains of a contract, whereby the traditional assumption both in neoclassical economics and in OM is that parties will engage in a contract provided it is mutually advantageous. Finally, Reactions refer to the human players' response to model parameter changes and include learning processes, responses to feedback, and perceptions of game changes. In traditional modelling response to a parameter change is static. For instance, when the probability distribution on an adverse event (say, a stock-out in inventory management) is known, the realization of that event should not change the decision maker's response to that risk. However, if managers act on the basis of the Representativeness heuristic (Tversky and Kahneman, 1974), they may overestimate the representativeness of a piece of information and draw inaccurate conclusions, thus over-reacting to the stock-out or disruption by over-ordering in the following periods.

Another way to classify behavioural effects from a different angle is provided by Mantel et al. (2006). Whereas Bendoly et al. (2006) focus on the behavioural hypotheses underlying modelling, Mantel et al. (2006) identify the possible causes of behaviour affected by psychophysical components, i.e. the sources of Bendoly et al.'s (2006) Actions and Reactions. These are classified in Personal Characteristics of the decision maker, Task, and Context. Personal characteristics include motivation, personal relevance, mood, and expertise that can influence the decision-making process. Task effects refer to perceived changes in the complexity of the task (e.g. number of alternatives considered, time pressure), or in the presentation of the task (e.g. information formality and presentation) to the decision maker, or to the type of response needed (a choice versus a valuation). Context effects concern the way in which the task relates to itself or to the environment (framing effects, reference points, group versus individual-level decisions).

Both frameworks provide useful perspectives for the study of behavioural effects in OM. Bendoly et al.'s (2006) approach highlights the impact of mismatches between prescriptive and descriptive models, thus pinpointing the consequences of ignoring behavioural effects. Mantel et al.'s (2006) identification of sources provides suggestions on how it is necessary to intervene (through training, communication, task design, etc.) in order to design systems robust to heuristics and biases.

According to Bendoly et al. (2010), behavioural OM draws from four separate bodies of research, namely cognitive psychology, social psychology, group dynamics, and system dynamics. Distinctions among these bodies of knowledge can be summarized by their typical unit of analysis (the individual in cognitive and social psychology, the individual and groups in group dynamics, and the group and the organization in system dynamics) and by their "preferred" methodologies (experimentation for individual level investigation, simulation for system dynamics, and surveys and case-studies for group and organizational level research).

While process modelling remains a prerequisite of any behavioural analysis of OM and SC management, the adoption of diverse approaches for empirical analysis has recently been advocated (Boyer and Swink, 2008). Whereas surveys, case studies, and simulation are well established methodologies of analysis in OM, only recently controlled human experiments have been acknowledged as an appropriate methodology for the collection of primary data in management and operations (Bendoly et al., 2006). The main advantage of controlled experiments is a high degree of internal validity, which is achieved by controlling the number of factors that may explain the relation between dependent variables and potential explanatory variables. There are several respects in which human experiments can inform OM as to the relevance of behavioural factors (Croson and Donohue, 2002): (i) by studying behavioural factors, keeping operational ones constant; (ii) by studying operational and organizational factors; (iii) by studying the interaction between operational and behavioural factors. Finally, experimentation provides a valuable instrument for observing choices and valuations in an incentive-compatible fashion, which adds reliability and validity to these measures with respect to standard survey methodologies.

BEHAVIOURAL ANALYSES OF SUPPLY CHAIN MANAGEMENT

Supply chain management is an example of a dynamic decision task that involves lagged feedbacks and multiple dependent decision makers. This task is known to be difficult for several reasons. According to Sterman (1989), when decisions have indirect and delayed feedback effects decision makers find it difficult to control the dynamics. Moreover, multiple agents are involved in the process, whose performance depends on the quality of other supply chain members' decisions, and therefore it is subject to coordination risk that may trigger instabilities in the system (Croson et al., 2005).

Research addressing SC management (SCM) from a behavioural perspective is still limited, though growing rapidly. Most of the extant studies are controlled human experiments studying ordering behaviour by means of well-known business games, such as the beer game (Forrester, 1958) and the newsvendor problem (Arrow et al., 1951). Little attention has been paid so far to SC risk issues, although this is one of the areas of SC management where the behavioural approach seems to be most promising, as the following sections will try to argue.

Before proceeding to the identification of behavioural assumptions that may contribute to explain observed behaviour and outcomes in SC risk management, we consider it useful to briefly present extant research in the wider perspective of SCM. Our aim is twofold: first to pinpoint topics in SCM research where behavioural studies are developing fastest, and second to explore whether results of these studies have implications that carry over to SC risk management.

Beer game experiments reproduce the ordering decisions of a four-echelon SC (retailer, wholesaler, distributor, and factory). In each period of the game (typically a week) buyers in each echelon decide how much to order from their immediate supplier in order to satisfy the orders placed from their immediate downstream customer. The bullwhip effect is a well-known empirical regularity that arises in the context of the beer game. The effect is described by the presence of oscillation of orders at each of the echelons, with oscillations amplified as one moves upward the SC. Operational causes of the bullwhip effect have typically been identified in demand signalling, inventory rationing, order batching, and price fluctuations (Sterman, 1989).

Beer-game human experiments have investigated the role of behavioural components in explaining SC instability (Croson and Donohue, 2002). Although these experiments are not directly related to SC risk management, they represent a powerful illustration of how a simple operational risk, such as lack of complete information about external demand, may trigger substantial SC volatility and sub-optimal performance, especially in a non-integrated SC.

Sterman (1989) posited that the bullwhip effect is attributable to the fact that players in the SC fail to account for the supply line. Thus, players tend to ignore that there are shipments in transit from one period to the next, due to non-zero lead times. By controlling for the four operational causes of the bullwhip effect, Croson and Donohue (2006) show that the bullwhip effect is resilient to this control, thus lending support to Sterman's hypothesis that behavioural factors (interpretable as cognitive deficiencies) are important in determining order fluctuations. Ancarani et al. (2010) show that order instability is further enhanced when risk within the SC has not only a downstream component (external demand) but also an upstream one, namely stochastic lead times.

Another issue that has been explored in beer game experiments is the impact of the type and degree of information about the SC and of the learning process of the actors involved on SC performance. For instance, Croson and Donohue (2003) study the impact of Point of Sale (PoS) data sharing and find that information sharing mitigates the bullwhip effect by reducing the oscillations of orders of upstream members. Similar results are obtained by Steckel et al. (2004). Gupta et al. (2002) study the beer game under three different demand scenarios (a step-up function, a S-shaped function, and a S-shaped plus error function) and show that PoS information results in improved performance only in the simplest scenario (the step-up demand). Machuca and Barajas (2004) find that significant savings can accrue from the implementation of an electronic data interchange (EDI) across the entire supply chain. Cantor and Macdonald (2009) show that information availability about the supply line (local vs. system-wide) interacts with the problem-solving approach (abstract/flexible rules versus concrete/fixed rules) in determining the performance of the supply chain. Their results suggest that individuals who adopt an abstract problem-solving approach perform better than individuals who adopt concrete problem-solving in settings where information available is local. No relevant difference exists when information is system wide. Wu and Katok (2006) study the effect of learning-by-doing on SC performance and find that experience of the game significantly reduces the bullwhip effect only when it is "system wide", i.e. it concerns the whole structure of the game, whereas ambiguous effects are reported when role specific experience is given to participants in the experiment. The implication is that training (i.e. repetition of the task) may improve individuals' knowledge and understanding of the system. However, it does not improve SC performance unless supply chain partners are allowed to communicate and coordinate through knowledge sharing.

In the newsvendor model, an agent decides the optimal amount of inventory each day. This decision has to be taken prior to the realization of demand. The marginal cost of acquiring each item and the selling price are constant and known. If the newsvendor runs out of inventory, he/she loses the expected profits from sales. Inventory in excess of demand might be sold for a salvage price, which in any case is lower than the marginal cost, and thus gives rise to losses on unsold units.

In the context of the newsvendor problem, Schweitzer and Cachon (2000) look for possible behavioural explanations of the observed pattern of orders whereby too much of low-profit products and too little of high-profit products is ordered. They find that this pattern is consistent with decision makers trying to minimize the gap between the quantities ordered and realized demand and with the anchoring and adjustment heuristic. This heuristic (Einhorn and Hogarth, 1985) implies that the decision maker anchors on a specific value, e.g. mean demand or prior orders, and then adjusts away from it. Bolton and Katok (2008) find evidence of a "law of small number" bias, whereby decision makers tend to take ordering decisions on the basis of too small samples (Tversky and Kahneman, 1971).

The effect of learning-by-doing has also been explored in the context of the newsvendor problem. Bolton and Katok (2008) find that knowledge gained through personal experience leads to a significant improvement in performance. Similarly, Ben-Zion *et al.* (2008) find that game experience is important in improving profits and leads to stationary orders. Although in the earlier stages of the game orders exhibited a bias towards mean demand, this effect was significantly reduced as the game unfolded. Bostian*et al.* (2008) test and find evidence in favor of a learning model with recency effects, i.e. in which subjects respond to recent gains and losses, and inertia. This model adds to previous studies since it incorporates demand chasing in a framework where expected payoffs also matter. Finally, Bolton et al. (2008), comparing the ordering behavior of students at different level of education with that of expert procurement managers, find the anchoring bias toward average demand is observable whatever the level of experience the subjects have. Rather than professional experience, it is the exposure to varying levels of information and task training that has a significant effect on performance.

A highly relevant area of SC research that has just started to be explored by behaviourally oriented research is contracting. Ho and Zhang (2008) study whether the loss-aversion model can explain "anomalies" in an empirical study of coordinating contracts. In this model, a buyer facing a two-part tariff frames the upfront payment as a loss (a negative change from the *status quo*) and frames the subsequent profit as a gain. The study shows that the introduction of fixed fee contracts fails to bring about higher efficiency with reference to a quantity discount contract. Katok and Wu (2009) find that, because of the anchoring and adjustment bias, buy-back contracts and revenue sharing contracts fail to achieve full efficiency. Whereas the above two studies focus on the impact of cognitive biases on contract efficiency, other experiments have explored the impact of social motives on behaviour in contract settings. Narasimhan et al. (2009) study how trust builds in lock-in situations, by means of an experiment in which pricing policies by suppliers and investment policies by buyers can act as signals for the promotion of long-term relationships. The authors use Social Exchange Theory (SET) (Blau, 1964) to derive the prediction that, in time, prices set by suppliers decline to signal intention to forego opportunistic profits and, likewise, investment by buyers in the diversification of supply falls. The experimental results support the predictions of SET. Loch and Wu (2008) develop a supply chain transaction model in which the partners care about each others' payoffs and have social preferences for status and reciprocation. A test of the model through a controlled experiment Shows that participants consistently deviate from self-interested profit-maximizing behaviour in all experimental treatments (that simulated different degrees of relationships). In particular, results suggest that a perceived relationship can induce collaborative behaviour and enhance performance with respect to perceived competition.

BEHAVIOURAL ISSUES IN SUPPLY CHAIN RISK MANAGEMENT

Issues at Hand

Understanding the psychological and social dimensions of risk taking is crucial in several respects. First, because by identifying biases in risk taking, these same biases can be taken account of or removed from decision making, i.e. SC managers can learn how to deal with risk (Croson and Donohue, 2006). Second, knowing supply chain managers' mental models can be used to appropriately design institutions, information systems, and incentive schemes (Sterman, 2006).

The experimental research on supply chains reported above only marginally makes inroads into SC risk management. In particular, in newsvendor and beer game experiments built-in risk is only represented by stochastic external demand, and supply risk stems from stock-outs caused by insufficient ordering by upstream suppliers.

In what follows, we shall draw examples from some well-established regularities in judgement and choice, either arising in individual decision making settings, or in relationships, with the aim to identify their potential implications for SC risk valuation and management. In particular, we shall discuss the implications for supply chain risk management of some features of Kahneman and Tversky (1979) Prospect Theory, such as probability weighting and reference point dependence. Next, we shall discuss the implications of uncertainty aversion, hyperbolic discounting, and overconfidence. Finally, we point out to the importance of trust and reciprocity in SC risk management.

Clearly, this list of deviations from the standard economic model is far from being exhaustive. A far larger discussion would to be needed to cover all topics relevant in supply chain risk management. The reader is referred to some recent surveys and methodological contributions to the field of behavioural OM (Carter et al., 2007; Loch and Wu, 2008; Gino and Pisano, 2008; Bendoly et al., 2010). The selection of behavioural assumptions presented has been guided by their potential relevance for explaining regularities in SC risk management that may be considered at odds with the standard OM theory. Our aim is to identify what are the relevant biases and what opportunities lay ahead to provide suggestions for the development of a theory of SC risk management that is robust to behavioural effects.

Risk Perception

There is plenty of empirical evidence suggesting that the view of perceived risk as a multiplicative combination of probability and magnitude of loss is misguided in managerial settings. Early work by March and Shapira (1987) shows that managers pay more attention to the size of loss than to its probability, while Yates and Stone (1992) argue that decision making under risk is a two stage process: in the first stage magnitude and probability of loss drive the overall perception of risk, in the second this overall perception determines choice. The latter model is supported by Ellis et al. (2010) who examine buyers' search for alternate suppliers, and show that both probability and magnitude of risk contribute to explain the overall subjective perception of the risk of disruption. Similarly, Mantel et al. (2006) show that the likelihood to outsource is strongly influenced by the perception of strategic vulnerability, defined as the level of risk associated to a given supplier alternative. According to their findings, perceived strategic vulnerability has greater influence than core competency on make-or-buy decisions, while information formality has a moderating role when strategic vulnerability and core competency conditions are mixed (high and low).

The above mentioned literature does not explain clearly how probability and magnitude of loss combine to yield an overall risk perception. Feeding on the results of psychological experiments, Prospect Theory provides an answer that implies two radical departures from standard theory. The first is that losses and gains are evaluated with respect to a subjective reference point. The second is that even when probabilities of outcomes are objectively known, the decision maker can weight them in a non-linear fashion. Thus, the overall perception of risk stems from the product of a probability weight and a value function.

These hypotheses can explain why decision makers often violate the principle of risk aversion (Cohen et al., 1985; Tverky and Fox, 1995; Di Mauro and Maffioletti, 2004, among others), i.e., why they are averse to risk for some ranges of pay-offs and of probabilities while risk loving for others. In particular, Prospect Theory predicts a fourfold pattern of risk attitudes (reflection effect): risk aversion for gains and risk seeking for losses at high probability, and risk seeking for gains and risk aversion for losses at low probability (Tversky and Wakker, 1995).

Risk seeking for high-probability losses is consistent with the tendency to undertake risk in order to avoid a sure loss. In fact, it implies that decision makers are more willing to risk a larger loss in exchange for the possibility that no loss will occur. In contrast, they are more likely to choose to accept the smaller sure gain rather than the possibility of a larger gain. Another implication of the reflection effect is that, if the likelihood of a disruption is perceived to be low, then the managers' willingness to invest in mitigation measures will be higher than the expected value of the loss that follows from the disruption. However, as the probability of loss increases, willingness to pay to protect against the loss will not increase proportionally. This pattern may explain why in spite of the fact that the perception of the risk of a major supply chain disruption on a global scale has increased among managers in the last decade, plans to mitigate the risk have lagged behind (Thun and Hoenig, in press).

Harrison et al. (2009) analyse supplier selection as a decision problem under risk, and examine the impact of a purchasing manager's risk attitude on final outcomes. Their experiment shows that managers are risk averse below a fixed reference point and risk seeking for pay offs above the reference point. No evidence is found of probability weighting. These results carry interesting implications for the choice of the purchasing budget: if the budget acts as a reference point, a high budget induces risk seeking behaviour while a low budget induces risk adverse behaviour.

Uncertainty Aversion

When decisions occur in the presence of vague or unknown probabilities of outcomes (usually defined uncertainty, as opposed to risk in which probabilities are objectively known), people tend to over-weight those outcomes whose probabilities are unknown or vague, thus displaying a behaviour known as uncertainty or ambiguity aversion.

The paradigmatic example of ambiguity aversion is Ellsberg's two-colour experiment (Ellsberg, 1961). Confronted with an urn containing 100 red and black balls in a ratio totally unknown to the decision maker (the ambiguous urn), and an urn with 50 red and 50 black balls (the risky urn), the decision maker prefers to bet on the latter whatever the colour. The Author defines ambiguity as "a quality depending on the type, amount, reliability and "unanimity" of information, and giving rise to one's degree of "confidence" in an estimate of relative likelihoods"(p. 657).

Frisch and Baron (1988) ascribe ambiguity aversion to the fact that the decision maker lacks the knowledge about some aspects of the stochastic structure of a problem that are unknown but could be known. Other authors have posited that reaction to ambiguity is part of a more general phenomenon that has been called source dependence. Preferences depend not only on the degree of uncertainty but also on the source of uncertainty (Tversky and Wakker, 1995). Heath and Tversky (1991) tie preference for one source of uncertainty to perceived competence about that source. Fox and Tversky (1995) find that the feeling of perceived competence may be enhanced by choice/valuation in a comparative setting in which the decision maker is made to feel more knowledgeable about one source than about another.

The psychological literature discussed above shows that the feeling of ambiguity is tied both to the source of information (e.g. formal vs. informal, perceived reliability) and to the amount of information (e.g. perceived sufficiency). Since the typical reaction to ambiguity is aversion (Camerer and Weber, 1992), this implies that SC managers may be willing to face higher costs in order to avoid ambiguous options. Mantel et al. (2006) offer evidence that the decision to outsource depends on the source, formality, and perceived sufficiency of the information the decision maker possesses about the potential suppliers.

Another implication of the uncertainty aversion literature is that the lower the amount of information and the less reliable, the more supply risk is perceived as ambiguous, and the more supply chain managers will respond to risk in chaotic fashions, leading to higher SC costs. Several models have underlined the role that uncertainty plays in affecting the performance of the supply chain. For instance, the literature on stochastic lead-times shows that the higher the variability of lead-times, the higher the cost of the supply chain, since managers facing uncertainty in orders shipping inflate inventories in order to avoid stock-out costs (Song, 1994; Chatfield et al., 2004; Kim et al., 2006).

Hyperbolic Discounting

When the outcomes of decision making take place over time, the standard assumption is that decision maker's trade off inter-temporal costs and benefits by a constant discount rate. Widely used formal decision methods, such as dynamic programming, build on the discounted utility framework that assumes that the decision maker has an exponentially discounted utility, with a constant discount factor. However, several studies have reported evidence that the discount rate declines over time, a phenomenon known as hyperbolic discounting (Camerer and Loewenstein, 2003; Ho et al., 2006; Della Vigna and Malmendier, 2006). Hyperbolic discounting arises from the fact that immediate costs and benefits are more salient than future ones, thus leading people to make "short-sighted" decisions that generate high immediate satisfaction but low long-term benefits (Loch and Wu, 2008b).

International supply network design is one area of SCM in which hyperbolic discounting may provide an explanation for the fact that firms are inter-temporally inconsistent in their choices. In fact, when firms decide whether to make or buy a product or a component, one of the most important decision criteria is the cost of the product. This means that an immediate expense reduction can induce managers to outsource the production to countries where costs are lower (labour, raw materials, etc.) because cost-savings in the short term are more salient (Nassimbeni and Sartor, 2006; Kremic et al., 2006). However, in the long-term it is possible that the disutility initially assigned to other costs (quality, supplier reliability, cultural issues, etc.) is revised, and this might lead to a reversal of the original outsourcing decision. Veltri et al. (2008) provide evidence that back-sourcing of information systems is driven by several reasons, among which overestimation of cost savings is one of the most important.

Over-Confidence

Overconfident individuals tend to believe that their information or their estimates are more accurate than they actually are, or that they hold superior skills than average (Moore and Healy, 2008). The concept of over-confidence is an umbrella under which two main psychological effects gather together, namely over-precision and over-estimation. Precisely, overconfidence as over-precision is used to refer to a subject's under-estimation of the variance of a relevant measure affecting performance (demand, costs, etc.). In some studies, when asked to state a 90 percent confidence interval for an uncertain variable, participants provide estimates in which the percentage of true values that fall outside the confidence interval are significantly higher than 10, thus suggesting that estimates are mis-calibrated. Conversely, the term over-estimation applies when the decision maker considers that either his skills or positive personality attributes are higher than average, or expresses unreasonable optimism about his chances of success (Glaser and Weber, 2003). While some studies have used proxies of overconfidence such as gender and past profits (Barber and Odean, 2001; Malmendier and Tate, 2005), others have measured over-confidence directly (Biais et al., 2005), and have provided evidence that different measures of over-confidence tend to be correlated (Glaser and Weber, 2003). What drives overconfident behaviour? Hilary and Menzly (2006) indicate that after making a short series of accurate predictions, financial analysts are more likely to be inaccurate than their skill and environment would predict. This suggests that overconfidence may be driven by experience rather than by lack of knowledge of the problem at hand.

The importance of over-confidence for management is that it has been shown to be a significant explanation of behaviour of traders in the stock market (Odean, 1998) and in other managerial settings (Malmendier and Tate, 2005), and its relevance for OM has been acknowledged (Bendoly et al., 2010).

Overconfidence may affect supply chain risk management both in the valuation phase and in the choice of risk mitigation strategies. In the valuation phase, over-confidence leads to risk under-estimation, whereby the decision maker believes that severe disruptions are less likely they actually are (miscalibration), that they can be managed ex post (illusion of control), and that he will do this better than competitors (better than average effect). The fact that in experimental studies alternative measures of overconfidence tend to be correlated, suggests the decision maker is bound to fall prone to all three. In terms of risk mitigation strategies, this entails that both supplier relationships and inventory management may be affected. If overconfidence is interpreted as over-precision (Moore and Healy, 2008), it may lead managers to under-estimate the variance of demand or of lead-time, thus inducing them to hold too little safety stock (Bendoly et al., 2010). Croson et al. (2008) develop a theoretical model that shows that overconfident newsvendors place suboptimal orders (which can be either higher or lower than optimal quantities) and earn lower profits than well-calibrated newsvendors. In particular, in high-profit industries, overconfident agents are likely to order fewer inventories than is optimal. In this case, the implication for contract design is that managers will be able to correct this biased behaviour by either increasing the salvage value of the good traded, or decreasing the marginal cost. In low-profit industries, overconfident agents are likely to order more inventory than is optimal. This biased behaviour can be corrected by decreasing the salvage value or increasing the marginal costs.

Overconfidence as overestimation of one's own abilities and skills may lead buyers to design their supplier network with a very limited supply-base, or to forego the use of appropriate procedures in the selection, evaluation and monitoring of external sources.

Social Preferences

Research in the social sciences has shown that individuals consistently deviate from rational behaviour not only because of cognitive biases but also because they hold social preferences, and that these preferences may be as important as incentives in affecting their behaviour in economic settings. Reciprocity, fairness, and trust are among the most studied facets of social considerations.

Reciprocity means that in response to friendly actions, individuals are more cooperative than predicted by the self-interest model. Conversely, they respond to self-interested or hostile actions by the same token (Fehr and Gachter, 2000; Fehr and Schmidt, 1999; Bolton and Ockenfels, 2000). Reciprocal responses take place even in the absence of present or future gains and even when they entail costs. The most well-known example of the pervasiveness of reciprocity comes from the so called ultimatum game. Consider two parties, A and B, who have to agree on the division of a fixed sum of money. A makes just one proposal on how to divide the amount. B can accept or reject the proposal. If B rejects, both receive nothing; if B accepts, the proposal is implemented. When A offers B less than 30% of the total sum, the frequency of rejections is very high. The feeling that the exchange is unfair leads to its rejection in spite of its being mutually advantageous.

There is strong evidence suggesting that reciprocity acts as a contract enforcement device. Reciprocity pushes opportunistic players to act cooperatively. For example, Fehr et al. (1997) show that even purely selfish employers make a generous job offer, if they expect sufficiently many workers to behave reciprocally. Similarly, even potentially shirking employees may provide a high effort in the expectation of a reward/punishment by the employer.

The literature on reciprocity is conceptually linked to the Organizational Behavioural literature on Distributive Justice and Procedural Justice, which is mainly applied to intra-firm relations and to supervisor-subordinate relationships (Colquitt, 2001). However, reciprocity is a wider concept that can be applied also to inter-firm relations, as it is the case for SC management. For example, cooperative purchasing is becoming more and more common practice. However, many cooperative initiatives end prematurely or do not thrive. Several studies have suggested that these problems may be related to the unfair allocation of gains (Xu&Beamon, 2006; Schotanus et al., 2008).

Evidence of the relevance of reciprocity in SC relationships is provided by Keser and Paleologo (2004) who study the performance of wholesale contracts by means of a controlled experiment. These contracts are akin to an ultimatum game: the supplier proposes the wholesale price and, thus, determines how the total profit will be distributed. However, he has to fear rejection or very low orders from the retailer. Results of the experiments show that the suppliers tend to offer wholesale prices that lead to an equitable distribution of profits, thus confirming the predictions of models of inequality aversion.

Interestingly, the impact of reciprocity has been found also in trust games (for example, McCabe et al., 1996), and not only in situations in which feelings of inequality aversion may arise. In a typical trust game, an individual A can send a chosen amount to another individual, B. The experimenter then triples the amount sent and B is free to return to A any proportion of the sum received. The modal response is that both A and B send money and the exchange is positively correlated with the initial amount of money sent by A. In SC management Ireland and Webb (2007) point out that although a fair distribution may not be necessary for trust to remain as a dominant characteristic of a supply chain's operations, allocating savings in a proportion that is consistent with partners' inputs enhances the feeling of trust.

Loch and Wu (2008a) build an experimental game between wholesaler and retailer in which the two agents choose their profit margins. By manipulating the level of relationship (no interaction/verbal interaction), they find that more salient relationships lead to lower prices, thus suggesting that participants pursue social motives and not only economic ones.

How can reciprocal relations aid supply risk management? Reciprocation may act as a counter factor for SC risk if it reduces the opportunistic tendencies of trading partners. In addition, given the interplay between reciprocity and trust, other benefits may arise from the reduction of inventory and logistics costs. When buyers consider their suppliers unreliable, they may order stock so as to have sufficient inventory to fulfil key-customers' demand. These inventory buffers then serve to further obscure supply chain visibility because the end-to-end pipeline is now longer as a result of the build-up of inventory (Mantel et al., 2006). From this it follows that trust may reduce chaos and costs in SC management.

We believe that social preferences in contract and network design are bound to become hot topics in SC research. Although the issues of trust, fairness, and reciprocity among the members of a SC network have received ample consideration in traditional SC literature, behavioural studies can provide new insights into the interplay among such issues. In particular, through controlled human experiments, it is possible to manipulate the degrees of reciprocity and relationship, and explore their impact on firm's behaviour, while isolating them from operational aspects.

SOLUTIONS AND RECOMMENDATIONS FOR SUPPLY CHAIN INNOVATION

In this chapter some of the main deviations from the standard model of behaviour have been identified along with their possible impact on SC risk evaluation and planning of mitigations actions. These deviations may consist of either irrational biases, or heuristics, or of other-regarding preferences that modify the objective functions of decision makers. The literature on the potential impact of deviations from rationality on SC risk management is far from being complete, and thus it is crucial to begin a systematic research effort aimed at building formal models that incorporate the presence of such deviations.

Field and experimental studies are crucial in order to put behaviourally based models to test. Empirical analysis may help disentangle biases and heuristics that are actually relevant for SC risk management from those that may hold in different areas of behaviour. This is not a negligible contribution since different biases may push risk management in different directions, for instance leading to insufficient risk planning (over-confidence) or to unnecessary costs in risk mitigation (ambiguity aversion).

To date, most behaviourally oriented OM research has focused on the consequences for operation systems of ignoring behavioural influences. While more research effort is needed in this direction, however significant practical contributions towards the innovation of the SC management will derive from the design of systems robust to heuristics and biases or to the presence of social preferences.

Hence, evidence of an impact of heuristics and biases on the performance of the SC must form the bases for the necessary de-biasing (Mantel et al., 2006). One way to minimise the impact of a behavioural bias may be simply to call attention to it. For example, we know that individuals evaluate outcomes on the basis of reference points. In this case the de-biasing process requires that the decision maker is told to consider carrying out a sort of sensitivity analysis, simulating the impact of alternative reference points.

The practical relevance of behavioural studies may carry over to innovative recruiting practises. Should empirical research prove that the actual managers' behaviour when facing risk reflects the impact of a single overarching deviation, personnel selection could take into account the psychological characteristics required for specific tasks and positions.

FUTURE RESEARCH DIRECTIONS

Behavioural studies generally isolate the effect of a single bias/heuristic on behaviour. However, individuals exhibit complex personalities, experiences, and attitudes that affect their behaviour. Thus, it is important to explore whether interactions exist among different biases and to identify their joint impact. This is a missing link in the literature that is particularly important in SC risk management since scenarios may be envisaged in which these joint effects lead to poor performance. For example, the choice to outsource the operations to low cost countries may be driven also by a combination of hyperbolic discounting, overconfidence, and low risk aversion, as suggested by the literature on back sourcing (Nassimbeni and Sartor, 2006; Kremic et al., 2006). A few empirical studies have addressed the problems of supply chain disruption risk and vulnerability, highlighting the need to explore the interplay between type and degree of information, perceived competence and perceived risk (Mantel et al., 2006; Ellis et al., 2010).

Next, it is important to ascertain how behavioural issues are affected by contextual factors, such as logistic issues, country-specific issues, and the ownership situation. One intuitive consequence for SC management of this interplay may be that these factors determine the reference point with respect to which gains and losses of a decision are calculated.

The final step of the research agenda is contract and systems redesign, "to either counter-act or at least provide accountability and adjustability for behavioural causes" (Bendoly et al., 2010). For instance, Croson et al. (2008) design a contract that may be used to incentivize overconfident newsvendors by means of the adjustment of either the salvage value or of the marginal cost facing the newsvendor.

The provision of answers to the research questions already raised in literature and summarized in this chapter will enrich OM theory, but also will suggest ways to effectively innovate the management of the supply chain.

CONCLUSION

There are multiple sources of supply chain risk: environmental, supply, and demand driven (Juttner (2005). Currently, the interplay of these sources makes supply chains increasingly complex and vulnerable both to normal operational risks and to major disruptions. Although formal models offer recipes for counterbalancing risks, there is plain evidence that both pro-active and reactive responses to risk (i.e. risk mitigations strategies and/or design of robust supply chain) are either chaotic, thus leading to unnecessary costs, or characterised by inertia, as in the case in which firms are slow to respond to unexpected risks.

Further, trends towards leaner supply chains have taken place at the cost of increased vulnerability due to fewer buffers. Since lean supply chains reduce the margin for human errors, it is more likely that severe disruptions occur as consequences of those errors.

One reason underlying such diverse,erratic and often ineffective responses is that the task to govern this system is assigned to bounded rational humans who must respond to continuous changes in incentives, information availability, and environmental parameters. Even when objective data is available to support rational decision-making, the subjective interpretation may bias the risk assessment process, due to imperfect perceptions. Subjective risk perceptions influence pro-active responses to potential and re-active responses to failures.

Innovative approaches that include behavioural analysis in supply chain design and management can significantly contribute to SC risk reduction by taking into account the individual attitudes and biases of the decision maker.

REFERENCES

Ancarani, A., Di Mauro, C., & D'Urso, D. (2010). A controlled human experiment of supply chain reaction to uncertainty in lead times. In J. Hallikas, A-K. Kähkönen, K. Lintukangas & V.M.Virolainen (Eds.), *Proceedings of the 19th Annual IPSERA Conference:* (pp. 517-529), Lappeenranta, Finland.

Anderson, E., Fine, C., & Parker, G. (2000). Upstream volatility in the supply chain: the machine tool industry as a case study. *Production and Operations Management, 9*(3), 239–261. doi:10.1111/j.1937-5956.2000.tb00136.x

Arrow, K. J., Harris, T., & Marschak, J. (1951). Optimal Inventory Policy. *Econometrica, 19*(3), 250–272. doi:10.2307/1906813

Atkinson, W. (2006). Supply Chain Management: New Opportunities for Risk Managers. *Risk Management*, Thursday, June 1, New York.

Baird, I. S., & Thomas, H. (1990). What is risk anyway? In Bettis, R. A., & Thomas, H. (Eds.), *Risk, strategy, and management* (pp. 21–52). London: JAI Press.

Banerjee, A. V. (1992). A simple model of herd behaviour. *The Quarterly Journal of Economics, 107*(3), 797–817. doi:10.2307/2118364

Barber, B., & Odean, T. (2001). Boys will be Boys: Gender, Overconfidence, and Common Stock Investment. *The Quarterly Journal of Economics, 116*(1), 261–292. doi:10.1162/003355301556400

Barnes, P., & Oloruntoba, R. (2005). Assurance of security in maritime supply chains: conceptual issues of vulnerability and crisis management. *Journal of International Management, 11*(4), 519–540. doi:10.1016/j.intman.2005.09.008

Ben-Zion, U., Cohen, Y., Peled, R., & Shavit, T. (2008). Decision-making and the Newsvendor Problem: An Experimental Study. *The Journal of the Operational Research Society, 59*(9), 1281–1287. doi:10.1057/palgrave.jors.2602470

Bendoly, E., Croson, R., Goncalves, P., & Schultz, K. (2010). Bodies of knowledge for research in behavioral operations. Production and Operations Management. *Journal of Operations Management, 19*(4), 434–452.

Bendoly, E., Croson, R., Goncalves, P., & Schultz, K. (2010). Bodies of knowledge for research in behavioral operations. *Production and Operations Management, 19*(4), 434–452. doi:10.1111/j.1937-5956.2009.01108.x

Bendoly, E., Donohue, E., & Schultz, K. L. (2006). Behaviour in operations management: assessing recent findings and revisiting old assumptions. *Journal of Operations Management, 24*(6), 737–752. doi:10.1016/j.jom.2005.10.001

Biais, B., Hilton, D., Mazurier, K., & Pouget, S. (2005). Judgemental Overconfidence, Self-Monitoring, and Trading Performance in an Experimental Financial Market. *The Review of Economic Studies, 72*(2), 287–312. doi:10.1111/j.1467-937X.2005.00333.x

Blaikie, P., Cannon, T., Davis, I., & Wisner, B. (1994). *At risk: natural hazards, people's vulnerability, and disasters*. London: Routledge.

Blau, P. (1964). *Exchange and Power in Social Life*. New York: Wiley.

Bolton, G. E., & Katok, E. (2008). Learning by Doing in the Newsvendor Problem: A Laboratory Investigation of the Role of Experience and Feedback. *Manufacturing & Service Operations Management, 10*(3), 519–538. doi:10.1287/msom.1060.0190

Bolton, G. E., & Ockenfels, A. (2000). ERC: a theory of equity, reciprocity and competition. *The American Economic Review*, *90*, 166–193. doi:10.1257/aer.90.1.166

Bolton, G. E., & Ockenfels, A. &Thonemann, U. (2008). *Managers and students as newsvendors: How out-of-task experience matters*. Working Paper No.39, University of Cologne, Working paper series in Economics.

Bostian, A. J. A., Holt, C. A., & Smith, A. M. (2008). Newsverndor "Pull-to-Center" Effect: Adaptive Learning in a Laboratory Experiment. *Manufacturing & Service OperationsManagement*, *10*(4), 590–608. doi:10.1287/msom.1080.0228

Boudreau, J., Hopp, W., McClain, J. O., & Thomas, L. J. (2003). On the interface between operations and human resource management. *Manufacturing and Service Operations Management*, *5*(3), 179–202. doi:10.1287/msom.5.3.179.16032

Boyer, K. K., & Swink, M. L. (2008). Empirical elephants—why multiple methods are essential to quality research in operations and supply chain management. *Journal of Operations Management*, *26*(3), 338–344. doi:10.1016/j.jom.2008.03.002

Camerer, C., & Loewenstein, G. (2003). Behavioral economics: past, present, future. In Camerer, C., Loewenstein, G., & Rabin, M. (Eds.), *Advances in Behavioural Economics* (pp. 3–52). Princeton, NJ: Princeton University Press.

Camerer, C. F., & Malmendier, U. (2007). Behaviour of economics of organizations. In Diamond, P., & Vartiainen, H. (Eds.), *Behavioral economics and its applications* (pp. 235–290). Princeton, NJ: Princeton, University Press.

Camerer, C. F., & Weber, M. (1992). Recent development in modeling preferences: Uncertainty and ambiguity. *Journal of Risk and Uncertainty*, *5*(4), 325–370. doi:10.1007/BF00122575

Cantor, D. E., & Macdonald, J. R. (2009). Decision-making in the supply chain: examining problem solving approaches and information availability. *Journal of Operations Management*, *27*(3), 220–232. doi:10.1016/j.jom.2008.09.002

Carter, C. R., Kaufmannn, L., & Michel, A. (2007). Behavioral supply management: a taxonomy of judgment and decision-making biases. *International Journal of Physical Distribution & Logistics Management*, *37*(8), 631–669. doi:10.1108/09600030710825694

Cavinato, J. L. (2004). Supply chain logistics risks: from the back room to the board room. *International Journal of Physical Distribution & Logistics Management*, *34*(5), 383–387. doi:10.1108/09600030410545427

Chatfield, D. C., Kim, J. G., Harrison, T. P., & Hayya, J. C. (2004). The bullwhip effect—impact of stochastic lead time, information quality, and information sharing: a simulation study. *Production and Operations Management*, *13*(4), 340–353. doi:10.1111/j.1937-5956.2004.tb00222.x

Childerhouse, P., & Towill, D. R. (2003). Simplified material flow holds the key to supply chain integration. *Omega*, *31*(1), 17–27. doi:10.1016/S0305-0483(02)00062-2

Choi, T. Y., & Krause, D. R. (2006). The supply base and its complexity: implications for transaction costs, risks, responsiveness, and innovation. *Journal of Operations Management*, *24*(5), 637–652. doi:10.1016/j.jom.2005.07.002

Chopra, S., Reinhardt, G., & Mohan, U. (2007). The importance of decoupling recurrent and disruption risks in a supply chain. *Naval Research Logistics*, *54*(5), 1–13. doi:10.1002/nav.20228

Chopra, S., & Sodhi, M. S. (2004). Managing risk to avoid supply-chain breakdown. *MIT Sloan Management Review*, *46*(1), 53–62.

Christopher, M., & Peck, H. (2004). Building the resilient supply chain. *International Journal of Logistics Management*, *15*(2), 1–13. doi:10.1108/09574090410700275

Cohen, M., Jaffray, J. Y., & Said, T. (1985). Individual behavior under risk and under uncertainty: An experimental study. *Theory and Decision*, *18*(2), 203–228. doi:10.1007/BF00134074

Colquitt, J. A. (2001). On the dimensionality of organizational justice: a construct validation of a measure. *The Journal of Applied Psychology*, *86*(3), 386–400. doi:10.1037/0021-9010.86.3.386

Craighead, C. W., Blackhurst, J., Rungtusanatham, M. J., & Handfield, R. B. (2007). The severity of supply chain disruptions: design characteristics and mitigation capabilities. *Decision Sciences*, *38*(1), 131–156. doi:10.1111/j.1540-5915.2007.00151.x

Croson, D., & Croson, R. &Ren, Y. (2008). How to manage an overconfident newsvendor. Working paper, Cox School of Business, Southern Methodist University, Dallas, TX 75275, USA.

Croson, R., & Donohue, K. (2002). Experimental economics and supply chain management. *Interface*, *32*(5), 74–82. doi:10.1287/inte.32.5.74.37

Croson, R., & Donohue, K. (2003). Impact of POS data sharing on supply chain management: an experimental study. *Production and Operations Management*, *12*(1), 1–11. doi:10.1111/j.1937-5956.2003.tb00194.x

Croson, R., & Donohue, K. (2006). Behavioral causes of the bullwhip effect and the observed value of inventory information. *Management Science*, *52*(3), 323–336. doi:10.1287/mnsc.1050.0436

Croson, R., Donohue, K., & Katok, E. &Sterman, J. (2005). Order Instability in Supply Chains: Coordination Risk and the Role of Coordination Stock. PSU Working Paper.

Della Vigna, S., & Malmendier, U. (2006). Paying not to go to the gym. *The American Economic Review*, *96*(3), 694–719. doi:10.1257/aer.96.3.694

Di Mauro, C., & Maffioletti, A. (2004). Attitudes to risk and attitudes to uncertainty: experimental evidence. *Applied Economics*, *36*(4), 357–372. doi:10.1080/00036840410001674286

Diamond, P., & Vartiainen, H. (2007). *Behavioral Economics and its applications*. Princeton, NJ: Princeton University Press.

Dooley, K. J., Yan, T., Mohan, S., & Gopalakrishnan, M. (2010). Inventory management and the bullwhip effect during the 2007–2009 recession: evidence from the manufacturing sector. *Journal of Supply Chain Management*, *46*(1), 12–18. doi:10.1111/j.1745-493X.2009.03183.x

Einhorn, I. J., & Hogarth, R. M. (1985). Ambiguity and Uncertainty in Probabilistic Inference. *Psychological Review*, *92*(4), 433–461. doi:10.1037/0033-295X.92.4.433

Ellis, S.C., Henry, R.M., & Shockley, J. (2010). Buyer perception of supply disruption risk: a behavioral view and empirical assessment. *Journal of Operations Management*, 28(_), 34-46.

Ellram, L. M. (1991). A managerial guideline for the development and implementation of purchasing partnerships. *International Journal of Purchasing and Materials Management*, *27*(3), 2–8.

Ellsberg, D. (1961). Risk, ambiguity, and the Savage axiom. *The Quarterly Journal of Economics*, *75*(4), 643–669. doi:10.2307/1884324

Fehr, E., & Gachter, S. (2000). Fairness and Retaliation: the economics of reciprocity. *The Journal of Economic Perspectives*, *14*(3), 159–181. doi:10.1257/jep.14.3.159

Fehr, E., Gachter, S., & Kirchsteiger, G. (1997). Reciprocity as a contract enforcement device: experimental evidence. *Econometrica*, *65*(4), 833–860. doi:10.2307/2171941

Fehr, E., & Schmidt, K. M. (1999). A theory of fairness, competition and cooperation. *The Quarterly Journal of Economics*, *114*, 817–868. doi:10.1162/003355399556151

Forrester, J. (1958). Industrial dynamics: a major breakthrough for decision makers. *Harvard Business Review*, *36*(4), 37–66.

Fox, C. R., & Tversky, A. (1995). Ambiguity Aversion and Comparative Ignorance. *The Quarterly Journal of Economics*, *110*(3), 585–603. doi:10.2307/2946693

Frisch, D., & Baron, J. (1988). Ambiguity and rationality. *Journal of Behavioral Decision Making*, *1*(3), 149–157. doi:10.1002/bdm.3960010303

Gino, F., & Pisano, G. (2008). Toward a theory of behavioral operations. *Manufacturing and Services Operations Management*, *10*(4), 676–691. doi:10.1287/msom.1070.0205

Glaser, M., & Weber, M. (2003). Overconfidence and trading volume. *The Geneva Risk and Insurance Review*, *32*(1), 1–36. doi:10.1007/s10713-007-0003-3

Gupta, S., Steckel, J. H., & Banerjii, A. (2002). Dynamic decision making in marketing channels. In Rapoport, A. (Ed.), *Experimental Business Research* (pp. 4–21). Boston: Kluwer Academic Publishers.

Harland, C., Brenchley, R., & Walker, H. (2003). Risk in supply networks. *Journal of Purchasing and Supply Management*, *9*(2), 51–62. doi:10.1016/S1478-4092(03)00004-9

Harrison, G. W., & Moritz, S. &Pibernik R. (2009). How Does The Risk Attitude of a Purchasing Manager Affect The Selection of Suppliers? unpublished manuscript.

Heath, C., & Tversky, A. (1991). Preference and belief: ambiguity and competence in choice under uncertainty. *Journal of Risk and Uncertainty*, *4*(1), 5–28. doi:10.1007/BF00057884

Hendricks, K. B., & Singhal, V. R. (2005). An empirical analysis of the effect of supply chain disruptions on long-run stock price performance and risk of the firm. *Production and Operations Management*, *14*(1), 35–52. doi:10.1111/j.1937-5956.2005.tb00008.x

Hilary, G., & Menzly, L. (2006). Does past success lead analysts to become overconfident? *Management Science*, *52*(4), 489–500. doi:10.1287/mnsc.1050.0485

Ho, T.-H., Lim, N., & Camerer, C. F. (2006). Modeling the psychology of consumer and firm behavior with behavioral economics. *JMR, Journal of Marketing Research*, *43*(3), 307–331. doi:10.1509/jmkr.43.3.307

Ho, T.-H., & Zhang, J. (2008). Designing price contracts for boundedly rational customers: does the framing of the fixed fee matter? *Management Science*, *54*(4), 686–700. doi:10.1287/mnsc.1070.0788

Ireland, R. D., & Webb, J. W. (2007). A multi-theoretic perspective on trust and power in strategic supply chains. *Journal of Operations Management*, *25*(2), 482–497. doi:10.1016/j.jom.2006.05.004

Jemison, D. B. (1987). Risk and the relationship among strategy, organizational processes, and performance. *Management Science*, *33*(9), 1087–1101. doi:10.1287/mnsc.33.9.1087

Juttner, U. (2005). Supply chain risk management—understanding the business requirements from a practitioner perspective. *International Journal of Logistics Management*, *16*(1), 120–141. doi:10.1108/09574090510617385

Kahneman, D., & Tversky, A. (1979). Prospect theory: an analysis of decision under risk. *Econometrica*, *47*(2), 263–292. doi:10.2307/1914185

Katok, E., & Wu, D. (2009). Contracting in supply chains: A laboratory investigation. *Management Science*, *55*(12), 1953–1968. doi:10.1287/mnsc.1090.1089

Kekre, S., Murthi, B. P. S., & Srinivasan, K. (1995). Operating decisions, supplier availability and quality: an empirical study. *Journal of Operations Management*, *12*(3/4), 387–396. doi:10.1016/0272-6963(95)00002-A

Keser, C., Paleologo, G.A., (2004).Experimental investigation of supplier-retailer contracts: the wholesale price contract. *IBM Research Report*, RC23424 (W0411-088).

Kim, J. G., Chatfield, D. C., Harrison, T. P., & Hayya, J. C. (2006). Production, manufacturing and logistics quantifying the bullwhip effect in a supply chain with stochastic lead time. *European Journal of Operational Research*, *173*(2), 617–636. doi:10.1016/j.ejor.2005.01.043

Kleindorfer, P., & Saad, G. (2005). Managing disruption risks in supply chains. *Production and Operations Management*, *14*(1), 53–68. doi:10.1111/j.1937-5956.2005.tb00009.x

Kremic, T., Tukel, O. I., & Rom, W. O. (2006). Outsourcing decision support: a survey of benefits, risks, and decision factors. *Supply Chain Management: An International Journal*, *11*(6), 467–482. doi:10.1108/13598540610703864

Ledyard, J. O. (1995). Public Goods: a survey of experimental research. In Kagel, J., & Roth, A. (Eds.), *Handbook of Experimental Economics*. Princeton: Princeton University Press.

Lee, H. L. (2004). The triple-A supply chain. *Harvard Business Review*, *82*(10), 102–112.

Lin, Z., Zhao, X., Ismail, K. M., & Carley, K. M. (2006). Organizational design and restructuring in response to crises: lessons from computational modeling and real-world cases. *Organization Science*, *17*(5), 598–618. doi:10.1287/orsc.1060.0210

Loch, C., & Wu, Y. (2008a). Social Preferences and Supply Chain Performance: An Experimental Study. *Management Science*, *54*(11), 1835–1849. doi:10.1287/mnsc.1080.0910

Loch, C., & Wu, Y. (2008b). Behavioural operations management. *Foundation and Trends in Technology Information and Operations Management*, *1*(3), 121–132. doi:10.1561/0200000009

Loewenstein, G. (1996). Out of control: Visceral influences on behaviour. *Organizational Behavior and Human Decision Processes*, *65*(3), 272–292. doi:10.1006/obhd.1996.0028

Machuca, J. A. D., & Barajas, R. P. (2004). The impact of electronic data interchange on reducing the bullwhip effect and supply chain inventory costs. *Transportation Research Part E, Logistics and Transportation Review*, *40*(3), 209–228. doi:10.1016/j.tre.2003.08.001

Malmendier, U., & Tate, G. (2005). CEO overconfidence and corporate investment. *The Journal of Finance*, *60*(6), 2661–2700. doi:10.1111/j.1540-6261.2005.00813.x

Mantel, S. P., Tatikonda, M. V., & Liao, Y. (2006). A behavioral study of supply manager decision-making: factors influencing make versus buy evaluation. *Journal of Operations Management*, *24*(6), 822–838. doi:10.1016/j.jom.2005.09.007

March, J. G., & Shapira, Z. (1987). Managerial perspectives on risk and risk taking. *Management Science*, *33*(11), 1404–1418. doi:10.1287/mnsc.33.11.1404

McCabe, K. A., Rassenti, S. J., & Smith, V. L. (1996). Game theory and reciprocity in some extensive form experimental games. *Proceedings of the National Academy of Sciences of the United States of America*, *93*(23), 13421–13428. doi:10.1073/pnas.93.23.13421

Moore, D., & Healy, P. J. (2008). The Trouble with Overconfidence. *Psychological Review*, *115*(2), 502–517. doi:10.1037/0033-295X.115.2.502

Narasimhan, R., Nair, N., Griffith, D. A., Arlbjorn, J., & Bendoly, E. (2009). Lock-in situations in supply chains: a social exchange theoretic study of sourcing arrangements in buyer-supplier relationships. *Journal of Operations Management*, *27*(5), 374–389. doi:10.1016/j.jom.2008.10.004

Narasimhan, R., & Talluri, S. (2009). Editorial Special Issue: Perspectives on Risk Management in Supply Chains. *Journal of Operations Management*, *27*(2), 114–118. doi:10.1016/j.jom.2009.02.001

Nassimbeni, G., & Sartor, M. (2006). *Sourcing in China-Strategies, Methods, Experiences*. London: Palgrave Macmillan.

Odean, T. (1998). Volume, volatility, price, and profit when all traders are above average. *The Journal of Finance*, *53*(6), 1887–1934. doi:10.1111/0022-1082.00078

Paulson, U. (2004). Supply chain management. In Brindley, C. (Ed.), *Supply Chain Risk* (pp. 79–96). Aldershot, UK: Ashgate Publishing Company.

Quiggin, J. (1982). A theory of anticipated utility. *Journal of Economic Behavior & Organization*, *3*(4), 323–343. doi:10.1016/0167-2681(82)90008-7

Schmeidler, D. (1989). Subjective probability and expected utility without additivity. *Econometrica*, *57*(3), 571–587. doi:10.2307/1911053

Schotanus, F., Telgen, J., & de Boer, L. (2008). Unfair allocation of gains under the Equal Price allocation method in purchasing groups. *European Journal of Operational Research*, *187*(1), 162–176. doi:10.1016/j.ejor.2007.03.009

Schweitzer, M. E., & Cachon, G. P. (2000). Decision bias in the newsvendor problem with a known demand distribution: experimental evidence. *Management Science*, *46*(3), 404–420. doi:10.1287/mnsc.46.3.404.12070

Sheffi, Y. (2005). *The resilient enterprise: overcoming vulnerability for competitive advantage*. Cambridge, MA: The MIT Press.

Sheffi, Y., & Rice, J. Jr. (2005). A supply chain view of the resilient enterprise. *MIT Sloan Management Review*, *47*(1), 41–48.

Simon, H. (1957). *Models of man*. New York: Wiley.

Song, J.-S. (1994). The effect of leadtime uncertainty in a simple stochastic inventory model. *Management Science*, *40*(5), 603–613. doi:10.1287/mnsc.40.5.603

Steckel, J. H., Gupta, S., & Banerji, A. (2004). Supply chain decision making: will shorter cycle times and shared point-of-sale information necessarily help? *Management Science*, *50*(4), 458–464. doi:10.1287/mnsc.1030.0169

Sterman, J. (1989). Modeling managerial behavior: Misperceptions of feedback in a dynamic decision making experiment. *Management Science*, *35*(3), 321–339. doi:10.1287/mnsc.35.3.321

Sterman, J. D. (2006). The Bullwhip Effect in Supply Chains. In Carranza, O., & Villegas, F. (Eds.), *Operational and Behavioral Causes of Supply Chain Instability*. London: Palgrave McMillan.

Svensson, G. (2000). A conceptual framework for the analysis of vulnerability in supply chains. *International Journal of Physical Distribution and Logistics Management*, *30*(9), 731–749. doi:10.1108/09600030010351444

Svensson, G. (2002). A conceptual framework of vulnerability in firms' inbound and outbound logistics flows. *International Journal of Physical Distribution & Logistics Management*, *32*(2), 110–134. doi:10.1108/09600030210421723

Svensson, G. (2004a). Vulnerability in business relationships: the gap between dependence and trust. *Journal of Business and Industrial Marketing*, *19*(7), 469–483. doi:10.1108/08858620410564418

Svensson, G. (2004b). Key areas, causes and contingency planning of corporate vulnerability in supply chains: A qualitative approach. *International Journal of Physical Distribution & Logistics Management*, *34*(9), 728–748. doi:10.1108/09600030410567496

Tang, C. A., & Tomlin, B. (2008). The power of flexibility for mitigating supply chain risks. *International Journal of Production Economics*, *116*(1), 12–27. doi:10.1016/j.ijpe.2008.07.008

Tang, C. S. (2006). Perspectives in supply chain risk management. *International Journal of Production Economics*, *103*(2), 451–488. doi:10.1016/j.ijpe.2005.12.006

Thun, J.-H., & Hoenig, D. (2009). (in press). An empirical analysis of supply chain risk management in the German automotive industry. *International Journal of Production Economics*. doi:. doi:10.1016/j.ijpe.2009.10.010

Tversky, A., & Fox, C. R. (1995). Weighting risk and uncertainty. *Psychological Review*, *102*(2), 269–283. doi:10.1037/0033-295X.102.2.269

Tversky, A., & Kahneman, D. (1971). The belief in the law of small numbers. *Psychological Bulletin*, *76*, 105–110. doi:10.1037/h0031322

Tversky, A., & Kahneman, D. (1974). Judgment under Uncertainty: Heuristics and Biases. *Science*, *185*(4157), 1124–1131. doi:10.1126/science.185.4157.1124

Tversky, A., & Wakker, P. (1995). Risk attitudes and decision weights. *Econometrica*, *63*(6), 1255–1280. doi:10.2307/2171769

Veltri, N. F., Saunders, C. S., & Kavan, C. B. (2008). Information systems backsourcing: correcting problems and responding to opportunities. *California Management Review*, *51*(1), 50–76.

Von Neumann, J., & Morgestern, O. (1992). *Theory of games and economic behaviour*. Princeton, NJ: Princeton University Press.

Wagner, S. M., & Bode, C. (2006). An empirical investigation into supply chain vulnerability. *Journal of Purchasing and Supply Management*, *12*(6), 301–312. doi:10.1016/j.pursup.2007.01.004

Wagner, S. M., & Neshat, N. (2010). Assessing the vulnerability of supply chains using graph theory. *International Journal of Production Economics*, *126*(1), 121–129. doi:10.1016/j.ijpe.2009.10.007

Webster, N. (1983). *Webster's New Twentieth Century Dictionary*. 2nd ed. New York: Simon & Schuster.

Wilding, R. D. (1998). Chaos theory: implications for supply chain management. *The International Journal of Logistics Management*, *9*(1), 43–56. doi:10.1108/09574099810805735

Wu, D., & Katok, E. (2006). Learning, communication, and the bullwhip effect. *Journal of Operations Management*, *24*(6), 839–850. doi:10.1016/j.jom.2005.08.006

Xu, L., & Beamon, B. M. (2006). Supply Chain Coordination and Cooperation Mechanisms: An Attribute-Based Approach. *The Journal of Supply Chain Management*, *42*(1), 4–12. doi:10.1111/j.1745-493X.2006.04201002.x

Yates, J. F., & Stone, E. R. (1992). Risk appraisal. In: J.F. Yates (Ed.), *Risk-taking Behavior (pp.* 49-85). New York: John Wiley & Sons.

Yates, J. F., Stone, E. R., & Parker, A. M. (1994). Risk communication: absolute versus relative expressions of low-probability risks. *Organizational Behavior and Human Decision Processes*, *60*(3), 387–408. doi:10.1006/obhd.1994.1091

Yu, H., Zeng, A. Z., & Zhao, L. (2009). Single or dual sourcing: decision-making in the presence of supply chain disruption risks. *Omega*, *37*(4), 788–800. doi:10.1016/j.omega.2008.05.006

Zsidisin, G. A. (2003). A grounded definition of supply risk. *Journal of Purchasing and Supply Management*, *9*(5-6), 217–224. doi:10.1016/j.pursup.2003.07.002

Zsidisin, G. A., Ragatz, G. L., & Melnyk, S. A. (2005). The dark side of supply chain management. *Supply Chain Management Review*, *9*(2), 46–52.

Chapter 20
Risk Management:
A New Way to Improve Logistics Outsourcing

Thierry Sauvage
Aix-Marseille University, France

Mohamed Haouari
Aix-Marseille University, France

ABSTRACT

In recent years, logistics outsourcing has shown a strong development. However, despite the benefits associated with logistics outsourcing, there are many relationships that do not last as long as they were initially planned. In this chapter the authors tried to sketch a conceptual model of Risk Management applied to logistics outsourcing and supported by a case study within aerospace industry. Their results show that Risk Management could be an innovative tool favoring the success of logistics outsourcing by securing future performance and relationships between supply chain partners.

INTRODUCTION

Companies, whether industrial or commercial, have proceeded for about twenty years in the outsourcing of operations. In the 80's, the outsourcing of activities like data processing, telecommunications or logistics, considered as an integral part of the company, was perceived as a solution of last recourse for firms in bad financial health (Barthélemy 2004). Nowadays, many functions are totally or partially outsourced by firms (Chanson, 2003). Logistics follows this trend. Thus, according to the barometer of Ernst & Young Outsourcing (2008), 36% of European companies have outsourced at least whole or part of their "distribution, logistics and transport" function.

Indeed, brought by the constraints of flexibility, competitiveness and cost control, more and more companies are using the services of logistics providers. According to Byrne (2004), 78% of

DOI: 10.4018/978-1-60960-585-8.ch020

North American shippers, and 79% of European shippers, resort to logistics service providers. Thus, since the second half of the 1990s, logistics outsourcing has become a major strategic issue, making logistics service providers (LSP) as critical and indispensable partners for industry and trade (Paché and Sauvage, 2004). The LSP is no longer limited to merely providing transport services, but offer complete packages of logistics services with a higher value added. Alongside this trend, the relationship between shippers and service providers has also evolved. There is a change in the nature of the relationship among shippers and suppliers to an extent that logistics partnerships have replaced the simple sub-contracting practices (Murphy and Poist, 1996). This change can be explained on the one hand, by the potential benefits associated partnership, and also by the emergence of new logistics' strategies in line with supply chain management (Brulhart, 2002).

However, Lieb (2000) notes that despite of the benefits of logistics outsourcing, many relationships are not renewed at the end of their contract or do not last as long as they were initially expected.

Thus, our thinking lies at the heart of this fact. This paper aims to draft the stake in managing risk in a logistics' outsourcing process. Our approach constitutes an innovative and successful way of managing the supply chain. We try to propose a new Risk Management (RM) framework for managing relationships between shipper and LSP. Our paper will show how RM would allow better integration of the LSP driving to success.

The chapter is organized as following. Section 1 presents a literature review, definitions and key concepts used throughout the chapter. Section 2 presents the preliminary results of an empirical study that we conducted on a firm operating in the aerospace industry. These results allow developing an exploratory model. Supply chain innovation implications deriving from the model are then discussed. Finally, the concluding section presents some concluding remarks, research limitations and future research avenues.

DEFINITIONS AND LITERATURE REVIEW

Logistics Outsourcing

On a theoretical level, the concept of outsourcing has been the subject of many research and definitions. Today, the proliferation of research work on outsourcing has led to some stabilization of the concept. Barthélemy and Donada (2007) clearly identify three essential characteristics of outsourcing: 1) the activity is firstly provided by the customer, 2) the outsourced activity is frequently accompanied by a transfer of assets, 3) the relationship between the outsourcer and the provider is a relationship of long or medium term.

Transaction cost theory (TCT) is the main theoretical approach mobilized to analyze outsourcing. Inspired by the famous works of Coase (1937) and primarily developed by Williamson (1975), the TCT is considered by many authors as a "dominant" paradigm in organizations study. This theory gives support to outsourcing process through contractual cost minimization. TCT focuses on three key-factors affecting transaction costs in outsourcing: asset specificity, uncertainty and frequency of transactions (Chanson 2003).

The emergence of logistics' providers is historically linked to the need of some industrial firms to disengage from marginal activities to focus on the considered necessities (Paché, Sauvage, 2004). Precisely, logistics' service providers have appeared in 1970 in the United Kingdoms (Brulhart 2002). During this period, the industrial and commercial companies have begun to outsource transportation (Brulhart 2002). Then in the 1980s, providers have benefited from the deregulation of transport service entrusted with the storage and other more complex operations such as picking or supply just in time (Sheffi, 1990). Finally, from the 1990s, complete supply chain functionalities have been outsourced.

Today, the popularity of managerial practice for the logistics outsourcing phenomenon continues to grow. Thus, according to Byrne (2004), 78% of

North American shippers, and 79% of Europeans' work with logistics' service providers. According to the outsourcing barometer of Ernst & Young (2008), logistic, distribution and transport come in the second most outsourced activities by European companies.

Factors Affecting Logistics' Outsourcing Success

What are the factors contributing to the success of a logistics partnership? According to Brulhart (2006), on the whole the measurement of the success in a partnership is prone to debate. There is no truly consensus on the performance measurement of alliances. The concept of satisfaction degree of each part with regard to the relationship seems to be the most relevant measurement for assessing the success of a logistics partnership. The success can be defined by the achievement of key results expected. The results can be economic, organizational or social. Frequently, the length of the relationship is regarded as a proof of the success of the partnership.

There is an abundant empirical literature on the determinants of successful outsourcing. Aubert et al (1996) suggest that these determinants can be grouped into two categories: a) the characteristics of the outsourced activity and b) characteristics of management of the relationship with the provider. Lee and Kim (2003) suggest that these variables can be grouped on psychological variables (*mutual benefits, commitment* and *predisposition*) and behavioral variables (*shared knowledge, mutual dependency* and *organizational linkage).*

In a logistics context, reliability of the service and the orientation towards the customer are perceived like the most essential items for a successful relation. Murphy and Poist (2000) insisted on the capacity of the service provider to be adapted to the requirements of the customers and conceive a proposal according to his holdings. Other authors proposed other factors which explain the success of the logistics partnerships. According to Lambert et al (1999) the durability of the relationship is explained by the implementation by the shipper of common processes based on joint scheduling of the activities and establishment of an effective communication). Knemeyer et al (2003) enforce that the shipper can increase the performance of the relationship by fostering trust, engagement, cooperation and the management of the conflict with their service providers. Brulhart (2006) adds that trust, engagement and equity have a direct impacton the success of the partnership, while underlining the indirect role of communication and information system integration.

In spite of the benefits associated with a logistics outsourcing, many are the relations which are not renewed at the end of their contract or which do not remain for the length of time planned initially. Thus, according to Murphy and Poist (2000) about one third of the relations are broken by the shipper of anticipated way.

Ackerman (1996) suggests that the relationship between the LSP and his shipper is dedicated as much to the failure if the last one discovers that it loses money in the relation and that it cannot renegotiate the contract, that the failures in the service became intolerable, that the charger with promised to achieve services which it cannot finally achieve or sometimes because one or more managers at the shipper's company do not want to make the relationship work and maintain a well-hidden desire to see it fail. Lambert et al (1999) suggest that the absence of expected benefits, the very low profitability of partners, the concern of the shipper on the upset direct of the activities, or the incapacity of the partners to adapt to the changes of the market can also be the causes of a failure of the relation. Ellram (1995) explain the failure of the relation by the absence of scheduling of activities, the deficiency of communication between the partners, the lack of total directive of the relation, and the absence of objectives common to the two partners. Lastly, Tate (1996) adds that the lack of support of the senior executives, the absence of confidence, and the bad scheduling of the objectives are also causes of failures of the logistics partnerships. These various contributions suggest that the failure of the relationship is generally associated with two main groups of factors: the factors dealing with the bad performance /execution of the service inducing costs and the factors generated by the lack of a common vision preventing the improvement of the cooperation.

Risk in Logistics Outsourcing

The environment in which firms evolve is characterized by shorter delays, better quality, shorter production cycles, shorter commercial cycles and an increasing competitiveness between actors that are linked to a value chain. This phenomenon is caused by a more top-level change in general business conditions. In such context, companies are constantly evolving. Therefore change management is becoming an important issue. However, if change management enables firms to make and succeed proactive decisions, it doesn't enable to make the right choice, and firms remain exposed to different risks.

What is risk? The word risk appears to be widely used to define an event both in terms of probability of occurrence or consequences. In the literature, we do not really find consensus language, because there are many definitions of "risk". These definitions are often the subject of confusion and vary by field and the context in which risk is studied.

March and Shapira (1987) who relied on the contributions of decision theory, defines risk as "variation in the distribution of possible outcomes, their likelihoods and their subjective values" (p. 1404). This definition suggests that the risk is mainly related to the variance of the results (positive and negative), and their probabilities. Literature suggests that authors refer to risk in a supply chain context by using "supply risk" or "supply chain risk". Lavastre and Spallanzani (2008) suggest that the first (supply risk) is operational and is focused on the supply, delivery, and management controls operating very short-term flows, while the second (supply chain risk) is more strategic and cross-cutting concerns and management, establishment and organization of flows between partners in a supply chain and its effects will have consequences on the supply risk.

Zsidisin et al (2004) suggest that "supply risk is defined as the probability of an incident associated with inbound supply from individual supplier failures or the supply market occurring, in which its outcomes result in the inability of the purchasing firm to meet customer demand or cause threats to customer life and safety" (p. 222). This definition focuses on events that may occur upstream and can cause failure of the business to meet consumer needs or can have an impact on his life or safety. Harland et al (2003) suggested that logistics risk is one of 11 types of risk that may affect the activity of an organization. These authors adopted the definition of Meulbrook's (2000) who defines supply risk as an "adversely affect inward flow of any type of resource to enable transactions to take place; Also termed as a "input risk". This definition, which is located in the logic of the previous (upstream), incorporates both the idea of flows and limit the impact of risk to the company's inability to function, which prevents it logically meet consumer demand. Other authors have proposed definitions of supply risk based on the general definition of risk proposed by March and Shapira (1987), with resonances of direct decision theory. Thus, Jüttner et al, (2003) propose to define the supply risk as ''any risks for the information, material and product flows from begging to the original delivery of the final product for the end user''. From these various definitions, logistics risk, like risk generally appears as a multidimensional concept and as suggested Zsidisin (2003, p.222): ''supply risk is a multi-faceted concept, since its scope includes risk sources and outcomes''.

Definition of Risk Management

Risk management concept is not recent and has spread in the late 1950s in the United States in the financial field, in connection with insurance issues (Tchankova, 2002). Subsequently, the concept of risk management has been extended to other areas including the environment, project management, marketing and logistics. If risk management is sometimes regarded as a "buzzword", Lhabitant and Tinguely (2001) suggest that risk management as perceived today is distinctly different from that represented 50 years ago, in the sense that it has evolved from an internal approach to integrate strategic and external risks.This reflects the increased instability and uncertainty in environments in which organizations must operate, and for many companies the concept of a stable external environment has ceased to exist (Tchankova, 2002).

It seems to have a general agreement on what risk management process should be. Dickson (1989) defines risk management as "the identification, analysis and control of those risks which can threaten the assets or earning capacity of an enterprise". Similarly, Fone and Young (2000) see risk management as a general management function that seeks to assess and address risks in the context of the overall aims of the organisation. According to the Royal Society (1992), there is some dispute over whether it is an everyday part of business life or something which is brought and used as and when it is needed. Our argumentation goes against this definition. We think that risk management should be a continuous and developing process, which runs throughout the organisation's strategy and the implementation of that strategy. It must be integrated into culture of the organization with an effective policy and programme led by the most senior management. It must translate the strategy into tactical and operational objectives, assigning responsibility throughout the organisation with each manager and employee responsible for the management of risk as part of their job description. (IRM[1]/AIRMIC[2]/ALARM[3], 2002).

Tchankova (2002) maintains that "risk management has become a main part of the organisation's activities and its main aim is to help all other management activities to achieve the organisation's activities and its main aim is to help all other management activities to achieve the organisation's aims directly and efficiently". This definition is relevant owing to the fact that it brings out the fact that risk management is not another function that the organization has to cope with. Risk management is rather a support function that helps managers at every level of the organization in their day-to-day making decision process.

Risk Management Models

In recent years, researchers have begun to explore how models of risk management, derivatives of other disciplines can be applied in a supply chain (Harland and Brenchley, 2001; Harland et al, 2003).

For Beckett (2005), mapping the supply chain is a prerequisite for risk management in the supply chain as it helps to understand the structure, strategy and accountability of actors in the networks of supply chain. The main limitation of this grid is that it does not take into consideration the different perceptions in the network. For Stemmler (2007), the risk management process generally includes the identification of the sources of risk analysis and assessment of their impact, the measurement, and finally the control of risk. Another limitation in the two models from Harland et al. (2003) and Stemmler (2007), is the lack of mechanisms for monitoring and reviewing the various steps performed. Indeed, Risk Management is an iterative, cyclical and permanent process requiring an accuracy of assessments and relevant effectiveness in the measures adopted. In that way, Manuj and Mentzer (2008) propose a model of a risk management in the global supply chain consisting of five phases. That model proposes a process consisting in five iterative phases: Risk Identification, Risk Assessment, Strategy selection of appropriate risk Development of the risk management strategy and finally the reduction of risk of supply chain. The advantage of this model lies in the fact that he considers that Risk Management process is not only a sequential process in which an element only affects the next. It is a multidirectional, iterative process by which any element has an immediate and systemic influence on all others.

These various contributions suggest that each model of Risk Management must be based on a logical sequence beginning with the determining of the context of the risks. The next steps are to assess those risks and to develop actions to reduce and to influence the probability of risks occurring and their impacts. White (1995) suggests that the different Risk Management models proposed in the literature tend to follow an approach consisting of three phases:

- ***Risk Identification:*** Starting from an appreciation of context, its purpose is to identify all risks which are likely to occur.
- ***Risk Analysis:*** Its purpose is to understand and estimate the probability of occurrence and impact on the most significant risks.
- ***Risk Treatment*:** The goal is to decide the most appropriate action to be undertaken for each risk (or combination of risks) as well as the most appropriate for managing each risk identified.

As we suggested before, the actors of the supply chain realised the importance of the risks and their impact on their performances and their relations. However, there exists, to our knowledge, few studies which concern the risk management in particular in the relations between shippers and logistics' service providers. According to the results of the study carried out by Kersten et al (2007), only 9% of LSP and 3% of shippers regarded the risk management as important in 2000. According to the authors, these results were explained by the fact that this discipline was not very widespread in the scientific and professional circles, and only few researchers and companies were interested in. However, according to the same authors the interest with the risk management increased over the last few years, and the proportion of LSP and shippers which considered the risk management as important were about 27% in 2005 and they should reach about 38% in 2010.

After the presentation of these various factors, it is clear that the behaviours of the partners play a relevant role in the success, or failure of the partnership. Indeed, in addition to the factors related to the correct achievement of the service, and the compliance with the ultimate consumer, the various authors cited above insist on the role of the behavioural variables like confidence, the engagement, the communication and the cooperation. However, there has been limited research effort in the area of risk management in relation to logistics outsourcing. We have therefore tried to study the impact of the introduction of a risk management approach on the success of an outsourcing operation realised by an aerospace case company as detailed in the next section.

EMPIRICAL ANALYSIS: A CASE EXAMPLE OF A COMPANY OPERATING IN THE AEROSPACE INDUSTRY

Company Profile

Our research is based on a fieldwork conducted over several months in the field of risk management in a company that we call Alpha (for confidentiality reasons). Alpha is a major player in the aerospace industry suppliers in Europe. This sector is characterized by an attempt of reorganization, in the aim to consolidate it and bring out major suppliers (Tier 1). These new players must have a critical size and sufficient resources to be able to follow the major manufacturers (such as Airbus and Boeing) in their development strategies and especially to share industrial costs and technological risks.

Alpha has chosen to outsource the logistics of its purchasing materials. This choice is justified by its desire to refocus its heart craft, to improve its global acquisition costs and to benefit from the experience and knowledge of business experts. This choice is also justified by the research of flexibility, responsiveness and a better response to customer expectations. The project outsourcing approach initiated by Alpha has been accompanied by setting up a risk management approach. The presentation of this approach and the methodology of data collection will be developed in the next section.

Methodology

Our research can be defined as an action-research type intervention conducted in accordance with a constructivist approach. This research is the result of a desire of change and the intention of research (Lewin, 1947). It responds to a double objective to solve the problem of users (Alpha Company) and to advance basic knowledge as well (Liu, 1997). However, Argyris (1995) suggests that the main condition of successful action-research is the researcher's ability to produce theorical knowledge directly useful on the field. Our action research adheres to a constructivist view of knowledge, since, rather than targeting the discovery of a hidden pre-existing reality, it aims is to build representations of studied phenomena proven by experience, representations that are to construct an intelligibility to intervene intentionally in these phenomena (Martinet, 1993). Avenier (1992) suggests that the properties of the action-research confer legitimacy in constructivist epistemologies, through interaction that it provides the researcher with the environment. These interactions through which it can progress while ensuring the relevance of the knowledge generated (Avenier, 1992).

The technique adopted to select the supplier was bidding with prequalification. This technique consists on the assessment by a client of the suitability of firms to carry out a particular contract prior to being invited to submit a bid. For this technique only a small number of providers has been sought, insofar as the discipline is very specific. This technique allows benefiting from lower costs because the number of proposals is stripped lower. It also allows a lower dissemination of information about the outsourcing operation in progress and makes competition almost as strongly as the single tendering (where all potential suppliers are sought).

Since the decision to outsource was taken, Alpha has established a Risk Management approach. Table 1 indicates the key elements included in the different phase of the Risk Management process. We have identified several risks grouped into five categories:

- Financial Risk
- Risk of underperformance
- Dependence on the provider
- Loss of expertise and skills and
- Social Risk.

In addition to these risks, we identified three categories of risk, where Alpha will choose to use several (two or more) service providers: difficulties to pilot two or more providers at the same time, getting together with two providers with different skill level and performance, balance the power in the relationship between Alpha and its providers. Following the identification and analysis of these risks, actions have been implemented with the aim of influencing the probability of risk occurring, its impact or both.

Table 1. Key dimensions in the risk management process

Chapter	Description
General	Basic information on the bidder
Supply Chain	It aims to assess the bidder's supply chain approach, in order to gain confidence in the supply chain control concerning the work package
Project Management	Questions on the bidder's project management approach, in order to gain confidence into quality management within his project management
Capacity	Questions to assess the bidder's manufacturing capacity to fulfil the requirements of the work package
Capability	Questions to assess the bidder's manufacturing capability to fulfil the requirements of the work package
Risk	Questions to assess the bidder's risk management approach and its suitability for the work package
Skill	Contains questions to assess the bidder's employee's skills and his approach to assure sustainable human resource management
Suggestion	Questions related to areas of potential cost saving. Also used as a feedback page towards Alpha

The screening took place in three phases:

- **Phase 1**: A RFI (Request for information), which yielded the first data on the first providers in the pre-selected targets to select a reduced number for the second phase. One thing to note is that during this phase, the bidders have received a general description of the service but without detail. Data collection during this phase was done using a tool called CCR (Capacity, Capability and Risk). The CCR is presented with eight chapters including 126 questions. Table 1 sums up the main key dimensions analyzed.
  After receiving filled questionnaires from each candidate, a data processing was performed. After this, the candidates were ranked based on the quality of their response and on the level of satisfaction with the criteria established in advance by Alpha.
- **Phase 2**: RFP was aimed to receive the proposals of the bidders and how they planned to make the delivery. During this phase, the bidders have received more quantified detailed description of the service. Throughout this phase, visits and on-site assessments have been conducted to judge the real capabilities of candidates and accuracy of data submitted during the RFI. Two tools have been mobilized for this phase: the CCR through the issues that concerned this phase and a questionnaire used in on-site audits.
- **Phase 3**: Negotiations with the various bidders, after providing them with more detailed figures. This phase has permitted to decide between any of the flexibility of the various candidates in terms of price but also in the details of the offers (as regards the settlements planned to install the machines, the human resources), and to demonstrate the capacity and expertise to conduct a plateau phase.

MODEL AND RECOMMENDATIONS FOR SUPPLY CHAIN INNOVATION

Case Results and Discussions: Dynamics of Key Success Factors in Logistics' Outsourcing

The first results of our empirical study show a direct impact of Risk Management on the success of the Relationships and on the quality of that relationship. These results allowed us to propose an exploratory model presented in Figure 1. This

Figure 1. A causal model of risk management impact on outsourcing success

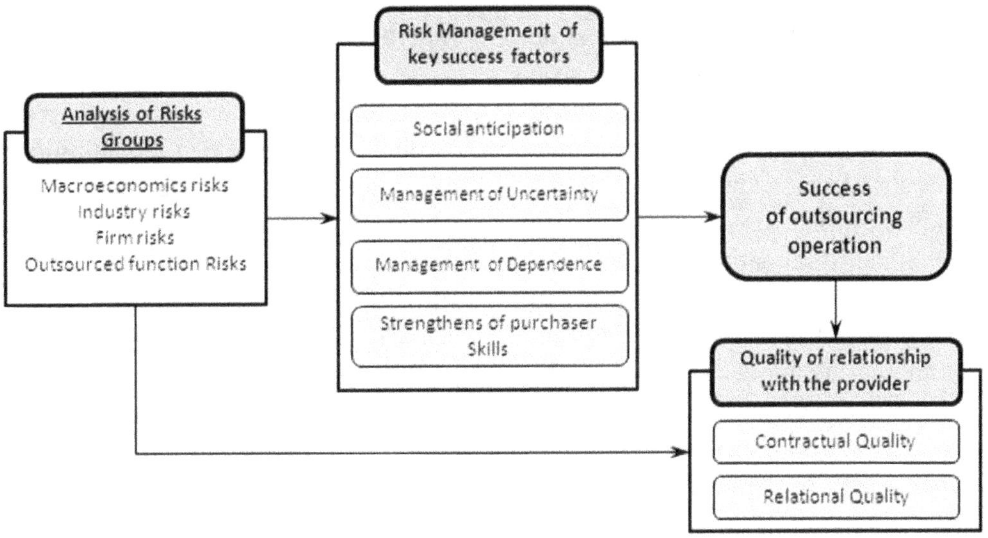

model is the result of empirical investigation. We support it by theoretical elements that we recovered from the literature review.

Before discussing this model, we must admit that the list of success factors is not exhaustive. We opt to retain the most significant ones. Regarding the evaluation of the success of the outsourcing process, in line with Brulhart (2006), we choose to analyse the achievement of the objectives expected by the client (Alpha) and the satisfaction of the two partners (Alpha and its service provider).

The macroeconomic risks reflect the degree of exposure to the external shocks, such as the economic growth, the inflation, the increase of price of raw materials, the interest rates and the exchange rates. *Industry risks* concerns uncertainties caused by the precise characteristics of the branch of industry in which a company operates. In the case of the company Alpha, this relies on the uncertainties brought,on the one hand, by the "Reorganization" of the sector of the aerospace equipment manufacturers, and the other hand by the variability on the international demand of planes. *Firm risks* are specific to a given company. In the case of the company Alpha these risks concern for example the uncertainties bound to the choice of setting-up of a new production site. More generally, *Risks* in an outsourcing process can be shared into the following five categories:

- Strategic risk concerning activities which outsourcing would endanger the survival of the company.
- The risk of dependence on the provider bringing to keep in house resources and skills to protect a minimum level of expertise.
- The risk of loss of control which generates hidden costs (including steering) and raising the bill for outsourcing.
- The legal risk bound to the recovery of the staff.
- The cultural risk (working habits, habit of short-term contractual relations, hegemony of the technical sphere)

Social Anticipation

The first key finding that emerges from our empirical study is the impact of the social anticipation on the result of outsourcing. Indeed, the firm such as a human construction ca not be insensitive to changes impact on human factor (economic, organizational and social) caused by the outsourcing. Our case study shows that the social anticipation and more specifically the quality of this anticipation is the key of a successful outsourcing. The non-inclusion of social advance can lead to cancellation of an outsourcing decision, due to the threats tied to the potential conflicts with organized staff representatives. Risk Management of Alpha consists in being prepared by firstly, identifying the potential risks, particularly risks of opposition from internal staff and secondly implementing preventing actions like the involvement of the staff in the change management. This is supposed to better prepare the staff and promote the success of outsourcing.

Management of Uncertainty

Regarding uncertainty, Barthélemy (2004) proposes to define the uncertainty surrounding an outsourced activity as a "the difficulty experienced by a company to predict its future needs in relation to that activity." Limiting to our literature findings, there is no empirical study which demonstrates the existence of an impact on the degree of uncertainty surrounding an outsourced activity, the performance of an outsourcing operation. On theoretical level, the literature suggests that outsourcing, considered as a hybrid organizational form, is less suited to handle situations with high uncertainty (Williamson, 1991). We can suggest that the existence of high uncertainty may have a negative impact on the success of outsourcing, and conversely low uncertainty would increase the chances of success. In this sense, the establishment of the risk management approach has reduced the uncertainty by providing, at best, the overall risk that may occur during the outsourcing process and during the lifetime relationship.

Management of Dependence

Regarding dependence, we must first distinguish its double meaning: first, organizational dependence between the outsourced function and the whole enterprise, and relational dependence between the firm and the service provider. In terms of organizational dependence, we chose to characterize the proximity to core business: more and outsourced activity is close to the "core business", more this dependence is high. Barthélemy (2004) suggests that over the outsourced activities are close to the "core business", less the results of outsourcing are positive. In the case of Alpha, the outsourced activity (logistics of general procurement) is rather far from his heart craft (design and manufacture of aero structures). We have therefore found no significant impact on the success of its outsourcing, and we have not seen the impact of risk management on this variable. Concerning the second type of dependence (relational), according to Lee and Kim (2003), it has a direct impact on the success of outsourcing. So we tried to find a possible link between the risk management and this variable. Our initial results have shown that risk management had no significant impact on the degree of dependence (low or high) but rather it allows better appreciating and identifying situations of dependence. In the case of Alpha, this dependence is exacerbated by the existence of high market concentration, the degree of specificity of the outsourced activity, and the high specificity of the assets necessary for its implementation. We must note that this type of dependence is more contingent sector: As providers are less numerous in a particular sector more outsourcing firm is likely to find themselves tied to a provider that it is little satisfying. Finally we assume that if the risk management did not have a significant impact on this variable; it may be because it (relational dependence) cannot really appreciate that in the long term.

Strengthening Purchaser Skills

The impact of strengthen of purchaser skills has been less discussed in the literature. Merminod and Retour (2006) note "the surprising absence of specific reference to buyers or purchasing department" in recent studies that have addressed key success factors of outsourcing (Barthélemy, 2004). Indeed, we found that few empirical studies that refer to strengthen of purchaser skills as a success factor in outsourcing, while the results of Monczka et al (2005) indicate that the purchasing department is "highly involved" in all three major phases of outsourcing to the tune of 64%, 79% and 48%. Our results in Alpha go in the same sense since we observed a strong impact of buyers skills and their previous experiences on the success of the operation. This observation may be justified insofar as the aerospace industry has enjoyed strong outsourcing in recent years, driven notably by the constraints of flexibility, competitiveness and cost control, which they have allowed them to accumulate knowledge on the subject. An interesting result that emerges from our empirical study is the existence of a reciprocal relationship between the risk management and the variable strengthen of purchaser skills. On the one hand, we found that the risk management had a significant impact on skills mobilized by purchasers (see Merminod and Back, 2006) by allowing them, for example, to better define the scope of delivery outsourced, well reflect the needs or the provider and to better prepare the negotiations. On the other hand, we found that the experience of buyers in turn had an impact on the process of risk management to the extent that it allowed benefiting from their prior knowledge to make better identifying risks and implement most appropriate actions to manage them.

Quality of Relationship with the Provider

After presenting the results for the first category of variable (social anticipation, uncertainty, dependence, strengthens of purchaser skills) we'll look at the relationship quality and its impact on the success of outsourcing. This categorization of the contract and relationship proposed by Barthélemy (2004) makes it easier to synthesize the various studies that have examined these two aspects of the relationship. Barthélemy (2004) suggests that the result of an outsourcing operation is "very strongly determined by the quality of the relationship with the provider". Our first results were in the same direction, but we believe, in contrast to Barthélemy (2004) that relational quality is not, primarily, determined by the level of trust between the company and its outsourcing provider but also by other variables such as collaborative communication and feed-back (Prahinski and Benton, 2004), bilateral/mutual cooperation and minimal interaction (O'Toole and Donaldson, 2000), implementation by the client (ordering party), of activity and common processes (Lambert et al, 1999), the organizational linkage (Lee and Kim, 2003) and finally confidence, engagement and equity (Brulhart, 2006). We found a significant impact of risk management on these variables, with different degrees. Another finding that emerged is that the success of outsourcing had a significant impact on the quality of relationships. Therefore, we suggest that outsourcing is more successful (achieving its objectives and enriched both partners), more relational quality will improve, which will translate into better levels of trust, cooperation, communication and interaction between the two partners, who will better sustain the relationship.

Regarding the quality of contract, many contributions have focused on the contract and its impact on the success of outsourcing and on establishing a good relationship between the two partners. Barthélemy (2004) suggests that "the use of a good outsourcing contract improves significantly the performance of an outsourcing operation." The quality of legal formalism of the contract and completeness are key success factors of outsourcing. Precisely on the completeness and quality of the contract we have seen a direct impact of risk management at Alpha. Indeed, the step of identifying risks identified conflict situations that may occur and to consider the contract terms best suited to these situations. We must also note that the variable strengthen of purchaser skills also has a significant impact on the quality of the contract, since it allows to benefit from their expertise and previous situations they have had to manage.

Solutions and Recommendations for Supply Chain Innovation

The results of this research allowed us to demonstrate the interest of the implementation of an approach of Risk Management during a Logistics Outsourcing Process. This analysis appears like an innovative way to manage the supply chain. It is consistent with the increasing role of logistics third party in the whole. The implementation of Risk Management contributes to the success of logistics outsourcing through building reliable relationships

Our research analyzed a process of Risk Management applied to logistics outsourcing. We underline the consequences in term of success and perennisation of the partnerships. We demonstrate that RM of Logistics Outsourcing prevents from the numerous reasons of failures and re-insourcing identified by Razzaque and Sheng (1998). Risk Management appears to give better control on the vulnerability of the the supply chain.

Others part, the implementation of risk management can improve the resilience of the supply chain. Several recent works present the resilience as means of reduction of the vulnerability of supply chains. For Peck (2006), resilience focuses on the "*ability of the system to return to is original or desired state after being disturbed*". In that way, Resilience is related to Risk Management and vulnerability. Haouari and *al* (2010) describe how Risk Management could affect the factors of resilience identified by Waters (2007) and targeting high reliability and agility.

The quest of agility through RM represents a real innovative way to manage the Supply Chain. In seminal literature, Agility has been defined as a strong ability in reconfiguring the value chain, particularly by preventing inertia (and stocks!) coming from conflicts and inappropriate behaviours (Christopher and Towill, 2000; Naylor et al, 1999). In the case of Alpha, RM of logistics outsourcing prepares the conditions of flexibility and reactivity critical to adapt to the current moving environment.

This research also participes in the construction of a model showing of the critical internal side of logistics outsourcing. The risk management approach promotes an internal vision of the factors of failure and success of outsourcing. The dynamic approach proposed consists of a number of sub-processes (risk identification, analysis and treatment) which allow to plan accurate mechanisms for the follow-up and the revision of the partnerships.

CONCLUSION

The chapter set out to explore the effect of risk management on logistics outsourcing success. We tried first to better understand the concepts of risk and risk management, and the aim of our research is born of a realization that we have drawn from the literature review. Indeed, it seems that if the work which investigates logistics in general, and logistics outsourcing in particular, have developed strongly in recent years, scientists and professionals agree that there are little studies that can provide conceptual frameworks and empirical findings for a better understanding and application of risk management in logistics outsourcing. We presented the case of a company in the aerospace industry. Our findings show the relationships between the application of an approach of risk management and the success of outsourcing operation by having a direct impact (at different degrees) on the various determinants of outsourcing successful. This suggests an important message for managers of outsourcing logistics that risk management is not just a fad but it could have a real effect on the success of outsourcing.

While studies based on action-research often have relatively low potential for generalization, but they allow to have better control over the sources of outside variations. Our choice allows to increase the internal validity, while recognizing the risk of degradation of external validity.

While we think this research makes an important contribution to the academic literature and provides the potential to influence managerial practice positively, there are nonetheless limitations that provide opportunities for further research. There are several areas where future outsourcing and risk management knowledge research is warranted. First, researchers should expand upon our work to examine the performance effects of risk management on outsourcing process because our work focuses on its results (success or failure). Second, researchers should examine the performance effects of risk-sharing on the quality and length of relationship. Researchers should also investigate the effects of risk management on supply chain performance.

Finally, futures research should concerns the impact of risk management on the suppleness and the flexibility of the supply chain. According to Fabbe-Costes (2007), whatever are their configurations, the contemporary supply-chain must be able to be at the same time adapted (to be effective and efficient) and adaptable (to face the instability and the turbulence). The author suggests that this double objective leads to look for a bigger integration of the supply chain while protecting its flexibility, in other words to make lean and agile supply chain. We think that it would be interesting to study in which measure the risk management could improve the capacity of supply chain to "plug and play" and to be more lean and agile.

REFERENCES

Abdur Razzaque, M., & Chen Sheng, C. (1998). Outsourcing of logistics function: a literature survey. *International Journal of Physical Distribution & Logistics Management*, *28*(2), 89–107. doi:10.1108/09600039810221667

Ackerman, K. B. (1996). Pitfalls in logistics partnerships. *International Journal of Physical Distribution & Logistics Management*, *26*(3), 35–37. doi:10.1108/09600039610115018

Argyris, C. (1995). *Savoir pour agir: surmonter les obstacles de l'apprentissage organisationnel*. Paris: InterEditions.

Aubert, B., Rivard, S., & Patry, M. (1996). A transaction cost approach to outsourcing behavior: some empirical evidence. *Information & Management*, *30*(2), 51–64. doi:10.1016/0378-7206(95)00045-3

Avenier M.-J. (1992), Recherche-Action et épistémologies constructivistes, modélisation systémique et organisation socio-économique complexes: quelques "boucles étranges" fécondes. *Revue internationale de systémique*, *6*(4), 403-420.

Barthelemy J. (2004, June). *La performance des opérations d'externalisation: Une analyse empirique des déterminantes*, Actes de la 13ème conférence de l'AIMS. Normandie. Vallée de Seine, France.

Barthelemy J., Donada C., (2007). Décision et gestion de l'externalisation. Une approche intégrée. *Revue française de gestion,* 33(177), 101-111.

Brulhart, F. (2002). *Les facteurs clés de réussite des partenariats verticaux logistiques: le cas de la relation chargeur agro-alimentaire - prestataire logistique*, Thèse de doctorat en science de gestion. Université de la méditerranée (Aix Marseille II).

Brulhart, F. (2006, June). *Performance des alliances logistiques: une proposition de typologie,* Actes des XVème Conférence Internationale de Management Stratégique, Annecy, Genève.

Byrne, P. (2004). Outsourcing and supply chain management: A natural marriage. *Logistics Management, 43*(4), 34–35.

Chanson G., (2003). Externalisation et performance dans la relation client-prestataire. *Revue française de gestion, 2*(143), 43-54.

Christopher, M., & Peck, H. (2004). Building the resilient supply chain. *International Journal of Logistics Management, 15*(2), 1–13. doi:10.1108/09574090410700275

Christopher, M., & Towill, D. R. (2000). Supply Chain Migration from Lean and Functional to Agile and Customized. *Supply Chain Management: an International Journal, 5*(4), 206–213. doi:10.1108/13598540010347334

Coase, R. (1937). The nature of the firm. *Economica. New Series, 4*(16), 386–405. doi:10.1111/j.1468-0335.1937.tb00002.x

Dickson, G. (1989). *Corporate Risk Management. Institute of Risk Management.* London: Witherby.

Ellram, L. M. (1995). Partnering pitfalls and success factors. *International Journal of Purchasing and Materials Management, 31*(3), 32–44.

Fabbe-Costes, N. (2007). La gestion des chaines logistiques multi-acteurs: les dimensions organisationnelles d'une gestion lean et agile. In Pache, G., & Spalanazani, A. (Eds.), *La gestion des chaines logistiques multi-acteurs: perspectives stratégiques. Presses universitaires de Grenoble.*

Fone, M., & Young, P. (2000). *Public Sector Risk Management.* London: Butterworth-Heinemann.

Haouari, M., Balambo, M., & Yuan, Y. (2010, May). *The relevance of a reflection on the resilience of Supply Chains: Perspectives for Global Supply Chains.* International Symposium in Logistics, Faculty Polydisciplinaire, El Jadida, Morocco.

Harland, C., Brencheley, H., & Walker, H. (2003). Risk In Supply Network. *Journal of Purchasing and Supply Management, 9*(2), 51–62. doi:10.1016/S1478-4092(03)00004-9

Harland, C., & Brenchley, R. (2001, June). *Risk in supply networks, Proceedings of the 8th International Conference European Operations Management Association,* (pp. 306-318), Bath, UK.

Institute of Risk Management/National Forum for Risk Management in the Public Sector/Association of Insurance and Risk Managers. (2002). *A Risk Management. Standard.* London: IRM/ALARM/AIRMIC.

Jüttner, U., Peck, H., & Christopher, M. (2003). Supply chain risk management: outlining an agenda for future research. *International Journal of Logistics: Research & Applications, 6*(4), 197–210. doi:10.1080/13675560310001627016

Kersten, W., Hohrath, P., & Böger, M. (2007). *An Empirical Approach to Supply Chain Risk Management: Development of a Strategic Framework.* Proceedings of the 18th Annual Conference of the Production and Operations Management Society Orlando, Dallas, USA, May 4-7.Available at: www.poms.org/conferences/poms2007 /CDProgram/Topics/full_length_papers_files/007-0507.pdf (Last access: April 2009).

Knemeyer, Corsi T.M., Murphy P.R. (2003). Logistics Outsourcing Relationships: Customer Perspectives. *Journal of Business Logistics*, *24*(1), 77–109. doi:10.1002/j.2158-1592.2003.tb00033.x

Lambert, D., Emmelhainz, M., & Gardner, J. (1999). Building successful logistics partnerships. *Journal of Business Logistics*, *20*(1), 165–181.

Lavastre, O., & Spalanzani, A. (2008, September). *Le Supply Chain Risk Management (SCRM): Etat des lieux et compréhension des pratiques*. 7èmes Rencontres Internationales de Recherche en Logistique (RIRL 08), (pp. 24-26) Avignon, France.

Lee, J. N., & Kim, Y. G. (2003, January). *Exploring a Casual Model for the Understanding of Outsourcing Partnership*. Proceedings of the 36th Hawaii International Conference on System Science. Big Island, HI, USA

Lewin, K. (1947). The channels of group life, social planning and action research. *Human Relations*, *1*(2), 143–153. doi:10.1177/001872674700100201

Lhabitant, F. S., & Tinguely, O. (2001). Financial Risk Management: An Introduction. *Thunderbird International Business Review*, *43*(3), 343–363. doi:10.1002/tie.1001

Lieb, R. C. (2000). *Third Party Logistics: a Manager's Guide*. JLK Publications.

Liu, M. (1997). *Fondements et pratiques de la recherche-action*. L'Harmattan, 351p.

Manuj, I., & Mentzer, J. T. (2008). Global Supply Chain Risk Management. *Journal of Business Logistics*, *29*(1), 133–155. doi:10.1002/j.2158-1592.2008.tb00072.x

Marasco, A. (2008). Third-party logistics: a literature review. *International Journal of Production Economics*, *113*(1), 127–147. doi:10.1016/j.ijpe.2007.05.017

March, J. G., & Shapira, Z. (1987). Managerial Perspective On Risk And Risk Taking. *Management Science*, *33*(11), 1404–1418. doi:10.1287/mnsc.33.11.1404

Martinet, A. C. (1993). *Les paradigmes stratégiques: l'éternel retour?* Actes du séminaire [Paris, Juin.]. *The Condor*, *V*.

Merminod, N., & Retour, D. (2006, November). *Un facteur clé de succès oublié de l'externalisation: les compétences mobilisées par les acheteurs*. Actes du XVIIe Congrès de l'AGRH, Reims, France.

Monczka, R., Markham, W., Carter, J., Blascovich, J., & Slaight, T. (2005). *Outsourcing Strategically for Sustainable Competitive Advantage*. Tempe, Arizona: Center for Advanced Purchasing Studies.

Murphy, P. R., & Poist, R. F. (2000). Third-party logistics: some user versus provider perspectives. *Journal of Business Logistics*, *21*(1), 121–133.

Naylor, J. B., Naim, M. M., & Berry, D. (1999). Leagility: Integrating the Lean Manufacturing Paradigms in the Total Supply Chain. *International Journal of Production Economics*, *62*, 107–119. doi:10.1016/S0925-5273(98)00223-0

O'Toole, T., & Donaldson, B. (2000). Relationship governance structures and performance. *Journal of Marketing Management*, *16*(4), 327–341. doi:10.1362/026725700784772862

Paché, G., & Sauvage, T. (2004). *La logistique: enjeux stratégiques* (3rd ed.). Paris: Vuibert.

Prahinski, C., & Benton, W. C. (2004). Supplier evaluations: communication strategies to improve supplier performance. *Journal of Operations Management*, *22*, 39–62. doi:10.1016/j.jom.2003.12.005

Royal Society. (1983). *Risk Assessment: A Study Group Report*. London: Royal Society.

Sheffi, Y. (1990). Third party logistics: present and future prospects. *Journal of Business Logistics*, *11*(2), 27–39.

Sheffi, Y., & Rice, J. B. Jr. (2005). A Supply Chain View of the Resilient Enterprise. *MIT Sloan Management Review*, *47*(1), 41–48.

Stemmler, L. (2007). Risk in the supply chain. In *Waters D., Global Logistics: new directions in supply chain management*. London: Kogan Page.

Tate, K. (1996). The elements of a successful logistics partnership. *International Journal of Physical Distribution & Logistics Management*, *26*(3), 7–13. doi:10.1108/09600039610115045

Tchankova, L. (2002). Risk Identification – Basic Stage In Risk Management. *Environmental Management and Health*, *13*(3), 290–297. doi:10.1108/09566160210431088

White, D. (1995). Application of system thinking to risk management: a review of the literature. *Management Decision*, *33*(10), 35–45. doi:10.1108/EUM0000000003918

Williamson, O. E. (1975). *Markets and Hierarchies: Analysis and Anti-trust Implications*. New York: The Free Press.

Zsidisin, G. A. (2003). A grounded definition of supply risk. *Journal of Purchasing and Supply Management*, *9*(5), 217–224. doi:10.1016/j.pursup.2003.07.002

Zsidisin, G. A., Ellram, L. M., Carter, J. R., & Cavinato, J. L. (2004). An analysis of supply risk assessment techniques. *International Journal of Physical Distribution & Logistics Management*, *34*(5), 397–413. doi:10.1108/09600030410545445

ADDITIONAL READING

Andersson, D., & Norman, A. (2003), *Managing risk when outsourcing advanced logistics*, in 12th International IPSERA Conference, Budapest, Hungary, 14-16 April.

Baratt, M. (2004). Understanding the meaning of collaboration in the supply chain, *Supply Chain Management. International Journal (Toronto, Ont.)*, *9*(1), 30–42.

Berglund, H. (2007). Risk Conception and Risk Management in Corporate Innovation: Lessons From Two Swedish Cases. *International Journal of Innovation Management*, *11*(4), 497–513. doi:10.1142/S1363919607001849

Christopher, M., & Peck, H. (2004). Building the resilient supply chain. *International Journal of Logistics Management*, *15*(2), 1–14. doi:10.1108/09574090410700275

Colin J. (1996, March), *La logistique, histoire et perspectives*, actes du colloque ARFILOG, Montluçon. France

Ellram, L. M. (1995). Partnering pitfalls and success factors. *International Journal of Purchasing and Materials Management*, *31*(3), 32–44.

Khan, O., & Burnes, G. (2007). Risk And Supply Chain Management: Creating A Research Agenda. *The International Journal of Logistics Management*, *18*(2), 197–216. doi:10.1108/09574090710816931

Menon, M. K., McGinnis, M. A., & Ackerman, K. B. (1998). Selection Criteria for Providers of Third-Party Logistics Services: An Explorary Study. *Journal of Business Logistics*, *19*(1), 121–137.

Nielson, N., Kleffner, A. E., & And Lee, R. B. (2005). The evolution of the Role of Risk Communication in Effective Risk Managemen. *Risk Management & Insurance Review*, *8*(2), 279–289. doi:10.1111/j.1540-6296.2005.00060.x

Quélin B., (2003) Externalisation stratégique et partenariat: de la firme patrimoniale à la firme contractuelle?, *Revue française de gestion*, 2(143), 13-26

Tapiero, C. (2008). Analyse Des Risques Et Prise De Décision Dans La Chaîne D'approvisionnement, *Revue Française. Gestion*, *6*(186), 163–182.

Zsidisin, G., Panelli, A., & Upton, R. (1999). Purchasing organization involvement in risk assessments, contingency plans and risk management: an exploratory study, *Supply Chain Management. International Journal (Toronto, Ont.)*, *5*(4), 187–197.

ENDNOTES

1 The Institute of Risk Management

2 The Association of Insurance and Risk Management

3 The National Forum for Risk Management in Public Sector

About the Contributors

Pietro Evangelista is senior researcher in logistics and supply chain management at the Institute for Service Industry Research (IRAT) of the Italian National Research Council (CNR). He carried out extensive research on economics and management issues associated with maritime logistics and logistics service industry. This is reflected in more than 100 articles published in national and international journals as well as chapters in books and papers in conference proceedings. His current scientific interest is focused on supply chain innovation with particular reference to the diffusion of ICT in the logistics service industry. On this topic he awarded a PhD in Logistics and Supply Chain Management by Heriot-Watt University (UK). He won the James Cooper Memorial Cup 2010 for the best PhD logistics dissertation by the UK Chartered Institute of Logistics and Transport. Pietro is lecturer in Business Economics and Management at the Department of Managerial Engineering of the University of Naples Federico II. He is member of the editorial board of the International Journal of Business and Systems Research and acts as peer reviewer for other leading international logistics and supply chain management journals. Pietro assists the EU Commission as an independent expert in evaluating transport and logistics projects for different programmes such as FP7, TEN-T and Marco Polo.

Alan McKinnon is Director of the Logistics Research Centre, which he set up in 1997. He has masters degrees from the universities of Aberdeen, British Columbia and a PhD from the University of London. He has been researching and teaching in freight transport and logistics for 30 years and is a frequent contributor to academic and business conferences on logistics around the world. In 2003 he received the Sir Robert Lawrence Award, the highest distinction of the UK Chartered Institute of Logistics and Transport for making a 'major contribution to transport and logistics over a sustained period'. Alan has been an adviser to several UK government departments, UK and Scottish parliamentary committees, the European Commission, the International Transport Forum, the International Energy Agency and OECD. In 2010, he was appointed Chairman of the World Economic Forum's Logistics and Supply Chain Industry Council. He is a visiting professor at universities in Sweden, Malaysia and China.

Edward Sweeney is Director of Learning at the National Institute for Transport and Logistics (NITL), based at the Dublin Institute of Technology (DIT). At NITL, he is responsible for the development and implementation of the integrated supply chain management (SCM) development programmes and carries out research and consultancy work on behalf of NITL client companies. Edward has held full-time academic posts at the University of Warwick (UK) and the University of Technology, Malaysia (UTM), as well as visiting positions in several Asian universities and institutes. He is an engineer by background and has worked and lectured in over 30 countries in Europe, North America and Asia. He is an experienced researcher with over 150 publications including books and book chapters, papers in international peer-reviewed academic journals, practitioner journal articles and conference papers. Edward's most recent book, *Supply Chain Management and Logistics in a Volatile Global Environment*, was published in 2009. The focus of his current work is on resilience and sustainability in global supply chains, with particular reference to the divergence between theory and practice.

Emilio Esposito is the chairman of the Management Engineering Degree Council and full professor of Business Economics and Organization at Faculty of Engineering of the University of Naples Federico II. He graduated in Aerospace Engineering and he was awarded a Ph.D. in Industrial Technology from the University of Naples Federico II. He is Head of the Aerospace Department of Odisseo (Centre for Organization and Technological Innovation of the University of Naples Federico II) and President of the association Campania Star-up (Association for entrepreneurship culture development). His research interests includes quality and technology management, technology and product evaluation in the aerospace industry, technological relationships between customer-supplier relationships, industrial organization in high tech industries (Aerospace and ICT), production organization in the aerospace industry, impact of ICT on the supply chain, e-government and e-procurement. He is author of more then 100 books and articles published in several national and international journals.

* * *

Julian Allen is a Senior Research Fellow in the Transport Department at the University of Westminster. His current research interests are urban freight transport, the impact of manufacturing and retailing techniques on logistics and transportation systems, and the history of freight transport.

Alessandro Ancarani is associate professor in Managerial Engineering at the University of Catania. He holds a D.Phil in Managerial Engineering from the University of Rome "Tor Vergata". He is President of the International Purchasing and Supply Education and Research Association, and co-Editor in chief of the Journal of Purchasing and Supply Management. His publications are in the areas of Public Service Procurement, Health organization and management, Behavioral Operations, Service Management.

Ng Wenwei Benjamin graduated with a Bachelor of Engineering (Mechanical) from Nanyang Technological University. He worked at Autodesk Asia Pte Ltd as a Software Quality Assurance Engineer during an internship in 2009. Currently Mr Benjamin Ng is working as an Industrial Engineer with GLOBALFOUNDRIES, Singapore.

Ruth Banomyong is currently an associate professor in the Department of International Business, Logistics and Transport Management at the Faculty of Commerce & Accountancy, Thammasat University in Thailand.He received his PhD in 2001, in the field of International Logistics within the Logistics & Operations Management Section (LOMS) at Cardiff Business School (UK). He was the winner of the James Cooper Cup in 2001 for the best PhD dissertation in logistics from the Chartered Institute of Logistics & Transport (CILT) in the United Kingdom. Ruth's main research interests are in the field of multimodal transport, international logistics and supply chain performance measurements. He has published over 70 papers and reports in such journals as International Journal of Physical Distribution and Logistics Management, International Journal of Logistics Research and Application, Asia Pacific Journal of Marketing and Logistics, Journal of Applied Sciences, Maritime Policy and Management, among others, and he has co-authored 10 books. Since 1995, Ruth has been a consultant for international agencies such as the United Nations Conference on Trade & Development (UNCTAD), the United Nations Economic and Social Commission for Asia and the Pacific (UN-ESCAP), The World Bank, The Asian Development Bank (ADB), The Association of South East Asian Nations (ASEAN), etc.

Maria Huge-Brodin is an Associate Professor of Logistics Management, Department of Management and Engineering, Linköping University, Sweden. Following a PhD-exam in 2002 (the dissertation was on logistics systems for recycling), she has specialised in research on the environmental impact of logistics system design and logistics management. Her areas of interest include strategic aspects of logistics decision making and business models to support a greening of logistics; product development; and innovation in logistics and supply chain management. She is the leader of the research group for Sustainable Logistics at Linköping University. Her research has been presented on conferences and has been published in e.g. the International Journal of Logistics Management, Logistics Management: an International Journal and International Journal of Logistics: Research and application.

Dermot Carey is an experienced management consultant, trainer and business coach. He is a Doctor of Business Administration where part of his research focused on the implementation of integrated Procurement & Supply Chain systems and structures in a complex business environment. He formed MRM Ltd. in 1990 in Ireland dedicated to supporting industry across vital business functions including Change Management, Business Process Re-Engineering with a specialist interest in Procurement & Supply Chain Management. His career spans 40 years, he has held a number of senior management positions in both the private and public sectors. In twenty years of consultancy he has successfully completed many major assignments in a variety of industries at home and overseas. He holds a number of strategic and advisory roles in SCLG Middle East and is responsible for regional development in Ireland the UK and across Europe and Scandinavia. He is also President of CSCMP Roundtable for Ireland. He is a regular speaker at conferences internationally. Dr. Carey's experience includes such sectors as Telecommunications, Software Development, FMCG, Pharmaceuticals, Aerospace, Construction Industry Federation, Aircraft Maintenance, Airlines, Defence, Financial Services, Computer Manufacturing, Education, Clothing, Confectionery, Electronics, Engineering, Government Departments, Healthcare, Logistics, Mail Order, Oil & Gas Exploration & Drilling, Print, Railways, Retail, Steel Manufacturing, Software Supplies, and Ship Building. This experience was gained in Ireland, UK, Europe, Middle East, Africa, Malaysia, and the USA.

Tom Cherrett (B.Sc., Ph.D, MCILT) is a Senior Lecturer within the Transportation Research Group, University of Southampton. His main research areas include developing sustainable strategies for the collection and disposal of wastes and the distribution of goods in urban areas, including distribution strategies for sustainable home delivery. He has considerable experience in the areas of incident detection and journey time estimation using urban traffic control infrastructure. He has management and logistics experience from working in the chilled distribution sector.

Marcella De Martino is researcher at Institute on Service Industry Research (IRAT) – National Research Council (CNR). Her main research field is port competitiveness according to managerial and organisational perspective. Others research interests include: service innovation and logistics integration for the competitiveness of the agri-food small and medium enterprises in Southern Italy. Extensive research in the field of supply chain management in the port context has resulted in a large number of national and international publications. Currently, she is carrying out a research project involving different European ports aimed at validating a new model for port competitiveness based on a network perspective.

Kym Fraser is currently an adjunct research fellow with the School of Advanced Manufacturing and Mechanical Engineering, University of South Australia. Before joining the university, Kym enjoyed 25 years of business and management experience in government and private enterprises, holding senior management positions in medium to large organisations within the automotive and rail industries.

John Gattorna is Executive Chairman of a Sydney-based specialist advisory business, Gattorna Alignment Pty Ltd, and he collaborates with a large community of supply chain enthusiasts, worldwide. He has spent a lifetime working in and around supply chains, in many different capacities – line executive, researcher, consultant/adviser, teacher and author. He is passionate about the subject – some might say obsessive.In the late 1980s, John became disenchanted with the lack of conceptual depth in the 'logistics' field; and as it turned out this did not improve much as logistics thinking morphed into 'supply chains' in the 1990s. So he started to search for a new model/framework that would better inform the design and operation of enterprise supply chains, seeking to satisfy customers and consumers. And he found it in *dynamic alignment.*

Mark Goh is a professor at the University of South Australia and the NUS Business School. He has published widely in the area of supply chain management. He sits on the Executive Board of Supply Chain Asia and has worked with various global agencies on trade logistics related to the Asia Pacific. He appears in Who's Who.

Mohamed Haouari, M.Sc., M.A., is a Phd student in CRET-LOG Research Center, *Aix-Marseille II University*, Aix-en-Provence, France. He holds a MSc in "Logistics Management and Strategy" of the Business and Economics Faculty of Aix-Marseille II University, and a MA in audit and management control, of ENCG National School of Business and Management, Marrakech, Morocco. He is currently engaged in completing a Ph.D in risk management in logistics outsourcing. His major fields of interest include risk management, uncertainty and resilience of Supply Chains. He also focuses on relationships between clients and logistics service providers.

Lisa Hüttinger is a PhD student at the School of Management and Governance (Department of Operations, Organization and Human Resources), University of Twente. Her research focuses on customer attractiveness, supplier satisfaction and the preferred customer concept.

Jacques Leonardi is a senior research fellow in the Department of Transport Studies, University of Westminster. His research specialities are related to urban freight transport, supply chain energy and carbon footprint, global logistics, surveys and survey methods, van use, new technologies, data management, and policy impact evaluation. Recent work in these areas includes research for Green Logistics (www.greenlogistics.org), Sustainable Urban Goods Logistics SUGAR (www.sugarlogistics.eu), Data and Knowledge Centre of TfL freight unit, and consolidation networks. He has published widely on these topics and also teaches at the University of Westminster.

Lee Ka Man is currently an assistant professor in the School of Mechanical and Aerospace Engineering, Nanyang Technological University. She obtained her PhD and B. Eng degree from The Hong Kong Polytechnic University. She was awarded Bronze Award of 16th China National Invention Exhibition Award in 2006 and Outstanding Professional Service and Innovation Award, The Hong Kong Polytechnic University in 2006. Her current research areas include logistics information management, manufacturing information systems, product development and data mining techniques. She focuses on applying computational intelligence such as genetic algorithm and artificial neural network for supply and demand chain management.

Alessandra Marasco is researcher at the Institute for Service Industry Research (IRAT) of the Italian National Research Council (CNR). Her areas of research include third-party logistics, supply chain management, innovation in logistics and service industries. She has published in leading journals and peer-reviewed conference proceedings. She has been involved in several research programs funded by the Italian Ministry of University and Scientific Research and she is currently in charge of a research project on open innovation in services.

Carmela Di Mauro is associate professor in Economics at the University of Catania. She holds a D.Phil in Economics from the University of York. Her publications are in the areas of experimental and behavioral economics and Health economics and Management.

Fraser McLeod (B.Sc., M.Phil) is a Research Fellow within the Transportation Research Group, University of Southampton, with 25 years experience of working on transport-related projects. In recent years his work has focused on ITS (Intelligent Transport Systems), freight distribution and on the logistics of collecting household and trade waste. The common theme of his research has been methods for improving transport efficiency and evaluating these through the use of simulation modelling, routeing and scheduling methods and mathematical analyses.

Alfonso Morvillo is Director of the Institute for Service Industry Research (IRAT) of the National Research Council in Naples. His research interests are wide–ranging, notably finance logistics and freight transport, supply chain management, shipping and port strategy. He has been scientific co-ordinator of several international and national research projects. His research has resulted in a large number of academic publications including "Training in logistics and the freight transport industry. The experience of the European Project ADAPT-FIT in Southern Italy" printed by Ashgate Ltd and "International Maritime Transport. Perspectives" printed by Routledge Ltd. He is also editor of a series of research monographs. He has lectured in shipping economies, management and finance at Parthenope University of Naples. As a Board Member he has been involved within scientific conferences around the world. He is member of the most important academic and practitioners Associations in the fields of Maritime Transport and Logistics.

Renato Passaro is full professor of Business Economics and Responsible of the Master in Supply Chain Management and Freight Transport at the University of Naples Parthenope. His research interests are in two main streams. The first deals with the impact of supply chain management and business logistics on the efficiency of business organization at firm, inter-firm and territorial level. The second addresses entrepreneurial characteristics and developing processes in small and medium sized enterprises. He is member of national and international academic organizations and he is author of several articles published on national and international scientific journals.

Shaligram Pokharel is an Associate Professor in the Department of Mechanical and Industrial Engineering, Qatar University, Doha, Qatar. Dr. Pokharel graduated as Mechanical Engineer from the University of Kashmir (India) and completed his Masters and PhD in Systems Design Engineer from the University of Waterloo, Canada. Dr. Pokharel worked in Nanyang Technological University before joining Qatar University. He conducts research in engineering management field, specially related to supply chains and energy management. Currently Dr. Pokharel is working on reverse logistics and emergency logistics related research.

Colm Ryan is a graduate of the Executive Supply Chain Masters programme of the National Institute of Transport and Logistics (NITL), Dublin, Ireland. He has extensive high-tech supply chain experience, having worked in Accenture, Gartner, EMC and Snap-on Inc. He is currently working in Apple Inc. in Cork, Ireland.

Thierry Sauvage is Professor in Purchasing and Supply Chain Management. He is Professor at Audencia Nantes Business School and Director of research at the Centre de REcherche sur les Transports et la LOGistique (CRETLOG) of the university Aix-Marseille II. His current research interests include Purchasing Risk Management, suppliers management and green purchasing.

Holger Schiele is chair of Technology Management at the School of Management and Governance of the University of Twente in Enschede, The Netherlands. He holds a PhD and the habilitation (venia legendi) from Leibniz Universität Hannover, Germany. Previous and in parallel to joining academia he has been working at the strategy department of Preussag AG, as a consultant for PricewaterhouseCoopers and as project manager with h&z business consulting. Apart from two best-selling management books, which climbed position 1 in the Financial Times list, he has extensively published academic papers in English language in such journals as Journal of Business Research, Research Policy, R&D Management, International Journal of Innovation Management, Industrial Marketing Management, International Journal of Physical Distribution and Logistics Management, Journal of Purchasing and Supply, Journal of Business Strategy, among others.

Jasper Veldman is an assistant professor at the School of Management and Governance (Department of Operations, Organization and Human Resources), University of Twente. His research focuses on product and process innovation in buyer-supplier relationships, technology management issues including maintenance management and process improvement concepts.

Claudia-Maria Wagner currently works as a lecturer with the Dublin Institute of Technology. Prior to that, she was Principal Researcher and Programme Director at the National Institute for Transport and Logistics in Dublin, Ireland. She has further worked with multinational companies on several industry-based research projects in China, Singapore, Malaysia, Finland, USA and Germany. Her research expertise covers ICT strategies and implementation challenges, with particular emphasis on B2B e-Marketplace diffusion in the transport industry and its impact on competitiveness and performance. Her research interests further include global procurement strategies in an SCM context, the role of ICT in the design of sustainable supply chain configurations, as well as transport policy and regulation.

Allan Woodburn is a Principal Lecturer in Freight and Logistics in the Transport Studies Department at the University of Westminster, London. He is involved in a wide range of teaching, research and consultancy activities in the field of freight transport, both within the UK and internationally. Allan completed his Doctorate examining the role for rail freight within the supply chain in 2000. Since then, his main research focus has been on rail freight policy, planning and operations, focusing specifically on efficiency and sustainability issues.

Index

E

F

G

H

I

J

R

S

T

U

V

W

Z

www.ingramcontent.com/pod-product-compliance
Lightning Source LLC
LaVergne TN
LVHW062139300926
849161LV00010B/2570